Kant and the Concept of Community

North American Kant Society Studies in Philosophy

General Editor
Robert B. Louden
University of Southern Maine

Editorial Board
Richard Aquila
Marcia W. Baron
Andrew Brook
Michael Friedman

Kant's Aesthetics (Vol. 1, 1991)
Edited by Ralf Meerbote

Minds, Ideas, and Objects (Vol. 2, 1992)
Edited by Phillip D. Cummins and Guenter Zoeller

Kant's Early Metaphysics (Vol. 3, 1993)
Alison Laywine

The Table of Judgments (Vol. 4, 1995/6)
Reinhard Brandt

Logic and the Workings of the Mind (Vol. 5, 1997)
Edited by Patricia A. Easton

Selected Essays on Kant (Vol. 6, 2002)
Lewis White Beck, Edited by Hoke Robinson

Kantian Virtue at the Intersection of Politics
And Nature (Vol. 7, 2004)
Scott M. Roulier

Understanding Purpose (Vol. 8, 2007)
Edited by Philippe Huneman

Kant and the Concept of Community (Vol. 9, 2011)
Edited by Charlton Payne and Lucas Thorpe

KANT AND THE
CONCEPT OF COMMUNITY

Edited by Charlton Payne and Lucas Thorpe

Volume 9
North American Kant Society
Studies in Philosophy

UNIVERSITY OF ROCHESTER PRESS

Copyright © 2011 North American Kant Society

First published 2011

University of Rochester Press
668 Mt. Hope Avenue, Rochester, NY 14620, USA
www.urpress.com
and Boydell & Brewer Limited
PO Box 9, Woodbridge, Suffolk IP12 3DF, UK
www.boydellandbrewer.com

ISBN-13: 978-1-58046-387-4

Library of Congress Cataloging-in-Publication Data

Kant and the concept of community / edited by Charlton Payne and Lucas Thorpe.
   p. cm. — (North American Kant Society studies in philosophy ; v. 9)
   Includes bibliographical references (p.) and index.
   ISBN 978-1-58046-387-4 (pbk. : alk. paper) 1. Kant, Immanuel, 1724–1804.
2. Communities. I. Payne, Charlton. II. Thorpe, Lucas.
   B2799.C66K36   2011
   193—dc22

2011005560

A catalogue record for this title is available from the British Library.

This publication is printed on acid-free paper.
Printed in the United States of America

An earlier version of chapter 9 was published as "Paradoxes in Kant's
Account of Citizenship," in *Responsibility in Context: Perspectives*,
ed. Gorana Ognjenovic (Dordrecht: Springer, 2009), 19–34.
Reproduced with kind permission from Springer Science+Business Media.

The editors gratefully acknowledge the graduate research program "The Figure of the
Third" at the University of Konstanz for travel support during the preparation of the
manuscript, the Boğaziçi University Bilimsel Araştırma Projeleri (BAP) Komisyonu
for financial support for the index, and Burak Erbora for compiling the index.

CONTENTS

Introduction

The Many Senses of Community in Kant

Charlton Payne and Lucas Thorpe

In recent years groundbreaking work has been done in Kant's philosophy of science, his practical philosophy, and his aesthetics. Unfortunately, due to the vast amount of specialized research, it has been difficult for scholars to keep up with developments in all of these distinct fields and Kant studies are fragmented. Kant was, however, a systematic philosopher, and so while this specialization is absolutely necessary, it makes it very hard for any one individual to grasp Kant's work as a system. This volume focuses on a single concept, the concept of community, which plays a central role in Kant's theoretical and practical philosophy, his aesthetics, and his religious thought. The articles by authors from various disciplines, who specialize in disparate aspects of Kant's work and take different approaches, will, we hope, not only fill a missing hole in the scholarship but also bring diverse approaches together and provide the reader with a more systematic view of Kant's work as a whole.

Community is a particularly good concept to focus on if one wishes to overcome critical divisions in Kant studies. There are many communities in Kant: the category of community introduced in the table of categories of the *Critique of Pure Reason*, the community of substances in the Third Analogy, the realm of ends as an ethical community, the state and the public sphere as political communities, the *sensus communis* of the *Critique of Judgment*, and the idea of the church as a religious community introduced in *Religion within the Boundaries of Mere Reason*. Community, then, is a major topic in Kant's theoretical, practical, and aesthetic writings. For a philosopher as systematic as Kant, we should not be surprised to find that commitments about the nature of community in one area affect his commitments in other areas. Our hope is that the papers in this volume, all on diverse and sometimes seemingly unrelated conceptions of community, will illuminate one another, perhaps in surprising ways.

In an important work on the table of judgments, Reinhard Brandt has argued that "whatever metamorphoses [his] other doctrines undergo, Kant never doubts the categories and thus the table of judgments as the foundation of his system as a whole. . . . All critique, transcendental philosophy, and

metaphysics (of morals and of nature) has its foundation in the table of judgments."[1] While many commentators may find this an exaggeration, it is defi-
nitely true that Kant himself thought the table of categories held a key place in
his system as a whole. We believe that many of Kant's conceptions of community are modeled on the concept of community found in the table of categories
and judgments, and we suggest that one can distinguish between a "core" set
of concepts of community, all of which are modeled on the category of community introduced in the first *Critique*, and a set of less central, perhaps derivative, concepts that are less clearly related to the core set of concepts.

Among the core concepts we include the *category* of community introduced in the first *Critique* and derived from the disjunctive form of judgment, the *scientific* idea of interaction introduced in the Third Analogy and
developed in the *Metaphysical Foundations of Natural Science*, the *metaphysical*
idea of a world mainly discussed in his precritical writings and the cosmology
sections of his metaphysics lectures, the *moral* ideal of a realm of ends, the
political ideal of a juridical community, and the *theological ideal* of heaven as
a community of holy beings (angels) in interaction. Among the less central
conceptions of community we would include the notion of an ethical community introduced in *Religion within the Boundaries of Mere Reason*, and the
notion of a *sensus communis* introduced in the *Critique of Judgment*. In claiming that these concepts of community are less central we do not wish to suggest that they are less important, merely that their relationship to the logical
category of community is less clear.

In the first *Critique* the concept of community is introduced at the third
category of relation, derived from the disjunctive form of judgment. It is significant that in his theoretical writing Kant often uses the words community and interaction interchangeably. This logical notion of community is
developed in his logic lectures. In his precritical writings and the cosmology
sections of his metaphysics lectures Kant provides an analysis of the metaphysical idea of a "world" understood as a community of individuals in interaction. In his works on ethics we find the idea of a realm of ends understood
to be an ideal moral community, and in his political writings the idea of a
political community governed by juridical laws. Finally, we find the theological ideal of a community of holy beings, which Kant sometimes calls "the
kingdom of heaven."[2] We believe, then, that Kant employs at least six "core"
notions of community:

1. The *category* of community. This is derived from the disjunctive form of
   judgment and Kant often identifies it with the concept of interaction.
2. The *scientific* notion of interaction. This concept is introduced in the
   Third Analogy and developed in the *Metaphysical Foundations of Natural Science*.

3. A *metaphysical* idea. The idea of a world of individuals (monads) in interaction. This idea was developed in his precritical period and can be found in his metaphysics lectures.
4. A *moral* ideal. The idea of a realm of ends.[3]
5. A *political* ideal. The idea of a political community (or community of communities) governed by juridical laws.
6. A *theological* ideal. What Kant calls "the kingdom of heaven," which can be thought of as a community of holy beings, or angels.[4]

It is clear that Kant believes that all of these notions of community are related in some way. Our suggestion is that all of these ideas are modeled on the category of community.

Kant wrote three *Critiques*, and, in organizing this volume, we have taken this division as our starting point, although we have divided the category of practical philosophy into two sections: ethics and political philosophy. However, for many of the papers it has been difficult to fit them neatly into one of these categories. This, however, is to be expected, and this difficulty merely confirms our belief that Kant's examination of the concept of community in one area can only be understood in relation to the others.

In this introduction we will give a brief survey of the various concepts of community in Kant, focusing on those core concepts that are likely to be less familiar to readers. In the first section, we give some arguments for believing that Kant has a core set of concepts of community that are modeled on the category of community. In part two we will discuss those concepts of community that do not seem to fit into the core set, and also suggest reasons for doubting that such a unified account of community can be given in the first place.

A Unified Account of Community

The Category of Community

The first three articles by Béatrice Longuenesse, Eric Watkins, and Lucas Thorpe focus on the concept of community in Kant's theoretical philosophy, and on three particular issues: first, the introduction of the category of community as the third category of relation; second, the argument of the Third Analogy; and third, the role of the concept of community in Kant's scientific writings.

One central question of these articles has to do with Kant's account of the relation between the disjunctive form of judgment and the category of community. Many commentators have seen Kant's arguments here as among the weakest in the *Critique of Pure Reason*. Thus Paul Guyer, for example, has noted that "as is often pointed out, Kant's connection of the real relation of reciprocal influence with the logical notion of exclusive disjunction is the most tenuous piece of his metaphysical deduction."[5] Longuenesse, Watkins, and Thorpe revisit this discussion and take the argument more seriously.

The category of community, as introduced in the table of categories in the *Critique of Pure Reason*, is the third category of relation. The structure of the table of categories is derived from the table of judgments. This table is divided into four classes: judgments of quantity, of quality, of relation, and of modality. The categories of relation, then, are derived from the judgments of relation. According to Kant there are three types of relational judgment: categorical judgments (A is B), hypothetical judgments (if p then q), and disjunctive judgments (p or q or r). The categories of substance and accident are derived from the categorical form of judgment. The categories of cause and effect are derived from the hypothetical form of judgment. The category of community, which either is or involves the idea of reciprocal influence, is derived from the disjunctive form of judgment.

A disjunctive judgment has the form: "x is A or B or C." Kant explains this form of judgment in the *Critique of Pure Reason* in the following terms: "In all disjunctive judgments the sphere (the multitude of everything that is contained under it) is represented as a whole divided into parts (the subordinate concepts)" (B112). A disjunctive judgment, then, is a judgment in which a number of judgments somehow restrict one another and fill up a logical space. In the disjunctive judgment, then, we find a number of judgments mutually excluding one another and completely filling a logical space. The conception of a logical space allows us to think of a "space" that has parts but that is not, unlike the space of intuition, infinitely divisible. We may thus think of a whole, the parts of which are simple. This will be important when we turn to the metaphysical idea of community, which Kant, in his metaphysical lectures, calls the idea of a "world."

In his commentary on the table of categories, Kant explains that the categories he has listed do not provide a complete list of the *a priori* concepts of the understanding, for there are also derivative concepts, which Kant calls "predicables," that can be derived from the categories (A81–82, B107). Under the category of community Kant lists two "derivative concepts" or predicables: presence and resistance (A82, B108). The concept of resistance plays an important role in Kant's account of community and interaction. The reason why Kant believes that resistance is a predicable of the category of community seems to be because he is conceiving of resistance in terms of exclusion, and thinks that our *a priori* understanding of exclusion is based upon our grasp of disjunction. Kant's thought here seems to be that in a disjunctive judgment the assertion of one member of the disjunction excludes the assertion of the other members, and that the retraction of the assertion can be thought of as a withdrawing resistance that allows for another member of the disjunction to be asserted. Thus, for example, suppose we assert a simple disjunctive judgment, "*x* is either a cat or not a cat." Given the assertion of this disjunctive judgment, the assertion of the judgment "*x* is not a cat" logically excludes the assertion of "*x* is a cat." Retracting the assertion of the judgment "*x* is not a cat" can be thought of as the withdrawal of resistance, or the removal of an impediment, that creates space for the assertion of the judgment "*x* is a cat."

According to Kant, then, the category of community lies at the base of the notion of a number of impenetrable individuals (concepts) filling a conceptual space (another concept) and excluding other individuals (concepts) from their part of the conceptual space, without any appeal to the space of intuition. The notion of resistance, and particularly the idea of the withdrawal of resistance, plays an important role both in Kant's account of interaction and his account of juridical law and the exchange of property.

The Third Analogy and *Metaphysical Foundations of Natural Science*

The Third Analogy is found in the section Analytic of Principles of the *Critique of Pure Reason*. The Analytic of Principles has to do with the application of the categories to objects of experience. This section of the *Critique* is divided into four subsections, and in the third subsection, the *Analogies of Experience*, Kant argues for certain principles governing the application of the categories of relation to experience. Thus, the Third Analogy deals with the application of the category of community to experience. Until recently, however, at least in the English speaking world, very few commentators have given it a sympathetic reading. Jonathan Bennett, for example, argues that in the Third Analogy Kant is making "the rather Spinozist claim that we could not know that two things coexisted in the same universe unless they had causal commerce (= community) with one another. His attempt to prove this, however, is a failure which is not even incidentally valuable except for a few flickers of light it throws on the second analogy."[6] In a similar vein, T. E. Wilkerson has argued that "The Third Analogy has a very shadowy existence. In part it reproduced material from the second Analogy, and in part it makes a nonsense of it."[7] In recent books however, Eric Watkins, Béatrice Longuenesse, and Jeffrey Edwards have provided far more sympathetic readings of the Third Analogy; and in this volume the contributions of both Longuenesse and Watkins add to our understanding of this difficult text.[8] One of the most exciting developments in Kant scholarship in recent years has been the high quality of the research into Kant's scientific writings such as the *Metaphysical Foundations of Natural Science* and the *Opus Postumum*. And Watkins's paper goes beyond the Third Analogy and examines the role of the concept of community in Kant's scientific project.

The Metaphysical Idea of a "World"

Kant frequently lectured on metaphysics, and would discuss the idea of a world in the cosmology sections of his lectures.[9] For the purposes of this introduction, there are two important features of Kant's account of the idea of a world. First, (a) Kant distinguishes between the idea of a world and a mere multitude of individuals. The idea of a world is the idea of a real whole consisting of individuals in real interaction. Second, (b) Kant believes that the only way of conceiving of real interaction between individual members of a world is in terms of the agent removing resistance that allows a "dead power" in the patient to become a "living power." We will briefly explain each of these features.

(a) For Kant our idea of a world is the idea of a substantial composite.[10] He makes his commitment to this position clear in the cosmology sections of his metaphysics lectures. The first point he makes is that our idea of a world is the idea of a whole. Thus he argues that "A *multitude* of substances without connection makes no world. One must thus not define world: the universe of substances, but rather the whole of them" (*Metaphysik Dohna*, 28:657). However, he also argues that for substances to constitute a world they must form wheat he calls a *real* as opposed to an *ideal* whole.

Kant believes that any composite must have both form and matter, and hence there are two conditions that distinguish a real from an ideal whole: a material condition and a formal condition. The material condition for the existence of a real whole is that the parts of a real whole must be true individuals. This condition, which Kant sometimes characterizes by saying that the world must be a substantial whole, implies, Kant believes, that spatial wholes, for example, are merely ideal wholes.[11] This material condition for real wholeness is a major motivation for Kant's claim that space is ideal. We also find similar claims in Leibniz.[12] The formal condition is that the unity of the whole must be "real" rather than "ideal" and the guarantee of the reality of the unity is the existence of "real" connection(s).

What is most significant here is his account of this formal condition; when we are talking of a world of monads it is assumed that the material condition is met, since the matter of the world are the individuals that make up the world. In explaining this formal condition, he writes: "Substances are the matter of the world, the formal aspect of the world consists in their connection (*nexu*) and indeed in a real connection (*nexu reali*). The world is thus a real whole (*totum reale*), not ideal" (*Metaphysik L2*, 28:581). Our idea of a world is the idea of a *real*, as opposed to an *ideal*, whole in this sense.

According to Kant an ideal whole is a whole that can be "represented in thought" as a whole (*Metaphysic Mrongovius*, 29:851). In such a whole the unity only exists in the mind of the observer. In a real whole, in contrast, the unity must be intrinsic to the whole. In his paper in this volume, Lucas

Thorpe argues that this implies that our idea of a world is the idea of a realm of ends. For if the individuals that constitute the whole must be responsible for the unity of the whole, and, given the fact that what supplies unity to a whole are laws, then a real whole will be one in which the individuals that make up the whole are the source of the laws that provide the whole with its unity. That is, the members of a real whole must be autonomous, and a world of autonomous being is the idea of a realm of ends.

(b) In his metaphysics lectures, Kant explains how one substance can act on another in terms of the withdrawal of resistance. In his metaphysics lectures from 1782–83 he explains the possibility of interaction in terms of the agent "determining the power" of the patient (*Metaphysik Mrongovius*, 29:823).

In a later passage he explains that one individual "determines the power" of another when it removes an impediment that allows a "dead" power to become a "living" power. Thus he argues that

> with a faculty we imagine only the possibility of power. Between faculty and power lies the concept of endeavor (*conatus*; *Bestrebung*). When the determining ground for an effect is internally sufficient, then it is a dead power. But when it is internally and externally sufficient, then it is a living power. *Power which is merely internally sufficient, without being able to produce the effect, is always opposed to an opposing power which hinders its effect, an impediment (impedimentum). Thus as soon as the impediment (impedimentum) is removed, the dead power becomes living.* (*Metaphysik L2*, 28:565; emphasis added)

A more detailed discussion of this topic can be found in Thorpe's paper. For the purposes of this introduction, what is important is that in these lectures Kant tries to explain interaction in terms of the removal of resistance, which Kant argues is a "predicable" of the category of community, and, as we shall see, the language Kant uses here is very similar to the language he will use in the *Metaphysics of Morals* in his account of the juridical condition and the exchange of property.

The Realm of Ends

In the *Groundwork of the Metaphysics of Morals*, with the third formulation of the categorical imperative, Kant introduces the idea of a realm of ends (*ein Reich der Zwecke*), and this is clearly the idea of some sort of community. But the exact nature of this community is unclear. In this volume, Lucas Thorpe attempts to identify the notion of a realm of ends with the theoretical idea of community. He argues that the idea of a realm of ends is modeled on the idea of a world found in Kant's metaphysics lectures and precritical writings, and that this idea is itself modeled on the category of community. Most readers believe that the idea of a realm of ends has more moral content than is posited by Thorpe, but there is no consensus on the exact nature of this content. Paul Guyer, for example, begins with the assumption that the idea of a realm of ends is clearly the idea of community of *moral* agents, and suggests, following Rawls, that such a realm is to be understood as the state of affairs that would be realized if everyone conformed to the categorical imperative. Onora O'Neill argues that the notion of an ethical community ultimately involves an appeal to the notion of public justification.

Political Community (Understood as a State Governed by Juridical Laws)

Understanding the nature and role of the political in Kant, and its relation to the ethical, is one of the most contentious issues in Kant studies. For Kant at least one sense of the political, however, involves the notion of a state governed by juridical laws that determine property rights, and it is our contention that Kant's conception of such a state is modeled on his account of a world and interaction developed in his metaphysical writings. Such a relationship is most noticeable in his account of the transferal of property. Thus, for example, Kant argues that

> my possession of another's choice, in the sense of my capacity [*Vermogen*] to determine it by my own choice to a certain deed in accordance with laws of freedom (what is externally mine or yours with respect to the causality of another), is a right (of which I can have several against the same person or against others); but there is only a single sum (system of laws), contract right, in accordance with which I can be in this sort of possession. (6:271)

The language here is very similar to the language he uses to explain action in his metaphysics lectures. There he argued that the agent must have a capacity to "determine the active power" of the patient. Here he claims that to have a right is to possess a capacity to determine the choice of another. And he argues that an individual can only possess such a capacity if there is a system of juridical laws and others recognize and affirm these laws. These laws are not physical laws but juridical laws, the existence of which depends upon them being freely taken up by each individual member of the community. Kant explains that "my capacity to determine another's choice by my own choices" is called a right and that it is the existence of juridical laws that makes rights possible and, consequently, allows one individual to act upon (determine the choice of) another. Laws that assign rights are called juridical (or coercive) laws. Such laws make interaction possible because they are the basis of resistance between individuals. Kant repeatedly stresses the relationship between juridical laws and the notion of resistance. For example, in his ethics lectures he argues that the universal law of reason can alone be the determining ground of action, but this is the law of universal freedom; everyone has the right to promote this, even though he effects it by *resisting* the opposing freedom of another, in such a way that he seeks to prevent an *obstruction*, and thus to further an intent. . . . The other, however, *obstructs* the action by his freedom; the latter I can curtail and *offer resistance* to, insofar as this is in accordance with the laws of coercion; so *eo ipso* I must thereby *obstruct* universal freedom by the use of my own. From this it follows that . . . the right to coerce the other consists in *restricting* his use of freedom, insofar as it cannot co-exist with universal freedom according to universal law; and this is the right of coercion. . . . Since nobody can exercise a right to coerce, who has not obtained a right thereto from a higher ground, which consists, however, in one's own freedom and its congruence with the freedom of everyone according to universal law, it is clear that the right to coerce can only be derived from the Idea of law itself. (*Ethik Vigilantius*, 27:523; emphasis added)

We should read such passages bearing in mind Kant's account of action in his metaphysical work, for he believes that all action should be understood in terms of the withdrawal of resistance. Here Kant argues that the right to coerce "consists in" (legitimately) resisting the freedom of others, and that such a right (i.e., the possibility of resistance) can only be derived from the "idea of law itself." In other words in this passage Kant is suggesting that it is juridical laws that make resistance, and hence interaction (being understood in terms of the withdrawal of resistance), possible. It is important to note that on this reading the notion of coercion has nothing to do with threats of violence.[13]

Only if such a community (or civil condition) exists can an individual really own property and "transfer" the property to another. In so doing, individuals are able to act upon one another through mutual consent. The activity of the agent (giver) is the withdrawal of an impediment, the activity of the patient (receiver) is an active uptaking. In the transferal of property, then, a property right does not flow from the giver to the receiver. Rather, in the context of a commonly willed set of property laws, one party renounces a right while the other party simultaneously uptakes the right actively. Kant is very careful to make it clear that in the "transferal" of property there has to be more than the mere abandoning or renouncing of a right by the giver, and we suggest that Kant's reason for stressing this is his commitment to the principle of active inherence. For the receiver to really possess a right she or he has to be the active ground of the right. Thus Kant explains that transferal of property

is only possible through a common will by means of which the object is always under the control of one or the other, since as one gives up his share in the common undertaking [*Gemeinschaft*] the object becomes the other's through his acceptance of it (and so by a positive act of choice.) Transfer of the property of one to another is alienation. An act of the united choice of two persons by which anything at all that belongs to one passes to the other is a contract. (6:271)

Just as, in general, a determination can only belong to a substance if the substance is the active ground of the determination, property can only belong to an individual if the individual is the active ground of the right. Acquiring a right to something cannot occur passively; one must be actively asserting a claim, even in the case of receiving a gift. In an act of exchange, then, it is not as if the donor actively gives and the recipient passively receives. Instead, the receiver must be actively asserting a claim to an object and the donor merely withdrawing her or his (legitimate) claim to it, withdrawing resistance to the recipient's claim. This is why Kant stresses that the recipient must accept the property "by a positive act of choice."

Such considerations lie behind Kant's claim that in the legal sense, all commissive acts, strictly speaking, are really omissive. Kant explains this in his lectures on ethics. He argues:

It must be noted . . . that all coercive or juridical laws are prohibitive, and rely on the principle of not withholding from the other what belongs to him (*neminem laede*). (For the fact that both commissive and omissive actions are equally necessary for the performance of actions in a physical sense, makes no difference, since all commissive actions are omissive, *in sensu juris*.) (*Ethik Vigilantius*, 27:512)

Thus, although on the phenomenal level an act such as paying a debt may appear to be an action on the part of the debtor,[14] on the legal level all that is happening is that the debtor is allowing the creditor to use what is legally the creditor's. In paying back the loan, the debtor has not really given the creditor anything. Kant believes that such an analysis can be applied to all property transactions and not merely to cases of repaying a debt. Thus he explains that "I cannot give the other anything—he already has what belongs to him; . . . you are to leave the other his own, take nothing, abstain from all actions whereby you would detract from his rights" (27:512).

Problems for a Unified Account of Community

Having discussed what we take to be Kant's core concepts of community, we will now briefly discuss the ways in which Kant's various concepts of community resist being understood as closely modeled on the category of community. We will begin by examining the various concepts of community in Kant's practical philosophy, including that contained in *Religion within the*

Boundaries of Mere Reason, and finish by discussing the conception of community found in the *Critique of Judgment*.

Community in Kant's Practical Philosophy (including the *Religion*)

Although this volume divides, rather artificially, the contributions on Kant's practical philosophy into two sections, ethics and political philosophy, the division does have its basis in Kant's own work. *The Metaphysics of Morals* is divided into a *Doctrine of Right* and a *Doctrine of Virtue*. As the essays in this volume nonetheless demonstrate, the dividing line between ethical and political community is hard to draw, as is the division between the aesthetic and the practical. We also had a problem deciding where to place the papers by Allen Wood and Michael Feola, both of which deal with the idea of religious community, as does a large section of Paul Guyer's paper. Does the idea of religious community in Kant deserve its own section? We believe this is not just a pragmatic organizational question, but that it also raises a serious question about the place of religion in Kant's work as a whole. Where does Kant's work on religion fit into his system? *Religion within the Boundaries of Mere Reason* is a major work, but it is not clear how it fits into the tripartite division of Kant's system into three *Critiques*. The same could be said about Kant's occasional works on history. Finally we decided to include these papers in the section on Kant's practical philosophy, as Kant does believe in a *practical* religion, but we leave it to the reader to judge whether this was the right decision. A central question here is how to understand the relationship between Kant's idea of a realm of ends and the notion of ethical community introduced in the *Religion*.

Within Kant's later, explicitly political writings, the concept of community takes many forms: the nation-state, civil society, the public sphere, humanity as a whole as a cosmopolitan ideal, and the notion of juridical state as a community of possession. If, as some contributors to this volume believe, Kant's aesthetic theory of judgment presents a version of community departing from the version derived from his practical philosophy, some commentators have argued that this movement away from ethical community is even more pronounced in the political writings, where Kant makes a fundamental distinction between ethics and right. However, the relationship between the ethical and the political in Kant is hard to draw. And it is not clear whether the ethical or the political has ultimate priority. On the surface it looks as if for Kant the ethical grounds the political. However, Kant's ultimate ethical ideal, the realm of ends, can itself be interpreted as a political idea, as shown in Guyer's discussion of the relationship between the legislation of perpetual peace and the virtue of the politicians who would institute global justice. Also, as previously noted, for constructivist readers of Kant, such as O'Neill, the ethical is ultimately grounded in the public sphere.

In terms of the state as a political community, Kant, following Rousseau, believes that government must rule in a republican spirit and that subjects should also be citizens. However, there is disagreement about the value of citizenship for Kant. Is citizenship ultimately a political or an ethical demand? This is the question that distinguishes between what Ronald Beiner, in his contribution to this volume, refers to as "low liberal" and "high liberal" readings of Kant. The high liberal believes that citizenship completes us in a moral sense, whereas the low liberal believes that our political engagement has a merely instrumental value. Kant seems to waver between these two views. However, if one accepts a high liberal reading of Kant, what are we to make of his acceptance of the distinction between "active citizens" who are not economically dependent on others and "passive citizens" such as servants, wage laborers, some peasants, and women?

In addition to offering a theory of the state and of rights in texts such as *What Is Enlightenment?*, Kant also develops a theory of the public sphere that has become increasingly influential in recent decades, in particular in the works of Jürgen Habermas, John Rawls, and Onora O'Neill. In her article in this volume, O'Neill examines the degree to which public reason plays a role in justifying ethical and political claims, thus raising once again the question of the relationship between the ethical and the political in Kant's work.

In addition to examining the state as a political community, Kant is also interested in the idea of the community of property owners. Kant's views on property are rather complicated. On the one hand he believes that a community of property owners is a necessary political, and perhaps ethical, ideal. On the other hand, he seems to suggest that any appropriation of property can only be through unilateral acts, and that such acts can never legitimate possession. In his contribution to this volume, Jeffrey Edwards attempts to unravel Kant's attempt to overcome this antimony.

Finally, we should not forget that Kant's politics ultimately transcends the political (understood in a narrow sense of the nation-state as the ultimate community), for in the end Kant's conception of political community is cosmopolitan. His strongest advocacy of this cosmopolitan ideal is found in *Perpetual Peace*, a work consisting of three articles that address the status of citizens in a state, nations in relation to one another, and citizens of the world as human beings, respectively. In the third article, Kant discusses cosmopolitan rights in terms of "universal hospitality," "the right of an alien not to be treated as an enemy upon his arrival in another's country."[15] This universal hospitality extends to the treatment that nations mete out to foreign lands, which is why Kant criticizes European colonialist practices for "the injustice that they display towards foreign lands and peoples (which is the same as *conquering* them)." Kant's theory of cosmopolitanism regards the global order as a community in which "a transgression of rights in *one* place in the world is felt *everywhere*."[16] As Susan M. Shell demonstrates in her contribution to this volume, Kant mixes his cosmopolitan view of the nation-state with a "religion of humanity": "In infusing the nation-state (and Europe generally) with an informing spiritual goal (that they had lacked in earlier liberal formulations), Kant breaks with earlier liberal thought by bringing a sort of 'religion of humanity' into the public sphere." Once again, however, we are forced to ask about the relationship between the ethical, political, and religious concepts of community in Kant's work.

Community in the *Critique of Judgment*

Within the *Critique of Judgment*, the most important discussion of community has to do with what Kant calls the *sensus communis* and the question of the universal communicability of our judgments of taste. Judgments of beauty, according to the third *Critique*, are always reflective judgments. They arise out of the free play of the faculties of imagination and understanding in making judgments about particulars for which there are no concepts, in contrast to determinate judgments that always move from concepts to particulars. The free play of imagination and understanding provide the basis for the universal validity of judgments of taste. Every judgment of taste assumes that others would likewise experience the free play of imagination and understanding when making judgments of taste about a beautiful phenomenon, that everyone would judge such an object as beautiful. Thus judgments of taste always implicitly refer to a virtual community of judges, which Kant calls a *sensus communis*. Kant argues that the possibility of the universal communicability of our judgments is always bound up in judgments of taste, and that an experience of pleasure results from our capacity as social beings to communicate with others.

Kant believed not only that his critical system reached its end with the *Critique of Judgment*, but that judgment was a key link between theoretical and practical reason. Whether Kant succeeds in unifying his philosophical system (and even precisely what that would mean) is highly contested. One could look at paragraph eighty-three of the section on teleological judgment, where Kant discusses forms of community that enable the purpose of culture for humanity—civil society and a cosmopolitan order of states—and in the argument in paragraph eighty-four that the final purpose of history cannot be human happiness but must be humanity under moral laws, thus showing that the supersensible realm is the final cause of the empirical realm, and so unifying the two.

Nevertheless, we find in Kant's discussion of the *sensus communis* an alternative to community understood as a realm of ends. Judgments of taste are the activities of a "situated" reason concretely embedded among sensory

objects (though not dependent upon them), yet involving imaginary rec-
ollections or productions of beauty not reducible to the chain of causality.
Their claims to universality rest on the activities of the cognitive faculties of
human beings, and are not based on supersensible acts of will complying with
moral law. This does not mean, however, that aesthetics abandons claims to
universality. Kant's antinomy of taste indicates the universal and particular
moments of judgments of taste: "Everyone has his own taste." "There is no
disputing taste" (*Critique of Judgment*, 5:338). In her essay in this volume,
Jane Kneller counters purely formalist accounts of Kant's theory of aesthetic
reflection, emphasizing instead the "profound contingency and unique character of aesthetic reflection." Furthermore, Kneller argues that Kant's theory
of judgments of taste enables us to conceptualize the experience of what
she terms "judgments of community"—community experiences that create
a communicable feeling of pleasure when contemplated. Judgments of taste
appeal to a communal reason that is implicitly dialogic, for their validity can
only be decided with reference to the judgments of others. Yet Jan Mieszkowski, in his contribution to this volume, questions the status of communication in Kant's aesthetic community, challenging interpretations of the
sensus communis that regard it as primarily a matter of communicability.

Moreover, there have even been important arguments for the political
relevance of the *sensus communis*. Hannah Arendt has been an important
advocate of the claim that the idea of the *sensus communis* lies at the foundation of Kant's political philosophy. In her *Lectures on Kant's Political Philosophy*, she argues that reflexive judgments create a political community out of
a specific form of political reason.[17] The contributions from Kneller, Payne,
and Mieszkowski, however, explore the possible alternative understandings
of community to which a focus on Kant's aesthetic community gives rise.
What are the specific characteristics of this community, and to what extent
can we understand the aesthetic community as a political community? For
instance, Charlton Payne's essay argues that, if we follow Arendt's reading,
the *sensus communis* offers a rather limited vision of political activity that
reduces participation within the political community to the role of spectatorship. With regard to Arendt's denigration of feeling in judgment, Kneller
emphasizes Kant's reference to feeling in judgments of taste or community.
And, as mentioned above, Mieszkowski challenges Arendt's equation of the
sensus communis with communication. The serious engagement of each essay
with Arendt's reading demonstrates the importance of her arguments for
contemporary discussions about aesthetic and political community.

All in all, we hope that this collection of essays shows the thriving state of
Kant scholarship at the present time and encourages readers to explore some of
the issues raised in this volume in greater depth. To this end, we have included
in the bibliography a selection of recent works on community in Kant. We

also believe that the essays included here show the central relevance of Kant and his concept of community for contemporary debates in a host of different fields. Kant is a systematic philosopher, and we suggest that his systematicity can be used as a thread to hold some of these seeming disconnected debates together.

Notes

1. Reinhard Brandt, *The Table of Judgments: Critique of Pure Reason A 67–76; B 92–101*, trans. Eric Watkins (Atascadero, CA: Ridgeview, 1995), 3.

2. This *theological* ideal of a kingdom of heaven should be sharply distinguished from the *religious* ideal of an "ethical community" discussed in *Religion*.

3. This idea should be distinguished from the idea of an ethical community introduced in *Religion*.

4. Or as a community of angels, where angels are understood as beings without needs. Kant often talks of angels, but this does not mean that he is in any way committed to the existence of angels. Instead, he thinks that the *idea* of an angel, or holy being, plays an essential role in our ethical thinking as an ideal. Similarly, our idea of heaven plays an important role as an ideal for Kant, but this is not to say that he believes in the existence of heaven. For the later Kant, metaphysical speculation has to do with the analysis of our ideas, not knowledge of the (putative) objects of these ideas.

5. Paul Guyer, *Kant and the Claims of Knowledge* (Cambridge: Cambridge University Press, 1987), 452.

6. Jonathan Bennett, *Kant's Analytic* (Cambridge: Cambridge University Press, 1966), 289.

7. T. E. Wilkerson, *Kant's Critique of Pure Reason: A Commentary for Students*, 2nd ed. (Bristol: Thoemmes Press, 1998), 70.

8. See Eric Watkins, *Kant and the Metaphysics of Causality* (Cambridge: Cambridge University Press, 2005), 185–229. Béatrice Longuenesse, *Kant and the Capacity to Judge* (Cambridge: Cambridge University Press, 1998), 375–93. Jeffrey Edwards, *Substance, Force, and the Possibility of Knowledge: On Kant's Philosophy of Material Nature* (Berkeley: University of California Press, 2000), 23–48.

9. Traditionally eighteenth-century German metaphysics was divided into general metaphysics (ontology) and special metaphysics, which consisted of three different sciences, each of which dealt with its own object: rational psychology, rational cosmology, and rational theology.

10. Kant calls our idea of a world "the intelligible world." In the *Critique of Pure Reason* he claims that "the *mundus intelligibilis* is nothing but the concept of a world in general, abstracting from all [i.e., spatio-temporal] conditions of intuiting it" (A433, B461). He makes a similar point in his metaphysics lectures from the same period when he claims that "a foreigner called it fantasy to speak of the *intelligible world (mundo intelligibili)*." But this is just the opposite, for *one understands by it not another world, but rather this world as I think of it through the understanding*" (*Metaphysik Mrongovius*, 29:850; emphasis added). All citations from Kant are located by volume

and page number of *Kants gesammelte Schriften*, ed. Königlich Preußische Akademie der Wissenschaften, 29 vols. (Berlin: de Gruyter, 1900–). The *Critique of Pure Reason* is cited by the page numbers of the first A and/or second B editions. Unless otherwise indicated, all translations are from *The Cambridge Edition of the Works of Immanuel Kant*, 13 vols., ed. Paul Guyer and Allen W. Wood (Cambridge: Cambridge University Press, 1992–), including *Practical Philosophy*, trans. and ed. Mary J. Gregor (1996); *Religion and Rational Theology*, ed. Allen W. Wood and George di Giovanni (1996); *Critique of Pure Reason*, ed. Paul Guyer and Allen W. Wood (1998); and *Critique of the Power of Judgment*, ed. Paul Guyer (2000). Since the Cambridge edition includes the Academy edition pagination in its margins, separate page numbers for the translations will not be given.

11. "The world is thus a substantial whole (*totum substantiale*), hence not merely ideal. We can think of diverse ideal wholes (*tota idealia*), but they do not constitute a world; e.g., I can represent to myself s syllogistic whole (*totum syllogismorum*), an accidental whole (*totum accidentale*), or a whole in space, etc., but these are mere ideal wholes (*tota idealia*), which consist of concepts. But the world is a real whole (*totum reale*), which consists of concepts" (*Metaphysic Mrongovius*, 29:851).

12. Thus, in a letter to Dangicout written shortly before his death, Leibniz writes, "Intellectual wholes have parts only potentially. . . . It is like unity in Arithmetics which is also an intellectual or ideal whole divisible into parts, such as into fractions for example, not actually in itself, otherwise it would be reducible into minimal parts which are not to be found in numbers, so as to produce assigned fractions. I therefore say that matter which is something actual is a result only of monads by which I mean simple, indivisible substances, but extension or geometrical magnitude is not composed of possible parts that can only be assigned there, nor is it resoluble into points, and points too are only extremities and must not be taken for parts or components of the line." Quoted from Jean-Baptiste Rauzy, "Leibniz on Body, Force, and Extension," in *Proceedings of the Aristotelian Society* 105, part 3 (1995): 382.

13. Such a reading of coercion in Kant has recently been defended by Arthur Ripstein. See Arthur Ripstein, "Authority and Coercion," in *Philosophy & Public Affairs* 32, no. 1 (2004): 2–35; Arthur Ripstein, "Kant's Legal and Political Philosophy," in *A Companion to Kant's Ethics*, ed. T. Hill (Oxford: Blackwell, 2009), 161–78; Arthur Ripstein, *Force and Freedom: Kant's Legal and Political Philosophy* (Cambridge: Harvard University Press, 2009).

14. "In terms of physical forces [i.e., on the phenomenal level], the payment of a debt is nothing else but an action *commissiva*" (27:512).

15. *Perpetual Peace and Other Essays*, trans. Ted Humphrey (Indianapolis: Hackett, 1983), 118.

16. Ibid., 119.

17. Hannah Arendt, *Lectures on Kant's Political Philosophy* (Chicago: University of Chicago Press, 1989).

I

KANT'S STANDPOINT ON THE WHOLE

DISJUNCTIVE JUDGMENT, COMMUNITY, AND THE THIRD ANALOGY OF EXPERIENCE

BÉATRICE LONGUENESSE

Kant claimed that the representation of the world by human beings depends on a system of fundamental categories or "pure concepts of the understanding." He also claimed that these categories are originally nothing other than elementary logical functions, which find expression in logical forms of judgment. Kant expounded these functions in a systematic "table" that then became the architectonic principle not only for the *Critique of Pure Reason* but also for the *Critique of Practical Reason* and the *Critique of Judgment*. In a famous footnote to the *Metaphysical Foundations of the Science of Nature* (1783), Kant claimed that as long as one accepted the two cornerstones of his doctrine—the merely sensible, receptive character of our intuitions, for which space and time are *a priori* forms; and the derivation of categories from logical functions of judgment—then it mattered little if the details of his proofs (in particular, the details of his transcendental deduction of the categories) failed to carry complete conviction in the minds of his readers, for the two main points of his demonstration, as far as he was concerned, were sufficiently established. Those two points are that (1) we have *a priori* concepts of objects originating in the understanding alone, and (2) these concepts can be applied in cognition only to appearances (that is, to objects given in accordance with the *a priori* forms of space and time), not to things as they are in themselves.[1]

The problem is that precisely the two purported pillars of the critical system are what consistently met, very early on, with the most radical skepticism on the part of Kant's readers. Kant's logic is charged with being archaic, caught within the narrow bounds of Aristotelian predicative logic. It is also charged with psychologistic fallacy: Kant is mistaken in supposing that logical forms are in any sense at all descriptions of acts of our minds. As for the role he assigns to *a priori* forms of intuition in grounding synthetic *a priori* judgments, Kant is charged with relying on a conception of arithmetic and geometry made obsolete by the development of non-Euclidean geometries and modern quantificational logic; he is also charged with a misguided absolutization of a Newtonian model of natural science made obsolete by revolutions in nineteenth- and twentieth-century physics.

In the present paper, I shall examine Kant's claims concerning the second of the two cornerstones mentioned above: the derivation of categories from logical functions. To do this I shall focus on one particular case: the category of community, its relation to the logical function of disjunctive judgment, and its application to appearances in the so-called Principle of Community, namely, the Third Analogy of Experience. This case is interesting for two main reasons. First, it is the most difficult to defend. Kant himself was aware of this, and took great pains to explain why even in this case, however implausible it might seem, the relation he maintained between logical functions and categories does in fact hold. The general view of Kant commentators, however, is that his defense remains utterly unconvincing. I shall argue, on the contrary, that the correspondence Kant wants to establish between the logical function of disjunctive judgment and the category of community is an important and interesting one, although indeed it is more complex than any other. But this very complexity is in fact my second reason for focusing on this case: what makes the category of community difficult to grasp is that it can be understood only in connection with the other two categories of relation (and even with the previous two "titles" of categories, quantity and quality). This being so, examining Kant's argument in this case should also give us some insight into his overall argument on the relation between logical functions, categories, and the application of categories to appearances.

In the first part of my paper, I shall briefly expound the relation Kant claims to establish between logical functions of judgment and categories. In the second part, I shall examine Kant's logical form of disjunctive judgment and its relation to the category of community or universal interaction. In the third part, I shall examine Kant's proof of the Third Analogy of Experience, namely, his proof that necessarily, things we perceive as simultaneously existing exist in relations of universal interaction or, in Kant's terms, of dynamical community.

The lesson of this examination, I shall suggest, is that neither Kant's general claim concerning the role of logical functions of judgment in generating our representations of objects, nor even his more particular claim concerning the relation between the form of disjunctive judgment and the category of community, deserve the summary dismissal they are often met with. Rather, Kant's argument provides an intriguing account of how elementary functions of minds such as ours might be responsible for the unity of our unsophisticated, ordinary perceptual world, as well as for the relation between this world and our more sophisticated, scientific worldview.

Finally, in the fourth and concluding part I shall suggest that paying the attention it deserves to the Third Analogy (the "principle of community"), and not just to the better known Second Analogy (Kant's response to Hume on the concept of cause and its objective validity), will give us important insights into the unity of Kant's critical system as well as its relation to its philosophical posterity.

Logical Functions and Categories: The Understanding as a Capacity to Judge (*Vermögen zu urteilen*)

In the *Critique of Pure Reason*, Kant explains that the understanding, or intellect as a whole—the intellectual faculty at work in forming concepts, combining them in judgments, combining judgments in inferences, and finally constituting systems of knowledge—the intellect that produces all this is essentially a *Vermögen zu urteilen*, a capacity to form judgments.[2] In other words, describing the features of the intellect that make it capable of forming judgments is by itself describing just those features that also make it capable of forming concepts, inferences, systems of thought and knowledge. This is because, as Kant puts it in the section that precedes his table of logical functions of judgment, if we start with the traditional notion that the understanding is a capacity for concepts, we soon find, upon examination, that we form concepts only for use in judgments, and this use itself involves implicit inferential patterns and their systematic arrangement.

Kant's explanation of this point can be summarized as follows. Concepts, as he defines them, are "universal and reflected representations." They are formed by comparing individual objects, focusing on the common features or marks of these objects and ignoring their differences. A concept is thus a conjunction of common marks under which one may recognize a class of objects as falling under the same concept. But this means that forming concepts is forming implicit judgments: for instance, forming the concept "tree" is forming the implicit judgment, "everything that has a trunk, branches, and roots, is a tree" (and conversely, "everything that is a tree has a trunk, branches, and roots"). On the other hand, forming such a judgment is forming the major premise for a possible syllogistic inference, for instance, "everything that has a trunk, leaves, and roots, is a tree; this tiny thing here has a trunk, branches, roots; therefore it is a tree." Judgments and syllogistic inferences, systematically arranged, give rise to universal hierarchies of genera and species under which individual things are classified into natural kinds; thus they give rise to systematic knowledge.

It is by virtue of their *form* that judgments can thus be the source of the systematic unity of knowledge. What Kant calls the form of a judgment is the way concepts are combined in judgment.[3] When we analyze the "mere form" of judgment, we have to consider concepts themselves as to their "mere form"; namely, their universality: their being combinations of marks common to a multiplicity of individual objects.[4] The "form" of a judgment is thus the way in which concepts, as universal representations, are combined in it. Kant's table of logical forms of judgment[5] is a table of just those modes of combination of concepts that are minimally necessary for the functions of intellect briefly outlined above to emerge: subsumption of individual objects under concepts, syllogistic inference, the systematic arrangement of knowledge and thought. I now want briefly to review this table, with only the degree of detail necessary to situate the particular function of disjunctive judgment within it.

Recall that concepts, in Kant's logic, are defined as "universal and reflected representations" (that is, as universal representations formed by comparing objects, selecting common marks, leaving aside particular marks by which the objects thought under the same concept nevertheless differ from each other). So considered, the kinds of combinations that concepts may enter into in judgment are exclusively what Kant calls "concept subordinations," where the extension of one concept (everything that falls under the concept) is, as a whole or only in part, included in, or excluded from, the extension of the other. The first two titles in Kant's table (quantity and quality, in their first two moments: universal and particular, affirmative and negative) describe precisely the four possible cases just mentioned: inclusion of the extension of a concept in the extension of the other, or exclusion there from (affirmative or negative judgment, *as are b* or *as are not b*), in totality or in part (universal or particular judgment, all/no *as are b*, some *as are/are not b*).[6] To these four possible combinations that exhaust the possible cases of concept subordination, Kant adds, under each of the first two titles (quantity and quality), a form of judgment that relates concept subordination to individual objects (singular judgment under the title of quantity), and to the unified logical space within which all spheres of concepts reciprocally limit each other ("infinite" judgment, A is not-B), respectively.

The *raison d'être* for the third title, that of "relation," is more difficult to elucidate. Kant notes that a judgment, considered according to the forms of relation, combines two concepts (categorical judgments) or two judgments (hypothetical judgment, where the connective is "if . . . then") or several judgments (disjunctive judgment, where the connective is "either . . . or").[7] This is hardly any explanation at all. We can do better if we consider the relation of judgment to syllogistic inference mentioned above. We saw that combining concepts in a universal *categorical* judgment (all As are B) was *eo ipso* obtaining the premise for a syllogistic inference in which one might attribute the predicate B to anything thought under the subject-concept A. This is why Kant calls a universal categorical judgment a *rule*, and the subject-concept in such a judgment the *condition* of a rule (for instance, the concept "man" functions as a condition of the rule "all men are mortal"). The term "condition" should here be understood as meaning "sufficient," not "necessary," condition: that some entity *x* be a man is a sufficient condition for its being mortal. Or, if *x* is a man, then *x* is mortal. Since being a man is a sufficient condition for being mortal, subsuming any individual *x* under the concept "man" provides a sufficient reason for asserting of it that it is mortal.[8]

However, there are other kinds of conditions for a rule. One is that of hypothetical judgment, the second title of relation in Kant's table. According to this form, a concept is not *by itself, on its own*, the condition for attributing a certain mark to an object thought under the concept. Instead, one can do so only *under an added condition*: "If *c* is *d* [added condition], then *a* is *b*" (and thus any object *x* subsumed under the concept *a* receives the predicate *b* under the added condition that some relevant *c* is *d*). Kant's example is the proposition: "If there is perfect justice, then the obstinately wicked will be punished." (Implicit possible subsumption: any individual falling under the concept "wicked" is doomed to be punished, *under the added condition* that the state of the world be one of perfect justice.) Or, to take up an example Kant uses in the *Prolegomena*, "If the sun shines on a stone, the stone gets warm." (Implicit possible subsumption: any individual falling under the concept "stone" gets warm, *under the added condition* that the stone be lit by the sun.)[9]

A third kind of condition for a rule is that expressed in a disjunctive judgment. The proper function of this form of judgment is to recapitulate, as it were, the possible specifications of a concept. According to this form, one *divides* a concept, say *a*, into mutually exclusive specifications of this concept, say *b, c, d, e*: *a* is either *b*, or *c*, or *d*, or *e*. There are two different ways in which one might consider it as a possible rule for subsumption, and thus a rule by virtue of which one might attribute some predicate to any individual thought under the condition of the rule. One is to say that the subject of the disjunctive judgment, say *a*, is the condition of the rule "*a* is either *b*, or *c*, or *d*, or *e*," so that being thought under *a* is a sufficient condition for being thought as falling under either *b*, or *c*, or *d*, or *e*. But this is not terribly informative. A more interesting way (corresponding to the classical inferences in *modus ponendo tollens* or *modus tollendo ponens*) is to consider the assertion of any one of the specifications (*b, c, d, or e*) of the divided concept *a*, as a sufficient condition for negating the others, and conversely considering the negation of all but one as a sufficient condition for asserting the remaining one: *a* is *b* under the condition that it be neither *c*, nor *d*, nor *e*; *a* is neither *c*, nor *d*, nor *e*, under the condition that it be *b*; and so on.[10] Note also the close connection between the forms of disjunctive and infinite judgment: these forms jointly contribute to the constitution of a unified logical space within which concepts delimit one another's sphere, and thus contribute to the determination of one another's meaning.

About the fourth title, that of modality, Kant explains that it does not add to the "content" of judgments. What Kant seems to mean is that the modal determinations of judgment do not determine a specific difference in the function of judging—by contrast with quantity, according to which one subordinates *all* or *part* of the extension of two concepts; quality, according to which the extension of the subject-concept is *included in* or *excluded from* the extension of the predicate-concept; relation, according to which one states that the predicate concept can be asserted of individual objects *under the condition that the subject-concept* itself be asserted of them, or *under an added condition*, expressed in the antecedent of a hypothetical judgment. Instead, the modality of a given judgment expresses only "its relation to the unity of thought in general." Correspondingly, Kant's modality of judgments finds no particular linguistic expression, contrary to quantity ("all" or "some"), quality ("is" *simpliciter* or "is *not*"), and relation ("is," "if . . . then," "either . . . or"). Instead, in the examples Kant gives for "problematic," "assertoric," or "apodeictic" judgments, modality is marked by no particular modifier but consists, he says, merely in the "value of the copula" in the judgment, as determined by its place in a hypothetical or disjunctive judgment or in syllogistic inferences.[11]

These remarks are certainly too brief to give a full account, even less an evaluation, of Kant's table. My hope is that they at least shed some light on the systematic character and, in the end, the simplicity of Kant's table: it displays forms (1) of concept subordination (first two moments of quantity and quality), (2) under either an "inner" or an "outer" condition (first two moments of relation), which also takes into account (3) the subsumption of singular objects under concepts (singular judgments, third moment of quantity), and (4) the unity of concept subordination in a system of genera and species (infinite and disjunctive judgments, third moments of quality and relation). Finally, (5) the place of each judgment in other judgments or in inferences (its "relation to thought in general") determines its modality. It is no whimsical choice on Kant's part to have presented these forms as a table. The tabular presentation makes perspicuous "at one glance" the systematic whole of elementary logical functions at work for the production of any of the judgments by means of which individual objects given in sensibility are subsumed under concepts.

Kant calls *analysis* the use we make of the understanding according to the logical forms laid out in his table. By analysis here he does not mean simply or even primarily analysis of *concepts*, i.e., the laying out of the marks that constitute the content of a given concept. He means the analysis of representations given in sensibility so as to *generate concepts from them*, by means of the aforementioned operations: comparing individual objects, focusing on common features or marks of these objects, and setting aside their differences.[12] Now, such analysis presupposes that the objects in question are combined together in some way, in order to be thus compared and subsumed under concepts. And not only this: they need to be recognized as a plurality of individual things that remain identical through time. For this, much more than simply bringing together objects for comparison is needed. What is needed is a process of generating the representation of these objects themselves as numerically identical individuals persisting through time. And for this, our representation of space and time themselves need to be unified and ordered. All of these operations of bringing together and ordering (which I list here in a regressive order, from the more derivative to the more *ursprünglich*): (1) *bringing together* individual things for comparison, (2) *generating the representation* of these individual things as numerically identical and persisting through time, (3) *bringing together the manifold of space and time* themselves—all of these operations Kant calls *synthesis*. For any *analysis* leading to concepts to take place, *synthesis* must already have taken place. And given that analysis proceeds according to the logical functions of judgment, synthesis too must take place in such a way that what is synthesized becomes susceptible to being brought under concepts according to the logical functions of judgment.

This relation between analysis and synthesis, finally, provides the key to Kant's definition of the categories. They are, he says, "universal representations of pure synthesis," or, according to the more extensive definition of the B edition, they are "concepts of an object, by means of which the intuition of this object is taken to be determined with respect to one of the logical functions of judgment."[13] This means two things: (1) categories are concepts that *guide* the syntheses of spatio-temporal manifolds *toward* analysis according to the logical functions of judgment; (2) categories are, like any other concept, "universal and reflected representations." What they "universally reflect," however, are not empirical features of objects, but just those syntheses by means of which manifolds given in (pure or empirical) intuition become susceptible to being reflected under concepts combined according to logical functions of judgment.

I said a moment ago that Kant's table of logical functions was meant to make available "at one glance" the system of elementary logical functions necessary to generate the least empirical judgment by means of which empirical objects are subsumed under concepts. I also suggested that the specific role of infinite and disjunctive judgments is to relate all concept subordination to the unified logical space within which concepts reciprocally delimit each other's sphere and meaning. If I am right, this means that correspondingly, the specific *synthesis* corresponding to these logical forms will be a synthesis by means of which the totality of objects belonging to a common logical sphere are reflected under concepts. The logical form of disjunctive judgment, and the corresponding category of community, thus provide the general structure, or ordering function, for the *standpoint on the whole* in the context of which any cognitive function is performed. I now want to show what this means by considering more closely Kant's exposition of the relation between logical form of disjunctive judgment and category of community.

Disjunctive Judgment and the Category of Community (*Gemeinschaft, Wechselwirkung*)

There are two ways in which Kant might choose to characterize the form of disjunctive judgment. He could characterize it by focusing on the relation of concepts considered in their *content*, or intension, and say that a concept *a* is determined, that is, specified, either by the specific mark *b* or by the specific mark *c*—for instance, an animal is either a human being or a beast, a rational or a nonrational animal. Or he might characterize the form of disjunctive judgment by focusing on the *extension* of concepts and say that in a disjunctive judgment, one states that a concept *a*, considered in its extension or sphere, is divided into two mutually exclusive and exactly complementary spheres, the sphere thought under concept *ab* and the sphere thought under concept *ac*.

Kant chooses the second description of the form of disjunctive judgment, focusing on the *extension* of concepts. This is particularly explicit in the *Jäsche* logic as well as in the *Reflexionen* on logic from the critical period. There Kant pictures the disjunctive judgment "*a* is either *b*, *c*, *d*, or *e*" by the division of a rectangular area *a* (representing the extension of the divided concept *a*) into four regions, *b*, *c*, *d*, and *e* (that respectively represent the extensions of the species of *a*). In a disjunctive judgment, says Kant, any "*x* thought under the concept *a*" belongs to one or the other of the divisions *b*, *c*, *d*, or *e*. He prefaces this explanation by a comparison between categorical and disjunctive judgment:

> In categorical judgments, *x*, which is contained under *b*, is also contained under *a*: In disjunctive ones, *x*, which is contained under *a*, is contained either under *b* or *c*, etc. Thus the division in disjunctive judgments indicates the coordination not of the parts of the whole concept, but rather of all the parts of its sphere.[14]

In the *Critique of Pure Reason*, Kant draws a surprising parallel between this logical form and the category of community: just as in a disjunctive judgment, the sphere of a concept (the class of objects thought under this concept) is divided into its subordinate spheres, so that these subordinate spheres are in a relation of mutual determination while at the same time excluding one another, so in a material whole, things mutually determine one another, or even in one material thing or body considered as a whole, the parts are in a relation of mutual attraction and repulsion.

> To gain assurance that [the category of community and the form of a disjunctive judgment] do actually accord, we must observe that in all disjunctive judgments the sphere (that is, the multiplicity [*Menge*] of everything that is contained under [the divided concept]) is represented as a whole divided into parts (the subordinate concepts); and that since no one of them can be contained under any other, they are thought as co-ordinated with, not subordinated to, each other, and so as determining each other, not in one direction only, as in a series, but reciprocally, as in an aggregate—if one member of the division is posited, all the rest are excluded, and conversely.
>
> Now in a *whole* which is made up of *things*, a similar connection (*Verknüpfung*) is being thought; for one thing is not subordinated, as effect, to another, as cause of its existence, but, simultaneously and reciprocally, is co-ordinated with it, as cause of the determination of the other (as, for instance, in a body the parts of which reciprocally attract and repel each other). (B112)[15]

What is surprising here is that Kant appears to assimilate a logical relation between concepts and a material relation between things: the mutual exclusion and complementarity of spheres or extensions of concepts is assimilated to the mutual determination, as by attraction and repulsion, of material bodies or parts of material bodies.

But this can't possibly be right. Assimilating in this way the relation of mutually exclusive concepts in a disjunctive judgment and the relation of things belonging to one world whole, or of parts making up one material thing, is *prima facie* precisely the kind of move Kant rejects throughout the *Critique*. As he insists in the Appendix (to the Transcendental Analytic) on the Amphiboly of Concepts of Reflection, this rejection is the core of his opposition to Leibnizian rationalist metaphysics. Leibniz's major metaphysical mistake, according to Kant, is to have thought that things could be distinguished and determined by concepts alone, specified all the way down to individuals, so that the latter are completely determined as *infimae species*, lowest specifications of concepts. Against this view Kant maintains, in the Amphiboly chapter, that two drops of water, for instance, may be identical as to their concepts; namely, as to the discursive representation of their internal determinations of shape, size, and quality, and nevertheless be numerically distinct, solely by virtue of their position in space.[16] Similarly, any two surfaces may be identical to one another as to their concept; namely, their internal determinations of size and shape, and nevertheless be numerically distinguished by their position in space as a whole.

Now, it seems that the parallel Kant draws, in the metaphysical deduction of the categories, between the logical relation of mutually exclusive and complementary concepts in disjunctive judgment on the one hand, and the relation of things expressed in the category of community on the other hand, is just the Leibnizian error Kant denounced in the Amphiboly chapter. This impression is only enhanced by the fact that in the text quoted earlier, Kant describes the reciprocal action between parts of things in terms of attraction and repulsion; namely, in terms of precisely the kind of external relation that he insists is quite distinct from the relation of internal determinations expressed in a logical disjunction of completely determined concepts, as Leibniz would have it.[17] This being so, the skepticism or even derision frequently directed at Kant's claim concerning the parallel between logical form of disjunctive judgment and category of community seems to be a very healthy one indeed, *by the terms of Kant's own doctrine*. For if this parallel displays the very confusion Kant himself denounces in the Amphiboly chapter, there is every reason for discounting this particular correspondence between logical form and category.

However, I want to argue that this suspicion, despite its seeming plausibility, is unwarranted. Kant's point is not that relations of things in space (the *a priori* form of external sense) are essentially the same as relations of concepts in logical space. If we follow the general thrust of his metaphysical deduction of the categories, we should understand his point as being, rather, that *the same act of the mind* that, by means of *analysis*, generates the form of disjunctive judgment and eventually the form of a unified system of such judgments, also generates, by means of the *synthesis* of spatiotemporal manifolds, the representation of a community of interacting things or parts of things— "*for instance*" (B112, quoted above) the relations of reciprocal attraction and repulsion of parts in a material body. And indeed, this is what Kant writes:

> The same procedure the understanding observes when it represents to itself the sphere of a divided concept, *it also observes* in thinking a thing as divisible; and just as, in the former case, the members of a division exclude each other, and yet are combined in one sphere, so the understanding represents to itself the parts of the latter as such that existence pertains to each of them (as substances) to the exclusion of the others, even while they are combined together in one whole. (B113, emphasis mine)

Note here how systematic the correspondence is. Just as the understanding represents to itself the subspheres (the extensions of the subconcepts) of a divided concept as *excluding* one another (if one of the specifications is *asserted* of the divided concept, the others are *excluded*), so it represents to itself the *existence* of an individual substance as *excluding* the existence of all others (where one exists, no other can exist at the same time). Just as the subconcepts are represented as combined together in one whole, so the things or parts of things are represented as constituting one material whole.[18] However, this *similarity* in the relations represented by the understanding should not lead us to forget—on pain of amphiboly—the *dissimilarity* between the two cases: the individuation of *things* in space cannot be represented by way of the specification of *concepts*. What we want to know, then, is *how* this individuation is represented by the understanding. Kant's answer, according to the metaphysical deduction of the categories cited in part one of this paper, is that individuation of things in space is represented by way of the acts of *synthesis* that are necessary if any *analysis* of the sensible given into concepts is to be possible.

I intend to show that Kant's argument in the Third Analogy is meant to lay out just those acts of synthesis by way of which things are individuated in space and time. According to Kant, those acts of synthesis are acts by means of which things are represented as being in relations of universal causal interaction. Only insofar as they are so individuated can they also be thought under concepts of natural kinds ordered according to the form of disjunctive judgment (and a system of such judgments).

If this is correct, one can perhaps complete Kant's elliptic statement in the passages just cited by saying the following. For a Leibnizian, the similarity between the understanding's representation of the mutual relation of disjunctive spheres of a divided concept on the one hand, and the mutual relation of things or parts of things in space on the other hand—this similarity goes all the way down: individual things just *are* ultimate specification of concepts. For Kant, by contrast, although there is indeed the systematic similarity described above between the understanding's representation of the two relations, one of them—the relation of concepts—is thought by way of analysis (of the sensible given into concepts, of concepts into higher concepts); the other—the relation of things—is represented by way of *synthesis* of manifolds in space and time, a synthesis that results in presenting things as individuated in space by their relations of universal interaction.

One mistake we should not make in trying to understand Kant's point is to lay too much weight on the example he gives, that of the reciprocal attraction and repulsion of parts of material bodies. For this example belongs, strictly speaking, to the context of the *Metaphysical Foundations of the Science of Nature* rather than to that of the *Critique of Pure Reason*. In chapter two of the *Metaphysical Foundations*, Kant explains that the concepts of repulsive and attractive forces are applications of the categories of reality and limitation to the empirical concept of matter as "the movable insofar as it fills space." In chapter three, he explains that the Newtonian principle of equality of action and reaction in the communication of motion is an application of the category of community (reciprocal action) to the empirical concept of matter as "the movable insofar as it is something having a moving force."[19] This means that, in order to form empirical concepts such as those of attractive and repulsive force, and to obtain the law of equality of action and reaction in the motions they generate, we must already possess the *a priori* concept of reciprocal action *and* presuppose the truth of the principle that all appearances are in universal relation of community or reciprocal action. I do not propose to examine Kant's argument on either of these points or to evaluate his claim concerning Newtonian science. What I do want to stress is that when Kant says, in the text of the *Critique* quoted earlier, that "the same procedure of the understanding" is at work in disjunctive judgment and in representing the parts of a material whole as being in reciprocal relations of attraction and repulsion, the point we should focus on is not the particular case of attraction and repulsion, but rather the general idea of *reciprocal action in general,* of which the action and reaction of moving forces (whether force of attraction or force of repulsion) is only a particular case. What we need to examine, then, is simply Kant's point that the same procedure of the understanding generates the logical form of disjunctive judgment and the representation of a thoroughgoing reciprocal action of substances, whatever the empirical determination of that reciprocal action happens to be.

Here again the Amphiboly chapter might help us clarify Kant's view—no longer as a warning against possible amphibolous interpretations of his point, but rather as a confirmation of the positive account I just gave of the correspondence between the logical disjunction of concepts and the category of community. Kant explains, in the Amphiboly, his opposition to Leibniz's view according to which substances are individuated by their internal determinations—determinations they have on their own, independently of any external relation to other substances. According to Kant, on the contrary, substances—material things whose essential properties persist while their accidental properties change—are recognized under concepts of *external* relations (mutual causal determination). This means, then, that the move from recognizing things as individuated in space and time, to thinking them under concepts of natural kinds, is a move from representing them in relations of *universal mutual interaction,* to thinking them under concepts of *relational properties.* Now, this is precisely the point Kant wants to *prove* in his argument for the Third Analogy of Experience: things are individuated in space and time and recognized under concepts only by their *relational* properties—properties that consist in their being related, by position and physical influx, to other things similarly individuated and recognized.[20]

Let me summarize my argument so far: it might seem that in relating the category of community, or universal interaction, to the logical form of disjunctive judgment, Kant is guilty of the very amphiboly that he denounces in Leibniz (confusion between the relation of mutual determination between spheres of *concepts* and the relation of mutual *causal* determination between *things*). However, I argue that Kant is *not* guilty of this confusion. Rather, Kant's point is that the concepts of natural kinds under which we know material things in nature (and thus, classify them under hierarchies of genera and species according to the form of disjunctive judgment) are concepts of *relational properties*—universal *causal interaction*. This being so, the category of *community*, Gemeinschaft, by virtue of which things are thought as belonging under one logical space of concepts, is also a category of *universal causal interaction, durchgängige Wechselwirkung*, by way of which they are thought as universally related in one empirical space (and time). To examine Kant's argument for this point, I now turn to the Third Analogy of Experience.

Kant's Proof of the Third Analogy: Simultaneity and Universal Interaction

In the Third Analogy of Experience, Kant argues that our experiencing the simultaneous existence of appearances is sufficient to attest that these appearances are in relations of thoroughgoing community (*Gemeinschaft*) or reciprocal action (*Wechselwirkung*). This is because, Kant argues, representing the simultaneous existence of appearances is *our doing*, and this representation is possible only if we represent appearances as being, with respect to one another, in relations of thoroughgoing reciprocal action. Thus the statement of the Analogy: "All substances, insofar as they can be perceived as simultaneous in space, are in thoroughgoing reciprocal action [*in durchgängiger Wechselwirkung*]."[21]

As students of Kant's Analogies of Experience know, the three Analogies should be read together as one argument that concerns the conditions of our representation of objective time determinations. Kant's question is: how do we come to have any representation at all of objective temporal determinations of appearances, since our apprehension of them is always successive, and since we have no given temporal framework that might allow us to situate events and states of affairs in time? In the Second Analogy, Kant explains how *subjective succession* in apprehension is interpreted as *objective succession* of states of things; in the Third Analogy, he explains how *subjective succession* in apprehension is interpreted as *objective simultaneity* of things and of their states. Prior to this, in the First Analogy he argued that any representation of objective temporal order (succession or simultaneity) rests on the *presupposition of something permanent*, as the substrate of objective temporal determinations. I do not propose here to evaluate Kant's overall argument in the Analogies of Experience.[22] What I am mainly concerned with is how discursive forms (forms of *analysis* or *reflection*) and forms of sensible *synthesis* relate, according to Kant, in the particular case of the Third Analogy.

Kant's reasoning proceeds, roughly, according to the following steps:[23]

1. The synthesis of our apprehension in imagination is always successive.[24]

2. We nevertheless perceive a subjective succession in apprehension as an objective simultaneity of things under specific states, if we are aware of the subjective succession as being order-indifferent. For example, we are aware that we could direct our gaze indifferently from the moon to the earth or from the earth to the moon; it is in this way that, even though we might never perceive at the same time the moon at its zenith and the surface of the earth, we do experience these objects as simultaneously existing.[25]

3. We have no perception of time itself that would allow us to derive from the simultaneity of objective states the order-indifference of subjective succession.[26]

4. Nor would the mere subjective succession suffice to generate either the representation of its order-indifference or the interpretation of this order-indifference as objective simultaneity. Subjective succession in apprehension would, by itself, give us only: one perception, then the other, and reciprocally, the latter, then the former. It would give use no access to the *simultaneity of things* as the necessary condition for the order-indifference of the perceptions.[27]

5. We are aware of the subjective succession as order-indifferent, and thus as a representation of objective simultaneity; just in case, in relating the subjective succession to objects, we form judgments such as: if object x (recognized under concept a) exists at time t at point $p1$, then object y (recognized under concept b) exists at that same time at point $p2$; and reciprocally, if the latter exists, then the former exists at the same time. We thus think x and y as being in themselves determined with respect to the logical form of a hypothetical judgment whose reciprocal converse is also thought to be true (if x, recognized under a, exists at $p1$ at t, then y, recognized under b, exists at $p2$ at t; and conversely if y recognized under b at $p2$ at t, then x under a at $p1$ at t). Thus a pure concept of the understanding is applied whenever we experience objective simultaneity.[28]

6. This concept is that of reciprocal action. Thus the simultaneity of substances in space can be known in experience (perceived) only under the presupposition that they are in relations of universal reciprocal action or community.[29]

7. So, all appearances, insofar as we perceive them as existing simultaneously, exist in relations of thoroughgoing reciprocal influence.[30]

Now, this conclusion is *prima facie* completely implausible. It is simply not true, one might object, that I perceive my desk and my chair as simultaneously existing only if I suppose a relation of interaction between them, and it is also not true that I perceive the earth and the moon as simultaneous only if I suppose reciprocal influence between them. However, this objection might be overcome if we remember that there is originally nothing more to the pure concept of cause than "the concept of an object, by means of which its intuition is regarded as *determined* with regard to . . . the logical function for hypothetical judgment."[31] Thus by "interaction" (namely, reciprocal *causal* action), Kant means nothing other than the relation between the states of one substance and the states of another, such that they can be regarded as *determined* with regard to the logical function of a hypothetical judgment whose reciprocal converse (the consequent taking the place of the antecedent, and reciprocally) is also taken to be true.

What Kant is saying is that interpreting two successively apprehended states, say *a*, *b*, as simultaneously existing states of objects, is thinking something like this: "If *x* (recognized under concept *a*) is part of the present whole of my experience, then *y* (recognized under concept *b*) is part of the same whole. And if *y* (recognized under concept *b*) is part of the whole of my present experience, then *x* (recognized under concept *a*) is part of the same whole." What we represent to ourselves as the *simultaneity* of things in space is then nothing other than the sensible (temporal) form; that is, the mode of ordering individuals in time, resulting from a *synthesis* guided by the capacity to *analyze* according to the discursive form of a hypothetical judgment whose reciprocal converse is also asserted to be true. In accordance with this discursive form, asserting the presence (existence, *Dasein*) of one of the objects perceived is represented as a sufficient condition for asserting the presence of the other, and conversely the presence of the latter is reflected as a sufficient condition for asserting the presence of the former. *Which* specific determinations condition one another (i.e., specifically *what* conditions *what*), we do not know. We shall acquire such determinate cognition only by means of the indefinite, never completed process of corrections and specifications of our discursive judgments in actual experience. Nevertheless, Kant's point is that this process finds its initial impulse in the mere consciousness of the *simultaneous existence of things in space*, because such consciousness *itself* already depends on a synthesis of sensible manifolds *guided by our capacity to judge*; namely, a synthesis oriented toward reflection according to the form of hypothetical judgments.[32]

Objects are thus individuated in space and time *by their reciprocal interaction*, and *concepts* of objects thus individuated are concepts of relational properties. The empirical-cognitive use of the form of disjunctive judgment has to be mediated by that of the form of hypothetical judgment, and thus the application of the category of community has to be mediated by that of *causal* interaction. This is why I said earlier that the category of community is the most complex of all. It cannot be understood *except* under the presupposition of the other relational categories, and thus under the presupposition of the empirical use of the logical forms *they* depend upon. I submit that this is why the third category of relation has two names: *Wechselwirkung* (reciprocal action, where the emphasis is on the relation of *causal* interaction) and *Gemeinschaft* (community, where the emphasis is on objects' belonging to one space, thus to one world whole and under one logical space of concepts).

Concluding Remarks

Kant's logic typically comes under heavy attack on two main grounds: it is suspiciously psychologistic and it is caught within the narrow bounds of an Aristotelian model of predication and syllogistic inference—a model relegated to irrelevance by Fregean/Russellian extensional logic. However, in light of the use Kant makes of his "logical functions of judgment" for solving the problems he addresses in the critical system, I would like to suggest that the charges of psychologism and archaism perhaps cancel each other. *Because* what Kant calls "pure general" or "formal" logic is exclusively concerned with the "universal rules of the understanding," and understanding is the faculty of *concepts* (defined as "universal and reflected representations"), Kant's logical forms of judgment are nothing but forms of concept subordination, and the forms of inference he is concerned with are merely the various ways in which concept subordination (*inclusion* or *exclusion* of the extensions of concepts, under an *internal* or *external* condition) allow for truth-preserving inference. And *because* his "pure general logic" is so narrowly defined, it can make a claim to being a description of the forms according to which minds such as ours are capable of making universal their representations—capable of combining their representations in such a way that they are susceptible to being reflected under concepts and thus related to objects, defined both *logically* as instances of concepts, and *intentionally* as what our representations are representations of (the intentional correlate of our representations). None of this makes Kant's "general pure logic" a part of psychology, for logic, as Kant puts it, is concerned not with the way we think, but with the way we *should* think: the normative rules of concept combination according to which our judgments are testable as to their truth and falsity.[33]

I pointed out earlier that in his explanation of logical forms of judgment—especially the form of disjunctive judgment—Kant gives pride of place to an *extensional* consideration of concepts and concept subordinations; that is, to the consideration of the classes or multiplicities (*Mengen*) of objects thought under concepts. This is because his main concern is to elucidate the ways in which forms of concept subordination are also forms according to which individual objects are subsumed under concepts, and thus extensions of concepts are constituted in the first place. And this in turn is related to the role Kant assigns to forms of intuition (space and time) as the forms according to which objects are individuated, distinguished from one another, and brought together, "synthesized" so that they become susceptible to being reflected under concepts. Examining and evaluating Kant's notion of a form of intuition is beyond the limits of this paper, as is examining Kant's account of the synthetic aprioricity of mathematics and its role in empirical science. Nevertheless, in light of my examination of Kant's logical form of disjunctive judgment and its relation to the category of community, I suggest that we should be attentive to the ways in which the notion of an *a priori* form *of intuition* is meant to account for an original capacity to represent (anticipate, generate) *homogeneous multiplicities* (multiplicities of objects thought under the same concept), just as Kant's table of logical functions is meant to account for an original capacity to form *universal concepts*. Kant did not anticipate logical or scientific revolutions to come, and certainly we have reason to wish he had been more circumspect in his remarks on Aristotelian logic, Euclidean geometry, or Newtonian science. But what he did provide was a striking model of how elementary functions of minds such as ours—functions of concept formation and functions of object individuation—might account for the unity of our unsophisticated, everyday perceptual world, and our sophisticated, scientific worldview.

He argued, moreover, that these same elementary functions, when related not to sensations, but to impulses and desires, are capacities to develop a moral standpoint (*Critique of Practical Reason*); and that both moral and theoretical standpoint are ultimately rooted in the peculiar nature of the living, pleasure-seeking, purposeful beings we are (*Critique of Judgment*). All three *Critiques* thus give us a view of human beings as having a peculiar capacity to develop what we might call a *standpoint on the whole*: a standpoint whose elementary discursive form is the form of disjunctive judgment, and whose grounding concept is that of community.

Just a few more words, before I close, about this concept of "community" and its further destiny in the critical system. In the first version of the Third Analogy, after developing his argument to the effect that substances are perceived as simultaneously existing only if they are in relations of universal reciprocal action, Kant notes that our own body is the mediator for our perception of the simultaneous existence of other bodies, or physical substances.

> From our experience it is easy to notice that only continuous influence in all places in space can lead our sense from one object to another, that the light that plays between our eyes and the heavenly bodies effects mediate community between

us and the latter and thereby proves the simultaneity of the latter, and that we cannot empirically alter any place (perceive this alteration) without matter everywhere making the perception of our position possible; and only by means of its reciprocal influence can it establish their simultaneity and thereby the coexistence of even the most distant objects (though only mediately).[34]

Because of this mediating role of our sensing body in our perception of the community of substances, the community of substances is also a community *of our standpoints* on substances, and on the world as a whole. Now, in the third *Critique*—the *Critique of Judgment*—Kant makes it one of the grounding maxims of the Enlightenment that we should strive to think "from the standpoint of everybody else." And he grounds our capacity so to think in what he calls a *Gemeinsinn*, a common sense, understood as *Gemeinschaftlicher Sinn*, a communal sense or one might say, a sense of community; namely, the capacity to develop a common standpoint on the whole (whether a common epistemic standpoint on the whole of objectively existing things, or a common normative/moral standpoint on the whole of interacting human beings). This *gemeinschaftlicher Sinn*, or sense of community, consists in our capacity to use imagination and understanding in such a way that each enhances the other in striving for a universal standpoint, albeit one premised on each of the particular standpoints we initially hold.[35]

We are more used to reading the critical system under the dominance of the concept of cause: from Kant's response to Hume's skeptical doubt in the first *Critique*, to his elaboration of the concept of free agency in the second *Critique*. And certainly, there is a lot to say for this line of reading. But I would like to suggest that from the community of substances in the first *Critique*, to the community of standpoints on substances, also in the first *Critique*, to the community of rational agents in the second *Critique*, to the *gemeinschaftlicher Sinn* of the third *Critique*, there is another line of reading, one that does not contradict the previous one but integrates it into a more complete view of Kant's philosophical project: relating, as he says, all cognition to "the essential purposes of human reason."[36]

Finally, I submit that it is also from the standpoint of this concept and its development throughout the critical system that we can best evaluate Kant's relation to his German idealist successors. It is quite striking, for instance, that in Hegel's *Phenomenology of Spirit* the progress from "Sense Certainty" to "Perception," to "Force and Understanding" (the first three chapters of the *Phenomenology*) be one in which we gradually become aware that only under a representation of universal interaction is the identification of any individual object of sense perception possible for a consciousness such as ours. Hegel thus appears to espouse just the kind of reasoning I have argued is Kant's own in the Third Analogy. And, like Kant, he goes on to examine what relations *between the conscious subjects themselves* are involved in the cognitive process just described (fourth chapter of the *Phenomenology*, "Self-Consciousness," and the dialectic of desire and recognition).

This being said, there are of course major differences between the ways each of them proceeds from there (not to mention the differences in the ways they arrive there). Where Kant thinks that the same discursive (intellectual) functions, by means of which we represent the community of spatiotemporal substances, can also serve to think a purely noumenal (atemporal and aspatial) region of being to which we belong as moral agents, Hegel, reasonably enough, denounces the hypostatization of an "inverted world" (end of the chapter on "Force and Understanding").[37] On the other hand, where Kant insists that our epistemic standpoint on the whole is irretrievably limited by the given spatiotemporal conditions of our human sensory knowledge, Hegel, unreasonably enough, strives to achieve a standpoint that would amount to "the presentation of God, as he is in his eternal essence before the creation of nature and of a finite spirit."[38] It is perhaps possible to interpret Hegel's grandiose statement as gesturing toward nothing more than some universal underlying logic of all concept formation and correction.[39] Just as it is perhaps possible to interpret Kant's talk of a "noumenal realm" as gesturing toward nothing more than our moral use of reason in achieving a fully autonomous determination of action. Perhaps we can come to this kind of reasonable reconstruction in both cases. Even so, I would suggest that the resistance Hegel opposes to Kant's "noumenal realm," on the one hand, and the resistance Kant opposes, preemptively as it were, to any ambition remotely resembling Hegel's logic of "absolute knowledge," are, from each of them respectively, a lasting legacy. But this is a matter for another paper.[40]

Notes

1. See *Metaphysische Anfangsgründe der Naturwissenschaft*, 4:475–76n; *Immanuel Kant, Metaphysical Foundations of Natural Science*, trans. J. W. Ellington (Indianapolis: Bobbs-Merrill, 1970), 11–14, n8. Works of Kant are cited from the Academy edition: *Kants gesammelte Schriften*, ed. Königlich Preußische Akademie der Wissenschaften, 29 vols. (Berlin: de Gruyter, 1900–) by abbreviated title, volume, and page number, followed by a reference in the relevant standard English translation. The *Critique of Pure Reason* is cited by the standard A and B pagination of the first (1781) and second (1787) editions.

2. See the *Critique of Pure Reason* (A69/B94, A81/B106).

3. See *Logik*, §18, 9:101; *The Jäsche Logic*, in *Lectures on Logic*, trans. J. Michael Young (Cambridge: Cambridge University Press, 1992), 518. See also *Refl.* 3039 and 3040, 16:628–29.

4. *Logik*, §2, §§4–8, 9:93–96, 591–94; *Refl.* 2855, 16:547; *Refl.* 2859, 16:549.

5. On Kant's notion of a "function" of judgment, see A68/B93. See also A70/B95. If we rely on Kant's explanations in these texts, logical *function* and logical *form* of

judgment seem to be distinguished as (1) the structure of an act—a structure that makes the act adequate to achieving a specific purpose, that of "ordering representations under a common representation," and (2) the result of the act: the mode of combination of concepts, or "form" of the judgment resulting from the act.

6. On these explanations and the privilege given to the point of view of *extension* in defining the form of judgment as to its quantity and quality, see *Logik*, §§21–22. Note that consideration of the *extension* of concepts, and of judgment as expressing the inclusion or exclusion of concepts' respective *extension* (*Umfang*), is also prominent in the explanations Kant gives in A71–72/B96–98.

7. A73/B98.

8. On the notion of the condition of a rule, see A322/B378; also *Logik*, §58, 9:120, 615. *Refl.* 3196–3202, 16:707–10. For a discussion of Kant's forms of relation in judgment, see Béatrice Longuenesse, *Kant et le pouvoir de juger* (Paris: Universitaires de France, 1993), 107–22, and Béatrice Longuenesse, *Kant and the Capacity to Judge* (Princeton: Princeton University Press, 1998), 93–104.

9. See *Prolegomena zu einer jeden künftigen Metaphysik, die als Wissenschaft wird auftreten* können, 4:312; *Prolegomena To Any Future Metaphysics That Will Be Able To Come Forward As Science*, trans. Paul Carus, rev. James W. Ellington (Indianapolis: Hackett, 1977), 54–55.

It is important here to keep in mind that Kant's logical form of hypothetical judgment is significantly different from our modern truth-functional material conditional. For reasons of length I cannot develop this difference in any detail. At least I want to stress two points:

(1) The truth of Kant's hypothetical judgment is the truth of the *Konsequenz*: the judgment is true just in case there is between antecedent and consequent a connection such that asserting the former entails asserting the latter. The meaning of the connective "if . . . then" thus grounds inferences in *modus ponens*—the antecedent of a hypothetical judgment being posited in the minor premise ("*a* is *b*"), the consequent should be posited in the conclusion ("so, *c* is *d*"), and *modus tollens*—the consequent being negated in the minor premise ("*c* is not *d*"), the antecedent should be negated in the conclusion ("so, *a* is not *b*"); (2) the two examples of hypothetical judgments I have just cited in the main text differ significantly from each other with respect to the nature of their *Konsequenz*, namely, the nature of the connection between antecedent and consequent. In the first ("If there is perfect justice, then the obstinately wicked will be punished"), the relation between the (added) condition ("there is perfect justice") and the conditioned ("the obstinately wicked will be punished") is analytic (it is part of our concept of perfect justice that the wicked be punished); in the second ("if the sun shines on a stone, the stone gets warm"), the *Konsequenz* is synthetic, and even a posteriori. This is why the question should be raised, according to Kant, of how the *Konsequenz* can nevertheless express a necessary connection. But of course this question is of no concern to "general pure" or "formal" logic. The latter considers only the form of judgment; namely, the nature of the connective and the forms of inference it grounds. On Kant's logical form of hypothetical judgment, see *Logik*,

§§25–26, 9:105–6, 601–2; Longuenesse, *Kant et le pouvoir de juger*, 118–22; and Longuenesse, *Kant and the Capacity to Judge*, 101–4. On the relation between hypothetical judgment and the concept of cause, see *Prolegomena*, §29, 4:312, 54–55; Longuenesse, *Kant et le pouvoir de juger*, 409–12; Longuenesse, *Kant and the Capacity to Judge*, 356–58.

10. Just as Kant's hypothetical judgment is different from our truth-functional material conditional, so Kant's disjunctive judgment is different from our truth-functional disjunction. First of all, as we just saw, Kant's disjunctive judgment is a disjunction *of predications*: a concept *a* is specified as either *b*, or *c*, or *d*, or *e* (and thus any object falling under a falls under either *b*, or *c*, or *d*, or *e*). Second, the disjunction is exclusive, not inclusive: what is asserted in a disjunctive judgment is that if one of the disjunct predicates belongs to the subject, then the others do not, and conversely. Thus the meaning of the connective "either . . . or" grounds the forms of inference in *modus ponendo tollens* and *tollendo ponens*: asserting one of the predicates is a sufficient reason for negating the others, negating all but one is a sufficient reason for asserting the remaining one.

11. See A74–76/B100–101.

12. On this notion of *analysis*, see A76/B102. So considered, analysis consists in the operations of "comparison, reflection, abstraction" described in *Logik*, §6, 9:94; *Refl.* 2876, 16:555.

13. See A78/B104; B128.

14. *Logik*, §29, 9:108, 604. See also *Refl.* 3096, 16:657–58.

15. When Kant talks about "the multiplicity contained in any one judgment" he means: the multiplicity *thought under each subspecies of the divided concept* (for instance, the multiplicity thought under *ab*, and the multiplicity thought under *ac*).

16. A264/B320. Cf. Gottfried Wilhelm Leibniz, *Nouveaux essais sur l'entendement humain*; *New Essays on Human Understanding*, trans. Peter Remnant and J. Bennet (Cambridge: Cambridge University Press, 1996), book 2, chap. 27, §3, 230–31.

17. See A265–66/B321, A274/B330. One may argue on Kant's behalf that he explains the form of disjunctive judgment in terms of the division of the *sphere* or *extension* of a concept into its subspheres, which is the division of a whole into its parts and thus grounds the parallelism with the division of a *whole of physical things* into its parts, or even the division of *one physical thing* into its parts (category of community). This is correct as far as it goes, but it is not sufficient to alleviate the charge of amphiboly. First, it remains that if things are represented as the ultimate parts of the *sphere of a concept*, then they are individualized as *ultimae species*, lowest specification of a concept, instead of being, as Kant claims they should be, individualized (represented as numerically distinct) by virtue of their position in space and time as forms of sensible intuition. Second, Kant invariably presents the category of community as a concept of the universal interaction of *empirical things*. We need more than a consideration of concepts according to their extension to explain how such an *interaction* might relate to the community of concepts under a higher concept, and thus clear Kant of the suspicion of amphiboly. And indeed, Kant does provide us with more justification than this, as I show below. See also Longuenesse, *Kant et le pouvoir de juger*, 375–93, and Longuenesse, *Kant and the Capacity to Judge*, 436–53.

18. I am grateful to Steve Engstrom for pressing me on this point and bringing to my attention the full measure of the structural similarities Kant underlines here. The limits of this paper unfortunately do not allow me to do full justice to the wealth of suggestions Engstrom offered me on this point.

19. See *Metaphysische Anfangsgründe der Naturwissenschaft*, 4:496–99, 544–47, 40–43, 106–9.

20. See A274–75/B330–31, A283–84/B339–40.

21. B256. In the first edition, the Analogy is stated as follows: "Principle of community. All substances, insofar as they are simultaneous, are in thoroughgoing community (i.e., reciprocal action among one another)." The formulation in B is superior in that it makes clearer that "simultaneous" means: "something *we* represent, or perceive, *as* simultaneous." Similarly, the argument in B is more clearly laid out as an argument about the conditions for *our* experiencing things *as* simultaneous. One may wonder how such conditions put any constraint at all on how things actually are. But the Transcendental Deduction is supposed to have established just this point: the conditions of possibility of experience are the conditions of possibility of the objects of experience. Evaluating the argument of the Deduction is of course beyond the scope of this paper. One should at least remember one essential aspect of its conclusion: the objects we are talking about here are objects *as appearances*—as individualized in space and time.

22. For an analysis and evaluation of Kant's Analogies of Experience, see Longuenesse, *Kant et le pouvoir de juger*, chap. 10; *Kant and the Capacity to Judge*, chap. 11.

23. There are two expositions of the argument in the Third Analogy. The first in A, remaining unchanged in B: A211/B258–A213/B260 (4:141[13]–42[14], 3:181[28]–82[26]). The second added in B: B256–58 (3:180[29]–81[27]). In my view, the exposition in B is the clearer of the two, for reasons similar to the ones I advocated in the previous note: the argument in B, just as the formulation of the Analogy itself, makes it clearer that what Kant is talking about are the conditions for *our experience of* objective simultaneity (which is also the only context in which the very notion of simultaneity has any meaning at all). In my reconstruction of the argument I will thus follow the order of the B edition. In an effort to limit the length of notes, I shall indicate the textual support for each step simply by the reference in B (for the 1787 version) and A/B (when the 1781 version provides useful additional textual support), and (in parentheses) the relevant pages and lines in AA 3. I shall not quote the texts themselves.

24. This premise is not explicitly stated in the argument of the B edition, but it is common to all three Analogies, and explicitly stated in the first and second: see A182/B225 (163[1–2]) (First Analogy), A189/B234 (167[20–21]), A198/B242 (172[13]) (Second Analogy); in the Third Analogy, this premise is implicit at B257 (181[2–5]).

25. B257 (180[29]–81[6]); A211/B258 (181[29–32]).

26. B257–258 (181[6–10]).

27. B257 (181[10–13]).

28. B257 (181[13–19]). In what I present as step 5, I am making explicit that the "pure concept of the understanding" needed to represent the reciprocal sequence as objective is the concept of an object, by means of which its intuition is considered as

determined with respect to the logical function of a hypothetical judgment together with its reciprocal converse. I hope to show later why it is helpful to stress this relation between the pure concept of the understanding and the corresponding logical function of judgment.

29. B257–258 (181[19–26]); also A212–13/B259–60 (182[11–21]).

30. B258 (181[26–27]); also A213/B259–60 (182[21–22]).

31. See above, note 13.

32. Note that Kant's reasoning here, just like his argument in the Second Analogy, displays a complex web of interdependence between subjective and objective temporality. On the one hand, awareness of the irreversibility or reversibility (order-determinateness or order-indifference) of the subjective succession of representations is *all* that perceiving (experiencing) the objective temporal order of appearances *amounts to*. So, the perception of *objective* temporal order depends on a specific feature of the *subjective* succession of representations. But on the other hand, what generates our awareness of such a feature of the subjective succession is just our act of relating our representations to an intentional object (an object they are the representation of). This is because relating our representations to objects is attempting to reflect objects under concepts according to the logical forms of categorical, hypothetical, and disjunctive judgment, and this in turn is what generates—depending on what is given to our senses—our awareness of the *irreversibility* of the subjective succession in case the pattern that emerges is that of a permanent object whose states change, or the *reversibility* of the subjective succession in case the pattern that emerges is that of several coexisting permanent objects whose states are interrelated. So, striving to relate representations to objects is what generates the awareness of the reversibility or irreversibility of the subjective succession, and this in turn is just what our awareness of the objective temporal order (succession *or* simultaneity of states of things) amounts to. Thus Kant's Analogies of Experience should be understood as being essentially an explanation of how we relate representations to objects in general: an explanation of intentionality and, *as a result*, a theory of what makes it possible to apply concepts such as those of causal connection and causal interaction to the objects of an empirical science of nature.

33. See A54/B78; also *Logik*, Einl. I, 9:14, 529.

34. A213/B260.

35. See *Kritik der Urteilskraft*, AAV, 293; *Critique of the Power of Judgment*, trans. Paul Guyer and Eric Matthews (Cambridge: Cambridge University Press, 2000), 173.

36. A839/B867.

37. Hegel, *Phenomenology of Spirit*, trans. A. V. Miller (Oxford: Oxford University Press, 1977), 79–105; G. W. F. Hegel, *Werke in Zwanzig Bänden*, vol. 3, *Phänomenologie des Geistes* (Frankfurt-am-Main: Suhrkamp Verlag, 1979), 107–36.

38. Hegel, *Science of Logic*, trans. A. V. Miller (New York: Humanities Press, 1976), 50; G. W. F. Hegel, *Werke in Zwanzig Bänden*, vol. 5, *Wissenschaft der Logik I*, 44.

39. This kind of reading is defended by Robert Brandom. See "Some Pragmatist Themes in Hegel's Idealism: Negotiation and Administration in Hegel's Account of the Structure and Content of Conceptual Norms," in *European Journal of Philosophy* 7, no. 2 (1999): 164–89.

40. See my "Point of View of Man or Knowledge of God: Kant and Hegel on Concept, Judgment, and Reason," in *The Reception of Kant's Critical System in Fichte, Schelling, and Hegel*, ed. Sally Sedgwick (Cambridge: Cambridge University Press, 2000), 253–83.

2

MAKING SENSE OF MUTUAL INTERACTION

SIMULTANEITY AND THE EQUALITY OF ACTION AND REACTION

ERIC WATKINS

The notion of community (*Gemeinschaft*), or mutual interaction (*Wechselwirkung*), has experienced a rather ambivalent reception in the scholarly literature devoted to Kant's thought. On the one hand, one must acknowledge that it is a central principle of Kant's entire Critical project. It is a pure concept of the understanding, or category, that he uses, along with the other categories (B109), to confer a distinctive formal structure onto both his theoretical and his practical philosophy in the *Critique of Pure Reason*, *Metaphysical Foundations of Natural Science*, and *Critique of the Power of Judgment*, as well as in the *Critique of Practical Reason* and *Metaphysics of Morals*.[1] It also plays an obvious and crucial role in the content of his moral philosophy, since the kingdom of ends referred to in one prominent formulation of the Categorical Imperative is nothing other than a particular kind of moral community (whose members are related by means of mutual love and respect); and it is not difficult to see, at least in principle, that it can take on a parallel function in his theoretical philosophy insofar as the world of experience, whose conditions he is exploring in the *Critique of Pure Reason*, is simply a world of mutually interacting objects (e.g., in the guise of Newtonian universal gravitation). It must therefore be admitted that an adequate understanding of Kant's philosophy requires a proper appreciation of the category of community as one of the fundamental concepts that he deploys in a comprehensive and systematic way throughout his Critical philosophy.

On the other hand, commentators have typically maintained that the category of community is—despite Kant's claims to the contrary—an optional, if not downright unfortunate, element of his philosophy. Many of the other categories, especially that of causality, have garnered significantly more attention as genuinely crucial components of his system, and it is a rather rare occurrence when commentators suggest that the category of community either has a special significance in Kant's philosophy or is indispensable for the attainment of one of its fundamental goals.[2] Instead, the majority of discussions devoted to the category of community conclude with negative assessments. It is objected, for example, that the category of community cannot in fact be derived from the disjunctive form of judgment, that one should "banish the concept of mutual interaction from metaphysics" due to a contradiction in its very notion, and that Kant's argument for the necessity of the category of mutual interaction in the Third Analogy of Experience is riddled with "equivocation" and must be viewed "a failure which is not even incidentally valuable."[3]

In the present paper I attempt to show that a greater appreciation of the precise meaning of the category of community and of the unique role that it plays at various junctures in Kant's theoretical philosophy allows us to see that these negative assessments and the ambivalence that they engender are themselves optional and, in fact, unfortunate occurrences. To clarify the meaning of the category of community and to show that it plays an ineliminable role in certain parts of Kant's philosophy, I discuss in greater detail (1) Kant's explicit comments on the category of community following the table of categories, (2) its relation to the notion of simultaneity discussed in the Schematism and the Third Analogy of Experience, and (3) the way in which it is both clarified and articulated further in Kant's *Metaphysical Foundations of Natural Science*, especially in his account of the equality of action and reaction. Specifically, I show that Kant's notion of community is not contradictory, but rather much more sophisticated and interesting than has been recognized. In fact, we see that it is unique both in its content, since the notion of reciprocal determination that it contains distinguishes it from the categories of causality and substance, and in the role that it plays in his broader system, since it is necessary to make possible certain fundamental kinds of experience of the world, such as simultaneity, the filling of space by matter, and the communication of motion.

The Category of Community in the *Critique of Pure Reason*

The Table of Categories

Kant introduces the category of community in §§10–11 of the *Critique of Pure Reason*, in his table of categories. It is listed under the third heading, the heading of relation:

> Of Inherence and Subsistence (*substantia et accidens*)
> Of Causality and Dependence (cause and effect)
> Of Community (mutual interaction between the agent and the patient).
> (A80/B106)

According to the Metaphysical Deduction, all twelve categories can be discovered by focusing on the primitive logical functions of the understanding in judgment that are listed in the table of judgments in §9; to get each
category, one attends to the basic function that is used when concepts are
unified in judgment, adds a "transcendental content," and obtains a function whereby a (sensory) manifold is unified in an intuition according to a
concept of an object (A79/B104–5).[4] In accordance with this procedure, the
category of community, the third relational category, is to be obtained from
the disjunctive form of judgment, the third kind of relational judgment, just
as the first two relational categories of inherence and subsistence and causality and dependence are to be gained from the categorical and hypothetical
forms of judgment.

In the second of three remarks on the table of categories—which may
have "considerable consequences with respect to the scientific form of all
rational cognition" (B109)—Kant explains why there are precisely *three* categories under each of the four headings. It would be natural, he suggests, to
expect two rather than three categories for each heading, since *a priori* conceptual division typically occurs by way of dichotomies (an object being, for
example, either F or not-F). In the case of the categories, however, it is different because "the third category arises everywhere from the combination of
the second with the first of its class" (B110). He then immediately illustrates
how this works for the third category that falls under each heading. For the
relational categories, he explains, "community is the causality of a substance
in determining another reciprocally" (B111). That is, the category of community arises from combining the categories of substance and causality.

However, if the category of community results from a combination of the
categories of substance and causality, why should it appear as a separate entry
in the table of categories, whose members must, Kant repeatedly insists, be
"elementary," "root," and "primitive," i.e., irreducible to any others? That is,
if it simply arises from combining the categories of substance and causality,
would it not obviously be derivative and what he calls "a predicable" (A82/
B108)? Later in the same paragraph Kant addresses this question directly
by claiming that the kind of combination in question involves "a special
act (*Actus*) of the understanding, which is not the same as the one that is
exercised in the first and second [categories under each heading]" (B111).
Specifically, "*influence (Einfluß)*, i.e., how one substance can be a cause of
something in another substance, is not immediately comprehensible (*zu
verstehen*) when I combine the concept of a *cause* with that of a *substance*.
Hence it is clear that a special act (*Actus*) of the understanding is required
for this" (B111). Kant's claim is thus that there is something special about
the category of community that distinguishes it from a simple combination
of the categories of substance and causality.

In his third remark on the table of categories, Kant acknowledges the need to explain the category of community in greater detail, since its "agreement" with the disjunctive form of judgment may not be "as obvious as in the other cases" (B112). He begins by describing several of the distinctive features of disjunctive judgments. In a disjunctive judgment, all of its members are coordinated with one another so as to be subordinated as parts are to a whole. For this to be possible, they must determine one another not unilaterally, as would occur in a series (e.g., of numbers, with each one determining the next higher member), but rather reciprocally such that positing one excludes all of the others. What Kant has in mind here is a very restrictive understanding of disjunctive judgment, according to which all of the parts that constitute a (disjunctive) whole are logically opposed to one another (i.e., do not overlap) and yet jointly exhaust all of the possibilities (i.e., "exhaust the sphere of cognition proper" [A73/B99]). Thus, if a disjunctive judgment asserts that A, B, or C is the case, then (1) A, B, and C have no members in common, i.e., if an element is a member of one of them (e.g., B), then it is not a member of either of the others (A and C), and (2) no options other than A, B, and C, are possible, i.e., every element of the entire class must be a member of either A, B, or C.[5]

Kant then describes how the category of community is similar to the disjunctive form of judgment:

> Now a connection similar [to that found in disjunctive judgment] is thought in a **whole of things**, since the one is not **subordinated**, as an effect, to the other, as the cause *of its existence*, but rather **coordinated** at the same time and reciprocally as cause *with respect to the determination* of the other . . . which is a kind of connection completely different from what is met with in the mere relation of a cause to an effect (of a ground to a consequence), in which the consequence does not reciprocally determine the ground in turn, and for that reason does not constitute with it a whole (as the creator of the world with the world). (B112, italics added)

This passage clarifies a number of important issues. First, Kant's description here makes clearer (at least at a certain level of generality) what is distinctive about community, or mutual interaction. He maintains that community, or mutual interaction, differs from causality by involving *coordination* rather than *subordination* and *reciprocal* rather than *unilateral determination*. The precise meaning of these terms must still be elucidated, but it is nonetheless significant that Kant explicitly provides a more specific description of the content that is supposed to be unique to community.

Second, these remarks indicate that in the Metaphysical Deduction Kant is attempting merely to draw attention to a *similarity* between disjunctive judgment and the category of community and not, strictly speaking, to *derive* the one from the other.[6] What they have in common, he thinks, is that they both represent their members as reciprocally coordinated with one another such that these members are parts that come together to constitute a whole. But similarity on these points is perfectly consistent with significant differences, such as the fact that the members of a disjunctive judgment *exclude* one another logically such that only one of them may be true, whereas entities standing in mutual interaction do not.[7] As a result, one can acknowledge important differences between the two notions without having to concede that Kant is guilty of equivocation or some other logical blunder in deriving the one from the other. In this case, due diligence to what Kant says shows that he is committed not to an obvious mistake, but rather to a somewhat more modest goal than is presupposed by the standard objection to his position.[8]

Third, a careful reading of this passage reveals why mutual interaction does not involve an obvious contradiction.[9] It is crucial to note exactly which terms Kant uses to describe the relata of mutual interaction. What Kant says here is that in mutual interaction each substance is the cause not of another substance, or of its existence, but rather of a determination, or state, of another substance. If one substance were the cause of another substance, or of its existence, this would have to be, he points out, an instance of unilateral causation involving subordination, not mutual interaction (i.e., coordinated reciprocal causation). For if one substance causes another substance, or its existence, the second substance cannot also cause the first substance, or its existence, since the second substance depends on (i.e., is subordinate to) the first substance and consequently cannot, in turn, be what the first substance depends on (i.e., is subordinate to) for its very existence.[10] That is, if we were to take causation to be between substances, mutual interaction would involve a contradiction (just as his critics had claimed), since it would entail the mutual existential dependence of (independently existing) substances.[11] If, however, we take causation to obtain not between substances (or with respect to their existence), but rather between substances and their states, or determinations, just as Kant says, then substances are not subordinate to each other with respect to their very existence; instead, they can, at least in principle, be coordinated with each other and this can occur by way of each one (reciprocally) determining the state of the other. Understanding causality as relating substances and their states (rather than substances themselves, or with respect to their very existence) thus shows that mutual interaction does not involve a contradiction (given that it is understood in terms of coordination and reciprocal determination).

Attending to Kant's remarks about the category of community or mutual interaction early in the *Critique* allows us to appreciate that (1) this category is distinct in a genuine and weighty sense from the categories of causality and substance insofar as it involves coordination and reciprocal determination, (2) Kant's "derivation" of this particular category need not be viewed as especially problematic once the relatively modest goal of his argument has been duly noted, and (3) mutual interaction need not involve a contradiction if its relata are properly identified. However, what still remains to be seen, at this point, is the precise sense in which mutual interaction involves coordination and reciprocal determination and, equally important, why Kant thinks that mutual interaction is uniquely necessary to achieve fundamental goals within his broader philosophical project.

The Schematism and Third Analogy

Since Kant employs the category of community in different ways in different parts of his philosophical system, further clarification of the notions of coordination and reciprocal determination mentioned above requires that we consider these notions in the more specific contexts in which they occur; the members of a specifically moral community are coordinated very differently from the way in which mutually interacting bodies are, even if they both involve reciprocal determination. Likewise, establishing the necessity of mutual interaction within Kant's overall project obviously requires discussion of the particular goals for which it is held to be necessary. For these reasons, I restrict myself to addressing the meaning and function of mutual interaction in certain parts of Kant's theoretical philosophy, starting with his discussion of that notion in the Schematism and the Third Analogy of Experience.

The need for schemata for the categories in general arises from the following situation. Since the Metaphysical Deduction obtains the table of categories from the table of judgments, which is a part of general logic, the categories are, at this point in Kant's argument, purely intellectual concepts, having nothing in common with particular objects that human beings might experience. As such, they *cannot* be applied to objects given in sensible intuition. However, the very next section in the *Critique*, the Transcendental Deduction, argues that the categories *must* be applied to sensible objects if cognition is to be at all possible. In the Schematism, Kant attempts to resolve the apparent inconsistency between these doctrines by identifying representations that have something in common with both the categories and sensible intuitions, and requiring that the categories refer to sensible objects *indirectly* by means of these intermediary representations, or schemata. To this end Kant identifies the schemata with what he calls "transcendental time determinations," which are, in effect, a set of temporal meanings for the categories. Because time contains an *a priori* manifold in pure intuition and determination requires a rule, transcendental time determinations, or schemata, have a number of features in common with the categories: they are all pure, general (*allgemein*), and rule-dependent (A138/B178). At the same time, they still have something in common with sensible objects, since all objects that we could sense must be temporal (A139/B178). Therefore, due to the intermediary role of the temporal meanings associated with the categories, the schemata allow the categories to refer to sensible objects, just as the Transcendental Deduction requires.

The schema that Kant then provides for the category of community is of particular interest in the present context, since the temporal meaning that it contains can be used to clarify what reciprocal determination involves in one theoretical context that is of central importance within the *Critique*. According to Kant, the schema of community "is the simultaneity of the determinations of the one [substance] with those of the other, in accordance with a general rule" (A144/B183–84). That is, the schema of community states that if two (empirically knowable) substances stand in mutual interaction, then their states (or determinations) must be *simultaneous*. What is especially salient about simultaneity here is that it is a perfectly symmetrical temporal relation. If state A is simultaneous with state B, then state B is simultaneous with state A as well. But if simultaneity is a symmetrical temporal relationship, it would also seem to be reciprocal, which suggests that at least part of what makes mutual interaction reciprocal is the temporal relation of simultaneity that obtains between the determinations (or states) of the substances that stand in mutual interaction.

If Kant thus holds that the *determinations* of substances standing in mutual interaction are reciprocal because they are simultaneous, the following question immediately arises: In what sense are the *causes* of these simultaneous determinations reciprocal as well? They might be reciprocally related in a minimal sense if, for example, (1) one substance causes a (change of) state in another substance, and (2) the second substance causes a (change of) state in the first substance. For in such a case there is a legitimate sense in which one can speak of their standing in mutual interaction, given that each substance does act on the other.

However, it is clear that mutual interaction cannot be understood in such a minimal way. First, one would have difficulty explaining why it would require a special act of the understanding. For merely applying the categories of substance and causality twice does not seem to be sufficient to warrant the claim that a special, irreducible act of the understanding must be involved; the two causal relations are not coordinated with each other in this case and therefore the special notion of reciprocal determination that is supposed to be distinctive of mutual interaction is absent. Second, if mutual interaction between two substances were to require simply that each substance cause a state in the other, we would not have explained why the resultant states must be simultaneous. For if we know only that one substance causes a state of the other and the other causes a state in the first substance, we would not know that their states must be simultaneous. Perhaps the first substance is causally efficacious several seconds, or minutes, before the second substance reciprocates. In other words, the simultaneity of determinate states is a reciprocal temporal relation and whatever causes such a relation must itself be reciprocal in some stronger sense, too. Thus if the resultant states are to be simultaneous and if mutual interaction is to involve a special act of the understanding that is not reducible to a simple two-fold application of the categories of substance and causality, the causality of both substances, and not just their states, must somehow be coordinated so as to be reciprocal. But how?

One might try to answer this question by maintaining that for mutual interaction to occur, one substance must cause a (change of) state in a second substance *at the same time* that the second substance causes a (change of) state in the first substance. For in this case one could easily discern why mutual interaction would be more than a simple two-fold application of the categories of substance and causality (i.e., why it requires a special act of the understanding); the causal efficacy of each substance must be coordinated with the other temporally. One could also see why the states caused by substances standing in mutual interaction might be simultaneous; if two causes act at the same time, it would be natural to infer that their effects exist at the same time as well. That is, the reciprocity of the simultaneous states is grounded in what would seem to be an appropriately parallel reciprocity in what causes them. Moreover, this solution can be supported by textual evidence from Kant's third remark on the table of categories quoted above, since he explicitly says there that both causes must be coordinated with each other "at the same time" for mutual interaction to occur (B112).

Despite the various advantages this interpretation enjoys, however, it turns out to be inconsistent with how the category of mutual interaction is employed in the Third Analogy of Experience. The Third Analogy asserts that mutual interaction is a necessary condition of our knowledge of the simultaneity of the states of objects. Since we can neither perceive "time itself" (B257) nor infer the temporal relations of objects directly from the order in which we happen to apprehend them, we must appeal to some other means to secure such knowledge. Kant's reasoning here, in rough outline, is that the means necessary for such knowledge must involve mutual interaction, because knowing the simultaneity of two states requires knowing the place in time of both of these states and knowing the place in time of both of these states is possible only on the basis of a two-way causal relation between them (with each "way" of the causal relation determining the place in time of a different state).[12]

The problem arises, however, that if mutual interaction is understood as requiring that the causes constituting mutual interaction be simultaneous, then the Third Analogy would simply be presupposing simultaneity (in the guise of mutual interaction) in order to account for simultaneity (at the level of the determinate states it causes). That is, if Kant's Third Analogy were interpreted in accordance with the model proposed above, his argument would be circular, since one could know the simultaneity of two substances' states, according to the Third Analogy, only if one knew that mutual interaction obtained; but if mutual interaction is understood as the simultaneous causal efficacy of two substances, one would already have to know simultaneity in order to establish simultaneity. As a result, if this interpretation were correct, the Third Analogy would be an egregious failure.[13] Rather than accept such a conclusion, the conception of mutual interaction initially proposed must be rejected; we must, instead, seek a different understanding of mutual interaction, one that explains simultaneity without presupposing it.

The crucial idea for understanding mutual interaction properly, I suggest, is that the substances involved must *jointly* determine their states. More specifically, in mutual interaction the causal activity and efficacy of one substance depends on the causal activity and efficacy of the other, and vice versa. For although substances, along with their grounds or causal powers, are independent of and thus, in some sense, distinct from each other, when they act, or exercise their causal powers, in a particular situation, what each substance does depends on external circumstances and conditions, including, particularly, on what the other substance is doing. As a result, their causal activities and the effects that result from them must be taken together in mutual interaction, and the causal contribution of one substance can be determined only by first considering the end result (i.e., the whole effect) and then ascertaining what each substance has contributed to it on the basis of its nature, its causal powers, and how they could combine with each other in those circumstances to bring about that end result.[14]

Something of the unique nature of joint (or reciprocal) determination underlying mutual interaction can be illustrated in common sense by means of an analogy with ballroom dancing or tug-of-war. For in both of these cases, what we see (i.e., the effect) cannot occur (or be made sense of) as such without the causal activity and efficacy of a plurality of parties acting jointly. Two people must move together in choreographed ways to form one pair of dancers doing the fox trot just as two teams must both be pulling on the same rope in opposite directions for it to be a game of tug-of-war. If only one person tried to perform these activities, one would be either moving around in strange ways or dragging a rope behind oneself for no apparent reason. These examples thus make clear that the *joint* causal activity of a plurality of agents is required for these events to occur and for us to understand them as such.

However, even if these examples do illustrate how it is that the joint activities of a plurality of distinct agents are required for certain kinds of events to occur, they do not clarify one central feature of mutual interaction that was under discussion. For part of the difficulty lay in how to understand mutual interaction without assuming that two agents (or substances) are acting *at the same time*. And on that count, these examples appear to be of no help: people must, it seems, be moving together or pulling a rope in opposite directions *at the same time* for dancing or tug-of-war to occur.

While this objection does reveal the limitations of the commonsense examples used to illustrate certain central features of mutual interaction, it does not show that Kant's position is untenable or that there is no room for a coherent understanding of mutual interaction. Shortly, we turn to Kant's account of matter in the *Metaphysical Foundations of Natural Science* to illustrate in more concrete ways how mutual interaction can be understood, but one should keep in mind that Kant's views regarding the temporality of the causal bonds forming mutual interaction are embedded in a larger context of transcendental idealism (even if that context cannot be treated in detail here in light of the controversial nature of the various complexities it involves).[15] For it can still be helpful to recall the importance Kant attaches to distinguishing between (1) what is temporally determinate; namely, events in the phenomenal world, and (2) what is not, whether it be atemporal beings—e.g., noumenal substances—or temporally indeterminate beings—e.g., phenomenal substances (which, though permanent, are not temporally determinate as their particular states are) and the causal activity by which events in the phenomenal world are determined (which are, like phenomenal substances, temporal in some sense, but not in a determinate way). In light of these distinctions, one can perhaps begin to form a preliminary notion of how Kant approaches this issue. If the joint causal activities constitutive of mutual interaction (as a special kind of causal activity) are temporally indeterminate, then they would not presuppose simultaneity, though they are still responsible, as causal factors, for determining the simultaneity of the states of substances.[16] As a result, although the commonsense examples used to illustrate mutual interaction are limited in certain respects, especially with regard to their temporal features, aspects of transcendental idealism may be in a position to make up for their inadequacy in that regard.

Near the end of the Third Analogy, Kant makes several explicit remarks about the different meanings the term "community" has that are relevant to what has been argued so far. He notes: "the word 'community' is ambiguous in our language, and can mean either *communio* or *commercium*. We use it here [in the argument of the Third Analogy] in the latter sense, as a dynamical community, without which even local community (*communio spatii*) could never be empirically cognized" (A213/B260). This passage confirms the distinction we have been drawing between the communal relations that obtain between the determinate states of substances (*communio*) and the causal relations that make up mutual interaction (*commercium*). Moreover, Kant seems to understand here that the nondynamical (or purely kinematic) communal relations that obtain between the states of substances include not only temporal relations (e.g., of simultaneity) but also spatial relations (e.g., of contiguity), and he suggests that (dynamical) mutual interaction is as necessary for the one as it is for the other, such that he is committed to (some version of) a causal theory not only of time but also of space.

It is interesting, however, that Kant also speaks of a "community (*communio*) of apperception" as a subjective community that representations have by virtue of being associated with each other in a mind. His reason for introducing this term is that it allows him to extend the scope of a claim made earlier (in the Transcendental Deduction and Second Analogy of Experience) that the subjective order (of our representations) depends on the objective order (of the states of objects).[17] Specifically, he wants to state here that if representations associated in a mind are supposed to represent objective reality, then there must be not only causality but also specifically *commercium* (dynamical mutual interaction) between the objects they represent. For we would otherwise have no reason not to ascribe the succession that occurs in all of our representations to the states of the objects they represent, even if those states happen to be simultaneous (in which case our representations would be erroneous). As a result, Kant's remarks toward the end of the Third Analogy both confirm the interpretation advanced so far and broaden the reach of one of the epistemological claims he makes in the *Critique*.

Accordingly, what we find in the *Critique of Pure Reason* regarding mutual interaction is the following. After listing community, or mutual interaction, in the table of categories as the third category under the heading of relation, Kant makes a series of remarks that delineate certain of its basic features: it is irreducible to any other category, despite arising from the categories of substance and causality, it possesses significant similarities (but also some differences) with the disjunctive form of judgment, and it involves coordination (rather than subordination) and reciprocal (rather than unilateral) determination. The temporal meaning ascribed to the category of mutual interaction in the Schematism could then be used to clarify part of the reciprocal content of mutual interaction, since the simultaneity of the states that are caused by dynamical mutual interaction between substances is a kind of temporal reciprocity.

Finally, the argumentative structure of the Third Analogy of Experience established that mutual interaction should not be understood as requiring that one substance causes its effect *at the same time* that the other substance causes its effect, since that would give rise to circularity in the argument (given that one would have to know simultaneity—in the guise of mutual interaction—in order to know simultaneity—with respect to the states of two substances). Instead, mutual interaction must be understood in terms of substances *jointly* determining their states in such a way that the causal activity of the one depends on that of the other (and vice versa) and the contribution of each cannot be determined before establishing their entire effect in a particular situation. This understanding of mutual interaction could be illustrated with common sense examples, but only to a certain extent. Some of these limitations might be addressed with certain features of transcendental idealism and Kant's distinctive understanding of time, but one could still rightly desire concrete examples that would illustrate and clarify further all of the basic features of mutual interaction, as Kant understands it. As a result, we must look beyond the *Critique* to the *Metaphysical Foundations of Natural Science*.

The Category of Community in the *Metaphysical Foundations of Natural Science*

Kant's explicit goal in the *Metaphysical Foundations of Natural Science* is to provide natural science with an underlying "special metaphysics" of nature, since the kind of apodictic certainty that a body of knowledge must satisfy to count as properly scientific can be supplied, he thinks, not by science itself, but rather only by metaphysics. Kant attempts to obtain such a special metaphysics from the "general metaphysics" established in the *Critique* by applying the transcendental principles it develops in an abstract way to the specific class of objects that are relevant to natural science, namely, objects of outer sense, or matter; in this way, he contends, one can derive the apodictic certainty and necessity of the properties of matter from the principles laid out in the *Critique*. Since community, or mutual interaction, is one of the central concepts established in the *Critique* and the *Metaphysical Foundations* is structured by the same principles, one can expect the *Metaphysical Foundations* to provide more specific illustrations of this concept in its explanations of the various properties of matter. Fortunately, this expectation is in no way disappointed; in both the Dynamics and the Mechanics chapters Kant argues that a particular instance of mutual interaction must be invoked to explain how it is possible that matter can fill a space and communicate motion, respectively.

Mutual Interaction in the Dynamics

In the Dynamics, Kant claims that matter must be endowed with attractive and repulsive forces to fill a determinate region in space. We need not concern ourselves with the details of the argument he gives in support of this claim—roughly, if matter had only repulsive force, it would expand so as to encompass all of space, whereas if it had only attractive force, it would contract to a single point, so that only a balance between the two forces can account for the determinate region of space that matter fills. What is important to recognize here is that it is through the mutual interaction of (repulsive) forces that matter fills a determinate region in space.

Consider, for example, what is the case, according to Kant, with two bodies that attempt to fill some determinate region of space. According to "the balancing argument" sketched above, each one has an expansive force by means of which it would fill all of space if nothing were to prevent it from doing so. But since this case involves two bodies, not one, and each one necessarily has an expansive force, there *is* something that prevents each one from filling all of space, namely, the other body, and what it is about each body that prevents the other from filling all of space is its expansive force. For the one body could fill all of space only if it completely penetrated the other (since without complete penetration there would be some space that it did not fill), but complete penetration is impossible, since a body that was completely penetrated would have to lack the expansive force that is, on Kant's view, essential to it.[18] What happens, then, in the case of two bodies that attempt to fill some region of space is that the very same expansive force by means of which each one attempts to penetrate the other is what resists the other's attempt at penetrating it. In other words, a body's expansive force (by means of which it attempts to penetrate another) is also its repulsive force (by means of which it attempts to resist being penetrated by others).[19]

Now the degree to which each body is (and is not) able to penetrate the other (and thereby fill a determinate region of space) will depend not only on the distance between them but also on the strength, or magnitude, of the expansive (or repulsive) force of each body. Accordingly, there will be a point (or series of points) somewhere between them that marks the boundary between the spaces they fill. Kant calls this "common boundary" (*gemeinschaftliche Grenze*) the point (or line) of contact, and describes it in the following terms: "Physical contact is the mutual interaction of repulsive forces at the common boundary of two matters" (4:512). Accordingly, two bodies can fill a determinate region of space, Kant claims, only if, through their expansive (or repulsive) forces, they stand in mutual interaction with each other.

Kant's account of how matter fills a determinate region of space is important in the current context because it illustrates two of the more striking aspects of the notion of mutual interaction that were introduced, but, as we saw, not fully clarified in the *Critique*. First, it is clear that the expansive (or repulsive) forces of two bodies must *jointly determine* the common boundary between them that marks off the region of space that each one fills. That is, one cannot, so Kant thinks, determine the region of space that a body fills, as an atomist might, by considering it in isolation from the forces of other bodies.[20] Rather, the expansive forces of the two bodies must jointly bring about a single effect, namely, the common boundary that demarcates the region that each one fills. For when the bodies exercise their expansive powers, what each body does depends not only on external circumstances and conditions (such as the distance between it and the other body) but also on what the other body is doing, i.e., how it is exercising its expansive force.

Second, Kant's account of how matter fills a space illustrates in an especially lucid way how mutual interaction exemplifies the kind of part-whole relation found in disjunctive judgment. For this example shows particularly clearly how mutual interaction can give rise to the kind of relation between parts that suffices to generate a given whole. In a whole, each part must be related to every other in such a way that they jointly suffice to constitute that whole and a change in any one part would require a corresponding change in the other. The example at hand reveals precisely this kind of structure, since given a certain point of contact between two bodies, the force exerted by the one must correspond in a very specific way to the force exerted by the other and a change in the force of the one would require a change in the force of the other. As a result, Kant's account of how matter fills a determinate region of space shows not only that bodies must *jointly* exercise their expansive forces but also that the exercise of these forces must be *coordinated* with each other in a *specific way* for a given effect to result, just as parts must be coordinated with each other in a specific way for a given whole to be constituted.

However, Kant seems to take one more step in this context than he had in his previous descriptions, since he invokes a new set of terms with which to understand contact, terms that will allow us to clarify mutual interaction further. For he asserts: "Contact in the physical sense is the immediate action and reaction of *impenetrability*" (4:511). What is novel here is his use of the concept pair of action and reaction.[21] Unfortunately, Kant provides no helpful descriptions of what he means by action and reaction in the Dynamics, but in the Mechanics, by contrast, Kant explicitly argues for the equality of action and reaction and clarifies how action and reaction should be understood. As a result, it is the Mechanics that promises to provide a detailed instance of mutual interaction that can be used to clarify this notion further.

Mutual Interaction in the Mechanics

Kant's primary goal in the Mechanics is to explain how matter can communicate motion, e.g., through impact, and his main contention is that this can happen only if his three "laws of mechanics" obtain. The "first law" of mechanics states that in all communication of motion the total quantity of matter must remain the same, while the "second law" of mechanics asserts that all changes in matter must have an external cause (an assertion that is similar to Newton's law of inertia). The "third law" of mechanics states: "In all communication of motion, action, and reaction are always equal" (4:544). It is thus Kant's third law of mechanics that is most immediately relevant to his account of the equality of action and reaction.

The first point to note is that Kant recognizes two different versions of the third law. On the one hand, he is sometimes interested simply in establishing the principle that the *relative motions* of bodies *toward each other* must be equal in the communication of motion, since the motion of one body relative to another entails the motion of the other body relative to it, i.e., "no body impacts another that is at rest *relative to it*" (4:548). The official proof that he gives for the third law seems to be concerned primarily (though not exclusively) with this issue, since the fundamental assumptions that it relies on are the rejection of absolute space (and therefore of any notion of absolute motion that would be directly based on it) and the perfect symmetry of the relative motions of bodies toward each other. In his second note on the third law, he explicitly remarks: "This is thus the *mechanical law* of the equality of action and reaction, which depends on the fact that no *communication* of motion takes place, except insofar as a *community* of these motions is presupposed" (4:548). What is distinctive of this type of principle is that it is purely kinematic and "mechanical" in the narrow sense insofar as it is concerned simply with how to attribute particular motions to matter as such.

On the other hand, Kant is also interested in how the equal motions posited by the mechanical law could be caused, and, to that end, asserts that there is, in addition to the mechanical law, a "*dynamical* law of the equality of action and reaction, not insofar as one [matter] communicates its motion to another, but rather originally *imparts* it to the latter and at the same time brings it about in itself through the resistance of the latter" (4:548). The idea here is that just as the changes in the relative motions of two bodies must be equal in impact, so, too, must the causal activities of the two bodies that bring these changes about. That is, the causal activity of the one body must be equal to that of the other such that "pressure and counterpressure are always equal to each other" (4:549).

Second, Kant explicitly contrasts his own understanding of the communication of motion with alternative proposals. Against the view of those whom he calls transfusionists, he maintains that the communication of motion does not occur literally by means of a transfer or "pouring" of motion from one body to another, on the grounds that this view would, in effect, "eliminate all reaction, that is, all reacting force of the impacted body on the impacting one" (4:449), and would also not *explain* so much as *presuppose* the communication of motion (4:550). He also makes clear that reaction is not to be understood as analytically entailed by action, as is the case on views according to which every active power analytically entails a corresponding passive power (such that if, e.g., fire has the power to melt gold, then gold must have the power to be melted). That is, reaction for Kant is not simply action described from the passive point of view of the patient; instead, it is a genuine force distinct from action.[22] As Kant states: "One cannot at all think how the motion of a body A must be necessarily combined with the motion of another body B, except by thinking forces in both that pertain to them (dynamically) prior to all motion (for example, repulsion)" (4:550). Action and reaction are the joint exercise of two separate (but equal) dynamical forces, where what distinguishes action from reaction is the recipient and the direction of the motion that each one causes, not some change in point of view.

Third, Kant's particular understanding of the equality of action and reaction can be illustrated nicely by means of the head-on collision of two billiard balls, A and B. What happens when A and B collide is that A acts on B, thereby forcing B to move in the direction in which A was originally moving. But on Kant's account, B must also act on A, since A stops moving in the direction in which it had originally been moving and, by the second law of mechanics, there must be some external cause for that change. Therefore, just as A acts on B, causing it to move, so, too, B acts on A, causing it to move in the opposite direction; the action of the one requires the reaction of the other. Moreover, this example illustrates not only the necessity of action and reaction as distinct forces, but also their *equality*. Action and reaction must be equal (though opposite), Kant argues, because the change in the motion of the one body caused by the action of the other must be equal (and opposite) to the change in the motion of the other body (given the mechanical version of the third law).

This account of Kant's understanding of the equality of action and reaction reveals that action and reaction display precisely the features that were discovered above to be constitutive of mutual interaction in the Schematism and Third Analogy. First, the distinction between the mechanical and dynamical versions of the third law corresponds to the distinction between *communio* and *commercium* and thus to that between simultaneity and the dynamical causal relation that makes simultaneity possible. Second, since action and reaction are distinct forces that nonetheless require each other, they jointly cause the communication of motion between two bodies, just as two substances jointly determine each other's states to be simultaneous in mutual interaction. Moreover, the way in which action and reaction cause the communication of motion displays the same kind of part-whole relation that is required for mutual interaction. For the communication of motion from one ball to another (and vice versa) is the whole effect, which action and reaction must bring about by being coordinated with each other in a *specific way*, namely, such that they are equal to each other; if the action was different, then the reaction would also have to be different, given that they must be equal in the communication of motion.

However, this account also clarifies further several features of mutual interaction. First, Kant's explanation of the communication of motion reveals the necessity of reciprocal causal determination more clearly than does his argument concerning simultaneity. For although simultaneity is obviously symmetrical, it is perhaps less clear that it is also a reciprocal relation and one might therefore suppose that a cause acting alone (rather than two separate but jointly acting causes) would be able to cause such a symmetrical relation. That is, one might think that if a single cause can bring about successive states, it could just as easily bring about simultaneous states.[23] Now Kant holds that succession and simultaneity are distinct modes of time (A177/B219) and cannot be defined in terms of each other, which leads him to assert that fundamentally different types of causality must be responsible for these different kinds of temporal relations; but even if Kant is correct on these points, focusing on the communication of motion can still allow one to see more perspicuously the necessity of both causes in mutual interaction. For if only one of the bodies was responsible for the change in motion of both bodies, then a body would cause a change of motion in itself. However, matter is, Kant thinks, essentially inert or lifeless, and asserting that matter can cause motion in itself is a clear violation of the second law of mechanics (and of Newton's law of inertia) that would spell "the death of all natural philosophy" (4:544). To avoid such consequences, it is evident that one must view both bodies as causes of the communication of motion.

Further, Kant's account of the communication of motion illustrates more clearly not only why two causes are required but also how they must *jointly* bring about their effect in mutual interaction, and thus what *reciprocal* determination can mean in this instance. What makes the communication of motion richer and thus more illustrative of the content of mutual interaction than simultaneity is the notion of equality it employs. As we saw above, the mechanical version of the third law states that the change in the motion of one body must be equal to (though in the opposite direction of) the change in the motion of the other. However, the equality of the relative motions of bodies brings with it as a consequence the equality of the dynamical action and reaction that causes these motions (in the guise of the dynamical version of the third law). That is, equality at the kinematic level requires equality at the dynamical level, but the equality of action and reaction in the communication of motion is a very specific aspect of two substances, reciprocally determining each other's states, that is more robust than what is required for, say, simultaneity. For equality is a feature that derives from the distinctive content of what it is invoked to explain, namely, the communication of motion, due to the distinctive fact that the relative motions of bodies must be equal to each other in the communication of motion. By contrast, not all causes that constitute mutual interaction must be equal, since some causes may not have a quantitative dimension and the question of whether such causes are equal would not even arise. But even if this notion of equality is not applicable to all cases of mutual interaction, it can still provide a clearer sense of how reciprocal determination can be understood.

Finally, the case of the communication of motion illustrates in a concrete and intuitively plausible way the unusual temporal status of the causal activities that constitute mutual interaction. As we saw above, the causal bonds that constitute mutual interaction are to be viewed not as simultaneous (at least not in the context of the Third Analogy), but rather as temporally indeterminate. But one might naturally wonder how a cause can be temporally indeterminate (especially if its effect is determinate)? What the case of the communication of motion brings out is that we are willing to accept that there is a distinction between a change in motion and the exercise of force that brings about this change. We can, in some intuitive sense, directly perceive the former and can therefore determine that it occurs at a particular time, whereas we cannot with respect to the latter—a point that leads Hume to deny the existence of forces altogether.[24] What Kant does is incorporate this distinction into his philosophy in such a way that motions are given in intuition and can therefore be known to occur at determinate times. Forces, by contrast, are not given in intuition and thus must be represented instead by the categories (e.g., of causality and mutual interaction), which are used to determine the properties of sensible objects. As a result, Kant holds that we can only infer their existence, nature, and specific magnitude on the basis of our determination of motions in intuition (4:537), but—and this is the crucial point—such an inference cannot deliver specific knowledge of the particular time at which these forces are exercised. That is, unlike the case of motions, we have no reason to postulate these forces as existing at one specific moment in time rather than at another; they are temporally indeterminate in that sense. Accordingly, Kant's account of the communication of motion shows how we can attain a plausible understanding of his claim that the causal activities that constitute mutual interaction are temporally indeterminate.

Conclusion

Focusing on the category of community, or mutual interaction, and on the role it plays in various parts of Kant's theoretical philosophy has lead to two important results. First, attending to Kant's explicit remarks about the category of community and several of the contexts in which it is employed have provided us with a fuller and clearer conception of its content such that (1) various objections that have been made against it can be rejected as being based on misunderstandings, and (2) its similarities and differences with the category of causality can be understood properly.[25] In its basic form, mutual interaction does not arise from two (or more) substances causing each other's existence, but occurs rather when two (or more) substances jointly determine each other's states in such a way that the causal activity of each one depends on the other in bringing about a certain kind of effect, akin to the way in which parts are coordinated in forming a whole. This basic meaning can then take on different forms, depending on the particular issue being addressed, whether to explain the possibility of our knowledge of simultaneity, the filling of space, or the communication of motion.

Second, we now have a much better sense of the reasons that lead Kant to introduce mutual interaction, i.e., why he thinks this kind of causality is necessary in contexts that are otherwise very different from each other. For what has become clear is that simultaneity, the filling of space, and the communication of motion all involve some kind of symmetrical relation, whether temporal, spatial, or kinematic, and Kant consistently holds that what causes these relations must also be symmetrical and reciprocal, since causes lacking reciprocity would be unable to account for the symmetry of the determinate relations. Hence arises the need for specifically mutual interaction.

Kant may or may not be correct in maintaining the necessity of mutual interaction for knowledge of certain kinds of symmetrical relations, such as simultaneity or the communication of motion. That issue can be settled definitively only after the specific arguments involving mutual interaction have been reconstructed and evaluated as to their merits, a task that is perhaps in progress, but certainly not complete. However, we can see more clearly now what is the core content of mutual interaction, what the systematic importance is of arguments that assert its indispensability, and what the fundamental principle is that motivates these arguments.[26]

Notes

1. Quotations from Kant's *Critique of Pure Reason* will be cited according to the standard A and B pagination for the first (1781) and second (1787) editions, respectively. Quotations from other works are cited from *Kants gesammelte Schriften*, ed. Königlich Preußische Akademie der Wissenschaften, 29 vols. (Berlin: de Gruyter, 1900–) by volume and page number. All translations are my own.

2. Notable exceptions to this are Béatrice Longuenesse, *Kant and the Capacity to Judge* (Princeton: Princeton University Press, 1998); Jeffrey Edwards, *Substance, Force, and the Possibility of Knowledge: On Kant's Philosophy of Material Nature* (Berkeley:

University of California Press, 2000); and Margaret Morrison, "Space, Time, and Reciprocity," in *Proceedings of the Eighth International Kant Congress*, vol. 2, ed. Hoke Robinson (Milwaukee: Marquette University Press, 1995), 187–95.

3. These quotations are from Arthur Schopenhauer, *Die Welt als Wille und Vorstellung*, vol. 2 of *Sämtliche Werke*, ed. Arthur Hübscher (Wiesbaden: Eberhard Brockhaus Verlag, 1972), 1: 544; Peter F. Strawson, *The Bounds of Sense: An Essay on Kant's Critique of Pure Reason* (London: Methuen, 1966), 140; and Jonathan Bennett, *Kant's Analytic* (Cambridge: Cambridge University Press, 1966), 219.

4. Without going into detail, the important point here is that the understanding uses one and the same set of functions in two different contexts, and the identity of the set of functions can be obscured by the differences in context. For in the case of judgments, the functions' inputs are concepts (or propositions) and their outputs judgments, whereas in the case of the categories, their inputs are intuitions and their outputs determinations of objects. Given the differences in their inputs and outputs, how can these functions truly be the same? Kant's answer is, roughly, that there are acts of unification that are the same in each case, despite the differences in what it is that is unified.

5. I have explained the part-whole relation embodied in disjunctive judgment in extensional rather than intensional terms, but nothing turns on this point for the present purposes.

6. This interpretation is, I believe, supported by the central argumentative passage of the Metaphysical Deduction at B104–5, where Kant asserts that one and the same understanding brings about unity in judgments and concepts by means of one and the same set of functions, given that the understanding can apply the same function of unification in different ways to different kinds of objects for a different set of ends. What the argument thus requires is merely a similarity in structure, not a derivation of the one from the other.

7. That is, the exclusion relationship that obtains between the members of a disjunctive judgment is different from the nonexclusive causal relationship that obtains between members standing in mutual interaction, but, this difference notwithstanding, both exhibit reciprocal determination. But even describing the situation in this way could be a bit misleading; namely, if it suggested that the only (or primary) difference between the two was whether the reciprocal determination was exclusive or not. For the notion of determination each one employs is very different too. Disjunctive judgment involves logical determination, whereas mutual interaction involves ontological (or a certain kind of causal) determination. This kind of difference can be seen quite easily by noting the difference between the logical notion of dependence expressed in hypothetical judgments and the causal notion of dependence expressed in causal claims.

8. See Béatrice Longuenesse's "Kant's Standpoint on the Whole: Disjunctive Judgment, Community, and the Third Analogy of Experience" (in this volume) for discussion of the parallels between the disjunctive form of judgment and the category of community.

9. Schopenhauer states the problem as follows: "Only insofar as state A precedes state B in time, but their succession is necessary, not contingent . . . only to that extent is state A the cause and state B the effect. The concept of mutual interaction

contends, however, that both are the cause and both the effect of the other: but this means the same as that each one is both the earlier and the later event: which is absurd [*ein Ungedanke*]. For that both *states* are simultaneous, and necessarily so, cannot be accepted: because as necessarily correlated and simultaneous, they constitute only *one* state" (*Die Welt als Wille und Vorstellung*, 1: 545).

10. This is part of what Kant is trying to express when he refers to causal relations between God and finite substances constituting the world; whereas finite substances belonging to the same world can act on each other mutually, God is the unilateral cause of the existence of finite substances, which do not cause anything in him and are therefore subordinate to him. Kant repeats this point in his metaphysics lectures, e.g., 28:196.

11. Or else, as Schopenhauer points out, not a relation between the states of two distinct substances, but rather a single state.

12. For a fuller discussion of Kant's argument in the Third Analogy, see my *Kant and the Metaphysics of Causality* (Cambridge: Cambridge University Press, 2005), chapter 3.

13. One can avoid this difficulty by understanding the claim of the Third Analogy as a hybrid of epistemological and metaphysical elements, asserting that *mutual interaction* rather than *knowledge* of mutual interaction is required for knowledge of simultaneity. Though the purely epistemological reading of the Analogies (developed most forcefully by Guyer) has been widely accepted, in chapters 3 and 4 of *Kant and the Metaphysics of Causality* I develop the hybrid version of the argument (and the model of causality it presupposes) in detail. If circularity can be avoided as I suggest, one might think that the causal bonds forming mutual interaction could be simultaneous and the notion of mutual interaction correspondingly clear. However, the matter is complicated for other reasons. For the causal bonds forming mutual interaction to be simultaneous, something would have to determine them to be such, but this seems to lead to an infinite regress (given that whatever might cause them to be temporally determinate would have to be itself either temporally indeterminate or temporally determinate). In short, regardless of how one reads the Analogies, further clarification of mutual interaction will be necessary. I thank Samuel Rickless for pressing me to be clearer on this point.

14. Note that there is an important contrast here between the cases of succession and simultaneity. Kant holds that in the case of succession only a single causal determination is required, whereas in the case of simultaneity the joint activity of two substances is needed. This contrast is due to differences in the structure of succession and simultaneity.

15. For extended discussion of these issues, see *Kant and the Metaphysics of Causality*, chapters 4 and 5.

16. For more detailed discussion of this point, see *Kant and the Metaphysics of Causality*, chapter 4.

17. See, e.g., B140 and A193/B238.

18. "One matter, in its motion, penetrates another, when it completely removes the space of its [the latter's] extension through compression" (4:500), and "Matter can be compressed to infinity, but can never be penetrated by matter, regardless of how great the compressing force may be" (4:501).

19. Attractive force is still necessary to keep bodies from repulsing each other further and further away, which would destabilize space.

20. For Kant's discussion of atomism, see, e.g., the General Remark on the Dynamics, 4:523–25.

21. Kant does, however, refer to action (*Handlung*) as a predicable in the *Critique* at B108.

22. Kant explicitly acknowledges this point in his metaphysics lectures at, e.g., 28:51–53.

23. In the Third Analogy, Kant assumes that a substance cannot determine its own place in time, but one might question the argument he develops in support of this assumption.

24. For assertions that we cannot perceive powers, forces, or their exercise directly, see 28:563, 565.

25. The categories of causality and mutual interaction share a basic notion of real, causal determination whereby the state of a substance is determined (or becomes determinate) at a particular time. Their differences arise from the special joint, or reciprocal, nature of the determination in the case of mutual interaction. However, these differences do not preclude their joint instantiation. That is, it is by no means impossible that one substance can cause a change of state in another at the same time that that cause also forms part of a causal configuration constituting mutual interaction. Consider, for example, universal gravitation. The sun is the cause of the change of motion of the earth such that it moves in its specific orbit (i.e., the sun determines the successive states of the earth). The sun and the earth can, however, be determined to exist at the same time, and it is, in part, by means of this very same attractive force that this determination occurs.

26. I thank Samuel Rickless, Donald Rutherford, Peter Thielke, James Messina, Susan Castro, Kory Schaff, Ryan Hickerson, and Lucas Thorpe for comments on this paper or for discussions of its content. I also acknowledge the Templeton Foundation for their support of a larger research project of which this is part. All errors are my own.

3

KANT ON THE RELATIONSHIP BETWEEN AUTONOMY AND COMMUNITY

LUCAS THORPE

The central idea behind this paper is the claim that Kant's moral idea of a realm of ends is modeled on the category of community examined in his theoretical works, and that understanding Kant's account of the category of community helps us understand certain features of the idea of a realm of ends, and in particular the fact that a member of a realm of ends must be an autonomous agent. For Kant the idea of a community is essentially the idea of a multitude of individuals in interaction and in this paper I will attempt to show why Kant believes that only autonomous individuals can interact.

Central to Kant's mature ethics is his belief that it is impossible to refute the solipsist theoretically, for from the theoretical perspective (the perspective of the *Critique of Pure Reason*), we can have no knowledge of the existence of other individuals.[1] According to Kant, if I believe that other human bodies are merely lumps of unconscious flesh to be used and abused for my own pleasure, I am not making a theoretical mistake but rather a moral choice. At the heart of Kant's ethics, then, is the belief that each individual faces a fundamental moral choice: one can either choose to be a solipsist, thinking of oneself as a solitary individual alone in the world and facing no external constraints, or one can choose to think of oneself as a finite individual in interaction with other such individuals. Choosing the second alternative involves recognizing and respecting others, who must simultaneously be thought of as radically *distinct from* but also, nevertheless, somehow *connected to* and *interacting with* oneself. To be moral, then, is to choose to be a member of a community and to *really* interact with others.[2]

Kant often distinguishes between what he calls ideal interaction (of which Leibnizian preestablished harmony is an example) and real interaction,[3] and the central thesis of this paper is that for Kant, *we can only think of a community of individual substances in real interaction if we think of each individual member of the community as autonomous*. Therefore, to reject solipsism and to choose to interact with others is to choose to be autonomous. For Kant, this is not primarily an ethical claim but rather a theoretical, conceptual claim, rooted in his metaphysics. If my reading of Kant's metaphysics is correct, then, in stark contrast to the standard reading of his ethics, Kant does not value autonomy primarily because he values self-mastery, but because he values the idea of being a member of a community and really interacting with others.[4]

Before examining the details of Kant's position and its development, let me briefly point to some textual evidence for my interpretation from the *Groundwork of the Metaphysics of Morals*. Here Kant explains that "by a realm I understand a systematic union of various rational beings through common laws . . . what these laws have as their purpose is just the relation of these beings to one another as ends and means" (4:434). Kant makes it clear that the purpose of laws in a realm of ends is to provide the "glue" that gives a community of individuals some sort of unity. And he continues by explaining that the only way to be a member of such a community is through being autonomous, that is by being (individually) the source of the laws that provide the community with its unity. Thus he explains that "a rational being belongs as a *member* to the realm of ends when he gives universal laws in it but is also himself subject to these laws" (4:434). Here Kant seems to be quite explicit about the fact that being autonomous is the membership condition for belonging to a realm of ends. And the best way of making sense of this claim is in the argument that a world of intelligible beings can only have real unity if the individuals that are members of the world are the source of the laws that provide the laws with its unity. Kant seems to be quite clear about this a few pages later, where he argues that "in this way a world of rational beings (*mundus intelligibilis*) as a realm of ends is possible, through the giving of their own laws by all persons as members" (4:438). Kant makes it quite clear that it is the giving of laws by the members of a world that makes the world possible.[5]

It should be clear by now that I am advocating a particular conception of autonomy. To be autonomous, on this interpretation, is not merely to "give laws to oneself" but also to give a particular type of law to oneself. To be autonomous is to give laws for a possible ideal community, laws that bind both oneself and others. One could, however, imagine a solipsistic egoist who wants to give some unity to his life and so chooses to act only on certain principles or laws. Such an egoist attempts to give laws to himself, but the only law he attempts to submit himself to is an intrapersonal law. Kant suggests that Wolff (1679–1754) can be thought of as advocating such an ethical principle, for the principle of perfection demands that we unify our desires and inclinations, but not necessarily in a way that makes them compatible with the desires and inclinations of others.[6]

Such an individual, who attempts to give unity to his inclinations by subjecting them to some intrapersonal law, might be thought of as taking Leibniz's (1646–1716) conception of a monad as his moral ideal. The Leibnizian believes that the only type of finite individual we can conceive of is a solitary individual.[7] Such an individual is essentially active and its activity is that of having representations. A Leibnizian monad, then, can be thought of as a series or stream of representations. This stream, however, is essentially unified. What unifies the representations of an individual is that they are subject to a law, and Leibniz calls this law, which provides the representations of an individual their unity, the "law of the individual" or the "law of the series." The law of the series can be thought of as the source of the series of representations and, Leibniz believes, accounts for the unity of the individual. Such a law, however, should be regarded purely as an internal law.

An egoist, then, who takes such a conception of an individual as his ideal would try to unify his representations (or desires) but would think that it could be done purely by reference to some law internal to himself, perhaps the "law of his genius." The rational solipsist (or a rational hedonist), then, can be thought of as attempting to subject himself to purely *intrapersonal* laws that make no reference to other individuals. Such an individual may claim that it is striving to be autonomous, claiming that it subjects itself to its own laws, or perhaps that it subjects itself to the law of its own genius. An autonomous agent in Kant's sense, however, legislates and subjects itself to *interpersonal* laws, that is, to laws of a possible (ideal) community. To be autonomous in the Kantian sense, then, is not merely to legislate for oneself but for a (potential) community.[8]

The paper is divided into five sections. In section one I examine Kant's account of the category of community in the *Critique of Pure Reason*. In section two I explain his account of community in his metaphysics lectures. In section three I sketch the historical background to Kant's views, and in particular the debate between proponents of preestablished harmony and physical influence. In section four I explain how Kant attempted to conceptualize the possibility of real interaction. Finally, in section five, I show how his account of interaction implies that only autonomous beings can really interact.

The Concept of Community in the *Critique of Pure Reason*

In the *Critique of Pure Reason*, Kant introduces the category of community as the third category of relation. The structure of the table of categories is derived from the table of judgments, and this table is divided into four classes, into judgments of quantity, of quality, of relation, and of modality. The categories of the third class, then, are derived from the judgments of relation. According to Kant there are three types of relational judgment: categorical judgments (A is B), hypothetical judgments (if p then q), and disjunctive judgments (p or q or r). The categories of substance and accident are derived from the categorical form of judgment, the categories of cause and effect are derived from the hypothetical form of judgment, and the category of community, which either is or involves the idea of reciprocal influence, is derived from the disjunctive form of judgment.[9]

Kant believes that the category of community (and as a result the notion of interaction) is to be sharply distinguished from that of cause and effect, for they are derived from different forms of judgment. We understand the importance of this claim by considering an alternative way of conceptualizing interaction. Defenders of such an alternative conception of interaction would argue that we can fully capture what is involved in interaction in the following terms: when two entities, say x and y, interact, x has a causal relation to y and y has a causal relation to x. Kant does not deny that this partially captures what is involved in the relation of interaction,[10] but he does not believe that it is the full story,[11] for he believes that when a number of entities interact they (a) constitute a *whole* and (b) mutually *exclude* one another. These two factors are essential to the relation of interaction and cannot be captured by appealing to the ideas of ground and consequence or to the hypothetical form of judgment. Thus, in his commentary to the table of categories in the *Critique of Pure Reason* Kant compares the causal relation to the relation of interaction/community and points out that in the case of simple causation the relation is one of *subordination*, whereas in the case of interaction the relation is one of *coordination* (B112).

What he means is that in a causal relation the consequence is subordinated to the ground. For this reason the ground-consequence relation is the principle of the series, for the relation of ground and consequence can provide us with a well-ordered chain of causes and effects. The relation of community, on the other hand, cannot be understood in terms of the idea of subordination, for when a number of entities are members of a community they are not subordinated to one another but are coordinated with one another and the concept of coordination cannot be understood in terms of mutual subordination. When entities are coordinated with one another they are parts of a whole and mutually exclude one another. Thus Kant explains that the relation of community/interaction

> is an entirely different kind of connection from that which is to be found in the mere relation of cause to effect (of ground to consequence), in which the consequence does not reciprocally determine the ground and therefore does not constitute a whole with the latter (as the world-creator with the world). The understanding follows the same procedure when it represents the divided sphere of a concept as when it thinks of a thing as divisible, and just as in the first case the members of the division exclude each other and yet are connected in one sphere, so in the later case the parts are represented as ones to which existence (as substances) pertains to each exclusively of the others, and which are yet connected in one whole. (B113)

In the first sentence of this passage Kant distinguishes the concept of causation from that of interaction, and focuses on the fact that in the case of interaction the entities "constitute a whole."[12] To understand the second sentence it is necessary to have a closer look at Kant's account of the disjunctive form of judgment. A disjunctive judgment has the form: "*x* is A or B or C."[13] Kant explains this form of judgment in the *Critique of Pure Reason* in the following terms: "In all disjunctive judgments the sphere (the multitude of everything that is contained under it) is represented as a whole divided into parts (the subordinate concepts)" (B112). He makes his point a little more clearly in his logic lectures. In *Jäsche Logic*, for example, he explains that "disjunctive judgments represent various judgments as in the community of a sphere and produce each judgment only through the restriction of the others in regard to the whole sphere" (9:107).

A disjunctive judgment, then, is a judgment in which a number of judgments somehow restrict one another and fill up a (logical) sphere. In *Jäsche Logic* Kant gives the following example of a disjunctive judgment: "A learned man is learned either historically or in matters of reason" (9:108).[14] Here the concept "learnedness" is divided into "parts." The concept "learnedness" is in this case the logical "sphere" that is to be divided into parts. The parts of this sphere are "learned historically" and "learned in matters of reason." These parts mutually exclude one another in the sense that insofar as one is "learned historically" one is not "learned in matters of reason," and, Kant believes, taken together they completely "fill the sphere" of the concept of learnedness in the sense that they exhaust the concept. In other words, Kant maintains that the "or" in a disjunctive judgment is an exclusive "or," and that in such a judgment the members of the disjunction exhaust the concept. In the disjunctive judgment, then, we find a number of judgments mutually excluding one another and completely filling a logical space. The conception of a logical space allows us to think of a space that has parts but that is not, unlike the space of intuition, infinitely divisible. We may thus think of a whole, the parts of which are simple. This will be important when we turn to the idea of community.

It is, then, from the disjunctive form of judgment that we get the concept of "exclusion." Kant makes this clear in his commentary to the table of categories. In this section he compares the disjunctive form of judgment with the hypothetical (if . . . then) form of judgment, and asks us to

> note that in all disjunctive judgments the sphere (the multitude of everything that is contained under it) is represented as a whole divided into parts (the subordinate concepts), and since none of these can be contained under any other, they are thought of as *coordinated* with one another, not subordinated, so that they do not determine each other *unilaterally*, as in a *series*, but *reciprocally*, as in an *aggregate* (if one member of the division is posited, all the rest are excluded, and *vice versa*. (B112)

Earlier in his commentary on the table of categories, Kant explains that the categories he has listed do not provide a complete list of the *a priori* concepts of the understanding, for there are also derivative concepts, which Kant calls "predicables," that can be derived from the categories. Thus, Kant explains that

> for the sake of the primary concepts it is therefore still necessary to remark that the categories, as the true *ancestral concepts* of pure understanding, also have their equally pure *derivative concepts*, which could by no means be passed over in a complete system of transcendental philosophy, but with the mere mention of which I can be satisfied in a merely critical essay. (A81–82/B107)

Under the category of community Kant lists two "derivative concepts" or predicables: presence and resistance (A82/B108). The reason why resistance is a predicable of the category of community is because our (pure, unschematized) concept of resistance is to be understood in terms of exclusion, and we understand the notion of exclusion *a priori* through our grasp of the disjunctive form of judgment. What we mean if we claim that one thing resists another is that if (or, insofar as) the thing is posited all the rest are excluded. As we shall see, the fact that resistance is a predicable of the category of community has important implications for Kant's account of interaction, for he conceives of interaction in terms of the withdrawal of resistance, which, given his analysis of community, implies that only members of a community can interact.

The category of community, then, allows us to understand the notion of a number of impenetrable individuals (concepts) filling a conceptual space (another concept) and excluding other individuals (concepts) from their part of the conceptual space, without any appeal to the space of intuition.

The Concept of Community in the Metaphysics Lectures

Before examining Kant's account of interaction and community in his metaphysics lectures it would be helpful to understand something about how metaphysics as a discipline was structured in eighteenth-century Germany. At that time German metaphysics textbooks divided metaphysics into general metaphysics (ontology) and special metaphysics. Special metaphysics was divided into three special sciences corresponding to the three objects of rational cognition, namely, rational psychology, rational cosmology, and rational theology. Rational psychology was concerned with rational cognition of the *soul*, rational cosmology dealt with rational cognition of the *world*, and rational theology dealt with rational cognition of God. Although Kant rejected the possibility of rational cognition—that is, cognition of objects through pure reason—the structures of the *Critique of Pure Reason* and the metaphysics lectures follow this traditional plan. Thus, although Kant rejects the possibility of ontology in the traditional sense, the first half of the *Critique of Pure Reason* can be understood as corresponding to the traditional role of general metaphysics, although ontology, in the strict sense of the "science of being," has been replaced by a "transcendental analytic." Kant believes that a science of being is not possible, for the intellect can give us no access to things in themselves.[15] As Kant explains in his lectures on metaphysics, "Ontology is a pure doctrine of all our *a priori* cognitions; or it contains the summation of all our pure concepts that *we* can have *a priori* of things" (*Metaphysik L2*, 28:541).[16]

Thus, in the *Critique of Pure Reason* and the metaphysics lectures Kant identifies three ideas of pure reason: the thinking subject, which is the object of *psychology*, the world, which is the object of *cosmology*, and God, which is the object of *theology*.[17] Kant's discussion of interaction and community is found principally in his cosmology lectures, which focus on the idea of a world.

As I will show, Kant, like Leibniz, believes that the idea of a world must be the idea of a multitude of essentially active individual substances, or monads. Unlike Leibniz, however, Kant believes that the idea of a *world,* as opposed to a mere multitude of individuals, is the idea of a *community* of such individuals in interaction. For Kant the idea of a world is, by definition, the idea of a community, and the distinguishing feature of a community for Kant is the *real* interaction of its members.

Questions about interaction were central to Kant's development. Much of his published work in the 1750s and 1760s was an attempt to explain how it is possible to conceive of real interaction between windowless monads. One of his earliest published works, the *Physical Monadology* of 1756, is an attempt to develop a monadology in which there is real interaction. And in his *Inaugural Dissertation* of 1770 he argues that

> the hinge . . . upon which the question about the principle of the form of the intelligible world turns is this: to explain how it is possible that a plurality of substances should be in mutual interaction with each other, and in this way belong to the same whole, which is called a world (2:407).[18]

Lying behind this question is Kant's recognition that Leibniz himself had huge, and I believe insoluble, problems with the idea of a world of monads. On the one hand, Leibniz's philosophy requires the idea that a world of monads makes sense, as the idea of possible worlds is central to his philosophy; on the other hand, like many commentators, I can see no way he can make any sense of the notion of a *world* of monads while he denies that monads can interact.[19] Kant had the same worries and realized that the idea of a world of monads requires some sort of real interaction between them.

Kant's commitment to this position can be traced back to his precritical period. Thus, in his metaphysics lectures from the mid-1770s he claims that

> the aggregation of the substances in which there is no community still does not constitute a world. Reciprocal determination, the form of the world as a composite (*compositi*), rests upon interaction (*commercio*). If we thought substances without real connection (*absque nexu reali*) and without interaction (*commercium*), where every substance would be in and for itself and they would have no community with one another, then that would indeed be a multitude (multitude), but still not a world. . . . Thus the connection (*nexus*) of substances that stand in interaction (*commercio*) is the essential condition of the world. (*Metaphysik* L2, 28:196)

Central to Kant's thoughts here is the belief that our idea of a world is, by definition, the idea of a whole. Kant states this explicitly and frequently in his metaphysics lectures. For example, in his metaphysics lectures from 1792 to 1793, a series of lectures given more than ten years after the publication of the first *Critique*, he argues that "a multitude of substances without connection makes no world. One must thus not define world: the universe of substances, but rather the whole of them" (28:657). He makes it clear that he believes we can think of a whole of substances only if we think of the substances as connected and interacting, for he continues by introducing the distinction between the form and matter of a world and arguing that while the "*material of the world are substances*," the formal element "*is the real connection (nexus realis) of these substances*. Real connection is reciprocal influence (acting and suffering) . . . a *multitude* of substances without connection makes no world" (*Metaphysik Dohna*, 28:657).

The idea of a world, then, is the idea of a whole of (individual) substances, and we can only think of a whole consisting of individuals if we think of the whole as a community and the individuals that constitute the whole as really interacting. As a consequence of this definition of a world, the idea of a member of a world is the idea of "an individual in real interaction with other individuals."[20]

Kant, then, makes it quite clear that the distinction between a world and a mere multitude is that for a set of individuals to constitute a world there must be some "real connection" between them, that they must interact and constitute a community. The idea of an intelligible world, then, is the pure idea of a community of individual substances (or monads) in interaction. The problem with this definition of a world is that, given Kant's Leibnizian conception of individuals as essentially active, there are good reasons to think that the idea of a community of such individuals in interaction is incoherent; indeed, this is precisely the conclusion that Leibniz had drawn. Kant, however, does not draw the conclusion that windowless monads cannot interact, but to understand his account of what is involved in interaction it is necessary to understand in a little more detail why there is a *prima facie* problem with interaction for someone who is attracted to an essentially Leibnizian conception of individual substances. It is to this topic I will now turn.

Occasionalism, Preestablished Harmony, and Physical Influx

When Kant was a young man, German metaphysics was dominated by debates about the nature and possibility of interaction and the development of Kant's account of interaction has to be placed in its historical context. In eighteenth-century German metaphysics textbooks, and in particular in Alexander Gottlieb Baumgarten's *Metaphysics* of 1739 (the textbook Kant used for his metaphysics lectures), the question of interaction was dealt with under two headings: Psychology and Cosmology. The psychological question is about a particular type of interaction, namely, that between mind and body, and is more familiar to contemporary philosophers. It developed in response to Cartesian dualism. For Descartes the mind and body are two radically different types of substances, and the *psychological question* has to do with understanding how two such radically different substances can interact with each other. The cosmological question, in contrast, is more general, and asks how substances in general, even substances of the same type, can interact with one another. The cosmological question, although not as prominent today, was a major topic of debate in the eighteenth century and remained of central importance to Kant throughout his career. This debate was not about ethics, but about metaphysics and the status of scientific laws.

By the time Kant began his philosophical career, there were three standard answers to the cosmological question of interaction: preestablished harmony, occasionalism, and physical influx or influence. This tripartite division can be traced back to Leibniz. In a letter of 1696 to Henri Basnage de Beauval, Leibniz, in the context of a discussion about the psychological question of mind/body interaction, famously elucidates the three possible accounts of interaction by drawing an analogy with a pair of clocks.[21] Leibniz writes,

> Consider two clocks or watches in perfect agreement. Now this can happen in *three ways*: the *first* is that of a natural influence. . . . *The second way* to make two faulty clocks always agree would be to have them watched over by a competent workman, who would adjust them and get them to agree at every moment. *The third way* is to construct these two clocks from the start with so much skill and accuracy that one can be certain of their subsequent agreement. . . . *The way of influence* is that of the common philosophy; . . . *The way of assistance* is that of the system of occasional causes. But, I hold, that is to appeal to a *Deus ex machina* in a natural and ordinary matter, where, according to reason, God should intervene only in the sense that he concurs with all

other natural things. Thus there remains only my hypothesis, that is, *the way of pre-established harmony*.[22]

Pierre Bayle in his *Historical and Critical Dictionary* (1697) popularized this tripartite taxonomy of theories of interaction. There are various ways of characterizing the difference between these three positions. The simplest is to explain it in terms of a finite substance's responsibility for (internal and external) change.[23] Thus, the theory of *(physical) influence* (or real interaction) asserts that individuals can cause changes both in themselves and in others—that is, they can cause both internal and external change. The theory of *occasionalism* denies that finite substances are the cause of change either in themselves or in others.[24] The theory of *preestablished harmony* asserts that finite substances are the cause of changes in themselves, but not in others.

In the early eighteenth century the dominant account of "physical influx" involved (as the name suggests) the idea of the accidents of one substance "flowing into" another substance. Following Kant I will refer to this position as the theory of *crude physical influence*. Although Kant is a defender of physical influence broadly understood, he firmly rejects the theory of crude physical influx. Some commentators have doubted whether any philosopher actually advocated the idea of crude physical influence. Leibniz seems to trace the theory of crude physical influence back to the Spanish Jesuit philosopher Francisco Suárez (1548–1617), but it is clear that this attribution does not stand up to close scrutiny.[25] It seems that many Cartesians misread the Aristotelian account of perception as a crude influctionist account of body-mind causation, and it seems to me that this is what Kant has in mind when he talks of crude physical influence. According to this misreading, perception involves *sensible species* flowing from the perceived object and into the mind of the perceiver. However, as Dennis Des Chene has pointed out, "despite the language of giving and receiving, [for Aristotle] nothing is literally transmitted from agent to patient."[26] Instead, despite what "Aristotle's own occasional analogy of wax and stamp, or statue and mould, might lead one to think. . . . The formal cause of change is always intrinsic to the patient; the role of the efficient cause is not to impose a form of the patient from outside . . . but to determine just how a certain mode of being in the patient, as yet potential and indeterminate, will become actual."[27] Thus, although it is common to trace back the crude influctionist position to the Peripatetics, it is clear that the Aristotelians were not proponents of the view.

Aquinas traces the influctionist position back to the Atomists, arguing that "Democritus claimed that every operation [*actionem*] is by way of an influx [*influxionem*] of atoms."[28] And Eileen O'Neill has convincingly shown that we can find an influctionist model of causation among Atomists and

Corpuscularians, which can be traced back to Roger Bacon, and which was influenced by Neoplatonic ideas of emanation.[29] As examples of advocates of such a position she points to Kenelm Digby, Walter Charlton, John Sergeant, and, perhaps best known to us today, Pierre Gassendi. For example, according to Digby's account of perception "there is a perpetuall fluxe of little partes or atomes out of all sensible bodies that . . . can not choose but gett in at the dores of our bodies, and mingle themselves with the spirits that are in our neves."[30] The idea of little particles flowing into our bodies through "doors" is clearly the type of view Leibniz is rejecting when he claims that monads are windowless.[31]

Whatever the provenance of the crude doctrine of physical influence, it is clear that in our everyday language we do often use influctionist metaphors, which involve the notion of something being transferred from the agent to the patient. For example, we talk of motion being *transferred* from one object to another, and of the *transference* of property rights from one individual to another.[32] Many people also see successful communication as the transference of ideas. A similar story can be told about popular views on education; knowledge is transferred from the teacher to the pupil. If the influctionist account of causation turns out to be incoherent, then there is a good reason to try to avoid all of these metaphors. Such examples should help convince a skeptical reader that our metaphysical views do have practical consequences, and so ethics, as a discipline, should not exist in a bubble as an autonomous discipline divorced from the rest of philosophy.

By the mid-eighteenth century, at least in the German-speaking world, the exhaustive tripartite taxonomy of theories of interaction was pretty much taken for granted. Thus, as Eric Watkins notes, by 1723 Georg Berhand Bilfinger could claim that occasionalism, preestablished harmony, and physical influence were the *only* three possible theories of interaction.[33] And it seems fair to say that in the German milieu in which Kant developed philosophically, only two of these answers were regarded as serious contenders: preestablished harmony and physical influence. Following Leibniz, Wolff and his school tended to be defenders of preestablished harmony. On the other hand, a number of important philosophers such as Johann Christoph Gottsched (1700–1766), Christian August Crusius (1715–75), and Martin Knutzen (1713–51) (who was one of Kant's teachers in Königsberg) had written tracts advocating physical influx. Occasionalism was no longer taken seriously; following Leibniz, most German metaphysicians of the period conceived of substances, even finite substances, as essentially active.

Leibniz rejects occasionalism because he is committed to the position that substances (which for Leibniz are, by definition, individuals) are essentially active. Thus, for example, he argues in his *New Essays on Human Understanding* that "activity is the essence of substance in general,"[34] and in a letter to Bayle in 1702 he claims that "without an internal force of action a thing could not be a substance."[35] As a result of his belief that substances are necessarily active centers of force or activity, he concludes that the occasionalist position amounts to a denial of the existence of finite substance. In effect, then, Leibniz believes that the occasionalist position collapses into Spinozism. Thus, in a letter to Jacques Lelong in 1712 Leibniz argues that

> without force there will be no substance; and one will fall despite oneself, into the opinion of Spinoza, according to whom creatures are only passing modifications. It is necessary, therefore, to say that God gives the force, and that he does not replace it, in order to preserve the substances outside of him.[36]

Kant himself rejects occasionalism without much discussion and I suggest that this dismissal was motivated by the fact that, like Leibniz, he regarded individual substances as essentially active (or by the critical period as agents), which led him to see occasionalism (understood as a doctrine that denies the real agency of finite individuals) as essentially a denial of the possibility of finite individuality and hence as akin to Spinozism.

Leibniz has a number of problems with physical influence, and his rejection of crude physical influx lies behind his famous claim that monads are "windowless." Individual substances have no windows through which anything can "flow in," nor, as Digby suggests, do they have doors. One obvious problem with the theory of crude physical influence is that it suggests that determinations (or, in the traditional vocabulary, "accidents") are the sort of things that can "float around" and exist independently of individual substances. Both Leibniz and Kant have a problem with this notion. A defender of crude physical influence, however, might just bite the bullet and accept the coherency of the idea of accidents existing independently of substances.

A more serious problem, however, with the doctrine of crude physical influx is that it is unclear in what sense a determination can really be thought of as being a determination of either the agent or the patient. For if accidents or determinations are the sort of things that can detach themselves from individuals and float from one individual into another, then we need some account of the way in which an accident can really "stick to" or really "belong to"[37] a particular individual in a way strong enough to make the accident an accident *of* that individual. If accidents are the sort of things that can be detached from an individual, we need to give some account of the real unity of accident and individual. As I hope to show in the following section, both Kant and Leibniz agree that the proponent of crude physical influx has no way of accounting for inherence. Kant, following Leibniz, rejects the theory of crude physical influence, for he believes that the only way an accident can truly belong to (or be unified with) a substance is if the substance is the (active) ground of the accident. That is to say, Kant agrees with Leibniz that individual substances must be windowless. However, he does not believe that this implies that individual substances cannot really interact with one another. Thus although Kant consistently rejected the theory of crude physical influx, Kant began and ended his philosophical career as a defender of real interaction.[38]

How Can Essentially Active Substances Interact and, in So Doing, Constitute a World? Kant's Solution to Leibniz's Problem

The problem with conceptualizing interaction is fairly simple. Following Leibniz, Kant thinks that the idea of an individual (substance) is the idea of something essentially active. There is, however, a problem in explaining how two essentially active beings can act upon one another, for we must be able to give an account of how an essentially active substance can suffer or be passive. Any account of interaction, then, must be able to explain how an agent can be a patient. Kant himself explicitly addresses this problem in his lectures on metaphysics. He explains, "That substance suffers (passive) whose accidents inhere through another power." He then asks, "How is this passion possible, since it was said earlier that it [i.e., the passive/suffering substance] is active insofar as its accidents inhere" (*Metaphysik Mrongovius*, 29:823).

The problem, then, is not merely that Kant conceives of individual substances as essentially active, but that, following Leibniz, he is committed to a particular conception of inherence. Namely, he is committed to the view that an accident (or, more generally, what Kant refers to as a "determination") can only truly inhere in or belong to a substance if the substance is the active cause or ground of the accident. I name this doctrine the *principle of active inherence*.[39] It is Leibniz's acceptance of this principle that lies behind his claim that monads are windowless and lies behind Kant's rejection of physical influence. If we accept the principle of active inherence, though, it is not clear how one individual can ever be the cause of any change in another individual. If a determination can only be a determination of individual *b* if *b* is the active ground or cause of the determination, how can another substance ever be the cause of a change in *b*? Leibniz's solution was to admit defeat and conclude that one substance cannot be the cause of a change in another.

Kant's solution to this problem will be to claim that we can understand the idea of an individual being acted upon without appealing to the untenable notion of accidents flowing into the individual in terms of the agent "determining the active power of the substance being acted upon" (29:823). This account of action does not violate the principle of active inherence, because the patient's determination inheres in the patient (since it is a result of the patient's power). This power, however, has been determined by the agent. It is not clear, however, what we should make of this notion of the agent "determining the power" of the patient.

The model Kant introduces to clarify the notion of one individual determining the power of another is that of the withdrawal of resistance. One individual substance (the agent) is the cause of a change in another individual substance (the patient) if the change in the patient is the result of the agent withdrawing its resistance. The patient remains, however, essentially active, for the determination is the result of its power. Thus each individual is essentially active in that everything that happens to a particular individual (everything a particular individual does or suffers) is the result of its own power or potentiality. But much of what we do occurs only when other individuals remove impediments.[40] On this model, if individuals are to interact they must already resist one another. In section one of this paper I explained the dependence of the concept of resistance on the concept of community; why, for Kant, individuals can only resist one another if they constitute a community. In the next section of this paper I will explain how Kant believes such resistance is possible. Kant argues that resistance must be the result of law and that the only possible source of *real* resistance between individuals is a law that has been "given" by each and every member of the community. I will, however, first present some textual evidence for my reading and will also examine some of the details of Kant's position.

Kant explains in his lectures on metaphysics from 1782–82:

> We can never be merely passive, but rather every passion is at the same time action. . . . Every substance is self-active, otherwise it could not be substance; . . . The substance being acted upon (*substantia patiens*) is acting in itself (*eo ipso agens*), for the accident would not inhere if the substance had no power through which it inhered in it, hence it also acts; influence (*influxus*) is therefore an unfitting expression, as it implies that the accident migrated out of a substance. What then is genuine passivity? The acting substance (*substantia agens*) determines the power of the substance being acted upon (*substantiae patientis*) in order to produce this accident, therefore all passivity (*passio*) is nothing more than the determination of the power of the suffering substance by an outer power. (*Metaphysik Mrongovius*, 29:823)

Here Kant spells out his commitment to the principle of active inherence: "an accident would not inhere if the substance had no power through which it inhered in it." And he believes that commitment to this principle rules out the possibility of crude physical influence. However, he does not believe that it necessarily rules out any commitment to real interaction, for it still allows for some account of passivity. An individual can be a patient, that is, can be acted upon, if another individual "determines the power of the substance being acted upon in order to produce the accident."

In a later passage he explains that one individual "determines the power" of another when it removes an impediment that allows what he calls a "dead" power to become a living power. Thus he argues that

> with a faculty we imagine only the possibility of power. Between faculty and power lies the concept of endeavor (*conatus; Bestrebung*). When the determining ground for an effect is internally sufficient, then it is a dead power. But when it is internally and externally sufficient, then it is a living power. Power which is merely internally sufficient, without being able to produce the effect, is always opposed to an opposing power which hinders its effect, an impediment (*impedimentum*). Thus as soon as the impediment (*impedimentum*) is removed, the dead power becomes living. (*Metaphysik L2*, 28:565)

Here Kant distinguishes between the idea of a faculty and the idea of a power. A faculty is a mere capacity, whereas a power is already a striving or endeavor. *Conatus* is a term that Kant has borrowed from calculus. Imagine a ball at rest. It has the faculty or capacity to move in a straight line. Now, imagine a ball attached to a rope being swung around a fixed point (or better, imagine the moon attracted to the earth by the force of gravity and circling it). At each particular moment the ball "wants" to move in a straight line, at a tangent to the circle it is describing. This is what Leibniz termed *conatus* and what Kant refers to in German as "endeavor" (*Bestrebung*). Thus, although the ball is actually moving in a circle, at any particular moment it is "endeavoring" to move in a straight line along the tangent. At any particular moment it would move along the tangent if all external forces were removed. Kant calls this "endeavor" to move along the tangent a "power"; it is more than what Kant calls a capacity or faculty, for even an object at rest has the capacity to move along a straight line. We can, however, distinguish between a "dead" power and a "living" power. The power of the ball (to move along the tangent) will remain a "dead power" unless the rope is cut. If the rope is cut, the impediment is removed, and the ball will move off along the tangent. Upon the cutting of the rope the dead power becomes a living power. The cutting of the rope "causes" the ball to fly off in a straight line—but this cutting merely allows for the actualization of the ball's dead power. So the motion of the ball along the tangent really is the ball's motion.

Thus, a static (physical) point has the *capacity* or *faculty* to move along a straight line. If it is moving in a circle around a center of gravity at every moment it is "striving" to move along the tangent. In such situations, at each moment it has a *dead power* to move along the tangent. If the force of gravity is removed it will move along the tangent along a straight line. In moving along a straight line it is exercising a *living power*. Although the movement along the straight line is due to its own power, the removal of the force of gravity is the *cause* of its motion in a straight line. Kant suggests that all interaction between substances can be understood in an analogous way.

Why Only Autonomous Individuals Can Interact

In the previous section I argued that Kant believes that if individuals are to interact they must resist one another. I will now explain how this resistance between individuals is possible. I will make two claims. First, Kant believes that the source of resistance between individuals are laws. Second, Kant distinguishes between real interaction and ideal interaction. If the individuals are to *really* interact the resistance must be "real" and this is only possible if the individuals themselves are the source of the laws that create the resistance. That is, if individuals are to really interact, they must be autonomous.

The example of the ball was an essentially spatiotemporal example. Kant however, believes that the idea of a community of individuals in interaction is intelligible,[41] and hence must be conceivable in essentially nonspatiotemporal terms. So, in order to conceive of real interaction between intelligible individuals we must be able to strip the analogy of its spatiotemporal elements. Kant believes that this can be done because (as we saw in section one of this paper) he believes that the concept of resistance is not a phenomenal concept, but is instead an *a priori* concept of the understanding derived from the table of categories of the first *Critique*. In Kant's terminology the concept of resistance is a "predicable" of the category of community. In the *Critique of Pure Reason* Kant explains that the category of community is derived from the disjunctive ("*x* is *a*" or "*x* is *b*" or "*x* is *c*") form of judgment. The notion of resistance is a predicable of the category of community because our (pure, unschematized) concept of resistance is to be understood in terms of exclusion, and, Kant believes, we understand the notion of exclusion *a priori* through our grasp of the disjunctive form of judgment. One individual resists another individual by excluding it from a "space." Kant believes that we *understand* the notion of one individual excluding another from a "space" without any appeal to intuitive space, in terms of the way in which, given a disjunctive judgment, the assertion of one of the disjuncts excludes the assertion of the other disjunctions. Given p or not-p, the assertion of p excludes the assertion of not-p. The category of community, then, allows us to understand the notion of a number of impenetrable individuals (concepts) filling a conceptual space (another concept) and excluding other individuals (concepts) from their bit of the conceptual space, without any appeal to the space of intuition, and he believes that this notion of logical exclusion is the basis of our concept of resistance. Given p or not-p, the withdrawal of the assertion of p removes the resistance to the assertion of not-p. This, Kant believes, is the basis for our capacity to think of intelligible individuals as resisting one another and hence as capable of interaction, without being subject to spatiotemporal conditions.

Kant, then, believes that interaction between active individuals is conceivable only in terms of the withdrawal of resistance; hence interaction is only possible between individuals that (already) constitute a community. The idea of a community, however, is the idea of a totality or whole, so individuals can only interact if they somehow constitute a totality or whole. If we accept this claim then we need to make only one more step to arrive at Kant's conclusion that only autonomous agents can really interact: namely, the claim that *only autonomous agents can constitute the right kind of whole.* Kant's final step, then, is to argue that if individuals are to really interact, the whole or totality they constitute must be "real" as opposed to "ideal" and that only autonomous individuals can constitute such a whole.

The mature Kant, then, reached the conclusion that what distinguished the idea of real interaction from that of ideal interaction is that in the case of real interaction the individuals constitute a *real,* as opposed to an *ideal,* whole. Thus, Kant explains in his lectures of 1790–91 on metaphysics that "substances are the matter of the world, the formal aspect of the world consists in their connection (*nexu*) and indeed in a real connection (*nexu reali*). The world is thus a real whole (*totum reale*), not ideal" (*Metaphysik L2,* 28:581). Our idea of a world is the idea of a *real* as opposed to an *ideal* whole. Elsewhere in the same lectures, Kant is more explicit about this distinction. He explains that

> the connection (*nexus*) is ideal if I merely think the substances together, and real if the substances actually stand in interaction (*commercio*). . . . The form of the world is a real connection (*nexus realis*) because it is a real whole (*totum reale*). For if we have a multitude of substances, then these must also stand together in a connection, otherwise they would be isolated. Isolated substances, however, never constitute a whole (*totum*), then they must also be a real whole (*totum reale*). For were they ideal, then surely they could be represented in thought as a whole (*totum*), or the representations of them would constitute a whole (*totum*); but things in themselves would still not constitute a whole on this account. (*Metaphysik Mrongovius,* 29:851)

An ideal whole is a whole that can be merely "represented in thought" as a whole. In such a whole the unity exists only in the mind of the observer. As a consequence, the resistance between the individuals really exists only in the mind of the observer. In a real whole, in contrast, the unity must be intrinsic to the whole, and hence the resistance between the individuals would also be real. And, although Kant himself does not explicitly make this claim, I suggest that the best way of making sense of what Kant means is that the individuals that constitute a real whole must somehow be responsible for the unity of the whole. Now, in the case of a community or world, what unifies the whole, and in so doing creates resistance between the individual members of the whole, are *laws* (or practical principles), and so the individuals must be thought of as the source of those laws that provide the community with its unity. Kant is explicit about the role of laws (or principles) in providing a world with its unity. Thus, he explains in an unpublished note from the 1780s that "the unity of the intelligible world [is] in accordance with practical principles, like that of the world of sense [is] in accordance with physical laws" (19:297, #7260). I am suggesting, then, that Kant believes that there can only be an intelligible world (or realm of ends) if each individual member of the world is the source of the unity of the world. Now, as laws (or principles) are what provide the world with its unity, each individual must be thought of as (concurrently) the source of these laws.

I have suggested, then, that the proponents of preestablished harmony and real interaction can be thought of as disagreeing about the nature of the unity of any possible community of individuals. Defenders of preestablished harmony can be thought of as claiming that the unity of the world is ideal in the sense that it exists merely in the mind of the ideal observer, God, whereas the defender of real interaction believes that its unity is real, that it constitutes some fact about the world itself. A "real" community is to be distinguished from an "ideal" community in that the unity of a real community is *intrinsic* to the community. The members of a real community must, by definition, themselves be the source of the relations (or laws) that provide the community with its unity. In other words, the members of a real community in which real interaction is possible must be autonomous.

Kant believes that it is possible to conceive of a community of individuals in interaction only if we think of the members of the community as governed by laws, and we can think of the members of a community as *governed* by laws only if we think of each individual member of the community as the *source* or *giver* of these laws. Kant believes that a world is essentially unified, for it is this unity that distinguishes the idea of a world from that of a mere multitude. In addition, he believes that a multitude of individual substances can only be unified or "held together" by laws. So the idea of a world is the idea of a multitude of individuals unified by laws. Now, if the unity of a world is to be "intrinsic" to the world, rather than merely existing in the mind of some ideal observer observing the world; that is, if there is to be *real interaction* between the members of the world rather than a mere *constant conjunction* between the state of one substance and that of another (à la Hume),[42] then the members of the world must be responsible for the unity of the world, and Kant believes that this is possible only if each individual member of the world is the source of, or "the giver of," the laws that provide the world with its unity. In other words, each member of a world must be autonomous. That is, in the language of his mature ethics, *we can think of a community of individuals in interaction only if we think of each individual member of the community as autonomous.* And to be autonomous is not merely, or even primarily, to rule oneself, but rather to be the source of the laws of a possible community.[43]

Notes

1. Indeed, Kant believes that from the theoretical, phenomenal perspective the solipsist is right, insofar as he rejects the existence of a plurality of independent substances. One indication of this is his belief that if the phenomenal world were all there is, Spinoza would be right. Thus, for example, in one set of metaphysics lectures he argues that "if we assume space as real we assume Spinoza's system" (*Metaphysik Dohna* 28:666). And in another set Kant argues that "those who assume space as a matter in itself or as a constitution of things in themselves, are required to be Spinozists, i.e., they assume the world to be a summation of the determinations of a united necessary substance, and thus only one substance" (*Metaphysik Vigilantius* 29:1008–9). He makes a similar claim in the *Critique of Practical Reason* (5:102). Elsewhere he makes a clear connection between Spinozism and egoism, arguing that "dogmatic egoism is a hidden Spinozism" (*Metaphysik L2*, 28:207). Kant's belief that immorality is to be thought of as a type of solipsism can be traced back at least to the 1760s; Kant writes in an early unpublished fragment that "action from the singular will is *moral solipsism.* Action from the communal will is moral justice" (2:246; my emphasis). References to Kant's writings, lectures, and correspondence are given by abbreviated title, volume, and page number of *Kants gesammelte Schriften*, ed. Königlich Preußische Akademie der Wissenschaften, 29 vols. (Berlin: de Gruyter, 1900–). The *Critique of Pure Reason* is cited by the standard A and B pagination of the first (1781) and second (1787) editions. Unless otherwise stated, translations are from *The Cambridge Edition of the Works of Immanuel Kant*, 13 vols., ed. Paul Guyer and Allen W. Wood (Cambridge: Cambridge University Press, 1992–). Since the Cambridge edition includes the Academy edition pagination in its margins, separate page numbers for the translations will not be given.

2. One indication that this is Kant's position is the fact that he often identifies the opposite of being moral and doing one's duty with what he calls "moral egoism" or "solipsism." He makes this clear in *Anthropology*, where he argues that "the moral egoist limits all purposes to himself; as a eudaemonist, he concentrates the highest motives of his will merely on profit and his own profit and his own happiness, but not on the concept of duty. . . . All eudaemonists are consequently egoists. Egoism can only be contrasted with pluralism, which is a frame of mind in which the self, instead of being enwrapped in itself as if it were the whole world, understands and behaves itself as a mere citizen of the world" (7:130). In his ethics lectures Kant identifies moral egoism with solipsism and argues that "the rule: *Be not selfish,* or *the duty in regard to solipsism,* is twofold" (my emphasis) and he explains that the second rule is: "Act unselfishly, i.e., act not from the principle of utility, merely, but also from that of duty" (27:620–21). See also 27:604.

3. He explains this distinction in his metaphysics lectures in the following terms: "The connection (*nexus*) is ideal if I merely think the substances together, and real if the substances actually stand in interaction (*commercio*)" (*Metaphysik Mrongovius*, 29:851). What this distinction actually amounts to will be an important topic of this paper.

4. Sam Kerstein has raised the objection that Kant merely draws an *analogy* between egoism (a moral concept) and solipsism (a metaphysical concept) rather than identifying the two. The main justification for my interpretation is that it provides a way of understanding puzzling aspects of Kant's ethics. Kant himself does at times, however, seem to explicitly identify solipsism and egoism. For example, in his lectures on metaphysics he defines the "egoist" as "one who assumes here that he is the only existing being" (*Metaphysik Dohna*, 28:657).

5. I believe that Kant tries to make a similar point in the *Critique of Practical Reason*, although there he is not so clear. For example, he argues that "supersensible nature . . . is nothing other than *a nature under the autonomy of pure practical reason*. The law of this autonomy, however, is the moral law, which is therefore the fundamental law of a supersensible nature and of a pure world of the understanding" (5:43). And he seems to repeat, or at least allude to the idea, that autonomy is a condition for the possibility of an intelligible world. So, for example, he argues that "the moral law is, in fact, a law of the causality through freedom and hence a law of the possibility of a supersensible nature" (5:43), and that "freedom considered positively" can be defined as "the causality of a being insofar as it belongs to the intelligible world" (5:132).

6. Nietzsche also at times seems to advocate a sort of egoistic, solipsistic autonomy. For example, in *Thus Spoke Zarathustra*, in the section *Of the Way of the Creator*, Zarathustra asks: "Do you call yourself free? I want to hear your ruling idea, and not that you have escaped from a yoke. . . . Free from what? Zarathustra does not care about that! But your eye should clearly tell me: free *for* what? Can you furnish yourself with your own good and evil and hang up your own will above yourself as a law? Can you be judge of yourself and avenger of your law?" Friedrich Nietzsche, *Thus Spoke Zarathustra*, trans. and with an introduction by R. J. Hollingdale (London: Penguin, 1961), 89. Nietzsche seems to suggest that we must be creative in the sense of creating our own individual intrapersonal law.

7. Leibniz famously argues in the *Discourse on Metaphysics* that "each substance is like a world apart, independent of all other things, except for God." G. W. Leibniz *Philosophical Essays*, ed. and trans. Roger Ariew and Daniel Garber (Indianapolis: Hackett, 1989), 47.

8. In claiming this I am disagreeing with Martin Schönfeld, who argues that "Leibniz's pre-established harmony permits the autonomy of souls." Martin Schönfeld, *The Philosophy of the Young Kant* (New York: Oxford University Press, 2000), 141.

9. Kant's account of the disjunctive form of judgment has received a rather bad press in the contemporary literature. Thus Paul Guyer, for example, writes that "as is often pointed out, Kant's connection of the real relation of reciprocal influence with the logical notion of exclusive disjunction is the most tenuous piece of his metaphysical deduction of the categories." Paul Guyer, *Kant and the Claims of Knowledge* (Cambridge: Cambridge University Press, 1987), 452.

10. "The third category always arises from the combination of the first two in its class" (B110). In the case of the category of relation, which is the third category of relation, the first and second categories are substance and causation. So community involves substances in causal relations, but cannot be reduced to the notion of mutual causation.

11. "But one should not think that the third category is therefore a merely derivative one and not an ancestral concept of pure understanding. For the combination of the first and second in order to bring forth the third concept requires a special act of the understanding, which is not identical with that act performed in the first and second" (B111).

12. This is not the case in the ground-consequence relation. He appeals to the example of God, the "world creator." God is the ground or cause of the world, but God and the world do not constitute a whole. If God was thought of as interacting with the world, however, God and the world would constitute a whole. Here I disagree with Jerome Schneewind, who argues that Kant advocates the "astonishing claim . . . that God and we share membership in a single moral community only if we all equally legislate the law we are to obey." Jerome B. Schneewind, *The Invention of Autonomy: A History of Modern Moral Philosophy* (New York: Cambridge University Press, 1998), 513; see also 554.

13. Or, perhaps more accurately: "*x* is A or *x* is B or *x* is C."

14. This is, perhaps, not a particularly good example, as Kant makes it clear that disjunction is to be understood exclusively; that is, Kant is making the assumption that a learned man could not be learned *both* historically and in matters of reason. I suspect that Kant chose this particular example in an attempt to introduce a light-hearted moment into his lecture. A sympathetic reader of Kant could imagine his students having a quiet chuckle at this point.

15. Having rejected the rationalist claim that noncontradiction is a sufficient criterion for real possibility, Kant believes that pure theoretical speculation can tell us nothing positive about the nature of being (or beings).

16. According to the critical Kant, then, ontology cannot tell us anything about being or about things in themselves. Instead, it only provides us with information about our own cognitive capacities and faculties, and the contents of these faculties. In addition, although reason in its pure use cannot provide us with knowledge of objects, it can tell us something about its own limits. The *Transcendental Dialectic*, on the other hand, corresponds to the traditional disciplines of special metaphysics and is structured according to the traditional division of special metaphysics into three special sciences. Whereas traditional German metaphysicians understood these three special sciences to be concerned with three distinct types of objects, which could be cognized by the human intellect, in Kant's *Transcendental Dialectic* these three "objects" are merely objects of thought and can be examined purely as ideas. These ideas are possible as objects of our thought, but we have no way of knowing if there are, or even if there possibly could be, "real" objects corresponding to them.

17. And, as we have seen, these ideas are "pure" in the sense that they have no sensible content. It is not merely that they have no empirical content (which would make them merely *a priori*); they are also ideas of pure reason, and as such, by definition, have no content provided by the faculty of intuition. As Kant explains, "A

pure concept is one that is not abstracted from experience but arises rather from the understanding even as to content" (9:92). In addition, these ideas of pure reason, although they are possible objects of thought, are not possible objects of experience (or intuition), and as a consequence they are not possible objects of cognition.

18. Although by his critical period Kant had come to see that answering questions about the form of the intelligible world would leave us no less the wiser about the nature of the world we experience, answering such questions does have a function in that it helps us understand the moral law, for, as he explains in the *Critique of Practical Reason*, the moral law "is to furnish the sensible world (*Sinnenwelt*) . . . with the form of a world of the understanding (*Verstandeswelt*)" (5:43). Therefore to understand the moral law we must understand the form of the *Verstandeswelt*, and Kant continues to conceive of the form of such a world in terms of a plurality of substances in mutual interaction with one another.

19. Leibniz himself believes that we can understand the notion of a world of monads through the purely logical notion of *compossibility*. Monads are members of the same world if they are compossible. However, it is unclear to me how we can understand the notion of *compossibility* (or more precisely the notion of *incompossibility*) if we reject any real connection between monads. If monads are not connected, how can any two monads be incompossible? For more on this, see G. H. R. Parkinson, *Logic and Reality in Leibniz's Metaphysics* (Oxford: Clarendon Press, 1965); Hidé Ishiguro, *Leibniz's Philosophy of Logic and Language* (London: Duckworth, 1972; 2nd ed., Cambridge: Cambridge University Press, 1990); and Margaret Dauler Wilson, *Leibniz' Doctrine of Necessary Truth* (New York: Garland, 1990).

20. Similarly, in his lectures from the early 1780s Kant once again distinguishes between the idea of a world and that of a mere multitude and argues that "a great multitude of isolated substances would not constitute a world (isolated substances are only the stuff for a world), because they would not constitute a whole, but rather each of them would be entirely alone and without any *community* with the others" (*Metaphysik Mrongovius*, 29:853; my emphasis). Once again, Kant makes it quite clear that substances can only constitute a world if they are in community with one another. Similar passages are not hard to find. See, for example: 28:581–82, 28:45, 29:851–52, 29:868, 29:1006–7.

21. Kant himself seems to have been aware of this passage and refers to this analogy while explaining Leibniz's position in his lectures on metaphysics. See *Metaphysic Mrongovius*, 29:866–67.

22. Leibniz, *Philosophical Essays*, 147–48. It should be noted that in this letter Leibniz is discussing the psychological question of mind-body interaction and not the cosmological question of interaction in general. In his lectures, however, Kant appeals to this analogy during his discussion of the cosmological question. And Leibniz himself ultimately regards the psychological question as a special instance of the cosmological question.

23. In explaining the distinction in this way I am following Eric Watkins; see "The Development of Physical Influx in Early Eighteenth-Century Germany: Gottsched, Knutzen, and Crusius," in *The Review of Metaphysics* 49 (1995): 295–339.

24. It is not clear if this reading is fair to the French Cartesian Nicolas Malebranche. In Germany in the eighteenth century it seems that the standard reading of

Malebranche was that he denied all activity to finite substances. Malebranche himself seems to have believed that finite individuals do have wills in that they possess the capacity to assert or deny. I think most of his readers in the post-Leibnizian tradition took this to mean that Malebranche denied that finite substances were active *in any meaningful sense.*

25. Suárez does explain action in terms of influence rather than dependence; however, for Suárez *influere* is a transitive verb the direct object of which is *esse* (being); the patient being acted upon is taken as the indirect object of this verb. Suárez does not, then, suggest that in interaction something (say an accident) is transferred from the agent to the patient; instead the agent "flows being into" the patient. What Suárez actually meant by the notion of the agent "flowing being into" the patient is unclear. See Disputation 12 on causality, *De causis entis in communi*, of his *Disputationes Metaphysicae* (*Metaphysical Disputations*, 1597), trans. and annotated by Shane Duarte (unpublished). Leibniz himself seems to have attributed the notion of influence to Suárez, and to have recognized that for Suárez *influere* was a transitive verb with a direct and an indirect object, for he writes that "on the invention of this last word [*influere*] Suárez prides himself not a little. . . . Introducing the phrase 'flow in' ('influx'), he defined a cause as what flows being into something else—a quite barbarous and obscure expression. Even the construction is inept, since *influere* is transformed from an intransitive into a transitive verb; and this *influx* is metaphorical and more obscure than what it defines. I should think it an easier task to define the term 'cause' than this term *influx*, used in such an unnatural sense." From "Preface to an Edition of Nizolius" (1670) in G. W. Leibniz, *Philosophical Papers and Letters*, 2nd ed., ed. and trans. Leroy E. Loemker (Dordrecht: Reidel, 1969), 126.

26. Dennis Des Chene, *Physiologia: Natural Philosophy in Late Aristotelian and Cartesian Thought* (Ithaca: Cornell University Press, 1996), 62.

27. Ibid., 62–63. Here Des Chene is talking about Zabarella; however, a similar story could be told about most of the other Aristotelians, including Aquinas. Aquinas makes it quite clear that he rejects an influctionist model of causation, pointing out that "a natural agent does not hand over its own form to another subject, but it reduces the passive subject from potency to act." Saint Thomas Aquinas, *Summa Contra Gentiles*, vol. 1, book 3, trans. Pegis et al. (Notre Dame: Notre Dame University Press, 1975), 28. Hereafter cited as SCG. The late scholastics advocated a position based upon Aquinas's position that the agent somehow triggers something in the patient that allows a potentiality in the patient to be actualized. As we shall see, this is, interestingly, very close to the view of the mature Kant.

28. Aquinas, *Summa Theologiae*, trans. Fathers of the English Dominican Province (New York: Benziger, 1974), part 1, q. 84, art. 6.

29. See Eileen O'Neill, "*Influxus Physicus*," in *Causation in Early Modern Philosophy: Cartesianism, Occasionalism, and Preestablished Harmony*, ed. Steven Nadler (University Park: The Pennsylvania State University Press, 1993). O'Neill argues that "the most important difference between the [Neoplatonist and Corpuscularian model] concerns the ontological status of what is transmitted in the flow. On the Neoplatonic model, what inflows is distinct from the substance of the agent; on the corpuscular model, the efflux is continuous with this substance" (45). The Corpuscularians believe that the agent is diminished by the efflux, as tiny particles are actually

shed by the agent, whereas the Neoplatonists deny that the agent is diminished in any way by the efflux. Another difference seems to be that Neoplatonists believe that the effect lasts only as long as the agent continues with its activity, whereas as least some Corpuscularians seem to think that the effect can remain in the patient even after the agent has stopped acting.

30. Kenelm Digby, *Two Treatises: In the One of Which, the Nature of Bodies, in the Other, the Nature of Man's Mind, is Looked Into* (Paris: Gilles Blaizot, 1644; facsimile reprint by Garland, 1978), 278.

31. The Corpuscularians clearly do not restrict this influctionist account to explanations of perception; a good example is Gassendi's explanation of magnetism in *De Motu* (1642).

32. I believe that much of Kant's account of property rights in the *Metaphysics of Morals* is an attempt to develop an ontology of property that does not involve an influctionist account of interaction. For Kant, property rights cannot, literally, be transferred.

33. Eric Watkins, "Kant's Theory of Physical Influx," in *Archiv für Geschichte der Philosophie* 77 (1995): 285.

34. G. W. Leibniz, *New Essays on Human Understanding*, ed. and trans. P. Remnant and J. Bennett (Cambridge: Cambridge University Press, 1981), 65.

35. G. W. Leibniz, *Die Philosophischen Schriften von G. W. Leibniz*, vol. 3, ed. C. I. Gerhardt (Berlin: Weidmann, 1875–90), 3:58.

36. A. Robinet, ed., *Malebranche et Leibniz: Relations Personelles* (Paris: J. Vrin, 1955), 421. Quoted in Donald P. Rutherford, "Natures, Laws, and the Roots of Leibniz's Critique of Occasionalism," in *Causation in Early Modern Philosophy*, 139.

37. This idiom may help the reader understand why Kant's engagement with this question had an important impact on his ontology of property.

38. That is, he was and remained a defender of "physical influence" broadly understood.

39. Kant's commitment to this principle can be traced back at least to the *New Elucidation* of 1755. Here Kant argues that "the inner determinations, which already belong to the substance, are posited in virtue of inner grounds which exclude the opposite. Accordingly, if you want another determination to follow, you must also posit another ground. But since the opposite of this ground is internal to the substance, and since, in virtue of what we have presupposed, no external ground is added to it, it is patently obvious that [4] the new determination cannot be introduced into the being" (1:140). In the *New Elucidation*, in advocating the principle of active inherence, Kant agrees with the Leibnizians that individual substances must be thought of as windowless; he agrees that the determinations of a substance must be due to inner grounds. His position, however, diverges from Leibniz's in that he believes that this does not imply that a *change* of determinations must also be due to grounds internal to an individual substance. This allows him to claim that although monads must be windowless, real interaction between them is possible, for one monad may be the cause of *change* in another monad. Here I disagree with Rae Langton, who argues that in the *Physical Monadology* Kant claims that "monads are not windowless, but open to the influence of others." Rae Langton, *Kantian Humility: Our Ignorance of Things in Themselves* (Cambridge: Cambridge University Press, 1998), 105.

40. As we shall see, however, there is at least one thing that we can do that is not the result of another agent withdrawing resistance; namely, "giving laws." It is the giving of laws that creates the resistance between individuals in the first place.

41. At this point I should remind the reader that I believe that for Kant the "idea of a community of individuals in interaction" is what he elsewhere calls the "intelligible world" and "the realm of ends."

42. Who, of course, was strongly influenced by Malabranche's occasionalism.

43. For comments on previous versions of this paper, I would like to thank Paul Guyer, Samuel Freeman, Eric Watkins, Andrea Rehberg, Sam Kerstein, Rae Langton, Ken Westphal, Shane Duarte, Michael Rohlf, Myrna Gabbe, and audience members at the third meeting of the Turkish Kant Working Group, held at Bogaziçi University in November 2004, and at the 2004 APA Eastern Division meeting.

4

Kantian Communities

The Realm of Ends, the Ethical Community, and the Highest Good

Paul Guyer

In his practical philosophy, Kant employs a number of conceptions of community among moral agents, the meanings of which and the relations among which are contested. The realm of ends that Kant introduces in his third formulation of the categorical imperative in the *Groundwork for the Metaphysics of Morals* is clearly a conception of a community of moral agents of some sort: a realm is "a systematic union of various beings through common laws," and a realm of ends is a "whole of all ends in systematic connection (a whole both of rational beings as ends in themselves and of the ends of his own that each may set himself" (G, 4:433).[1] The highest good, which Kant discusses in each of the three *Critiques* (1781/1787, 1788, and 1790) as well as in *Religion within the Boundaries of Mere Reason* (1793) and in the essay "On the Common Saying: 'That May Be Correct in Theory, but It Is of No Use in Practice'" (1793), is clearly a condition of a community of moral agents of some sort, at least in some of Kant's versions of this concept, as when he defines it as "universal happiness combined with and in conformity with the purest morality throughout the world" (TP, 8:279). But what is the relationship between the realm of ends and the highest good? Some authors hold that the concept of the highest good is identical to or follows directly from that of the realm of ends,[2] while others argue that they are quite distinct and that the concept of the highest good as the complete object of morality cannot even be derived from that of the realm of ends.[3] In a section of the "Canon of Pure Reason" in the *Critique of Pure Reason* that is entitled "On the Ideal of the Highest Good," Kant also introduces the concept of the "moral world" as that of a "system of self-rewarding morality" (A809/B837). Is the moral world the same concept as that of the highest good or a different concept? Further, in the *Religion*, Kant speaks of an "ethical community," and contrasts it as an "ethico-civil society" to a political community or "juridico-civil society" (RBMR, 6:94–95); yet while some authors accept this distinction, and insist that an ethical community "may have nothing resembling a *political constitution*,"[4] others argue that the ethical community is fully realized in the condition of international perpetual peace, which according to Kant must be the product of a league of nations that one would have thought does have a political constitution.[5] More generally, some philosophers think that Kantian ethics requires a focus on the agent's own virtue that eliminates a genuine concern for the well-being of others,[6] while other philosophers think that Kantian ethics is so exclusively focused on what is universally owed to others that it allows neither duties attached to particular stations nor any place for a genuine concern with an agent's own projects.[7] Some think that "For Kant, true community involves the collective pursuit of ends set in common with others"[8] and that the ends of morality can only be achieved through collective effort, while others interpret Kant to believe that the achievement of morality is always up to the individual. What is one supposed to make out of such a welter of concepts and conflicting interpretations?

We can make no headway on such issues without a careful analysis of what Kant means by the various concepts that have been mentioned. This paper will thus be an analysis of just what Kant means by the realm of ends, the moral world, the highest good, an ethical community, and the juridico-civil state to which the latter is contrasted, and will trace out some of the relations between these concepts. I will argue in particular that Kant's conception of the highest good underwent some considerable changes from 1781 to 1793, that is, from the *Critique of Pure Reason* to the essay on "theory and practice" and the *Religion*, and that different interpretations of the relation between the concepts of the highest good and the realm of ends can arise from Kant's different conceptions of the highest good. I hope by means of this narrative to bring some order to the current confusion of beliefs about the various concepts of community in Kant's practical philosophy.

The Realm of Ends

The first candidate for a conception of a community of moral agents that Kant introduces into his specifically moral writings is the realm of ends.[9] The realm of ends is the culminating conception in Kant's sequence of formulations of the categorical imperative,[10] and is introduced in the position of a criterion or goal for the selection of maxims, depending perhaps on exactly how one translates the word *zu*: using the concept in the formulation of an imperative, Kant writes that "*alle Maximen aus eigener Gesetzgebung zu einem möglichen Reiche der Zwecke, als einem Reiche der Natur, zusammenstimmen sollen*" (G, 4:436), which Mary Gregor translates as "all maxims from one's own lawgiving are to harmonize with a possible kingdom of ends as with a kingdom of nature,"[11] treating the concept of the realm of ends as a criterion against which one's particular maxims are to be tested, while Allen Wood translates it as "all maxims ought to harmonize from one's own legislation into a possible realm of ends as a realm of nature,"[12] treating it as a goal that is to be achieved through the sum of one's maxims. I find the translation of *zu* as "into" more natural, and thus read the realm of ends as the goal that is to be aimed at in the selection of all of one's maxims. This is also a natural conclusion to draw from the fact that Kant says that this "fruitful concept" follows from the preceding requirement that "every rational being . . . must regard himself as giving universal law through all his maxims" (G, 4:433). The realm of ends is the state of affairs that would be realized if everyone were to conform to this formulation of the categorical imperative as the fundamental norm or command of morality, and is thus the goal, object, or ideal for each agent in his or her selection of maxims in accordance with the fundamental principle of morality. To borrow John Rawls's terminology, the realm of ends is thus the concept of the condition that will be "constructed" in accordance with the categorical imperative, although that does not imply that the preceding formulations of the categorical imperative are to be interpreted "constructivistically," whatever exactly that is supposed to mean.[13]

Now, as already noted, Kant defines the realm of ends as "a whole of all ends in systematic connection (a whole both of rational beings as ends in themselves and of the ends of his own that each may set himself)" (G, 4:433). This suggests that what moral legislation is to aim at is a state of affairs in which every agent who could possibly be affected by one's own choice of maxims is treated as an end and never merely as a means (thus showing that the concept of the realm of ends is firmly anchored in Kant's second formulation of the categorical imperative, which requires precisely that; see G, 4:429), and in which the particular ends set by each such agent, including oneself, are realized to the extent that they are consistent with the treatment of every agent as an end and not merely a means and with each other. As Allen Wood, for example, puts it, "Rational beings constitute a *realm* to the extent that their ends form a *system*. This happens when those ends are not only mutually consistent, but also harmonious and reciprocally supportive. . . . The laws of a realm of ends are such that universally following them would result in the agreement and mutual furthering of the ends of all rational beings in a single unified teleological system"[14]—although if it is not already clear from the expression "a single unified teleological system," I would make it explicit in the last of these sentences that the laws of a realm of ends would result in the agreement of the ends of all those rational beings *who can actually interact with one another* and are thereby residents of a single world. However, immediately prior to the phrase that I am taking as the definition of the concept of the realm of ends, Kant says that "Now since laws determine ends in terms of their universal validity, if we abstract from the personal differences of rational beings as well as from all the content of their private ends we shall be able to think of" a realm of ends in the sense defined (G, 4:433). This could suggest that the realm of ends has no concern with particular ends at all, but is simply the condition in which each agent regards all others as ends in themselves and therefore adopts only maxims that could be accepted by all others, thus only maxims that could be collectively universalized. On this account the realm of ends would simply be a community of autonomous moral legislators but would imply nothing about their ends.

John Rawls might be thought to suggest such an interpretation when he says that "we now come back to viewing ourselves not as subject of the moral law, but as legislators, as it were, of the public moral law of a possible realm of ends," and that "what we legislate, viewed as a moral law for a possible realm of ends, is the whole family of general precepts . . . that are accepted by the [categorical imperative] procedure."[15] However, I take Kant to mean that while adopting only maxims that treat all others as ends in themselves may require that one cannot regard one's own particular ends as sufficient and conclusive reasons for the adoptions of maxims, *what it is* to treat rational beings as ends and not merely as means is precisely to regard all of their ends as worthy of promotion just because they have been set by those rational beings in the exercise of the rational and free agency that gives them their dignity as ends in themselves. This I take to follow from Kant's statement that "Rational nature is distinguished from the rest of nature by this, that it sets itself an end" (G, 4:437).[16] Since the underlying moral requirement is to treat rational beings as ends and never merely as a means *in one's own person as well as in that of others*, the realm of ends formulation of the categorical imperative therefore requires that the particular ends of *oneself and others* be promoted insofar as they form a consistent system, not because of the particular contents of one's own ends or of anyone else's and the particular attachments anyone may have to these ends, but simply because they have been freely chosen by rational beings. And in fact Rawls too recognizes that the realm of ends requires the promotion of particular ends when he writes:

> To understand what Kant means by a whole of ends in systematic conjunction, we should also take into account the next paragraph. Thus, as [Kant] says there (4:433), the systematic conjunction of a realm of ends arises when all reasonable and rational persons treat themselves as well as others as such persons and therefore as ends in themselves. From the second formulation [of the categorical imperative], this means that everyone not only pursues their personal (permissible) ends within the limits of the duties of justice (the rights of man) but also gives significant and appropriate weight to the obligatory ends enjoined by the duties of virtue. These duties, to state them summarily, are to promote one's moral and natural perfection and the happiness of others.[17]

This way of explicating the concept of a systematic whole of ends, however, depends upon the derivation of the duties of justice and the duties of virtue from the requirement that rational nature always be treated as a means and not merely as an end, a derivation that is only sketched in the *Groundwork* (4:422–23 and 429–30) and is not provided in any detail until the much later *Metaphysics of Morals*. Moreover, by employing the latter work's specification of the only ends that are also duties as one's own *perfection* and the happiness of *others* (MM, Doctrine of Right, introduction, §§4–5, 6:385–88), this way of deriving the requirement of the realm of ends potentially creates a problem about the place of *one's own* particular ends in the realm of ends. My analysis, that treating *all* rational being, *both* oneself and others, as ends in themselves directly implies treating the freely set ends of all of those agents as ends for all insofar as that can be consistently done, avoids the dependence on the specific derivations of duties that Rawls's approach requires and the problem about the place of one's own ends in the realm of ends that this approach may bring. But since Kant himself, in spite of his arguments that one's own happiness cannot be an end that is also a duty, ultimately does recognize that "since all *others* with the exception of myself would not be *all* . . . the law making benevolence a duty will include myself, as an object of benevolence, in the command of practical reason" (MM, Doctrine of Virtue, §27, 6:451; emphasis added), he does finally recognize the place of one's own particular ends in the systematic whole of ends required by the realm of ends even on the approach that derives the realm of ends from the ends that are also duties. Rawls's interpretation and the one offered here are thus ultimately coextensive.

Now since virtue is "the moral strength of a *human being's* will in fulfilling his duty, a moral *constraint* through his own lawgiving reason" (MM, Doctrine of Right, introduction, §13, 6:405), what duty requires is that we choose our maxims with the goal of establishing a realm of ends; a realm of ends requires the promotion of all of our individual ends insofar as they are consistent with one another and with the treatment of each agent as an end in him- or herself, maximal happiness consists simply in the satisfaction of a maximally consistent set of ends (see for example, CPrR, 5:124), and the highest good is "universal happiness combined with and in conformity with the purest" virtue or "morality throughout the world" (TP, 8:279), it would seem as if the conceptions of the realm of ends as the goal of morality and the highest good as the object of morality are identical, or at least so closely related that the highest good is the condition that would obtain in a realm of ends so far as that is fully realized. And so I have myself previously suggested.[18] As we saw, however, a commentator like Rawls holds that the conceptions of the realm of ends and the highest good are quite distinct. So we can see that the story of their relationship is going to be at the very least more complicated, and we are going to have to examine each of Kant's chief conceptions of the highest good in order to unravel it. In order to get started on that task, however, we will have to look at another concept of a moral community that Kant introduces in the first *Critique*, the concept of a "moral world"; for it is his exposition of that concept that leads directly to his first concept of the highest good.

The Moral World

Kant defines a moral world as "the world as it would be if it were in conformity with all moral laws (as it *can* be in accordance with the *freedom* of rational beings and *should* be in accordance with the necessary laws of morality" (CPR, A808/B836). Since the realm of ends would be the outcome of "conformity with all moral laws," a world in which the goal of the realm of ends was realized would be a moral world; the concept of the realm of ends is thus one way and, given that this conception culminates Kant's exposition of the categorical imperative in the *Groundwork*, it is perhaps the best way of characterizing the idea of which a moral world would be the realization. Although he has not yet introduced the term "realm of ends," Kant seems to suggest the close connection between the two notions as he continues:

> The idea of a moral world thus has objective reality, not as if it pertained to an object of an intelligible intuition (for we cannot even think of such a thing), but as pertaining to the sensible world, although as an object of pure reason in its practical use and a *corpus mysticum* of the rational beings in it, insofar as their free choice under moral laws has thoroughgoing systematic unity in itself as well as with the freedom of everyone else. (A808/B836)

The exotic expression of a "*corpus mysticum* of rational beings" seems to mean the same as a realm of rational beings each of whom treats all beings as ends and not merely as means, and the "thoroughgoing systematic unity" of "their free choice under moral laws" seems to imply that they would use their free choice to choose a consistent set of particular ends as well as maxims. A *corpus mysticum* of rational beings therefore seems to be the same as a realm of ends, and our duty to make the sensible world agree as far as possible with the idea of a moral world thus seems to be the same as the duty to make it as far as possible into a realm of ends.

To be sure, Kant immediately adds that the concept of a moral world abstracts "from all conditions (ends) and even from all hindrances to morality in it (weakness or impurity of human nature)," and that it is therefore "a mere, yet practical, idea, which really can and should have its influence on the sensible world, in order to make it agree as far as possible with this idea" (A808/B836). I have already suggested how Kant's requirement of abstraction from ends should be dealt with: it should be interpreted as requiring abstraction from one's own personal ends as motives for the adoption of maxims that can harmonize with or into the idea of a realm of ends, but not the irrelevance of particular ends in the determination of what maxims consistent with the moral law require of us and thus in the realization of the realm of ends. Kant's second point, that in the concept of a moral world we abstract from hindrances to morality arising from human weakness or impurity, is what leads to his introduction of the concept of the highest good.

The Highest Good in *The Critique of Pure Reason*

Kant introduces the concept of the highest good into the *Critique of Pure Reason* in a tortuous way. He first appeals to a claim that all who have made themselves *worthy of happiness* by moral conduct should be able to *hope* for happiness:

> I say . . . that just as the moral principles are necessary in accordance with reason in its **practical** use, it is equally necessary to assume in accordance with **reason** in its theoretical use that everyone has cause to hope for happiness in the same measure as he has made himself worthy of it in his conduct, and that the system of morality is therefore inseparably combined with the system of happiness, though only in the idea of pure reason. (A809/B837)

One of Rawls's objections to any equation of the concepts of the realm of ends and the highest good is that the principle that anyone who has proven worthy of happiness by moral or virtuous conduct should be happy does not itself seem to be part of the fundamental principle of morality.[19] One might be tempted to admit this but to maintain at least that as an assertion about *worthiness* this principle must itself be normative, and thus must still be a principle arising from practical reason, even if independently from the fundamental principle of morality. But here Kant seems to suggest that it is a principle of *theoretical* reason. How can this be understood?

Kant may reveal what he has in mind in the next paragraph:

> Now in an intelligible world, i.e., in the moral world, in the concept of which we have abstracted from all hindrances to morality (of the inclinations), such a system of happiness proportionately combined with morality, since freedom, partly moved and partly restricted by moral laws, would itself be the cause of the general happiness, and rational beings, under the guidance of such principles, would themselves be the authors of their own enduring welfare and at the same time that of others. (A809/B837)

This suggests that the principle that those who have proven themselves worthy of happiness by virtuous behavior should be able to hope for happiness is a principle of theoretical reason because it is grounded in a *causal* claim: in ideal circumstances, in which no one's commitment to the principles of morality and their execution was weakened or undermined by refractory inclinations (Kant does not seem to worry about any interference with the efficacy of morality coming from *outside* of *human* nature), happiness would be the causally necessary consequence of moral conduct, and indeed a *system* of happiness or *general* happiness would be the causally necessary consequence of systematic or general morality or virtue, that is, universal compliance with the moral law. This supposition makes sense, of course, only if the realization of particular ends is included in the concept of a moral world, and thus if the concept of a moral world is related to the idea of a realm of ends as it has here been interpreted, since it is the realization of particular ends that produces happiness. Given that assumption, Kant's idea seems to be that theoretical reason's demand that causes should have their proper effects leads to the expectation that universal morality should be accompanied by general happiness. Of course, one might also suppose that practical reason has an independent conception of moral worth and independently holds the normative principle that worthiness to be happy should be accompanied with happiness, and thus that the demands of theoretical and practical reason coincide in the conception of the highest good.

Alas, human beings do have refractory inclinations that can weaken or destroy their commitment to do as morality requires, and so in the sensible world the conditions are not ideal for the realization of the moral world. Here Kant's argument may then seem to take a turn toward an *individualistic* conception of the conjunction between virtue and happiness, in which a normative conception that worthiness to be happy should be accompanied with happiness plays an indispensable role: that is, he seems to be launching an argument that even though in the real conditions of human existence we cannot expect universal compliance with morality and therefore cannot expect general happiness, at least those individuals who are actually virtuous should be able to expect their *own* happiness under some realizable condition:

> But this system of self-rewarding morality is only an idea, the realization of which rests on the condition that **everyone** do what he should. . . . But since the obligation from the moral law remains valid for each particular use of freedom even if others do not conduct themselves in accord with this law, how their consequences will be related to happiness is determined neither by the nature of the things in the world, nor by the causality of actions themselves and their relation to morality; and the necessary connection of the hope of being happy with the unremitting effort to make oneself worthy of happiness . . . cannot be cognized through reason if it is grounded merely in nature, but may be hoped for only if it is at the same time grounded on a **highest**

reason, which commands in accordance with moral laws, as at the same time the cause of nature. (A809–10/B837–38)

Kant then calls the idea of "such an intelligence, in which the morally most perfect will, combined with the highest blessedness, is the cause of all happiness in the world, insofar as it stands in exact relation with morality (as the worthiness to be happy), **the ideal of the highest good**," but more precisely the "ideal of the highest **original** good" that would ground the "practically necessary connection of both elements of the highest derived good, namely of an intelligible, i.e., **moral** world" (A810–11/B839–40). To the highest original good, Kant argues, in an argument he will repeat in each of the three *Critiques*, we must ascribe all but those properties that are necessary for it to ground the highest derived good, namely, omnipotence, omniscience, omnipresence, and eternity (A815/B843; see also *CPrR*, 5:139, and *CJ*, §86, 5:444); we must thus postulate God so defined as the ground of the highest derived good. Kant also holds that since the "sensible world" does not offer the necessary connection of both elements of the highest derived good, we must assume the moral world in which these elements will be joined "to be a world that is future for us," and thus "God and a future life are two presuppositions that are not to be separated from the obligation that pure reason imposes on us in accordance with principles of that very same reason" (A811/B839).

I say that Kant seems to be offering an individualistic conception of the highest good (that is, the highest derived good, but I will usually leave that qualification out) here because his argument starts from the premise that one cannot count on *everyone* behaving morally in the sensible world, where morality would be self-rewarding only if everyone did. He then apparently urges each one of us to fulfill individually our moral obligations nevertheless; that is, regardless of the noncompliance of others, in the hope that the "unremitting effort to make oneself worthy of happiness" will be rewarded with happiness in a future life by a God who in his omniscience knows what we have attempted to do even if because of the noncompliance of others our virtue will not be rewarded in our normal lifetime.

However, Kant repeatedly states that what we must believe to be possible in a future life is a moral *world*, not simply our individual happiness. He says that "Morality in itself constitutes a system, but happiness does not, except insofar as it is distributed precisely in accordance with morality. This, however, is possible only in the intelligible world, under a wise author and regent" (A811/B839). Borrowing Leibniz's expression, he calls this future life "the **realm of grace**" (A812/B840), where the word "realm" suggests that *all* will be moral and happy. He says that "happiness in exact proportion with the morality of rational beings, through which they are worthy of it, alone constitutes the highest good of a world in which we must without exception transpose ourselves in accordance with the precepts of pure but practical reason" (A814/B842), thus indicating that what we must believe in is a whole world in which all rational beings worthy of happiness are rewarded with it, not just the possibility of our own happiness.

And finally he refers to the highest good as "this systematic unity of ends in this world of intelligences" (A815/B843). Kant's view thus seems to be not that the individual who does the right thing throughout his earthly life must be able to hope for his own happiness as a reward in spite of the refractory behavior of others around him, and that the individual's commitment to morality will be weakened if he cannot expect this reward; rather, his view seems to be that a genuinely moral agent must aim at the morality and the happiness of all, and that his commitment to morality will be weakened if he cannot believe in the possibility of the realization of this complete object of morality. Kant says that "without a God and a world that is not now visible to us but is hoped for, the majestic ideas of morality are, to be sure, objects of approbation and admiration but not incentives for resolve and realization, because they would not fulfill the whole end that is natural for every rational being and determined *a priori* and necessarily through the very same pure reason" (A813/B841). The end that is natural for every rational being might be only his or her own happiness, but the end that is determined *a priori* and necessarily for every rational being through pure reason is surely the morality of all and the happiness of all as a consequence of that morality, so all rational beings must be able to believe in the possibility of this end for all in order to maintain their moral resolve.

In spite of some language that might initially suggest otherwise, then, even in the first *Critique* Kant's conception of the highest good is clearly communalistic rather than individualistic: that is, it postulates the realization of a moral world as the condition that would obtain if the categorical imperative were universally observed and thus the harmonization of all of our maxims into a realm in which all are treated as ends in themselves and all of their lawful and consistent particular ends are realized, not a condition in which just some individuals who happen to have been virtuous are rewarded with their own happiness. Further, in spite of some remarks that might be taken otherwise, Kant's ideal of a moral world as the highest good seems to be generated by pure reason's demand for completeness. As we saw, Kant's generation of this ideal may be meant to invoke both practical and theoretical reason, the latter demanding that the consequences of the actions demanded by the former actually come to pass; but then again, Kant may mean that pure practical reason alone demands both virtue from all and happiness for all as a product of that virtue, and the postulation of the conditions necessary for the realization of this highest good may depend only on that interpretation of the demand of morality plus the general canon of rationality that what ought to be the case must be able to be the case. Either way, Kant's argument for the highest good would *not* seem to depend upon an independent *normative* principle that virtue should be accompanied with its just reward, contrary to what Rawls, for example, supposed.

Also, contrary to some popular views,[20] there is nothing in Kant's suggested grounds for the ideal of the highest good that would require that we postulate the existence of God in order to guarantee the provision of divine *punishments* in strict proportion to human *vice*. Kant's statement that "happiness in exact proportion with the morality of rational beings, through which they are worthy of it, alone constitutes the highest good" (A814/B842) is often taken to mean that in a morally ideal world the virtuous would be rewarded with happiness in proportion to the exact degree of their virtue and the vicious punished in exact proportion to their vice, thus that a divine judge is necessary to ensure that each of these conditions will be met, and indeed Kant may fall into that thought elsewhere; but there is nothing about punishment in the present argument at all. The argument is simply that morality requires the happiness of all within its own limits, that under ideal conditions morality would be self-rewarding, or automatically produce that happiness, that conditions are not ideal in the sensible world, but that our resolve to do what morality requires would be weakened if we had to believe that it is unfeasible, therefore we must postulate life in a future world grounded by God in order to maintain our resolve to do what morality demands.

One last point. Kant's conception of the highest good in the first *Critique* is often called a "religious" conception rather than a "secular" or even "political" conception of the highest good.[21] Any simple contrast between "religious" and "secular" conceptions of the highest good is, however, seriously misleading. Kant's conception of the highest good in the first *Critique* clearly supposes that morality will be self-rewarding with happiness only in a *future life*, and postulates God as the condition of morality's self-rewarding production of happiness in that future life. In subsequent accounts, Kant will suggest that we must be able to suppose that morality will produce happiness in *this life*, or more precisely, if not in the earthly life of a particular human being then at least in the earthly course of the human species. So we might distinguish between *future-life* and *present-life* conceptions of the highest good, *transcendent* and *immanent* conceptions, or perhaps most simply between *heavenly* and *earthly* conceptions of the locus where both the morality and the happiness demanded by the ideal of the highest good will be realized. But wherever or whenever it is supposed to occur, Kant always supposes that we will need to postulate the existence of God as the *ground* of the conjunction of virtue and happiness, and if belief in the existence of God is sufficient to make anything dependent upon it religious, then to that extent Kant's conception of the highest good is never anything other than religious. This is so even if the set of rational beliefs needed in order to ground conviction in the possibility of the highest good does not always include belief in a future life. Either a heavenly or an earthly conception of the highest good remains religious as long as it involves the postulation of the existence of God.

While clearly both heavenly and religious, Kant's conception of the highest good in the first *Critique* nevertheless seems incoherent. This is because he argues that we must postulate God as the author *of nature* (A810/B839), even though God is postulated to ensure that our collective efforts to be moral will be accompanied with collective happiness in a future, that is to say, *nonnatural* life. Yet there is no reason why we would need to postulate God as the author of nature if s/he were needed to deliver a result only in a nonnatural world. Kant's argument could be saved from incoherence if it was meant to claim that God must be postulated as the only ground for the possibility of our collective compliance with the demands of morality in *this* earthly life; that is, as the only possible ground for our *virtue*, even though that compliance is to be rewarded with happiness only in a future, heavenly life. As we will subsequently see, in *Religion within the Boundaries of Mere Reason* Kant does apparently argue that God must be postulated as the ground of the possibility of the "ethical community," which is in turn a condition of the possibility of the achievement of virtue in this life, and so does argue for the first part of the position just described. But in the first *Critique* he seems to postulate the divine author of nature only as the ground for a heavenly realization of happiness, so his position does seem to be incoherent.

The Highest Good in the *Critique of Practical Reason*

Kant makes only two passing references to the highest good in the *Groundwork for the Metaphysics of Morals* (4:409, 412), the first of which is a reference to God, thus to the highest original rather than derived good. But of course the concept of the highest good is the crux of the "Dialectic" in the *Critique of Practical Reason*, which is Kant's most extended discussion of the postulates of pure practical reason. Here Kant's exposition may seem to suggest an individualistic conception of the highest good even more strongly than did his discussion in the first *Critique*, although after some pages of tension he may also come down in favor of a communalistic conception even more clearly than he previously did. His account remains what I am calling a heavenly rather than earthly conception of the highest good, although in this case it is clearly the perfection of virtue rather than the deliverance of happiness that Kant postpones to a future life. This might seem to remove the incoherence of postulating God as an author of nature who makes its laws (which govern the deliverance of happiness) consistent with the laws of morality, when happiness is supposed to be delivered only in a nonnatural afterlife rather than in the natural life of human beings, whether individually or collectively. But Kant's account remains incoherent, since there is no reason why happiness should need to be delivered within nature or consistently by its laws if virtue is to be perfected only in a nonnatural future life, and it would indeed seem premature for happiness to be delivered within nature if virtue can be realized only beyond nature.

Kant introduces the concept of the highest good into the *Critique of Practical Reason* in a way that strongly suggests that it must include the ideal of the happiness of all insofar as that is consistent with and the product of universal morality. He states that "pure practical reason . . . seeks the unconditioned for the practically conditioned (which rests on inclinations and natural needs), not indeed as the determining ground of the will, but even when this is given (in the moral law), it seeks the unconditioned totality of the object of pure practical reason, under the name of the **highest good**" (CPrR, 5:108). Here Kant does not, as in the *Critique of Pure Reason*, suggest that a separate appeal to theoretical reason is necessary to explain reason's interest in the unconditioned: practical reason itself suffices as the source for the demand for not only complete compliance with the moral law but also for the complete realization of the consequences of such compliance, namely, the realization of the particular ends set by ends in themselves and the happiness that would be the natural consequence of such realization.

Since the moral law demands that all rational beings who can be affected by one another's choice of maxim be treated as ends in themselves, and therefore that all their particular ends and, by consequence, the happiness of all of them be promoted, a communalistic rather than individualistic conception of the highest good is obviously grounded. Kant confirms the intimate connection between the moral law and a happiness that can therefore only be the happiness of all in concluding the opening chapter of the "Dialectic of Pure Practical Reason": while he has been insisting that "the moral law is the sole determining ground of the pure will," he adds that it is "evident that if the moral law is already included as supreme condition in the concept of the highest good, the highest good is then not merely **object**: the concept of it and the representation of its existence as possible by our practical reason are at the same time the **determining ground** of the pure will" (CPrR, 5:109). This statement can only be explained on the assumption that promoting the morally permissible and consistent ends of all, and therefore the happiness that would result for all from the realization of those ends, is itself enjoined by the moral law requiring that all be treated as ends in themselves, and the ensuing argument should then be that the conditions for the realization of this objective must be postulated as conditions for the coherence of attempting to do what morality demands.

The second chapter of the "Dialectic," however, might seem to introduce grounds for an individualistic rather than communalistic conception of the highest good. Here Kant begins by suggesting that their own, individual happiness is a natural desire of "rational finite beings," that is, human beings who have both pure reason and natural desires, and that "to need happiness, to be also worthy of it, and yet not to participate in it cannot be consistent with the perfect volition of a rational being that would at the same time have all power" (*CPrR*, 5:110). Such a perfectly rational being might seem to be willing in accordance with the principle that anyone who proves worthy of happiness by his or her own virtue should be rewarded with happiness, regardless of what others have done or will receive; and this, moreover, would seem to be the sort of independent normative principle not derivable from the moral law itself that leads Rawls to argue that the concept of the highest good must be distinct from the concept of an ideal that can be derived from the fundamental law of morality itself, namely, the realm of ends and its realization in a moral world.

However, Kant continues the passage just cited by saying that "inasmuch as virtue and happiness together constitute possession of the highest good in a person, and happiness distributed in exact proportion to morality (as the worth of a person and his worthiness to be happy) constitutes the **highest good** of a possible world, the latter means the whole, the complete good, in which, however, virtue as the condition is always the supreme condition, since it has no further condition above it" (*CPrR*, 5:110–11). The contrast between the highest good of a person and the highest good of a possible world, together with the claim that the latter means the whole, complete good, strongly suggest that Kant invokes an individual conception of the highest good only in order to introduce the communal conception, and that it is the whole that is in fact the proper object of morality, which must be shown to be believable through the postulates of pure practical reason in order to prevent the commitment to morality from becoming undermined. Of course, the happiness of any individual, that is, the satisfaction of his or her particular but lawful ends, will also be part of the communal highest good.

Yet this impression might itself seem to be undermined a page later, when Kant writes that

> it is clear from the Analytic that the maxims of virtue and those of one's own happiness are quite heterogeneous with respect to their supreme practical principle, and even though they belong to one highest good, so as to make it possible, yet they are so far from coinciding that they greatly restrict and infringe upon one another in the same subject. Thus the question, *how is the highest good possible?* still remains an unsolved problem. (*CPrR*, 5:112)

This might seem to suggest once again that the concept of the highest good is that of an individual's virtue rewarded with happiness, regardless of the condition of others. However, that would be a misinterpretation of the passage. Kant has shown in the "Analytic" of the *Critique of Practical Reason* that the *maxim* of virtue and the *maxim* of one's own happiness are utterly heteronomous; thus, that there is no moral value in wishing or aiming for one's own happiness for its own sake and that such a maxim is utterly incompatible with a commitment to the moral law for its own sake. But the ultimate resolution of the problem about the relation between one's own virtue and happiness will ultimately be solved precisely by the recognition that one's own happiness is part of the happiness of all; thus, that insofar as the virtuous commitment to the fundamental principle of morality in fact requires the promotion of universal and systematic happiness, it in fact also requires the promotion of one's own happiness, although not on the immediate ground that one's desire for happiness makes it unconditionally valuable, but rather on the indirect ground that this is a consequence of what is required by the fundamental moral requirement to treat all humanity, in one's own person and that of every other, as an end and never merely as a means. Kant subsequently makes this clear when he writes that

> although in the concept of the highest good, as that of a whole in which the greatest happiness is represented as connected in the most exact proportion with the greatest degree of moral perfection (possible in creatures), **my own happiness** is included, this is nevertheless not the determining ground of the will that is directed to promote the highest good; it is instead the moral law (which, on the contrary, limits by strict conditions my unbounded craving for happiness). (CPrR, 5:129–30)

This is Kant's ultimate resolution between morality's insistence on the unconditional value of all rational beings and one's natural desire for one's own happiness: one is allowed to will and strive for one's own happiness, but only as part of the systematic and universal happiness that one must will and strive for as a consequence of the moral law itself. Thus Kant's ultimate solution to the tension between the demands of morality and the demands of nature in the second *Critique* depends squarely on a communalistic rather than individualistic conception of the highest good.

That being said, elements of an individualistic rather than communalistic conception of the highest good do remain in the second *Critique*. One place they do *not* remain is in any suggestion of the view that virtuous individuals should be rewarded with happiness and vicious individuals should be punished with unhappiness, and that an omniscient and omnipotent God must be postulated in order to ground our assurance that this will happen. In spite of Kant's use of the term "exact proportion," there is no basis in the argument of the second *Critique* for the ascription of such a view to Kant, because, as we have just seen, he unequivocally states that the concept of the highest good is "that of a whole in which the greatest happiness is represented as connected in the most exact proportion with the greatest degree of moral perfection (possible in creatures)." Morality requires the virtue of all together with the happiness of all as its ideal consequence, or "self-reward" in the language of freedom; it simply says nothing about punishment.

However, an individualistic conception of the highest good does rear its head in Kant's argument that immortality must be postulated as the condition for the realization of the "greatest degree of moral perfection." A key difference between the argument of the first *Critique* and that of the second is that while in the earlier work a future life was postulated as the locus for the realization of the happiness that is supposed to follow from virtue, in the second *Critique* immortality is postulated as the condition for the possibility of the perfection of human virtue in the form of holiness. Thus Kant writes that in a will determinable by the moral law,

> the **complete conformity** of dispositions with the moral law is the supreme condition of the highest good. . . . Complete conformity of the will with the moral law is, however, **holiness**, a perfection of which no rational being of the sensible world is capable of at any moment of his existence. Since it is nevertheless required as practically necessary, it can only be found in an **endless progress** toward that complete conformity, and in accordance with principles of pure practical reason it is necessary to assume such a practical progress as the real object of our will.
>
> This endless progress is, however, possible only on the presupposition of the **existence** and personality of the same rational being continuing **endlessly** (which is called the immortality of the soul). (CPrR, 5:122)

Here Kant supposes that each person committed to morality must believe that he or she has adequate time to perfect his or her own virtue by attaining the state of holiness, and therefore that he or she is immortal. There is no reference to any community of beings collectively perfecting their virtue in an endless future life. And if the perfection of virtue is an individual affair, then presumably the happiness that will somehow accompany that perfection—we cannot quite say that it will be realized at the end of an endless progress, like a pot of gold at the end of a rainbow—is also an individual affair.

Perhaps this lapse into individualism is just a manner of speaking, not something that should really undermine the communalistic character of Kant's conception of the highest good in the second *Critique*. There are nevertheless two profound problems with Kant's treatment of the postulate of immortality. The first is simply that he gives no reason for the demand that the perfection of human virtue take the form of *holiness*, which on Kant's account is the condition of a will that simply has no inclinations contrary to the requirements of morality, "an accord of the will with the pure moral law becoming, as it were, our nature, an accord never to be disturbed (in which case the law would finally cease to be a command for us, in which case we could never be tempted to be unfaithful to it)" (CPrR, 5:82). Kant himself, as we have seen, finally states that the concept of the highest good is that of the greatest happiness in exact proportion with the greatest moral perfection *possible in creatures*, and Kant gives no reason why we should think of the latter as consisting in anything other than refusing to act upon any inclinations contrary to the moral law in one's natural lifetime. Indeed Kant himself suggests precisely that when he says that "The moral law is . . . for the will of a perfect being a law of **holiness**, but for the will of every finite rational being a law of **duty**, of moral necessitation and of the determination of his actions through **respect** for this law and **reverence** for his duty" (5:82). Finite rational beings should thus be able to perfect their virtue by maintaining this respect and reverence throughout their natural life spans, and there is no need for immortality in order to attain the highest degree of moral perfection possible for creatures. In this regard, Kant's argument for the postulate of immortality in the second *Critique* seems even worse than his argument for it in the first.

Kant's position on the necessary conditions for the conjunction of virtue and happiness in the second *Critique* also seems incoherent in the same way as his position in the first *Critique*. In the first *Critique* there seemed to be no reason for Kant to insist upon the postulation of God as an author of laws of nature that would make happiness a consequence of virtue when he also insisted that happiness would be realized only in a nonnatural future life. In the second *Critique* Kant is even more insistent that God is postulated precisely as an author or "supreme cause" of nature, the laws of which make possible happiness proportioned to morality (CPrR, 5:124–25), but there is again no need for happiness proportioned to morality to be possible in nature if morality itself can be perfected only in a nonnatural afterlife.

Kant's conception of the highest good in the second *Critique* is basically communalistic rather than individualistic. It lapses into both individualism and incoherence when it requires individual immortality for the perfection of virtue, although even then it does not suggest that the highest good consists in the apportionment of rewards and punishments in response to individual virtue and vice. It is incoherent in requiring God as an author of laws that make happiness the consequence of virtue within nature when it postulates the perfection of virtue only beyond nature. But that leaves room for a requirement of God as the ground for the conjunction of virtue and happiness on a conception according to which both of those must be achieved by and for the human community within nature. That is essentially the earthly but still religious form that Kant's conception of the highest good takes in his works of the 1790s, although even then we shall see that Kant sometimes emphasizes the postulation of God as the condition for the realization of the happiness of the human species once it has perfected its virtue as far as is possible for finite creatures, and other times emphasizes God as the condition for the possibility of the perfection of virtue itself—in this way mirroring the distinction between the roles assigned to the postulate of immortality in the first and second *Critiques*.

The Highest Good and the Ethical Community in the 1790s

As did the first two *Critiques*, the *Critique of the Power of Judgment* also culminates with the argument that the highest good is the necessary object of morality and the foundation for an "ethicotheology" (CJ, §86, 5:442). Kant adds little to his previous attempts to explain why morality makes the highest good its object, except to emphasize that the ends that rational beings can choose to set for themselves are suggested by nature, for that reason fall under the rubric of happiness, and that the highest good at which morality aims is therefore properly described as "the **highest good in the world** possible through freedom" (§87, 5:450). There is no room here for a conception of the highest good as something that can be completed only in a nonnatural afterlife, and any such conception would be especially inconsistent with Kant's objectives in the "Critique of Teleological Judgment," which is to complete his philosophy *of nature* by arguing that although we can explain phenomena in nature only by mechanical laws, we must also be able to conceive of those laws themselves as having been designed to make it possible for us to realize our "final end," the development of our freedom and the achievement of our happiness through our own freedom (see also §84, 5:435), *within* nature. And for this reason, Kant's standard argument that we can specify the properties of God only as the conditions of the possibility of the realization of the highest good emphasizes that God's properties ground the possibility of the realization of the highest good in nature:

> In relation to the **highest good** possible under his rule alone, namely, the existence of rational beings under moral laws, we will conceive of this original being as **omniscient**, so that even what is inmost in their dispositions (which is what constitutes the real moral value of the actions of rational beings *in the world*) is not hidden from him; as **omnipotent,** *so that he can make the whole of nature suitable for this highest end*; as **omnibenevolent** and at the same time **just,** because these two properties (united in **wisdom**) constitute the conditions of the causality of a supreme *cause of the world* as a highest good under moral laws; and likewise all of the remaining transcendental properties, such as **eternity, omnipresence**, etc. (for goodness and justice are moral properties), which must

be presupposed in relation to such a final end, must also be thought in such a being. —In this way **moral** teleology makes good the defect of **physical** teleology, and first establishes a **theology**. (CJ, §86, 5:44; italics added)

That Kant describes the conditions for the realization of the highest good as a *moral teleology* makes it clear that the highest good is supposed to be realized in nature even though we must believe it to have a divine ground: Kant's view here is thus clearly what I have called an earthly but religious view. Kant does mention eternity, but only as a property of God, not of human beings. He makes no use of the argument of the first *Critique* that we must postulate our own immortality to give us time for the realization of our happiness nor of the argument of the second *Critique* that we must postulate immortality in order to give us time for the perfection of our virtue. References to immortality, and thus to a heavenly rather than earthly conception of the highest good, recur only at the end of the third *Critique*, where Kant is analyzing the "kind of affirmation produced by means of a practical faith" (§91, 5:467), and formulaically repeats his earlier thesis that the existence of God and the immortality of the soul are **"matters of faith"** because they are **"the sole conditions"** of the possibility of the highest good (5:469), without any argument that would show why immortality is among these conditions (see also 5:470, 5:471, and 5:473, where the reference to immortality is ritualistically repeated). Kant does not explicitly surrender his heavenly conception of the conditions for the realization of the highest good, but it is inconsistent with his claim that only a moral teleology can ground moral theology.

Kant returned to the topic of the highest good in his two important publications of 1793, the essay "On the Common Saying: 'That May Be Correct in Theory, but It Is of No Use in Practice'" and the book *Religion within the Boundaries of Mere Reason*. The first is a seminal work in which Kant first published the main themes of his political philosophy, but its first section is a polemic with Christian Garve, who had argued that Kant's theory of the highest good could undermine his insistence that moral motivation must be pure, because it makes the promise of individual happiness a motivation for morality, and that the only way for Kant to avoid this is to remove any consideration of ends and therefore happiness from morality altogether (TP, 8:280–81).[22] Kant vehemently objected to both parts of Garve's charge. He argued that the human being must *abstract* from his individualistic natural end of his own happiness in determining his duty and not make his own happiness "the **condition** of his compliance with the law prescribed to him by reason," but that he "is not thereby required to **renounce** his natural end" (TP, 8:278–79), and he then argued that "this concept of duty does not have to be grounded on any particular end but rather **introduces** another end for the human being's will; namely, to work to the best of one's ability toward the **highest good** possible in the world (universal happiness combined with and in conformity to the purest morality throughout the world" (8:279). Kant insists that "not every end is moral (e.g., that of one's own happiness is not)," but that a truly moral end must be "unselfish," thus, in the language I have been using here, communalistic. But a human will must have an end, and thus a moral human will must have an unselfish end, and this gives rise to the necessity of the object of the highest good as a communalistic "whole of all ends":

> The need for a final end assigned by pure reason and comprehending the whole of all ends under one principle (a world as the highest good and possible through our cooperation) is a need of an unselfish will **extending** itself beyond observance of the formal law to production of an object (the highest good). This is a special kind of determination of the will; namely, through the idea of the whole of all ends, the basis of which is that **if** we stand in certain moral relations to things in the world we must everywhere obey the moral law, and beyond this there is the duty to bring it about as far as we can **that** such a relation (a world in keeping with the moral highest end) exists. . . . A determination of the will that limits itself and its aim of belonging to such a whole to this condition is **not selfish**. (TP, 8:279–80n)

Kant's claim that the idea of the highest good is that of a whole of all ends that is not selfish implies that it includes one's own ends, but only as part of the ends of all with whom we may stand "in certain moral relations . . . in the world." Thus one does not need to renounce one's own ends and the desire for their fulfillment in one's own happiness, but to abstract from them as an *incentive* in making the highest good one's *object* (8:279)—and then the concept of the highest good will itself make one's own happiness part of one's object.

Kant maintains that the realization of the highest good "is within our control from one quarter but not from both taken together," and that for this reason we must believe "in a moral ruler of the world and in a future life" (8:279). Presumably he means that our virtue is within our own control, but our happiness is not, and that we must postulate both God and immortality to ensure the possibility of the latter—which would bring him back to the position of the first *Critique*. But this way of talking may be just a matter of habit here; his primary concern is to make clear that the highest good is not a conception of individual reward but a communal object of communal effort.

He gives somewhat more attention to the postulate of immortality in *Religion within the Boundaries of Mere Reason*, but only as part of a complex argument that suggests that the idea of immortality is a *subjective* way of *representing* the moral conversion from evil to good and thus the perfection of virtue, but *cannot* be considered a genuinely necessary condition for the perfection of virtue. Thus, in spite of what one might expect from a book that purports to argue that among the historical religions Christianity most closely approximates the contents of the religion of reason, Kant's *Religion* may diminish the importance of the postulate of immortality even more than the third *Critique* and the essay on theory and practice had already done. At the same time, the *Religion* adds to Kant's "ethicotheology" the positive argument that the existence of God must be postulated as the condition of the possibility of the existence of the "ethical community," which is an earthly condition of cooperation that facilitates the development of individual and thereby collective virtue. Thus Kant finally concludes that the perfection of virtue required by the highest good is a collective goal to be achieved within the natural life of human beings, and that God is necessary as the condition of that possibility—which finally makes his conception of the perfection of virtue coherent with his view held since the second *Critique* that the collective happiness of human beings required by the highest good is to be realized within nature, and that God must therefore be postulated as the author of laws of nature consistent with the moral law. Kant thereby arrives at a coherent conception of the highest good as an earthly condition that would realize the normative ideal of the realm of ends and a moral world, but that requires the postulation of a divine condition of its possibility.

The present discussion of the *Religion* will therefore touch upon its treatments of the highest good, immortality, and the ethical community. Kant's preface to the *Religion*, composed within a few months of the composition of the essay on theory and practice as well as the four essays that comprise the new book, begins by reiterating the point of the first part of the former: Kant distinguishes again between pure moral *motivation*, which abstracts from all ends except for rational beings as ends in themselves, and the *object* of morality, which has a "necessary reference to" ends "not as the ground of its maxims but as a necessary consequence accepted in conformity to them" (*RBMR*, 6:4). Kant holds again that "in the absence of all reference to an end no determination of the will can take place in human beings at all," so that "it cannot possibly be a matter of indifference to reason how to answer the question, **what then is the result of this right conduct of ours?**" (*RBMR*, 6:4–5). He then states that although the idea of the highest good is not the "foundation" of morality, it does *rise out* of morality, because what it does is to unite "within itself the formal condition of all such ends as we ought to have (duty) with everything that is conditional upon ends that we have and that conforms to duty (happiness) proportioned to its observance" (*RBMR*, 6:5). Using Kant's subsequent exposition of his theory of duties in the *Metaphysics of Morals* to interpret this statement,[23] we can understand it to mean that through the direct requirements of duty, morality requires us to make our own perfection, including our moral perfection, and the happiness of others our end, while morality allows us to pursue our own happiness as far as doing so is consistent with the duties just enumerated. And from this we can derive the conclusion that *each* of us must make our *own* virtue and the happiness of *all*—our own *and* that of all others—our object, while *together* we must make both the virtue of all and the happiness of all our own insofar as that is required by and consistent with morality. Thus morality generates an entirely communalistic conception of the highest good as its object and, ideally, necessary consequence. And Kant also emphasizes that this end must be achieved within nature:

> It cannot be a matter of indifference to morality, therefore, whether it does or does not fashion for itself the concept of an ultimate end of all things (although, to be sure, harmonizing with this end does not increase the number of morality's virtues, but rather provides these with a special point for the uni- fication of all ends); for only in this way can an objective practical reality be given to the combination, which we simply cannot do without, of the purpo- siveness from freedom and the purposiveness of nature. (*RBMR*, 6:5)

Thus the *Religion* begins with a clear statement that the highest good is a communal condition, realizing the aims of morality and thus the norma- tive conception of the realm of ends or a moral world, that must be realized within nature—although of course, given the character of the work, within a nature that itself must be conceived as having a divine ground.

Kant touches only briefly upon immortality in the *Religion*, and his posi- tion is not easy to interpret. Kant introduces the idea of immortality in the second part of the *Religion*, where he considers the Christian image of the Son of God as a model for persuading ourselves that we human beings can do what we know we ought to do. As in the second *Critique*, he interprets the moral goal of the perfection of our virtue as the attainment of holiness, and assumes that "the distance between the goodness that we ought to effect in ourselves and the evil from which we start is . . . infinite and, so far as the deed is concerned—i.e., the conformity of the conduct of one's life to the holiness of the law—is not exhaustible in any time" (*RBMR*, 6:66). How- ever, instead of next arguing that we must therefore postulate that we have an infinite time in which to achieve holiness in our disposition, Kant instead says that we must *nevertheless* assume the possibility of a change of heart from evil into a disposition entirely committed to "the universal and pure maxim of the agreement of conduct with the law, as the germ from which all good is to be developed—which proceeds from a holy principle adopted by the human being in his supreme maxim" (6:66).

Kant then adds that "according to our mode of estimation" (*nach unserer Schätzung*), "unavoidably restricted to temporal conditions in our conceptions of the relation of cause to effect," we may conceive of our moral conversion only "as a continuous advance *in infinitum* from a defective good to something better," in which our action is "**at each instance** inadequate to a holy law," but that in the view of "him who scrutinizes the heart (through his pure intellectual intuition," our moral conversion *can* be seen as "a perfected whole even with respect to the deed (the life conduct)"; thus a human being "can still expect to be **generally** well-pleasing to God, *at whatever point in time his existence is cut short*" (*RBMR*, 6:67; final emphasis added). Thus the imperfection of our knowledge of our own motivation combined with our inability to foresee the moment of our own death, which leaves an indefinitely extendable although not infinite series of actions open for us, may lead us to see our own moral conversion as an indefinitely extended progress, but God can see that our moral conversion *has actually been completed*. A non-natural infinite lifespan is therefore unnecessary for us to prove our worthiness of happiness, although a nonnatural *judge* may be necessary to see that we have proven that worthiness in our natural and therefore finite lifespan.

Kant then adds that "*if* after this life another awaits" a human being who as far as he can see has made steady improvement in his moral conduct, then he can reasonably hope that he will persevere in this progress in that second life, "for on the basis of what he has perceived in himself so far, he can legitimately assume that his disposition is fundamentally improved" (*RBMR*, 6:68; emphasis added; see also 6:77). But this is not to argue that we must believe that a future life is necessary in order to complete our moral conversion from evil to good; on the contrary, it is merely to observe that if there is a future life then we can believe that the moral conversion that we have in fact, but not to our own certain knowledge, completed in this life will continue to determine our disposition. This may well represent a radical change from Kant's earlier argument for the postulation of immortality: here he is merely showing how the Christian belief in immortality can be added to his own conception of moral conversion, but he is not arguing that we must believe in immortality in order to believe in the possibility of complete moral conversion from evil to good.

Part Three of the *Religion* turns to the possibility of "the victory of the good principle over the evil principle," which would lead to "the founding of a realm of God *on earth*" (*RBMR*, 6:93; emphasis added), the very title of the part, thereby making it clear that Kant now unequivocally holds that the moral world must be achieved within nature although we must believe in a divine condition of its possibility. The two key steps to Kant's argument here are that the individual perfection of virtue requires the support of an ethical community, and that we can only believe that the possibility of such a community itself depends upon the existence of God; in what is really Kant's final statement of his theory of the postulates of pure practical reason, the postulate of the existence of God thus serves as the condition of the possibility of the greatest *virtue* of human beings rather than, or at least prior to, serving as the condition of the possibility of their *happiness*. In this regard Kant reverts to the approach of the second *Critique*, although not as part of an argument for personal immortality.

Neither step in Kant's argument, I hasten to add, is well-developed. Although his concept of ethical community has recently drawn a considerable amount of favorable press,[24] Kant is actually extremely vague about its role in the perfection of virtue. He begins Part Three with a quick argument (or allusion to a Rousseauian argument) that a human being will become vicious only when he is "**among other human beings**," thus creating opportunities for envy, addiction to power, avarice, and the malignant inclinations associated with these" (RBMR, 6:93–94). Obviously, the presence of others is necessary to create *opportunities* for the development of such vices, but Kant must also be assuming that the presence of others creates a *tendency* to the development of these vices. (In this argument Kant says nothing about the origin of purely self-regarding vices, such as sloth or gluttony.)

Kant then says that without "a union that has for its end the prevention of this evil and the promotion of the good in the human being—an enduring and ever expanding society, solely designed for the preservation of morality by counteracting evil with united forces—however much the individual human being might do to escape from the domain of this evil, he would still be held in incessant danger of relapsing into it" (6:94). Although one might have expected Kant to argue that a community collectively committed to virtue would prevent such vices as envy and avarice from *arising* by providing pressures to virtue opposed to the pressures to vice that are otherwise prevalent in society, what this statement suggests is rather that the ethical community can only *reinforce* individual commitments to virtue rather than vice, thereby preventing *relapses* from individual conversions to the good. This might in fact be what one should expect given Kant's general theory of the absolute freedom of moral agents, but it does restrict the role of the ethical community, making it not a necessary condition for moral conversion, but rather possibly only one support for the maintenance of virtue once it has been achieved. But even if this is all that the ethical community actually does, that would at least obviate the obvious objection that the ethical community is nothing but the *product* of individual choices to be virtuous, playing no role at all in the individual choices to be virtuous. One thing that we should take away from Kant's discussion of individual moral progress in Part Two of the *Religion* is that although human beings may undergo true moral conversions within their finite life spans even if they can never be certain that they have in fact done so, their virtue is not complete at one moment but must be maintained throughout that lifespan. Communal support for that effort rather than pressure to undermine it would certainly be welcome.

Kant is also vague about just *how* the ethical community provides its support for its members' efforts to maintain their virtue. He says little more than that "In addition to prescribing laws to each individual human being, morally legislative reason also unfurls a banner of virtue as a rallying point for all those who love the good, that they may congregate under it and thus at the very start gain the upper hand over evil and its untiring attacks" (*RBMR*, 6:94). Kant emphasizes that it would be contradictory for the ethical community to advance the cause of virtue by providing coercive enforcement of moral laws—this must be left to the "**juridico-civil** (political) **state**" (6:95), which can of course coercively enforce only a small part of our moral duties, namely, our duties to avoid injury to the external freedom of others. But otherwise he seems to suggest only that the ethical community celebrates the commitment to the cause of virtue and by that means reinforces individual commitments to virtue or perhaps encourages individual conversions to virtue. One might have thought that the ethical community would play an indispensable role in moral *education*, being the means by which both the contents of our duties and examples of those who have fulfilled them are communicated to our young. But Kant does not explicitly make that assertion (here).

I will come back to the relation between the "juridico-civil state" and the ethical community or "ethico-civil state" in a moment, but first I want to comment on the second step of Kant's argument, namely, his claim that belief in the existence of God is a necessary condition for the existence of the ethical community and thus for the support of the individual conversion to virtue, whatever the details of that support. This step is not based on the supposition that always imperfect human efforts to be virtuous need to be completed by an act of divine grace, although Kant at least entertains that idea in Part Two of the *Religion* (6:74–75). It depends instead on the premise that laws will only be effective for us if they are attributed to a lawgiver. Kant then argues that the source of the laws of the ethical community cannot be the sovereign of a political state, however sovereignty is assigned, because such a sovereign legislates only laws "directed to the **legality** of actions, which is visible to the eye," not laws "designed to promote the **morality** of actions (which is something **internal**, and hence cannot be subject to public human laws)" (6:98–99). Since we cannot represent laws concerning the internal conditions for virtue as laws legislated by "the people, as a people," Kant infers that we can represent the "supreme lawgiver of an ethical community, with respect to whom all **true duties**, hence also the ethical, must be represented as **at the same time** his commands," only as "God as a moral ruler of the world. Hence an ethical community is conceivable only as a people under divine commands, i.e., as a **people of God**, and indeed **in accordance with the laws of virtue**" (6:99). The possibility of an ethical community depends upon a belief in the existence of God because God is represented as the source of the laws of such a community.

In drawing attention to this argument and the radical revision of the role of the postulate of the existence of God that it represents, I by no means intend to endorse it. Kant's argument in fact seems to depend upon an inference from the fact that a people as a *political unit* cannot be the source of purely ethical legislation to the unsupported idea that there is *no* form of association among human beings that can credibly promulgate and celebrate such legislation. Thus Kant's argument seems to be fallacious, and should be distinguished from his claim several years later in the unpublished *Opus postumum* that we (each) use the image of a divine lawgiver to represent the power of *our own* reason to legislate to the other side of our own existence, namely, our sometimes unruly and refractory desires, inclinations, and emotions.[25] In the *Opus postumum*, Kant also stresses that although we represent the "subject of the categorical imperative . . . as God," and "it cannot be denied that such a being exists," it also "cannot be asserted that it exists outside rationally thinking man. In him—the man who thinks morally according to our own commands of duty—we live (*sentimus*), move (*agimus*), and have our being (*existimus*)."[26] On this account the condition of the possibility of the ethical community would lie in nothing other than the quasi-divine power of human practical reason itself.

I shall not attempt to decide here whether Kant changed his mind about the postulate of the existence of God between 1793 and the end of the century, or merely changed his mind about what he would have been willing to publish after the liberalization of the Prussian regime that took place in 1797. My concern has been only to establish that in the *Religion* Kant has emphasized that we should think of the existence of God primarily as the condition of our own achievement of virtue. This at least suggests the highest good, which was the initial concern of the book, will take care of itself if we attend to our virtue, which is consistent with the idea that the universal happiness that should be the complement of universal virtue would be a consequence of that virtue rather than an externally granted reward for it. In any case, Kant does stress a strictly communalistic rather than individualistic conception of the highest good in his discussion of ethical community. He maintains that "since the duties of virtue concern the entire human race, the concept of an ethical community always refers to the ideal of a totality of human beings, and in this it distinguishes itself from the concept of a political community" (RBMR, 6:96). He then claims that in our duty to leave an "ethical state of nature" in order to establish an ethical community, "we have a duty *sui generis*, not of human beings toward human beings but of the human race toward itself," and thus that as a species we are "objectively—in the idea of reason—destined to a common good, namely, the promotion of the highest good as a good common to all" (6:97). He continues:

> But, since this highest moral good will not be brought about solely through the striving of one individual person for his own moral perfection, but rather requires a union of such persons into a whole toward that very end, toward a system of well-disposed human beings in which, and through the unity of which alone, the highest moral good can come to pass; yet the idea of such a whole, as a universal republic based on the laws of virtue, differs entirely from all moral laws (which concern what we know to reside within our power), for it is the idea of working toward a whole of which we cannot know whether as a whole it is also in our power. . . . We can already anticipate that this duty will need the presupposition of another idea, namely, of a higher moral being through whose universal organization the forces of single individuals, insufficient on their own, are united for a common effect. (6:97–98)

This crucial passage makes several points that may be regarded as central to Kant's final conception of the highest good. First, he clearly indicates that the ideal of the highest good arises directly from the idea of pure reason, here obviously pure practical reason. The highest good would thus simply be the realization of the pure practical ideas of a moral world and a realm of ends. Second, Kant makes it clear beyond all doubt that the highest good is not an individual good that can be brought about by the virtue of an individual, but the good of the entire human species, which can be brought about only by the virtue of all—"a system of well-disposed human beings." The highest good is thus a condition that must be realized by the human species rather than individually. Third, the biological reference to the human species clearly suggests that the highest good is to be realized within nature, not beyond nature, even though we must believe that its realization depends upon the existence of a "higher moral being." Finally, the claim that the role of this higher moral being is to organize the forces of single individuals is at least consistent with the general idea that God is postulated to explain the possibility of the collective development of virtue—however the details of that argument are supposed to go—and that if human beings with this assistance collectively organize the exercise of their virtue, happiness will at least eventually—*but in the life of the species*—take care of itself.

The Highest Good and the Highest Political Good

Kant's final position is thus that through an ethical community organized in accordance with the ideal of a moral world and realm of ends, the highest good of the species should emerge in its earthly course, although with divine support. Before I rest with this conclusion, however, I want to return at least briefly to the question of the relation between the ethical community and the "juridico-civil state," that is, to the relation between the highest good and politics. Philip Rossi has recently advocated that what Kant sometimes calls the "highest political good," namely, the establishment of perpetual peace, is the vehicle for the realization of the highest good properly speaking.[27] This seems to fly in the face of Kant's insistence that the concept of the ethical community, which he does maintain is the condition of the possibility of the realization of the highest good, is to be distinguished from that of the juridico-civil state.

In the conclusion of the "Doctrine of Right" of the *Metaphysics of Morals*, Kant does call perpetual or "universal and lasting" peace "the entire final end of the doctrine of right within the limits of mere reason" and the "highest political good" (MM, 6:355). Kant defines the political as the sphere within which duties and rights can be coercively enforced (see MM, 6:218–19), and infers that "it would be a contradiction (*in adjecto*) for the political community to compel its citizens to enter into an ethical community, since the latter entails freedom from its very concept" (RBMR, 6:95). An ethical community is one to which all members have freely chosen to belong and in which they have all freely chosen to commit themselves to virtue rather than vice, so it cannot be established or maintained by coercion. For that reason the "highest political good" would not seem to be able to contribute to the establishment of the highest good properly speaking through an ethical community, although one would certainly think the converse to be true, namely, that the highest good properly speaking would include the highest political good, perpetual peace. But there is no reason to think that the establishment of perpetual peace by political means should be a sufficient condition for the establishment of the highest good properly speaking, even if it would follow from it.

One might think to escape this objection to a position like Rossi's by observing that while in an early piece like the "Idea for a Universal History from a Cosmopolitan Point of View" (1784) Kant does seem to think of perpetual peace being achieved by a "system of united power, hence a cosmopolitan system of general political security, thus a federation with coercive powers of enforcement" (IUH, Seventh Proposition, 8:26), in *Toward Perpetual Peace* (1795) and the discussion of the "right of nations" in the "Doctrine of Right," he seems to advocate only a "congress" or "voluntary coalition of different states which can be **dissolved** at any time" (MM, "Doctrine of Right," §61, 6:351), and which does not have any enforcement powers. Thus one might claim that the condition of perpetual peace can only be produced by global good will, and must thus be considered as a product of a global ethical community even if it is not yet equivalent to or a sufficient condition for the highest good properly speaking. But that suggestion still seems to be inconsistent with Kant's position that perpetual peace is the ultimate goal of the doctrine of *right* or *justice*, which implies that it concerns the external relations of nations and their peoples, and does not concern the motivation and hence the virtue of those peoples at all. Further, Kant at least seems to suggest that perpetual peace can and will eventually be brought about by natural mechanisms, because the burdens of war and the benefits of trade will lead nations to become republics whose citizens will not be willing to pay for wars with their own blood or treasure; obviously the internal condition of virtue, which is a necessary component and indeed the ground of the highest good properly speaking, cannot be brought about by an external mechanism. While nature may compel mankind to seek the solution to the problem of "attaining a civil society that can administer justice universally" (IUH, Fifth Proposition, 8:22), nature cannot compel mankind to become virtuous. Indeed, perhaps that is why when Kant postulates God as the ground of the ethical community in the *Religion*, he is careful not to suggest that God does this through his authorship of the laws of nature, but only through his authorship of the moral law.

Yet there are two things that can be said in behalf of the proposal that the highest political good is in fact an indispensable factor in the establishment of the highest good properly speaking. First, although Kant suggests in the *Religion* that while the political community may be a stepping-stone toward the ethical community—he says that "without the foundation of a political community," the ethical community "could never be brought into existence by human beings" (6:94)—perhaps the political community should not be thought of as a stepladder that is simply left behind once the ethical community has been achieved. Remember that Kant has always characterized the highest good as the greatest happiness in exact proportion to the highest degree of moral perfection *possible for creatures*: it may be that while the idea of an ethical community founded entirely on the good will of its members is an admirable moral ideal for human beings, the highest degree of virtue *that we can reasonably expect to attain under natural conditions* is the creation of political conditions that will at least enforce outward compliance with the demands of morality. The greatest degree of happiness *that we could then reasonably expect* would then be that degree of happiness that can be created through the best possible administration of justice together with the always lesser degree of human virtue that we can expect, and the conjunction of *that* degree of happiness with *that* degree of virtue would then be the highest good possible, as Kant so often says, *in the world*, that is, in the natural conditions of human existence. The maintenance of perpetual peace, even if this should involve the use of coercion at the national or even the international level, would then be not merely a stepladder to a higher degree of virtue, which can be left behind once it has fulfilled its purpose, but would remain an essential component of the highest good actually possible for human beings.

It should also be mentioned that Kant may not mean that the political condition of perpetual peace can be mechanically created merely by natural means in the first place. Although the interpretation of this passage is certainly controversial, in the first appendix of *Toward Perpetual Peace* Kant may mean to argue that although the coercive means for the establishment of justice at the national level and the appropriate means, whatever they are, for the establishment of peace at the international level can be *devised* or *described* even by a "nation of devils" (8:366), they can in fact be *instituted* and *maintained* only by "moral politicians" (8:372), who will themselves make the choice *out of their own virtue* to institute coercive laws by means of which even those who are not themselves virtuous can be compelled to act in at least outward compliance with at least those demands of morality concerning the maintenance of external freedom and to enforce those laws justly.[28]

In other words, although the political condition uses coercive means to maintain justice, even a just political condition does not itself come into existence automatically, but rather depends upon the free and virtuous choice of those who have in one way or another (itself usually not just) come into power to institute a condition of justice. *And perhaps a condition in which some virtuous individuals choose to institute a political system in which others can be coerced into at least outward compliance with some of the demands of morality is the highest degree of virtue that the human species can actually expect.* In this case, the degree of happiness that would be possible in and result from such a political system and the imperfect exercise of further ethical duties would be the greatest happiness that is actually possible for human beings, and the conjunction of that degree of virtue with that degree of happiness would in fact be the highest good, properly speaking, possible for human beings.

Conclusion

We thus reach the following conclusions about the relations among Kant's several conceptions of community. The concept of the realm of ends characterizes the goal of our moral choice of maxims in the most abstract terms, by enjoining us to treat all rational beings with whom we may interact as ends in themselves and to seek a systematic union of the particular ends freely chosen by all such rational beings, including of course ourselves, as a consequence of the moral status of those who choose those ends. The idea of a moral world is the idea of the realization of the goal of the realm of ends, in principle in any kind of world but in practice in the sensible world. The idea of the highest good is the idea of the condition that would result from the realization of a moral world and therefore of the realm of ends under ideal conditions, in which virtue would not merely make those who have it worthy of happiness, but rather the virtue of all would make all happy as far as is possible consistently with the demands of morality. Although Kant sometimes makes it seem that those particular individuals who are worthy of happiness must be able to believe that they will eventually become happy regardless of the moral failings of other agents, his predominant view from the first *Critique* to the *Religion* is that the goal of the highest good is that of the virtue of all combined with, indeed as the source of, the happiness of all, and that each agent must be able to believe that the realization of *this* goal is possible for the attempt to be moral to be rational and for the commitment to be moral not to be undermined.

In the first and second *Critiques* Kant argues, although for slightly different reasons, that we can conceive of the two components of the highest good as realized fully only in a future life, and on those accounts the realm of ends and a moral world will be fully realized only in an intelligible rather than a sensible world. In all of his writings of the 1790s, however, even including the *Religion*, Kant argues that we must be able to believe that both components of the highest good, and thus the moral ideals of the realm of ends and a moral world, can be fully realized in the sensible world by the human species, at least over the course of its existence as a species. This earthly conception of the highest good remains a religious conception, however, because Kant continues to maintain that we must postulate God as the condition of the possibility of its realization.

Finally, although the concept of the condition of global justice in the form of perpetual peace that constitutes the highest political good is not equivalent to the concept of the greatest happiness in exact proportion to the highest degree of virtue, the condition of the highest political good cannot be produced without the virtuous motivation of at least some human beings, namely, moral politicians. And it may be that the degree of virtue that would be represented by the highest political good, and the addition of an always imperfect fulfillment of ethical duties, together with the degree of happiness that would result from that, may be the highest good that is *possible for human beings*, so in that way the concepts of the highest political good and the highest good may be almost intensionally, even though not extensionally, equivalent.

Notes

1. All citations from Kant are located by volume and page number of *Kants gesammelte Schriften*, ed. Königlich Preußische Akademie der Wissenschaften, 29 vols. (Berlin: de Gruyter, 1900–). The *Critique of Pure Reason* is cited by the page numbers

of the first A and/or second B editions. Unless otherwise indicated, all translations are from *The Cambridge Edition of the Works of Immanuel Kant*, ed. Paul Guyer and Allen W. Wood, 13 vols. (Cambridge: Cambridge University Press, 1992–), including *Practical Philosophy*, trans. and ed. Mary J. Gregor (1996); *Religion and Rational Theology*, ed. Allen W. Wood and George di Giovanni (1996); *Critique of Pure Reason*, ed. Paul Guyer and Allen W. Wood (1998), hereafter cited in text as CPR; and *Critique of the Power of Judgment*, ed. Paul Guyer (2000), hereafter cited as CJ. The translation of *The Groundwork of the Metaphysics of Morals* (hereafter cited as G followed by volume and page numbers from the Academy edition) is from *Practical Philosophy*, 37–108. The *Critique of Practical Reason* (hereafter CPrR) is also from *Practical Philosophy*, 133–272; *The Metaphysics of Morals* (hereafter MM) is from *Practical Philosophy*, 353–604; "On the Common Saying: 'That May Be Correct in Theory, but It Is of No Use in Practice'" (hereafter TP) is from *Practical Philosophy*, 273–310; *Religion within the Boundaries of Mere Reason* (hereafter RBMR) is from *Religion and Rational Theology*, 39–216; and "Idea for a Universal History with a Cosmopolitan Aim" (hereafter IUH) is from *Anthropology, History, and Education*, ed. Robert Louden and Günter Zöller (2008), 107–20. Since the Cambridge edition includes the Academy edition pagination in its margins, separate page numbers for the translations will not be given.

2. Gordon E. Michalson Jr., *Kant and the Problem of God* (Oxford: Blackwell, 1999), 106.

3. John Rawls, *Lectures on the History of Ethics*, ed. Barbara Herman (Cambridge, MA: Harvard University Press, 2000), 313–17.

4. Allen W. Wood, *Kant's Ethical Thought* (Cambridge: Cambridge University Press, 1999), 315.

5. Philip J. Rossi, S.J., *The Social Authority of Reason: Kant's Critique, Radical Evil, and the Destiny of Humankind* (Albany: State University of New York Press, 2005), 99.

6. For example, Carol Gilligan and other "care theorists"; for references and discussion, see Sally Sidgwick, "Can Kant's Ethics Survive the Feminist Critique?" in *Feminist Interpretations of Immanuel Kant*, ed. Robin May Schott (University Park: The Pennsylvania State University Press, 1997), 77–100, at 77–78.

7. Bernard Williams, *Ethics and the Limits of Philosophy* (Cambridge: Harvard University Press, 1985), 7.

8. Wood, *Kant's Ethical Thought*, 315.

9. Like John Rawls, I prefer "realm" rather than "kingdom" as the translation for *Reich* because it does not so clearly imply the existence within the realm of a lawgiver who is not also a subject of those laws, i.e., a king.

10. For the idea that Kant's sequence of formulations of the categorical imperative should be considered as a systematic exposition of the full contents of a single moral principle, see Allen W. Wood, "The Moral Law as a System of Formulas," in *Architektonik und System in der Philosophie Kants*, ed. H. F. Fulda and J. Stolzenberg (Hamburg: Felix Meiner Verlag, 2001), 287–306, and Wood, *Kant's Ethical Thought*, chaps. 3–5.

11. *Practical Philosophy*, ed. Gregor, 86. Here Gregor follows the older translations of Thomas K. Abbot, *Immanuel Kant, Groundwork for the Metaphysics of Morals*, ed. and rev. Lara Denis (Peterborough: Broadview, 2005), 94, and H. J. Paton, *Immanuel Kant, Groundwork of the Metaphysic of Morals* (London: Hutchinson, 1948), 104, and is followed by Arnulf Zweig, *Kant, Groundwork for the Metaphysics of Morals*, ed.

Thomas E. Hill Jr. and Arnulf Zweig, trans. Arnulf Zweig (Oxford: Oxford University Press, 2002), 237.

12. Wood, *Kant's Ethical Thought*, 54.

13. See Rawls, "Kantian Constructivism in Moral Theory," in *John Rawls, Collected Papers*, ed. Samuel Freedom (Cambridge: Harvard University Press, 1999), 303–58.

14. Wood, *Kant's Ethical Thought*, 166.

15. Rawls, *Lectures on the History of Ethics*, 204–5.

16. See also the introduction to the "Doctrine of Virtue" in the later *Metaphysics of Morals*, where Kant makes the same claim about "humanity," which in this context is simply the incorporation of rational being or nature in biologically human form (6:387, 392)—the only case of rational being, of course, with which we are actually acquainted.

17. Rawls, *Lectures on the History of Ethics*, 208–9.

18. See Paul Guyer, *Kant on Freedom, Law, and Happiness* (Cambridge: Cambridge University Press, 2000), 340.

19. Rawls, *Lectures on the History of Ethics*, 314.

20. See Frederick Beiser, "Moral Faith and the Highest Good," in *The Cambridge Companion to Kant and Modern Philosophy*, ed. Paul Guyer (Cambridge: Cambridge University Press, 2006), 588–629. But many authors have supposed this to be part of a "religious" conception of the highest good.

21. See Yirmiahu Yovel, *Kant and the Philosophy of History* (Princeton: Princeton University Press, 1981); Andrews Reath, "Two Conceptions of the Highest God in Kant," in *Journal of the History of Philosophy* 26 (1988): 592-619; and Gordon Michalson, *Fallen Freedom: Kant on Radical Evil and Moral Regeneration* (Cambridge: Cambridge University Press, 1991).

22. Kant is responding to arguments Garve made in his *Versuche über verschiedene Gegenstände aus der Moral und Literatur* (Breslau, 1792), part 1, 111–16.

23. Thus taking the approach of Rawls.

24. See especially Sharon Anderson-Gold, "God and Community: An Inquiry into the Religious Implications of the Highest Good," in *Kant's Philosophy of Religion Reconsidered*, ed. Philip J. Rossi and Michael Wreen (Bloomington: Indiana University Press, 1991), 113–31; Gordon Michalson, *Kant and the Problem of God*, 100–22; Wood, *Kant's Ethical Thought*, 309–20; and Rossi, *Social Authority of Reason*, 87–112.

25. See, for example, *Opus postumum*, 7th fascicle, sheet 5, page 2, 22:251–53, in *Kant, Opus postumum*, ed. Eckart Förster, trans. Eckart Förster and Michael Rosen (Cambridge: Cambridge University Press, 1993), 211–13.

26. *Opus postumum*, 7th fascicle, sheet 5, page 3, 22:55, in *Kant, Opus postumum*, 213–14.

27. See Rossi, *Social Authority of Reason*.

28. Since originally writing this paper, I have argued for this position more fully in "The Possibility of Perpetual Peace," in *Kant's Perpetual Peace: New Interpretative Essays*, ed. Luigi Caranti (Rome: LUISS University Press, 2006), 161–82, and "The Crooked Timber of Mankind," in *Kant's Idea for a Universal History with a Cosmopolitan Aim: A Critical Guide*, ed. Amelie Oksenberg Rorty and James Schmidt (Cambridge: Cambridge University Press, 2009), 129–49.

5

RELIGION, ETHICAL COMMUNITY, AND THE STRUGGLE AGAINST EVIL

ALLEN W. WOOD

Religion and Subjectivity

In part four of *Religion within the Boundaries of Mere Reason*, Kant states his more or less official definition of religion: "Religion is (subjectively considered) the recognition of all our duties as divine commands" (*RBMR*, 6:153; cf. MM, 6:443).[1] To be religious, for Kant, is to view all of one's duties as commands issued to oneself by God. Kant's wording of this definition, apparently restricting the definition to religion "subjectively considered," might suggest that there could be another, "objective" way of considering religion, and this "objective" consideration might present a different definition of religion. But in fact Kant never offers a definition of that sort. In fact, Kant had already put forward the same official definition in part three in the following words: "Religion is the moral disposition (*Gesinnung*) to observe all duties as [God's] commands" (*RBMR*, 6:105). There is no suggestion here that this is a definition of only one kind of religion, to which another kind might be opposed. Instead, there is only a further emphasis on the subjectivity of *all* religion (as consisting in a special kind of "moral disposition"). A reasonable (and I think correct) inference from these facts is that Kant, like Kierkegaard, regards all religion as entirely a matter of "subjectivity." It has to do with one's way of regarding one's duties, and with one's moral disposition or attitude in fulfilling duties. The "objectivity" of religion, at least for beings like ourselves, would be a contradiction in terms.

Religiousness, then, is solely a matter of a person's subjective attitude toward the moral life. A moral agent is religious if she associates her moral duties with the thought that they are commanded by God, and observes her duties in that spirit. She might do so, for instance, by thinking about the moral life in terms of her personal relationship with God. Thus she might think of her moral transgressions as troubling that relationship, and her resolve to do better in the future as an attempt to repair that relationship, by giving God a reason to forgive her. This clearly is the way Kant represents the moral life of the individual in part two of the *Religion*, which deals with "the battle of the good against the evil principle for dominion over the human being" by invoking Kantian interpretations of the traditional Christian doctrine of justification (6:66–84).

The idea that religion for Kant is an entirely "subjective" matter may, however, also give rise to the thought that he regards it as an entirely optional matter whether one regards one's duties as divine commands. This is certainly true in the sense that Kant thinks that it would be a basic violation of right to *compel* anyone to regard them in this way, as when people are forced or pressured into participating in religious services or making confession of a religious creed. It would be even more repugnant if they were forced or terrified into thinking about their moral duties as commands of God, since the whole moral point of their doing so will be lost unless they do it freely and spontaneously.

But the "subjectivity" of religion for Kant might also be taken to imply Kant regards it as in general a matter of moral indifference whether one thinks about one's moral life religiously or not: that there is nothing in rational morality itself that might justify or even provide strong moral reasons for looking at one's moral life in a religious light. It might also be interpreted to mean that for Kant religion is entirely an individual and private matter— that "religion" has to do solely with the way people (when they happen to be so disposed) choose to think privately about their personal duties. On this interpretation, Kant's conception of religion would make religion consist solely in optional private thoughts and feelings individuals might have about their duties. In that case, nothing people might do outwardly or collectively could have anything distinctively "religious" about it, since for religion to have that sort of existence would be to make it into something "objective," which would be foreign or even inimical to the nature of religion as Kant conceives it. What we might call this "extreme liberal" interpretation might be reinforced by noting that Kant found formal religious creeds morally objectionable and regarded religious services as "counterfeit service of God"; he himself always refused on principle to participate in religious services of any kind, even when such participation was (at least an informal) component of his duties as rector of the University of Königsberg. It might lead to the further thought that Kant's insistence on the "subjectivity" of religion might really represent a desire on his part to exclude religion altogether from the collective or shared life of human society.

It is my purpose here to show that the extreme liberal interpretation of Kant's conception of religion described in the last paragraph is mistaken. By this I do not mean only that it is exaggerated or one-sided, but rather that it is fundamentally wrong—that it gets Kant's view of religion about as wrong as it could be gotten. For it is a basic and not a marginal misinterpretation of Kantian ethics to regard religion even as incidental to rational morality (much less as morally superfluous or undesirable). It is the very reverse of the truth to interpret Kant's emphasis on the "subjectivity" of religion, and his insistence that religious activities must always be voluntary, never coerced, to mean that he regards religion as properly a private rather than a public thing. Probably the deepest error of all is to think that because Kant disapproved of creeds and traditional religious rituals, he must have regarded public or organized religion as of doubtful or negative value. This is to impose on an eighteenth-century thinker our twentieth-century prejudices about what religion is, then letting these prejudices constrain what we take that thinker's options to consist in, and consequently forcing on him a choice he would not have made. It is rather like saying of the ancient Israelites (as some of their shortsighted, prejudiced, and unimaginative contemporaries might have said) that because they disapproved of the worship of idols, they must therefore have been atheists. In Kant's case, I mean to argue, the whole point of religion is its relation to human community. Religion for Kant represents the free and subjective aspect of human community under moral principles—or rather, it represents the communal aspect of moral principles themselves, which is essential to them, when they determine our subjective disposition in the right way.

Why Should My Duties Be Regarded as God's Commands?

The right place to begin our inquiry, I think, is with the question: *Why* does Kant think moral agents might choose subjectively to regard their duties as divine commands? Obviously this *cannot* be because this way of regarding them plays any role in determining the *ground* of obligation. For Kant is emphatic that "theological morality" (or divine command theory) cannot give us a satisfactory account of the categorical obligation attaching to duty. Taken in one way, divine command theory is a theory of heteronomy, which must rest obligation on a contingent volition (e.g., on our love or our fear of God), thus undermining the categorical character of obligation (G, 4:443; CPrR, 5:40–41). On a more sympathetic interpretation of divine command theory, this theory regards God's commands as obligatory because it is contained in our rational concept of God that God has a perfect will, hence that God necessarily wills all and only that which is in itself right (i.e., categorically obligatory). A divine command theory of that kind, I think, is not considered by Kant to be a form of heteronomy, but is in fact a position Kant himself holds—at least as often as he has reason to think about morality in its relation to a possible *ens realissimum*, or God. But this would still not explain why God's perfect volitions should have to us the determinate character of *commands*. Even if we solved that problem, however, we would still need an account of what categorical obligation consists in; only a theory of autonomy of the will, and not divine command theory, will suffice for a satisfactory account of obligation. If Kant still rejects divine command theory (sympathetically interpreted) as a fundamental account of obligation, it is really for that reason, and not because it involves a moral system of heteronomy.

For this reason, however, thinking of our duties as divine commands cannot play a fundamental role in the proper *motivation* for doing our duty. On the contrary, the only pure motive for doing our duties is the motive of duty itself, or, as Kant restates this motive in the *Groundwork*, the worth of rational nature in the person of the finite rational being to whom we owe the duty (4:427–29). God himself, as a being with a pure will, must will that we should perform our duties from this motive rather than, say, from fear of his power, or hope of his favor, or even love of his person; for any of these motives would compromise the autonomy of our will, something a good God could not will that we do.

Just as little could the thought that our duties are divine commands play any role in determining the *content* of our duties. For he holds that we have no special duties *to* God (MM, 6:443–44). Nor could our authentic acquaintance with duty come from any special divine revelation. We can have no empirical acquaintance with any being corresponding to our concept of God, since this concept is an idea of reason to which no experience could ever be adequate. Instead, things must work just the other way round; our only possible acquaintance with what God wills or commands must come from our rational awareness of the content of duty, and the thought that God, as a supremely perfect being, must necessarily will that our duties be performed.

Kant does not even think that we have to believe that there really is a God who wills that we perform our duties. Even a religious person, who regards her duties as divine commands, need not be certain that her duties are in fact commanded by God. For religion, Kant says, "no assertoric knowledge (even of God's existence) is required, [but] only a problematic assumption (hypothesis) as regards speculation about the supreme cause of things"; the "faith" that is strictly indispensable to religion "needs merely the *idea of God* . . . only the minimum cognition (it is possible that there is a God) has to be objectively sufficient" (RBMR, 6:153–54). To be religious, then, I do not even have to believe in the existence of God. Religion requires that I have duties, that I have a concept of God (as a *possible* supreme cause of things), and that my awareness of duty is subjectively enlivened by the thought that if there is a God, then my duties are God's commands to me. We are still trying to find out, however, why Kant thought that a moral agent—even one who is agnostic about God's existence—might have a good reason subjectively to regard her duties as divine commands.

Kant's most explicit answer to our question consists in appealing to our pursuit of the highest good (*summum bonum*), and our need to conceive this pursuit in relation to the will of God. The highest good requires a correspondence of happiness to worthiness to be happy, and Kant famously maintains that we can conceive of such a correspondence only by supposing that the world is governed by a being that is omniscient (so as to know our worthiness to be happy), omnipotent (so as to be able to grant happiness in proportion to worthiness), and perfectly good (so that it wills, both justly and benevolently, that beings who have made themselves worthy of happiness should partake in it). Accordingly, Kant answers our question as follows: "[Our duties] must be regarded as commands of the supreme being because we can hope for the highest good . . . only from a morally perfect . . . will, and therefore we can hope to attain [the highest good] only through harmony with this will" (CPrR, 5:129).

This answer, however, is as it stands highly unsatisfactory—or at least incomplete, and for at least three reasons. First, it seems to appeal to Kant's moral arguments for believing in the existence of God (as the sole way of conceiving the possible reality of the highest good); it therefore fails to explain why Kant might suppose that even someone who is agnostic about God's existence might nevertheless regard her duties as divine commands. Second, although we may hope to attain the highest good only if our will is in harmony with God's will, it has not yet been explained why we should think of this harmony specifically as our *obedience to commands* issued by God's will. Third, even if we could solve these problems, the answer would still be incomplete in that it merely shifts our attention to another big question we may have about Kantian ethics: Why in any case do we have to regard the highest good as a necessary object of our pursuit?

This is also the point at which to articulate another worry we may have about Kant's entire account of religion, as we have seen it so far. This account seems legalistic in a way that is probably unappealing to most of us, and may even seem inconsistent with certain parts of Kant's own doctrines. As an object of religious attitudes, God seems to be conceived exclusively as a moral legislator, a powerful holy being who issues commands. As religious people, our subjective attitude toward God seems to be that of the subject of a cosmic monarch, to whose will we are supposed to conform in order to attain the highest good (that is, to obtain the happiness of which our conduct has made us worthy). It must be admitted, of course, that this way of representing God, as a cosmic lawgiver, and of our love to him, as obedience to his commands, is quite traditional—it is basic to much theology in both the medieval and early modern periods. Yet Kant's theory of moral obligation as grounded on autonomy seems attractive to many of us precisely because it distances itself from this picture, repudiating the divine command moralist's conception of obligation as based on cringing obedience to the orders of a cosmic despot and regarding moral agents instead as self-governing rational beings, who are bound to the moral law by their sense of their own dignity as self-legislators.

My thesis in this paper will be that there is a common solution to all these problems, consisting in the fundamental role played in Kant's conception of religion by the idea of an *ethical community*.

Evil and Sociability

But our route to this solution must take yet another apparent detour, through Kant's doctrine of the radical evil in human nature. Kant holds that two sorts of incentives present themselves to the human will: incentives of inclination, referring to our natural desires, and incentives of reason, referring to our dignity as self-governing rational agents; the latter incentives always have rational priority over the former, especially when these rational incentives take the form of categorically valid moral imperatives. Yet Kant also holds that we find in human beings an innate propensity to invert the rational order of these incentives, preferring incentives of inclination over those of reason, choosing the satisfaction of empirical desires over the rational commands of duty (RBMR, 6:36–39). The human being, in his view, is an *animal rationabile*, an animal capable of reason, but not an *animal rationale*, a being in which this capacity is typically exercised successfully (APPV, 7:321–22).

Kant calls this propensity the *radical* evil in human nature, because it lies at the *root* of all the particular evil we do. It shows itself not only directly in the form of "depravity"—the direct preference of natural desires over rational principles—but also in the two lesser degrees of "fragility" (the tendency not to abide by good maxims we have adopted) and "impurity" (the need for empirical incentives in order to do what reason commands) (RBMR, 6:29–30). It shows itself in the "bestial" vices of gluttony, drunkenness, and wildness (6:26–27), and in the crude vices of brutality and cruelty toward other human beings (6:33), but also equally, or perhaps to an even greater extent, in the better concealed "civilized" vices, engendered by jealousy and rivalry between human beings, such as envy, deceitfulness, ingratitude, and malicious gloating over the misfortunes of others (6:27, 33–34).

Since the incentives that we tend to prefer to moral ones come from our natural inclinations, it might be thought that in the struggle between good and evil, the enemy for Kant is natural desire as such. But this would certainly not follow, since evil on Kant's account of it does not lie in either the fact or the particular content of natural inclinations, but rather in our tendency to give them greater motivational weight than they rationally deserve. Kant sees things this way too, since he is quite explicit, moreover, in maintaining that natural inclinations are in themselves good. He takes the Stoics to task for viewing the moral struggle as a contest between reason and natural desire: "Those valiant men mistook their enemy, who is not to be sought in the natural inclinations, which merely lack discipline and openly display themselves unconcealed to everyone's consciousness, but is rather as it were an invisible enemy, one who hides behind reason and is hence all the more dangerous" (*RBMR*, 6:57). The common misinterpretation of Kantian ethics, which regards it as hostile to "the body" or "animal desire," is here repudiated as explicitly as it could possibly be.

Kant distinguishes three "predispositions" in human nature: (1) "animality," the source of our natural desires relating to the survival of the individual and the species, and to our sociability; (2) "humanity," the ground of our capacity to set ends according to reason and to take the sum of our inclinations as a comprehensive end under the name of "happiness"; and (3) "personality," the ability to give and obey laws through reason alone, hence the ground of our moral accountability (*RBMR*, 6:26). All are in themselves good, but two of them are also incapable of being the source of evil. Personality cannot be, since for it the moral law alone is an incentive, and animality, though it can have vices "grafted onto it," cannot be the source of these vices because it has to do solely with instinctive desires, not with comparison between incentives and the choice of one over another, in which evil consists. The source of evil, therefore, must lie in our predisposition to humanity, which contains "a self-love which is physical and yet *involves comparison* (for which reason is required)" (6:27).

The reason involved in our humanity is "comparative," however, not only in the way it treats desires (uniting them into a comprehensive end of happiness, and choosing to satisfy one rather than another) but also in the way it regards the *self* of the rational being who makes such choices and pursues happiness: "that is, only in comparison with others does one judge oneself happy or unhappy. Out of this self-love originates the inclination to *gain worth in the opinion of others*" (6:27). Originally, and innocently, this is merely a desire to be equal to others, but our anxiety that others may seek an ascendancy over us turns it gradually into "an unjust desire to acquire superiority for oneself over others. Upon this, namely, upon *jealousy* and *rivalry*, can be grafted the greatest vices of secret or open hostility to all whom we consider alien to us" (6:27). Our desire to be happy, therefore—to form the idea of a comprehensive good, encompassing all our inclinations—is a product of rational humanity, not of our animal nature; and its fundamental rationale is to assist us in comparing ourselves to others, where the comparison is motivated by a competitive desire to be worth more than they are, in their eyes and therefore in our own.

Kant thinks nature uses this natural antagonism between human beings to prod us to develop the faculties of our species (*RBMR*, 6:27). This Kant calls our "unsociable sociability" (*TP*, 8:20–22). It makes us sociable creatures, insofar as we need the comparison with others, and their opinion of our self-worth, as a measure of our own well-being, but at the same time it is an unsociable tendency, since it leads us to seek an unjust superiority over others who, as rational beings, are really our equals. From a moral standpoint, therefore, unsociable sociability is identical to a propensity to evil. For the moral law tells us in effect that all human beings are of equal worth as ends in themselves (G, 4:429), and that we must adopt only those ends that can be brought into harmony with others in a "realm" of ends (4:432). But owing to our natural propensity to seek superiority over others, we tend to treat our own inclinations as having greater worth than those of others; we have, in other words, a propensity to "self-conceit," that is, to claim a preeminent worth for ourselves prior to our conformity to the moral law, and thus to treat our own inclinations as if they were legislative in place of the moral law of reason (CPrR, 5:73–74).

Evil for Kant is therefore a product of human reason under the natural conditions of its full development, which are found in the social condition. The radical evil in human nature is an inevitable accompaniment of the development of our rational faculties in society. Kant regards this fact as crucial in determining the way we must struggle against evil:

> The human being is in this perilous state through his own fault; hence he is bound at least to apply as much force as he can muster in order to extricate himself from it. But how? That is the question. If he searches for the causes and circumstances that draw him into this danger and keep him there, he can easily convince himself that they do not come his way from his own raw nature, so far as he exists in isolation, but rather from the human beings to whom he stands in relation or association. It is not the instigation of nature that arouses what should properly be called the *passions*, which wreak such great devastation in his originally good predisposition. His needs are but limited and his state of mind in providing for them moderate and tranquil. He is poor (or considers himself so) only to the extent that he is anxious that other human beings will consider him poor and despise him for it. Envy, addiction to power, avarice, and the malignant inclinations associated with these, assail his nature, which on its own is undemanding, *as soon as he is among human beings*. (RBMR, 6:93–94)

The Need for Ethical Community

The source of evil, Kant concludes, is *social*. The struggle against it, he concludes, if it is to be effective, must therefore also be social.[2] It is our original or natural social relation to others—a hostile or competitive relation involving our own subjectivity, our free will, and hence our responsibility—that makes us evil. The struggle against evil, therefore, must consist in a different subjective relationship to others, based on mutual respect for human dignity and on a community of ends (a "realm of ends") rather than conflict or competition among human ends, and hence on a different form of society among human beings than the natural one determined by evil or unsociable sociability.

This means that the struggle against evil requires as its prerequisite that we enter subjectively into a new and different kind of community with other human beings. Kant thinks that if we imagine the struggle against evil individualistically, in the form of isolated individuals each struggling heroically against our own inclinations and propensity to evil, then we are only concocting a recipe for the ignominious defeat of morality. In this sense, nothing could be farther from the truth than the all too common characterization of Kantian ethics as "individualistic." There may be truth in this characterization if it refers to Kant's view that we are responsible as individuals for the evil that we do (and cannot blame our misconduct on other people or on "society"). Or it may correctly express the point that for Kant our dignity requires us to think for ourselves rather than blindly following the thoughts dictated to us by others (authorities or traditions or books). But if people infer from either of these points that Kant thinks the moral life must be carried out by isolated individuals, each struggling inwardly with himself, or that Kantian principles either reject or neglect the importance of our being in community with others, then they have gotten Kantian ethics about as far wrong as they possibly could (just about as far wrong as if they said that Kantian ethics regards "desire" or "animal nature" or "the body" as the source of evil).

In fact, Kant makes this anti-individualistic point about the struggle against evil both repeatedly and emphatically; it is central to the argument of the last two books of the *Religion*, and it is the note on which he chooses to end his textbook on anthropology, with which he ended his career. Hence it could, literally and without exaggeration, also be called Kant's *last word* about the human condition as a whole:

> If no means could be found to establish a union which has for its end the prevention of this evil and the promotion of the good in the human being, [then] however much the individual human being might do to escape from the dominion of this evil, he would still be held in incessant danger of relapsing into it. . . .
>
> The highest good cannot be achieved merely by the exertion of the single individual toward his own moral perfection, but instead requires a union of such individuals into a whole working toward the same end—a system of well-disposed human beings, in which and through whose unity alone the highest moral good can come to pass. (RBMR, 6:94, 97–98)

> In working against the [evil] propensity [in human nature] . . . our will is in general good, but the accomplishment of what we will is made more difficult by the fact that the attainment of the end can be expected not through the free agreement of *individuals*, but only through the progressive organization of citizens of the earth into and toward the species as a system that is cosmopolitically combined. (*APPV*, 7:333)

We need, however, to understand a little more clearly why Kant thinks an ethical community is needed in the struggle against the evil in human nature. His reason is apparently that the origin of evil is social, and therefore the struggle against it must take the form of a certain kind of society. But taken in one quite natural way, the form of that argument is not at all convincing. For if we were to decide that all evil in human nature is due to hatred or greed, it would not therefore be natural or reasonable to conclude that what we require to combat evil is some special form of hatred or greed. Looking at the matter this way, if we decide that evil is social in its origin, then the most natural inference from this might be that the struggle against it should take the form of self-isolation (the solution of the hermit). The hermit's attitude, however, is one that Kant utterly rejects, calling it "negative misanthropy," a "flight from humanity" (*LE*, 27:672). Even if such a person wishes others well, his "timidity" or "anthropophobia" (*Leutescheuen, Anthropophobie*) is contrary to the duties of love that we have toward other human beings (*MM*, 6:450).

The point of Kant's argument that the struggle against evil requires a moral community can be seen more clearly if we think about his account of evil in greater detail; and this will also give us a clearer indication of the nature of the community that is needed. Our unsociable sociability is evil because, seeking superiority over others by competing with them for such things as money, honor, and power, we set ends that are not only contrary to the ends others actually set, but are also in conflict with the very possibility of a system of ends that might unite all rational beings on the basis of mutual respect for their equal dignity as ends in themselves. To combat this tendency directly consists in adopting ends that do in fact agree (or even coincide) with the ends of other human beings, and that do so by directly fulfilling the idea of a "realm" in which all ends form an organic unity or mutually supporting system. Such a system would constitute a "community" (*Gemeinschaft*) of ends in the technical metaphysical sense of that term (as it is used, for example, in the table of categories, A80/B106). That is, between the ends of rational beings there would be a *reciprocity*, so that the pursuit of each end would advance the pursuit of others, and human ends would constitute a self-organizing whole, combined into a unity like the parts of a living organism. That is what Kant means, at the end of the *Anthropology*, when he speaks of "the progressive organization of citizens of the earth into and toward the species as a system that is cosmopolitically combined" (*APPV*, 7:333). The kind of society we need in order to struggle against evil is one that "progressively organizes" all human beings so that they gradually become a cosmopolitan community of this kind. In the *Religion*, Kant's name for this sort of society is "ethical community" (*ethisches gemeines Wesen*) (*RBMR*, 6:94).

Several things follow directly from the fundamental nature of ethical community. First, such a community cannot be conceived on the model of a juridical commonwealth or political state, whose function is to protect the right of human beings through coercion. A juridical community or political state determines which actions we may rightfully perform, and it protects the right by guaranteeing their performance through the use of external force. The state's rightful power extends only to compelling me by force to restrict my actions so that they are consistent with everyone else's freedom according to universal law (*MM*, 6:230). A juridical community cannot determine the ends set by human beings, because setting ends is an act of freedom; and for it to attempt to do so would even be contrary to the right it is supposed to protect. The closest the state could come to making me adopt an end would be to compel me to perform actions that serve the ends adopted by someone else (i.e., the state's despotic ruler); and to do that would be contrary to the right of the state, since it would violate my right as a free and rational being. It follows that membership and participation in an ethical community must always be entirely voluntary, never subject to external compulsion of any kind (*RBMR*, 6:94–95).

Second, since the aim of ethical community is the combination of all human beings into a single system or realm of ends, the ethical community cannot be subject to any sort of limitation as to its extent, as by restricting it to people who live in a certain geographical area or belong to a specific race or heredity. For the same reason, it may not bind itself to any specific practices or creeds that would exclude part of the human race from belonging to it.

This means, third, that it can recognize only ends and motivations that are ethical (deriving from laws of reason, which are in their concept freely yet universally binding). And that entails, fourthly, that the constitution of this community (the principles of its union) must be unchangeable, which requires at the same time that the rules of its administration must remain completely flexible and open to constant modification in order to reflect the free, rational judgment of its members and in order to enable it to pursue the end of progressively including more and more of the human race, since its members of necessity include in principle all rational beings without exception.

Kant organizes these four features of the ethical community in accordance with the four headings of his table of categories (A80/B106):

Quantity (of the community itself): *Unity*, guaranteed by the universality of its extent.

Quality (of the incentives motivating membership in it): *Purity*, depending solely on moral incentives of reason.

Relation (between its members): *Freedom*, admitting no coercive government either by a juridical state or by a class of officials within the ethical community itself.

Modality: *Unchangeableness* (of its constitution), but freedom and openness of its mode of administration. (RBMR, 6:101–2)

Ethical Community and Religion

We are now in a position to use Kant's conception of ethical community to solve the problems about his concept of religion that earlier perplexed us.

We wondered, to begin with, why Kant thinks that we should regard our duties as divine commands. The answer to this lies in a thesis he holds about the ethical community, namely, that it is best conceived as "a people of God" under pure moral laws of virtue (RBMR, 6:99). Kant distinguishes the *legislator* of a law, the one who issues a command and may attach positive or negative sanctions to it, from the law's *author*, the one whose will imposes the obligation to obey it. In these terms, Kant thinks only the idea of the rational will of every rational being as such can be regarded as its *author*, because the content of the law depends on the nature of rational will, or the idea of the rational will (its pure concept, to which no finite human will can ever be fully adequate) (G, 4:431, 448). But this is only a way of regarding the matter: properly speaking, the moral law, which is binding on us in itself or as lying in the nature of things, has no author. It is binding on us in itself and, like the truths of mathematics, the moral law lies in the nature of things rather than being a positive statute laid down arbitrarily by a will (LE, 27:261–62, 282–83, 29:633–34; cf G, 4:439).

Our own will may likewise be regarded as the *legislator* of the law, since it provides us with the moral incentive to obey the law (and this is the basic idea behind the Kantian conception of *autonomy*). But this too is only a way of considering or regarding the matter. The moral law in itself has no legislator either. If, however, the moral law is to be regarded as a public law, binding on an actual community of human beings, then God's will is the only one fittingly regarded as its *legislator* (MM, 6:227; RBMR, 6:99). For (as required by the "quality" criterion of the ethical community) only this will is *pure* or holy, and universal in its extent. In the case of a juridical community, it is permissible and even necessary to think of the combined will of the citizens as the legislator; but a fallible and contingently restricted will of this kind would be inappropriate for a moral community. We should regard our duties as divine commands, therefore, because (and to the extent that) we ought to view ourselves as members of an ethical community, whose legislator is God.

The ethical community must be open even to agnostics, because Kant holds that no satisfactory theoretical proofs either of the existence or the nonexistence of a Deity can ever be given, and if membership in the moral community is to be truly universal, it has to extend at least to all those whose beliefs fall within the range of belief consistent with the state of the possible theoretical evidence. Moreover, even an agnostic is capable of forming the concept of God, and of recognizing the will of such a being as an appropriate legislator for the moral law when it is regarded as the law of a living human community. Thinking of the moral law as commanded by a (possible or actual) God whose free, moral sovereignty unites people in a universal human society is the best way for me to think of moral laws as having public recognition, and myself as belonging with others to an ethical community that is united by that recognition.

We were also puzzled by the fact that Kant links our conception of duties as divine commands to our pursuit of the highest good (*summum bonum*), as the sum total of all moral ends. We wondered why Kant thinks we need to regard ourselves as pursuing such an all-encompassing, universal end, at all, and also what role this pursuit was supposed to play in religion (the subjective recognition of all duties as divine commands). Now we see that what is fundamental to the ethical community is the fact that human beings should pursue in common a set of ends that are systematically united into a "cosmopolitical combination" or "realm," that is, an organic unity. When we try to think of this organic unity of all rational ends as a single end, what we are thinking of is just the highest good (*summum bonum*). Kant thinks we are bound to be assailed by doubts concerning the real possibility of ever achieving this end, but that we have an answer to such doubts in the form of a faith in God as a supreme legislator and governor of the world, through whose highest knowledge, absolute power, and perfect will the highest good is possible. Kant's conception of the highest good as perfect morality or virtue combined with happiness proportionate to it is, admittedly, very abstract. But this is because it is merely the general idea of the unity of all ends on which all rational beings can agree. Even agnostics can join in pursuit of it, and hopes for its achievement even provide them with subjective or moral grounds for believing in God (though such moral arguments constitute no theoretical evidence in favor of such belief).

Our worry that Kant's conception of religion is uncomfortably legalistic can now also be addressed. Kant conceives religion this way because, following much theological tradition, he thinks of God as a moral legislator, and of the ethical community as like a political community in being bound together by public recognition of a common legislation. But Kant's version of this tradition really turns it against itself, since a Kantian ethics based on autonomy removes "legalism" from the content of morality even as it expresses morality using the traditional legalistic forms. It is ironic, in fact, that we raise this objection against Kant at all, since his ethical theory is one of the primary developments through which we have come to see morality in ways that repudiate the whole tradition of legalistic command that provides the tradition within which his formulations are given.

Kant is very clear that the ethical community differs decisively from any political community in that membership in it must be wholly free and voluntary, and the only incentives to obey its laws must be purely moral, not externally coercive. For this reason, there is no room in the moral community as Kant conceives it for a religious hierarchy of any kind, or even any form of government (whether monarchical, aristocratic, or democratic) (*RBMR*, 6:99–100).

> It could best of all be likened to the constitution of a household (a family) under a common though invisible moral father, whose holy son, who knows the father's will and yet stands in blood relation with all the members of the family, takes his father's place by making the other members better acquainted with his will; these therefore honor the father in him and thus enter into a free, universal, and enduring union of hearts. (*RBMR*, 6:102)

Though Kant does not make this explicit, it is arguable that an even better analogy for the ethical community in Kantian ethical theory than the family would be *friendship*. For in friendship, people achieve trust and intimacy with one another through sharing their ends, and friends (according to Kant) even abandon the private end of their own happiness for the sake of a common or shared end in which the happiness of the friends is swallowed up (*RBMR*, 6: 469–73; *LE*, 27:423). Friendship and religion also have this in common: friendship and the ethical community are the only nonjuridical social relationships into which Kant says we have an ethical duty to enter.[3]

The Ethical Community and the Church

Kant's conception of the ethical community is obviously modeled on organized religion, and especially on the Christian church. More than this, Kant believes that (owing to a certain weakness of human nature) it is impossible for people directly to form a pure ethical community, but they must rather reach such a community through "ecclesiastical faiths" that are originally very different in spirit and conduct from pure religious faith, and approximate to a genuine ethical community only through a long process of historical progress, enlightenment, and reform.

Ecclesiastical faiths are typically based on a scriptural authority, guarded and interpreted by special scholars and a priestly hierarchy (*RBMR*, 6:100–103). Their "priestcraft" (*Pfaffentum*) rules over people's minds by a variety of ignominious means—superstitious fears, enthusiastic pretensions to mystical insight or empirical divine revelation, fetishistic attempts to invoke divine favor or aid through petitionary prayers or other forms of pretended magic and sorcery, and the "counterfeit service" (*Afterdienst*) of God through all sorts of morally indifferent rites and statutory observances (6:151–202). Kant looks forward to a time when the kernel of true religion will outgrow this empirical shell, lay aside its superstitious and fetishistic trappings, abolish "the humiliating distinction between laity and clergy," and approach the condition of a genuine ethical community, which (in Kant's view) it is the appointed historical task for organized religion someday to become (6:115–37).

Since Kant's fundamental conception of the human condition is that we are a species of rational beings destined to struggle in history against our innate propensity to evil, and since for Kant the ethical community is conceived as the indispensable focal point for this struggle, it is virtually impossible to overestimate the importance of organized religion in Kant's scheme of things. We also miss one of the main conceptions of Kantian ethics if we fail to appreciate how vital ethical community is to its conception of the moral life. Kantian ethics is fundamentally misconceived when it is portrayed only as a morality of cold duty and desiccated individuals struggling stoically against their natural desires. We take a step in the right direction when, with John Rawls, we see it "not as a morality of austere command but an ethic of mutual respect and self-esteem."[4] But we still miss the heart of it if we do not appreciate that the fundamental ideal of Kantian ethics is that of a universal community of free beings in which all are recognized and treated as equals and all work together toward human dignity and happiness as a single shared or collective end.

The Enlightenment View of Religion— And What It Means That We Fail to Understand It

Kant therefore is the first to admit (or even to proclaim) that the ethical community that grounds his conception of religion is very different from organized religion as it has ever existed. But here it will be instructive to compare Kant's conception of organized religion and its role in human history with his conception of the political state and its historical role. Kant's model in the real world for the community whose task it is to protect the rights of persons is the juridical community or political state. He recognizes that no existing state comes very close to fulfilling the rational idea of a juridical community, and in fact that most states are themselves among the chief perpetrators of injustice and violators of human rights. But he hopes that as people become more enlightened, existing states will shed the defects that now make them unjust, and over time gradually come to approximate that rational idea.

For Kant, the only political constitution that is really consistent with the idea of human rights is a *republican* one (TP, 8:349–50 and note). Most states in his time, including the one in which he lived, were fundamentally different from this republican ideal. But he thinks that even a state whose constitution is not republican can come to govern in the spirit of a republic, and over time it may even evolve into a republican form of government. Kant looks forward to the time when there will be a wide consensus among the members of the human race that no state can be legitimate unless it fully protects the rights of its citizens, and that the only truly satisfactory political constitution is a republican one. Looking back over the last two hundred years, I think we must admit that Kant's political hopes were not unreasonable; indeed, I think we have to be impressed with them as not only remarkably prescient, but even as hopes that decent people everywhere have come to share.

Analogously, Kant's model in the real world for the ethical community is the church, or organized religion. Organized religion is to our historical hopes for the moral improvement of the human race what the political state is to our hope to live with other human beings on terms of safety, peace, freedom, and justice. Yet perhaps it is hard for us to take the analogy seriously, because political institutions and our demands on them have evolved in the direction Kant had hoped they would, whereas religious institutions have not. On the contrary, nineteenth- and twentieth-century religion has often seen itself as engaged in a battle to preserve reverence for tradition, ethnic diversity, and a sense of the transcendent and mysterious in human life against enlightenment rationalism, universalist and humanist morality, and a liberal, cosmopolitan society, which it blames for the rootlessness, disorder, and moral degeneracy of modern life.

But we must not forget that the Enlightenment, especially in Germany, was much more a religious than a political movement, and a movement that was regarded as coming from *within* religion, not as a secular movement arrayed against religion. Until we are able to recapture the perspective on history and religion represented by Enlightenment thinkers such as Kant, we will be unable to understand what the Enlightenment was; we will be unable to grasp what its true aims were, and we will be unable to estimate, or even properly to see at all, the extent of its successes and failures—or, as I would prefer to put it, we will be unable to see how far humanity in the last two centuries has been impoverished by its failure to realize the ideals of the Enlightenment.

There are many in our century who have celebrated the failure of the Enlightenment view of religion, regarding it as shallow and unspiritual, and complacent in the thought that religious thinking and practice has left it behind forever. In the past twenty years, there have also been many who celebrate the failure of socialism in a similar spirit. Sometimes these rejoicers are even the same people—as well they should be, since the historical hopes whose defeat they welcome have a great deal in common. As someone who still cherishes those hopes, I confess I am torn between pitying those who are quick to bury them and being furious with these same people for their pernicious attitudes and aims. But I am also uncertain whether either attitude is healthy, since pity implies an unattractively superior stance and fury seems to imply a relation of implacable hostility and despair over the possibility of genuine community with them. I am entirely certain, however, that the future of the human race will be bleak indeed as long as it is left in the hands of people who think as they do.

Notes

1. Kant's writings will be cited parenthetically in the text by title abbreviation, volume, and page number of *Kants gesammelte Schriften*, Königlich Preußischen Akademie der Wissenschaften, 29 vols. (Berlin: de Gruyter, 1900–). The *Critique of Pure Reason* will be cited by A/B page numbers. Translations are taken from *The Cambridge Edition of the Works of Immanuel Kant*, ed. Paul Guyer and Allen W. Wood, 13 vols. (Cambridge: Cambridge University Press, 1992–). The translation of *The Groundwork of the Metaphysics of Morals* (hereafter cited in text as G followed by volume and page numbers from the Academy edition) is found in *Practical Philosophy*, trans. and ed. Mary J. Gregor (1996), 37–108. The *Critique of Practical Reason* (hereafter CPrR) is also from *Practical Philosophy*, 133–272; *The Metaphysics of Morals* (hereafter MM) is from *Practical Philosophy*, 353–604; "On the Common Saying: 'That May Be Correct in Theory, but It Is of No Use in Practice'" (hereafter TP) is from *Practical Philosophy*, 273–310; *Religion within the Boundaries of Mere Reason* (hereafter RBMR) is from *Religion and Rational Theology*, ed. Allen W. Wood and George di Giovanni (1996), 39–216; and *Anthropology from a Pragmatic Point of View* (hereafter APPV) is from *Anthropology, History, and Education*, ed. Günter Zöller and Robert B. Louden (2008), 227–429.

2. This "social" interpretation of Kant's doctrine of radical evil and the response to it can also be found in Sharon Anderson-Gold, "God and Community: An Inquiry into the Religious Implications of the Highest Good," in *Kant's Philosophy of Religion Reconsidered*, ed. P. Rossi and M. Wreen (Bloomington: Indiana University Press, 1991), 113–31. For a further discussion and defense, see my paper "Kant and the Intelligibility of Evil," in *Kant's Anatomy of Evil: Interpretative Essays and Contemporary Applications*, ed. Sharon Anderson-Gold and Pablo Muhnik (Cambridge: Cambridge University Press, 2009), 144–72.

3. See Allen Wood, *Kant's Ethical Thought* (New York: Cambridge University Press, 1999), chap. 9, §4.3.

4. John Rawls, *A Theory of Justice* (Cambridge: Harvard University Press, 1971), 256.

6

KANT'S CONCEPTION OF PUBLIC REASON

ONORA O'NEILL

The idea that public reason provides the basis for justifying normative claims, including fundamental ethical and political claims, has acquired new resonance in recent decades. Yet it is not obvious whether or how the fact that a process of reasoning is public can contribute to fundamental justification. Indeed, since conceptions of reason, of the public, and of the boundaries between public and private are various and strongly contested, any claim that public reason justifies is multiply ambiguous. Moreover, some popular conceptions of public reason are quite ill-suited to any justification of fundamental norms. I offer three contemporary examples.

First, reasoning might be thought of as public simply because it is actually done in public or by the public, for example, in a context of political debate or of discussion in the media. Publicity in this sense may be crucial for any proposal to have democratic legitimation, variously conceived; but it cannot supply fundamental justifications. Democracies presuppose bounded territories and distinctions between citizens and noncitizens and, more broadly, between members and nonmembers (aliens, resident, and other); democratic process presupposes at least a rudimentary range of institutions such as the rule of law and at least minimal personal and civil rights. All of these demarcations and institutions would themselves have to be justified before democratic legitimation could be seen as providing or contributing to any fundamental form of normative justification. Similar points are true of those more widely conceived forms of public reasoning or debate that are structured by powerful formative institutions—publishers, the media, telecommunications providers, educational institutions, to name but a few—whose nature and influences would once again themselves have to be justified before the processes of public debate they structure could be seen as providing or contributing to any fundamental form of normative justification.

A second view of public reason locates its justificatory power not in democratic process, narrowly or widely conceived, but in the shared, publicly accepted categories and norms of communities. In communitarian writing we find a version of the thought that the fundamental categories and norms (of a community, of a tradition) are constitutive of identities, so cannot coherently be questioned (they are *Nicht hintergehbar*), so by default achieve what must pass for the most fundamental sort of justification that can be mustered. Normative justification cannot but be internal to communities, since there is no way of engaging with the categories and norms that outsiders deploy. Such conceptions of justification may seem appealing among the like-minded, at least when they have no wish to query their like-mindedness, but are patently inadequate for an account of normative justification in a globalizing world in which there is constant interaction among those who are not like-minded. Far from revealing a secure grasp of social reality, communitarian and other relativist conceptions of normative justification take nostalgic flight from the world in which we now live.

A third conception of public reason has been put forward recently by John Rawls, particularly in *Political Liberalism*. The distinctive feature of his approach is that he takes seriously the thought that normative and cultural pluralism rather than homogeneous community is the natural outcome of free reasoning.[1] However, this conception of public reason too offers no fundamental justifications.

As Rawls sees it, no appeal to shared values will work in a world in which people with diverse categories and norms find themselves interacting: communitarian justification must fail. Nevertheless we can appeal to a certain conception of reasonable *persons*, who (in Rawls's view) are committed to a form of reciprocity: they "are willing to propose principles and standards of co-operation and to abide by them willingly, given the assurance that others will likewise do so."[2] Given that the facts of pluralism preclude the possibility of identifying such principles with comprehensive ethical norms, Rawls argues that reasonable persons "are ready to work out the framework for the public social world,"[3] and must construct rather than discover principles of justice by public reasoning among those who are fellow citizens: public reason as Rawls construes it is "citizens' reasoning in the public forum about constitutional essentials and basic questions of justice."[4]

Evidently this conception of public reason as reciprocity among members of the public relies on many of the background assumptions on which conceptions of democratic legitimation depend. For Rawls, public reason has its context in a "bounded society," which he views as "a more or less complete and self-sufficient scheme of co-operation . . . existing in perpetuity,"[5] whose citizens enter by birth and leave by death, and whose politics are democratic. Various considerations suggest that this essentially *civic* conception of public reason cannot justify fundamental norms. In the first place, the conception presupposes, so cannot justify, many fundamental social arrangements, such as boundaries, democracy, and citizenship. Second, it is left unclear whether reasonable action, as Rawls understands it, is intrinsically public: on the one hand he holds that "the reasonable . . . addresses the public world of others";[6] on the other hand he notes that "Not all reasons are public reasons, as there are the non-public reasons of churches and universities and of many other associations in society."[7] Presumably the idea is that reciprocity among a wide but nevertheless restricted range of reasoners (coreligionists, scholars) constitutes reasoning appropriate for the relevant limited domain, but that only reasoning among *all* fellow citizens, that abstracts from the differences between them, constitutes fully public reason and can achieve the public justification of political norms at which political liberalism aims. Third, the identification of reasonableness with commitment to reciprocity is itself open to questions, some of which Rawls leaves unanswered. For example, in *Political Liberalism* he shifts between a *motivational* and a *modal* conception of the reasonable: the motivational conception stresses the *willingness* of reasonable persons to seek and live by fair terms of cooperation, the modal conception stresses their *capacity* to do so. A conception of the reasonable might center on one, but hardly on both of these views.[8]

Scope and Authority: "Private" Reason and Polemic

The failures of these three conceptions of public reason do not show that every conception of public reason is irrelevant to fundamental justification; indeed they may provide clues for the construction of a more convincing conception of public reason. One important clue can be found in the way in which the failure of each conception arises from its attempt to draw on other powers, institutions, or practices and to enlist their authority on behalf of reason. In each case it is the appeal to claims that lack reasoned vindication that undermines the possibility of fundamental normative justification. Just as the novice cyclist who clutches at passing objects and leans on their stability to improve his balance thereby fails to balance at all, so a would-be reasoner who leans on some socially or civilly constituted power or authority that lacks reasoned vindication offers only conditional reasons.

Kant made this negative point with crystal clarity when he drew a famous, and in my view still too little appreciated, distinction between public and private uses of reason. He characterises uses of reason that appeal to rationally ungrounded assumptions, such as the civilly constituted authority of church or state, not as *public* but as *private*. In *What Is Enlightenment?* he speaks of the official reasoning of military officers, of pastors of the established church, and of civil servants as *private*: these functionaries hold and derive their authority from their civil or public office, and their communications when acting officially are not (fully) reasoned because they assume the authority and the edicts of that civil power. Kant states quite explicitly that "the private use of reason is that which one may make of it in a certain *civil* post or office with which he is entrusted" (WE, 8:37).[9] By the same token he would classify the sorts of reasoning achieved in processes of demo-cratic legitimation, as well as those advocated by communitarians and by late Rawlsians, as private, or at least as not fully public, in each case because they appeal to the authority of civilly and socially constituted institutions and practices. He contrasts such "private" uses of reason with "the public use of one's reason . . . which someone makes of it *as a scholar* before the entire public of the *world of readers*" (8:37), a scholar "who by his writings speaks to the public in the strict sense, that is, the world" (8:38).

Kant frequently uses a variety of idioms to convey the basic insight that fundamental reasons, and with them the authority of reason, cannot derive from or be subordinate to any other power or authority. For example, in pas-sages in the "Doctrine of Method" of the first *Critique* he makes the same point by insisting that reasoning must be *uncoerced*. There, he writes:

> If you grasp at means other than uncoerced reason, if you cry high treason, if you call together the public . . . as if they were to put out a fire, then you make yourself ridiculous. . . . It is quite absurd to expect enlightenment from reason and yet to prescribe to it in advance on which side it must come out. (A746–47/B774–75)

The Conflict of the Faculties reiterates this negative point: "reason is by its nature free and admits of no command to hold something as true" (CF, 7:20),[10] and elaborates its implications for the tasks of the university. Giv-ing up the "argument" from supposed authority is not easy matter. In fact the "higher" faculties of theology, law, and medicine live by arguments from authority: they derive their authority from the state, which institutes, regu-lates, and restricts them, and assigns them the task of professional education and practice. Like the state officials of *What Is Enlightenment?*, these facul-ties speak with a voice of duly constituted authority, namely, that of civ-illy constituted and regulated professions. Like the speech of those officials, the teaching of these faculties is in Kant's sense of the term a private use of reason. In these passages Kant depicts the "higher" faculties not as wholly abandoning reason, but as aiming for a conditional sort of reasoning that will reach only those who accept a common authority without reason. The audi-ence is (at most) "the people as a civil community" (7:34).

By contrast, Kant claims, the "lower" faculty of philosophy[11] has no com-mitment to professional education or practice, and is not or should not be regulated by the state; its discipline is that of reason:

> It is absolutely essential that the learned community at the university also con-tain a faculty that is independent of the government's command with regard

to its teachings; one that, having no commands to give, is free to evaluate everything, and concerns itself with the interests of the sciences, that is, with truth: one in which reason is authorised to speak out publicly (CF, 7:19–20).[12]

The teaching of the "lower" faculty is therefore "directed to a different kind of public—a learned community devoted to the sciences" (7:19–20). This theme is continued with considerable detail in the appendix to part 1 of *The Conflict of the Faculties*,[13] whose theme is the conflict between one of the "higher" faculties, that of theology, and the "lower" faculty. Here Kant revels in pointing out what their appeal to ecclesiastical authority costs the "biblical theologians" of the "higher" faculty, and points out that their task can be only to teach ecclesiastical faith dogmatically to an audience of the faithful. By contrast, he asserts, the "philosophical theologians" of the "lower" faculty, who rely on reason to interpret the world and texts, even the texts of Holy Scripture, can communicate not merely with restricted audiences but also with the world at large.

In these and many other passages Kant sets out a dilemma. If we appeal to any civilly or socially constituted powers or authorities, let alone to mere brute force, we limit our own attempts to reason, and achieve at best communication of restricted scope and authority. Like the novice cyclist who loses the very balance he seeks in clinging to stable objects, reasoners lose the very authority they aspire to in making such appeals. But have they any alternative? Neither the passages in the *Conflict of the Faculties* nor those in *What Is Enlightenment?* get beyond the negative point. They do not show whether or how the aspirations and responsibilities of the "lower" faculty can be achieved. An account of the proper procedure of the lower faculty and of its authority is still needed. By itself insistence that reason cannot be derived from powers or authorities of other sorts takes us only a limited distance. It leaves us in need of some positive account of the means by which some but not other uses of cognitive capacities, that are not derived from spurious sources, are to be counted as reasoned. Surely reasoned thought and action demand more than the rejection of or resistance to spurious sources of reasons.

Scope and Authority: The "Lawless" Use of Reason

An obvious response to the limitations of democratic, communitarian, and civic conceptions of public reason, and of the many other private uses of reason to which Kant draws attention, is to insist that serious reasoning should not be beholden to any civilly constituted authority, indeed to any contingent power or authority for which no justification is provided, and that this independence is the condition of reaching audiences of wider scope.

However, this response is easier to formulate than to understand. Kant's favored image of public reason is the reasoning of scholars, the reasoning of the faculty of philosophy communicating with the world at large. It has evident limitations. Perhaps in the eighteenth-century world of international correspondence and communication among the learned this example was as good an image as Kant could find for reasoning that is not beholden to the edicts and assumptions of bounded states and institutions, practices, and roles, and their coercive powers. But he certainly knew that the realities of scholarly life seldom lived up to this ideal. The burden of argument in *What Is Enlightenment?*, and of passages in many other texts, is the vulnerability of such communication; his aim is to show that states, even despotic states, have an interest in allowing scholars "The least harmful of anything that could even be called freedom: namely, freedom to make *public use* of one's reason in all matters" (*WE*, 8:36). In Kant's view, states and governments that refuse to accord their citizens this "most innocuous freedom" act to their own detriment. This argument is not convincing, since the interests of rulers, and especially of despots, even when they claim to be "enlightened," may well be threatened by the ferment of unrestricted intellectual inquiry.

However, the deeper question is not whether governments, including despotic governments, have a genuine interest in permitting free inquiry, but whether we can say anything about the requirements of reasoned communication other than asserting the negative point that it should not, indeed cannot, defer to the edicts and assumptions of civil or other powers or authorities. Is reasoning merely a matter of freedom from restrictions, of unfettered and unstructured words, of a market place, a bazaar, a babble—of utterances? Is there perhaps nothing beyond a postmodernist play of (quasi) signifiers?

Other texts make it clear that Kant does not think of freedom from interference as the sole requirement of reason, or specifically of public reason. Although the emphasis in *What Is Enlightenment?* is very much on the need for public uses of reason to be free from restraint or control by the civil powers, the text is far more than a banal and timid contribution to the literature on free speech. Indeed, by contemporary standards, Kant limits the domain of free speech severely—so severely that his image of "public" reason as modelled on scholarly communication may be read as suggesting only that rulers should allow those whose communication has little impact on civic life to say what they wish. But the text does not advocate a merely permissive view of the proper use of human cognitive capacities.

Even in *What Is Enlightenment?*, in which the freedom rulers accord their subjects is a central concern, Kant is far from viewing public reason as mere absence of constraint. He depicts those who make free public use of their reason not as abandoning all intellectual discipline, but as judging carefully, as attaining intellectual maturity and autonomy, as pursuing "the calling of each individual to think for himself" (*WE*, 8:36). Although wise rulers will leave subjects free to make public use of reason, Kant does not for a moment assume that uncoerced reason must amount to unconstrained babble.

The distinction Kant draws between acceptable and unacceptable uses of freedom to reason is more deeply explored in *What Does it Mean to Orient Oneself in Thinking?*, published the year after What Is Enlightenment? The earlier essay focuses on reasons why rulers should accord their subjects the freedom to speak and to communicate; the later on the proper use of this freedom, and the reasons why mere absence of constraint is not enough for reasoned thinking. Kant contends in *What Does it Mean to Orient Oneself in Thinking?* that nothing could deserve to be called reason if it was wholly without structure and discipline. He pointedly asks the critics of reason, "have you thought about . . . where your attacks on reason will lead?" (*WOT*, 8:144), and contends that if they assume that reason is no more than freedom in thinking they will find that the very freedom they prize stands in the way of communicating with others: we cannot communicate our thoughts or offer one another reasons for action without imposing a certain structure or discipline on our thought and speech.

Kant's initial move is to argue that freedom of thought cannot be separated from freedom to communicate. Thought, speech, and writing all presuppose possible audiences, hence pluralities of potential thinkers, speakers, and communicators:

> Freedom to think is opposed **first** of all to civil compulsion. Of course it is said that the freedom to speak or write could be taken from us by a superior power, but the freedom to think cannot be. Yet how much and how correctly would we think if we did not think as it were in community with others to whom we communicate our thoughts, and who communicate theirs with us! Thus one can very well say that this external power which wrenches away people's freedom publicly to communicate their thoughts also takes from them the freedom to think—that single gem remaining to us in the midst of all the burdens of civil life. (*WOT*, 8:144)

The option of solitary thinking is not open, in Kant's view. Even a private use of reason assumes some plurality. But if the background authorities and institutions that private uses of reason accept and depend upon are unvindicated, we must ask whether serious, public reasoning must be wholly unconstrained or "lawless." Kant's answer is an emphatic "no."

He uses a fierce and sometimes sarcastic rhetoric[14] to characterize those who purvey the illusion that reasoning could be without all structure or discipline, or imagine that such absence of structure and discipline could be liberating. He had clear targets in mind, including sundry purveyors of religious enthusiasm, superstition, and exaggerated views of the powers of genius. Today his targets might include sundry postmodernists, skeptics, and deconstructionists. All of these opponents of reason blindly fail to see where unstructured liberation by itself will lead:

> If reason will not subject itself to the laws it gives itself, it has to bow under the yoke of laws given by another; for without law, nothing—not even nonsense—can play its game for long. Thus the unavoidable consequence of *declared* lawlessness in thinking (of a liberation from the limitations of reason) is that the freedom to think will ultimately be forfeited and—because it is not misfortune but arrogance which is to blame for it— . . . will be *trifled away*. (WOT, 8:145)

The illusions of "lawless" thinking end not merely in confusion but in disaster:

> First genius is very pleased with its bold flight, since it has cast off the thread by which reason used to steer it. Soon it enchants others with its triumphant pronouncements and great expectations and now seems to have set itself on a throne which was so badly graced by slow and ponderous reason. Then its maxim is that reason's superior law-giving is invalid—we common human beings call this **enthusiasm,** while those favoured by beneficent nature call it illumination. Since reason alone can command validly for everyone, a confusion of language must soon arise among them; each one now follows his own inspiration. (WOT, 8:145)[15]

Such anarchic, "lawless" thinking yields mere babble and is defenceless in the face of the claims of dogma, rabble rousing, and superstition.

Scope and Authority: Autonomy and Public Reason

If "lawless" thinking ends not in freedom of thought and communication but in gibberish and isolation, even in superstition and cognitive disorientation, and vulnerability to tyrants and demagogues, and then any activity in human life that can count as reasoned must be structured. In particular it must have enough structure for us to distinguish thoughts and proposals that provide good reasons from those that provide only poor reasons, so enabling us to decide which we ought to accept and which we ought to reject. Reasoning, whether theoretical or practical, must have normative force.

How can this authority and normative force be found or constructed, if they cannot be borrowed from elsewhere? When thinking and acting are structured only by the borrowed categories and norms of particular civil or social institutions and practices, they can achieve only limited, conditional authority and normative force. As Kant sees it, such categories and norms can ground no more than partial, "private" uses of reason, which can reach and be followed only by those others who grasp and accept the same categories and norms. So if anything is to count as *more* than "private" reason, in Kant's sense of the term, if there is to be anything that is to count as *fully public reason*, then the structures and disciplines that constitute it cannot be derived from existing institutions and practices. But what provides the internal discipline or structure of fully public reasoning? Kant's answer is straightforward:

> Freedom in thinking signifies the subjection of reason to no laws expect those which it gives itself; and its opposite is the maxim of a **lawless use** of reason (in order, as genius supposes, to see further than one can under the limitations of laws). (WOT, 8:145)

Public uses of reason must have *lawlike* rather than *lawless* structure, but since they are not to derive their lawlikeness from any external sources, this lawlikeness will have to be *self-legislated.* Since the terms *self-legislation* and autonomy (in Kant's usage) have the same meaning, it follows that a commitment to public reason and to autonomy are one and the same. Kant is quite explicit: "The power to judge autonomously—that is, freely (according to principles of thought in general)—is called reason" (CF, 7:27).

This identification of reason with autonomy is initially startling because contemporary interpretations of autonomy see it largely as a matter of independence rather than of reason. Kant never equates autonomy with independence; unlike most recent "Kantian" writers he views autonomy or *self-legislation* not as emphasising a *self* that does the legislating, but rather legislation that is not done by others, that is not derivative. Nonderivative "legislation" cannot require us to adopt the actual laws or rules of some institution or authority; it can be only a matter of requiring that any principle we use to structure thought or action be *lawlike.* This is what it is to conform to "the principles of thought in general."

At the end of *What Does It Mean to Orient Oneself in Thinking?* Kant elaborates this interpretation of reason as autonomy by identifying reasoned thinking with the practice of adopting principles of thinking and acting that have the form of law, which can be adopted by all.

> The maxim of always thinking for oneself is **enlightenment**. Now there is less to this than people imagine when they place enlightenment in the acquisition of information; for it is rather a negative principle in the use of one's faculty of cognition. . . . To make use of one's own reason means no more than to ask oneself, whenever one is supposed to assume something, whether one could find it feasible to make the ground or the rule on which one assumes it into a universal principle for the use of reason. (WOT, 8:146n)

In this passage Kant again states quite clearly that autonomy, or thinking for oneself, as he conceives it, is never a matter of mere or "lawless" freedom in thinking or doing: we think, judge, and act autonomously only if we structure our freedom by adhering to and adopting principles that could be universally followed or adopted, which must therefore have the formal structure of a law, that is to say, the formal structure of a universal principle.

Kant's conception of autonomy builds on the notions of *plurality* and *law*. We think and act autonomously only if and to the extent that we think and act on principles that could be principles for all, rather than principles that are fit only for limited audiences as defined by some civil or other authority or ideology. The form of independence that counts for Kantian autonomy is not the independence of the individual "legislator," but rather the independence of the principles "legislated" from whatever desires, decisions, powers, or conventions may be current among one or another group or audience.

Reasoning, whether theoretical or practical, is only a matter of structuring thought and action in ways that others *could* follow. In one respect this conception of public reason as autonomy parallels various contemporary conceptions of public reason (as well as Kant's own conception of private reason): all conceptions of reason are thought of as requiring that thought and action be conducted on principles that others can follow or adopt. The single, but crucial, difference between recent conceptions of public reason (and Kant's conception of "private" reason) and Kant's conception of reason as autonomy is that the former all address **bounded pluralities,** defined by civic or social institutions, practices, and ideologies, whereas for Kant public reason requires thinking and acting that address an **unrestricted plurality,** the world at large.

If these considerations are convincing, Kant has connected the authority and the scope of reason, indeed he has vindicated a specific conception of public reason by requiring that it be serviceable across the widest scope. Reasoning is a matter of following patterns of thought or adopting principles of action that others too can follow or adopt. If we aspire to reach only local and like-minded audiences there will be shared assumptions enough from which to reason. But the result will be no more than a private use of reason, which is comprehensible and convincing only among the like-minded. If we seek to reach beyond restricted circles where there are shared authorities or shared assumptions that can carry the burden of reason-giving, we have to supply a structure that the members of a wider, potentially diverse and unspecified, plurality can follow, by adopting and following principles of thought and action that an unrestricted audience can follow. As Kant notes, "there is less to this than people imagine"; but what there is may still surprise us by its combination of normative authority and extensive scope in guiding thought and action.

Some Surprises of Reason

I finish with a few comments on ways in which, as I see it, Kant's account of reason may still surprise us. A bare list might include the following points. This is an account of reason that is neither individualistic nor anchored to a philosophy of consciousness; it is an account of reason that is equally relevant to thinking and to acting; it is an account of reason that is closely linked to Kant's view of autonomy and almost without connection to contemporary views of autonomy.

First, by approaching the nature and authority of reason in this way Kant has taken a straightforward view of the need of anything that is to count as reasoned to provide reasons to others. He conceives of reasoning as directed to an audience. Private uses of reason are directed to restricted audiences, public uses of reason are directed to unrestricted audiences. It would be misleading to label Kant's conception of reason dialogical, because he does not (unlike a number of contemporaries) think that it is the product of real time, of actual dialogue. Kant's arguments are about the necessary conditions for anything to count as a reason, and his most basic thought might be put quite crudely as the thought that we do not give others reasons unless we present them with a pattern of thought that can be followed, and that we do not give them unconditional reasons unless we give them patterns of thought that they can follow without adopting some arbitrary starting point.

Notes

1. "Pluralism is not seen as a disaster but rather as the natural outcome of human reason under enduring free institutions." John Rawls, *Political Liberalism* (New York: Columbia University Press, 1993), xxiv; cf. 47, 55.

2. Ibid., 49.

3. Ibid., 53.

4. Ibid., 10, And: "Public reason, then, is public in three ways: as the reason of citizens as such, it is the reason of the public; its subject is the good of the public and matters of fundamental justice; and its nature and content is public, being given by the ideals and principles expressed by society's conception of political justice, and conducted open to view on" (213).

5. Ibid., 18.

6. Ibid., 53.

7. Ibid., 213. See also the discussion of Kant's conception of private reason below.

8. For further discussion of these issues, see Onora O'Neill, "Political Liberalism and Public Reason: A Critical Notice of John Rawls's *Political Liberalism*," in *The Philosophical Review* 106 (1997): 411–28.

9. References to Kant's writings, lectures, and correspondence are given parenthetically in the text by abbreviated title, volume, and page number of *Kants gesammelte Schriften*, ed. Königlich Preußische Akademie der Wissenschaften, 29 vols.

(Berlin: de Gruyter, 1900–). The *Critique of Pure Reason* is cited by the standard A and B pagination of the first (1781) and second (1787) editions. Unless otherwise stated, translations are from *The Cambridge Edition of the Works of Immanuel Kant*, ed. Paul Guyer and Allen W. Wood (Cambridge: Cambridge University Press, 1992–). The translation of *An Answer to the Question: What Is Enlightenment?* (hereafter cited in text as WE followed by volume and page numbers from the Academy edition) is found in *Practical Philosophy*, trans. and ed. Mary J. Gregor (1996), 11–22; *The Conflict of the Faculties* (hereafter CF) is from *Religion and Rational Theology*, ed. Allen W. Wood and George di Giovanni (1996), 233–328; and *What Does It Mean to Orient Oneself in Thinking* (hereafter WOT) is from *Religion and Rational Theology*, 1–18.

10. Note also "when it is a question of the truth of a certain teaching to be expounded in public the teacher cannot appeal to a supreme command or the pupil pretend that he believed it by order" (7:27).

11. Kant conceives of the "philosophy" faculty as covering a wide range of humane studies; he divides it into departments concerned with *historical cognition* (history, geography, philology, humanities) and departments concerned with *rational cognition* (pure mathematics, pure philosophy, metaphysics of nature and of morals). See CF, 7:28.

12. See also, "the government reserves the right itself to *sanction* the teachings of the higher faculties, but those of the lower faculties it leaves up to the scholar's reason" (7:19), and "The lower faculty . . . occupies itself with teachings which are not adopted as directives by order of a superior . . ." (7:27–29).

13. CF, 7:36ff.; many of Kant's claims in this appendix have parallels in *Religion within the Boundaries of Mere Reason*.

14. A reasoned rebuttal of the deniers of reason would hardly be possible—as those who seek to engage reasonably with postmodernists often discover.

15. See also CPR (A707/B735).

7

ORIGINAL COMMUNITY, POSSESSION, AND ACQUISITION IN KANT'S METAPHYSICS OF MORALS

JEFFREY EDWARDS

Kant's theory of private law (or private right: *Privatrecht*) is presented in part 1 of *The Metaphysics of Morals*, the Metaphysical Foundations of the Doctrine of Right.[1] The theory treats the conditions under which external objects of the power of choice (*Willkür*) can be rightfully "mine and yours."[2] The Metaphysical Foundations of the Doctrine of Right is divided into three main parts, all of which concern the principles that ought to govern the power of choice in relation to anything that can be acquired as externally mine or yours.[3] The first part, the doctrine of possession (§§ 1–9), determines the general conditions under which one can have something external as "one's own [*das Seine*]." The second part, the doctrine of acquisition (§§ 10–35), establishes the way in which something external may be rightfully acquired. The third part, "Of Subjectively Conditioned Acquisition Through Decision by a Public Court of Justice" (§§ 36–42), gives an *a priori* account of basic contractual relations and other normative factors in keeping with which the public administration of justice should take place. In this chapter, I discuss the doctrine of possession in connection with the portion of the doctrine of acquisition in which Kant establishes the principles in accordance with which corporeal objects can become property (*Eigentum* or *dominium*). I therefore focus on the concepts of possession and acquisition as they apply to the law of things (*Sachenrecht* or *ius in re*).[4] The primary point of interest is the role played by the idea of an original community of possession, or original possession in common, in Kant's theory of acquisition. I treat this role against part of its historical background in early modern natural law theory, and I bring out its implications for modern theories of the foundations of property law.

Intelligible Possession and the Juridical Postulate of Practical Reason

The doctrine of possession revolves around two systematic factors: the exposition of the concept of intelligible possession, and the argument by which

Kant establishes the universal validity of the juridical postulate of practical reason. In this section, I will clarify these factors in order.

Kant defines what is "rightfully mine" (*meum iuris*) as something with which "I am so connected that another's use of it without my consent would wrong me" (MM, 6:245.9–11). In view of this definition, he stipulates that the subjective condition under which I can make use of anything is possession; and he holds that the possibility of my possessing (and hence using) something as rightfully mine presupposes that a clear distinction can be drawn between two basic meanings of possession.[5] It is necessary to distinguish between sensible or physical possession and intelligible or merely rightful possession (*bloß rechtlicher Besitz*).[6] These different meanings correspond to a distinction that underlies our thinking of objects, a distinction implicit in the expression "external to me." It is the distinction between an object conceived as something "merely distinct from me (the subject)" and an object regarded as something located in another position in space or existing in another time. The type of possession that corresponds to the first sense of externality—intelligible possession—is possession taken without limiting reference to the conditions under which something exists apart from me in space or time.[7] Since (according to Kant) these conditions are all sensible, intelligible possession leads to the understanding of rightful possession as purely rational possession (*Vernunftbesitz*).

Interpreted as intelligible or rational possession, rightful possession is not merely nonsensible. It is also nonempirical. Possession is empirical when a subject's relation to objects depends on the spatial and temporal limitations that are characteristic of physically having some object in hand or at hand.[8] As Kant puts this point: "Intelligible possession (if such is possible) is possession without *holding* [*Inhabung*] (*detentio*)" (MM, 6:245.27–246.2). Accordingly, the possibility of intelligible possession, as rational possession, has fundamentally to do with our capacity to abstract from the conditions of physical possession. As rational beings, we must be able to disregard the set of sensible conditions under which "empirical possession" denotes a subject's phenomenal relation to certain objects of choice (i.e., *possessio phaenomenon*). Intelligible possession must therefore denote a noumenal possessive relation to such objects (*possessio noumenon*), and the practical proposition that grounds the juridical possibility of intelligible (or nonphysical) possession is one which presupposes that *all* conditions of empirical possession in space and time can be set aside. For only in this way can possession without holding, i.e., intelligible possession, be affirmed as "necessary for the concept of something externally mine and yours" (6:250.13–14).

The practical proposition just referred to is the juridical postulate of practical reason. This postulate is given its primary formulation in § 2 of the Doctrine of Right.[9] The postulate states:

> It is possible for me to have any [*einen jeden*] object of my power of choice as
> mine; that is, a maxim by which, if it were to become a law, an object of choice
> would *in itself* (objectively) have to become something belonging to no one
> (*res nullius*) is contrary to right. (MM, 6:246.5–8)

Kant argues that the juridical postulate of practical reason provides us
with a permissive law (*lex permissiva*), a law that authorizes each of us to put
all other rational agents under an obligation that they would not otherwise
have, namely, the obligation to "refrain from the use of certain objects of our
choice because we were the *first* to take them into our possession" (6:247.2–
6; italics mine). He maintains further that the possibility of intelligible (i.e.,
nonphysical) possession must be "inferred" from the juridical postulate as an
immediate consequence of the latter.[10] As we will see, the combination of
these two factors—the interpretation of the juridical postulate as a permissive law that grounds obligation through first possession, and the view that
intelligible possession is grounded as a direct implication of the same postulate—determines the character of Kant's theory of the foundations of property law. But first we need to understand these factors in the context of the
doctrine of possession in which they are introduced.

Since the juridical postulate asserts that *any* object of my power of choice
is something that is possibly mine, we can see that physical possession cannot be the defining mark of the rightful possession that correlates with the
notion of rightfully mine.[11] Thus, if rightful possession is to be possible, the
spatiotemporal conditions that limit physical (or empirical) possession must
be set aside. And if this is true, we can readily understand how the possibility
of rightful possession (as intelligible possession) is anchored directly in the
categorical requirement of practical reason expressed by the juridical postulate. What is not so readily apparent, however, is how this grounding relation fits together with the interpretation of the juridical postulate as a law
that authorizes me (or anyone else) to obligate others to refrain from making
use of some object of my power of choice because I was the first to take it
into my possession.[12] To better understand this problematic, let us turn to §§
8–9 of the Doctrine of Right, where Kant treats the concept of provisional
rightful possession in connection with his account of the juridical and civil
condition (*Zustand*).

In the sections just cited, Kant establishes that a subject can be in the
state of having something external as her own only if she exists in a juridical condition (*rechtlicher Zustand*) with respect to other subjects, that is, in a
civil condition (*bürgerlicher Zustand*) involving a publicly legislative power.
Such a power requires a civil constitution that conforms with the universal
principle and *a priori* laws of right set forth as principles of natural law in
the Doctrine of Right.[13] This civil constitution is what represents the juridical condition in which everything that belongs to each person is secured for

every single person, respectively, as his own. Kant thus takes the civil constitution to be the fundamental guarantee of right with respect to everything that is externally mine and yours. At the same time, though, he insists that this guarantee *presupposes* a normatively valid possessive relation, and he links this presupposition to the assumption that something externally mine and yours must be possible even apart from the condition under which it is guaranteed:

> Any guarantee, then, already presupposes that something belongs to someone (to whom it secures it) [*setzt . . . das Seine von jemanden voraus (dem es gesichert wird)*]. Thus, prior to the civil constitution (or in *abstraction* from it), something externally mine or yours must be assumed as possible, and with it also a right to compel everyone with whom we could have any dealings to enter with us into a constitution in which what is externally mine and yours can be secured. (MM, 6:256.30–35)[14]

We thus arrive at the interpretation of rightful possession that furnishes the centerpiece of the description of the state of nature relevant to the theory of private right. Apart from the civil constitution, anything that can be conceived of as externally mine and yours must be understood as a merely provisional rightful possession.[15] In a provisional sense, possession can be rightful even for agents who are thought of as existing in a state of nature. Possession in this natural condition can be rightful in the sense that it permits anyone to resist those who are unwilling to enter into the civil condition and who would interfere with what one has come to possess. But this way of portraying what it is to have something as one's own in the state of nature must still be characterized in terms of *physical* (or *empirical*) possession. It qualifies as rightful possession only in a derivative sense: it has in its favor "the rightful presumption" that it will be *made* rightful possession "through unification with the will of all in a public lawgiving" (MM, 6:257.14–18). Thus, by treating the relationship between the different meanings of rightful possession, Kant brings to light the necessary connection between the concepts of rightful possession and universal will. But he also acknowledges, as a crucial component of his theory of private right, a "prerogative of right arising from empirical possession" (6:257.20).

Now consider again the problem addressed above, which concerns the interpretation of the juridical postulate as a permissive law by which the obligation-founding character of first possession is determined. In keeping with Kant's considerations thus far, we can understand first possession-taking (*Besitznehmung*) as the type of act that gives rise to empirical possession. We can also accept that the empirical possession achieved through first possession-taking has to be consistent with the deontic requirements of right that are developed from Kant's concept of universal will. On these assumptions, we are presumably in a position to grasp how possession-taking can establish a prerogative of right that necessarily correlates with the obligation of others (or more precisely: the obligation to be placed on others) to refrain from using objects of our choice *because* we were, each of us respectively, the first to take them into our possession. To see whether these conjectures bear out, however, we must move beyond Kant's treatment of rightful possession to his account of the possibility conditions for rightful acquisition. We thus turn to the theory of original acquisition.

Acquisition, Occupation, and Original Community

It will not be possible here to provide fully detailed analysis of Kant's arguments on rightful acquisition as they pertain to the law of things (*Sachenrecht*). My considerations on the doctrine of acquisition will therefore have to presuppose that Kant effectively substantiates the following points in the course of his reflections on the principles of private right. First, whoever wants to claim that he has a thing (*Sache*) as his own must be *in* possession of an object; for otherwise he could not be wronged by another's use of any object without his consent, and such use would for that reason not be contrary to right.[16] Second, the fundamental principle of external acquisition in general is fully consistent with the universal law of right, the juridical postulate of practical reason, and the juridical requirements of practical reason that are contained in the concept of universal will.[17] Third, only corporeal things can be originally acquired.[18] Fourth, the basic argument presented in the second paragraph of § 12 of the Doctrine of Right is sound. That is to say, Kant successfully establishes that first acquisition of a thing can only be thought of in terms of the acquisition of land if it is to have foundational significance for the law of things.[19] Finally, the possibility of originally acquiring an external object of the power of choice is the immediate consequence of the juridical postulate of practical reason.[20]

How exactly are we to understand the concept of original acquisition in accordance with the assumptions just stated, especially given Kant's position that the possibility of original acquisition is the *immediate consequence* of the juridical postulate? If, in keeping with this postulate, I am to acquire anything originally, then what I acquire must be something external that is not originally mine. For nothing external to me can be mine originally;[21] and whatever I can acquire originally *as* mine cannot be something acquired from anything that belongs to someone else as her own, since all acquisition from another person or persons is derivative, and so cannot be original.[22] Consequently, if original acquisition is to be possible as a rightful act, then two things must obtain. I must not only be able to think of myself as a subject that can relate itself to something external. I must also be able to think of this external something as a thing that can be neither originally mine nor possessed by another subject as something that is her own. According to Kant, thinking jointly in these ways is possible only if the following conditions are satisfied. Acquisition must take place through the act of bringing something corporeal under my control. The control-seizing act (*Bemächtigung*) by which things are brought under my control must be the result of *unilateral* choice. Yet such a unilaterally performed act of seizure, or occupation (*occupatio*), must be able to take place consistently with the understanding of universal will as an *omnilateral* will—that is, it must be compatible with the idea of a will that is "united not contingently but *a priori* and therefore necessarily, and because of this is the only will that is lawgiving" (MM, 6:263.26–27).

It is in view of the relation between action proceeding from unilateral choice and action performed in conformity with the idea of an omnilateral will that Kant articulates the three aspects or "moments" (*Momente*) of original acquisition through seizure or occupation: (1) the apprehension (*apprehensio*) of an object that belongs to no one, which is effected by a subject's taking possession of an object of choice in space and time, and which therefore results in *possessio phaenomenon*; (2) the designation (*declaratio*) of the possession of this object as mine and of my act of choice to exclude everyone else from it; and (3) appropriation (*appropriatio*) conceived as an act conforming to the idea of an externally and universally lawgiving will, whereby everyone is bound to agree with my choice.[23] Kant understands the connections between these different aspects of original acquisition in terms of the stages of syllogistic inference. The descriptions given for apprehension and designation provide, respectively, the contents of the major and minor premises. The conclusion asserts that what I possess by virtue of the acts described under (1) and (2) is merely rightful possession (or *possessio noumenon*).[24] Thus, the movement of thought from the first to the last conceptual moments of original acquisition makes the transition from empirical possession (*possessio phaenomenon*) to intelligible possession by an inference of reason. This inference is meant to demonstrate how, in accordance with the universality requirements of practical reason, "abstraction can be made from the empirical conditions of possession, so that the conclusion, "the external object is mine," is correctly drawn from sensible to intelligible possession" (MM, 259.8–10).

But here, of course, we must ask how anything that I come to possess empirically as the result of unilateral choice could be something that I *can* possess in conformity with the idea of an omnilateral will. Kant formulates this specific problem of original acquisition as follows:

> Original acquisition of an external object of the power of choice is called *seizing control* [*Bemächtigung*] (*occupatio*), and it can take place only with respect to corporeal things [*Dinge*] (substances). When it takes place, what it requires

as the condition of empirical possession is priority in time to anyone else who wills to seize control of a thing [*Sache*]. . . . As original, it is only the result of unilateral choice. . . . —Still, if an acquisition is *first*, it is not yet for that reason *original*. For the acquisition of a public juridical condition by the union of the will of all for universal lawgiving would be an acquisition such that none could precede it, yet it would be derived from the particular wills of each and would be *omnilateral*, whereas original acquisition can proceed only from a unilateral will. (MM, 6:259.12–18)

Thus, the specifically Kantian problem of original acquisition has to be understood in view of the following requirements of intelligibility. First, original acquisition has to be thought of as taking place only in connection with a condition of empirical possession, namely, the temporal priority of the act by which one wills to seize control of—occupy—corporeal entities. Second, original acquisition is conceivable only as the result of unilateral choice under this temporal condition. Third, because of its conceptual link to such a condition of empirical possession, the act by which original acquisition takes place must somehow be made consistent with the act to which it seems most radically opposed. We must be in a position to think of the act of seizing control (occupation) as compatible with the omnilaterally unifying and universally lawgiving act by which a public juridical condition is to be established.

By this point, then, we can see how Kant clarifies the concept of original acquisition by explicating the notion of *occupatio* (*Bemächtigung*). We can also see how this explicative work enables him to formulate the problem of original acquisition so as to make it the systematic centerpiece of the law of things. But the considerations on original acquisition summarized thus far do not yet provide an adequate platform from which to address the problem of obligation that emerges from the interpretation of the juridical postulate as a permissive law, i.e., from the interpretation of this postulate as the law that authorizes me (or anyone) to hold that everyone else *ought* to refrain from using some object of my power of choice *because* I was the first to take possession of it. Those considerations do, of course, confirm one of the conjectural assumptions mentioned above. If taking possession of an object of choice represents the initial aspect (or moment) of original acquisition, and if priority in time with respect to the occupying will of others provides the condition for empirical possession, then we are surely justified in regarding first possession-taking as the act that gives rise to empirical possession. Consequently, as long as it can be demonstrated that the achievement of empirical possession through first possession-taking is necessarily consistent with the categorical prescriptions of right involved in the concept of universal will, we should be able to grasp how this kind of acquisitive action establishes a prerogative of right corresponding to the obligation placed on others by the juridical postulate. The ground of this purported consistency, however, is precisely what is not yet evident. Indeed, the contrast that Kant brings out between the necessarily unilateral character of the procedure of original acquisition and the union of the will of all for universal lawgiving serves to highlight the problem of obligation that issues from the interpretation of the juridical postulate as a use-excluding permissive law. Just how is this problem to be solved in the context of a doctrine of acquisition that takes the possibility of original acquisition to be the immediate consequence of the juridical postulate of practical reason?

Kant holds that original acquisition, regarded as the result of unilateral choice, is possible as a rightful act because the original possession of an external object can *only* be possession in common.[25] Accordingly, he maintains that first possession-taking can be thought of as an act performed in agreement with the law of the external freedom of everyone only if it is conceived in connection with an "original possession in common [*ursprünglicher Gesamtbesitz*] (*communio possessionis originaria*) whose concept is nonempirical and independent of temporal conditions" (MM, 6:262.28–30). If one accepts, with Kant, that first acquisition must be thought of as the acquisition of land, it follows that the relationship between the subjects who possess something in common must be represented in terms of the "original community of land in general" (6:262.13–14).[26] Moreover, because the earth's surface is spherical, this community must extend to "the possession of the land of the entire earth" (6:267.4–5). This conception of the universal scope of original community is yielded when we take account of a fundamental material factor that conditions human existence on earth: the unending finitude, as it were, of the terrestrial globe's surface makes it physically impossible for human beings to be dispersed to the extent that they exist beyond the limits of possible community with one another.[27]

By specifying the notion of original possession in common in terms of the universal community of land, Kant introduces "a practical rational concept that contains *a priori* the principle in accordance with which alone human beings can use a place on earth in accordance with laws of right" (MM, 6:262.32–34). He thus bases his theory of rightful acquisition on the idea of "the possession of all human beings on earth that precedes every rightful act of theirs," a possession that is "constituted by nature itself" (6:262.2–28). By employing the idea of the original community of land, Kant seeks to explain how it is possible to think of first possession-taking as an act by which I (or anyone else) can come to use, in accordance with laws of external freedom, things that I *already* possess in common with all others. By means of his conception of original community, then, Kant wants to show that the act of physically taking possession of something (*apprehensio physica*) furnishes an "empirical title" of acquisition that correlates directly, and necessarily, with "the title to an intellectual possession-taking [*intellektuelle Besitznehmung*] (setting aside all empirical conditions of space and time)" (6:264.9–14). The latter serves as a principle of entitlement that authorizes my (or anyone's) control-seizing activity with respect to objects that can only be thought of as belonging to *everyone* once all *empirical* conditions of space and time are set aside. As such, it provides for "the rational title of acquisition" that "can lie only in the idea of the will of all united *a priori*" (6:264.17–18).

The analysis of this concept of universal will thus yields the warranting principle by which external acquisition is authorized. Accordingly, we can say that the idea of universal will must itself be presupposed as an indispensable condition for *all* external acquisition. For all external acquisition must accord with the requirements of reason developed from the concept of the unified will of everyone if the control-seizing activity that proceeds from a unilateral will is to place upon others the obligation to refrain from using the things that one has taken into one's possession and designated as one's own.[28] Otherwise, the rightful quality of derivative acquisition could have no strictly rational ground; and the possession-taking act required by original acquisition could not be consistent with the formal requirements of practical reason's universal lawgiving in the domain of external freedom of action.[29] With reference to this domain, the idea of original community is a conceptual representation that picks out the objective correlate of the idea of universal will. The employment of this idea of will in conjunction with its correlate leads to the theoretical insight that something external can be rightfully acquired only if its way of acquisition conforms to the specific requirements of the juridical or civil condition: *anything* external that I can have as mine must be acquired "in conformity with the idea of a civil condition" (MM, 6:264.24). For Kant, this means that whatever one chooses to seize (i.e., occupy) as one's own from the originally common possession of humankind must be something acquired *with a view to* the realization of the civil condition, but prior to its establishment. Original acquisition is therefore necessarily provisional;[30] and anything originally acquired in keeping with laws of external freedom must be thought of in terms of the provisional acquisition of land through occupation.[31]

In Kant's doctrine of acquisition, then, reference to the global unity of the earth's surface, i.e., reference to the consideration of the physically insurmountable unity exhibited by the universal object and material substrate of all possible originally acquirable particular things, puts us in a position to regard possession-taking as the type of act that can be performed in conformity with the idea of an *a priori* united will. Kant introduces the notion of "the unity of all places on the face of the earth as a spherical surface" (MM, 6:262.22–23) as an essential feature of the rational concept of an original community of possession. He employs this idea to show how every subject's possession-taking acts can be conceived as ultimately grounded in an authorization to occupy that fulfills the universality requirements of practical reason's external lawgiving. The idea of an original community of land thus furnishes an *a priori* conceptual representation that structurally corresponds to, and combines with, the idea of universal will as an omnilateral will. Although this rational concept of original community is nonempirical and independent of temporal conditions, its correlation with the idea of universal will allows for the determination of the sensible conditions—specifically, the spatial conditions—of external possession as well as the conditions under which empirical possession is established through a unilateral will to occupy:

> We have found the *title* of acquisition in an original community of land, and thus among the spatial conditions of an external possession. The way of acquisition [*Erwerbungsart*], however, we have found in the empirical conditions of an external possession-taking (*apprehensio*), joined with the will to have the external object as one's own. (MM, 6:268.3–7)[32]

There will be a good deal more to say below about the connection between original community and the spatial conditions for external possession. At this juncture, the major item of interest lies in the connection that Kant discerns between the empirical conditions of external possession-taking and the naturally given unity exhibited by the universal object of possible acquisition.

Original Community and Universal Possession

To clarify further the notion of the community of possession that the latter connection presupposes, I refer here to several passages from Kant's preliminary work on private right, as published in volume twenty-three of the Academy edition.[33] In these passages, Kant is concerned with two different views of universality involved in the idea of original possession in common. He distinguishes between disjunctively (or distributively) universal possession and collectively universal possession.[34] We must think of the earth as the disjunctive-universal possession (*disjunktiv-allgemeiner Besitz*) of humankind when we take account of the physical fact that the earth's spherical surface, and hence its finite magnitude, sets all of the earth's inhabitants "in a relation of thoroughgoing reciprocal possible influence." In virtue of this relation of possible causal reciprocity, every human being is potentially in possession of any place on the earth's surface. Each human agent is therefore "in a potential but only disjunctive-universal possession of all places on the earth's land [*Erdboden*]" (VAMS, 23:320.22–23). Regarded from this distributive viewpoint, i.e., from the point of view by which each human inhabitant of the earth is considered in relation to what any given agent can individually possess, the original community of possession is something more than a

merely spatial relation of human beings. It has to be understood as a relation
of possible causal community between all agents, that is, as a universal relation of possible reciprocal influence. We must therefore think of it in terms
of the dynamical community—the *commercium*—of all originally possessive
agents, and not just in terms of the spatial juxtaposition (*communio spatii*) of
separate human entities.[35] Now, because the possible reciprocal causal relation between these agents extends to their possessive relations to all places
on the earth's surface, the relation of community between the earth's inhabitants must itself be thought of in terms of a universal community of possession. Moreover, the form and scope of the relation of possessors is such that
this community of possession must be regarded from a collective point of
view as well as from the distributive point of view just characterized. Specifically, it must be thought of as the

> possession in common that, as collective-universal possession through resistance
> in occupying the space that everyone on earth requires, makes a rightful act pos-
> sible and practically, i.e., objectively, necessary—an act by which the possession
> of each is *determined* distributively. (VAMS, 23:320.30–31; italics mine)

Thus, the universal community of possession, the form of which consists
in the relation of possible reciprocal influence between all of the earth's
inhabitants, puts anyone in a position to possess any place on earth, which
is what it means to say that the earth is originally possessed in common. But
this is precisely why

> this possession must also be regarded as collectively universal, i.e., as the com-
> mon possession of the human species to which corresponds an objectively
> united will or will that is to be united; for without a principle of distribution
> (which can only be found in the united will as law) the right of human beings
> to be anywhere at all [*irgend wo zu sein*] would be entirely without effect and
> would be destroyed by universal conflict. (VAMS, 23:323.30–324.2)

Taken from the standpoint of its disjunctive universality, humankind's
original community of possession represents a state of nature. Since the
juridically salient feature of this natural condition is its potential for universal conflict, the specification of the properties of the disjunctive-universal
possession makes evident practical reason's demand for a principle of distribution by which the possession of each can determined as rightful possession. According to Kant, the practical rational ground of this principle can
lie only in the idea of an *a priori* united will that corresponds to the collective view of the originally common possession of all humanity.

Let us return to the published text of the Doctrine of Right. The considerations on disjunctively universal and collectively universal possession just

put forward are fully congruent with what Kant argues in his metaphysical exposition of the concept of the original acquisition of land (§ 16 of the Doctrine of Right). Given that all human beings are originally in common possession of the land of the entire earth, and assuming that each has the will to use this land, it follows that the "naturally unavoidable opposition of the power of choice of one in relation to another" would "do away with all use of it [the land] if that will to use it did not also contain the law by which a *particular possession* can be determined" (MM, 6:267.7–11). This law—the distributive law of mine and yours with respect to land (*das Austeilende Gesetz des Mein und Dein eines jeden am Boden*)—can issue only from the *a priori* united will that normatively underlies, and is realized in, the civil condition. Still, the account of the juridical state of nature as a condition of unavoidable opposition between human agents' powers of choice must include the "rightful capacity [*Vermögen*] of the will of everyone to recognize the act of possession-taking and appropriation as valid, even though it is only unilateral" (6:267.19–21). That is because original acquisition, understood as the provisional acquisition of land, "requires and has the favor of the law (*lex permissiva*) in view of the determination of the limits of rightful acquisition" (6:267.24–26). This favor (*Gunst*) of the law in question (that is, the favor of the permissive law by which the obligation-founding character of first possession-taking is determined) does not reach beyond the point at which the juridical condition is established. In other words, it obtains only with a *view to* the achievement of the condition in which the limits of the rightful acquisition on the part of each agent are determined in accordance with the principle of distribution that proceeds from an *a priori* united will of all. Nonetheless, that favor of law carries with it "all the effects of acquisition in conformity with right" (6:267.31).

It is essential to note here that the favor extended by *lex permissiva* with respect to external acquisition cannot derive from any consideration of need or equity that may pertain to the distribution of some good. This type of material consideration can play no grounding role in a doctrine of acquisition that is consistent with the general account of strict right (*ius strictum*) at issue in the Doctrine of Right as a whole. This account concerns *only* the conditions under which the power of choice of one can be united with the power of choice of another in accordance with a universal law of freedom. Within the systematic framework of the theory of these conditions, the concept of right "has to do solely with the external and practical relations of one person to another, insofar as their actions . . . can have (direct or indirect) influence on each other" (MM, 6:230.9–11). It concerns the "reciprocal relation of powers of choice" in which "no account at all is taken of the *matter* of choice, that is, of the end that each has in mind with the objects he wants" (6:230.16–17). The theory of the metaphysical foundations of right therefore treats only the formal conditions under which the relation of possible influence between subjects whose powers of choice are reciprocally related can be in accordance with practical reason's universally prescriptive lawgiving role.[36]

The strict formalism of Kant's foundational juridical position entails that this lawgiving role of reason, as clarified by means of the concept an *a priori* united will, furnishes the only possible basis for limiting the scope of original acquisition. To clarify this thought, Kant employs the idea of an original contract in conformity with which the juridical or civil condition is to be established. By introducing this conceptual device, Kant wants to show how a given agent's authorization to occupy land unilaterally is necessarily subject to restriction, given the deontic requirements developed from the concept of the united will of all. This restriction on the scope of original acquisition, however, is itself subject to a crucial qualification. According to Kant, it is not possible to specify, either quantitatively or qualitatively, the limits of what *can* be originally acquired unless the conditions that feature in the idea of the original contract actually apply to the whole human species:

> The indeterminacy with regard to quantity as well as quality of the external object that can be acquired makes this problem (of the sole, original acquisition) the hardest of all to solve. Still, there must be some original acquisition or other of what is external, since not all acquisition can be derived. So this problem cannot be abandoned as insoluble and intrinsically impossible. But even if it is solved through the original contract, such acquisition will always remain provisional unless this contract extends to the whole human race. (MM, 6:266.28–37)

What follows from the qualification just stated?

It is essential to bear in mind here that the contractualist idea at issue in this passage must in any event apply normatively to the entire human species, whether or not all acquisition is merely provisional. So the implication of Kant's qualifying claim must be this: no definite limits can be placed upon the unilateral act of occupation by which original acquisition occurs as long as the juridical condition of humanity as a whole is not *realized*. Apart from the universal realization of a juridical condition in accordance with the idea of an original contract that extends to the entire human species, original acquisition through unilateral occupation cannot be understood as the type of act that is subject to specific distributive restriction.

This interpretation follows from Kant's understanding of the relationship between the juridical state of nature and the civil condition. It is a required interpretation because the laws of juridico-practical reason prescribe the realization of the juridical condition of humanity, and because these laws therefore maintain their prescriptive force for human beings, as rational beings, no matter what the condition may be in which their powers of choice are in fact reciprocally related.[37] At the same time, though, that interpretation sheds light on a fundamental problem for Kant's theory of private right. Let me formulate this problem with reference to the disjunctively universal quality of the originally common possession of humankind and the dynamical nature of the original community of possession. According to Kant, *all* acquisition must satisfy one of two conditions. Either it must take place in view of the determination of the limits of rightful possession (that is, it must be thought of as taking place with a view to the establishment of the juridical condition), or it must occur in accordance with the distributive law of mine and yours that is actually operative in a universally realized juridical condition. But if this is true, why should original acquisition receive the favor of *any* law of right if we have to think of it as following from a unilaterally appropriative act of possession-taking, i.e., as something achieved by an act of occupation that *can* generate a condition of universal conflict by virtue of the nature-given form of the causal community of all human possessors? As we have seen, this is a condition characterized by the unavoidable opposition of the powers of choice of all appropriating agents; and this opposition is such that it would do away with *all use* of things already possessed in common if the will of each to use such things did not "contain" (in other words, were not capable of conforming with) a law by which the particular possession of each can be determined. We have also seen that the quantitative and qualitative indeterminacy of the object of external acquisition is what makes original acquisition a problem to be solved by means of the idea of an original contract. Why, then, should we accept that the type of act that gives rise to such indeterminacy with respect to particular possession is compatible with the categorical requirements of right that demand, in keeping with the contractualist idea, the realization of a universal juridical condition in which all indeterminacy of possession is overcome?

Dominium, Right, and the Reach of Cannons

In view of the problem just posed, let us consider several passages from the two segments of the doctrine of acquisition in which Kant concretely treats empirical conditions of external possession-taking. At the beginning of the remarks appended to the main argument in Doctine of Right§ 15, which establishes the provisional status of all acquisition in the state of nature, Kant writes:

> The question arises, how far does the authorization to take possession of land [*die Befügnis zur Besitznehmung eines Bodens*] extend? As far as the capacity for having it under one's control extends, that is, as far as whoever wills to appropriate it can defend it—as if the land were to say, if you cannot protect me,

you cannot command me. This is also how the dispute over whether the sea is *free* or *closed* would have to be decided; for example, within the range of cannon fire no one may fish, haul up amber from the ocean floor, and so forth along the coast of a territory that already belongs to a certain state. (MM, 6:265.1–10)

And in a similar vein, Kant puts forward the following claim as part of his remarks on the deduction of the concept of original acquisition in Doctrine of Right § 17:

My *possession* extends as far as I have the mechanical capacity, from where I reside, to secure my land against encroachment by others (e.g., as far as cannons reach from the shore) and up to this limit the sea is closed (*mare clausum*). But since it is not possible to *reside* on the high seas themselves, possession also cannot extend to them and the open seas are free (*mare liberum*). (MM, 6:269.31–36)

Both of these passages refer to a dispute in modern international law concerning the permissibility of acts and policies that would establish exclusive *dominium* in the seas. Hugo Grotius and John Selden set the terms of the dispute in the early seventeenth century. In order to determine with precision how Kant relates to these particular figures, it would be necessary to investigate various references (direct or indirect) to the *mare liberum v. mare clausum* controversy found in the eighteenth-century compendia on natural jurisprudence that Kant used in connection with his lectures on natural law. But we need not be concerned here with the philological details. For the dispute between Grotius and Selden was of fundamental importance for the whole development of modern natural law theories of property, and Kant makes it quite clear that he addresses an issue of international maritime law only because it pertains to a basic question of his general theory of original acquisition. In keeping with Kant's broader concern with this question about the limits of occupation, I will discuss Grotius and Selden in view of the problem of original acquisition that underlies the *mare liberum v. mare clausum* controversy.[38]

Selden's treatise against Grotius—*Mare Clausum*—is intended to establish that the high seas are just as much subject to exclusive appropriation and use as is landed territory. Selden's argument is based on an account of the principally unrestricted scope of the unilateral act of occupation. While Selden directly opposes Grotius on the question of *dominium* in the seas, his account of occupation makes use of the key elements of the theory of original acquisition that Grotius constructs in his *Mare Liberum* and in *De Jure Belli ac Pacis*.[39] Given our focus on Kant, Selden's critical employment of these elements will be the primary item of interest in this section. But before turning to this employment, a few comments on the Grotian theory of property are in order.

Grotius's account of the origins of property employs the notion of an originally common *dominium*. Since, according to Grotius, all human beings share this *dominium* in the earth and its products, every man may arbitrarily seize for his own use whatever may offer itself for consumption.[40] The result of this universally permissible seizure for use—physical possession—generally takes the place of property in the state of nature. The need for definite property relations arises only when primitive use is replaced by productive activity requiring the distribution of livestock and land.[41] Property as such is established by universal agreement:

> At the same time we learn how things came to be property. It was not by an act of the mind alone; for some could not know what others wanted to have their own so as to abstain from it, and many might want one and the same thing. Rather, it was by some agreement [*pactum*]—an agreement either expressed, as by division, or tacit, as by occupation. For it must be supposed that as soon as community was no longer satisfactory, and before any division was instituted, all agreed to this: that which anyone had occupied he should have as his own.[42]

Notice that the postulated agreement of all to dissolve the originally community of things takes no account of any distinction that can be drawn between the primitive use of things for the purpose of immediate consumption and the more developed forms of relationship between human beings and the natural world that emerge from productive activity and require the establishment of property. Grotius's postulate of universal agreement pertains *generally* to the universally (even if tacitly) accepted principle that whatever one *had* occupied should be something that one possesses as one's own. Selden's account of the normative grounds of acquisition hinges on this general point.

Selden's portrayal of the origins of property, as found in the fourth chapter of *Mare Clausum*, revolves around the ideas of common *dominium*, occupation, and universal agreement. His portrayal is similar to that of Grotius in this regard. But Selden employs those ideas in order to draw conclusions about the permissible scope of unilateral occupation that undermine Grotius's systematic intentions in the controversy over freedom of the seas. Selden holds that any viable theory of property must begin by supposing that all things were at first given to all human beings in common, and that the earth and its products therefore originally constituted humanity's common *dominium*. Given this theoretical requirement, he uses the idea of universal agreement (*consensus humani generis corporis seu universitatis*) to explain how people could relinquish their original common right to things (*ius commune*

pristinum) in such a way that exclusive individual *dominia* could be established in accordance with the law of nature.[43] Building on this explanation,
he offers an explicitly contractualist interpretation of the Grotius passage
quoted above. Selden thereby wants to show that the theory of the normative grounds of acquisition cannot place any restriction on the scope of unilateral occupation with respect to unoccupied things. The thrust of Selden's
argument is as follows.[44]

If all people were originally owners (*domini*) of what was given to everyone in common, then it seems that they must have retained their community of ownership with respect to anything not subject to distribution in the
first partition of things through universal consent. Yet, although it is true
that all humans must be regarded as joint owners of what was given to everyone in common prior to the first partition, we must still conclude that the
original common title and right to things given to everyone in common was
renounced in a way that any individual might become the owner of what
remained vacant (i.e., undistributed) after that consent-based partition. This
accords with a parity of reason (*parilis sane ratio*). For if we accept, with Grotius, that each should retain as his own whatever he *had* come to possess
before this partition, then we also have reason to conclude that anyone may
occupy any thing that was afterwards left vacant as *res nullius*.

Note well the implication of Selden's "parity of reason" argument: *all*
components of the originally common stock of things are subject to exclusive appropriation by way of first seizure or occupation. Exactly this is the
lesson that Selden is concerned to draw from the link that Grotius forges
between the concepts of universal agreement and *occupatio*. For Selden, the
unilateral act of occupation performed subsequent to the partition of humanity's common *dominium* is (*qua* act) conceptually indistinguishable from such
an act performed beforehand. Thus, there is no reason to employ the principle of universal agreement in order to restrict the quantitative or qualitative scope of occupation after the dissolution of the common *dominium* while
not placing any explicit restriction on it prior to this dissolution. For the
same universality principle that allows an agent to retain what he had seized
prior to dissolution must apply to all things not owned by particular subjects
afterwards. (This is the underlying point of Selden's parity of reason claim.)
And, according to Selden, there is no basis whatsoever for restricting the
scope of anyone's unilateral act of occupation prior to everyone's agreement
that whatever anyone had occupied should be something that one has as
one's own.

Selden holds, then, that every agent is entitled unilaterally to occupy
any given thing from the common stock of things available to humankind.
The *ius commune pristinum*, as Selden designates it, determines the character of the human agent's possessive relation to things seized before the first

partition. It also determines this agent's possible appropriative relation to everything afterwards left vacant. Thus, with regard to both the originally common *dominium* and all things that can qualify as *res nullius* subsequent to the dissolution of the original community, Selden's *ius commune* serves as the ground for unrestricted appropriation. It is, in effect, *ius commune in omnia*: a right of all to all things—at least to those things not previously subject to exclusive occupation and particularized distribution.[45]

It is on the basis of his doctrine of acquisition that Selden seeks to refute Grotius' arguments against the permissibility of exclusive appropriation of the world's oceans. In his most telling counterargument, Selden maintains that Grotius fails to comply with what is entailed by his own crucial claim, i.e., the claim that the seas do not present a proper object of acquisition.[46] Grotius insists that the seas are not, and never have been, subject to exclusive appropriation. Yet he also concedes that it is possible to establish *dominium* in certain parts of the maritime world (stretches near the shore, bays, and the like). As Selden points out, this concession implicitly reduces the whole problem of the permissibility or impermissibility of the oceans' exclusive appropriation to an empirical question about the pragmatically feasible reach of occupation—which is in fact to miss the philosophic import of the point in question. This point, after all, concerns the juridical possibility of unilateral occupation; and a coherent doctrine of acquisition—even one that takes its key elements from Grotius's own theoretical arsenal—must allow for the possibility of the unilateral and *global* occupation of the oceans. Selden grants, of course, that this global occupation would be an exceedingly difficult act to carry out unilaterally. But if such an act of occupation *could* be successfully performed, then the object of acquisition—the oceans and, indeed, the entire globe for that matter—would become part of the occupant's *dominium*;[47] and this would be entirely consistent with the requirements of natural law in its permissive sense.[48]

So much for the historical background to Kant's references to the *mare liberum v. mare clausum* debate. Having explored a bit of this background, we can see how Kant's claims regarding the extent of the seas' occupation are in keeping with the position that Grotius wanted to defend. It might be an interesting exercise to investigate the extent to which Kant actually understood his doctrine of acquisition as offering support for Grotius's attempt to set limits on the appropriation of the world's oceans. Our interest in this particular issue in international maritime law, however, extends only as far as it sheds light on a basic problem in Kant's theory of original acquisition. The problem, again, is this: why should acquisition through unilateral occupation receive the favor of any law of right if it represents the type of control-seizing act that can generate a condition of universal conflict by virtue of the dynamical community of all possessive agents? In view of this question, the focus of our interest in Grotius's and Selden's doctrines of acquisition has been the connection between the concepts of occupation and community of possession. Thus, in assessing the significance of those doctrines for Kant's theory of original acquisition, we need to bear in mind the following considerations.

The conceptions of common *dominium* found in Grotius's and Selden's doctrines fall under the Kantian heading of "primitive community [*uranfängliche Gemeinschaft*]."[49] According to Kant, the concept of primitive community, or primitive possession in common, underlies the quasi-historical and unavoidably fictional (*gedichtet*) descriptions of humankind's natural condition that Grotius and others put forward in order to depict the beginnings of property and juridical relations among human beings.[50] It is an empirical concept that depends on temporal conditions.[51] The theory of original acquisition, however, is not concerned with temporal conditions that underlie the description of supposed historical (or prehistorical) states of affairs. Rather, this theory aims to determine *a priori* the necessary conditions for all rightful acquisition. To achieve this aim, it requires a concept of the community of possession, but this must be a rational practical concept whose application in no way depends on empirically specifiable temporal conditions. No empirical concept of the community of possession can qualify as such a concept of reason, and the narrative portrayals of the beginnings of property that rely on this kind of empirical concept cannot meet the conceptual demands of the theory of original acquisition.

This Kantian criticism of traditional doctrines of acquisition certainly applies to Grotius's portrayal of the origins of property relations.[52] It also applies to Selden, at least to the extent that he follows Grotius in giving a historicizing depiction of the state of nature and the dissolution of primitive community. But we should notice as well an interesting implication of the "parity of reason" argument that Selden directs against the Grotian doctrine of acquisition. Selden contends that the contractualist principle of universal agreement can furnish no ground for restricting the quantitative or qualitative scope of unilateral occupation after the dissolution of primitive community if it does not place any explicit restriction on this occupation beforehand. But if this is true, then (*parilis sane ratio*) it must also be the case that there can be no such restriction on the scope of occupation prior to that dissolution either. This follows for two reasons: first, because there is no basis for restricting the scope of anyone's unilateral act of occupation apart from some principle of agreement to do so; and second, because the whole point of employing the principle of universal agreement is to establish that each occupying agent should have as his own whatever he had occupied prior to everyone's (tacit or expressed) agreement to restrict each agent's unilaterally occupying acts to those things not already occupied by another.

Selden himself does not bring out this implication regarding the unrestricted scope of occupation prior to universal agreement. His main line of attack against Grotius in *Mare Clausum* led him to concentrate instead on the temporal conditions under which the dissolution of primitive community leaves a world full of objects (including all the seas) that have *yet* to be occupied. But if the further inference step is taken, then the general upshot of Selden's parity of reason argument against Grotius becomes clear: apart from the determination of an occupying act's priority in the *order* of time, the specification of temporal conditions is not relevant to a theory of acquisition that employs a contractualist principle of universal agreement. As long as an agent's unilaterally occupying act is thought of as performed prior to the corresponding act of another, it makes no difference whether occupation occurs before or after the point in time at which universal agreement is supposed (imagined or stipulated) to take place. For the relevant conditions to account for in a theory of *original* acquisition are the conditions by which all occupying agents are set in community with one another in virtue of the relation of each of these agents to all of the outer objects that are subject to unilateral occupation.

It is (logically, if not historically) but a short further step to link the conceptual representation of the sum and the material substrate of these spatial conditions to the potential for universal conflict and the naturally unavoidable opposition of occupying agents' powers of choice. But it is precisely in view of this potential and this opposition that we must again consider the passages from Doctrine of Right § 15 and § 17 quoted at the outset of this section.[53] The general question that Kant poses is the question of the extent to which one is authorized to take possession of unoccupied land. His response, which is keyed to the *mare liberum v. mare clausum* controversy, is in keeping with his standpoint that the theory of original acquisition must not rely on the substantive specification of particular conditions of empirical possession apart from the condition of temporal priority in possession-taking. But notice that his treatment of the permissible extent of occupation under actual empirical conditions of possession-taking is entirely unilluminating as far as the pivotal task of that theory is concerned. To put the matter in terms as blunt as Kant's own: settling the permissible spatial scope of possession-taking (hence occupation) by calculating the range of one's weapons is unhelpful if the theoretical task is to clarify how the will of each to use humanity's originally common possession can lead to unilaterally possession-taking acts that are necessarily in keeping with the universality requirements of juridico-practical reason. That is because the insurmountable global unity of this object of possible use is such that the weapons of each *can* be within the range of everyone else's weapons, in which case the nature-given will of each to use the originally common object can give rise to a condition of universal conflict in which no one's use of that object is possible.

It will hardly do to think that an indispensable systematic component of Kant's doctrine of right depends on empirical assumptions about the limitations on human beings' technical capacity for the use-prohibiting mutual infliction of physical damage. There must be something still missing from our treatment of original acquisition. It is certainly not the possible existence of the cannon, which nowadays are real enough in any event.

Dynamical Community and the Formal Principle of Material Equality in Distribution

Section 17 of the Doctrine of Right gives Kant's "Deduction of the Concept of Original Acquistion" (MM, 6:28.2). The overall argument of the doctrine of acquisition prior to this deduction leads to the following results, which Kant summarizes in the passage translated at the end of section 2 above. The title of acquisition (*Title der Erwerbung*) is found in the original community of land, and thus "among the spatial conditions of external possession." The way of acquisition (*Erwerbungsart*), however, is found by taking account of empirical conditions of external possession-taking, and by conceptualizing how these conditions connect up with the will to have external objects as one's own. The remaining task—the actual deduction of the concept of original acquisition—is to "develop *acquisition* itself, i.e., the external mine and yours . . . from the principles of pure practical reason" (6:268.8–11). Perhaps, then, we can find the way to complete the pivotal task of the theory of original acquisition by carefully examining this deduction.

In the second paragraph of Doctrine of Right § 17, Kant explicates the concept of intelligible possession (*possessio noumenon*), showing that it contains as one of its features a representation that denotes "the connection of an external object with me insofar as this connection is the subjective condition of the possibility of the object's use" (MM, 6:268.18–19). Since it features in a concept of pure practical reason, this representation must itself be both nonempirical and intellectual. Specifically, it must be the *a priori* conceptual representation that signifies the property of "*having* an external object *under my control* [des in *meiner Gewalt Habens* . . . des äußeren Gegenstandes]" (6:268.18–20). Even as applied to sensible objects, the concept of having here at issue is one that abstracts from the sensible conditions by which possession appears as "a relation of person to objects that have no obligation" (6:268.22–23). Now when these sensible conditions of concept application are disregarded, possession proves to be "nothing other than the relation of a person to persons, all of whom are subject to the first person's *will* to *bind*" (6:268.23–28) to the extent that this first person's will accords with the principles of juridico-practical reason and the idea of the universally lawgiving function of the united will of all. In sum, the deduction of the concept of original acquisition involves the specification of the concept of intelligible possession in terms of "having an external object under my control"; and this specification is what furnishes the particular concept of having that we can employ to explain how one person's will to bind can actually place an obligation upon all other persons with respect to certain objects of the power of choice. By means of that specification, then, Kant wants to show how the concept of having that plays so central a role in the doctrine of possession also provides the key to understanding the justificatory basis of original acquisition.

Is Kant successful in this endeavor? The analytic procedure of Doctrine of Right § 17 clearly does show the way to think of the possession of objects as a relation of obligation between persons, instead of merely as a physical relation of persons to objects. It therefore sheds considerable light above all on the culminating aspect (or "moment") of original acquisition mentioned above. In particular, it allows for a proper understanding of what Kant means in § 10 when he asserts that appropriation is "the act of an externally and universally lawgiving will (in idea) through which everyone is bound to agreement with my choice" (MM, 6:259.2–4). Given its focus on an *a priori* concept of *having*, however, it is far from obvious that Kant's procedure in § 17 can even address what is fundamentally at issue in the required account of original acquisition as long as acquisition as such must be understood as an act of *acquiring* things in order to be in the state of having them. With regard to the use of these things, Kant's aim in § 17 is to show how all persons can be bound by the will of a first person, i.e., by the will of a unilaterally control-seizing agent who was the first to take possession of an object. The argument is that all persons are so bound *insofar* as that first person's will to have something under her control accords with the universality requirements of juridico-practical reason, and hence conforms with "the universal *lawgiving* of the will that is thought as united *a priori*" (6:268.25–26). Yet it remains entirely unclear how we are to go about determining the extent to which the way of acquisition (*Erwerbungsart*) can be in conformity with this universally prescriptive role of the *a priori* united will of all as long as that way of acquiring things is to be found in the empirical conditions of possession-taking that are joined with a person's will to have objects under her control.

The full import of this line of questioning becomes evident when we consider three things that Kant establishes in the sections that prepare the terrain for the deduction of the concept of original acquisition in Doctrine of Right § 17. As we have seen, Kant argues in §15 and § 16 that (a) taking possession of objects from the originally common possession of all human beings gives rise to quantitative and qualitative indeterminacy with regard to particular possession (*besonderer Besitz*); (b) each human being's nature-given will to use that common possession is unavoidably faced with the opposition of human powers of choice; and (c) this opposition would do away with all use of the common possession unless that will to use contained the law by which the particular possession of each can be determined. What, then, is the determining ground of the will that this law expresses? Kant makes it quite clear, of course, that the law itself must derive from the *idea* of an *a priori* united will of all. Consequently, the ground in question obviously cannot be found in empirical conditions of possession-taking. But neither the expository work on the concept of original acquisition that Kant undertakes prior to his deduction of this concept nor the deduction itself provides for the explanation of any *a priori* ground (or condition) by which the particular possession of each can be *determined*.

There is but one remaining path to take if we are to discover this kind of ground. It is the path that leads from the title of acquisition, not from the empirical conditions of an external possession-taking. Let us therefore examine more closely the "spatial conditions" (MM, 6:268.3) that feature in the *a priori* concept of the original community of land that furnishes the title of acquisition. This is best accomplished with reference to the considerations on disjunctively universal and collectively universal possession found in Kant's preliminary work on the doctrine of right. As we have seen (section 3 above), the thought that the earth furnishes the disjunctive-universal possession of humankind takes account of a physical factor that conditions human existence: the spatial properties of the earth's surface are such that all of the earth's inhabitants stand in a relation of possible reciprocal influence or possible dynamical community (*commercium*). In virtue of this relation, each human being is *always* potentially in possession of any place among *all* places on the earth's surface, which is what requires the collective view of the universal dynamical community of possession. The explication of this collective view shows both the possibility and the practical necessity of a rightful act "by which the possession of each is determined distributively" (VAMS, 23:320.36). Regarded from the collective point of view, the common possession of the human species must therefore be thought of as something the particularized distribution of which *can* coincide with "an objectively united will or will that is to be united." Apart from the consideration of this possible structural overlap, there is no way to ground the principle of distribution without which "the right of human beings to be anywhere at all would be entirely without effect and would be destroyed by universal conflict" (23:323.31–324.2).

All this is in keeping with the argument presented in the published version of the Metaphysical Foundations of the Doctrine of Right. Yet Kant's concern to highlight the causal features of the universal spatial community of possession allows us to discern the import of a key requirement of practical reason that is not readily apparent in the published text. On its collective view, the original community of possession may not be understood *simply* in terms of the reciprocal causal relation of all persons that can emerge from their possessive relation to usable objects. For in addition to its representing a universal relation of persons to persons, that original community must also be thought of as representing the relation of all persons to all possible objects that are subject to original acquisition in virtue of the fact that all such objects are constitutive components of the common possession of all human beings. It is this collective causal relation of *persons to objects*—that is, the possessive relation that persons have to usable objects of the power of choice on the basis of their possible reciprocal causal relations to the powers of choice of all other persons—that must be constituted in conformity with a principle of distribution that derives from the idea of a united and universally lawgiving will of all persons.

Now as regards acquired rights, all lawgiving in accordance with this idea of practical reason is subject to a fundamental requirement. It has to be consistent with a basic principle of juridico-practical reason involved in Kant's understanding of freedom as "the only original right belonging to every human being by virtue of their humanity" (MM, 6:237.32–33). The relevant principle is that of innate equality, i.e., "independence from being bound by others to more than one can also reciprocally bind them" (6:237.34). Kant's theory of private right, and hence his account of original acquisition, presupposes the practical objective validity of this principle of independence. The principle of distribution that applies to original possession in common, i.e., to the original community of land, must therefore accord with the constraint against the nonreciprocal imposition of obligation in terms of which the innate equality of human beings is defined.[54] With respect to the conditions of original acquisition, then, what Kant calls the "rightful capacity of the will to bind everyone" (6:267.19–20) must be governed by a principle that recognizes that *no* person's unilateral act of possession-taking and appropriation can bind other persons to more than that first person can be bound by them. With regard to all the things that can be acquired for use, this principle allows for indefiniteness or indeterminacy from the point of view of disjunctive-universal possession, i.e., from the point of view according to which every human being is potentially in possession of any arbitrarily chosen place on earth because of the possible dynamical community—the *commercium*—of all the planet's inhabitants. Yet Kant's understanding of original possession in common is such that the principle of distribution contained in the idea of the united will of all must be a principle of *equality* in distribution. For even if I am (originally) the first to *take* possession of something that I already possess in common with all others, I would violate the constraint against the nonreciprocal placement of obligation unless I limited the extent of my possession-taking in accordance with the following precept: we may place upon all others an obligation to refrain from using certain objects of our powers of choice because we were (each of us respectively) the first to take possession of these objects—but *only insofar* as this does not bind all others, in their use of objects, to refrain from *more* than we are reciprocally bound by all of them to refrain from using.

However quantitatively or qualitatively indeterminate the object of acquisition may turn out to be under empirical conditions of possession-taking, the consideration of the collective relation of all persons to the universal object and material substrate of all possible external acquisition gives rise to the following demand. The principle of distribution at issue in the conceptual determination of original acquisition must be a principle of equality. It must be the principle (or law) through which the *a priori* determinable condition of possession-taking is *specified as* the ground of equality in the distribution of things. This is the only way to establish that the will of each to use the originally common possession of humankind is necessarily consistent with the universal lawgiving at issue in the idea of an *a priori* united will of all. The normative basis for all derivative acquisition therefore lies in a distributive principle of original equality in use. This principle must retain its objective validity and practical necessity with respect to all conditions of possession-taking. That is to say: it must retain its universally prescriptive force independently of the extent to which the outcome of the unilaterally control-seizing activity of human beings in fact satisfies the imperative of reason that such a principle of equality yields.

We should bear in mind that the principle in question furnishes a law of practical reason that belongs to the theory of *ius strictum*. This is a law of right that concerns merely the reciprocal relations of powers of choice. Its derivation does not depend in any way on considerations of equity or human need;[55] and it takes no account of the matter of choice, i.e., the end that one may have in mind with whatever object one might want to have. The principle of distribution in question is therefore a strictly formal principle of equality. Nonetheless, it is a principle of *material* equality as far as the acquisition of objects is concerned. Only if it incorporates a formal principle of material equality can Kant's theory of original acquisition provide a coherent normative basis for property law.

Needless to say, this conclusion is hardly what one would expect to get from a classic modern theory of the foundations of property, and I hasten to emphasize that Kant himself by no means draws it in the Metaphysical Foundations of the Doctrine of Right. Yet there seems to be no defensible alternative conclusion—unless, that is, we are prepared to accept that a person's will to use and rightfully to have objects need not be in keeping with practical reason's *exeundum* prescription, that is, with its commandment to go forth from the juridical state of nature and leave it behind.[56]

Notes

1. Kant's works are cited parenthetically in the text by volume, page, and line number of *Kants gesammelte Schriften*, ed. Königlich Preußische Akademie der Wissenschaften, 29 vols. (Berlin: de Gruyter, 1900–). The translations of passages in Kant's *Vorarbeiten zur Metaphysik der Sitten* (hereafter VAMS), as published in volume 23 of *Kants gesammelte Schriften*, are my own. The renderings of passages taken from Kant's *Metaphysik der Sitten* (*Metaphysics of Morals*; hereafter MM) generally conform with Mary Gregor's English translation. See Mary J. Gregor, trans. and ed., *Practical Philosophy* (Cambridge: Cambridge University Press, 1996), 363–615. I have, however, substantially altered the Gregor translation whenever I have judged it appropriate to do so.

2. I translate *Willkür* as "power of choice" or simply as "choice." Despite the drawbacks inherent in the employment of "choice" in this regard, I know of no other English alternative rendering that better captures central aspects of the meaning of *Willkür* in most of the contexts in which Kant employs the term. For the purposes of this chapter, at any rate, my use of "will" and "(power of) choice" is always consistent with the distinction between *Wille* and *Willkür* as Kant draws it in the general introduction to his *Metaphysik der Sitten*; see MM, 6:213.14–25.

3. See MM, 6:245.5. For general discussion of the structure and systematic character of the theory of private right, see Hans Friedrich Fulda, *Zur Systematik des Privatrechts in Kants 'Metaphysik der Sitten,'* in *Recht, Staat, und Völkerrecht bei Immanuel Kant*, ed. Dieter Hüning and Burkhard Tuschling (Berlin: Duncker & Humblot, 1998), 141–56; Wolfgang Kersting, *Wohlgeordnete Freiheit: Immanuel Kants Rechts- und Staatsphilosophie* (Frankfurt am Main: Suhrkamp, 1993), 225–321. See also Paul Guyer, "Kant's Deductions of the Principles of Right," in *Kant's Metaphysics of Morals: Interpretive Essays*, ed. Mark Timmons (Oxford: Oxford University Press, 2002), 23–64.

4. On the relationship between *Sachenrecht* and the theory of property in Kant, see Rainer Friedrich, *Eigentum und Staatsbegründung in Kants 'Metaphysik der Sitten'* (Berlin: de Gruyter, 2004), 89–95. On modern theories of property and their developmental background, see Reinhard Brandt, *Eigentumstheorien von Grotius bis Kant* (Stuttgart: Fromman-Holzboog, 1974); Manfred Brocker, *Arbeit und Eigentum: Der Paradigmenwechsel in der neuzeitlichen Eigentumstheorie* (Darmstadt: Wissenschaftliche Buchgesellschaft, 1992); Stephen Buckle, *Natural Law and the Theory of Property: Grotius to Hume* (Oxford: Oxford University Press, 1991); Jeffrey Edwards, "Property and *Communitas Rerum*: Ockham, Suarez, Grotius, Hobbes," in *Societas Rationis: Festschrift für Burkhard Tuschling zum 65. Geburtstag*, ed. Dieter Hüning, Gideon Stienig, and Ulrich Vogel (Berlin: Duncker & Humblot, 2002): 41–60; Brian Tierney, *The Idea of Natural Rights: Studies on Natural Rights, Natural Law, and Church Law 1150–1625* (Atlanta: Scholars Press/Emory University, 1997); Brian Tierney, "Permissive Natural Law and Property: Gratian to Kant," in *Journal of the History of Ideas* 62 (2001): 381–99.

5. See MM, 6:245.13–21.

6. Whenever appropriate, I translate *rechtlich* as "rightful." Ordinarily, though, I use "juridical." This accords with Kant's own use of the cognate adjective when he

refers to *juridische Gesetgebung* and *juridischer Naturzustand*, and it avoids Gregor's circumlocutionary renderings (e.g., "postulate of practical reason with regard to rights" for *rechtliches postulat der praktischen Vernunft*), which on occasion can be misleading.

7. See MM, 6:245.23–27.

8. See MM, 6:245.16–27.

9. As has long been widely acknowledged, § 6 (Deduction of the Concept of the Merely Rightful Possession of an External Object [*possessio noumenon*]) of the Doctrine of Right was flawed by the insertion of a piece of text the content of which belongs to Kant's reflections on original acquisition. Bernd Ludwig, in his *Philosophische Bibliotek* edition of Kant's *Rechtslehre* (Hamburg: Felix Meiner, 1998), has maintained that the faulty insert should be replaced by transferring the entire text of § 2 to § 6. This is not the place to examine the extensive controversy in the secondary literature that has arisen in the wake of Ludwig's editorial work and publications relating to the textual reconstruction of the Doctrine of Right. While not insisting on the sanctity of the original text, however, I should at least state here my reasons for rejecting Ludwig's approach (especially since the recent Cambridge edition of the *Metaphysics of Morals* follows it). (1) I find that removing the faulty insert leaves no logical gap in the argument of § 6. (2) Because Kant asserts in §6 that the possibility of nonphysical possession is the immediate consequence of the juridical postulate (see MM, 6:252.17–21), the deduction of the concept of nonempirical possession (in § 6) presupposes the soundness of the argument by which Kant establishes the juridical postulate. Transferring this argument from its original location (in § 2) to the middle of § 6 threatens to make Kant's deduction of the concept of merely rightful possession circular and question-begging. (I owe this point to Rainer Friedrich, *Eigentum und Staatsbegründung in Kants 'Metaphysik der Sitten,'* 104.) (3) The argument of § 2 grounds the juridical postulate by appealing to the formal coherence of the concept of external freedom, and by determining pure practical reason's lawgiving role in relation to the use of external objects of the power of choice. It makes no reference to the concept of nonempirical or nonphysical possession, the possibility of which Kant holds to be an immediate consequence of the juridical postulate as a synthetic *a priori* practical proposition. Thus, even if there is a logical gap in § 6, we cannot fill it or bridge it by transferring § 2 from one textual location to another. In sum: apart from removing the considerations belonging to the doctrine of acquisition from the doctrine of possession, I see no plausible reason for assenting to any conjectural rerouting of Kant's line of argument in the Doctrine of Right.

10. See MM, 6:252.17–21.

11. Kant defines object of choice [*Gegenstand der Willkuer*] as "something that I have physically in my power [*Macht*] to use" (MM, 6:246.9–10). Thus, the concept of rightfully mine at issue in the juridical postulate applies to any object (and indeed to all objects) that I *can* have physically in my power to use irrespective of the limitations of my actual physical possession of any particular object (or objects) that is (or are) spatially distinct from me at any given point of time.

12. Kant holds that the authorization to place such an obligation on others cannot be obtained "from mere concepts of right" (MM, 6:247.2–3)—i.e., from the fundamental understanding of right as "the sum of the conditions under which the power of choice of one can be united with the power of choice of another in accordance

with a universal law of freedom" (6:230.24–26). This standpoint is fully consistent with Kant's position that the juridical postulate furnishes a synthetic *a priori* proposition that cannot be derived analytically from the universal principle or the universal law of right, even though the proof of practical reason's capacity to lay down synthetic *a priori* propositions "can . . . , in a practical respect, be adduced in an analytic way" (6:255.20–21). (Regarding this position, see further 6:230.29–31, 6:231.10–11, 6:249.30–250.17, 6:251.37–252.30, 6:255.13–20, 6:396.4–11.) But just why should the *possibility* of my having any object of my power of choice as something rightfully mine warrant the exclusion of others from the use of an object because I *was* the first to take possession of it? In other words, the question is why the juridical postulate (as the synthetic *a priori* practical proposition that asserts the possibility of the merely rightful possession of external objects) does not necessarily abstract from the temporal priority of possession-taking acts if we must set aside all conditions of empirical possession.

13. On the significance of Kant's account of private right for natural law theory, see, e.g., MM, 6:242.3–19, 6:256.22–35, 6:257.14–19.

14. The analytic connections between the concepts of right and compulsion or constraint [*Zwang*] are established in §§ D and E of the introduction to the Doctrine of Right (see 6:231.22–233.25). The argument that Kant presents in Doctrine of Right § 9, incidentally, does not establish that public right is *based* on the account of the externally mine and yours that is at issue in the theory of private right. On this, see the critical discussion of Reinhardt Brandt, Wolfgang Kersting, and Bernd Ludwig in Friedrich, *Eigentum und Staatsbegründung in Kants 'Metaphysik der Sitten,'* 12–17, 55–57, 69–71, 174–81.

15. See MM, 6:256.35–257.6.

16. See MM, 6:247.10–13.

17. "The principle of external acquisition is as follows: that is mine which I bring under my control [*Gewalt*] (in accordance with the law of outer *freedom*); which, as an object of my power of choice, is something that I have the capacity [*Vermögen*] to use (in accordance with the postulate of practical reason); and which, finally, I *will* that it is to be mine (in conformity with the idea of a possible united will)" (MM, 6:258.22–27).

18. See MM, 6:258.22–25.

19. See 6:262.1–10; cf. Karl Marx, *Grundrisse der Kritik der politischen Ökonomie* (Berlin: Dietz Verlag, 1974), 391–92.

20. See 6:263.12–19.

21. According to Kant, everything that is originally mine (or yours) falls under the heading of "inner mine and yours (*meum vel tuum internum*)." It is therefore a feature of freedom understood as the single innate right of human beings. As such, it cannot be a systematic component of the account of acquired right to which the theory of private right belongs. See MM, 6:237.13–32; cf. VAMS, 23:295.33–296.18, 23:297.10–20, 23:302.27–303.30, 23:309.4–7.

22. See MM, 6:256.1–11, 6:259.17–20.

23. MM, 6:258.28–259.4. For discussion, see Wolfgang Kersting, *Wohlgeordnete Freiheit*, 264–67; Bernd Ludwig, *Kants Rechtslehre*, 127–33.

24. MM, 6:259.4–7.

25. See MM, 6:258.9–14.

26. See also MM, 628.3–4. It is natural to think of *"ursprünglicher Gesamtbesitz"* as the term to use when referring to the object possessed in common (that is, when referring to the relation of possessors *to* their common object). It is also natural to think of *"Gemeinschaft des Bodens"* as the expression for the mutual relations that possessors have by virtue of their relations to that common object. Kant, however, seems to use the two terms interchangeably. In any event, nothing in his arguments on original acquisition hinges on the distinction just mentioned.

27. See MM, 6:262.20–26.

28. See MM, 6:264.17–22, 6:265.19–30.

29. See MM, 6:259.17–20, 6:260.33–261.14.

30. If it were thought of as acquired at the same time as or subsequent to the establishment of the civil condition, it would have to be understood as a derivative acquisition. It would depend on a type of acquisition that cannot be original. See MM, 6:259.23–28, 6:264.23–28.

31. See MM, 6:264.29–35.

32. See also MM, 263.4–12.

33. See Loose Leaf 58, especially the following passages: VAMS, 23:320.19–321.8, 23:323.26–324.2.

34. Regarding Kant's conception of the relationship between distributive and collective universality, see 3:392.1–9, 427.19–32; 4:526.15–18, 4:563.39–564.9; 6:323.31–324.7; 8:371.6-14; 14:287.1–288.2; 17:397.7–12, 17:442.10–23, 17:570.26–571.2, 17:703.7–11; 18:238.26–28, 18:366.28–29, 18:528.6–9; 21:586.8–24, 21:603.4–9.

35. These terms are, of course, taken from the *Critique of Pure Reason's* Third Analogy of Experience (see 3:182.27–31; cf. 6:352.6–22). For discussion, see Jeffrey Edwards, *Substance, Force, and the Possibility of Knowledge: On Kant's Philosophy of Material Nature* (Berkeley: University of California Press, 2000), 20–21, 37–43.

36. Which is *not* to say that this theory disregards the force of moral requirements derived in view of need, or that it assigns no place to the determination of equity in the public administration of justice. See MM, 6:235.6–11; MM, 235.16–236.7.

37. See note 57 below.

38. For more extensive treatment of both Grotius and Selden, see Jeffrey Edwards, "Natural Right and Acquisition in Grotius, Selden, and Hobbes," in *Der lange Schatten des Leviathan. Hobbes' politische Philosophie nach 350 Jahren*, ed. Dieter Hüning (Berlin: Duncker & Humblot, 2005), 153–78.

39. For a succinct account of the exceptionally interesting (not to mention complicated) publication histories of the works mentioned in this paragraph, see Richard Tuck, *Philosophy and Government: 1572–1651* (Cambridge: Cambridge University Press, 1993), 169–70, 190–92, 211–14.

40. On Grotius's conception of originally common *dominium* and for discussion of its broader historical context, see Jeffrey Edwards, "Property and *Communitas Rerum*," 52–56; Brian Tierney, *The Idea of Natural Rights*, 316–42.

41. Hugo Grotius, *The Freedom of the Seas*, trans. Ralph Van Deman Magoffin (1609; repr., Oxford: Oxford University Press, 1916), 25. (Reference is to the pagination of the Latin text of Grotius's *Mare liberum*, which was published in conjunction

with the Magoffin translation.) See also Hugo Grotius, *De Jure Belli ac Pacis Libri Tres*, ed. J. B. Scott (1625; 2nd ed., 1631; a photomechanical reproduction of 1746 Latin text, Washington DC: Carnegie Institute, 1913), II.2 §2.25. (In keeping with standard citation practice, my references to Grotius's *De Jure Belli ac Pacis* [1625; 1631] and *Mare Liberum* [1609] are to the relevant book, chapter, and section numbers.)

42. "Simul discimus quomodo res in proprietatem iverint: non animi actu solo; neque enim scire alii poterant, quid alii suum esse vellent, ut eo abstinerent; et idem velle plures poterant: sed pacto quodam aut expresso, ut per divisionem, aut tacito, ut per occupationem. Simulatque enim communio displicuit, nec instituta est divisio, censeri debet inter omnes convenisse, ut quod quisque occupasset id proprium haberet." *De Jure Belli ac Pacis*, II.2 § 2.

43. See John Selden, *Opera Omnia* (1636; London, 1726), 2: col. 1197. (My references to Selden are to the volume and column numbers of the eighteenth-century edition of his collected works.)

44. "Jam vero si communiter & pro indiviso fuere universi domini ante partium aliquot distributionem, earum quae in distributionem non venerant, ut manerent pariter universi, quemadmodum ante, pro indiviso domini, necessum est ut existimemus; nisi pactum aliquod intervenerit, quo pristino omnimodo communionis titulo jurique ita renunciatum fuerit, ut deinceps eorum, quae vacua manerent, seu in distributionem non venirent, domini fierent singulares quicunque primo animo possidendi, insistendi, utendi furendi, corporaliter occuparent. Neque aliter in cassua sociorum aut cohaeredum (quales in rerum communione homines fuisse videntur universi) fingi potest, quomodo ea quae in distributionem non veniant, non ut antea maneant communia. Itaque pactum ejusmodi primariis dominii privati initiis intercessisse, . . . Adeo ut non minus de distributione per assignationem, quam de occupatione rerum derelictarum ad libitum, pactum universale, sive verbis difertis sive tacite ex morum usu, initum esse decernamus. Quod ipsum sane amplecti videtur V. C. Hugo Grotius: *Res,* inquit, *in proprietatem* (de cujus exordio loquitur) *ibant, non animi actu soli (neque enim scire alii poterant, quid alii suum esse vellent, ut eo abstinerent; et idem velle plures poterant) sed pacto quodam aut expresso, ut per divisionem, aut tacito, ut per occupationem. Simulatque enim communio displicuit, nec instituta est divisio, censeri debet inter omnes convenisse, ut quod quisque occupasset id proprium haberet.* Parilis sane ratio etiam ejus quod quisquam postea, ex eo quod derelictum erat, occuparet" (ibid., 2: cols. 1197–98).

45. For recent discussion of Selden in connection with Thomas Hobbes's account of natural right and the state of nature, see Richard Tuck, *The Rights of War and Peace: Political Thought and the International Order from Grotius to Kant* (Oxford: Oxford University Press, 1999), 16–50.

46. See Selden, *Opera Omnia*, 2: col. 1274.

47. "Et sane ut occuparetur totius oceanus, nemo existimare potest non esse difficillimum. Si tame occuparetur, ut fretum aut finus, ut totus orbis veteribus occupari a principibus dictus est, aeque etiam in dominium occupantis posset transire" (ibid.).

48. Selden lays out his conception of universal permissive natural law (*ius permissiva*) in chapters 5–7 of *Mare Clausum*.

49. See MM, 6:258.14–21, 6:262.26–34.

50. See MM, 6:251.1–13. Regarding this passage's underlying references to Grotius and Pufendorf, see Jeffrey Edwards, "Disjunktiv- und kollektiv-allgemeiner Besitz: Überlegungen zu Kants Theorie der ursprünglichen Erwerbung," in *Recht, Staat, und Völkerrecht bei Immanuel Kant*, 127n17.

51. See MM, 6:262.28–31.

52. For extended discussion of the medieval and modern background relevant to pre-Kantian doctrines of acquisition and theories of property, see Annabel Brett, *Liberty, Right, and Nature: Individual Rights in Later Scholastic Thought* (Cambridge: Cambridge University Press, 1997); Manfred Brocker, *Arbeit und Eigentum*; Jeffrey Edwards, "Property and *Communitas Rerum*," 41–60; Brian Tierney, *The Idea of Natural Rights*; Brian Tierney, "Permissive Natural Law and Property," 381–99.

53. A more thorough discussion of the historical background covered thus far would, of course, have to consider Kant's relation to Hobbes as well as Hobbes's relation to Grotius and Selden. I must forego this discussion in the chapter at hand, but see Edwards, "Disjunktiv- und kollektiv-allgemeiner Besitz," 126–35, and Edwards, "Property and *Communitas Rerum*," 56–60.

54. Which is not to say that this principle can be *derived* from Kant's account of the innate notion of freedom.

55. In this regard, the position that I take on what is required by Kant's doctrine of original acquisition may well differ significantly from Guyer's approach to the same set of issues. See Paul Guyer, *Kant on Freedom, Law, and Happiness* (Cambridge: Cambridge University Press, 2000), 253–58; Paul Guyer, "Life, Liberty, and Property: Rawls the Reconstruction of Kant's Political Philosophy," in *Recht, Staat, und Völkerrecht bei Immanuel Kant*, 273–92.

56. Marcus Willaschek argues that Kant denies the prescriptive character of the laws of right (or juridical laws). See "Which Imperatives for Right? On the Non-Prescriptive Character of Juridical Laws in Kant's *Metaphysics of Morals*," in *Kant's Metaphysics of Morals: Interpretive Essays*, ed. Mark Timmons (Oxford: Oxford University Press, 2002), 65–87. According to Willaschek, "we are forced to the paradoxical conclusion that, in a Kantian framework, juridical laws cannot be prescriptive in the sense that they do not issue in prescriptions meant to direct the behaviour of their addressees" (71). While juridical laws are normative in the sense that they define a nonfactual standard of rightness, "they cannot *prescribe, command*, or *require* that their addressees act in accordance with that standard" (71). Thus, in adhering to Kant's theory of *ius strictum*, we end up with "a purely non-prescriptive conception of Right" (85) that makes no room for categorical imperatives of right. I find this antiprescriptivist interpretation of Kant's juridical laws remarkably interesting, especially since it represents a frontal assault on the type of interpretive approach taken in this chapter. It seems to me, however, that Willaschek's approach stems from a failure to take proper account of how Kant's crucial distinction between laws for *actions* and laws for *maxims* of actions relates systematically to the ways in which Kant differentiates between juridical and ethical lawgiving, internal and external lawgiving, internal and external actions, and "the law of *your* own will" and "the law of will in general, which could also be the will of others" (see MM, 6:219.17–221.3 and 6:388.32–389.11). This is not the place to sort out all these factors, so I will limit my critical comments to two central components of Willaschek's argument:

(1) In order to show the nonprescriptive character of juridical laws, Willaschek must claim that the only way to *obey* these laws would be to "obey them for their own sake," which is of course incompatible with Kant's position that "juridical laws require only external compliance, not compliance for the sake of the law" (72). Apparently, Willaschek bases this key claim on his previously presented argument that the only way to obey a categorical imperative is to obey it for its own sake, assuming that not obeying such an imperative for its own sake is "a conceptual impossibility" (70). But even if we were to accept that this first argument is sound, it would still not follow that the only way to obey a juridical law is to obey it for its own sake. It is possible (and indeed necessary) for anyone to obey a juridical law *because* this obedience is what this law demands *just insofar* as it requires external compliance. If one acts in this way, then one's obedience to law satisfies the requirement (and standard) of external compliance even if one does not obey the law for its own sake (i.e., even if in obeying the law one does not think of it as the law of one's own will, as distinguished from the law of will in general, which can also be the will of others [see MM, 6:388.34–389.6]). Thus, contrary to what Willaschek seems to assume (see 70–72), "obeying a law (or imperative) for its own sake" and "obeying a law because this is what the law demands" are not equivalent descriptions for the same type of act, although both of these descriptions presuppose the prescriptive character of law. That is because the law to which the two descriptions refer is necessarily of the type that it requires, or demands, obedience whether or not it is obeyed for its own sake. It a practical law, that is, a law that represents the *necessity* of an *action* (see MM, 6:222.7–8); and such a law represents this necessity of action whether it is a juridical law or not.

(2) Kant states in *DR* § E that strict right is "based on everyone's consciousness of obligation in accordance with a law" (MM, 6:232.16–18). He also argues that this consciousness of obligation may not, and cannot, be appealed to as an incentive for the determination of the power of choice if strict right, as external right, is not to be mingled with prescriptions of virtue (*Tugendvorschriften*). In view of this argument, Willaschek contends that the obligation in question "does not have any prescriptive force, and therefore we 'may not and cannot' . . . appeal to it in order to motivate others to act in accordance with Right" (80). Now, we can agree that this kind of motivational appeal to obligation (or more precisely: to *consciousness* of obligation) is not relevant to the theory of *ius strictum*. We can agree to this even if Kant does assert that strict right is *based* on everyone's consciousness of obligation in accordance with a law. Yet this gives us no reason at all to think, as Willaschek seems to assume it does, that juridical laws lack prescriptive force. For it certainly *is* a conceptual impossibility that any practical law—that is, any law belonging to the set of laws that includes all juridical laws—could lack prescriptive force for human beings as long as (a) it specifies a duty that furnishes "the matter of obligation" (MM, 6:222.32), (b) obligation is defined as "the necessity of a free action under a categorical imperative of reason" (6:222.4–5), (c) the categorical imperative that expresses obligation with respect to actions is "a mor-

ally practical law" (6:222.36–223.1)—in other words, is a law that specifies a duty, i.e., a categorical *ought*, as the matter of obligation, and (d) every morally practical law is a "proposition that contains a categorical imperative (a command)" (6:227.10–11). The fact is, I think, that the prescriptive import of all of Kant's laws of morally practical reason (*Sittengesetze*) is so transparent that I am simply at a loss to see what the problem could be with the prescriptivity of the laws of right. But this may be just my limitation.

8

COMMUNITY AND NORMATIVITY

HEGEL'S CHALLENGE TO KANT IN THE JENA ESSAYS

MICHAEL FEOLA

Historians of philosophy face a difficulty in conceptualizing the relationship between Kant and his Idealist successors, for the latter offer a wide range of options—from completing the architectonic of reason (by offering a single principle from which it could be deduced), to overcoming entirely what they take to be the deep contradictions of the critical project. This ambivalence is nowhere more evident than in the writings of the young Hegel, which swing from one pole to the other within the span of a few years. In his Berne (1795) essay on Christianity, Hegel attributes to Jesus a thinly veiled Kantian gospel of pure reason and moral legislation. And this enthusiasm is only corroborated in contemporaneous letters to Schelling and Hölderlin, which demonstrate that all three thinkers had sworn to transform corrupt social conditions by working toward the Kingdom of God familiar to them from Kant's *Religion within the Limits of Reason Alone*.[1] Hegel's earliest published writings, however, take an acerbic tone when they denounce Kantian morality as self-domination and the wider critical system as an "unphilosophy" that eventuates in the "total crushing of reason."[2] My question in this essay is, then, what did Hegel take to be particularly objectionable about Kant's practical philosophy that would not only threaten human freedom but also vitiate its claim to rationality altogether? While many critics have detailed Hegel's critique of the moral law or the incentive of duty, I will focus on an area of their dispute that is underrepresented in the literature: their disparate visions of the relationship between freedom, community, and reason.[3]

It will be instructive to begin with an interpretation that (no matter its popularity) proves unsustainable. That is, when Kant bases morality within the agent's motivational life, he endorses a monological relationship to the moral law, which forecloses the possibility that our intersubjective attachments could play a significant role in our ethical practice.[4] If Kant's founding error is meant to be his individualism, Hegel (we are told) overcompensates by absorbing the agent into an ethical community [*Sittlichkeit*] whose participants enjoy the solidarity absent within Kant's system at the cost of their reflective autonomy.[5]

To understand why such a reading, though superficially plausible, is nevertheless misleading, we must register a shift in critical approaches to Kant's practical philosophy. There is a familiar, textbook version of Kantian deontology that rejects any appeal to substantial moral goods, as they would instrumentalize the will and thus foreclose its capacity to legislate its own ends.[6] Once Kant takes this strongly antiteleological stance, the story continues, he reduces the moral good to the formal conditions under which individual willing could serve as universal law—classically expressed in the categorical imperative. Increased attention to the full range of his practical texts, however, has disclosed the imperative, which appears as early as the *Critique of Pure Reason*, that we strive to bring about substantial ends that are posited by reason itself. Most important for present purposes is one specific end: we must create a "moral world" that would be "an object of practical reason in its practical employment, that is, as a *corpus mysticum* of the rational beings in it, so far as the free will of each being is, under moral laws, in complete systematic unity with itself and with the freedom of every other."[7] This moral world is thus not a neutral arena in which we happen to pursue our individual moral projects; rather, it is an ideal set by reason that suggests our highest practical vocation can be realized only when we are bound to others, in some kind of rationally structured, interconnected whole.

While these brief hints will require further development, they suffice to indicate that there is at least *some* meaningful appeal to community in Kant's work, against widespread suspicion that he is an arch-individualist who subordinates all ethically significant relationships to the moral law. To perform a similar defense of Hegel's criticism might seem rather more perverse at this point of the essay, so I will suggest that these charges by Hegel of "domination," "unreason," or "tyranny" will become more readily intelligible if we consider them indictments of the normative logic that frames Kant's practical thought. On the one hand, moral consciousness is defined by its capacity for universal legislation, bound by rational norms; on the other hand, we understand ourselves as particular agents, playing nonfungible roles within life narratives made up of singular projects, commitments, and entanglements with others. Though Hegel offers various critiques of Kantian practical philosophy in these Jena texts, I take them to center around the basic proposition that Kant does not successfully mediate this universal (which alone is taken to be legitimately authoritative in our thought and communication) with the particular that it governs. Hegel's 1802 essay, *Faith and Knowledge*, makes this connection explicit when it argues that the "contradiction between empty universality and living particularity" that defines the critical system produces a "formalism of legal theory and morality . . . which is without vitality and truth."[8]

The meaning and implications of this "contradiction" will guide the remainder of this essay. I will thus begin by reconstructing Kant's vision in such a way as to trouble the standard account sketched above, and dedicate the second half of the essay to Hegel's charge that a community founded upon these premises would undermine a wide variety of practical goods— including a wholesale evisceration of reason. This brings us to a final preliminary consideration. While Hegel is often presented as a polemical critic of Kant, I will follow recent trends in the literature to suggest that he does not sacrifice his predecessor's commitments to autonomy, so much as radicalize them to overcome what he takes to be Kant's fatal limitations. To rearticulate this point from a critical perspective, what Hegel describes as the irrationality and coercion of Kantian practical philosophy is a *symptom* of a more fundamental error that his predecessor commits regarding the "location" of those norms that govern human thought and action.

Formalism and Recht: Preliminary Questions

As Hegel is a well-known critic of Kant's metaphysical dualism, it would be natural to interpret this charge of formalism (i.e., a "formalism of legal theory and morality") as targeting a similar dualism between the legal and the moral. In fact, Hegel's *Naturrecht* essay (1802/3) seems to take such a stance when it argues that the "absoluteness of difference" that defines Kantian philosophy risks dividing our normative lives into two distinct modalities, each of which becomes objectionably abstract without its relation to the other.[9] On the one hand, we belong to a Kingdom of Ends [*Reich der Zwecke*] through our mutual legislation of the moral law; on the other hand, we are subject to civic legislation that regulates our action, so as to prevent our pursuits from encroaching excessively upon others. Unless these two models come to inform one another, however, they threaten to develop into pathological forms; our actions would be governed by purely instrumental criteria of order, and our moral aims would remain merely inner, unable to find purchase within an institutional sphere dedicated to security.

On a quick reading, this kind of interpretation might seem to capture the deep logic of Kant's juridical texts. The opening pages of the 1797 *Rechtslehre* define right as the "sum of those laws for which an external lawgiving is possible," which signals his intention to distinguish the object of right—the external relations between juridical agents—from the internal mandates of morality.[10] And, this distance gains greater bite through a technical distinction by which Kant opens the work. That is, all practical legislation possesses two components: first, a law that commands certain ends or forbids their performance; second, an incentive that would ensure compliance with these orders. Once this formal commonality has been articulated, Kant argues that moral and juridical lawgiving are distinguished not by the ends they demand (which may well be identical), but rather by the kinds of incentives that are attached to their realization. As any student of Kant knows, morality requires that duty alone serve as the incentive for the will; because right limits itself to external freedom, however, legal commands must leave aside the motivational springs of action and limit themselves to *external* incentives (i.e., the threat of coercion).[11]

With this conceptual groundwork in place, the final piece of evidence for the dualist reading would appear to be provided by Kant's political anthropology. As his memorable account of "unsocial sociability" suggests, human sociality is marked by an antithetical tendency: the incapacity of the subject to meet the full range of its needs forces it toward cooperation with others; however, this interdependence is accompanied by a desire to promote individual flourishing over shared autonomy. To curb the excesses of this unsociability without courting paternalism, Kant assigns this task to the state, which regulates our external freedom through external means. As he argues in *Toward Perpetual Peace*:

> The problem is not the moral improvement of human beings but only the mechanism of nature, and what the task requires one to know is how this can be put to use in human beings in order so to arrange the conflict of their unpeaceable dispositions within a people that they themselves have to constrain one another to submit to coercive law and so bring about a condition of peace in which laws have force.[12]

From this unstinting rejection of moral training, it would seem that Kant has conceptualized the state as little more than a technical problem—more specifically, to master the problem of social antagonism. And, if this is the case, coercive legal sanctions would be subject to no justificatory criteria other than the state of unmediated conflict that would result in their absence.

Although isolated passages within Kant's essays might corroborate this instrumentalist view, any meaningful engagement with the *Rechtslehre* demonstrates its limits, as he denies from the outset that the doctrine of right could be conceptualized as a response to *any* social factor (whether good or ill). As a branch of the metaphysics of morals, right is founded upon *a priori* concepts, which means that it "cannot be based on anthropology but can still be applied to it."[13] This theme is developed further in the engagement with legal positivism that opens the work, where Kant distances himself from those who would reduce right to what has been posited as legally binding by parties authorized to issue such orders. If the positivist might be able to reproduce the norms governing conduct in a "certain place and at a certain time," he or she could not offer a judgment as to their *substantial* right (i.e., their normative warrant) without presupposing a rational standard against which they would be judged (thereby abandoning the positivist commitment altogether).[14]

And, once Kant introduces the possibility of such a criterion, he quickly supplies one of his own that (to distinguish between legal prescriptions and legitimate right) must be located in reason alone: "Right is therefore the sum of the conditions under which the choice of one can be united with the choice of another in accordance with a universal law of freedom."[15] At first glance, this appeal to choice offers little more than liberal boiler-plate—establishing the privilege of the right over the good, such that we could pursue whatever material ends we wish, so long as they do not interfere with the pursuits of others. When framed by our guiding question, however, Kant's recourse to the law of freedom as a suprapositive basis for legitimation demonstrates that this procedural neutrality cannot signal an indifference to moral concerns altogether. Rather, the coercive sanctions of the state find their justification in our sole "original right"—freedom from determination through the choices of others[16]—the value of which can be established only through a *moral* commitment to a certain ideal of personhood.

This is an admittedly hasty reconstruction that elides many features of Kant's wide-ranging doctrine and the interpretive controversies it raises. For instance, the language of a "universal law" that would reconcile our shared freedom has understandably generated questions about the relationship between the principle of right and the categorical imperative—more specifi-cally, whether the former can be deduced from the latter (with any meaning-ful degree of determinacy),[17] and what kinds of difficulties follow once we observe the conditions governing a deduction in the strict sense.[18] As such debates would bring us far beyond the scope of this essay, however, I wish to return to the question with which we began: unless Hegel makes a crude interpretive blunder, his charge cannot be that Kant has simply sundered legal from moral concerns in an "absolute" sense. Rather, a more productive staging ground for this dispute will be gained by taking seriously the "moral world" encountered at the very outset of the essay—a shift in perspective that leads us to a number of important questions. More specifically, can the appeal to community be reduced to an institutionally secured practice of noninterference between essentially independent agents; or, does Kant's pro-vocative language of a *corpus mysticum* suggest a tie between agents that is richer than their shared subjection to common, external laws? And, if widely shared intuitions regarding this term incline us toward the latter option, then some positive considerations must be addressed. To wit, what *kind* of bond leads Kant to adopt this mysterious language of communal participa-tion? How can it be reconciled with the irreducible individuality of moral experience? And what role does it play within the broader critical system?

Ethical Community and Moral Regeneration

To unpack this moral world (and its quasi-organic rhetoric of belonging) it is necessary to look elsewhere in the literature. Where Kant's juridical texts offer a technical project in the service of moral ends, we receive a rather different vision when we turn our attention to the Kingdom of God [*das Reich Gottes*] that so affected Hegel as a young seminarian. To understand Kant's project within the *Religion* essay, we must recall the "scandalous" question that opens the book: how is it possible to overcome the "radical evil" that afflicts humanity? And, to avoid any confusion that may attend this theological language, it is critical to note that this evil denotes neither a fact of moral fallenness nor a natural property (both of which would violate what it *means* to be a rational agent on Kantian premises),[19] but rather our propensity (through a somewhat mysterious ur-decision) to invert the motivational incentives of the will, such that self-love would trump the moral law as its motivational ground.[20]

It is clear, then, that we have entered a very different problematic. No longer is Kant concerned with the potentially destructive effects of choice within a contested social field, but rather with reorienting the fundamental maxim of the will toward the moral law, and thus with generating the motivational conditions under which virtue would be possible for finite agents. It follows from the considerations above that juridical measures are inadequate to bring about this "revolution" of the will, as conformity to law would leave the central, motivational problem intact.[21] And this dismissal of external norms might lead us to suspect that this transformation could only take place within a private, inner space—a conclusion spurred on by Kant's tendency to frame the activity of the will through a language of interiority. He flouts this expectation, however, at the beginning of the third essay when he argues that our motivational hierarchy possesses an *essentially* social dimension:

> Envy, addiction to power, avarice, and the malignant inclinations associated with these, assail his nature, which on its own is undemanding, *as soon as he is among human beings*. Nor is it necessary to assume that these are sunk into evil and are examples that lead him astray: it suffices that they are there, that they surround him, and that they are human beings, and they will mutually corrupt each other's moral dispositions and make one another evil.[22]

To grasp the full significance of this passage, it will be helpful to distinguish its diagnostic and prescriptive senses. If Kant's idealist commitments mean that we cannot conceptualize this motivational inversion on naturalist grounds (i.e., driven by brute desires or passions),[23] this relational account pushes the argument further—so as to suggest that the exertions of a single agent would be inadequate to resist the influence of a corrupt social world.

As the following passage makes clear, those gains that we might make in isolation would be undermined by our continued contact with others.[24]

> Human beings mutually corrupt one another's moral predisposition and, even with the good will of each individual, because of the lack of a principle which unites them, they deviate through their dissensions from the common goal of goodness, as though they were *instruments of evil*, and expose one another to the danger of falling once again under its dominion.[25]

This analytic thesis—that the subject's motivational order is mediated by her relations with others—thus leads Kant to frame the reformist project in socially "thick" terms. Because the tendency toward evil is located in our other-relations, the possibility of regaining our "original predisposition to good" cannot be limited to some transcendental act of freedom, locked away in the space of interiority; rather, it must also be addressed at this same, suprapersonal level. Or, to put the argument in terms that were surely significant for the young Hegel, only an ethical *community* [*ein ethisches gemeines Wesen*], bound by laws of virtue, can secure the conditions under which the moral agent could engage in the communication demanded by reason and yet resist temptations to will on the basis of maxims that would not meet the criterion of universalizability.[26]

If Kant's exposition leaves us with many questions regarding just what *degree* our individual capacity for moral regeneration (or, for that matter, our tendency toward evil) is bound to others, this communalist framework for reform raises significant problems for those individualist readings that I introduced at the outset. Additionally, the strong thesis of moral sociality complicates those more nuanced critiques that acknowledge Kant's demands for a rational union, yet deny it the status of a "genuine" community due to his tendency to mediate these social models through a third term, the moral law.[27] Admittedly, such Hegelian reservations might find a foothold within the rhetoric surrounding the Kingdom of Ends, whose agents are bound by their "mutual legislation" of the moral law (and their respect for this capacity in others)—though even here there are grounds for a more measured reading. For instance, recent literature (Korsgaard, O'Neill) has suggested that this relation "to the moral law" is something of a discursive red herring, as it denotes nothing other than a particular stance toward others, whereby we limit our pursuit of ends that would undermine their capacity to lead a self-directing life and we act only on those reasons that could, plausibly, be adopted by all other agents. On such a reading, Kant's admittedly misleading language does not suggest a shared contribution to some hypostasized legal fiction that substitutes for a "direct" relation to others, but rather a relational ideal that would foster the maximal degree of freedom and dignity for all its members.[28]

For present purposes, it is not necessary to settle this interpretive dispute. No matter the insights or difficulties of this revisionist account, the ethical commonwealth offers a significant contribution to Kant's social ontology—particularly from a Hegelian perspective. Although both "kingdoms" present a systematic union of rational agents, bound through moral laws, the *Religion* essay proposes that the agent's motivational order has not only an orientation toward others but also intersubjective *conditions* that subtend its very possibility—or, conversely, contribute to its pathological distortion. To bring out what I take to be the significance of this point, the moral disposition toward good or evil cannot be safely delimited within some "primal scene" of the will—even if Kant suggests precisely this kind of reading in the early installments of the text. Rather, if we take seriously the intersubjective grammar developed in the later sections, two potentially surprising conclusions follow: (a) the agent's dispositional quality is radically inflected by its relations to others, and (b) the social domain within which such relations take place imbues them with a determinate character. To give this episode what would otherwise seem to be an arch-Hegelian twist, this means that the possibilities for moral consciousness are intimately bound up with our social membership, and thus to be addressed at the interpersonal level.

The Kingdom of God: Religion, History, and Praxis

It is not difficult to recognize that this vision represents a more sensitive phenomenology of subjecthood than is characteristic for Kant's texts; and, it surely contains more promising resources for an intersubjective "moral world" than the atomistic grammar of noninterference found within the *Rechtslehre*. Before moving further, however, it will be useful to examine more closely the form this union takes within the *Religion* essay. For, Kant does not elaborate a vision of ethical community in the abstract, nor a broad thesis on social ontology—but proposes, more specifically, a religiously inflected Kingdom of God. The question that naturally arises, then, is the following: if moral aims require some kind of rational, social union, why must it be negotiated through these theologically freighted terms? What implications does the deity have for the community that bears its name, and what light can this religious framework shed upon our central concerns?

Because any adequate discussion of Kant's God would far exceed the limits of this essay, we can gain a more focused avenue into these concerns through the linguistic formula of this community (*das Reich Gottes*). It will be helpful to begin by framing the term *Reich* through a terminological note from the *Groundwork*: "By a kingdom [*Reiche*] I understand a systematic union of various rational beings through common laws."[29] And, from this definition, the important issues hinge upon what *type* of laws bind its participants into this systematic unity, whence they derive their authority, and how they relate to their subjects. Kant's answer, here, is unequivocal. For, if allusions to the *civitas Dei* in *Aufklärung* political thought (e.g., Thomasius, Pufendorf) typically emphasize its political pedigree in order to suggest a civic order that would bring order to warring sectarian interests, Kant's version excludes the political, in principle: "an ethical community, then, in the form of a church, i.e., as a mere *representative* of a state ruled by God, really has nothing in its basic principles resembling a political constitution."[30] That is, moral community may be coterminous with the political order, though their respective principles of union differentiate them according to the familiar distinction between public laws of coercion and inner laws of virtue—the latter of which unify its members as a free "union of hearts" [*Herzensvereinigung*].[31]

Now, this gives us only half the story, for if Kant disavows the external bonds of right, he owes us an argument as to how this nonpolitical union is to be conceptualized in a positive sense. At the very least, the text's wide-ranging language of Protestant inwardness allows Kant to argue that the divine is *uniquely* qualified to bind such a community given the conditions elaborated thus far. While human legislation can regulate only external freedom, through external sanctions, this God that "knows the heart" offers conceptual resources to account for laws that would be motivationally oriented (i.e., "inner") and yet still bind its agents within a shared, common world.[32] At this point, however, we may suspect that Kant has traded one difficulty for another. For, if this appeal to inwardness provides nonjuridical (and yet normatively binding) resources for social union, his persistent language of divine "rule" or "dominion" begs some more serious concerns—readily apparent in the following passage: "religion is (subjectively considered) the recognition of all our duties as divine commands."[33] On a quick read, this moral solidarity of the *Reich Gottes* may seem to be purchased at prohibitive cost (i.e., submission to a transcendent will). Closer attention to the linguistic cues in the cited passage, however, offers resources to defuse the difficulty: this consciousness of command is an interpretive stance that *we* take upon moral duties. And it is this delimitation that allows Kant to propose a form of religiosity better able to negotiate the demands of rational autonomy. To put the argument in quick and brutal terms, the divine provenance of these duties does not suggest that they must be obeyed *because* of their source; rather, this divine status reflects the way that agents conceptualize the nonnegotiable force of the obligations that bind them to one another—obligations, moreover, that will come to be recognized (through a process sketched below) as grounded within, and accessible through, reason.[34]

To this point, I have offered a "thin" reading of Kant's appeals to the divine. And, if this minimalist account exhausted the argument, Kant's God might strike the reader as an empty placeholder or piecemeal stopgap, designed to provide *whatever* resources are demanded for the argument to run. Our interests will be advanced, however, by examining how the traditional attributes of the divine introduce some rather more substantive constraints into the form that this social model will take. Most important for present purposes, Kant deploys the universality of the Christian deity to argue that the ethical commonwealth must extend to the same totality: "a multitude of human beings united in that purpose cannot yet be called the ethical community as such but only a particular society that strives after the consensus of all human beings (indeed, of all finite rational beings) in order to establish an absolute ethical whole of which each partial society is only a representation or schema."[35] Given Kant's commitment to the categorical authority of moral duties, this scope may not initially seem significant. The impetus toward universality, however, carries a number of implications for the shape and features of this community—two of which merit particular attention with regard to our guiding questions.

First, the approach to the "universal church" charts not only a process of numerical expansion or inclusion—but rather a parallel movement of enlightenment, such that ecclesiastic religions (i.e., those based upon revelation and statutory law) will be superseded once we can recognize pure reason (and thus the moral law) as the authoritative ground of our duties and obligations.[36] And, this movement toward the "one true church"—mapped along an axis of futurity—introduces a broader point that will be of some significance for the argument to follow. If critics have long taken at face value Kant's formulations that reason does not enter into history or take on different shapes,[37] recent scholarship has persuasively argued that their relation is rather more complex.[38] Because of our finitude, human reason is not given in its fully elaborated, systematic form from the outset, but rather relies upon a process of self-unfolding that reserves for history [*Geschichte*] an essential role toward the realization of moral ends.[39] To distinguish Kant's narrative, however, from the eschatological models that he evokes, he consistently maintains that we cannot rely upon a preestablished harmony between reason and world that is ineluctably worked out through a providential "cunning" of history. Rather, such a coincidence must be *created* through human activity.

This *praxical* demand leads to the second point: the active language of "establishment" and "striving" in the cited passage indicates that this soteriological figure does not entail a messianic intervention by which we would be delivered from moral evil and social antagonism through some act of grace. Rather, Kant's persistent emphasis on our *preparation* for the Kingdom of God details a commitment to ethical praxis from the potential member of this state.[40] Just as Kant argues elsewhere that it is our duty, as rational beings, to work toward the highest good,[41] the "coming" [*Annäherung*] of the *civitas Dei* does not proceed from a transcendent will that would be independent of human endeavor; rather, it represents *our* approach to this ideal through our collective labor on ourselves and the world around us, even if we cannot ever know whether the *de facto* corruption of social life will permit us to succeed.[42] In the most generous formulation, we might say that the God of this kingdom is meant to name (if in rhetorically displaced fashion) the human capacity to reorient moral consciousness by constructing a systematically ordered inter-subjective space wherein our relations with others would both instantiate and affirm the motivational conditions of virtue.[43]

At an exegetical level, these considerations help to dispel a number of the anxieties that attend this divinized language—in which a transcendent lawgiver threatens to relieve human agents of their moral autonomy or responsibility for transforming their world toward rational ends. To push the argument forward, however, we can close this section by noting the degree of overlap between Kant's ethical community and what are typically viewed as "Hegelian" commitments. Minimally, I have proposed that Kant's thesis on the sociality of evil complicates some standard assumptions regarding the Kantian subject: moral goodness cannot be secured (in any sustainable fash-ion) through some stoic withdrawal into the space of interiority; rather, it must take root within those practices and relationships that give shape to our values, needs, and motivations. And, a closer look at the Kingdom of God has revealed another Hegelian resonance: these intersubjective conditions for moral ideals will come to pass only through our historically articulated labor upon ourselves and the social space that binds us—a thesis that intro-duces a substantial role for history within the moral project. These consid-erations go some way toward explaining the attraction this relational model held for the young Hegel. As we will see in the following section, however, this common ground should not be overextended, as it is *precisely* this imbri-cation of history, sociality, and community that leads us to the heart of Hegel's critique. It is to this long-overdue question that we will now turn.

Moralität and *Sittlichkeit*

There is much here to complicate the traditional lines of dispute between these philosophical antagonists—where Kant is meant to be some brand of ahistorical individualist, and Hegel the historicized communitarian. Indeed, Hegel admits at various points that these avatars of the highest good (the Kingdom of God, the Kingdom of Ends, the moral world) demonstrate that his predecessor caught a glimpse of reason's imperative to form the world in accordance with its own principles—though it remains *only* a glimpse, sig-naled by Kant's telling description of this ideal as "sublime."[44] Just as the *Critique of Judgment* deploys this term to mark the excess of the rational idea over the subjective conditions of experience, so too is the moral community of the *Religion* essays figured as "infinitely removed" from the agents who are duty bound to work in its service.

Hegel's well-known indictment of any such perpetual "ought" (what, in his mature works, he terms a "bad infinity") offers a preliminary avenue to grasp his turn from this Kantian model in favor of an alternate doctrine of "ethicality" [*Sittlichkeit*]. As much of the literature demonstrates, it is tempting to figure the argument through a fashionable rhetoric of openness and closure.[45] That is, Hegel's desire to close the outstanding gap between the good and its realization means that he locates the actualization of reason within the institutions, norms, and practice of a given community, rather than some "continual approximation"[46] to a universal church (or a cosmopolitan federation of nations) that rests within an asymptotic future.[47] Furthermore, this thesis on the "location" of ethical rationality possesses substantial implications for subjecthood and agency—we derive our duties not from some formalized, evaluative procedure, but rather from those roles that we inhabit within the lifeworld and the expectations that attend their performance.[48]

Once the problem is cast in these terms, it is easy to appreciate the suspicions that have long attended this Hegelian rejoinder. Most broadly, critical literature has charged that his attempt to resituate normative authority within our customs and practices threatens two unsavory possibilities. On the one hand, we are told that Hegel solves this Kantian distance between the "ought" and the "is" a bit too well by *reducing* the former to the latter, thereby discarding the normative ideal of rationality (and its critical potential) in favor of an uncritical submission to the *status quo*.[49] On the other hand, this unattractive legitimist argument is thought to be compounded by an atavistic reduction of what it means to be a moral subject—which (at least within modernity) demands that my commitments be evaluated, endorsed, and understood as "mine" in some meaningful sense. In Hegel's model, this evaluative dimension is ostensibly eliminated, so as to condemn the agent to carry out the mandates associated with its social roles without the capacity to negotiate their claims in light of competing allegiances and obligations.[50]

Because any resolution of these difficulties would bring me far beyond the scope of this essay, I will not attempt to address them in head-on fashion. Rather, they can be engaged more obliquely by examining how this apparently anachronistic model contributes to the argument that Hegel stages with Kant over reason and community. To this end, we might ask how is *Sittlichkeit* meant to restore a kind of ethical reason that is foreclosed by Kant's practical philosophy? And, the concern can be brought into greater focus by situating the inquiry one step further back: what, exactly, is the problem this model of community is meant to answer—that is, just *how* do Kantian premises threaten the reason appropriate to ethical practice?

To grapple with such questions, it is necessary to press a bit harder upon Kant's developmental narrative, as it would surely overstate the case to ascribe to him a blanket thesis on the historicity of reason. Though I have claimed that progressivist themes play a central role within the critical system, the relationship between history and practical reason is characterized by a central ambivalence: on the one hand, the movement toward the Kingdom of God (or the other manifestations of the moral world) represents an imperative for reason to work over the world so as to bring it into accordance with rational ends; on the other hand, Kant consistently presents historical norms as mere artifacts of what a specific community contingently happened to value, and thus incapable of justifying their authority on rational grounds. This deficiency is clearly articulated in a parenthetical remark within the *Rechtslehre*: "the German word *Sitten*, like the Latin *mores*, means only manners and ways of life."[51] To parse the argumentative force of this "only" [*nur*], I will hazard the following formula: while practical reason demands that we create a rational social order through conscious, collaborative *praxis*, it does not redeem the social world from a moral point of view, for Kant is uncompromising in holding that rational principles cannot be *derived* from our shared practices. The temporalized advance that Kant charts toward the "true church of reason" is thus the course of its *purification* or "freeing" [*losgemachen*] from historical norms in favor of a collective binding through the moral law.[52] Or, to put the point in directional terms, we could say that Kant posits a unilinear relationship of influence from *a priori* principles to the social world, as the customs, traditions, and practices of the latter have been denied any claim to rational normativity.

It is precisely this dissymmetry that Hegel targets in the *Naturrecht* essay when he claims that any community structured according to Kantian premises brings about "so-called" reason, "natural wrong" [*Naturunrecht*] and *Unsittlichkeit* (which I will leave in the German in order to acknowledge the challenge it poses to English translation). This final term cannot seamlessly be rendered as "immorality," as such a translation would remain within the conceptual horizon that Hegel attempts to delimit by opposing the Latinate *Moralität* to the Germanic *Sittlichkeit* in the following passage.

> We also note in this connection a linguistic indicator which, though dismissed in the past, is completely vindicated by the foregoing—namely, that it is in the nature of absolute ethical life [*Sittlichkeit*] to be a universal [*Allgemeinheit*] or an *ethos* [*Sitten*]. Thus, both the Greek word for ethical life and the German word express its nature admirably, whereas the newer systems of ethics, which make a principle out of being-for-itself and individuality [*da sie ein für sich seyn und die Einzelnheit zum Princip machen*], cannot fail to reveal their relation in these words. Indeed, this internal indicator proves so powerful that, in order to define *their own* enterprise, these systems were unable to misuse the words in question

and adopted the word "morality" [*Moralität*] instead; and although the latter's derivation points in the same direction, it is more of an artificial coinage and consequently does not so immediately resist its debased meaning.[53]

Although we may have serious questions regarding Hegel's philological rigor, his polemical intent is clear: *Moralität*—at least in its Kantian guise—is not a neutral conceptual vocabulary to represent practical concerns, but is rather a specialized interpretation that "debases" the more fundamental, ethical domain. To represent morality as a privative form of ethicality [*Un-Sittlichkeit*] thus suggests that it is a form of the same that nonetheless distorts the practice upon which it is parasitic—a charge that requires us to investigate the argumentative grounds for assigning these normative models to the respective categories of the primordial and derivative.

There is a quick answer to be found in Hegel's criticism of Kantian moral legislation. While Hegel's critique of the moral law for its alleged emptiness is well-known, a corollary of his argument is instructive here—because this formalized mechanism for evaluating maxims cannot generate any determinate duties, we are forced to supplement its vacuity with the conventions that we *already* follow as agents located within a particular, historical community. And, to sharpen the point a bit, this means that we are forced into a kind of systematic "falseness," as we persistently borrow such content from a domain whose legitimacy cannot be recognized on Kantian premises. When we step back from the question of individual moral reasoning, however, a broader argument suggests itself. Put somewhat crudely, we might say that this etymological claim attempts to reverse the directionality between normativity and community presupposed by the Kantian model. By emphasizing the semantic link between the German words for community [*die Gemeine*] and universality [*das Allgemeine*], Hegel wants to argue that our normative bonds do not follow from imposing an *a priori* principle upon a recalcitrant or wayward social domain. Rather, we are born into a world that already makes rational claims upon us through the traditions and practices [*Sitten*] that articulate the meaningful ends of human life, as particularized within this community [*Sittlichkeit*].

Without further development, this argument must strike us as unconvincing. The retrospective gaze of history reveals no shortage of brutal or degrading elements within institutions that avow a rational warrant—and claims from semantic affinity should do little to convince any other than the most inveterate Hegelian. As Robert Pippin has argued in a series of recent texts, however, this methodological weakness should not obscure a genuinely philosophical point regarding the provenance of ethical rationality for beings who (a) act and (b) justify their actions on the basis of reasons.[54] To explain this position, we can begin with a fairly uncontroversial claim, drawn from recent debates over agency and deliberation. Although a reason must always count as such for *me* (the acting agent), it must nonetheless meet a minimal condition of shareability. For something to perform this work only for myself (which could not be communicated to, or recognized by, others) means that it could not intelligibly be understood *as* a "reason" within an intersubjectively shared space of action, persuasion, and evaluation.[55]

If this first premise could be readily admitted by Kant, a more controversial moment of the argument comes in its second step—how do the specificities of human subjectivity and agency place constraints upon what we could *recognize* as a reason? According to Hegel's Idealist commitments, human agents are not fundamentally defined by their relation to natural desires, a divine word, or a noumenal law, but rather through those traditions that articulate what it means to conduct a meaningful life in a world shared with others. And, to give a further turn to the screw, such customs and institutions are not simply the brute heritage of the past—as they represent our collective interpretations over personhood, agency, and value. These practices are thus orientational in the phenomenological sense. Once taken up as categories of self-interpretation, they are constitutive of how the world shows up for us as members of a certain community, what kinds of relations we could intelligibly adopt toward others, what expectations are attached to the roles we perform, and what norms would be authoritative for our deliberations and appeals.[56] To locate rational "universality" within these shared practices thus does not commit Hegel to a kind of premodern, tribal conventionalism. Rather, he wants to suggest that, for something to do the motivational and justificatory work associated with rationality, it must be identifiable as a move within the "space of reasons" into which we have been acculturated—and it is only by virtue of these situated practices of meaning that anything could possibly appear to us *as* possessing ethical salience in the first place, and thus as noble or base, normal or degenerate, right or wrong (and this set of evaluative possibilities is hardly exhaustive).

This argument may sound familiar from communitarian texts, which argue that the kind of agent required by liberalism (particularly its neo-Kantian variant) is insufficiently sensitive to the role of our social membership.[57] However, Hegel's doctrine of *Sittlichkeit* gains its real teeth by coupling its historicized, relational phenomenology of selfhood with an argument about normativity. That is, this prominent role for *Sitten* is inadequately conceived as a "conceptual scheme" interpolated between subject and subject-independent facts, whether epistemic or moral, as this intermediary status would tacitly preserve the realist commitments that any post–Kantian Idealist would reject out of hand. Because these norms and customs are constitutive of what could intelligibly matter to me as a member of this historico-linguistic community, they could not, somehow, be "gotten behind" in order to access some nonmediated, ethical truth of the matter that could then be used as an independent standard to judge the codes that we contingently happen to endorse. Nor, Hegel argues, can we place our faith in a proceduralized discursive tool that would somehow strip away the historical dross in order to access a "genuinely" rational standard for common life. Although we may certainly wish to revise our norms and institutions, any such challenge must come from *within* our historically and culturally thick conceptual space, as it is only in these terms that we can recognize what counts as a good argument or what the ends of such disputation ought to be in the first place.

This argument against an ethical in-itself [*Ansich*], long associated with Hegel's allergy toward any form of metaphysical realism, allows us to address his most fundamental challenge: Kant's attempt to bind community through the moral law (accessible through *a priori* reason), and his attendant disqualification of our lived ethical traditions, reverses the ontological order of priority between *Sittlichkeit* and *Moralität* once the latter is recognized as the practice of ethical self-understanding *specific to* bourgeois civil society.[58] Notwithstanding the strident tone of Hegel's early essays, then, he does not abstractly *oppose* Kant in a kind of one-sided, philosophical polemic, so much as he pursues a genealogical strategy: by exposing Kantian morality as a *kind* of ethical practice, grounded within specific social conditions and a specific interpretation of personhood (i.e., evacuated of historical and cultural content), Hegel acknowledges its legitimate right, even while relativizing its claim to normative absoluteness.[59]

On this reading that proved so influential for the Left Hegelian tradition, the most intractable problem of Kantian practical philosophy cannot be limited to its emptiness or formalism. Rather, these difficulties might be viewed as symptomatic of Kant's effort to present the normative ground of morality as somehow "separate" from the lifeworld that offers its material condition of possibility.[60] We can now offer the following answer to what Hegel means with his charges of "untruth" or "so-called reason": because Kant does not sufficiently appreciate the degree to which sociality is constitutive of our thought, values, and reflection, his metaphysics of normativity comes on the scene "too late"—by which I mean that it is unable to account for the substantial, historical grounds that it, nonetheless, presupposes. Or, stated in such a way as to fully emphasize its contradictory character, *Moralität* is the *Sitte* that disavows its status as such.

Final Reflections: *Sittlichkeit*, Freedom, and Modernity

As the previous section should suggest, there are at least two lines of argument that characterize the early Hegel's challenge to Kant. At one level, Hegel pursues a well-known critique over moral agency: attempting to live according to the strictures of the moral law would leave us disoriented, unable to generate any determinate duties, and ultimately its rigorist tendencies require us to sacrifice those particular commitments that render our lives *ours* in a meaningful sense (i.e., as agents with singular projects and ties to concrete others). Though much critical debate has focused upon these questions of agency, identity, and deliberation, I want to close by extending a point from the argument over norms and reason—one that will allow us to flag (though we can hardly do more than this) the stakes behind Hegel's indictments by situating them within recent discussions over the legacy and challenge of modernity.

At bottom, Hegel charges Kant with a kind of reflexive blindness, in that the moral enterprise cannot account for its own constitutive conditions. However, this effort to redescribe *Moralität* as a social practice already foreshadows Hegel's mature challenge over a form of self-determination appropriate to modernity—particularly when framed by the project announced by Kant himself (i.e., reason would be fully self-determining when bound only by its own mandates). It is here that the argument over the "location" of reason bears its ultimate fruit. While Kant's commitment to rational autonomy leads him to refuse attempts to ground obligation upon, say, conformity to divine will or the proper objects of the will (those that are authoritative for us independent of our choosing them), his recourse to nonderivable, *a priori* principles, abstracted from the domain of sociality, leads Hegel to conclude that he has not fully come to grips with modernity's self-grounding project. Given traditional concerns over why certain kinds of norms should be considered authoritative for us, a legitimating strategy naturally presents itself: the seriousness of our obligations can be maintained only if they are based upon a standard that transcends our contingent desires or tastes (whether at an individual or collective level) and can thus serve as an ultimate ground of their value. Thus, when Kant attributes the force of morality to an inscrutable *Faktum der Vernunft*, that we simply *must* recognize—or he invokes a moral law that "forces itself upon us"—Hegel wants to suggest that this cannot be construed as a simple rhetorical slippage.[61] Nor is it *simply* a sign that *Moralität* is insufficiently attentive to its rootedness within specific social practices and models of subjecthood. Rather, these discursive moves are symptomatic that Kant has succumbed to such anxieties and is unable to follow this grammar of autonomy through to its conclusions.

Ultimately, then, these arguments over community do not simply explore the terrain of social ontology and personhood. Rather, Hegel's turn to *Sittlichkeit* represent a move in this argument over the provenance of our norms and its implications for a doctrine of freedom appropriate to modernity—one that ultimately radicalizes the Kantian thesis on autonomy: the free will would subject itself to no authority other than reason itself. Where

Kant wants to locate the criteria for self-legislation within the formal structure of the will, Hegel counters with the following strategy, elaborated in recent neo-Hegelian scholarship (Pippin, Pinkard): autonomy is no "fact" to be reconstructed, but rather a social accomplishment that results from an increasingly reflective understanding that our sources of normativity exist nowhere other than our collectively instituted practices of setting, evaluating, and revising those norms through which we give intelligible shape to social space.[62] If this is correct, then to be "at home" [*Zuhause*] in the social world (to employ Hegel's language) need not suggest an unreflective submission to the communally bounded *status quo* and thus a foreclosure of rational autonomy; rather, this metaphor enjoins social participants to recognize that their norms are social "all the way down," without recourse to a kind of normative facticity whose power they could only acknowledge.[63] And, such institutions will be amended not by measuring them against some extrasocial, *a priori* standard, but (as his *Phenomenology* makes clear) by whether they are ultimately sustainable in the terms that they set out for themselves.[64]

This claim regarding the "location" of normativity brings us full circle on the question that opened this essay: what might Hegel mean when he represents Kant's practical philosophy as alternately incoherent and tyrannical? While I hope to have shown that Kant is surely no individualist who jettisons the ethical significance of our relations with others, Hegel wants to argue that his normative grammar betrays the deepest stakes of the Idealist project, inaugurated by Kant himself. That is, if modernity is founded upon the insight that our norms receive their authority from our *taking* them to be authoritative, then Kant commits a rearguard act of mystification when he attempts to bind social life through a law that we could not interrogate or resist, but only acknowledge. As Terry Pinkard has put this point, Hegel's apparent rejection of Kantian themes is perhaps better described as a strategy to "get out of Kant by way of Kant."[65] That is, Hegel accepts an antirealist, self-grounding framework for normativity, but denies that Kant was ultimately faithful to his own founding insight. We may question whether Hegel adequately grasped Kant's recourse to a peculiar "fact" of reason[66]— and we can only find his faith in such things as the nation-state or the rational course of history to be naïve (if not outright dangerous). That said, his suspicion toward any such attempts to bring the lifeworld under the rule of alien authority—from scientistic myths of "the natural" to theocratic revelation—surely retains its urgency today.

Notes

1. This Kantian allegiance is further reflected in their promise to consider the "invisible church" their point of union [*Vereinigungspunkt*] when next they were to

meet. This vow appears in a letter to Schelling, written at the beginning of 1795, shortly after Hegel left the Tübingen *Stift*. G. W. F. *Hegel: Briefe von und an Hegel, Band 1: 1785–1812*, ed. Johannes Hoffmeister (Hamburg: Felix Meiner Verlag, 1952), 18.

2. This passage appears in *Glauben und Wissen*, located in the *Gesammelte Werke*, ed. Hartmut Buchner and Otto Pöggeler (Hamburg: Felix Meiner Verlag, 1968), 4:338 (hereafter *GW*). The English version that I use for the remaining references is the translation by H. S. Harris and Walter Cerf, *Faith and Knowledge* (Albany: State University of New York Press, 1977), (hereafter *FK*).

3. A notable exception is Burkhard Tuschling, who also seeks to dispel the putative "individualism" of Kantian moral practice—even if he may overstate the case by describing this "universal relationship toward fellow human and rational beings" as a kind of being-for-others. See his "*Rationis Societas*: Remarks on Kant and Hegel," in *Kant's Philosophy of Religion Reconsidered*, ed. Philip Rossi and Michael Wreen (Bloomington: Indiana University Press, 1991), 181–205. In what follows, I do not wish to contest Tuschling's findings, so much as argue for a dimension of Hegel's criticism that is largely absent from his essay.

4. Jürgen Habermas has argued for precisely this kind of interpretation: "[Hegel] sees through the concept of autonomous will that appears to constitute the essential value of Kant's moral philosophy. He realizes that this concept is a peculiar abstraction from the moral relationships of communicating individuals. . . . The intersubjectivity of the recognition of moral laws accounted for *a priori* by practical reason permits the reduction of moral action to the monologic domain. The positive relation of the will to the will of others is withdrawn from possible communication, and a transcendentally necessary correspondence of isolated goal-directed activities under abstract universal laws is substituted. To this extent moral action in Kant's sense is presented, *mutatis mutandis*, as a special case of what we today call strategic action." This passage is found in *Theory and Practice by Jürgen Habermas*, trans. John Viertel (Boston: Beacon Press, 1973), 151.

5. This conclusion has been drawn even by typically sensitive commentators. See, for instance, Ernst Tugendhat's *Self-Consciousness and Self-Determination* (Cambridge: MIT Press, 1986), 314–18.

6. For a reading that contests this tendency through an extended investigation of Kant's engagement with various teleological models, see Thomas Auxter, *Kant's Moral Teleology* (Mercer: Mercer University Press, 1982).

7. This passage is found in *Critique of Pure Reason*, trans. Norman Kemp Smith (New York: St. Martin's Press, 1965), 637–38.

8. *FK*, 153/*GW*, 4:387.

9. "One concerned with the oneness of the pure concept and the subjects (or the morality of actions), the other with their non-oneness [*Nichteinssein*] (or legality), but in such a way that if, in this division of the ethical realm into morality and legality, these two become mere possibilities, they are both for that reason equally positive." Through the course of this essay, references to the *Natural Law* essay (*NL*) will be to the English translation of H. B. Nisbet, "On the Scientific Ways of Treating Natural Law," in *Political Writings*, ed. Laurence Dickey and H. B. Nisbet (New York: Cambridge University Press, 1999). On the occasions in which I have found it

necessary to alter the translation or provide one of my own, I have made reference to the original in *GW* (*NL*, 131/*GW*, 4:442).

10. This passage appears in *The Metaphysics of Morals*, trans. Mary J. Gregor, in *Practical Philosophy*, trans. and ed. Mary J. Gregor (Cambridge: Cambridge University Press, 1996). All references to this essay (hereafter MM) will be to the Gregor translation. Corresponding references to the German original (hereafter Ak) are to *Kants gesammelte Schriften*, ed. Königlich Preußische Akademie der Wissenschaften, 29 vols. (Berlin: de Gruyter, 1900–). MM, 386/Ak, 6:229.

11. "Duties in accordance with rightful lawgiving can be only external duties, since this lawgiving does not require that the idea of this duty, which is internal, itself be the determining ground of the agent's choice; and since it still needs an incentive suited to the law, it can connect only external incentives with it" (MM, 383–84/Ak, 6:219).

12. This passage is found in *Perpetual Peace* (hereafter PP), translated by Mary J. Gregor, in *Practical Philosophy* (PP, 335/Ak, 8:366).

13. MM, 372/Ak, 6:217. Earlier in the text, Kant elaborates the dangers of allowing a moral anthropology to enter into the formulation of a doctrine of right. While anthropological considerations might aid in the application of the principles of right, they "must not precede a metaphysics of morals or be mixed with it; for one would then run the risk of bringing forth false or at least indulgent moral laws, which would misrepresent as unattainable what has only not been attained just because the law has not been seen and presented in its purity (in which its strength consists) or because spurious or impure incentives were used for what is itself in conformity with duty and good" (ibid.).

14. "He can indeed state what is laid down as right (*quid sit iuris*), that is, what the laws in a certain place and at a certain time say or have said. But whether what these laws prescribed is also right, and what the universal criterion is by which one could recognize right as well as wrong (*iustum et iniustum*), this would remain hidden from him unless he leaves those empirical principles behind for a while and seeks the sources of such judgments in reason alone, so as to establish the basis for any possible giving of positive laws (although positive laws can serve as excellent guides to this)" (MM, 386–87/Ak, 6:229–30).

15. MM, 387/Ak, 6:230.

16. MM, 393/Ak, 6:237.

17. Robert Pippin, for instance, argues that generating substantive legal norms requires Kant to supplement the categorical imperative with teleological considerations regarding the meaningful *exercise* of autonomy. See "On the Moral Foundations of Kant's *Rechtslehre*," in Robert B. Pippin, *Idealism as Modernism: Hegelian Variations* (New York: Cambridge University Press, 1997), 56–91.

18. See, for instance, Marcus Willaschek, "Why the *Doctrine of Right* Does Not Belong in the *Metaphysics of Morals*," in *Jahrbuch für Recht und Ethik* 5 (1997): 205–27. For a rival interpretation, see Paul Guyer, "Kant's Deductions of the Principles of Right," in *Kant's Metaphysics of Morals: Interpretive Essays*, ed. Mark Timmons (Oxford: Oxford University Press, 2002), 23–64.

19. To invoke Henry Allison's well-known "incorporation thesis," Kant's commitment to a particular form of moral idealism means that natural inclinations cannot

immediately determine me to action, no matter their force. While the finitude of the human agent means that she is subject to competing motivational grounds, a natural desire can only determine her to action insofar as the will has chosen to "incorporate" it as its maxim—thus eliminating any directly "causal" theory of motivation.

20. *Religion within the Boundaries of Mere Reason*, trans. and ed. Allen Wood and George di Giovanni (New York: Cambridge University Press, 1998), 59 (Ak, 6:36); hereafter *RWL*. It should further be noted that the radicality of this evil does not denote simply a tendency to privilege maxims of self-love over the moral law, but rather a distortion of what Kant calls the "first ground of the adoption of maxims" or, alternately, the "supreme maxim"—that is, a self-given rule to *systematically* invert these incentives of the will. A helpful discussion of the difficulties surrounding this inscrutable "decision" can be found in Gordon E. Michalson Jr., *Fallen Freedom: Kant on Radical Evil and Moral Regeneration* (Cambridge: Cambridge University Press, 1990), 52–70.

21. *RWL*, 67/Ak, 6:47.

22. *RWL*, 106/Ak, 6:94.

23. Shortly before the cited passage, Kant claims, "If he searches for the causes and the circumstances that draw him into this danger and keep him there, he can easily convince himself that they do not come his way from his own raw nature, so far as he exists in isolation, but rather from the human beings to whom he stands in relation or association" (*RWL*, 105/Ak, 6:93).

24. The passage I cited above continues: "If no means could be found to establish a union which has for its end the prevention of this evil and the promotion of the good in the human being—an enduring and ever expanding society, solely designed for the preservation of morality by counteracting evil with united forces—however much the individual human being might wish to escape from the dominion of this evil, he would still be held in incessant danger of relapsing into it. —Inasmuch as we can see, therefore, the dominion of the good principle is not otherwise attainable, so far as human beings can work toward it, than through the setting up and the diffusion of a society in accordance with, and for the sake of, the laws of virtue—a society which reason makes it a task and a duty of the entire human race to establish in its full scope" (*RWL*, 105–6/Ak, 6:94).

25. *RWL*, 108/Ak, 6:97.

26. *RWL*, 106/Ak, 6:94. It should further be noted that Kant's holistic language suggests that this community would be inadequately conceived as an aggregate of individuals, each of whom has made the choice for virtue on their own, and then banded together: "Since this highest moral goodwill not be brought about solely through the striving of one individual person for his own moral perfection but requires rather a union of such persons into a whole [*ein Ganzes*] toward that very end, toward a system of well-disposed human beings in which, and through the unity of which alone, the highest moral good can come to pass" (*RWL*, 109/Ak, 6:97–98).

27. Robert Pippin, for instance, has argued the following: "Kant is quite clear that the good life is the one that best realizes human freedom, the distinctive human capacity worthy of respect. Since this freedom can best be realized in subjection to a universal, rational principle, 'community' is simply a result of such necessarily equal

subjection. We relate to each other by virtue of our relation to the moral law; certainly an indirect, a more 'Leibnizean,' one might say, than Aristotelian or Hegelian 'community.'" In "Hegel, Ethical Reasons, Kantian Rejoinders," *Idealism as Modernism*, 123.

28. This kind of reading has been pursued—in very different ways—by Onora O'Neill and Christine Korsgaard. See O'Neill's *Constructions of Reason: Explorations in Kant's Political Philosophy* (New York: Cambridge University Press, 1989), particularly the essay "Reason and Politics in the Kantian Enterprise," 3–27. For Korsgaard, see *Creating the Kingdom of Ends* (New York: Cambridge University Press, 1996), particularly chapter 7.

29. GW, 83/Ak, 4:433.

30. RWL, 112/Ak, 6:102, translation modified.

31. RWL, 106/Ak, 6:94; RWL, 112/Ak, 6:102.

32. This distinction between divine and human lawgiving come out clearly in an aside within the *Rechtslehre*: "Just because ethical lawgiving includes within its law the internal incentive to action (the idea of duty), and this feature must not be present in external lawgiving, ethical lawgiving cannot be external (*not even the external lawgiving of a divine will*), although it does take up duties which rest on another, namely an external, lawgiving by making them, *as duties*, incentives in its lawgiving" (MM, 384/Ak, 6:219; emphasis added).

33. RWL, 153/Ak, 6:153. While this language of "command" might rankle those with even a passing acquaintance with Kant's moral doctrine, he is clearly assuming the further qualification offered in the *Critique of Practical Reason*: "religion, that is . . . the recognition of all duties as divine commands, not as sanctions—that is, chosen and in themselves contingent ordinances of another's will—but as essential laws of every free will in itself . . ." (Ak, 5:129).

34. In more technically sound terms, these two options reflect Kant's distinction between revealed and natural religion: "That religion in which I must know in advance that something is a divine command in order to recognize it as my duty, is the *revealed* religion (or the one standing in need of a revelation); in contrast, that religion in which I must first know that something is my duty before I can accept it as a divine injunction is the *natural* religion" (RWL, 153/Ak, 6:153).

35. RWL, 107/Ak, 6:96. Earlier he describes this social task as "a duty *sui generis*, not of human beings toward human beings but of the human race toward itself" (RWL, 108/Ak, 6:97).

36. "It is therefore a necessary consequence of the physical and, at the same time, the moral predisposition in us—the latter being the foundation and at the same time the interpreter of all religion—that in the end religion will gradually be freed of all empirical grounds of determination, of all statutes that rest on history and unite human beings provisionally for the promotion of the good through the intermediary of an ecclesiastical faith" (RWL, 127/Ak, 6:121).

37. A symptomatic case can be found in the *Critique of Pure Reason*, where Kant claims that "reason is present in all the actions of men at all times and under all circumstances, and is always the same; but it is not itself in time, and does not fall into any new state in which it was not before" (A 556/B 584).

38. The most committed attempt to elaborate the historical dimension of the critical system is Yirmiahu Yovel's *Kant and the Philosophy of History* (Princeton: Princeton University Press, 1980).

39. Kant makes a significant technical distinction between *Geschichte* and *Historie*, which is elided in the English language. By the former, he typically refers to the temporal process by which reason articulates itself into a completed architectonic; he typically uses the latter to disparage methodological approaches that compile empirical data without mediation through rational principles. For a discussion of this distinction, see Yovel, 240.

40. For instance, when Kant argues that the ethical commonwealth must take the form of a church, he claims that "the wish of all well-disposed human beings is, therefore, 'that the kingdom of God come, that his will be done on earth'; but what preparations must they make in order that this wish come to pass among them?" (*RWL*, 111/Ak, 6:101).

41. This imperative comes out clearly in other texts. For instance, in the *Theory* essay, Kant argues that "*if* we stand in certain moral relations to things in the world we must everywhere obey the moral law, and beyond this there is added the duty to bring it about as far as we can *that* such a relation (a world in keeping with the moral highest ends) exists" (TP 282–83/Ak, 8:280).

42. Such an emphasis upon *our* contribution to this divine kingdom can be found in the following passage: "Yet human beings are not permitted on this account to remain idle in the undertaking and let Providence have free rein, as if each could go after his private moral affairs and entrust to a higher wisdom the whole concern of the human race (as regards its moral destiny). Each must, on the contrary, so conduct himself as if everything depended on him. Only on this condition may he hope that a higher wisdom will provide the fulfillment of his well-intentioned effort" (*RWL*, 111/Ak, 6:101).

43. Philip Rossi puts this point well: "Human beings must *work together* to establish the *social* conditions that enable each and every member of the ethical commonwealth to develop and sustain the disposition to work for this common destiny for the human species." See *The Social Authority of Reason: Kant's Critique, Radical Evil, and the Destiny of Humankind* (Albany: State University of New York Press, 2005), 53. For reasons that I will argue below, I have doubts regarding the degree to which Kant's reason can meaningfully be described as "social" or what its "social authority" might be.

44. In the *Encyclopedia Logic*, Hegel argues that "this contradiction [between reality and the "ought"] may seem to be disguised by adjourning the realization of the Idea to a future, to a *time* when the Idea will also be. But a sensuous condition like time is the reverse of a reconciliation of the discrepancy; and an infinite progression—which is the corresponding image adopted by the understanding—on the face of it only repeats and reenacts the contradiction." This passage is found in *Hegel's Logic*, trans. William Wallace (New York: Oxford University Press, 1975), 91.

45. In *Faith and Knowledge*, Hegel takes this infinite progress as evidence of the "bad infinity" that follows from Kantian metaphysics: "Practical reason, which takes refuge in this infinite progress and means to constitute itself as absolute in freedom,

confesses its finitude and its inability to validate its absoluteness precisely through this infinity of the progress" (*FK*, 84/*GW*, 4:337).

46. *RWL*, 128/Ak, 6:122.

47. Hegel is characteristically hostile toward any such notion of a numerically universal community in political terms as well—evinced in the *Naturrecht* essay when he derides the "shapelessness [*Gestaltlosigkeit*] of cosmopolitanism, or . . . the vacuity [*Leerheit*] of the rights of man or the equal vacuity of an international state or a world republic" (*NL*, 179/*GW*, 4:484).

48. This point is clearly expressed in the *Naturrecht* essay, where Hegel sets the "truth" of ancient thought against the abstractions of modern moral philosophy: "the ethical consists in living in accordance with the ethics [*Sitten*] of one's country" (*NL*, 162/*GW*, 4: 469).

49. This charge finds its putative justification in Hegel's elliptical statement in the preface of the *Philosophy of Right* that "what is rational is actual, and what is actual is rational [*Was vernünftig ist, das ist wirklich; und was wirklich ist, das ist vernünftig*]." Fortunately, this habit of reading the *Doppelsatz* as a kind of ideological justification of prevailing social conditions has begun to recede in the face of recent scholarship, based upon the technical distinction between *Wirklichkeit* (i.e., actuality in conformity with the concept) and *Realität* (i.e., the domain of mere existence, regardless of its rational content). While there are virtually no specialists who would commit this interpretive error, I do not mean to suggest that there are no grounds for arguing that Hegel has mistaken certain elements of the social world for rationally backed features, necessary for the realization of freedom—as many features of the state evince this precise confusion. A helpful discussion of this passage can be found in Michael Hardimon, *Hegel's Social Philosophy: The Project of Reconciliation* (New York: Cambridge University Press, 1994).

50. This kind of anxiety has been expressed by Ernst Tugendhat, who argues that "the possibility of an independent and critical relation to the community or the state is not admitted by Hegel" such that his philosophy "is consciously and explicitly the philosophy of the justification of the existing order, quite irrespective of how this existing order may be constituted." These passages are found in *Self-Consciousness and Self-Determination*, trans. Paul Stern (Cambridge: MIT Press, 1986), 315 and 317. A definitive response to Tugendhat can be found in Ludwig Siep, "The *Aufhebung* of Morality in Ethical Life," in *Hegel's Philosophy of Action*, ed. Lawrence Stepelevich and David Lamb (Atlantic Highlands: Humanities Press, 1983).

51. MM, 371/Ak, 6:216, translation modified.

52. We can find rhetorical evidence for this anxiety in Kant's insistence that the Kingdom of God must be "freed" [*losgemacht*] from statutory, historical laws in order to unify its members through *a priori* laws of pure reason: "It is therefore a necessary consequence of the physical and, at the same time, the moral predisposition in us—the latter being the foundation and at the same time the interpreter of all religion—that in the end religion will gradually be freed of all empirical grounds of determination, of all statutes that rest on history and unite human beings provisionally for the promotion of the good through the intermediary of an ecclesiastical faith" (*RWL*, 127/Ak, 6:121).

53. *NL*, 159/*GW*, 4:467.

54. Perhaps the most developed reading is presented in *Idealism as Modernism,* particularly the essays "Hegel's Ethical Rationalism" and "Hegel, Ethical Reasons, Kantian Rejoinders."

55. The difficulties surrounding the opposite premise—that reasons are initially something "private" that must somehow be made public—have been well treated by Christine Korsgaard, particularly chapter 10, "The Reasons We Can Share: An Attack on the Distinction Between Agent-Relative and Agent-Neutral Values," in *Creating the Kingdom of Ends.*

56. Hegel's privileged example for such an ethical "orientation" is, of course, found in Antigone's performance of what it means to be a sister in the world of the classical *polis.* Her unreflective allegiance to the conventions of Greek sisterhood hardly exhausts the kind of nomological orientation I am trying to describe here, as Hegel makes clear in the *Phenomenology* that this lack of self-consciousness is a deficiency in the Greek form of *Sittlichkeit,* and must be replaced by a modern model that would allow for reflective identification with the roles of the community.

57. For the most well-known of these objections, see Michael Sandel, *Liberalism and the Limits of Justice,* 2nd ed. (New York: Cambridge University Press, 1998).

58. *NL,* 160–61/*GW,* 4:468.

59. "But however vacuous these abstractions and the relation of externality to which they give rise may be, the moment of the negatively absolute or infinity . . . is a moment of the absolute itself that must be identified in *absolute ethical life*" (*NL,* 139–40/*GW,* 4:449).

60. This argument is particularly clear in Hegel's description of how a philosophical position may become "positive" even if it is based upon a legitimate claim to truth: "insofar as what is ideally opposite and one-sided, and has reality only in absolute identity with its own opposite, is isolated, posited as existing independently, and declared to be real . . . it is possible not only for a purely formal abstraction to be fixed and falsely regarded as a truth and reality (as indicated above), but also for a true idea and genuine principle to be misunderstood with regard to its limit, and posited outside that area in which it has its truth, thereby forfeiting its truth altogether" (*NL,* 169/*GW,* 4:475–76). What Hegel is trying to argue here, then, is that the limited right of morality, as a particular, historically appropriate form of ethical consciousness (as well as the limited right of civil society), is forfeited when it absolutizes its claim so as to deny its social conditions.

61. As Hegel sardonically describes this moral fact in the *Lectures on the History of Philosophy,* its surdlike quality renders it "the last undigested log in our stomach, a revelation given to reason." Rüdiger Bittner has made similar charges in *What Reason Demands,* trans. Theodore Talbot (New York: Cambridge University Press, 1989), 89–90. A rather more sympathetic reading of this curious "fact," that attempts to remove its dogmatic character, can be found in Henry Allison's essay, "Justification and Freedom in the *Critique of Practical Reason,*" in *Kant's Transcendental Deductions: The Three Critiques and the Opus postumum,* ed. Eckart Förster (Stanford: Stanford University Press, 1989), 114–30.

62. A helpful discussion of these themes can be found in Robert Pippin's essay, "Hegel and Institutional Rationality," in *Southern Journal of Philosophy* 39 (2001):

1–25. See also Terry Pinkard, "Historicism, Social Practice, and Sustainability: Some Themes in Hegelian Ethical Theory," in *Neue Hefte für Philosophie* 35 (1995): 56–94.

63. For a focused discussion of what this vision of freedom would entail, see Robert Pippin, "What Is the Question for Which Hegel's Theory of Recognition Is the Answer?" in *European Journal of Philosophy* 8 (2000): 155–72.

64. I borrow this criterion of "sustainability" from Terry Pinkard, "Historicism, Social Practice, and Sustainability," 65–72.

65. See Terry Pinkard, "Virtues, Morality, and *Sittlichkeit*: From Maxims to Practices," in *European Journal of Philosophy* 7, no. 2 (1999): 217–38.

66. For a discussion of the factors that led Kant to postulate the existence of this "fact," as well as the difficulties to which it gives rise, see Dieter Henrich's influential essay, "The Concept of Moral Insight and Kant's Doctrine of the Fact of Reason," in *The Unity of Reason: Essays on Kant's Philosophy*, ed. Richard Velkley, trans. Jeffrey Edwards et al. (Cambridge: Harvard University Press, 1994).

9

PARADOXES IN KANT'S
ACCOUNT OF CITIZENSHIP

RONALD BEINER

What are we to make of Kant as a philosopher of citizenship? In order to begin answering this question, we need to determine how exalted Kant intends the status of citizen to be, especially in relation to the forms of moral experience that for Kant are decisive in conferring moral worth upon us as rational beings; and clarifying this turns out to be anything but a simple matter. In a very direct sense, our status as citizens constitutes a nonmoral status, for the domain of politics per se refers to forms of civic behavior that can be regulated by laws—i.e., state coercion—and therefore civic life doesn't (and cannot) touch that which for Kant *defines* moral experience: the quality of our intentions or of our ultimate motivation. This is why Kant famously says that a race of intelligent devils could in principle devise a perfectly satisfactory political constitution: as long as we, for instance, pay our taxes, what is demanded of us in the *political* aspect of our life is fulfilled (even if the *moral* worth of these civic performances is precisely zero).

Kant offers one of the most powerful accounts of moral equality available within the Western philosophical tradition. Yet his account of *citizenship* is anything but egalitarian or universalistic. On the face of it—and probably also with respect to our final judgment—this would appear deeply to discredit Kant's moral egalitarianism. How can one coherently champion the radical equality of all rational beings (and therefore all human beings) while refusing to draw the entailment of a robust *civic* equality. But the issue of whether nonequality of citizenship poses a severe problem for Kant's liberalism (or of how severe a problem it poses) hangs on where one locates Kant as a theorist of citizenship between what I'm going to call (adapting terms introduced by Richard Flathman)[1] "high-liberal" and "low-liberal" interpretations of citizenship. According to what I'm calling the low-liberal view, politics is conceived as an instrumentality for securing a system of laws that allows each of us to get on with our individual purposes without unnecessary interference by the state, and citizenship is simply the title assumed by all those who participate in this arrangement. There is no "moral community" at stake in citizenship so conceived. According to what I'm calling the high-liberal view, our dignity as human beings is itself implicated in our civic identity, and hence our lives as citizens count for a great deal in establishing or expressing our moral status. For convenience, let's assign the low-liberal view of citizenship to Hobbes, and assign the high-liberal view to Hegel.[2] If the "intelligent devils" passage in *Perpetual Peace* exhausted Kant's thinking about politics, then of course his conception of citizenship would fall foursquare within the low-liberal view. But in fact I want to suggest that his conception of citizenship occupies an unstable position between Hobbes and Hegel in the relevant sense, and therefore it is not entirely easy to pin down how damaging or how damning his views about citizenship are in relation to his liberalism.

Before turning to the texts in which Kant addresses most directly the issue of citizenship, I want to look more closely at the "intelligent devils" text, which again presents, in a fairly stark depiction, the low-liberal side of Kant's reflections on the meaning of civic membership. Kant writes:

> The *republican* constitution is the only one that is completely compatible with the right of human beings. . . . Many assert it would have to be a state of *angels* because human beings, with their self-seeking inclinations, would not be capable of such a sublime form of constitution. But now nature comes to the aid of the general will grounded in reason, revered but impotent in practice, and does so precisely through those self-seeking inclinations, so that it is a matter only of a good organization of a state (which is certainly within the capacity of human beings), of arranging those forces of nature in opposition to one another in such a way that one checks the destructive effect of the other or cancels it, so that the end result for reason turns out as if neither of them existed at all and the human being is constrained to become a good citizen even if not a morally good human being. The problem of establishing a state, no matter how hard it may sound, is *soluble* even for a nation of devils (if only they have understanding) [*selbst für ein Volk von Teufeln (wenn sie nur Verstand haben)*]. . . . Such a problem must be soluble. For the problem is not the moral improvement of human beings but only the mechanism of nature.[3]

This surely presents itself as a classic statement of the low-liberal view. But is Kant really as Hobbesian as he sounds in this passage? It would seem that his more standard line is that our dignity as human beings plays out strictly in the domain of private (especially moral) doings, and politics merely coordinates and regulates interaction in the society such that citizens don't infringe on each other's autonomous sphere of action in the private domain. This is still a low-liberal view, as I have defined it, for it sees little at stake with respect to the civic dimension of our lives in relation to what confers dignity and moral status upon individuals. Yet it is importantly different from Hobbes's view, for Hobbes would of course regard it as a piece of silly superstition to talk of something like the dignity of human beings, whether located in the private domain or in the domain of civic life.

The basic thesis that I want to explore, both in relation to this text and in relation to the other writings relevant to Kant's doctrine of citizenship, can be formulated as follows: If, *for political purposes*, we are all just atomistic monads trying to avoid colliding into each other, and thus we contrive a set of political arrangements that secures this objective, then Kant's violation of his own egalitarianism through the denial of full citizenship to large classes of adult human beings seems somehow less egregious. If, on the other hand, citizenship is itself the affirmation of an important moral status, it is hard to see how Kant could fail to discern that *civic* antiegalitarianism would taint or impugn his *moral* egalitarianism. The decisive issue, then, is whether citizenship is itself a form of *moral community*, and although Kant leaned heavily toward the view that it isn't,[4] there are significant intimations of the contrary view, which therefore suggests an important tension in Kant's account of citizenship.

There is at least a minimal sense in which the state *is* a "moral community" for Kant. It is a crucial aspect of Kant's version of social contract theory that the formation of a state is not the contingent outcome of reasoning about our best interests, as it is for Hobbes[5] and Locke; rather, exit from the state of nature is *morally compulsory*.[6] In that sense, membership in a political association, an association of citizens, is already an expression of our moral nature. Recognition of the equality and moral autonomy of our fellow citizens is likewise a *moral* recognition.[7] So the "intelligent devils" view *does not* capture Kant's broader conception of citizenship. If the state's ultimate job is to acknowledge and protect the autonomy of its members, which is indeed Kant's conception, then the state is doing more than just treating us as devils with understanding.

As we move from the "intelligent devils" text to Kant's discussions of citizenship proper, the "moral" relevance of civic membership comes more to the fore. Kant offers parallel analyses in the two works where our topic is addressed—namely, sections 43–49 of the "Doctrine of Right" portion of *The Metaphysics of Morals*, and part 2 of his essay "Theory and Practice." The texts here are compact but nonetheless damning. The basic thrust of both texts is to argue that while the civil commonwealth must respect the freedom and equality of all its subjects *as human beings* and as subjects of the state, this doesn't necessarily entail equal rights *as citizens*. In fact, Kant's main purpose in these texts is to argue that one must distinguish two fundamentally different kinds of political status within the state: "active" citizens versus "passive" citizens, or those who are recognized by the state as possessing civil personality versus those who are not recognized as being in possession of civil personality. "Passive citizens" include children, women, and those who are economically dependent on a "master" (e.g., apprentices or domestic servants).[8] Those who fail to satisfy the criterion of "being one's own master"[9] are entitled only to a subordinate form of citizenship: they are "subjects" of the state,[10] "mere associates in the state,"[11] "co-beneficiaries of [the state's] protection,"[12] reduced to the status of being a "part" [*Theil*] of the commonwealth without being a "member" [*Glied*] of it.[13] On the other hand, "active citizens," citizens in the full sense, are "co-legislators" of the state.[14]

What is most remarkable about Kant's version of the argument in TP, as becomes evident from his discussion in the conclusion of part 2, is that he's not really talking about *actual* civic status, but merely *hypothetical* citizenship as providing a regulative idea for judging the legitimacy of laws or a legal regime that is not expected to emanate at all from the exercise of civic powers by citizens: What is at stake is "*only an idea* of reason, which, however, has its undoubted practical reality, namely, to bind every legislator to give his laws in such a way that they *could* have arisen from the united will of a whole people and to regard each subject, insofar as he wants to be a citizen, as if he has joined in voting for such a will."[15] What's truly bizarre about the exclusions of citizenship laid out in TP, read in the light of the passage just quoted, is that they serve *not* to distinguish those who vote as citizens from those who don't (and don't have a claim to vote). *Rather*, what is being distinguished, it seems, are those who deserve to be taken into consideration *as if* they participated in voting, as opposed to those who don't even have status as *hypothetical* citizens! Conceding active citizenship to all adults would not actually confer voting rights on *anyone*, since Kant is more concerned with "binding the legislator" according to an *idea* of the will of an hypothetical citizen body than with actually distributing civic powers—hence, Kant's civic exclusions in the TP account seem utterly gratuitous. What matters is the judgment of the *legislator*, not the judgment of the *citizens*.[16] In that sense, again, the impressive-sounding talk of citizens as "co-legislators" of the state is really a kind of phantom citizenship.

The MM version of the argument seems different: here Kant speaks of citizenship as "being fit to vote," which entails "want[ing] to be not just a part of the commonwealth but also a member of it."[17] It implies "the right to manage the state itself as *active* members of it."[18] So in the MM account, by contrast to the TP account, it seems that real civic status is at issue. And tailors have it whereas woodchoppers don't; wig makers have it but barbers don't; leasehold farmers have it but tenant farmers don't; teachers have it but tutors don't; men have it but women don't.[19] With respect to the second term in each of these pairs, Kant has made the judgment that they "are mere underlings [*Handlanger*] of the commonwealth because they have to be under the direction or protection of other individuals, and so do not possess civil independence."[20]

In order to judge how dubious is the theoretical grounding of Kant's distinction between active and passive citizens, it might be worth considering the fact that, in both the TP and MM versions of the argument, Kant takes care not to let go of *his own* civic status or civil personality.[21] It is obviously no accident that teacher versus tutor constitutes one of Kant's active/passive pairs. But since teachers and tutors may have identical skills (many of the major figures within the history of political thought were tutors or secretaries for well-to-do families, including Kant himself!), it is not at all obvious why teaching for the state makes one a citizen but teaching within a private household disables one for citizenship. Also, as several of Kant's examples indicate, his account seems to privilege self-employment; but again, those who are on the payroll of the state are *not* self-employed.

The implied technical reason why employment by the state doesn't disqualify one from active citizenship is that one should be subject to no *master apart from the commonwealth,*[22] and therefore if *the state* is one's master, this doesn't constitute serving two masters.[23] Yet this strikes one as a bit of a dodge, since being a servant of the commonwealth *qua* employee of the state *does* run in some tension with the crucial qualification, which is: "*being one's own master.*"[24] It seems that part of what Kant has in mind is the notion that human beings who are basically unskilled sell in effect their brute labor power, and *therefore* they can't help but be dependent: "*being one's own master* [implies] having some *property* (and any art, craft, fine art, or science can be counted as property) that supports him."[25] But how can we assess in the abstract whether day laborers, barbers, and tutors are bereft of skills in the relevant sense? Why does Kant say that wig makers or tailors, by virtue of their craft, own property in their own person, whereas tutors, for instance, are mere servants? In any case, Kant is certainly aware that the whole analysis is rather shaky: "It is, I admit, somewhat difficult to determine what is required in order to be able to claim the rank of a human being who is his own master."[26]

Perhaps the issue of how Kant's own citizenship fares in relation to his status as an employee of the state is too *ad hominem*. A deeper objection is that his denial of civil personality to those who are economically subordinate betrays the principle that Kant himself articulated so powerfully in *Religion within the Limits of Reason Alone*: "I cannot really reconcile myself to [expressions such as] 'The bondmen of a landed proprietor are not yet ready for freedom.' . . . For according to such a presupposition, freedom will never arrive, since we cannot *ripen* to this freedom if we are not first of all placed therein (we must be free in order to be able to make purposive use of our powers in freedom)."[27]

Whatever one may make or fail to make of Kant's arguments for the civic exclusion of those who are economically dependent, his treatment of the civic rights of women seems an even more blatant violation of egalitarian principles. Unlike the criterion of exclusion applied to apprentices and servants, Kant describes the restriction of the franchise to male adults as the *"natural"* quality requisite to full citizenship.[28] With respect to the status of *subjecthood* (our subjection to shared coercive laws), Kant says that it would be an unacceptable injustice for facts of birth to be a ground of inequalities, since birth is not a "deed" for which we can assume responsibility but simply something that befalls us.[29] Committing crimes may alter our equality as subjects, but differences owing to birth cannot do so.[30] Yet it appears that the same principle does not apply to our claims to participate in full and active citizenship. At least in the case of *men* who are disenfranchised, Kant can claim that more concerted exercise of their talents might have qualified them for active citizenship; so to some extent, he could argue, they have themselves to blame for their limited citizenship. (He states that rising to a condition of independence is a matter of "talent," "industry," and "luck," so the responsible actions of these individuals are at least part of the story here.)[31] But this isn't the case with respect to *women*: if they are denied full civic status for *natural* reasons, there is no suggestion that this has anything to do with deeds or omissions for which they are responsible; they simply lack the *nature* of civic beings.

As Susan Mendus has highlighted well in her analysis of Kant's account, all of this has the effect of rendering all adult men at least *candidates* for (eventual) full citizenship: the door is in principle unlocked and *must* be kept unlocked as a matter of liberal justice, which is not the case for women. This is in fact a key difference between the two main kinds of passive citizens (servants and women).[32] A central component of Kant's argument that the economically dependent are to be restricted to passive citizenship is Kant's insistence on the *right* of the latter not to be hindered in their efforts to rise to civil personality through the winning of economic independence. This is where Kant gets to wave the flag of his own liberalism even within his doctrine of passive citizenship: an essential aspect of the universal moral equality that Kant affirms is "that anyone can work his way up from this passive condition to an active one."[33] No commonwealth can satisfy standards of right if its laws entrench perpetual economic subordination: "Every member of a commonwealth must be allowed to attain any level of rank within it (that can belong to a subject) to which his talent, his industry and his luck can take him; and his fellow subjects may not stand in his way by means of a *hereditary* prerogative (privileges [reserved] for a certain rank), so as to keep him and his descendents forever beneath the rank."[34] That is, not only must access to full citizenship remain open in principle to the economically dependent, but the state must also see to it that institutionalized obstacles blocking such access are removed.[35] Again, there is no corresponding notion of a right on the part of women to exercise future opportunities to ascend to civil personality. *Their* lack of citizenship, unlike that of social classes who are disenfranchised on account of their position within the economy, applies in perpetuity.

Kant makes no effort to spell out the reasons why women as women are "naturally" excluded from active citizenship, but of course it's implicitly related to his sexist arguments concerning marriage in sections 24–27 of The Doctrine of Right.[36] According to Kant, marital *equality* is not contradicted by the need for the wife to obey the husband as her "master." The reason, such as it is, is that dominance by the husband is said to be based on the husband's "natural superiority . . . to promote the common interest of the household"; and since the "unity and equality" of the marital relationship is constituted by this end, deference to the husband's judgment in some sense serves rather than contradicts equality.[37] Two observations are in order here. First, one may well conclude that this conception expresses a fairly perverse allegiance to the principle of marital equality, yet, however deeply it may violate egalitarian principles, it is distinct from the question of the implications of marriage for *civic* equality. Still (and this is the second point), one can't help noticing that with respect to *both* spheres of social life, domestic and political, Kant claims to be *upholding* the idea of equality (the equality of husband and wife, the equality of all subjects within the state) while nonetheless giving huge weight to notions of *natural inequality* between men and women.

One cannot resist asking: If women are civically incapacitated insofar as wives are dependent upon husbands, parallel to the way in which servants are dependent on employers, why can't women maintain their civil personality simply by refusing to marry? It is striking that Kant nowhere considers this as a possibility. In the MM version of the argument, Kant specifies that "*all* women" [*alles Frauenzimmer*] are denied civil personality,[38] which clearly suggests that the married or unmarried status of women doesn't affect their prospects of full citizenship. Mendus writes: "Kant tells us that by entering into marriage the woman, unlike the man, renounces her civil independence."[39] If so, then the question, why marry? is a reasonable one, for loss of civil personality is a substantial price to pay for marriage. This indeed is what one would *expect* the structure of the argument to be, given the strong emphasis that Kant places on dependency as a disqualification from citizenship. Yet Kant nowhere states explicitly that marriage brings about a loss for women of antecedent civil personality—that is, he nowhere concedes that unmarried women *have* a civil personality that is forfeited in marriage.[40] Again, the door to citizenship for women is locked shut, regardless of contingent circumstances.

In this context, it is interesting to consider Kant's relationship to Rousseau, for of course Kant claimed that it was from Rousseau that he drew his appreciation of the importance of human equality. Rousseau, as Kant famously put it, "set me straight" [*hat mich zurecht gebracht*], because he showed him that the vanities of scholars are as nothing in comparison with the common dignity of the ordinary man.[41] Why didn't this egalitarianism issue in a doctrine of citizenship that recognized men and women as equal citizens? When one asks of Kant, How can a thinker who is the source of such an exalted egalitarianism and universalism in his moral philosophy rest content with such a stunted civic vision in his political philosophy?, in a way the puzzle is even deeper with respect to Rousseau, for Rousseau also articulated an exalted *civic* egalitarianism, and *still* he excluded women from citizenship. *Neither* Rousseau *nor* Kant were as successful at applying their egalitarianism to the civic equality of men and women as one might hope, but ultimately, I want to suggest, Kant sins more grievously against egalitarian citizenship. Since it's much more common for feminist theorists to target Rousseau than to target Kant,[42] this requires some explanation.

For all the feminist fire against Rousseau, it's striking how little ammunition is drawn from the work of Rousseau's that is the direct counterpart of Kant's *Rechtslehre*, namely, the *Social Contract*. Without doubt, feminists have found much to complain about in Rousseau's political thought with respect to gender stereotypes. Yet they've had to content themselves with *reconstructing* his presumed exclusion of women from citizenship on the basis of other Rousseauian texts (especially *Emile*) because it is never spelled out as an element of his "official" *doctrine of citizenship*. For instance, Lynda Lange argues that participation in the general will requires meeting a high standard of rationality and autonomous judgment, and we know from the other texts that Rousseau had a very dim view of women's capacity for rationality and autonomy; therefore he *must* have intended to exclude them from civic participation in the general will.[43] But this is an extrapolation, rather than something explicitly professed as an article of Rousseau's civic doctrine. If this was Rousseau's view, why didn't he spell it out?[44] The same goes for other feminist critiques directed at Rousseau: theorists such as Susan Okin,[45] Carole Pateman,[46] and Jean Ehlstain[47] analyze the sexism of *Emile*, *La Nouvelle Héloïse*, the *Second Discourse*, the *Letter to d'Alembert*, the *Geneva Manuscript*, and the *Discourse on Political Economy*. None of these critics of Rousseau cites the *Social Contract* as evidence of his sexism, for the simple reason that there's nothing in the text that explicitly excludes female citizens. As Margaret Canovan says, "In the *Social Contract* Rousseau did not mention female citizenship even to refute it."[48] *Why not?*

All of this serves to cast in an even starker light Kant's categorical and incontrovertible statements of female subordination in *his* doctrine of citizenship. Now it may well be that for Rousseau and his eighteenth-century readers, the ineligibility for citizenship status of women was so obvious—

as obvious as it was for Kant—that it seemed redundant to spell it out. On this interpretation, Kant, with his greater honesty and forthrightness, simply made explicit what to Rousseau seemed not to require articulation in his authoritative treatise on citizenship. (Or maybe Rousseau thought that while an understanding of deep gender differences was highly relevant to reflection on ways of living, it *wasn't* relevant to a treatise laying out "principles of political right"?) In any case, I think it makes a significant theoretical difference when one makes a decision to lay down as official doctrine, so to speak (which Kant does but Rousseau doesn't) a view of citizenship that so blatantly contradicts one's moral egalitarianism. In omitting to *spell out* the limits of citizen status in his doctrine of right, it's as if Rousseau leaves room for eligibility for citizenship status to be renegotiated at some future point in the history of citizenship.[49] One could say that Kant does just the opposite: he tries to lay out a principled argument (however unconvincing) for explicit restrictions on citizenship.

As Mendus points out, Kant himself more or less *concedes*, at the very point at which he first articulates the distinction between active and passive citizens in MM, that "the concept of a passive citizen seems to contradict the concept of a citizen as such" [*mit der Erklärung des Begriffs von einem Staatsbürger überhaupt im widerspruch zu stehen scheint*].[50] Of course, he hastens to say that the apparent contradiction between the notion of passive citizenship and "the concept of a citizen as such" is a mere "difficulty" [*Schwierigkeit*] that can be "removed" [*zu heben*] by considering examples of these two categories of citizenship (full citizen and partial citizen). But really, the cat has been let out of the bag: although Kant denies it, the telling admission that passive citizenship stands *prima facie* in contradiction with "the concept of a citizen as such" lets slip that freedom, equality, and independence actually form an integral moral package. This is what the reference to "the definition of the concept of a citizen as such" conjures up—the inextricability of our moral status and our civic status. What generates the "apparent" contradiction that Kant acknowledges is precisely the intuition that freedom, equality, and independence are inseparably bound up together as aspects of a single moral "package," built into the very logic of the concept of citizenship.[51] Hence, in claiming that his examples "resolve the difficulty," Kant is attempting to resist the implicitly civic implications of his own moral thinking—a kind of inevitable "spillover" from his moral philosophy into the domain of civic life.

In order to resist or roll back this spillover from his moral philosophy to his civic philosophy, Kant must somehow detach independence from the broader egalitarian package: associating *freedom* with the *humanity* of members of the state and *equality* with their status as *subjects* is Kant's way of allowing for a mode of citizenship that is *not* a guarantee of full freedom and equality (hence: "this [civic] inequality is . . . in no way opposed to their freedom and equality *as human beings*").[52] Independence, rather than being an *entailment* of citizenship as a properly moral status, instead becomes the *condition* of an experience of full citizenship that is available to some but not available to others. This line of argument only works if citizenship is not itself implicated in our moral status as free and equal. We can sum up our suspicions about Kant's theoretical strategy by saying that "civil personality" has the "look" of a moral status, or at least a quasi-moral status, hence it seems implausible that one could deny civil personality to members of the state without simultaneously detracting from their freedom and equality (i.e., their moral dignity).[53] In conceding that the definition of the concept of a citizen as such appears to be in tension with the notion of a division into full and partial citizens, it's as if Kant is anticipating the trajectory of his thought from moral to civic equality, and taking countermeasures to defeat this trajectory.

Kant could perhaps respond that we are interpreting freedom, equality, and independence as more moral than he intends; he could say that he's using these terms in a *political* sense that's strictly distinct from their meaning in his moral philosophy. Liberty—in the context of the doctrine of right—means that it's not for the *state* to decide what will make its citizens happy. Equality means all subjects of the commonwealth are subject to the same system of laws defining a community of right. Independence means we have proven ourselves worthy of participating actively in the representation of our own civic personality. Insofar as these ideas compose a package, it's a *political* package, quite distinct from autonomy, equality, and self-responsibility in the sphere of morality. One's *moral* status is not at stake in a set of arrangements that allow different individuals to pursue their own happiness in their own way, and that mandates shared subjection to laws that enable this scheme of reciprocal liberty.

If Kant's "low-liberal" account of membership in a state was the whole story, then I think this response might well be sufficient. But I'm convinced that there's also a "high-liberal" dimension to Kant's thinking about citizenship (even if he himself tacitly denies it)—that is, a notion of the *dignity* of the citizen as someone who belongs to the community of right, the notion of the inner worth of those who participate in a "sublime," because rightful, organization of civic life. And we get a better sense of the latter by glancing sideways at what autonomy, equality, and inner worth mean in Kant's account of moral life.

The above analysis may prompt the following response: Why should anyone *expect* Kant, living in the nonliberal Prussian state of the late eighteenth century, to endorse strongly egalitarian civic norms? Offering one version of such a response, Susan Shell argues that, *relative to political norms then prevailing in Europe* (apart from postrevolutionary France), Kant's civic vision is still a radical one, for it defines *self-employment* ("labour[ing] at self-imposed tasks") rather than *leisure* as the criterion of full citizenship; he thereby shifts the political horizon (in accordance with the spirit of the French Revolution) from the nobility to the bourgeoisie.[54] This may well be true; yet the ultimate philosophical standard for judging Kant's political philosophy is not whether it looks liberal or reactionary in relation to his own context, but rather the standard set by his own philosophy (i.e., the rigorously egalitarian principles of his moral philosophy). If there is an incoherency between his moral philosophy and his political philosophy, Shell's contextualist defence of Kant's liberalism doesn't seem sufficient. One can also ask more generally whether Kant himself would welcome defenses of his political thought that take the position that one must adjust one's critical judgment of his politics in the light of what one could pragmatically hope for in Kant's own (illiberal) political context. After all, Kant himself of course insists throughout his political writings that politics is not about pragmatism but about *right*— that is, *timeless* rather than context-bound principles of what is owed to citizens by virtue of the source of their moral dignity. "True politics can . . . not take a step without having already paid homage to morals. . . . The right of human beings must be held sacred. . . . One cannot compromise here and devise something intermediate, a pragmatically conditioned right (a cross between right and expediency); instead, all politics must bend its knee before right."[55]

To return to the argument that we started with: lack of full citizenship status may perhaps seem less of an injustice if citizens are merely devils with understanding who contrive a mechanism that allows them to pursue their self-seeking inclinations without colliding into each other. The injustice is substantially greater if citizenship is actually a crucial expression of our human dignity. Ultimately, it's hard to see how Kant can avoid opting for the more elevated of these two conceptions of the civic condition. As we saw above, even in the "intelligent devils" passage itself, Kant speaks of the republican constitution as a "sublime form of constitution" [*einer Verfassung von so sublimer Form*] because it alone embodies "the right of human beings" [*dem Recht der Menschen*]. According to the civic vision laid out by Kant, the state acknowledges our *freedom* as human beings and grants us *equality* as subjects. But as for *independence*, the token of full civic status, it is something whose achievement or nonachievement reposes on us as responsible individuals. Therefore, unlike freedom and equality, independence is not a given but something that certain individuals *achieve* (although it seems that this achievement is, for reasons that Kant doesn't specify, beyond the reach of women per se). To be capable of freedom, equality, *and* independence is what constitutes a complete civic existence for human beings, whereas many or most individuals even in a liberal society as Kant conceptualizes it will have to satisfy themselves with an incomplete civic existence. This accomplishment of civic completion is what Kant calls civil personality [*der bürgerlichen Persönlichkeit*], and we are never given satisfactory reasons why any free and equal human being should ever settle for less than this.

One hopes that Kant's sexism is effectively dead as a theoretical option for political philosophers, and that no contemporary theorist would try either to justify Kant or to come up with their own version of his unattractive arguments. But what is perhaps *not* a closed question for political philosophers is the relationship between "civil personality" and moral personality, and it is on account of its relevance for *that* question that we thought it might be worthwhile to take one last look at Kant's outmoded and discredited sexual politics.

Notes

1. See Richard E. Flathman, "Citizenship and Authority: A Chastened View of Citizenship," in *Theorizing Citizenship*, ed. R. Beiner (Albany: State University of New York Press, 1995), 105–51. Flathman presents Rousseau and Hannah Arendt as exemplars of "high citizenship," and Hobbes and Michael Oakeshott as exemplars of "low citizenship." Flathman himself aligns himself with the low citizenship view.

2. As far as Hegel is concerned, consider his statement that "the individual . . . finds that, in fulfilling his duties as a citizen, he gains protection for his person and property, consideration for his particular welfare, and satisfaction of his substantial essence, the consciousness and self-awareness of being a member of the whole," in *Elements of the Philosophy of Right*, ed. Allen W. Wood (Cambridge: Cambridge University Press, 1991), 285; I have slightly amended the translation. The phrase "satisfaction of his substantial essence" [*die Befriedigung seines substantiellen Wesens*] clearly points to a quite elevated high-liberal view. As for contemporary theorists of citizenship, it's possible to view John Rawls as the exponent of a fairly ambitious version of high-liberal citizenship. Consider the suggestion by Rawls that what political liberalism basically means is that "the values of the special domain of the political . . . normally outweigh whatever values [associated with other domains of social life] may conflict with them," where it can be presumed that *citizenship* is the specific status conferred and upheld by the domain of the political, over against subordinate moral identities made available within other subdomains. John Rawls, *Political Liberalism* (New York: Columbia University Press, 1996), 139; cf. 157. I owe this citation, as well as the interpretation that highlights its importance, to William Galston. See William A. Galston, *The Practice of Liberal Pluralism* (Cambridge: Cambridge University Press, 2005), 38–40. See also note 53 below.

3. *Toward Perpetual Peace*, in *Practical Philosophy*, trans. and ed. Mary J. Gregor (Cambridge: Cambridge University Press, 1996), 335; (8:366). All citations from Kant are located by volume and page number of *Kants gesammelte Schriften*, ed. Königlich Preußische Akademie der Wissenschaften, 29 vols. (Berlin: de Gruyter, 1900–). Unless otherwise indicated, translations are from *The Cambridge Edition of the Works of Immanuel Kant*, 13 vols., ed. Paul Guyer and Allen W. Wood (Cambridge: Cambridge University Press, 1992–). Hannah Arendt, *Lectures on Kant's Political Philosophy*, ed. R.

Beiner (Chicago: University of Chicago Press, 1982), 17–18, lets Kant off the hook much too easily when she interprets this passage as expressing Kant's impulse to insulate public life from "moralistic" concerns ("he kept away from all moralizing"). For the question is why citizenship isn't related to, or doesn't participate in, the moral status, and therefore moral dignity, of human beings, and this question has nothing to do with the issue of how to avoid "moralism."

4. Consider, for instance, Kant's formulation in *Religion within the Limits of Reason Alone*, trans. Theodore M. Greene and Hoyt H. Hudson (New York: Harper & Row, 1960), 87: "In an already existing political commonwealth all the political citizens, as such, are in an *ethical state of nature* and are entitled to remain therein," because one can gain entry to an *ethical* commonwealth only by a free exercise of virtue, by contrast to the coercive character of the state; "woe to the legislator who wishes to establish through force a polity directed to ethical ends!" (6:95–96).

5. To be sure, we encounter a bit of a complication in characterizing Hobbes's account of the social contract in this way, insofar as Hobbes has his own version of the Kantian doctrine that we are (morally) *obliged* to exit from the state of nature. This comes in Hobbes's doctrine of the "law of nature," which states precisely that we are obliged to move from the insecurity of the natural state to the security offered by the civil state: "men are commanded to endeavour Peace" (*Leviathan*, chapter 14). But since Hobbes doesn't really allow us to distinguish what is dictated as a matter of moral obligation from what is dictated by our interests, the appeal to "laws of nature" is something of a rhetorical trick, as I think Hobbes himself realizes (as he indicates at the end of *Leviathan*, chapter 15).

6. In *The Metaphysics of Morals* (hereafter MM), Kant offers the following formulation: The constitution of the state "is that condition which reason, *by a categorical imperative*, makes it obligatory for us to strive after." In *Practical Philosophy*, ed. Gregor, 461 (6:318).

7. This (not minimal but fairly robust) moral dimension of the state is acknowledged by Kant in the passage quoted above when he refers to the republican constitution as "a sublime form of constitution" because it expresses, uniquely, "the right of human beings." One should add that, alongside Kant's "low-liberal" and "high-liberal" conceptions of citizenship, there are corresponding "low-liberal" and "high-liberal" conceptions of *right*. In one place, Kant defines right as "the limitation of the freedom of each to the condition of its harmony with the freedom of everyone"— clearly a "low-liberal" definition. "On the Common Saying: 'That May Be Correct in Theory, but It Is of No Use in Practice'" (hereafter TP), in *Practical Philosophy*, ed. Gregor, 290 (8:289–290); cf. 293 (8:292). But if republicanism is a "sublime" form of constitution, then it must instantiate a more elevated conception of right than this definition conveys.

8. TP, 295 (8:295); MM, 458 (6:314–15).

9. TP, 295 (8:295).

10. TP, 292–94 (8:291–94).

11. MM, 458 (6:315).

12. TP, 294 (8:294).

13. MM, 458 (6:314). It's possible to interpret the last of these characterizations as implying a lower status than the others. This is what is intimated in TP, 291 (8:290),

where Kant refers to "the *independence* of every member of the commonwealth" [*Die Selbstständigkeit jedes Gliedes eines gemeinen Wesens*], which suggests that those who have not risen to independence are not really members of the commonwealth at all. Indeed, one way of formulating what the distinction between active citizens and passive citizens means is that the former are the real *citizens* (lawgivers); the latter, mere *subjects* of the commonwealth (subject to the law and enjoying the law's protection). So interpreted, this would be a real break with Rousseau's idea of citizenship, since it would annul the reciprocity between being sovereign source of the law (at least in some sense—obviously in a more attenuated sense in Kant than in Rousseau) and being subject to its provisions.

14. MM, 458 (6:314).

15. TP, 296–97 (8:297).

16. TP, 297n. (8:297): "they [the subjects] are not entitled to appraise this [e.g., a war tax]."

17. MM, 458 (6:314).

18. MM, 459 (6:315).

19. MM, 458 (6:314–15); TP, 295n. (8:295).

20. MM, 458 (6:315). The phrase "*blos handlanger des gemeinen Wesens*" can also be translated: "mere odd-jobbers of the commonwealth"—which reinforces the point that their status as "underlings" follows from their lack of an established (i.e., middle-class) trade.

21. For a similar observation (namely, that Kant is lucky enough to hold a form of employment that constitutes a happy exception from his general principle of civic exclusion), see Hans Reiss, "Kant's Politics and the Enlightenment: Reflections on Some Recent Studies," in *Political Theory* 27, no. 2 (1999): 250; and "Postscript," in Immanuel Kant, *Political Writings*, ed. Hans Reiss, 2nd enl. ed. (Cambridge: Cambridge University Press, 1991), 257.

22. TP, 295 (8:295): what makes the citizen fully a citizen is that "he *serves* no one other than the commonwealth."

23. Note the crucial exemption, "except the state," in MM's account of how being in the service of others is a civic disqualification: MM, 458 (6:314).

24. TP, 295 (8:295).

25. Ibid. Applying this mode of analysis to the distinction between teachers and tutors, one would have to say that teachers have a skill that *they* own that can be sold like a commodity; whereas tutors, on the other hand, *sell their labor*, which is precisely tantamount to selling themselves. But again, one wonders: is Kant as a state-employed teacher fully master of his own labor?

26. TP, 295n. (8:295).

27. *Religion within the Limits of Reason Alone*, 176n. (6:188).

28. TP, 295 (8:295).

29. TP, 293 (8:293).

30. Ibid.

31. Ibid.

32. See Susan Mendus, "Kant: 'An Honest but Narrow-Minded Bourgeois'?," in *Essays on Kant's Political Philosophy*, ed. Howard Lloyd Williams (Chicago: University of Chicago Press, 1992), 166–90, esp. 170–74. Cf. Susan Moller Okin, *Women in*

Western Political Thought (Princeton: Princeton University Press, 1979), 6: for Kant, "the only characteristic that *permanently* disqualifies any person from citizenship in the state . . . is that of being born female" (my italics).

33. MM, 459 (6:315).

34. TP, 293 (8:292); cf. 293 (8:293): "There can be no innate prerogative of one member of a commonwealth over another as fellow subjects, and no one can bequeath to his descendants the prerogative of the *rank* which he has within a commonwealth. . . . [Those who are economically superior] may not prevent [those who are economically inferior from exercising their right] to raise themselves to like circumstances if their talent, their industry, and their luck make this possible for them."

35. On the other hand, Kant also insists that disadvantaged members of the society should expect no help from the state in raising themselves up to this condition of economic independence. As Roger Scruton has I think rightly argued, as a theorist of justice Kant is certainly far closer to Hayek than to Rawls. See Scruton, "Contract, Consent, and Exploitation: Kantian Themes," in *Essays on Kant's Political Philosophy*, 213–27.

36. Also relevant, as Lucas Thorpe has helpfully pointed out to me, is what Kant sees as the differential attitudes toward work on the part of the two sexes: men need to be industrious, whereas women need merely to be "occupied," that is, busied with amusements, however idle. See Immanuel Kant, *Lectures on Ethics*, ed. Peter Heath and J. B. Schneewind (Cambridge: Cambridge University Press, 1997), 164–65 (27:396).

37. MM, 428 (6:279); cf. TP, 292: "a wife [must obey] her husband" (8: 242).

38. MM, 458 (6:314); my italics. "Frauenzimmer" is a derogatory term for women in current German usage, but it was a neutral term in older German usage. (A rough counterpart in English would be "dame," which is a coarse term in contemporary usage but a genteel term in archaic usage.) Mendus claims that Kant places a less severe clamp upon female citizenship in MM than in TP ("Kant: 'An Honest but Narrow-Minded Bourgeois'?," 170–72), but this text suggests otherwise.

39. Mendus, "Kant: 'An Honest but Narrow-Minded Bourgeois'?" 176.

40. However, the view that Mendus attributes to Kant *is* expressed by Rousseau: see Okin, *Women in Western Political Thought*, 165.

41. "*Bemerkungen zu den Beobachtungen über das Gefühl des Schönen und Erhabenen*" (20:44). Kant says that prior to being inspired by Rousseau to become an egalitarian, he "despised" [*verachtete*] the "ignorant rabble" [*den Pöbel der von nichts weis*]. This phrase gives one a good sense of just how big a leap Kant needed to make in order to get from his preegalitarian self to his egalitarian self.

42. Okin, for instance, devotes no less than four chapters of *Women in Western Political Thought* to Rousseau, yet she makes only passing references to Kant.

43. Lynda Lange, "Rousseau: Women and the General Will," in *The Sexism of Social and Political Theory: Women and Reproduction from Plato to Nietzsche*, ed. Lorenne M. G. Clark and Lynda Lange (Toronto: University of Toronto Press, 1979), 41–52. Carole Pateman makes a similar argument in *The Sexual Contract* (Stanford: Stanford University Press, 1988), 100–102. Lange refers to the unforgettable story of the Spartan mother narrated by Rousseau near the beginning of *Emile* (Lange, 50), but, strangely, she doesn't see this as evidence that Rousseau was able to imagine women as exemplary citizens. See Jean-Jacques Rousseau, *Emile or On Education*, trans. Allan Bloom (New York: Basic Books, 1979), 40. Cf. Margaret Canovan, "Rousseau's Two Concepts of

Citizenship," in *Women in Western Political Philosophy*, ed. Ellen Kennedy and Susan Mendus (Brighton: Wheatsheaf Books, 1987), 89, 90. The closest that Rousseau comes to an explicit exclusion of women from citizenship is in *Emile*, 362–63: "In his *Republic*, Plato gives women the same exercises as men. I can well believe it! Having removed private families from his regime and no longer knowing what to do with women, he found himself forced to make them men. . . . [Plato's fatal mistake consisted in] that civil promiscuity which throughout confounds the two sexes in the same employments and in the same labors and which cannot fail to engender the most intolerable abuses. I speak of that subversion of the sweetest sentiments of nature, sacrificed to an artificial sentiment which can only be maintained by them—as though there were no need for a natural base on which to form conventional ties; as though the love of one's nearest were not the principle of the love one owes the state; as though it were not by means of the small fatherland which is the family that the heart attaches itself to the large one; as though it were not the good son, the good husband, and the good father who make the good citizen!" Jean Bethke Elshtain's summary of Rousseau's teaching concerning gender in book 5 of *Emile* is apt: "boys . . . are in training for citizenship, and girls . . . are preparing for their roles as virtuous and noble wives." *Public Man, Private Woman: Women in Social and Political Thought*, 2nd ed. (Princeton: Princeton University Press, 1993), 160. See also Jean-Jacques Rousseau, *Politics and the Arts: Letter to M. d'Alembert on the Theatre*, trans. Allan Bloom (Ithaca: Cornell University Press, 1968), 87: "Even if it could be denied that a special sentiment of chasteness was natural to women, would it be any the less true that in society their lot ought to be a domestic and retired life"?

44. The view that Lange and others attribute to Rousseau, namely, that women are naturally incapable of autonomy, is made more or less explicit at the beginning of "What Is Enlightenment?," where Kant associates "the entire fair sex" with self-incurred tutelage: "An Answer to the Question: What Is Enlightenment?," in *Practical Philosophy*, ed. Gregor, 17 (8:35). The response to this passage by Kant's friend, J. G. Hamann, seems on target: Kant "slanders [women] like an old bachelor"; see Johann Georg Hamann, "Letter to Christian Jacob Kraus," trans. Garrett Green, in *What Is Enlightenment? Eighteenth-Century Answers and Twentieth-Century Questions*, ed. James Schmidt (Berkeley: University of California Press, 1996), 148.

45. Okin, *Women in Western Political Thought*, chaps. 5–8, esp. chap. 7. Okin (167) highlights the text in *Emile*, p. 448, where Emile is informed by his tutor: "When you become the head of a family [*chef de famille*], you are going to become a member of the state"—implying that only heads of households (i.e., males) become citizens.

46. Pateman, *The Sexual Contract*, 53–54, 96–102.

47. Elshtain, *Public Man, Private Woman*, 148–70. Elshtain and Okin both cite a strong statement of female subordination from the *Geneva Manuscript*, which is clearly dropped from the final version of the *Social Contract* (the corresponding text in the latter work refers only to the relationship between fathers and children). This in itself suggests that Rousseau thought that it was inconsistent with the purposes of the *Social Contract* to distinguish sharply between the status of men and women. The same text is used by Rousseau in his *Discourse on Political Economy* (in fact, Rousseau may have simply borrowed the passage in the *Geneva Manuscript* from the latter work). In any case, in both works, the explicit context is the radical *difference* between relationships

of authority in the household and those in the political community, so even if Rousseau had a sexist and patriarchal view of the household, by his own argument, nothing follows for principles of political rule from the fact that "the father should command *in the family*." Rousseau himself makes this explicit: "Nothing of this kind [i.e., command by the head of the household over his wife, his children, and his servants] exists in political society." Elshtain, 158; Okin, 146–47; Jean-Jacques Rousseau, *On the Social Contract*, ed. Roger D. Masters, trans. Judith R. Masters (New York: St. Martin's Press, 1978), 170 ("Geneva Manuscript"); 47 ("On the Social Contract"); 210 ("Discourse on Political Economy").

48. Canovan, "Rousseau's Two Concepts of Citizenship," 85.

49. Why would Rousseau implicitly leave space for citizenship to be later renegotiated? Jean Elshtain provides a possible answer to this question. She argues that Rousseau *knew* that women would be unlikely to be happy in the private household to which he confines them, and that the patriarchal family, even as he celebrates it, is ultimately "doomed." See *Public Man, Private Woman*, 162. The question then becomes: if women themselves ultimately reject the domestic roles that Rousseau wants to persuade them to embrace, what do "principles of political right" say about refusing or conceding the civic rights they then demand?

50. MM, 458 (6:314). See Mendus, "Kant: 'An Honest but Narrow-Minded Bourgeois'?," 169–70.

51. It's significant that in the MM account of citizenship, unlike the TP account, freedom, equality, and independence are all given a *civic* meaning. For instance, freedom is associated with "the attribute of obeying no other law than that to which [the citizen] has given his consent" (MM, 457; 6:314). If so, then those denied citizenship by virtue of lacking independence are *also* thereby denied freedom.

52. MM, 458 (6:315).

53. This is expressed, for instance, in John Rawls's account of personhood *cum* citizenship: "a person is someone who can be a citizen, that is, a fully cooperating member of society over a complete life." "Justice as Fairness: Political not Metaphysical," in John Rawls, *Collected Papers*, ed. Samuel Freeman (Cambridge: Harvard University Press, 1999), 397.

54. Susan Meld Shell, *The Rights of Reason: A Study of Kant's Philosophy and Politics* (Toronto: University of Toronto Press, 1980), 158.

55. *Toward Perpetual Peace*, in *Practical Philosophy*, 347 (8:380). I've pushed this argument pretty hard. On the other hand, Lucas Thorpe has made the helpful point to me that if Kant's sexism in his theory of citizenship is a case of "bad application of good principles," then attention to Kant's historical context might be a reasonable way of trying to understand why Kant didn't apply his egalitarian principles more coherently. Cf. Charles Taylor, *Modern Social Imaginaries* (Durham: Duke University Press, 2004), 146: "The people of [the late eighteenth century] can easily seem to us to be inconsistent, even hypocritical. Elite males spoke of rights, equality, and the republic, but thought nothing of keeping indentured servants . . . and kept their women, children, their households in general under traditional patriarchal power. Didn't they see the glaring contradiction?" Taylor's response is that our late-modern view of this expresses a failure to appreciate how deeply patriarchy shaped the "social imaginary" of that epoch.

Kant's Conception of the Nation-State and the Idea of Europe

Susan M. Shell

Conceptual and moral difficulties surrounding the question of Europe are often both signaled by appeals to Immanuel Kant. From the ambiguously Kantian "ode to joy" that the European Union has made its anthem, to Derrida's and Habermas's joint reference to what they call "the Kantian hope in a global domestic politics,"[1] to the invocation by Joseph Weiler, Gerald Delanty, and others of the Kantian principle of "autonomy" as a grounding norm of European commonality—one is constantly encountering what one good European famously called the "the great Chinaman of Königsberg."[2] Indeed, political analyst Robert Kagan has gone so far as to call the aspiration of many Europeans today a "Kantian paradise"—in contrast with what he regards as the sounder "Hobbesianism" of the United States.[3]

In what follows I will attempt to show that some, though not all, such identifications of Kant with current visions of Europe are misplaced, or at least based on a misunderstanding of Kant's own, and arguably superior, solution to the problems of the nation-state with which current theorists are grappling. In particular, I will argue that some of the tensions, or polarities, between affective identity and rationalization (or eros and civilization, as Joseph Weiler has wittily put it)[4] were more satisfactorily addressed by Kant prior to the emergence of romantic nationalism. Subsequent postmodern efforts to deal with the excesses of romantic (and postromantic) nationalism have failed to appreciate Kant's own solution, as it were, before the fact, a solution that the romantics, for reasons of their own, may have too precipitously discarded. This failure of understanding is deepened rather than corrected by postmodern appropriations of Kant's mantle. Such problematic invocations typically replace Kantian moral norms in their original sense with an ethic of "otherness" (as if one could have one's universals while denying them too.) A further consequence of my analysis is to suggest that there may be fewer genuine differences of principle between Europe and the United States than sometimes appears. Old-fashioned conflicts of interest currently dividing Europe and the United States may masquerade in both directions in a misleadingly idealized dress. The United States is more "Kantian" in its self-understanding than either Europe or the United States is inclined to realize or acknowledge. And Europe, to the extent that it wishes to uphold human rights in a roughly Kantian sense, cannot deem itself as different from the United States as some might like.

At the same time, I would not want to deny that Kant's conception of the nation-state, and a related understanding of the possibilities and limits of a united Europe, give rise to their own dilemmas and negative temptations. In infusing the nation-state (and Europe generally) with an informing spiritual goal (that they had lacked in earlier liberal formulations), Kant breaks with earlier liberal thought by bringing a sort of "religion of humanity" into the public sphere. The results were not altogether benign, as his own flirtations with racism and anti-Semitism make clear. But such temptations, as I will try to argue, are resistible on Kantian grounds rather than overriding.

Europe, of course, has meant many things to many people, as Professor Delanty masterfully shows in his *Inventing Europe*.[5] I will not try to recapitulate his findings. But it will be useful (since our orientations and purposes are somewhat different) to outline a few stopping points in the intertwinement of ideas of Europe with the development of modern political thought more generally, to better understand the problem of Europe as Kant himself understood it:

First: a premodern period, in which the term "Europe" is mainly used to designate a general geographic region extending northward and westward from the western shores of the Mediterranean.

Second: an early modern period in which the term "Europe" is also increasingly used as a synonym for Western or Roman Christendom, especially by those (such as Francis Bacon) who regard Christianity as deeply problematic, both in itself and in its political and moral effects. For such early modern thinkers, "Europe" is a convenient label for an area of particular distress and opportunity, whose fractious politics make "new modes and orders"[6] possible and necessary.

Third: a later modern period in which the idea of Europe is entwined with new notions of man's historical malleability (no doubt partly stimulated by the discovery of the Americas). Increasingly, I would argue, Europe is conceived (by Montesquieu, Rousseau, and others) as the peculiar site from which human history decisively originates, be it owing to peculiarities of climate and related sexual practices (Montesquieu), or an accidental conjunction of plentiful natural supplies of wheat and iron (Rousseau), or other factors entirely. For Rousseau especially, of course, this process is decidedly ambiguous. Europeans may, as a consequence, have enjoyed the best and most long lasting political orders (at least prior to the emergence of Christianity); but they were also cut off sooner and more irrevocably than peoples of other continents from the prepolitical or tribal condition he calls "the happiest and most durable known to man."[7]

Rousseau's most comprehensive, albeit largely palliative, solution for a Christian and post-Christian Europe in which true citizenship is, for the most part, no longer possible is sketched out in his *Emile*, an educational novel that ought to constitute, he says, the "history of the species."[8]

This very brief account brings us, finally, to Kant, whose germinal "idea" of Europe first appears in an early (and very popular) work that explicitly takes up Rousseau's challenge. *Observations on the Feeling of the Beautiful and the Sublime*, published in 1762, almost twenty years before the appearance of the first *Critique* and almost thirty before the French Revolution, represents a high-water mark of Kant's early, quasi-romantic hopes for "an aesthetic education of the human race," i.e., for what he will later call "communication."[9]

> [Now that] the human genius [displayed in ancient Greece and Rome] has happily lifted itself out of an almost complete destruction [in the Middle Ages] by a kind of palingenesis, we see in our own times the proper taste for the beautiful and noble bloom in the arts and sciences as well as with regard to the moral; and there is nothing more to be wished for than that the false brilliance, which so readily deceives, should not distance us unnoticed from noble simplicity, but especially that the as yet undiscovered secret of education should be torn away from the old delusion in order early to raise moral feeling in the breast of every young world citizen. (2:256)[10]

The key to such an education, according to Kant, is a combined feeling for the beautiful and the sublime or noble—a feeling that is unique to European nations, as expressed above all in the peculiar idealization that there attends the relation of the sexes. On the basis of this relation (a generalized version of the courtship of Emile and Sophie), the "flower" of Europe (as he puts it elsewhere) can be restored and made transparent to itself—once the secret of education is "torn away" from the ancient illusion.

The history of Europe, at this stage of Kant's thinking, is the palingenetic story of the "human genius," whose medium is an all too protean "taste."[11] Kant's effort to fix that medium (in moral feeling) founders here on a still undisclosed "secret" of civil and moral education—a problem that his later work will claim to solve. What is especially noteworthy for present purposes is the special role for Germany that Kant carves out in this his own signal contribution to an emerging literary German language. The vitality of the human genius arises through a balancing of the various humors peculiar to each European nation, an aesthetic task for which Germans seem especially well suited. Lacking in both the effeminate beauty of France and the too masculine sublimity of England, Germany excels, somehow, in sublimity and beauty in balanced combination. As such, it seems poised to do for Europe (by way of harmonizing the extremes) what Europe does for mankind as a whole. Germany, in short, replaces Greece (whom Aristotle had held up as a model) in furnishing a mean in which humanity takes on its richest and most vital form.[12] As Germany reconciles the humoral extremes of Europe (whose mixture of the beautiful and the sublime is otherwise out of balance), so Europe reconciles the humoral extremes exhibited on other continents (whose peoples do not combine a feeling for the beautiful and the sublime at all). This lack, it must be said, leads Kant, at this time, to doubt non-Europeans' capacity for genuine moral feeling—a status, to be sure, they share with the vast majority of European men and perhaps all women.

How can such an idea of Europe (not to speak of women and the vast majority of European men) be reconciled with the moral universalism of his later work, with its emphatic insistence on the equal dignity of every human being as a co-legislator of the moral law? Is it a youthful experiment, which Kant subsequently drops (with his discovery of the categorical imperative rooted in the principle of human autonomy)? Or does it linger on, in subtle and not so subtle forms? The answer, I believe, is complicated.

Kant's early idea of Europe as the unique vehicle of man's spiritual advancement is never altogether put to rest. Indeed, in some ways it reaches an even higher pitch—as in his later theories of race (of which he proudly claimed to be the first to form a "philosophic concept"), and in opinions he advanced orally in his courses on anthropology or—in a form even more extreme—committed to private notes. Kant's politics are exposed, one might say, to an early and lingering continentalist (and later racialist) temptation. It is a temptation, however, to which—or so I will claim—his politics need not, and for the most part, does not, give way.

Kant's continentalism is most dubious when it flirts with biological determinism (as it sometimes does, albeit only once in print (if we limit our inquiry to his later work), and then only in a brief remark, in which the inferior moral capacities of non-Whites is advanced as an unproven and perhaps improvable suspicion.)[13] But there is another version—another view of the superiority of Europe—that is entirely consistent with his official moral teaching and the account of history that accompanies it. On this view, the political and spiritual advantage of Europe is merely cultural and altogether temporary. What is more, it cuts both ways. Kant's official view of Europe—the one that he publicized—takes both optimistic and pessimistic forms. Europe's advantages also make it vulnerable to unprecedented moral and political deformities. Europe, according to Kant's official teaching, is (almost) as likely to destroy humanity as to fulfill it.

I have written elsewhere about Kant's darker vision of a potentially self-cannibalizing Europe, a vision clearest in certain passages from *Perpetual Peace* in which one can almost smell the smoke of Verdun.[14] Kant's official view of Europe shows its sunnier face in several of his well-known essays on history. In the "Idea for a Universal History," for example, he gives pride of place to Europe, not because nothing politically noteworthy can have happened elsewhere, but because only in Europe has there existed unin-terruptedly (beginning with Thucydides) an "educated public" that can "authenticate" the ancient accounts (8:29). Europe is the "historical" conti-nent par excellence in the sense that it alone has a continuous public mem-ory. Beginning with the Greeks, peoples of Europe have kept track of their own doings in a way that allows them to transmit the fruits of their political experience to later generations. Entrance into that collective memory marks the beginning of the "true history" of other peoples (such as the Jews), whose isolated and episodic reports would otherwise gain little credit, and which constitute a kind of "terra incognita."[15]

A concluding passage from Kant's *Critique of Aesthetic Judgment* (1790) contains a related discussion of the political history of Europe, a passage that responds so neatly to the conclusion of the *Observations* written thirty years earlier as to suggest that Kant had the earlier work specifically in mind. I quote the passage nearly in full:

> The propedeutic to all fine art, insofar as it concerns itself with the highest degree of its perfection, seems to lie, not in precepts but in the culture [Cul-tur] of the forces of the mind through that foreknowledge that we call the humanities [humaniora], presumably because humanity [Humanität] signifies, on the one hand, the feeling of universal sympathy [Theilnehmungsgefühl], and on the other, the capacity to be able to communicate [mittheilen] universally and very intimately. When these two qualities are combined they constitute a sociability suited to our humanity [Menschheit], and distinguish it from animal limitedness. The age, as well as the peoples, in which the strong drive toward lawful sociability, through which a people constitutes a lasting commonwealth [gemeines Wesen], wrestled with the great difficulties that surround the hard task of uniting freedom (and thus equality) with a compulsion (more that of respect and submission from duty than that of fear). Such an age and such a people would have had to first discover the art of reciprocal communication of the ideas of the most artificial part with the crude; they would have had to first discover the attunement [Abstimmung] of the expansion and refinement of the former to the natural simplicity and originality of the latter, and in this way that mean between high culture and sufficient nature, a mean that also constitutes the correct measure, given by no universal rule, even for taste, as common human sense.
>
> Later ages will make this model dispensable only with difficulty, for they will be ever further from nature; so that without enduring examples, they will hardly be in a condition even to form a concept of the happy combination, in one and the same people, of the lawful compulsion of the highest culture with the force and rightness of a free nature that feels its own worth.

However, taste is fundamentally a capacity of judging the rendering sensible of ethical ideas (by means of a certain analogy of reflection over both). The pleasure that taste declares valid for mankind as such . . . must indeed derive from this and from the resulting increase in receptivity to . . . moral feeling. It is thus clear that the true propedeutic for the grounding of taste is the development of ethical ideas and the culture of moral feeling; for only when sensibility is brought into harmony with moral feeling can genuine taste accept a determinate, unalterable form [*Form*]. (5:355–56)

In sum: ancient Greece, whose "strong drive" toward "lawful sociability" wrestled with the "hard task" of uniting "freedom" with "compulsion," presents a *nearly* indispensable model of republican endeavor. And the main reason to study the humanities (which transmits such models) is to help to educate free citizens at a time (like the present) when the natural love of freedom is increasingly occluded by civilized ways. The point is not the natural superiority of Europe (in which Kant may have privately believed) but its public commemoration and transmission of the spirit of civic life. Peoples other than the Greeks may have chanced upon the same discovery; they are not remembered.

There is another matter worthy of note: Kant admits the natural originality of peoples but he also doubts that that originality will long survive the onslaught of civilization. Peoples of the future will find themselves ever farther removed from the immediate sources of their original "wholeness." As Rousseau complains, there are no longer English, Italian, or French; there are only Europeans.[16] The solution, for Kant, is neither the historical pessimism of Rousseau nor the fanciful nostalgia of the romantics, but rather a bringing to full awareness of heretofore unconscious processes of national formation. The secret of Greek civic life lay in reciprocal communication between the educated and the popular classes, i.e., between a studied concern with coercive rules and a naïve sensualization of the rational idea of a community of free and equal beings. The symbiosis of rules and an original love of freedom—a symbiosis that marks the highest levels of individual artistic genius—also defines the genius of a people, making the ancient Greeks joint artists in their own national invention.[17] But ancient Greek civic life was not *merely* an invention, in the sense of arbitrary fiction; it was rather a particular embodiment—imperfect yet alive—of the rational idea of justice, an idea of which even the most philosophic of the Greeks were not yet fully conscious, as Kant's critique of Plato aims to show.[18] In bringing the republican idea to full rational clarity, Kant makes obsolete the naïve artistry of nation building at which the Greeks excelled, a natural simplicity that is no longer, in a Christian and post-Christian age, either possible or necessary.

What, then, is to replace Greece's naïve political artistry, beyond studying the humanities, a study that preserves Greek civic genius as a model for reflective judgment.[19] That question is addressed in Kant's later explanation, in *Anthropology from a Pragmatic Point of View*, of the difference between a people and a nation, a difference that has gone largely unnoticed in the literature. By the term "people" [*Volk, populus*], says Kant,

> we mean a group of human beings united in a territory, insofar as it constitutes a whole. This group, or the part of it that recognizes itself as united into a civil whole by common derivation, is a called a nation [*Nation, gens*]. That part that excepts itself from these laws (the savage [*wilde*] group in this people) is called rabble [*Pöbel, vulgus*], which, uniting against the law, becomes a mob [*Rottiren, agere per turbas*]—behavior that excludes them from the quality of a citizen. (7:311)[20]

So a lawless mob is, by definition, excluded from the nation, though it still may constitute a portion of the people, whose peculiar "wholeness" is a matter I'll return to. What is most significant for present purposes is that nationhood, unlike mere *Volkstum*, implies mutual recognition of submission to a common coercive legal framework that constitutes them as cocitizens:

> The human beings who constitute a people [*Volk*] can be represented as born from the soil [*Landeseingeborne*] according to an analogy of reproduction from a common ancestral stem [*Elterstamm*] (*congeniti*), even though this isn't so: yet in an intellectual and juridical sense, they can be represented as born from a common mother (the republic), so as to make up, as it were, a family (*gens, natio*), whose members (state citizens) are of equal birth, and who avoid, as ignoble, any commingling with those (savages [*Wilden*]) who may live around them in a state of nature. (MM, 6:343)

Unlike the ancient Greeks, who felicitously combined a taste for rules (associated with the few) with a taste for freedom (associated with the many), modern human beings are directly ennobled by the republican idea, an idea that Kant's philosophy first brings fully to light.

States are the vehicle through which a people becomes a nation. All states are nation-states. The double analogy of a "common derivation" both from the soil, as it were, and from the commonwealth (or *gemeines Wesen*) helps explain the transformation of human beings into citizens with distinct and potentially overriding rights and duties from which other human beings might be properly excluded. (The process also works the other way: when Kant wants to explain natural organic form, he compares it to the organization of a state.)[21] Citizenship implies a reciprocal, coercively enforced obligation to uphold the rights of other citizens—an obligation that does not apply with the same force and in the same way to others.

Citizens, according to Kant's adaptation of an ancient and a more recent political conceit, are familially related in a double sense: first, as still-savage children, as it were, of a common soil; second, as jointly ennobled sons of the republic. Without this shared double "natality," for which being human is not enough, men, in their capacity as purely moral beings, would hover over the world like angels (to borrow a conceit from Pierre Manent). Juridical man is embodied man (a "child of the earth") who takes up space and thus comes potentially into conflict with other human beings. Everyone excludes others from some portion of the globe, beginning with the place where he or she is born. Peoples arise, in both fact and right, from the debt of support that parents owe their children. Kant's account of citizenship acknowledges this debt (to which myths of "autochthony" fictionally attest), while subordinating to an ideal of civic re-creation.

In sum: the education of "young world citizens" no longer involves a mysterious and peculiarly European sublimization of the relation of the sexes (as in Kant's earlier work). Instead, it rests upon a new conception of the state, as the unity of law and freedom brought to life in the peculiar "spirit" of a nation, and accessible, in principle, to peoples everywhere.

This is not the place to develop fully a Kantian account of citizenship. It must suffice to note the following principles:

1. All human beings have rights to life, liberty, and the acquisition of property.
2. One cannot be coercively compelled to recognize the rights of others unless they are similarly compelled to recognize one's own.
3. A civil community consists of persons who recognize themselves to be reciprocally so obligated.
4. Obligations of citizenship include the duty to sacrifice one's own life and property when necessary (as determined by a fair and representative legislative process) for the survival of the civil community.

These principles may seem harsh by the standards of some contemporary humanitarians, who would like to blur the line between what we owe our fellow citizens and what we owe to others, and who are happy to impose heavy taxes on the rich while denying that anyone can be compelled to join the army.[22] These principles are crucial, however, to a proper Kantian understanding of the conditions of civic order, an order dependent on the existence of independent, sovereign states (with a right and willingness to defend themselves), and absent which so-called world citizenship is at best an idle dream. Sovereignty matters because its breach is an injury, in principle and in fact, to the rights of citizens to be self-governing. At the same time, Kant regards the state so conceived (i.e., as the sole arrangement under which we can be forced to give up our property and even, at times, our life, without doing violence to our rightful freedom) as the best possible school for inculcating respect for humanity at large. The state can best cultivate world citizenship by not seeking to assimilate it prematurely.

How does such a conception of citizenship articulate with the primary, territorially rooted ethnic affinity that Kant associates with peoples? If civil ordering converts peoples into nations, can states include a plurality of peoples, or is national unity necessarily linked to that of a single *populus*? What defines a *populus* as a "whole"? And what happens when two or more peoples claim a common territory? Kant indirectly addresses such questions by conceding that each of the "nations" of Europe is composed of many peoples. Over time, at least, separate peoples can come to form a single nation, whose members regard themselves as "co-descended," inasmuch as the union of the members is (presumed) to be inherited (6:343). This is all the more the case, inasmuch as Kant regards the key constituents of *Volkstum* to be language and religion (plus race, according to an unpublished draft).[23] To what extent can our civic "rebirth" as citizens override such popular, or *völkstümlisch* differences?

Kant had an opportunity to resolve this question decisively on the side of civic, over *völkstümlisch*, identity; and he had, I think, the moral and intellectual resources to do so. But in the end, he blinked, or at least equivocated, with arguably portentious consequences for the history of Germany and Europe. Jews represented, according to Kant's thinking, both a nation and a people. Could Jews and Germans be civically united? Could the Jewish physician Marcus Herz, whom Kant once called his most perceptive student, become a full-fledged Prussian citizen? Kant's answer was inconclusive. He did not say outright that Jews could not be Prussian citizens; but he did say that their acceptance of what he calls "the religion of Jesus" would mightily help their case. Thus Kant applauded, as a favorable moral and civil development, the (apparent) decision of Lazarus Ben David to adopt the Gospel (along with Jesus):

> We can consider [*halten*] the proposal of Ben David, a very good mind [*Kopf*] of that nation, to publicly accept the religion of Jesus (presumably with its vehicle, the Gospel), not only very fortunate but also the only proposal [*Vorschlag*] whose carrying out would soon make this people noticeable [*bemerklich machen*] as one that is learned, well-civilized and ready for all civil rights [whose faith could also be sanctioned by the government] without their having to amalgamate with others in [morally inessential] matters of faith. (7:53)

Adoption of the religion of the Gospels (interpreted in their own way) would make the Jewish people "noticeable" as one "ready for all civil rights," and this without having to fully amalgamate [*vermischen*] with others (i.e., German Christians). Prussia, so conceived, would unite two peoples in a single nation. Such a divided union would be conditional on the adoption of both peoples of a single moral faith, which Jews might still interpret in their own way. Thus: "[Jews] would surely have to be left free to interpret the Bible

[Torah and Gospels] so as to distinguish the way that Jesus spoke as a Jew to Jews from the way he spoke as a moral teacher of men in general" (ibid.).

Convinced of the political necessity, for the foreseeable future, of moralized religion as a vehicle of civic education, and of the need to clothe it in institutions adapted to the peculiar genius of a people, Kant goes so far as to suggest that Jews lend their special gifts as skilled interpreters to a common civic enterprise, albeit at the price of renouncing Judaism as such.

This is not the place to examine Kant's tendentious understanding of Judaism as a faith devoid of true moral religion.[24] Whatever his thinking on this score, his treatment of the problem of Jewish emancipation opens up a promising possibility for national (or civic) unity among a plurality of peoples. Unlike contemporary formulas of "union in diversity" Kant does not emphasize respect for "otherness" as such, but instead stresses the differing positive contributions of each people (according to its own individual gifts) to a common national project.

Republican self-government, according to Kant, cannot flourish without what Lincoln later called a "political religion." Tolerance is not enough;[25] and it is, in any case, not possible without damaging the essence of republican citizenship. Citizens need not constitute a single people; but they must be able to accept subpopulations (like the Jews) as cocontributors to a common civic purpose and as cosubscribers to a related national creed—not as irritations to put up with. Tolerance, as Kant once put it, is for despots.

One senses that a precious opportunity was lost, with Kant's conditional and hesitant endorsement of Jewish emancipation, to include them as full members of a republican Germany without requiring them to renounce their Jewish faith and without denying the special role of Christianity in defining Germans as a people. As Kant was tempted by new and dangerous doctrines of race, so he was tempted by a new sort of spiritual anti-Semitism. Judaism as a faith is devoid, for Kant, of moral content and, as such, is an enduring spiritual burden, both for the Jews themselves and for others with whom they are in contact. The moral progress of humanity is thus linked, for Kant, with a specific project of de-Judaization. This notion found fertile ground, in Fichte and others, for whom the German nation came increasingly to be defined by a specific exclusion of the Jews along with all things Jewish.[26]

But the temptation was not, I am claiming, a necessary one, given the general outline and direction of Kant's thought. Kant's conception of the nation-state (unlike that of, say, Herder, not to speak of Fichte) is supple enough to support the existence of multiple peoples within a common constitutional framework.[27] But it also requires, if that framework is not to be a hollow one, a common national creed—an historically adapted vehicle of civic spirit.

Where does this leave Europe, from a Kantian perspective? Kant has much to say about Europe, not all of it flattering. Europe is at once mankind's first best hope (or, as he privately suspects, its only hope), and the most likely source of humanity's undoing. In works like *Perpetual Peace*, Europe emerges as the continent that uniquely threatens to combine the lawlessness of savages with the technique of the enlightened, who differ from cannibals only in knowing more destructive ways to dispose of enemies than by eating them (8:354–55). In their manifest contempt for law, modern rulers (and their advisors) turn the ancient European genius on its head. Only in Europe is it presumed that states can "marry" (as if a state were somehow equivalent both to its ruler and to the land on which it sits). Such a perverse conception of the state ignores its Kantian definition as a sovereign "society of human beings" that "no one other than itself can dispose of or command" (8:344). It denies, in short, his understanding of the essential relation, as he conceives it, between state and nation.

What Europe can do is to initiate the federation of republican states of which Kant is famously the champion. Is the new Europe the federation Kant envisions (as is often claimed)? Insofar as it seeks to "pool sovereignty," or otherwise submit members to a common juridical jurisdiction, the answer, I think, must be no. Is, then, the new Europe on its way to becoming a Kantian nation-state in its own right, informed by a thick sense of common spiritual mission (as Ortega y Gasset once famously hoped)? Or, finally, does it propel us beyond the nation-state and its archaic attachment to notions like national sovereignty and civic patriotism? Is Europe increasingly what Habermas calls a "postnational constellation"?[28]

To partially address such questions, I will turn, briefly, to a recent work by Joseph Weiler, one of the most thoughtful proponents of a "postnational" or "supernational" Europe. What does it mean, today, to be a "citizen" of Europe? As Weiler astutely notes, the European Union constitutional draft has much to say about the "rights" of citizens, but little to say about their "duties."[29] According to the drafted version: "Every national of a Member State shall be citizen of the Union. Citizenship of the Union shall be additional to national citizenship; it shall not replace it."[30]

Weiler notes the telling ambiguity of a text that asserts the civic preeminence of Europe, and then rushes to deny it, i.e., that wants to have it both ways. The Treaty of Rome, undertaken in the initial stages of the integrative process, had nothing to say about a common citizenship. The purpose of European integration was and apparently remains "laying the foundations for an ever closer union among its peoples [in the plural]. Not the creation of one people, but the union of many." Adding European citizenship to the "discourse of integration" seems to constitute a fundamental "change of telos" culminating in the creation of a single European people.[31]

Where, then, does the loyalty of a citizen ultimately rest? With Europe or with the nation-state? This question is not so much answered as avoided by an understanding of citizenship that identifies it, primarily, with subjective feelings of "belonging." If one grants this understanding, the (alleged) postmodern insight that individuals have multiple, contestable identities, means that one can "belong" in many ways and at many levels. But if the primary purpose of the nation-state is to guarantee the lives and property of citizens, the ambiguity fades. I may have multiple identities, but I have only one life to live or lose.

We have already seen how Kant would solve the problem of reconciling many peoples in a single civic nation: a course arguably taken by countries like the United States and Canada. This is not to say that Kant would favor a single European nation-state, but only that from a Kantian point of view, one cannot have it both ways. Citizenship implies not only a willingness to pay taxes or affective feelings of belonging but also, first and foremost, a reciprocal right and duty of mutual defense, a spirit of "all for one and one for all" whose imagery is typically co-natal. (It is, from a Kantian viewpoint, no accident that Americans call becoming a citizen "naturalization.")

Weiler's solution is, instead, to separate the affective ties associated with the nation from a new understanding of citizenship as a celebration of the postmodern self. This partial decoupling of nationhood and citizenship (or eros and civilization) turns on the premise that older notions of sovereignty have been rendered obsolete by the inability of states "even to pretend to have control over their most classical functions, the provision of material welfare and personal and collective security."[32] But is this really so? Kantian sovereignty, in his own understanding at least, does not turn on the perfect attainment of these ends, but expresses, instead, the conditions of legitimating consent absent which they may not rightly be pursued coercively. As with an individual human being, a state's right to defend itself does not rest on its ability to do so successfully.

Weiler prefers to tie citizenship, not with consent that legitimates coercion (which is scanted, for obvious reasons, in the new European constitution), but with "the fragmented sovereignty" of "porous" states, and the "fractured" selves of the individuals comprising them.[33] As an alternative to the "consumerist" "bread and circuses" approach to citizenship offered by official constitutionalist discourse, which, as he tellingly notes, mentions "duties" while failing to name any,[34] he proposes the "reconstruction" of what he calls a "European ethos" based on "supernational" premises.

By "nationhood" Weiler, following Herder and Mazzini (but not Kant!), has primarily in mind two "fundamental human values": "belongingness" and "originality." It would, indeed, be fair to say that Weiler's "nation" is something like Kant's "people," albeit without Kant's doubts that peoplehood can serve as an enduring source of "originality" or, as Weiler later has it, "sponteneity and authenticity." Like Herder (and unlike later fascist champions of a United Nations of Europe), Weiler believes that peoples, in their belonging

and originality, can flourish authentically without impinging on the flourishing of others: difference without inferiority or oppression. The history
of European states has, however, been tragically otherwise. The solution,
for him, is not a European nation-state (which would only reinscribe the
errors of the past), but a new, postmodern ethos of authentic difference. The
purpose of a European polity, on Weiler's view, is not only to "control the
excesses of the modern nation-state" (a purpose it would share with Kant's
international federation of Europe) but also, and more radically, to express
and help internalize this ethos.[35]

Nationality, according to Weiler, is not "the thing itself," not a "spontaneous expression" of what it "signifies," but rather a "highly stylized artifact."
By preventing "discrimination" on "state-national" grounds, supernationalism makes the artificial boundaries of national exclusion and inclusion more
flexible and porous. "At an intergroup level," Weiler says, "it pushes for cultural differences to express themselves in their authentic, spontaneous form,
rather than the codified statal legal forms."[36]

Here, at last, we come to the heart of the matter (or the thing itself),
which Weiler (rather strangely) calls its "first Kantian strand": a replacement
of the "false consciousness" that "nationalism may create" by a "nonformal"
sense of "sharedness" and belonging.

As he continues:

> Kantian moral philosophy grounds moral obligation on the ability of humans
> not simply to follow ethical norms . . . but to determine for themselves the laws
> of their own acting, and to act out of internal choice according to these norms.
> Supernationalism . . . favors national culture when, indeed, it is authentic,
> internalized, a true part of identity.[37]

Autonomy, on this view, is no longer, as it was for Kant, a capacity to
act out of respect for universal law (or formalism if there ever was one);
the spontaneity of each harmonizes with the spontaneity of the others, for
Weiler, not by virtue of common submission to a universal law of one's own
making, but instead through the mutual decoupling of a sense of national
belonging from the "formality" of state institutions.

But Weiler's invocation of Kant goes further, becoming more "formal"
where Kant himself is less so. Like the "cosmopolitan right" that Kant calls
an "unwritten codex to the law of nations," the supernationalism of the new
constitution, in guaranteeing transnational intercourse, is said to embody
the Enlightenment ideal of "rising above" one's "national closet."[38] How,
then, is one to overcome the potential for angst and alienation believed to
have given rise to national excesses in the first place?

Weiler's answer, finally, is a dual conception of the European demos,
which reaches both inward, where it engages feelings of organic culture and

belongingness, and outward, where it embodies "transnational affinities and values." Here, in his dual conception of the demos, Weiler comes closest to Kant's own distinction between a people and a nation. But he abandons Kant when he goes on to stress—not the material contributions of each people to a common civic project, but the sheer (emptily formal) opportunity that "difference" provides in educating the "I" to "reach out to the other."[39] What finally unites the peoples of Europe is not some shared positive ideal or goal, but only a negative tolerance or forbearance—a common relinquishment of the "drive" toward "an overarching organic-cultural national identity" displacing that of other member states. Citizenship proceeds, not directly, through participation in a common civic project, but only indirectly, through a reciprocal unwillingness to foist the conditions of one's own sense of belonging upon others.

Tellingly, Weiler cites not Kant, but the neo-Kantian Hermann Cohen, according to whom one first discovers one's humanity through observation of a duty to protect the stranger (343). But is it by being forced to tolerate and support the foreigner in one's midst that one comes to recognize the duty of humanity? Or is it not rather, as Kant would insist, recognition of that duty that leads one to protect the stranger?

One can applaud Weiler's praise of a "construct" tending to promote virtues of tolerance and humanity. But one also wonders whether that constitutional construct can prevail without the loyalty—the affective ties—that he associates almost exclusively with the nation. Weiler wants an eroticized "demos" without the demons. But the result is a Europe without spirit, a Europe unable and unwilling to defend itself. Kant wondered whether human vitality, reflected in rivalry and competition among nations, would survive the spirit of commerce. Weiler rather more hopefully believes such rivalry to be unnecessary and unhelpful.

Is nationhood, then, best understood as primarily a matter of "belonging" and "originality" [*à la* Herder], qualities that can be decoupled from the supernational institutions that both secure and police the boundaries of authentic national expression? It would seem that one either faces, once again, the problem of divided political and religious loyalties (out of and against which the modern idea of Europe arguably emerged), or one decouples affective ties of loyalty from the institution charged with protecting them. The Kantian alternative, whatever its weaknesses, need not succumb to this dilemma. Kantian nationhood is not primarily defined by a subjective sense of "belonging" but by allegiance to shared civic institutions, formal and informal, and the idea of justice they embody.

Let me conclude, then, with the following tentative hypothesis: If Europe cannot be a federal nation-state (along U.S. lines), it would be better off as a federation of nation-states along genuinely Kantian lines.

The current "constellation" of Europe hovers uneasily between a nation-state (where coercion is legitimated by the mutual consent of citizens) and a federation (where the absence of coercion makes civic consent less important and less salient). Current European attitudes seem at once too trusting (as if the world harbored no enemies that might require citizens to make the ultimate sacrifice of dying for their country) and not trusting enough (hence the unwillingness of the members of each nation to place themselves in one another's hands, when it comes to common legislation). As Delanty suggests, Europe's greatest enemies have mainly been internal. Now that Europe is internally at peace, many in Europe, it seems, want fervently to believe that war itself is obsolete. Kant (who cautions that in the best of times "war constantly threatens to break out") was not so sanguine.

Some practical implications of this hypothesis:

1. A clear reassertion of the principle of national sovereignty (which has never really been relinquished by the member states, who, for example, retain an unimpeded "right of succession").
2. Franker recognition of the ongoing salience of self-defense and of collective security against internal and external aggression as the central mission of the state.
3. A lessened tendency to define the role of Europe as one of checking the United States (rather than making an alternative contribution to the joint project of promoting and securing a liberal world order). Indeed, European anti-Americanism often sounds like a reversion to the sort of old-fashioned, balance-of-power politics Kant fiercely criticized. A more Kantian European federation would, in short, be comfortable in NATO, or more comfortable, at least, than the current European constellation. Nothing, of course, would prevent the countries of Europe from collectively supporting and embodying a different understanding of liberal government, including, but not limited to, more generous social welfare benefits, than is typical for the United States.
4. A potentially healthier way for European states to deal with religious and other minorities. Viewed in a more Kantian light, integration of such groups would be understood less as a painful if salutary exercise in "difference ethics," and more as a matter of recognizing and encouraging the peculiar contributions, actual and potential, of such communities to civic life at large. Such recognition and encouragement might be made all the easier by a fuller recognition of the historic contributions of Muslims, Jews, and others to Europe's shared cultural and spiritual capital.[40]

A final point: according to Robert Kagan, the European Union, as "a confederation of free states that subject themselves to interference with their sovereignty," fulfills the "vision of Kant" rather than of Grotius.[41] I respectfully disagree. Far from qualifying the principle of national sovereignty, Kant's famous federation of republics is, for him, the one international arena in which that principle can be realized in full. Far from embodying Kant's vision, the European Union as currently conceived and constituted obscures some harsh political realities that Kant does not hesitate to grant—realities that, for Kant, underlie that right of nations to resort unilaterally to preemptive war, and may even justify regime change where no threat is imminent.[42] If Europe and the United States disagree on principles, it is not because Europe is more "Kantian" than the United States. Appreciation of this fact cannot mend the current Atlantic rift, but it might remove one source of mutual misunderstanding among nations that should, if Kant is right, be allies if not friends.

Notes

1. Jürgen Habermas and Jacques Derrida, "February 15, or What Binds Europe Together: A Plea for a Common Foreign Policy, Beginning in the Core of Europe," in *The Derrida-Habermas Reader*, ed. Lasse Thomassen (Chicago: University of Chicago Press, 2006), 270–77.

2. Friedrich Nietzsche, *Beyond Good and Evil: Prelude to a Philosophy of the Future*, trans. Walter Kaufmann (New York: Vintage, 1989). 210.

3. Robert Kagan, *Of Paradise and Power: America and Europe in the New World Order* (New York: Knopf, 2003), 3–5.

4. Joseph H. H. Weiler, *The Constitution of Europe: "Do the New Clothes Have an Emperor?" and Other Essays on European Integration* (Cambridge: Cambridge University Press, 1999), 324.

5. Gerard Delanty, *Inventing Europe: Idea, Identity, Reality* (London: Macmillan, 1995).

6. Niccolò Machiavelli, *Discourses on Livy*, trans. Harvey C. Mansfield and Nathan Tarcov (Chicago: Chicago University Press, 1996), 5.

7. Jean-Jacques Rousseau, *Discours sur l'origine et les fondements de l'inégalité*, *Oeuvres complètes*, vol. 3 (Paris: Gallimard, 1964), 171.

8. Jean-Jacques Rousseau, *Emile*, trans. Allan Bloom (New York: Basic Books, 1979), 416.

9. Unlike Habermas, who claims a Kantian provenance for his own notion of "communicative discourse," Kant distinguishes, both here and later, the aesthetic function of "communication" from the civil and philosophic role of public argument. Not by accident, in Habermas, public reason giving tends to eclipse the qualities of civic and intellectual independence (or "enlightenment" in Kant's peculiar sense) to which, for Kant, public "reason giving" is a tool, not (as with Habermas) a community-establishing substitute. (See, for example, Habermas, *Moral Consciousness*

and Communicative Action, trans. C. Lenhart and S. W. Nicholson (Cambridge: MIT Press, 1989) [German 1983].

10. All references to Kant in parentheses are to the Academy edition, *Kants gesammelte Schriften*, ed. Königlich Preußische Akademie der Wissenschaften, 29 vols. (Berlin: de Gruyter, 1900–). The translations are my own.

11. For an insightful discussion of palingenesis and metamorphosis as political metaphors in Kant, see Howard Williams, *Kant's Critique of Hobbes* (Cardiff: University of Wales Press, 2003), chapter seven. In general, *metamorphosis* signifies a gradual change of form in a living being (Kant's later favored model of political transformation), whereas *palingenesis* signifies an abrupt termination of life followed by rebirth (or, in political terms, violent revolution).

12. Germany (and Europe more generally, of which Germany is deemed the center) thus displaces Greece, which Aristotle had famously described as constituting a desirable mean between the spirited crudeness of Europe and the spiritless refinement of Asia. See Aristotle, *The Politics*, trans. Carnes Lord (Chicago: University of Chicago Press, 1984), 1327bl, 24–38; 1285al, 18–20. "The nations in cold locations, especially in Europe, are filled with spiritedness, but relatively lacking in thought and art; hence they remain freer, but lack [political] governance and are incapable of ruling their neighbors. Those in Asia, on the other hand, have souls endowed with thought and art, but are lacking in spiritedness; hence they remain ruled and enslaved. But the stock of the Greeks shares in both—just as it holds the middle in terms of location. For it is both spirited and endowed with thought, and hence both remains free and governs itself in the best manner and at the same time is capable of ruling all, should it obtain a single regime. The nations of the Greeks also display the same difference in relation to one another. Some have a nature that is one-sided, while others are well blended in relation to both of these capacities" (24–45). Aristotle's characterization of Greece is qualified by his praise of the non-Greek city of Carthage.

13. See his essay, *On the Use of Teleological Principles in Philosophy* (8:174n).

14. Susan Meld Shell, *Kant and the Limits of Autonomy* (Cambridge: Harvard University Press, 2009), chapter six.

15. Kant attributes the survival of Jewish national memory to Christian institutions and a related educated public. See, *Religion within the Boundaries of Bare Reason* (6:136n). And he seems to have a related point in mind when he asserts that Europeans (including the "European Turks") are the only peoples who "travel to study human beings and their national character" (*Anthropology from a Pragmatic Point of View*, 7:312n). Still, he attributes to the Jews at least one genuine contribution to human history: the invention or reception of biblical scripture, whose ambiguous but ultimately hopeful spiritual legacy constitutes the main subject of Kant's late religious work.

16. Cf. *Emile*, trans. Allan Bloom (New York: Basic Books, 1979), 453: "The Europeans are no longer Gauls, Germans, Iberians and Allobroges. They are nothing but Scythians who have degenerated in various ways."

17. For the Rousseauian antecedents, see *Emile*, 469ff. The idea of savage community to which Kant implicitly appeals bears a striking resemblance to the so-called Golden Age described in Rousseau's *Second Discourse*.

18. *Critique of Pure Reason*, A316/B372–73 (3:247).

19. This argument is famously expanded in Schiller's theory of naïve and sentimental poetry.

20. Kant's usage, however, is not always altogether consistent on this score.

21. See *Critique of Judgment*, 5:375n.

22. Habermas, for example, suggests that "military duty" and "capital punishment" (but not "compulsory taxation") is indefensible, given the premises of today's "enlightenment culture." See Jürgen Habermas, *The Postnational Constellation: Political Essays*, trans. Max Pensky (Cambridge: MIT Press, 2001), 101.

23. *Vorarbeiten zum ewigen Frieden* (23:170).

24. I differ with Michael Mack's otherwise richly perceptive discussion of Kant's hostility toward the Jews. Unlike Mack, I do not regard anti-Semitism as an inevitable consequence of Kant's overall philosophic project. For a fuller treatment of Kant's attitude toward Jews and Judaism, see Susan M. Shell, "Freedom and Faith in Kant's *Religion Within the Limits of Bare Reason*," in *Essays on Freedom*, ed. Richard Velkley (Washington, DC: Catholic University of America Press, 2008).

25. Kant claims that an "enlightened" prince, who considers it his duty, in religious matters, not to prescribe anything to his people, "will reject the arrogant name of *tolerance*." See "What Is Enlightenment?" (8:40). From a Kantian point of view, mere tolerance (implying as it does an evil one chooses to put up with) would not be enough, while "celebration" of difference for its own sake (as some contemporary ethicists urge) would be excessive.

26. For an informative and insightful discussion of Fichte's attitude toward Jews and Judaism, see Anthony La Vopa, *Fichte: The Self and the Calling of Philosophy, 1762–1799* (Cambridge: Cambridge University Press, 2001), 131–49. The "Marcionic heresy," which denies any connection between "true" Christianity and Judaism, has, of course, a long theological history.

27. See especially his "Nachschrift eines Freundes," which explores that possibility with respect to the Lithuanian and Polish minority populations of a recently expanded Prussia (8:445). For a fuller discussion, see Shell, "Nachschrift eines Freundes: Kant on Language, Friendship, and the Concept of a People," in *Kantian Review* 15, no. 1 (2010): 88–117.

28. Jürgen Habermas, *The Postnational Constellation*, trans. Max Pensky (Cambridge: MIT Press, 2001). Habermas revisits the question of postnationalism in *Europe: The Faltering Project*, trans. Ciaran Cronin (Malden: Polity Press, 2009). As he there notes, the anthem, which the failed EU Constitution of 2004 had specifically named, is not mentioned in the Lisbon Treaty of 2008 (81).

29. See Weiler, *The Constitution of Europe*, 333–34.

30. Ibid., 333. Weiler is referring to the 1997 draft Amsterdam Treaty (modifying the Maastricht Treaty of 1992). According to the Amsterdam draft, as quoted by Weiler, "Citizenship of the Union shall complement and not replace national citizenship" (324). The phrase reappears in slightly altered form in the Treaty of Union of 2008 (The Lisbon Treaty) at II: 20: "Every national of a member state shall be a citizen of the Union. Citizenship of the Union shall be additional to national citizenship and shall not replace it." See: http://www.deljpn.ec.europa.eu/union/showpage_en_union.history.1.php; and http://www.openeurope.org.uk/research/comparative.pdf. Neither text specifically mentions the duties of citizens.

31. Weiler, *The Constitution of Europe*, 327–28.

32. Ibid., 328.

33. Ibid., 329.

34. Ibid., 335.

35. Ibid., 341.

36. Ibid., 342–43.

37. Ibid., 343.

38. Ibid.

39. Ibid., 346.

40. Weiler explores such a possibility in his more recent ¨Un'Europa Cristiana: Un saggio esplorativo* (Milan: BUR Saggi, 2003).

41. Robert Kagan, "America's Crisis of Legitimacy," in *Foreign Affairs* (March/April 2004): 79.

42. See *Metaphysics of Morals* (6:349).

Kant's Parergonal Politics

The Sensus Communis and the Problem of Political Action

Charlton Payne

In *Lectures on Kant's Political Philosophy*, Hannah Arendt advances a number of convincing arguments for why Kant's discussion of aesthetic judgment provides the basis for a kind of political reason.[1] However, once we begin to read the third *Critique* as offering a theory of political community, I contend we find that Kant's emphasis on judgment would reduce political agency to the role of the spectator, and thereby exclude creative activity from this model of communal interaction. Using Arendt's reading as a starting point will lead us through Kant's discussion of taste and genius to demonstrate how productive action only emerges as the activity of the creative artist. The upshot of this focus on the interaction of genius and taste is that if we want to find in Kant's "common sense" (*Gemeinsinn* or *sensus communis*)—which Kant defines as the effect arising from the free play of our cognitive powers that is always presupposed in judgments of taste[2]—a model for an interactive political reason, we must also reckon with the implications.

Kant's critique of genius and taste rests on a fundamental reliance upon the genius as producer that must also exclude the genius from the more proper activity of the *sensus communis*, that of judging. For this reason, I follow Henry Allison's appropriation of Derrida's terminology in calling genius parergonal to Kant's theory of taste.[3] By treating genius as a parergon in Kant's discussion, I insist on genius' extrasystematic status vis-à-vis Kant's critique of the *sensus communis*. Genius emerges as the ternary element that must function within the community of taste, if we are to have beautiful representations for judgment, yet must also be kept at bay for fear that genius might confound the integrity of taste by indulging in too radically innovative activity. Really, then, genius operates as both within and external to the theory of taste. This predicament is especially paradoxical, considering that the very constituent that is beyond (*para-*) the work (*ergon*) of the community is the very one whose works (beautiful art) are fundamental to the constitution of a theory and community of taste.

If we argue by analogy that genius and taste can be translated into the political categories agency and community, we are left with a problematic political philosophy in which creative political action is parergonal to judgment, and hence the actor is parergonal to the political community, or *sensus communis*. This leaves us with the task of how to handle Arendt's trenchant conclusion that "Kant does tell one how to take others into account; he does not tell one how to combine with them in order to act" (44). Obviously a lot hinges on what we define as political action; in this essay, political action will mean the ability of an agent within a political community to create new conditions out of the existing legal structure. Kant leaves us in a complicated bind if we seek to construct a theory of political community out of the third *Critique*. For one thing, it is a theory of political community without creative political action, in which case it is obviously limited as a political philosophy. In order to find action, we thus have to turn to his theory of genius, in which case we enter into yet another bind. First, genius can lead to both good and bad results (hence the necessity of taste), and second, only the sovereign can act as a political genius in Kant's political theory, as my analysis of the parallels between the theory of taste and Kant's political writings will show. Ultimately, my argument is mostly critical in its explication of the limits of an attempt to construe a political community out of the theory of taste, but I will end on a more positive note with the proposal that we try to articulate a theory of political genius that doesn't come from the sovereign, but rather from the public, and that can influence taste.

Arendt and Kant's *Sensus Communis*

First, I want to review Arendt's arguments for why the *sensus communis* can be understood as a political community, to see what type of community is implied in such a model. Arendt's appropriation of Kant's theory of taste focuses on the fact that for Kant taste consists of individual and collective judgments. Judgments of whether an object is beautiful are reflective insofar as they encounter particular aesthetic objects that prevent the beauty of such objects being judged according to conceptual criteria; instead of subsuming the particular beautiful objects under a concept of the object (I perceive a chair and judge its suitability to my general understanding of what a chair is), our faculty of judgment reflects back upon itself, upon the very act of judgment, and the individual judging such aesthetic phenomena experiences pleasure in the harmony of his or her faculties of imagination and understanding when judging a beautiful object. This pleasure coincides with a reflection upon the harmony induced by the very act of judgment.

More important for Arendt, though, is the public aspect of judgment, its always being embedded within a community of others who judge. While the individual judging a beautiful phenomenon experiences a certain pleasure in harmony, this pleasure is moreover linked to reflection upon the fact that others may experience such harmony too. In section 40 of the third *Critique*, titled "On Taste as a Type of *sensus communis*," Kant argues that whenever we judge something as beautiful we always presuppose a "faculty of judgment" (*Beurteilungsvermögen*) common to everyone else. In the moment of an aesthetic judgment this faculty assumes that the same reflection on an object could occur with others, enabling it "to compare its judgment with the collective Reason of humanity" (*KU*, 174). When we judge whether an object is beautiful we always hypothetically compare our judgment to the possible judgment of others as a form of reality testing, so to speak, that prevents us from succumbing to private illusion; as Kant says, we put ourselves in the place of others whenever we judge (174).

This appeal to a shared human faculty of judgment is the precondition for belonging to a *sensus communis*, or is what Kant says is what it means to have "taste": "We could even define taste as the faculty of judging that which makes universally communicable, without the mediation of a concept, our feeling in a given representation" (177).[4] For Kant, then, taste is above all tied in with the human ability to communicate the pleasant feelings produced by the free accord of imagination (*Einbildungskraft*) with understanding (*Verstand*) when judging an object as beautiful. One belongs to a community of taste to the extent that one communicates that one is judging an object to be beautiful. Community as it emerges out of the third *Critique* depends on a *universally* shared human faculty of judgment. Potentially everyone who can experience the harmony of imagination and understanding in reflexive judgments belongs to the *sensus communis*.

Arendt sees in this public dimension of taste the fundament for a model of citizenship rooted in reflexive judgment. Her analysis is moreover invested in an understanding of the *sensus communis* that insists that acts of judgment imply communication.[5] Furthermore, Arendt weakens Kant's criteria for membership in the *sensus communis* by transforming the sense of "common" from universality to a more empirical generality. To continue her lifelong dedication to understanding the nature of a public life conditioned by the sensual world, Arendt renders Kant's *sensus communis* into a more specifically context-bound historical organization. This distinction becomes more clear when, in support of her conceptual move from universality to generality, Arendt distinguishes between three meanings of "man" in Kant: human species, rational (moral) man, and, most important for Arendt, "men as actual inhabitants of the earth" (26). Arendt defines this generality of men as follows:

> Men = earthbound creatures, living in communities, endowed with common sense, *sensus communis*, a community sense; not autonomous, needing each other's company even for thinking ("freedom of the pen") = first part of the *Critique of Judgment*: aesthetic judgment. (27)

We don't just judge as human beings, but rather as historical communities judging particular phenomena within specific settings.

Nevertheless, for Arendt the universally shared faculty of judgment provides the commonality required for earthbound men to interact with one another as thinking members of an actual community. According to Arendt:

> The "enlargement of the mind" plays a crucial role in the *Critique of Judgment*. It is accomplished by "comparing our judgment with the possible rather than the actual judgments of others, and by putting ourselves in the place of any other man." The faculty that makes this possible is called imagination. . . . Critical thinking is possible only where the standpoints of all others are open to inspection. Hence, critical thinking, while still a solitary business, does not cut itself off from "all others." To be sure, it still goes on in isolation, but by the force of imagination it makes the others present and thus moves in a space that is potentially public, open to all sides; in other words, it adopts the position of Kant's world citizen. (42–43)

Arendt emphasizes the "enlargement of the mind," or stepping into the minds of others as the maxim of judgment, at the expense of Kant's other two premises of human understanding and reason, namely, thinking for oneself as the maxim of understanding and thinking consistently as the maxim of reason. This is because Arendt wants to move beyond Kant's preoccupation with autonomy into a heteronomous realm of public interaction. Thanks to the imagination's ability to allow us to anticipate what others might be thinking the faculty of judgment provides Arendt a basis for communal interaction. Arendt transforms common sense from a universal cognitive faculty into the generality of a shared community.[6] In making this tendentious interpretive leap from the *a priori* nature of Kant's *sensus communis* to an empirical sociality of community—a process that Ronald Beiner describes as "detranscendentalization"[7]—Arendt stands Kant on his head, just as she did Lessing in the lecture delivered upon her acceptance of the Lessing Prize, as part of a reevaluation of Enlightenment philosophy driven by the same problems influencing her lifelong philosophical output.

The Kant lectures are concerned with the relation between the *vita activa* and the *vita contemplativa*.[8] Toward the end of her life, Arendt hoped to culminate her project in a three-volume magnum opus on thinking, willing, and judging; the Kant lectures would form the beginnings of the judgment part. For Arendt, one thinks and wills alone, but one judges with others;

the former belong to theory, and the latter to practice. Above all, Arendt insists on the collective and practical nature of judgment, and in the process attempts to divorce it as much as possible from the requirements of autonomy. Thus, Arendt leaves us with a version of the *sensus communis* based on interaction through the enlargement of the mind in the activity of the imagination, at once context-bound and invested in a belief that one actually communicates something when making reflective judgments.

Arendt seems content with Kant's emphasis on reflection as the ground of a political community. But I suggest that we examine this emphasis more critically. If Kant has indeed described a communal interaction that could form the basis of a political philosophy derived from the experience of the aesthetic, he faces the problem that the emphasis on judgment underlying this political philosophy is grounded in the position of the spectator. The *sensus communis* thus far has been characterized as something like a community of art appreciation, just as Kant's public sphere would consist of people judging, but not acting politically. In fact, even Arendt acknowledges this point in the lectures. Kant distrusts actors because as participants in the events they are unable to glance the meaningful whole, unlike the spectators who reflect on the deeds of these actors from a distance. However, as I will now proceed to argue, within Kant's deduction of pure aesthetic judgments we find the potential for productive action in the activity of the genius.[9] By turning to Kant's discussion of genius in the *Critique of Judgment*, we can pursue, as a thought experiment, the argument by analogy introduced by Arendt's own reading of Kant's aesthetics as a political philosophy. Kant's theory of genius contains the kernel of a theory of political action, whose parergonal status connects on another level with the status of political action in Kant's political writings. In fact, a denigration of the *vita activa* mirrors the fate of the genius in Kant's theory of taste. Both are treated with suspicion, even though they are equally important for the functioning of their respective domains of politics and art; because they function as included-excluded elements, the sovereign political agent and the creative genius remain parergonal to Kant's aesthetic and political communities.

Genius

If beautiful art is artificial, and Kant says beautiful art appears to be nature while maintaining our perception of its artifice, then it must be *produced*.[10] Someone has to fashion such a work of art. Hence, section 46, "Beautiful Art is Art of Genius," launches an important discussion of the conditions of production of beautiful art. Since beautiful art must resemble the purposiveness of nature, genius is the "talent" (*das Talent*) that gives "rules" to art, and for this reason beautiful art is only possible as the product of genius (*KU*, 193).[11]

But what exactly are the traits that define genius? According to Kant, the essential characteristic of genius is that it is a productive talent to which no determinable rule can be given, hence "originality must be its primary characteristic"; but this originality is restricted by a second characteristic: that the products of genius be patterns (*Muster*) that are exemplary, serving others as a measure of estimation, though genius does not itself spring from imitation (194).[12] Genius must be original, rather than imitative, but in a way that sets the standard, so to speak, for future works of genius. Genius imitates other geniuses when it creates original works of beautiful art and thereby inspires other original creations from other geniuses. To be more precise, Paul Guyer has pointed out how the genius creates precedents, rather than works to be imitated, and so is more properly creating according to a logic of succession or influence, as Kant himself describes it in section 32. By establishing precedents through its own originality, genius influences future geniuses to produce original works of fine art.[13]

These two characteristics of genius—originality and exemplarity—may not at first glance appear to be at odds with each other. But in fact the passage from the first to the second characteristic, from which we arrive at the definition of genius as exemplary originality, is decisive for Kant's critique of genius and its relation to the community of taste. On the one hand, Kant insists on the originality of genius as its "essential" characteristic, but he then immediately qualifies such originality by emphasizing that its products be exemplary. Kant's retreat from the originality of genius here is entirely consistent with his constriction of the creative originality of genius in the discussion of genius that unfolds over the course of his argument as he further describes the traits contributing to genius' construction of a work of art.

Among these other contributors to artistic production comprising the activity of genius Kant names "spirit" (*Geist*). Spirit, he says, is the invigorating impulse behind artistic production capable of finding an expression for an aesthetic idea: "the faculty of the presentation (*Darstellung*) of aesthetic ideas" (*KU*, 202). As the faculty of presentation, it plays a crucial role in relation to the imagination in the creation of beautiful works of art. The imagination is the faculty that enables genius to create an alternative nature out of the nature that is actually given to it. Kant says, "The imagination (as productive faculty of cognition) is very powerful in the creation of another nature out of the material that actual nature gives to it" (202). Spirit, though, finds form in the manifold play of imagination, so that spirit and imagination work together and belong on the side of genius' originality. And, Kant says, imagination's productive faculty of cognition, which strives for a realm beyond the merely phenomenal, is most properly characteristic of *poetry* (*Dichtkunst*) (212). Poetry is privileged here because of its use of metaphor, the mode of presenting aesthetic ideas.[14] Yet because poetry, as beautiful art *par excellence*, attempts to present aesthetic ideas in sensible form (through metaphor), and because of this restriction demands that the products of genius serve as a measure, the imagination must always return to understanding, albeit in as indeterminate a cognitive way as possible.[15] Aided by spirit, genius becomes the talent that finds representations for ideas (*Ideen*) and expresses them so that they may be communicated to others, who may in turn experience the pleasure induced by the free harmony of imagination and understanding (206–7). With this emphasis on the communication of aesthetic ideas and the formal pleasure they incite, we have returned to the act of judging within a *sensus communis* in which every member of the community of taste communicates his or her pleasure in judging poetic works as beautiful, and reflects upon the possibility that others too may do the same.

In this dynamic interchange between the creation of original works of art and the presentation of such works to a community of judges, then, taste and genius always work together in the production of beautiful art. Yet if imagination, understanding, spirit, and taste are the four characteristics of beautiful art, taste is, as Kant points out in a footnote to paragraph 50, the unifying term (*KU*, 210). This is because for Kant the demands of the *sensus communis* remain fundamental to the experience of the beautiful: though beautiful art does not exist without the "spirit" that the imagination of the genius lends to the product, it is only beautiful when judgments are being made about it. Taste, as the community of judges, is the "discipline" (*Disziplin*) of genius in that it tells genius how far the imagination can go, yet still remain purposive (210). Only as form can beautiful art "stand before the power of judgment" (197). This form that the genius arrives at via taste, which is the realm of "common sense," is no less than communication itself—in short, taste enables genius to communicate, and for that reason genius must always be "sacrificed" (*aufgeopfert*) to the demands of taste (210). Kant's discussion of genius and taste in sections 46 to 50 reveals a struggle between these two components of beautiful art. Nevertheless, in the end, Kant subordinates genius to the imperative to communicate—the creative artist as genius can only belong to the *sensus communis* if he or she conforms to the demands of form by exposing his or her representations or products to the power of judgment.

Although genius (or production) is always intertwined with taste (or judgment), genius emerges as the necessary yet dangerous precondition of judgment, and hence of belonging to the community: it is necessary for creating beautiful art, but if allowed too much free play of the imagination it can threaten the accord of the faculties necessary for taste.[16] The community of taste relies upon genius to provide it with aesthetic ideas in the form of an artwork so that there is beautiful art to present to the faculty of judgment and thereby constitute a community of judges, but it has to limit the activity of genius or risk the disarticulation of taste when imagination exceeds understanding and hence threatens to unravel form. Occupying this role of necessary but insufficient condition, or even as the element that must be included and simultaneously excluded, genius functions as a parergon to Kant's community of taste.

Spectatorship and Action

We have already seen how Kant's argument constructs a theory of community of taste by making the condition of inclusion within the community dependent upon a crucial exclusion of excessive imagination on the part of genius. Likewise, Arendt's rendering of Kant's theory of taste into a model for political interaction repeats this fundamental gesture of inclusion and exclusion, because the *sensus communis* or public sphere situates its members as spectators, not actors. To exercise one's judgment for Kant and Arendt means assuming the stance of the spectator who observes and evaluates from a distance. If we consider Kant's political theory, we see that he insisted on collective judgment not only in matters of art but also in the realm of politics. Turning now to Kant's more explicitly political writings, we can push the analogy with which I'm experimenting here even further to see how well Kant's aesthetic and political theories map onto one another. Fully aware of the need for actors, his view of collective activity in political life nevertheless was modeled on the public sphere of taste. As Arendt points out, Kantian politics, like art, requires both actors and spectators. Yet this leads to a troubling sense of what political action entails, a problem that plagues Kant's political theory. Arendt quotes this passage from *The Metaphysics of Morals*:

> Moral-practical reason within us pronounces the following irresistible veto: *There shall be no war.* . . . Thus it is no longer a question of whether perpetual peace is really possible or not, or whether we are not perhaps mistaken in our theoretical judgment if we assume that it is. On the contrary, we must simply act as if it could really come about . . . even if the fulfillment of this pacific intention were forever to remain a pious hope . . . for it is our duty to do so (54).[17]

Action as Kant understands it here is on the level of practical morality. Issuing from the imperatives of reason, perpetual peace is something we merely have to do out of duty. We would demonstrate our freedom as moral subjects in our acting "as if" peace could really come about. There is no reflection upon this action, and it could just as well be done alone. And yet such action is not so easily undertaken as Kant may present it here. Commenting on this passage, Arendt says:

But these maxims for action do not nullify the aesthetic and reflective judgment. In other words: Even though Kant would always have acted for peace, he knew and kept in mind his judgment. Had he acted on the knowledge he had gained as a spectator, he would, in his mind, have been criminal. (54)

More than only dutiful activity, politics is intrinsically bound to the reflection of the spectators, whose "disinterestedness" is what prevents the imagination of the actors from running astray of sound judgment, or good taste. But what is especially curious about this passage is the barring of the spectator from becoming a political actor. The spectator who acts on his knowledge is a "criminal." Arendt points out that this is so because

> it should be clear that Kant could conceive of action only as acts of the powers-that-be (whatever they might happen to be)—that is, governmental acts; any actual action from the side of the subjects could consist only in conspiratorial activity, the acts and plots of secret societies. In other words, the alternative to established government is, for him, not revolution but a coup d'état. (60)

Kant believed that the proper behavior within a public sphere was to be found in the role of judging among a community of spectators. (Of course this is the message of "What Is Enlightenment?": public reason=academic freedom v. private reason=obey.) Not a revolutionary, Kant encounters the difficulty of accounting for collective political action on the side of the members of the political community, resulting in a restriction of political action to the exceptional acts of the ruler.

Arendt cites examples from "The Contest of the Faculties" and "Perpetual Peace" (47–48), yet nowhere is Kant's strict demarcation of public opinion from legitimate governmental acts more apparent than in Kant's "Theory and Practice" essay, written in 1793 at the height of revolution in France.[18] In this essay, Kant develops a distinction between right and coercion, according to which right means the limitation of each person's freedom so that it is compatible for everyone, whereas coercion entails more simply the limitation of freedom of the will by another (TP, 72). Always related to freedom, right and coercion for Kant take priority over considerations of happiness within the civil state. According to Kant, we perform our roles as subjects within the civil state when we exercise our duty and right to coerce and be free, as an equilibrium of effect and countereffect conforming to universal laws of freedom that limit everyone's will (74). Our actions within the civil state, in other words, should be guided by the rights that secure our freedom as autonomous wills. Therefore, we enter into a contract with the sovereign to secure our freedom, and our membership to the political community is based upon this right; every public law should be formulated based on the possibility that all might consent, which in turn is based on the inviolable right of the citizen to have its right secured against external and internal enemies (78). For Kant, securing the state of right against internal and external enemies is the primary requirement for prosperity. That is, happiness should never govern the constitution of a civil state, because its empirical, temporally labile nature prevents it from ever serving as a foundation derived from reason:

> For both the temporal circumstances and the deeply conflicting and thus continually changing illusions in which each person places his happiness (though no one can prescribe for another where he should place it) make all fixed principles impossible, and happiness is in itself unfit as a principle underlying legislation. (TP, 78)

Kant refuses to allow happiness to propel legislation and the participation of subjects within the commonwealth. Furthermore, whether a law benefits the happiness of the commonwealth should be left to the judgment of the legislators and not to the subjects. Kant says, "the foremost issue is the rights that are thereby secured for everyone, which is the supreme principle, limited by no other, from which all maxims concerning the commonwealth must be derived" (TP, 78). The subjects have entered into a contract with the sovereign body of legislators to secure these rights, and in so doing have agreed that no citizen may coerce the sovereign. Kant is very clear on this: in order to insure the legitimacy of the civil constitution, the ruler (which Kant understands as a republican conglomerate of materially independent citizens) must be excluded from the system of coercion. Consequently, the subjects have no legitimate claim to rebel against a ruler who they believe has injured either their happiness or even their rights. Kant believes rather sanguinely that the public use of reason—through the freedom of the pen, whereby the acts of the ruler are submitted to the reflective judgments of the citizenry—can suffice as "the sole protector of the people's rights" (82). A piece of legislation or an act of the state "is subject to general and public judgment, but resistance to it in word or deed must never be mustered" (83).

Kant's civil state resembles the *sensus communis*, especially as it emerges out of Arendt's appropriation. It consists of a supreme creator of legislation, the ruler, which presumably would be limited in its productive acts by the requirement that its legislation be subject to the judgment of the political community. Just as the *sensus communis* is constituted by and regulates the activity of the genius, the members of the civil state can protect the people's rights by communicating to one another their judgments of the sovereign's actions. Translated into a model for political life along the lines offered by the "Theory and Practice" essay, the activity of the genius takes the form of the activity of the ruler. Moreover, its activity exists as an exception, and as such is again parergonal to the community. Every member of the political community can be subject to coercive laws, but the community is bound together by the power of the sovereign to coerce and to secure the rights upon which the community is founded, without itself being coerced.

As a parergon, genius functions as a structuring limit to Kantian aesthetics, and to a theory of political community based on both the political writings and the *Critique of Judgment*. With respect to the *sensus communis*, genius operates as a necessary and dangerous element, whereas as a category of political philosophy, genius as a figure for the legislator, or the criminal, divides the political community into a legitimate actor in the form of the sovereign, and a legitimate citizenry consisting of spectators who circulate public opinion regarding the acts of the sovereign. Productive action on the side of the citizenry gets marked as illegitimate, or as Arendt calls it, "criminal": those who belong to the political community can either reflect on the actions of the sovereign or simply obey them. Agency within the political community is limited to the judgment of the members of the public as spectators.

One problem with Kant's political philosophy is this seemingly gaping divide between the universality of rights and the ephemeral nature of happiness. Kant's foremost concern in political life is with the preservation of the autonomy of the individual within the political community; consequently, his political community relies on an inviolable contract that so narrowly insists upon the right to freedom of each member of the community as to limit the potential for collective political action. In contrast, Arendt sees in reflective judgments, which are always bound up with particular phenomena, the possibility for a model of community mediated by the temporality of communal life. In other words, her version of public life attempts to tie the inherently empirical nature of political judgments to the foundation of the community. Her attempt falls short, however, because it remains too Kantian in its treatment of the creative acts of genius. Arendt seems just as unwilling or incapable to integrate genius into the political community.

However, as I have argued, Kant's discussion of beautiful art in the third *Critique* introduces the problem of what constitutes collective action, once we interpret the *sensus communis* as a model for political interaction. As the talent capable of producing an alternative reality inspired by aesthetic ideas, which nonetheless always creates within the sensible world of a community of taste, poetic genius would seem to offer a model for the political actor. If perpetual peace is an idea of pure reason, only the poet (or the criminal) would be able to produce a beautiful art that would give us an experience anywhere near it, that could then be subject to interactive judgment. Such beautiful art would be inscribed within the form of the *sensus communis*. However, the criminal/genius belongs to the community as the necessary but dangerous condition upon which membership relies.

Action produces those beautiful representations that enable a *sensus communis* but must always remain subordinate to the demands of taste, i.e., public opinion. So while Kant's *sensus communis* offers a kind of community based on a political reason grounded in reflective judgment, it does so in a way that locates creative political action on the side of the ruler and maintains a gap between the members and the exceptional status of the ruler(s) of the political community.

I have focused on the slippery role of genius in Kant's account of community as elaborated in the third *Critique* in order to suggest that it poses a problem for those who celebrate the *sensus communis* as a positive model for community formation. It seems we never quite overcome the impasse best identified by Paul Guyer between the integrity of individual agency, or the autonomy of production, and the integrity of the community realized in taste. On the one hand, as Guyer has shown, we find a potentially radical dialectic buried within the third *Critique* between the imperatives of the originality of genius and the tradition of the artistic canon out of which taste grows.[19] This radicality is, of course, only implicit in Kant's text, hidden beneath his explicit attempt to stabilize this dialectic by sacrificing genius to taste. Taken as a theory of art, then, the third Critique holds the potential for a rather revolutionary view of art as a process of production and reception, when we consider the full implications of genius for Kant's aesthetics, even if Kant's subordination of genius to taste shies away from the full implications implicit in his aesthetic community. However, once we follow Arendt's path, and begin to think about the *Critique of Judgment* as a political philosophy, Kant appears far more conservative as political agency gets reduced to spectatorship.

The problem lies perhaps in the fact that Kant is most radical when discussing the autonomy of the individual artist or ethical actor. Kant's emphasis on individual autonomy may serve art and morality well, but what about as a politics? The moment he turns to politics, Kant sacrifices the full potential of the integrity of the individual, or, in the case of art, the unstable dialectic between part and whole, to the demands for organizational coherence necessary to an aesthetic community on the one hand, and to the sanctity of the civic contract upon which the political community is based on the other. This disjunction between the radical nature of individual acts of genius within the aesthetic community and the conservative preservation of individual autonomy within the political community leads to Arendt's poignant diagnosis that Kant doesn't tell us how to act together to create new works from within the community. He doesn't tell us how a community can maintain that same dialectic of originality and tradition that Guyer uncovers as the lasting contribution of Kant's theory of genius and art appreciation. Kant gives us radical action for the individual, but he doesn't give us a theory of productive collective action as we get in his discussion of the dialectic of genius and taste.

My focus on the parergonal status of genius suggests a possible answer to Arendt's claim that "Kant does tell one how to take others into account; he does not tell one how to combine with them in order to act" (44). The question is whether the ternary function of action in political life can be better integrated into a theory of community, in which case the exceptional status of agency capable of producing an alternative political reality would not be restricted to the ruler alone, but would instead impute creative agency to the entire community. The community might then be constituted through a reciprocal dynamic of acting and judging that doesn't reduce the citizenry, public, or members of the community to spectators, but instead paves the way for collective political action. We could even turn to contemporary political life for an example. Recent events in San Francisco and Boston display acts of political genius on the side of the citizenry that both challenge the law of the sovereign and the current "common sense" view of marriage as a union between a man and a woman. Seizing upon an opportunity afforded by San Francisco mayor Gavin Newsom's decision to allow his county clerk to wed gay and lesbian couples, gay and lesbian couples simply lined up outside of courthouses and began to wed. These spontaneous acts caused a national debate about how to define marriage and whether to change the existing laws. These acts of genius led to a change of "taste" regarding marriage on the local level, and have at least influenced the political community in the United States nationally. Perhaps their actions will lead to a gradual change among members of the national community, such that in the future both common sense and laws concerning same-sex marriage in the United States will no longer restrict marriage to traditional notions of a union between a man and a woman.

To base a political community on a generalized concept of genius—according to which genius is not merely "sacrificed" to the demands of taste, but rather reciprocally transforms taste—might free Kant's political philosophy from its conservative investment in the existing sovereign as guarantor of autonomy, and thereby allow a temporal dimension to enter the community that, rather than enslaving the members of the community to heteronomy, would in fact make each member happy that he or she acts with the greatest integrity.

Notes

1. Hannah Arendt, *Lectures on Kant's Political Philosophy* (Chicago: The University of Chicago Press, 1989); henceforth cited parenthetically in the text by page number. More recently, John McCumber's *Poetic Interaction* has celebrated the model

of freedom to be found in the third *Critique* as a basis for community. John McCumber, *Poetic Interaction: Language, Freedom, Reason* (Chicago: The University of Chicago Press, 1989), 259–74.

2. All references to Kant's *Critique of Judgment* are from Immanuel Kant, *Kritik der Urteilskraft* (Hamburg: Felix Meiner Verlag, 2001), 96. Hereafter cited parenthetically in the text by abbreviated title (*KU*) and page number. The translations are mine.

3. I am working with the definition of a *parergon* as that which is an ornamental accessory, a subsidiary work, or supplement or byproduct. Kant uses the term *parerga* (the German word is *Zieraten*) himself in section 14, when he says that ornaments exist as an element "that does not belong to the entire presentation of the object as an internal constituent, but only as an external addition" (78–79). Derrida picks up on this statement and shows how it operates within Kant's analytic of the beautiful as symptomatic of philosophical discourse itself: "A *parergon* comes against, beside, and in addition to the *ergon*, the work done, the fact, the work, but it does not fall to one side; it touches and cooperates within the operation, from a certain outside. Neither simply outside nor simply inside." See Jacques Derrida, *The Truth in Painting*, trans. Geoff Bennington and Ian McLeod (Chicago: University of Chicago Press, 1987), 54. Applying Derrida's term, Allison claims fine art and genius have an "extra-systematic" status vis-à-vis Kant's theory of taste. Henry E. Allison, *Kant's Theory of Taste: A Reading of the Critique of Aesthetic Judgments* (Cambridge: Cambridge University Press, 2001), 272. The use of the word *parergon* to describe the central problem driving my thesis in this paper is particularly apt because the ancient Greek term *ergon* meant both "work" and "deed."

4. "Mann könnte sogar den Geschmack durch das Beurteilungsvermögen desjenigen, was unser Gefühl an einer gegebenen Vorstellung ohne Vermittlung eines Begriffs allgemein mitteilbar macht, definieren" (177).

5. Compare Lyotard's denial of communicative rationality in favor of emotion in Jean-François Lyotard, *Lessons on the Analytic of the Sublime*, trans. Elizabeth Rottenberg (Stanford: Stanford University Press, 1994).

6. See Beiner and Nedelsky's introduction to *Judgment, Imagination, and Politics: Themes from Kant and Arendt*, ed. Ronald Beiner and Jennifer Nedelsky (Lanham: Rowman & Littlefield, 2001), xi.

7. Ronald Beiner, "Rereading Hannah Arendt's Kant Lectures," in *Judgment, Imagination, Politics*, 96.

8. See Hannah Arendt, *The Human Condition* (Chicago: University of Chicago Press, 1998).

9. Arendt touches very briefly on Kant's discussion of genius in *Lectures*, 62–65.

10. Henry E. Allison's *Kant's Theory of Taste* is good at elucidating the tortuous distinctions between beautiful nature, art, and fine art, especially as they revolve around "representation" (272–301).

11. Kant says genius "is the innate talent of the mind (*ingenium*) through which nature gives the rule to art" (*KU*, 193).

12. The third characteristic: genius cannot describe or demonstrate scientifically how it produces; and fourth: through genius nature prescribes rules to art rather than science and only insofar as art is beautiful (194). Kant has to qualify

the first condition with the second for fear of genius indulging in "originary non-sense" (the grotesque). For a discussion of nonsense in the *Critique of Judgment* see Winfried Menninghaus, *In Praise of Nonsense: Kant and Bluebeard*, trans. Henry Pick-ford (Stanford: Stanford University Press, 1999), 15–31. Menninghaus uncovers the function of nonsense within a logic of the "included Excluded" in the third *Critique*, a structural logic similar to that which I am describing as parergonal regarding genius/action within the aesthetic community.

13. Paul Guyer, *Kant and the Experience of Freedom: Essays on Aesthetics and Morality* (Cambridge: Cambridge University Press, 1996), 296–97.

14. For a careful description of spirit's production of metaphors, see Brigitte Sassen, "Artistic Genius and the Question of Creativity," in *Kant's Critique of Taste: Critical Essays*, ed. Paul Guyer (Lanham: Rowman & Littlefield, 2003), 171–79.

15. "I understand an aesthetic idea to be a representation of imagination that occasions much thought, but for which there is not some determinate thought, that is concept, adequate to it, so that consequently it cannot be fully captured and made understandable by language. —One sees easily that it is the counterpart of an idea of reason, which vice versa is a concept to which no intuition [*Anschauung*] (representation of imagination) can be adequate" (*KU*, 202).

16. Allison sees in Kant's discussion a "thick" and a "thin" conception of genius. The "thin" version of genius sides with the imagination, and must be "sacrificed" (Kant's word) to make room for the "thick" version of genius, the genius of "exemplary originality" in which understanding, judgment, and imagination all work together to produce aesthetic ideas and fine art. Of course, Allison champions this thick sense of genius and doesn't insist on the problematic status of such a genius. Allison, *Kant's Theory of Taste*, 298–301. In contrast, Guyer champions a dialectic of taste with this "thin" version of genius that doesn't dilute the radical activity of genius into a thick solution: Guyer, *Kant and the Experience of Freedom*, 291–303.

17. Arendt cites: *Kant, Political Writings*, ed. Hans Reiss, trans. H. B. Nisbet (Cambridge: Cambridge University Press, 1991), 174.

18. Kant, "The Contest of the Faculties": "These rights [to be co-legislators] . . . always remain an idea that can be fulfilled only on condition that the means employed to do so are compatible with morality. This limiting condition must not be overstepped by the people, who may not therefore pursue their rights by revolution, which is at all times unjust." "Perpetual Peace": "The rights of the people are injured, [then] no injustice befalls the tyrant when he is deposed. There can be no doubt on this point. Nevertheless, it is in the highest degree illegitimate for the subjects to seek their rights in this way. If they fail in the struggle and are then subjected to severe punishment, they cannot complain about injustice any more than the tyrant could if they had succeeded." My text follows the English translation of "On the Proverb: 'That May Be True in Theory, but It Is of No Practical Use'" (1793), in *Perpetual Peace and Other Essays*, trans. Ted Humphrey (Indianapolis: Hackett, 1983), 61–92 (hereafter cited in the text as TP).

19. Guyer, *Kant and the Experience of Freedom*, 275–303.

AESTHETIC REFLECTION
AND COMMUNITY

JANE KNELLER

> To solve the relationship between the singular and the universal, this kind of dialogue ["a dialogue of cultures"] could make use of Kant's theory of aesthetic judgment, which would understand culture and forms of life as singular experiences that have the pretension or hope of being universally shared.
>
> Juan Christóbal Cruz Revueltas, "Philosophy as a Problem in Latin America"

In an essay addressing communities of philosophers outside the European context, Juan Revueltas outlines the difficulties of self-definition and the construction of a uniquely Latin American philosophical community.[1] The problem as he explains it is to find a way between the horns of the dilemma of a colonizing universalism on the one hand and of a "false particularism" on the other. Revueltas argues that in describing or constructing a uniquely Latin American philosophical community it is necessary to avoid the occupation of indigenous communities by dominant European systems, since the latter tend to normalize and mask their own built-in cultural biases via claims to universal validity. His point is backed by a burgeoning literature critiquing the tendency of Western philosophy for its colonization of world philosophical communities and calling on these communities to define themselves.[2] On the other hand, Revueltas argues, it is equally necessary to refrain from characterizations that claim authenticity based on a regionalism that in his words "ignores the fact that an individual or community is a contingent historical phenomenon and forgets that individual communities are not monolithic realities but mobile groups of multiple identities."[3] Benedict Anderson's conception of "imagined communities" makes the same point:

> In fact, all communities larger than primordial units of face-to-face contact (and perhaps even these) are imagined. Communities are to be distinguished not by their falsity/genuineness, but by the style in which they are imagined.[4]

The dilemma posed by Revueltas is ubiquitous in multicultural theoretical contexts, even recently including discussions of the value—or disvalue—of aesthetic theory in illuminating community and cultural differences.[5] In light of this work, Revueltas's suggestion to turn to Kant, a grand patriarch of Western philosophy, for a solution (and an aesthetic one, no less) may seem surprising. I want to argue that it is in fact plausible, but only when one recognizes the profound contingency and unique character of aesthetic reflection as Kant understands it.

The relationship between aesthetic judgments and judgments evaluating cultural "objects" or practices have yet to be developed in detail. Adapting a Kantian account of aesthetic judgment to cultural judgments further complicates that task, given the lack of general agreement about the correct interpretation of Kantian judgments of taste. Moreover, from the perspective of the ideology critiques used to theorize multiculturalism, the very idea of a nonbiased aesthetic judgment appears compromised beyond repair. Pierre Bourdieu, for one, has famously rejected the "judgment of taste" conceived along roughly Kantian lines, as a bourgeois instrument of domination masquerading as "pure." "The eye," he says "is a product of history reproduced by education. . . . The 'pure' gaze is a historical invention linked to the emergence of an autonomous field of artistic production. . . ."[6] One can grant the importance of these criticisms of modernism and of biases inherent in Western theoretical analyses, however, while still maintaining that if serious cultural disagreements are to be adjudicated at all, there must surely be a place for judgment by first hand experience, "enlarged" imagination, and genuine individual attempts to communicate feelings.

If cross-cultural communication is to be possible at all, these judgments cannot be rejected from the outset as merely "a product of history reproduced by education." There is no doubt that aesthetic, historical, and educational practices produce and reproduce class, gender, race, and a host of other interests and biases, as these very authors so convincingly show. Kant's theory is no exception. But there is more to Kant's account of aesthetic reflection than many standard readings allow. Bourdieu and others typically adopt one interpretation of Kant's aesthetics, basically a formalist reading, while overlooking or minimizing certain aspects of the theory that might be taken to offset and even undermine the ideological uses of the theory. In what follows, I argue that Kant's analysis of the judgment of beauty, an "aesthetic reflective judgment," is a reasonably plausible account of how people can communicate particular feelings.

My conclusion, in part 2, will be to flesh out Revueltas's suggestion by showing how the aesthetic reflective judgment can be usefully extended to reflection upon the nature of particular community practices, traditions, and beliefs as they manifest themselves in particular cases, while avoiding the attendant twin dangers of universalism and particularism. This argument, if successful, will point to an entirely new sort of judgment, what I will call "judgments of community" that are closely related to pure judgments of taste, and may even be considered a subcategory of these. Judgments of community, I will argue, are "pure" in Kant's sense: they are disinterested, particular, and about the relationship of the subject's feeling to natural objects. The difference is that these "objects" are cultural and community experiences: events or artifacts that create a communicable feeling of pleasure when contemplated.

Revueltas's suggestion relies upon two central aspects of Kant's account, namely, the *singularity* of the judgment and also its *regulative*, or *nonconstitutive* nature. A third and fundamental element of these judgments is relevant to judgments of community as well, viz., that they are aesthetic: about feeling. Hannah Arendt, who first looked to Kant's critical theory of reflective aesthetic judgment for insights into political judgment and community, did not consider the reference to feeling in Kant's account to be of central importance in extrapolating a model for political judgment.[7] Yet Kant himself, following Baumgarten, clearly intends the term *aesthetic* to refer to a nonconceptual state of the subject, a state that, prior to his work on the *Critique of Judgment*, he did not believe could be based on universal principles *a priori*. Arendt understands the aesthetic judgment primarily in terms of the disinterestedness of the spectator, which in turn she interprets in light of Kant's discussion of the maxim of judgment or enlarged *thinking*. "Critical thinking is possible only when the standpoints of all others are open to inspection." Arendt's insight is to see the crucial role of imagination in political judgment:

> To be sure, it still goes on in isolation, but by the force of imagination it makes the others present and thus moves in a space that is potentially public, open to all sides; in other words, it adopts the position of Kant's world citizen. To think with an enlarged mentality means that one trains one's imagination to go visiting.[8]

Yet in the same passage, at the same time, she insists that this exercise in imaginative travel is not about shared feelings: "The trick of critical thinking does not consist in enormously enlarged empathy through which one can know what actually goes on in the mind of all others." Arendt understands Kant's aesthetic theory to be useful to politics insofar as it attributes disinterest, or enlarged thought, to judgment, but she makes relatively little reference to pleasure and the *felt* aspect of the judgment of beauty.

Ronald Beiner continues Arendt's project of extrapolating a theory of political judgment from Kant's aesthetics, and his account also downplays the role of feeling in the judgment of taste.[9] Yet the strength of Kant's aesthetics lies in his giving a plausible account of the legitimate claims that can be made upon the feelings of others. If he can provide such an argument without violating his own ban on demanding "pathological," i.e., contingent and *merely* subjective feelings of others, then a plausible case can be made for extending this account to what I am going to call "aesthetic judgments of community."

Judgments of Taste and Reflective Judgments

An extension of Kant's account of aesthetic reflective judgment from objects of aesthetic value to community practices and values requires an explanation of the former, as well as an argument for the extension of Kant's account of aesthetic experience of beauty to aesthetic experience of community.[10] It is to these two tasks that I now turn, beginning with a closer look at the unique aesthetic reflective character of judgments of taste. In order to make the second argument it is important to have a grasp of the basics of Kant's complex account of the judgment of taste. The basic elements will then be extended to an account of judgments about community and culture.

All of the characteristics of judgments of taste are united in the notion of a particular class of judgments that Kant calls "nondetermining" or "reflective" judgment. In the *Critique of Pure Reason* he characterizes the power of judgment generically as "the faculty of subsuming under rules" (A132/B171) and in the First Introduction to the *Critique of Judgment* as "the ability to subsume the particular under the universal" (20:201).[11] He contrasts the power of judgment with other aspects of our "ability to think," namely, our ability to *understand* (the ability to know universals/rules) and to *reason* (the ability to draw inferences (derive particulars) from universals/rules). For Kant, judging is an element of cognitive activity that is not *itself* conceptual or inferential.[12] Rather, it is merely the relating or mediating of instances and concepts "given from elsewhere" (20:202).

This is not to say that nothing guides this mediating process of judgment, however, and it is the aim of the third *Critique* to specify judgment's reflective process.[13] Kant calls reflection a power of assessing (*beurteilen*: to estimate or review; and he even claims that animals reflect, though only instinctively): "When we *reflect*, we need a principle just as much as we do when we determine, where the underlying concept of the object prescribes the rule to judgment and so takes the place of the principle" (20:211).

In other words, even though we are not determining an object of experience, either empirically or *a priori*, reflection is not random association.[14] In the case of judging natural systems, where the aim is to make a judgment about the conditions of the possibility of a *particular* experience *a priori*, Kant recognizes the need for a special sort of guidance *a priori*.

This principle is what he calls a "concept of a purposiveness of nature for the sake of our ability to cognize nature" (20:202).[15] But the principle of purposiveness is merely *regulative*; it does not "constitute" knowledge, as do the categories of the understanding:

> This lawfulness *in itself is contingent* (in terms of all concepts of the understanding). Judgment (only for its own benefit) presupposes it in nature, *as a presumption*. This lawfulness is a formal purposiveness in nature that we simply *assume* in it; it provides no basis for a theoretical cognition of nature, nor for a practical principle of freedom, but it does give us a principle for judging and investigating nature: a principle by which to seek, for particular experiences, the universal [empirical] laws we must follow in engaging in such experiences. (20:204, first two emphases added)

The principle of reflective judgment, which Kant also refers to as "the concept of nature as art" and "the concept of the technic of nature regarding its particular laws," yields "no basis for any theory, no cognition of objects and their character. . . . It gives us only a principle by which we [can] proceed in terms of empirical laws, which makes it possible for us to investigate nature" (20:204–5). And he adds that a critique of the power of reflective judgment will include a "concept of a technic of nature, as a *heuristic* principle for judging nature" (20:205, emphasis added).

In sum, reflective judgment, the activity of judging particular cases without applying concepts of the understanding, proceeds according to a heuristic principle that merely presumes that nature's forms are in harmony with our ability to apprehend them. This same guiding or regulative principle of the power of judgment is also the basis for aesthetic reflective judgments of taste/beauty, where the "heuristic" applies not to the investigation of natural systems but to very state of the subject when judging: *It applies to the inner state of the human mind when its operations are poised to run optimally, a state that occurs when a given presentation is "figuratively" or "formally" purposive for our cognitive powers.*[16] The heuristic principle of the technic of nature allows a reference to the conditions—the natural forms—that give rise to this pleasurable subjective state by presuming that this particular pleasure is somehow rooted also in the world, not just in the human mind. The principle of reflective judgment thus defines our reflective process as a feeling of nature's purposive forms.

Aesthetic Reflective Judgments

The Kantian judgment of taste is a reflective judgment about the beauty of an object in nature. As with all natural properties for Kant, what constitutes beauty is in large part a function of the human subject's constitution and it's capacities for exerting itself about what is given to it in experience. Taste in its primary sense for Kant is an account of one of these capacities. In a footnote to the first use of "taste" in the body of the "Critique of Aesthetic Judgment," Kant says that "The definition of taste on which I am basing this [analysis] is that it is the ability to judge the beautiful" (5:203). It is then characterized by four "moments" in the third *Critique*. As many scholars have pointed out, this categorization is strained. Kant forces it on his subject matter in order to reproduce the original table of judgments and categories of the first Critique, and also to recapitulate the organizational format of both the second and the first *Critiques*. (The four "categorical" headings appear in the Analytic, followed by an "antinomy of taste" in the section on the Dialectic.) Yet to the extent that Kant was mildly obsessive about maintaining the presentational structure of the first two *Critiques*, his explicit deviation from the format gains significance: Quality is placed first, and out of standard order in the table of judgments, because, Kant tells us, "an aesthetic judgment about the beautiful is concerned with it first." It is followed by Quantity, Relation, and Modality.

Quality: Aesthetic Judgment

Kant transgresses his own classification system to emphasize the peculiar nature of judgments of beauty. Qualitatively, these judgments are first and foremost *aesthetic*. The term is obviously not new for Kant, but the sense here has changed from his usage in the first *Critique* to include inner feelings as well as sensations given in pure and empirical intuition.[17] Kant says that an aesthetic judgment is one "whose determining basis *cannot be other than subjective*" (5:203). In the First Introduction he defines it as follows:

> We may define an aesthetic judgment in general as one whose predicate can never be cognition (i.e., concept of an object, though it may contain the subjective conditions for cognition as such). In such a judgment, the basis determining [it] is sensation. There is, however, only one so-called sensation that can never become the concept of an object: the feeling of pleasure and displeasure. This sensation is merely subjective, whereas all other sensation can be used for cognition. Hence an aesthetic judgment is one in which the basis determining it lies in a sensation that is connected directly with the feeling of pleasure and displeasure. (20:224)

Aesthetic judgments do not predicate a *concept* of an object. They do not make claims about the object's empirical properties, about its moral value, or its utility, all of which assume a concept either cognitive or practical. Rather they reference an object (or the perception or representation of it) only in terms of its causal relation to a feeling of pleasure or displeasure in the judging subject. What such judgments are primarily or "directly" (5:208) about is the feeling state of the subject who is making a judgment as a result of perceiving the object. Put as simply as possible, aesthetic judgments are claims about the feelings produced by an object in a subject via the latter's perception of the former.[18]

Kant distinguishes two kinds of aesthetic judgment: If I claim that my perception of something *immediately* produces pleasurable feelings in me, the resulting judgment is in Kant's terms a "judgment of sense" (20:224; 4:214). It is a direct report on my feelings and is "merely" subjective. On the other hand, if my perception is related to my feelings as a result of contemplating or reflecting upon the object, that is, as a result of a more complex sustained attentiveness to the object, then according to Kant the pleasure that arises is "disinterested" and the judgment is "of taste."[19] It is the result of an act of reflection involving the interplay of imagination and understanding. That is, it is a claim that expresses this special pleasure that could only arise from thinking reflectively about, as opposed to responding reflexively to, the object. It is about a pleasure not merely stimulated by my perception (though perception is necessary), but a pleasure caused in me by my deliberate, conscious, and imaginative attentiveness as I linger over the perception.

It is in this sense that Kant can assert that disinterested pleasure is not "connected with the presentation of an object's existence" (5:204). That is, he contrasts pleasure in the beautiful with pleasure in the merely "agreeable," where the latter is a pleasure that is at the same time a desire to "have" the object. "When I speak of the agreeable, I am not granting mere approval: the agreeable produces an inclination" (5:207). Judgments of sense are in this regard similar to nonaesthetic ("determining" or "logical") judgments. Both, according to Kant, produce an interest. Cognitive judgments involve an interest in the correct application of a concept to a particular, a "recognition interest," so to speak. Judgments about the good, though practical, are also conceptual inasmuch as we do not simply react to a stimulating sensation, we also recognize that a presentation falls under a concept of what that sort of thing *ought* to be. Still, just as in judgments of sense, we also express an interested liking for the object of our judgment: we "want" the good to be the case.

Thus Kant concludes that what distinguishes judgments of taste from both aesthetic nonreflective judgments and nonaesthetic, cognitive judgments is that they "judge an object, or a way of presenting it, by means of a liking or disliking *devoid of all interest*. The object of such a liking is called *beautiful*" (5:211). Commentators have pointed out that it does not follow from this view that the judging subject cares not at all for the object contemplated.[20] If I find a mountain landscape beautiful, I am expressing a pleasure it gives me by virtue of its intrinsic features, not a desire to call my real estate agent to see if it is for sale, nor to slake my thirst in its streams, nor even to admire it for some preconceived notion of perfection (as a mountain climber might assess the value of the vertical surfaces for her adventures, or a geologist might assess its value for researching certain formations, etc.). In other words, it is the very "form" of the mountain that is pleasurable to contemplate.

Quantity: Subjective Universality

The quantity, or scope, of the judgment of taste follows from its disinterested quality, according to Kant (5:211). If a judgment expresses my liking for something apart from personal, moral, or cognitive interest, then I "cannot help judging that it must contain a basis for being liked [that holds] for everyone" (5:211). The scope of the judgment of taste thus ranges over all human beings and is in this sense universal. Because I feel "completely free" of subjective interest with respect to my liking for the object of my judgment, Kant says, I will talk about this free reflection and the resulting pleasure as if it were a characteristic of the object itself. What warrants this way of talking is the intersubjective validity that I assume results from my disinterested stance: if I feel this way, anyone in the same disinterested position will too. At the same time, my claim to the agreement of others is based on a feeling, not an objective concept:

> It follows that, since a judgment of taste involves the consciousness that all interest is kept out of it, it must also involve a claim to being valid for everyone, but without having a universality based on concepts. In other words, a judgment of taste must involve a claim to subjective universality. (5:212)

These judgments lack "objective" universal validity. They are not, logically speaking, universal generalizations, but instead are claims about an actual feeling of one particular object's effect on oneself, viz., the reflective pleasure to which it gives rise. For this reason Kant says they must be logically singular: ("*This* rose is beautiful")—and no general rule can help me *prove* the judgment by allowing an inference to the beauty of the object judged. This is why, Kant says, "We want to submit the object to our own eyes, just as if our liking of it depended on that sensation" (5:216).

"And yet," he continues, "if we then call the object beautiful, we believe we have a universal voice, and lay claim to the agreement of everyone . . ." (5:216). If upon aesthetic reflection on it an object produces pleasure in me, I "cannot help but judge" that others reflecting aesthetically upon that very object will feel this way too. This projection of my own particular feeling in judging an object present to my senses accounts for that element of what Kant calls an "aesthetic universal validity" or an "aesthetic quantity of universality" (215) in the judgment. In making these judgments I do not assume that everyone will agree, but rather "require"—in the sense of "expect"—

that they will share my feeling. Such a judgment may thus find confirmation [*Bestätigung*] in the agreement of others, but is not thereby proven as if I were to say "All roses are beautiful." If I do not find universal agreement, Kant suggests here, then I have reason to reconsider whether my judgment was indeed disinterested in the first place, i.e., whether I might have made an erroneous judgment of taste. If, however, I am sure that I have "observe[d] these conditions [of disinterest]," I may feel certain that I can count on the agreement of others (216).

The universal scope of a judgment of taste is thus a function of the fact that its conditions are quite generic, and that it occurs at a level of subjectivity involved in all cognition:

> A presentation that, though singular and not compared with others, yet harmonizes with the conditions of the universality that is the business of the understanding in general, brings the cognitive powers into that proportional attunement which we require for all cognition and which, therefore, we also consider valid for everyone who is so constituted as to judge by means of understanding and the senses in combination (in other words for all human beings). (5:219)

Subjective, aesthetic generality here is elaborated in Kant's well-known account of the "state of the *free play* of the cognitive powers" (5:217). Typically, i.e., in cognition, the imagination and the understanding work together for the purpose of combining given intuitions (configured and reproduced in imagination) to be united in a determinate concept (supplied by the understanding), a relation described in excruciating and opaque detail in the *Critique of Pure Reason*. What is new in the "Critique of Aesthetic Judgment" is Kant's focus on the general state of the subject in the process of cognition: a state that requires an account of a cooperative interaction between the capacity to imagine and the capacity to conceive. No cognition can arise without this interaction, but that interaction may occur without resulting in cognition.[21] In this case a presentation may give rise to a feeling (of pleasure in the free play of imagination and understanding) apart from any determinate concept. Because this pleasure is the result of the presentation being processed by conditions that hold for "cognition in general," it must be assumed that these conditions are common to all human beings. At this point, Kant says, we postulate nothing more or less than a "universal voice" (5:116), i.e., the universal *communicability* (not the actual communication) that makes valid aesthetic judgments possible.

Relation: Purposiveness Without Purpose

The moment of "relation" for Kant's analysis refers, as it does in the first *Critique*, to the sort of connection the judgment makes between the object judged and the judging subject. But the difference here is that in dealing with the power of judgment, whose sole function is to relate or mediate representations at all levels of generality, nothing is determined by this relating—no object is constituted and no action is commanded or forbidden. If it is the function of understanding and reason to provide rules for relating representations, then the fundamental relation predicated in a purely reflective judgment of taste is "merely the relation of the presentational powers [imagination and understanding] to each other, so far as they are determined by a presentation."[22] Judgments of taste involve a complex of relations: first, the subject's own internal relation of harmonic play between imagination and understanding, and second, the relation of that harmony to the object that first occasions it. Hence the phrase "so far as they are determined by a presentation" is important: when we judge something to be beautiful, we *thereby* judge that our disinterested pleasure was caused by the perceived object. Because the pleasure is based on reflection, and we are not "interested" in it for any particular purpose, we cannot readily articulate why we find *the object* so pleasing except to point out that its form fits and facilitates our reflective capacities. Nothing in the mechanically determined world of objects guarantees that some of them should be so perfectly suited to our contemplation, causing us to linger over them (5:222). So, Kant argues, we cannot identify the beautiful by any simple property of the object; instead, we elliptically refer to that quality in the object that makes it so well-suited to our generic capacity for perception and understanding. We might call this relational property "being *as if* created for the purpose of our aesthetic reflective capacity."

The relational character of beauty is for Kant a kind of formal as opposed to substantive or specific purposiveness. It is purposiveness without a definite purpose, a notion that captures the essentially reflective nature of these judgments. The principle of reflection, as we saw, claims that nature's forms are meant to further our cognitive capacities. This claim, no more than a heuristic device or assumption, is necessary if aesthetic reflection is to be possible in the first place. It is the basis for nothing more (or less) than the hope or presumption that such objects can be found and it provides the guiding thread that helps us seek and find these experiences in the first place.[23]

Because of its hopeful account of our relationship to the world, the judgment of taste, according to Kant, can give rise to further judgments that are not themselves "pure" disinterested judgments, but that express concern for the beautiful object. The disinterested judgment of taste might lead us to further judge that the beautiful object *should be* reproduced and/or preserved. It might lead us to judge that the object is valuable intrinsically, and that it *ought* to exist whether or not it occasions disinterested pleasure in anyone. So although the pure pleasure in the beautiful is itself merely contemplative and not action guiding, it may provide the *impetus* for what Kant calls "applied" judgments of taste. Applied judgments of taste, for their part, "can never be purely aesthetic" (5:236).[24]

Modality: Exemplary Necessity

Judgments of taste assert a kind of necessity. I urge my judgment upon others, and expect that if they judge in a properly aesthetic reflective way, then necessarily, they will also feel the pleasure I feel in reflecting on the beauty of the object. For Kant, judgment in general brings with it the possibility of pleasure, and is always accompanied by some feeling or other.[25] Pleasure in the conceptual recognition of something is always possible for human beings, even if particular circumstances preclude or overwhelm that pleasure. A physical stimulus produces an immediate pleasure (or pain) whose *actuality* the subject reports in what Kant calls "judgments of sense." And there is a certain intellectual satisfaction that according to Kant *necessarily* accompanies making the right moral choice. But the pleasure I take in the beautiful is of a special sort. I claim necessity for my judgment about it, not because everyone *will* feel this pleasure in the object: taste is notoriously difficult to get agreement upon precisely because it is so hard to set up the conditions under which it may occur. Neither am I demanding that everyone necessarily behave in a certain way toward the object of my judgment (although my judgment might lead me to make an "impure" or "applied" judgment that does make such demands, e.g., for the conservation, preservation, or restoration of the beautiful thing). Rather, in the judgment of taste, my claim is that *if* another human being were to view the object in an aesthetic reflective way, that person *would* agree with my judgment. I thus hold my judgment up as an example of judgment in accordance with a universal principle, Kant says, and in this sense demand of everyone their agreement. Such "exemplary necessity" is "a necessity of the assent of everyone to a judgment that is regarded as an example of a universal rule that we are unable to state" (5:237).

The necessity of the judgment is conditional on the assumption of a common ability to appreciate things that "feel" purposive to us, even though we cannot identify any purpose. In other words, we assume that we share a sense in common with others.

Justifying the Assumption of a Common Aesthetic Sense

In section 21 of the third *Critique* Kant argues that we do indeed have reason to suppose a common aesthetic sense. In completing his analysis, Kant intends to "unite all these [elements] ultimately in the idea of a common sense" (5:240, sec. 22), and it is clear that the notion of a common aesthetic sense is a fundamental assumption and leading premise in his argument for our right to make claims on the agreement of others in making judgments of taste. The right to presuppose a common sense is argued for in section 21 and becomes the cornerstone of the deduction of taste in sections 38–40. In an important footnote at the beginning of the deduction "proper" (section 38, "Deduction of Judgments of Taste"), Kant reduces the justification of judgments of taste to two assumptions:

> (1) that in all people the subjective conditions of this power are the same as concerns the relations required for cognition as such between the cognitive powers that are activated in the power of judgment, and this must be true, for otherwise people could not communicate their presentations to one another, indeed they could not even communicate cognition: (2) that the judgment has taken into consideration merely this relation (and hence the *formal condition* of the power of judgment) and is pure. . . . But even if a mistake is made on the latter point, this amounts to nothing but an incorrect application in a particular case, of an authority given to us by a law, and in no way annuls the authority [itself]. (5:290, n15)

That everyone shares a common sense is an assumption or an "idea"—nothing can prove its existence, but an argument has been given that justifies it on the basis of its being a necessary condition of the very possibility of communication in general. In this respect the universal communicability of the judgment of taste has been "deduced." The second assumption that Kant claims is necessary for judgments of taste to be justified is one based on the principle of reflection already discussed, namely, the heuristic principle (the "law," mentioned at the end of the note, that nature produces forms that are suited to our capacity for reflection).

Here the two "assumptions," *sensus communis* and the principle of reflective judgment, are placed on equal footing. In spite of his argument for the *a priori* necessity of the assumption of common sense, Kant emphasizes its regulative, heuristic nature. Judgments of taste are not judgments about natural objects, but are rather about the *relationship* of our cognitive abilities to natural objects. Such judgments always already assume that something underwrites this relationship. That "something" is inarticulable for the simple reason that it lies outside the realm of the sensible:

> It is impossible to provide a determinate, objective principle of taste that would allow us to guide, to test, and to prove its judgments, because then they would not be judgments of taste. As for the subjective principle—i.e., the indeterminate idea of the supersensible in us—as the sole key for solving the mystery of this ability [i.e., taste] concealed from us even as to its sources, we can do no more than point to it: but there is nothing we can do that would allow us to grasp it any further. (5:341)

In sum, Kant's analysis and deduction of aesthetic reflection on beauty provides an account of a judgment that may claim universal necessity but that is always deeply contingent: it depends on a heuristic assumption about the uniformity of nature as well as upon the assumption of a shared ability to feel our own cognitive processes. *If* these assumptions are plausible, and *if* we have proceeded to apply the judgment properly (under conditions specified by the analysis itself, of disinterested contemplation), then, and only then, can we claim universality and necessity for our judgments. Given this conditional and, for that very reason, more plausible account, Kant's analysis holds out the possibility of a very different sort of judging: one that bridges the gap between dogmatic (apodictic) assertion based on constitutive universal principles and mere statement of opinion. Such a model of judgment is especially promising, as Revueltas suggests, in the case of understanding our judgments of community and culture.

From Judgments of Taste to Judgments of Community

Kant's analysis of taste distinguishes between "pure" and "applied" judgments of taste where the latter are judgments that embody an interest in the existence of the object judged. In extending Kant's account to judgments of community it might initially seem more plausible to turn to an "applied" model. That is, judgments involving the perception and appreciation of community practices, events, and objects are so closely and obviously tied to individual interests that it seems these should be construed as either judgments of sense or cognitive/moral judgments rather than "disinterested" aesthetic reflections. I want to resist this move. Although an account of applied judgments of community can also be developed along Kantian lines, Revueltas's suggestion that judgments about community values should be understood along the lines of pure judgments of taste promises an innovative and potentially fruitful way to look at the question. Indeed, if the Kantian model is correct, the applied judgments necessary for practical, moral decisions about community will depend upon pure judgments of community for their plausibility. Moreover, using the applied model from the start would import moral content, or empirical agreement, into our reflections, and this would invite the problems mentioned at the outset of preemptive universalism or false particularism. I will argue that Kant's account allows an extension from the disinterested to the moral that can avoid these problems. To show how this extension works, I will turn to each of the characteristics of pure judgments of taste in turn.

Reflective Judgments of Community

Although judgments about the value of a communal experience or outlook are often "merely" subjective, they may be reflective, just as are judgments of taste. Recall that Kant believes that in reflective judgment "what is presupposed is that nature, even in its empirical laws, has adhered to a certain parsimony suitable for our judgment, and adhered to a uniformity we can grasp; and this presupposition must precede all comparison, as an *a priori* principle of judgment" (20:213). At the same time this presupposition of "a purposiveness of nature for the sake of our ability to cognize nature" (20:202) is regulative and only a presumption. It is this assumption that, in the case of aesthetic reflective judgment, guides my search for objects that occasion "free play" of my cognitive faculties—a pleasurable mental "enlivening" as a result of reflection upon them. Analogously, in judging an "object of community" (e.g., a ritual, tradition, or other community "event"), I must also assume from the start that natural "forms of community" are suitable for occasioning a similar mental "awakening." Before I can appreciate it aesthetically and without "interest" I must presume, for heuristic purposes, that shared forms of community life are possible. Otherwise there would be no point in reflecting. So I must assume the possibility that something in this community will make me want to watch, linger over, and appreciate it.

Here a comment about the "community" under discussion is in order: I do not want to attempt a definition or even give an account of necessary conditions of community; for the purposes of this paper, I will simply use the term in its broadest connotation. I may reflectively appreciate community from within, i.e., when I contemplate my own community's practices (and of course I will belong to more than one community, some of which may overlap and some of which may not), or I may contemplate a community that is entirely distinct from my own. The point, however, is that in order for my contemplation to be aesthetic and reflective, I will be distancing myself from both in ways that put them, ideally, on a par with each other. The difficulties attendant upon achieving disinterest, both as an insider and as an outsider to any given community, may be acknowledged without succumbing to skepticism about the very possibility of such an achievement. Judgments of community, even more than judgments of taste, are always presumptuous for this reason, and it is important that we remain critical at all times of our claims to disinterested judgment. But absolute skepticism need not follow.

Just because it is so presumptuous, the judgment about community cannot claim objectivity in the sense of being a determinate claim to truth about the object. Like all reflective judgments it will be a "nonjudgmental" judgment. While I certainly intend more by it than that it be taken simply as a report of my feelings, and I expect or "require" that others make the same judgment when they experience its object, in the end this sense of requirement or expectation is really little more than a hope. I know that I can only point others in the direction of my experience, ask them to assume they will find it, and urge them to try for themselves.

Aesthetic Quality of "Pure" Judgments of Community

As in judgments of taste, so in the case of my judgment about community: first hand perceptual experience is essential. I am not simply a rational observer. Kant's own travel behavior notwithstanding, judging community "objects" requires on this model that one *actually* experience the object or event. So, to paraphrase Kant's own sort of example, I might read about a certain community festival and the dances and practices involved, and on the basis of a concept of what is "good" or "appropriate" I may *conclude* that this or that behavior or practice is good or appropriate, or not. This sort of judgment courts the evil of dogmatism because it is neither aesthetic nor reflective. On the other hand, my judgment would be truly aesthetic and reflective if I actually attend the festival, and at some point during the proceedings distanced myself and reflected on the general form of the event. If my judgment is not anthropological, moral, or just plain selfish, but rather expresses the pleasure I feel in reflecting upon the event and the expectation that others in my circumstance would enjoy it too, I then assert a "pure" aesthetic judgment of community and I exhibit what could be called "cultural taste."

For this judgment to fit Kant's analysis of an aesthetic judgment, it would have to meet the criteria of disinterestedness already described. This is illustrated in the example by the fact that no scientific enterprise is being pursued, no moral agenda is motivating the judgment, and it is not, in the reflective moment, prompted even by a desire to have fun.[26] All or any of these might explain why I find myself in the situation in the first place, just as I might experience the natural beauty of a mountain stream as I gather samples for an entomology project. The judgment itself, however, is without any of this baggage. In the midst of the merriment, ritual, or dance, I may suddenly find myself reflecting on the "form" of the event, something that prompts me to express my pleasure and my admiration for it, and my expectation that others would experience this as well.

Disinterest is not a cold, distanced, and abstracting attitude in Kant's account of beauty and it need not be in the case of cultural taste, either. Although Kant occasionally speaks of the need to abstract from my particular interests in order to enter into this frame of mind, the frame of mind itself is that of "free play." In the case of judgments of community, it is aptly described as a kind of open-mindedness, following what Kant calls the maxim of judgment: "to think from the standpoint of everyone else" (5:294). Regardless of their intellectual talents, Kant argues, persons can use what abilities they do have to produce a "broadened mind" if they override . . . the private subjective conditions of [their] judgment, into which so many others are locked, as it were, and reflect . . . on [their] own judgment from a *universal standpoint* (which [they] can determine only by transferring themselves to the standpoint of others). (5:295)

Arendt refers to this passage in her account of political judgment and it is the basis for her claim that as a critical thinker one must "train one's imagination to go visiting." What is missing in her account is discussion of the crucial passage that follows in this section, in which Kant defines taste as a kind of *sensus communis* (5:295). Here he explicitly distinguishes *thinking with* from *feeling with* others, arguing that there is more reason to call feeling a common *sense* than there is to refer to thinking in this way. In judgments of taste, the presentation communicates itself *not as a thought, but as an inner feeling* of a purposive state of mind. This is a perfect description of what is communicated in judgments about community "presentations" as well. It is not that I am attempting to think with others, but rather to express the universally shareable nature of my feelings about something in the community. What enables me to do so is that I was able to put myself in the position of any imaginative, feeling person in experiencing it, that I was, in other words, disinterested in my reflection.

Maria Lugones's work on "playfulness," "world-travel," and "loving perception" is closer to the account of judgments of community I am suggesting than is Arendt's. She emphasizes the nonagonistic nature of the "playful attitude" and the necessity of giving up reliance on rules, pointing out the difficulties in entering another's space for the sake of creatively and constructively experiencing it:

Playfulness is, in part, an openness to being a fool, which is a combination of not worrying about competence, not being self-important, not taking norms as sacred, and finding ambiguity and double edges a source of wisdom and delight.[27]

This account of letting go of one's self-consciousness and defensiveness, of dropping the reverence for norms, and of appreciating the multiple sources of complexity and combination in the cross-cultural experience is perfectly compatible with Kant's view of the state of mind required for disinterested free play of the imagination: I must cease to be self-centered around my own interests (the disinterest requirement), I must not rely on even the most established rules of criticism (the aesthetic requirement—I must "see" for myself), and I must open my imagination to free play with an array of presentations without trying to bring them under a single unified concept (the nondetermining nature of aesthetic reflection—its focus on the interplay of forms).

Subjective Universality of Judgments of Community

Since I realize that there is nothing but my own feeling about an object prompting this judgment, and yet at the same time I expect that others agree with me, my judgment is, in Kant's terms, subjectively universal. It is also the case that the experience, as already mentioned, must always be *singular*. In judgments of taste, "beauty" is never a determinate concept, i.e., a definition or generalization; the judgment is always that this or that *particular* case is beautiful. And so in the reflective aesthetic community judgment: the claim would be that this event/case produces reflective pleasure in anyone open, i.e., disinterested enough to appreciate it. It is not deduced from a prior concept or belief of what is "good community"—it is about *this* case.

Relation to the Object in the Judgment of Community

The guiding thread for experiencing community aesthetically, as for judgments of beauty, is the reflective principle of "purposiveness without purpose" or, as Kant also calls it, "formal purposiveness" attributed to the object of the aesthetic reflective judgment. If, in a moment of disinterested imaginative free play, I find that an object/event causes a pleasure in me that can only be attributed to a kind of harmony between the object/event and my (reflective) self, such that I seek to return to and prolong the experience, then I would have to say that there is something appropriate for human reflection in this experience. Although this "something" is only felt, and as a feeling it is not discursively specifiable, still I judge that there really is something there that is *as if* meant to harmonize with my reflective capacities. This relationship between the object and myself in turn leads me to want and, based on the assumption that we all share a common aesthetic sense, to expect others to be able to feel this harmonious relationship too. Thus the principle of reflective judgment guides me toward and puts me in relationship with others.

However, relations expressed in the *pure* judgment of taste or community are not "interested" ones. In itself the judgment does not prompt action or claim knowledge. Reflective judgments of community, like judgments of taste, may prompt other judgments that do lead to action. That is, they may prompt "applied" or interested judgments about their objects. Just as Kant argues that the appreciation of natural beauty may be tied to a love for nature's value in its own right (5:298–303, sec. 42), it seems equally plausible to suppose that aesthetic reflective appreciation of community objects/events may eventuate in a love for and concern for the preservation of those objects/events. But as with judgments of taste, the universality of the original aesthetic reflective judgment of community depends on the noninvolvement of those interests.

Exemplary Necessity of Judgments of Community

An aesthetic reflective judgment claims to be necessarily true in the very mit-
igated sense of being held up as an example of the use of a principle, universal
in scope, that cannot be articulated except as a "perhaps" (5:340): "perhaps"
there is something that transcends individual human experience and stands
behind the human condition. So also "exemplary necessity" makes sense as
a description of the judgment of community that I want to construct: I hold
my judgment up to the light of everyone's scrutiny, claiming it is an example
of the application of a universal principle. I expect agreement because I have
judged under the appropriate aesthetic reflective conditions. I am therefore
sure that my judgment transcends my individual experience in its reference
to the world of common human experience generally, a world in which we
presume that nature cooperates with our ability to judge. At the same time
it is necessary because I have every reason to assume (in fact I must assume)
that all human cognition, in general, is capable of the reflective pleasure
that my experience, and hence my statement of it in a judgment, exemplifies. I simply hold my judgment up to examination by others and expect, on
the basis of the way I have judged, that they will make the same judgment in
my circumstances. This is why enthusiastic travelers will urge you to make
the trip yourself, or "wish you were here" to experience it with them.

Justifying the Assumption of a Common Aesthetic
Sense for Community

Finally, as with the judgment of taste, there are two basic assumptions at
work in an aesthetic reflective "judgment of community": first, that we all
share a common ability to feel the same pleasure in reflection, and second,
that I have not erred in believing that the judgment is a result of the conditions of disinterested reflection. Because neither of these conditions is easy
to achieve—reflection requires leisure, a calm state of mind, and being absolutely certain that I have left my own cultural and personal interests aside—
these judgments in their "pure" form will be rare. Hence, when made, they
must always be adopted with a sense of their fallibility.

In this section I have begun a sketch of what the aesthetic reflective judgment of community might look like. I will conclude the argument for this
expansion of the concept of reflective judgment by pointing to one more
useful parallel to Kant's argument justifying judgments of taste, namely, the
antinomy of taste.

Kant's account of the antinomy, or apparent contradiction, in the concept
of taste is strongly analogous to the problem Revueltas mentions and that
many others have belabored in their accounts of the shared and disparate

claims of communities. The antinomy of taste begins with common sayings reflective of popular opinion about taste: first, that it is merely subjective, "everyone has their own taste," and second, that "there is no disputing about taste." (Kant sets these claims in opposition, since the former asserts that opposing tastes express merely subjective opinion and thus cannot be a source of conflict, whereas the latter asserts that people do in fact quarrel about taste, even though no objective dispute is possible.) Kant sets up the antinomy as follows: the thesis "a judgment of taste is not based on concepts" captures the first bit of common wisdom, while the antithesis "a judgment of taste is based on concepts" captures the underlying assumption of the second, namely, that judgments do in fact conflict.

In his second "Comment" on the antinomy, Kant elaborates by contrasting the relativism of the thesis with the absolutism of the antithesis. In relativism the issue is resolved by giving up on any possibility of underlying consensus in human aesthetics:

> so that we hold that all claim to necessary universal assent is a baseless, vain delusion and [hold that] a judgment of taste deserves to be considered correct only insofar as there *happen* to be many people agreeing on it; . . . because . . . there is a contingent uniformity in the organization of [different] subjects. (5:345)

The antithetical case supposes that some objective quality, or "perfection" is discoverable in the thing itself, "so that basically the judgment is teleological, and we call it aesthetic only because of the confusion that here attaches to our reflection."

The analogy to judgments of community is easy enough to draw. Relativism about judgments of the value of community practices, institutions, etc. is standard fare not only in common opinion but also in theoretical accounts. Attempts to combat it tend toward versions of teleological responses[28] and often end up sounding, on the surface at least, something like the perfectionist accounts Kant criticizes. The problems with both are clear from the opening discussion of this essay. Absolutist accounts, because they claim objective knowledge about what constitutes "good" or "ideal" communities, cannot really be aesthetic reflective judgments (they may even be true, but they are not judgments based on firsthand experience and feeling). For this reason they are prone to dogmatism and are extremely dangerous in their application. Examples abound in religious and political communities. Relativism, on the other hand, is hardly less dangerous since it gives up altogether the hope of shared intercommunity judgments.

Kant's solution in the case of taste, couched in the language of "*a priori* principles" and the "supersensible," is unfortunately easy to dismiss. But I hope to have shown that the contingent, regulative nature of the aesthetic reflective judgment has little to do with metaphysical speculation. The supersensible that Kant refers to in these judgments is no more or less than the "principle of nature's subjective purposiveness for our cognitive power," or "the concept of a general basis of nature's subjective purposiveness for our power of judgment" (5:340) and these, as we saw, are in the first case a purely heuristic principle, adopted as a guiding thread for aesthetic reflection, and in the second, a "postulate" necessary for explaining the possibility of cognition generally. These assumptions enable us to gesture toward the feeling we are having in the presence of beauty as one that is more than momentary and personal.

Analogous feelings may also accompany reflective firsthand experience of community. These are the experiences that the traveler seeks and, in the seeking, assumes she can find in the world. She cannot give up *a priori* on the possibility of a consensus of feeling, and so assumes, however implicitly, that nature has arranged things such that vastly different cultures and societies exhibit some unity of feeling and purpose. Not being a dogmatist, she refuses to claim to know what that purpose is, even though on occasion she finds herself so positioned as to feel *as if* it existed. The "supersensible" here is only a principle assumed for the sake of a hope that she may, perhaps, discover a genuine harmony of community purposes in the world. These "supersensible" assumptions are a hermeneutic strategy. Together they provide a solution to the problem of intercommunity discourse because without them there is not even a hope of finding a nondogmatic, noncoercive approach to judging one's own and others' communities.

Conclusion

In *The Human Condition*, Hannah Arendt says:

> The activity of taste decides how this world, independent of its utility and our vital interests in it, is to look or sound. . . . For judgments of taste, the world is the primary thing, not man, neither man's life nor his self.[29]

The last sentence might seem to belie the importance of intersubjectivity in judgments of taste and of the subjective, but Arendt is of course not denying this. The point in the passage is that the perspective taken in the judgment of taste projects the individual into a public sphere where the emphasis is no longer on the individual's peculiar needs and interests, not even her moral ones. The judgment of taste is directed toward "deciding" how and where human beings fit into their world. If the argument of this essay holds, then we can specify a second sense of "taste," one that may be called social and cultural, but that is best characterized as predicating human community of certain features of the world, in a way analogous to the predication of beauty of objects of nature and art.

There is no word analogous to "beauty" for instances of positive community value, and the analysis of this essay might help explain why: such a term would have to indicate a disinterested feeling attributed universally on the basis of a regulative, not constitutive, principle of purposiveness. Making disinterested judgments about community is not an easy matter. It can be exceedingly difficult to put oneself into a state of mind free of prejudice and the baggage of one's own community. Nevertheless the difficulty of finding and maintaining the standpoint should not count against trying, and as Kant himself says, "nothing could be more natural," really, than making the effort. It is, after all, one of life's great pleasures to be able to reflect upon uplifting experiences one has in community, whether one's own, or that of others. The more distant and difficult to understand, the greater the reflective pleasure when moments of genuine attunement occur.

Positioning oneself to make these judgments and have these feelings requires literally putting oneself in the places of others, traveling to their community spaces, leaving behind as far as possible one's partisan side to attempt to experience the position from an "other" side. Just as experiencing the beauty the world has to offer sometimes requires the sacrifice of familiarity and ease, so too experiencing other forms of community may require not only physical displacement but also a potentially unsettling displacement of one's own interests and psychological props. For reasons both within and outside their control, not everyone can or will achieve such judgments. But when they are successfully made, their value is immense. To paraphrase Arendt, such judgments "will decide how human community is to look and sound." Ultimately, it should be added, such judgments will decide how human community feels. They will "make the world community the thing, not individual lives and selves."

Notes

1. Juan Christóbal Cruz Revueltas, "Philosophy as a Problem in Latin America," in *What Philosophy Is*, ed. Havi Carel and David Gamez (New York: Continuum, 2004), 116–25.

2. Postcolonial studies collections that contain some of the most significant works to date include *The Post-Colonial Studies Reader*, ed. Bill Ashcroft, Gareth Griffiths, and Helen Tiffin (New York: Routledge, 1995), esp. parts 1 and 2. This anthology focuses on literatures primarily, but the issues raised are effectively similar in the case of philosophies, and ultimately for the larger debate about universality and difference in human community. For an excellent introduction to the philosophical issues for philosophy itself, see *Postcolonial African Philosophy: A Critical Reader*, ed. Emmanuel Chukwudi Eze (Oxford: Blackwell, 1997), especially Eze's introduction, 1–21, and, for the purposes of this paper especially, his essay "The Color of Reason: The Idea of 'Race' in Kant's Anthropology." For a sustained and rigorous critique of classic

European contractarian philosophy, see Charles Mills, *The Racial Contract* (Ithaca: Cornell University Press, 1997).

3. Revueltas, "Philosophy as a Problem in Latin America," 118.

4. Benedict Anderson, *Imagined Communities* (London: Verso, 1983, rev. ed. 1991), 6. The book's focus is on the "community" of the nation-state and nationalism, but as this quotation shows, his notion of "imagined communities" holds for much smaller units as well.

5. See *The New Aestheticism*, ed. John J. Joughin and Simon Malpas (Manchester: Manchester University Press, 2003). Andrew Bowie's essay, "What Comes After Art?" is especially relevant to the topic of this paper. See in particular his response to Adorno's reductive view of aesthetic universalism: "The question is, though, whether a wholesale rejection of [Kant's aim of universality in aesthetic judgment] does not obviate the *point* of the critical perspective that gives rise to the rejection. If there is no access to what could be understood in some way as taking us *beyond* our being determined by objective social pressures, the sense that these pressures are a problem at all becomes hard to understand" (75).

6. Pierre Bourdieu, *Distinction: A Social Critique of the Judgment of Taste*, trans. Richard Nice (Cambridge: Harvard University Press, 1984), 3; originally published as *La Distinction: Critique sociale du jugement* (Paris: Les Éditions de Minuit, 1979). See also Martha Woodmansee, *The Author, Art, and the Market: Rereading the History of Aesthetics* (New York: Columbia University Press, 1994), and Terry Eagleton, *The Ideology of the Aesthetic* (Oxford: Basil Blackwell, 1990), for analyses of the broad cultural and economic forces driving the modern concept of the autonomy of art, a concept that is often taken to be central to Kant's aesthetics.

7. See Hannah Arendt, *Lectures on Kant's Political Philosophy*, ed. Ronald Beiner (Chicago: University of Chicago Press, 1982); Ronald Beiner, *Political Judgment* (Chicago: University of Chicago Press, 1983); and Dieter Henrich, *Aesthetic Judgment and the Moral Image of the World* (Stanford: Stanford University Press, 1992).

8. Arendt, *Lectures*, 43.

9. Ronald Beiner, *Political Judgment*. Beiner calls for a substantive account (Aristotelian) of teleology and community "ends" that Kant would reject for reasons that will shortly be explained. It is interesting that in his list of characteristics of the judgment of taste the role of feeling is submerged and, as with Arendt, the strictly aesthetic aspect of these judgments is subordinated to other features (38–39). The concern for the formal and procedural in politics—for fairness and equity—may explain why even those theorists interested in Kant's account of taste for a model of political judgment tend to skirt the empathic and the pleasurable in Kant's account in favor of a more intellectualized reading. And indeed, no philosopher has been more skeptical than Kant about the right to demand a feeling of anyone (hence his commitment to the view that the Christian commandment to love thy neighbor can only be understood as a command to respect their humanity).

10. Kant's account of aesthetic reflective judgment is complex and unwieldy. Although his aesthetics is generally acknowledged as profoundly important in the development of the field, exactly why it is considered important varies dramatically from scholar to scholar. Thus his aesthetic theory has been interpreted as formalist, subjectivist, individualist, bourgeois, expressivist, and (proto) hermeneuticist, among

others things. Reconstructions of the judgment of taste abound in the literature, but however interesting these may be in their own right, for the purposes of this essay I will skirt the myriad exegetical and philosophical particulars in favor of providing a brief account of the nature of reflective judgment for Kant.

11. *Critique of Judgment*, trans. Werner Pluhar (Indianapolis: Hackett, 1987). Page numbers cited in this paper will refer to the Academy edition of Kant's works, *Kants gesammelte Schriften*, ed. Königlich Preußische Akademie der Wissenschaften, 29 vols. (Berlin: de Gruyter, 1900–), which are incorporated into both the Pluhar translation and other translations.

12. The motivation for this account already is provided in the first *Critique*, where Kant points out the paradox of judging if the activity is rule-governed: In order to judge a rule would be required, but for judging what rule is needed a further rule would be required, and so on *ad infinitum*. See CPR (A133/B172).

13. "Judgment can be regarded . . . as mere[ly] an ability to *reflect*, in terms of a certain principle, on a given presentation so as to [make] a concept possible. . . . To *reflect* (or consider [*überlegen*]) is to hold given presentations up to, and compare them with, either other presentations or one's cognitive power [itself], in reference to a concept that this [comparing] makes possible" (20:211).

14. Even in objective *a priori* judgments, where a determinate schema is applied, judgment requires a principle—Kant says in this case it "is already [contained] in the concept of nature as such" (20:212).

15. "But for concepts that must first be found for given empirical intuitions, and that presuppose a special [*besonder*] natural law in terms of which alone *particular* experience is possible, judgment needs for its reflection a principle of its own, a principle that is also transcendental . . . what is presupposed is that nature, even in its empirical laws, has adhered to a certain parsimony suitable for our judgment, and adhered to a uniformity we can grasp; and this presupposition must precede all comparison, as *a priori* principle of judgment" (20:213).

16. Kant uses the term "figurative purposiveness" in the First Introduction (20:233–34) to describe the guiding principle of reflection as applied in aesthetic judgment of natural forms. He distinguishes the "figurative purposiveness" from the "organic" as two types of the technic of nature (20:234).

17. For an extended account of Kant's "aesthetics" throughout the critical system, see Gary Banham, *Kant and the Ends of Aesthetics* (New York: St. Martin's Press, 2000), esp. chapter 1.

18. Dieter Henrich, in *Aesthetic Judgment and the Moral Image of the World* (Stanford: Stanford University Press, 1992), 38, emphasizes the dependence of judgments of taste upon perceptual processes, and the connection of this aspect of aesthetics to imagination, a capacity that is central to, and largely constitutive of, perception.

19. The term is not Kant's own. It is most likely Shaftesbury's use of the term that influences Kant most directly. See Jane Kneller, "Disinterestedness," in *Encyclopedia of Aesthetics*, vol. 2, ed. Michael Kelly (Oxford: Oxford University Press, 1997), 59–64.

20. See, for instance, Paul Guyer's discussion in *Kant and the Claims of Taste* (Cambridge: Harvard University Press, 1979), 191–202.

21. This occurs in the case where a singular presentation is given but not compared with others for the sake of describing it via an empirical concept. In this case

a presentation may be more or less suited to the general conditions of "cognition in general," i.e., to the conditions of cooperation between the imagination and the understanding. Dieter Henrich provides a helpful account of the difficulties of the notion of free play in Kant's theory, as well as a compelling solution, by appealing to Kant's notion of *Darstellung* (exhibition) as a mode of empirical concept formation that does not involve comparative, i.e., determinate, judgment. *Aesthetic Judgment and the Moral Image of the World*, 44–50.

22. See also section 35 of the third *Critique*, 5:387.

23. Kant never doubts that we do indeed make such judgments. His critical philosophy begins with what we manifestly *do* experience. In his account of cognition, or empirical knowledge, he begins with ordinary human experience of a unified and mostly coherent world of nature. In the practical philosophy he assumes as given that we are agential beings: actors in our world. Here in the third *Critique* Kant is assuming as a given that all human beings are capable of experiencing the pleasure of mental liveliness. He argues that judgment of any kind depends on the interaction of imagination with our ability to understand and to reason and that, if conditions for reflection are met, we are capable of experiencing this "play" of cognition as a pleasure. Reflective experience is not a universal fact in the way that cognition and agency are for human beings, but its possibility is universal. Aesthetic reflection, when it occurs, produces and is maintained by the pleasurable feeling of optimal mental activity. The feeling of mental "attunement" is how Kant describes this state, and it is accessible in principle to all. (Kant's claim is a sufficiency claim. If we are in the proper frame of mind for experiencing the beautiful, we will experience a quickening of our powers. Other frames of mind may also suffice. He does not argue that aesthetic reflection is a necessary condition for the quickening of the mind, and is careful to state that it is "*a* basis," or cause, of this state.)

24. Kant introduces the notion of an "applied judgment of taste" at 5:231. In this section he argues that "pure" judgments of taste refer to "free" beauty while applied judgments of taste are about "adherent" or "accessory" beauty. Applied judgments, he says in the next section, "can never be purely aesthetic" (5:236).

25. See the section on "Opining, Knowing, and Believing in the Doctrine of Method" of the *Critique of Pure Reason*.

26. The fact is that upon reflection I might find it unpleasant to dwell upon the event. It could turn out to be the cultural analog of "the ugly."

27. Maria Lugones, "Playfulness, 'World'-Traveling, and Loving Perception," in *Pilgrimages/Peregrinajes: Theorizing Coalition Against Multiple Oppressions* (Lanham: Rowman & Littlefield, 2003), 96.

28. Martha Nussbaum's neo-Aristotelian accounts of flourishing and Richard Boyd's fallibilist realism about homeostatic property clusters are two recent and otherwise very different versions of this. Martha C. Nussbaum, *Women and Human Development: The Capabilities Approach* (Cambridge: Cambridge University Press, 2000). Richard Boyd, "How to Be a Moral Realist," in *Essays on Moral Realism*, ed. G. Sayre-McCord (Ithaca: Cornell University Press, 1988), 181–228.

29. Hannah Arendt, *The Human Condition* (Chicago: University of Chicago Press, 1958), 222.

13

Social Demands

Kant and the Possibility of Community

Jan Mieszkowski

Theoretically, the tendency to the tyrannical can be detected in
almost all great thinkers. (Kant is the great exception.)
Hannah Arendt, *Letters 1925–1975, Hannah Arendt and Martin Heidegger*

Virtually every account of the history of Western political philosophy
accords Immanuel Kant a prominent place among the thinkers responsible
for our conceptions of liberty, justice, and the social contract. Although best
known as a metaphysician or aesthetician, Kant remains at least as central
to ongoing debates about rights and equality as Locke, Rousseau, or Mill.
His commitment to deontological ethics and to a substantive link between
morality and reason, his insistence on treating people as ends rather than
means, and his affirmation of individual autonomy as a key to understanding
human praxis are all widely accepted positions that seem to fit comfortably
into the paradigms of self-interested agency prevalent in contemporary liberal democratic theory and neoclassical economics.

The legacy of Kant's political thought is somewhat complicated by the
fact that he is frequently cited as an authority by critics undertaking a wholesale reevaluation of his positions. Nowhere is this tendency to celebrate
Kant's work by transforming it more in evidence than in the perceived need
to revise our characterizations of social dynamics by unsettling the preeminence he accords the autonomous individual. Characteristic of this trend,
Jürgen Habermas has argued that the legacy of Idealist subject philosophy
and its spontaneously singular actant constitutes a substantial stumbling
block on the road to a truly intersubjective model of human experience.
While Habermas acknowledges that Kant takes nothing for granted when
it comes to examining the workings of the solitary mind, he maintains that
Kant situates this thinking entity in an empirical realm populated by similar entities without adequate concern for the problem of what gives rise to

or sustains this social field. The Kantian conception of autonomy atomizes human society, turning it into a field of parts not essentially dependent on a greater whole. The result, Habermas concludes, is that the more fundamental question of whether the social sphere might in some respect preexist or make possible the emergence of individuality is never addressed.[1]

The goal of this paper is to demonstrate that such criticisms of Kant are misguided insofar as they underestimate the degree to which his understanding of sociality is not wholly grounded in interactions between self-governing beings. Like many who seek to revise him, Kant offers a full-fledged theory of community, but its crucial elements are often overlooked, perhaps because it is incompatible with current liberal paradigms of sociality as communication. Like Habermas, possibly the most influential contemporary critic of Kant, Kant's approach to communal existence is guided by an analysis of human beings as intrinsically linguistic entities. Unlike Habermas, Kant is vigilant in never allowing the polity to become an unexamined empirical given.

We will begin by focusing on a passage from a 1784 essay in which Kant describes the advent of human society, highlighting the extent to which an irreducible antagonism is vital to his argument. We will then turn to the *Critique of Judgment* and consider its more extended investigation of what it means to speak of people as existing "in common." Exploring the account of community in the third *Critique*, particularly the connection described between community and communicability, will allow us to grasp the profound differences between Kant's and Habermas's conceptualizations of the relation between language and politics.

The great challenge that confronts the study of community and the question of the commons in general—in Latin, that which is *communis*: "the shared, the public, the universal"—is the difficulty of examining this constellation of concepts without implicitly relying on the very dynamic under scrutiny. The first step in an exploration of the common must thus be to ask whether it can be adopted as an object of inquiry from any position other than within a *common* space, idiom, or argumentative framework. If not, then its analysis becomes merely an exercise in exemplifying what it makes (or has already made) possible. Even the effort to conceptualize radical particularity or singularity is at risk of proving to be coherent only insofar as it presents itself as a discourse motivated by common utility, governed by common standards, and pursued within a common linguistic field.

In his writings on ethics and politics of the 1780s and 1790s, Kant leaves little doubt that the commonality that obtains between peoples is intimately connected with, if not dependent on, our propensity for domination, violence, and war. Nowhere is this clearer than in a well-known passage from the essay "Idea for a Universal History from a Cosmopolitan Point of View," written in 1784, between the first *Critique* and the *Groundwork for the Metaphysics of Morals*:

> The means employed by nature to bring about the development of all the capacities of men is their antagonism in society, so far as this is, in the end, the cause of a lawful order among men. . . . By "antagonism" I mean the unsocial sociability [*ungesellige Geselligkeit*] of men, i.e., their propensity to enter into society, bound together with a mutual opposition [*Widerstand*] which constantly threatens to break up the society. Man has an inclination to associate with others [*sich zu vergesellschaften*] because in society he feels himself to be more than man, i.e., as more than the developed form of his natural capacities. But he also has a strong propensity to isolate himself from others, because he finds in himself at the same time the unsocial characteristic of wishing to have everything go according to his own wish. Thus he expects opposition on all sides because, in knowing himself, he knows that he, on his own part, is inclined to oppose others. This opposition awakens all his powers, brings him to conquer his inclination to laziness and, propelled by vainglory, lust for power, and avarice, to achieve a rank among his fellows whom he cannot tolerate but from whom he cannot withdraw. Thus are taken the first true steps from barbarism to culture, which consists in the social worth of man; thence gradually develop all talents, and taste is refined. ("Idea," 15)[2]

While it may be tempting to read this argument in the context of other late eighteenth-century descriptions of the social division of labor and the efficiency of groups informed by decentralized agents, Kant places special emphasis on the difficulty of transcending the inevitable conflicts he locates at the heart of communal relations. What makes society what it is also threatens to tear it apart. Society is a binding through self-division, a potentially tortured dynamic that is organized by the fact that every individual anticipates resistance to forming a connection with others, resistance from itself as well as from everyone else. The most individualistic capacity of the individual is thus its ability to recognize itself in the other—identifying there a similar propensity to defy restraints on self-volition. The ensuing interdependence, which individuality cannot countenance despite the fact that it *must* do so ("his fellows whom he cannot tolerate but from whom he cannot withdraw"), brings with it a profound risk. The individual becomes most individual insofar as it puts into jeopardy what is most uniquely its own—its autonomy and integrity as an agent—by entering a realm in which circumstances, i.e., other people, may compromise its independence. Only in gambling with its autonomy, that is, in anticipating opposition from those with whom it will socialize and in seeking to protect itself by finding a place of rank among its fellow antagonists, can the individual strive to realize its full potential and thereby effect the emergence of humanity from barbarism.

Kant's presentation of social existence is notably ambiguous about the ultimate worth of individualism as an ideal. In acting in its own interests as well as in anticipation of clashes with others, the individual effectively demonstrates an antagonism toward individuality itself—toward individuality both as a principle of self-contained self-sufficiency and as a state of harmony among equals who are careful not to step on each other's toes. This is a society of competition as endless strife, not competition that leads to cooperation or consensus. "Man," writes Kant, "wishes concord, but nature knows better what is good for the race; she wills discord" ("Idea," 16).

Kant leaves no doubt that the dynamic tensions among individuals that characterize the social polity manifest themselves on the macro-political level as well:

> The same unsociability which drives man to [the creation of a commonwealth] causes any single commonwealth to stand in unrestricted freedom in relation to others; consequently, each of them must expect from another precisely the evil which oppressed the individuals and forced them to enter into a lawful civic state. ("Idea," 18)

Relations between societies mirror the relations between individuals because Kant presents society as a person fashioned on a larger scale. As the individual individuates itself by threatening to lose its own individuality, so a state comes into its own by entering into antagonistic relations with other states. Although both the individual and the state exist in and as a dynamic of mutual dependence and hostility, the parallelism between them is never questioned. In giving expression to their belligerent drives, individuals inexorably underwrite the existence of the greater social order. In the form in which Kant describes it, then, the antagonism that is the guiding force of the human condition, however destructive it may be, appears to have clear limits—that is, it does not threaten the basic identity of the forms—the individual, the society—that it shapes. What would it mean if this homology between the social and the individual were no longer guaranteed, or if the violence that for Kant is the essence of social connections failed to produce a state of affairs in which the individual and society were identical in their internal machinations? As we will subsequently see, Kant's approach to the concept of community in the *Critique of Judgment* proceeds along somewhat different lines—in part, we may surmise, in order to avoid subordinating political morphology to an individual-group dichotomy rooted in a hierarchical schema of general and particular.

These questions about the relationship between the individual and society are complicated by the curious mix of optimism and pessimism that organizes "Idea for a Universal History" as well as Kant's short essays on politics and government through the 1790s. Despite his gloomy account of the evil that oppresses the individual in the so-called progress of nature toward civic society, Kant is confident about future gains, averring that the wars and revolutions that necessarily accompany the growth of human civilization will ultimately lead to a league of nations. Humanity, he proclaims, will eventually give up its freedom in exchange for the safety and security of stable constitutional rule. Whether in "Idea for a Universal History" or in "To Perpetual Peace" a decade later, it is hard to decide how serious Kant is about such prognostications. Especially in the latter essay, the argument—at times playful, at times mournful—seems to be in the grips of an irony whose implications are far from clear.[3]

Recent discussions of Kant by liberal democratic theorists have tended to avoid these difficulties by focusing less on his ideas about world history and the evolution of society and more on the parameters of his ethics. Such interpretations are motivated by a conviction that Kant never goes beyond the fundamental individuality of his social model, a claim that seems to be consistent with our reading of "Idea for a Universal History," in which the conflicted inner workings of the self are mirrored on both the national and the international level. In what follows, however, we will show that the understanding of community in the *Critique of Judgment* presents an alternative both to the argument of Kant's earlier text and to the current view of Kant as insufficiently concerned with human sociality. Particularly where Kant's ethics and aesthetics are concerned, misconceptions about his theory of language produce misleading accounts of his work.

The objection to Kant's excessive individualism has been a central motive in the development of what has come to be known as communication or discourse ethics. Stressing that the goal is to understand moral deliberation not in terms of the solitary soul-searching of an isolated consciousness but as something that takes place in an irreducibly plural medium, Seyla Benhabib summarizes the transformation of Kant that occurs in writers such as Habermas and Karl-Otto Apel:

> Instead of asking what an individual moral agent could or would will, without self-contradiction, to be a universal maxim for all, one asks: What norms or institutions would the members of an ideal or real communication community agree to as representing their common interests after engaging in a special kind of argumentation or conversation? The procedural model of an argumentative praxis replaces the silent thought-experiment enjoined by the Kantian universalizability test.[4]

Much of Habermas's work is devoted to explaining precisely what this "special kind" of argumentative praxis might be. In the process, he describes society as governed not by Kant's "discord," but by a search for consensus in which social agents come "to an understanding with one another so as to coordinate their actions [and] pursue their particular aims."[5] Although Habermas presents his philosophy as an ethicopolitical doctrine, he frequently bypasses the dilemmas that constitute the central domain of ethical inquiry in the *Groundwork for the Metaphysics of Morals* and the *Critique of Practical Reason*. For Kant, the will becomes a moral agent by divorcing itself from every particular interest or desire and acting solely on the basis of a form of universal lawgiving. Only in this way can the subjective principle or "maxim" of the self's action reveal itself to be an objective principle of reason, universal because it cannot by definition conflict with any other individual's interests or desires. The resulting moral act is a paradoxical event whereby a singular being gives itself a universal law as if it already possessed this law.[6] Sidestepping these difficulties with his notion of community consensus, Habermas effectively dispenses with any debate about the nature of the human will, thereby renouncing Kant's theory of freedom entirely. Far from completing the rationalist Enlightenment dream of harmoniously fusing ethical theories and political institutions, Habermas fashions a pragmatic model of social interaction by ignoring the central query underlying Kant's moral thought: How can a human being have knowledge of and take responsibility for the actions it calls its own? While the political philosophy Habermas offers may provide an account of how people might relate to one another in society, none of the social contract theorists Habermas could identify as his forerunners—Locke, Rousseau, or Hume, let alone Kant—would be nearly as quick to dismiss the question of how the power of compacts is related to the vicissitudes of practical human spontaneity.

Perhaps it is precisely metaphysical conceits such as the "freedom of the will" with which we should dispense if we seek to develop a concept of society that is no longer based on a paradigm of discrete individuality. Still, it is far from obvious that the social model Habermas terms a "communication community" is free of metaphysical features. Examining the arguments he makes for his revision of Kant, we encounter a decisive difference between the two when it comes to the question of founding postulates. Habermas writes:

> Discourse ethics replaces the Kantian categorical imperative by a procedure of moral argumentation. Its principle postulates that only those norms may claim to be valid that could meet with the consent of all affected in their role as participants in a practical discourse.[7]

Kant's doctrine of the categorical imperative is first and foremost a consideration of what it means to postulate and how a postulate establishes its authority. To give oneself a universal law *as if* it were a law one already possessed is nothing if not to accord oneself the right to found principles. Habermas's discourse ethics is grounded in the postulate of the possibility of a correspondence between norms and a consensus that is reached about them. Yet what guarantees that such a correspondence is possible—and more important from the Kantian perspective, what insures that a norm is a rational statement or demand? For Kant, for whom the question of the categorical imperative is the question of whether a discourse of universal reason is possible at all, one cannot properly speak of morality without considering the force—the violence—that gives a norm a form or mode in virtue of which its very normativity becomes recognizable as such.

The authority Habermas accords to consensus is *postulated*—it is certainly not arrived at by consensus. However, he gives no account of how the power (antagonism?) that enables such a postulate will affect subsequent efforts to make consensus possible, or why it should be the case that the deliberations of participants in a practical discourse will necessarily produce propositions that will assume the (as yet unclarified) form of norms. What Habermas seeks to dispel is arguably not just the primacy of the autonomous subject, but what Kant and the German Idealists addressed as the power of language to posit (*setzen*). Habermas aims to bring theories about pragmatic language use to bear on a tradition that he regards as having been all too willing to avoid practical considerations. In so doing, however, he ignores the theory of language already at work in the ethical and political texts of that tradition.

Of course, Habermas argues that Kant makes the same mistake in reverse: "The singularity of Kant's transcendental consciousness simply takes for granted a prior understanding among a plurality of empirical egos; their harmony is pre-established. In discourse it is not. . . . There are no shared structures preceding the individual, except the universals of language use."[8] Habermas charges Kant with being unable to account for the individual's status as always already social. Yet where discourse in particular is concerned, precisely what Kant never takes for granted are the "universals of language use." In his writings on ethics, language is anything but a preestablished system. If the exercise of the categorical imperative is an effort to establish a form in virtue of which a singular speech act can articulate universal laws, this form does not preexist the act by which a free will seeks to establish it, but rather manifests itself only in the course of each individual instance of human spontaneity. This is why Kant characterizes each articulation of the categorical imperative as a unique attempt at *giving* the moral law, insisting that the law is never something that precedes the self, like a standard or regulation that one would obey or disobey.[9]

One may grant such shortcomings in Habermas's criticisms of Kant and nonetheless maintain that Kant never comes to terms with the intersubjective dimension of the human condition. My argument, however, is that Habermas's conception of his break from Kant rests on the mistaken conviction that any communitarian theory has to regard Kant and his supposed individualism as a potential foe. To appreciate the issues at hand, we must examine more closely the model of communicative community that Habermas outlines, particularly the relationship he proposes between community and communication. According to Habermas, the value of the practical discourse in which the members of his community interact derives from the belief that in social exchanges "the unforced force of the better argument" will prevail.[10] Granting that this assumption may be dubious, he nonetheless avers that to abandon it as a guiding presupposition would be to give up on the very idea that human beings can relate to one another in a rational manner. The formulation "unforced force" may sound similar to the "unsocial sociability" of "Idea for a Universal History." Yet Kant's odd locution underscores precisely the intractability of the negativity at work in social identity formations, whereas Habermas seems to be moving in the opposite direction: the force in question is a force precisely insofar as it is not one. How can we be confident that an argument is even recognizable as an argument, much less as the better argument among several, if it is devoid of any "forced force"? Habermas's further claim that participants in communal discourse are motivated "solely by the revisionary power of *free*-floating reasons" heightens the contrast with Kant's identification of antagonism as the core of humanity's collective existence. This attempt to expel strife from the heart of the social order is made, moreover, by reclassifying freedom as an attribute of reasons rather than of agents, with no indication of what this tells us about the relationship between thinking and acting. If for Habermas thoughts are free, this may be because he believes that people are not.

Insofar as violence remains overtly present in Habermas's model, it is the violence of idealization. He writes:

> No matter how misleading the image of an ideally extended communication community (Apel) that reaches a warranted mutual agreement under ideal epistemic conditions (Putnam), before an ideal audience (Perelman), or in an ideal speech situation (Habermas), we can in no way forgo making some such idealizations.[11]

For Habermas, the viability of a polity organized under liberal democratic ideals cannot be legitimated in its own terms, i.e., by the inherent value of the pragmatic speech acts that are said to make up "everyday life." Only with reference to a language situation that is neither "practical" nor "everyday" does the worth of communal exchange become clear. This necessary (if, by Habermas's own admission, "misleading") idea of an idealized language is grounded in one of the most basic tenets of his theory—one that perhaps most starkly distinguishes him from Kant—namely, the assertion of an outright identity between community and communication. "In his capacity as a participant in argumentation," Habermas argues, "everyone is on his own and yet embedded in a communication context. This is what [Karl-Otto] Apel means by an 'ideal community of communication.'"[12] In his theory of communicative action, Habermas is explicit that "the human species maintains itself through the socially coordinated activities of its members" and that "this coordination has to be established through communication."[13] This communication is the grounds of sociality—in fact, communication is sociality:

> Linguistically and behaviorally competent subjects are constituted as individuals by growing into an intersubjectively shared lifeworld, and the lifeworld of a language community is reproduced in turn through the communicative actions of its members. This explains why the identity of the individual and that of the collective are interdependent; they form and maintain themselves together.[14]

Any question of whether individuals preexist their social interactions with others or vice versa is subordinated to the underlying claim that communicative intersubjective activity gives rise to individuals and the collective alike. On both the micro- and the macrolevel, human community manifests itself in and as communicative praxis. Community is communication. Communication is community.

The suggestion that communication is a, if not the, privileged medium of human praxis may sound eminently reasonable to us today, at a time when the ability to generate and transport data is celebrated as the very essence of economic activity. One may be skeptical that communication alone is enough to facilitate harmony between diverse individuals or cultures, and one may doubt that on balance it fosters peace more than strife or serves liberation more than oppression. Nonetheless, even those models of community that seek to challenge the implicit equality between people seemingly posited by Habermas in his vision of communicative relations are unlikely to disturb the more fundamental identity he postulates between community and communication.

We thus find ourselves returning to the difficulty inherent to all discussions of the common: Must not the analysis of community presuppose the existence of a coherent community dynamic within which such an analysis can occur? Likewise, must our analysis of communication not presuppose that communication is possible in order to make such an analysis feasible in the first place? To do otherwise, that is, to explore the relationship between community and communication without taking their functionality and mutual support for one another for granted, we must proceed in a way that at least allows for the possibility that both community and communication are in part postulates, ideals, or constructs—stable or unstable as the case may be—rather than absolute givens.[15] Otherwise, it will be impossible even to characterize a discursive space that is not simply a commons within which community and communication interchangeably facilitate and reinforce one another.

To ask what it would mean to develop a model of community that would not be merely an affirmation of the authority of the common, we must think further about the implications of Habermas's generalization of communication. For him, communication always takes place as an act aimed to facilitate understanding. As a model of society, such a theory necessarily excludes anything that cannot be universally grasped or shared.[16] Indeed, once communicability is established as the standard for participating in the activity of "social coordination" that for Habermas is everyday life, any individual intervention must be reducible to or presentable in codes and schemas that preexist it. For Theodor W. Adorno, it is imperative that we not capitulate to the tyranny of this "liberal fiction of the universal communicability of each and every thought."[17] Under its reign, only that which is always already assimilated to and understood by the dominant discourse will even be identifiable as a social act. An instance of "communicative action" can prove its legitimacy only by revealing its status as something that can be unproblematically transmitted to and understood by every—again in Habermas's language—"linguistically and behaviorally competent" subject. Novel, obscure, or outlandish thoughts are by definition antisocial, to the point that society will not even recognize them as existing, much less as protests against the status quo. The reification of universal communicability obliterates any pretense to a pluralistic tolerance of "difference" (or "differing opinions"). "Everyone," argues Habermas in the quote above, "is on his own and yet embedded in communication context," but this turns out to mean that everyone participates in social "argumentation" only by deferring to standards and norms that prefigure and predefine what will be understood, i.e., what will be tolerated as "social." A community of pure communicability is a community that commits itself to expelling anything unfamiliar or other, anything that might compromise the intercourse of understanding between known quantities and their equally well-known counterparts.

The question of what cannot be universally communicated brings us at last to a properly Kantian perspective on these problems, for a concern about what communication can communicate about its own conditions of possibility lies at the heart of the *Critique of Judgment*. To understand both what the book has to say about the connection between communication and community and how its argument constitutes a critique of Habermas's philosophy, we must proceed somewhat indirectly. What is overtly under discussion is not a concept of *Gemeinschaft* or *Gesellschaft*, but what Kant in Latin terms a *sensus communis*, or as he also calls it in German, a *Gemeinsinn*. The figure of *sensus communis* emerges as Kant is attempting to explain the peculiar features of a judgment of taste. A judgment about a specific thing—

"*this* flower is beautiful"—is said to take place in such a way that although the judgment is not based on concepts or on the sensuous perception of an empirical object, it nevertheless proclaims its own universal validity, as if all people would say exactly the same thing about this specific flower. At certain points, Kant comes close to suggesting that such a judgment is a reflexive claim about the act of judging itself rather than a judgment of something in the world, as when he writes that a judgment of taste "is posited merely in the form of the object for reflection in general" (*Judgment*, 30).[18] At other moments, he insists that aesthetic judgments are singular judgments, proclamations about a "singular empirical representation" (154).

The authority for such a judgment is said to lie not in the pleasure that accompanies it as it is made, but in the "universal validity of the pleasure . . . that we present *a priori* as [a] universal rule for the power of judgment, valid for everyone" (*Judgment*, 154). Kant continues:

> Only under the presupposition, therefore, that there is a common sense [*Gemeinsinn*] (by which, however, we do not mean an outer sense, but the effect arising from the free play of our cognitive powers)—only under the presupposition of such a common sense can judgments of taste be made. (87)

Jacques Derrida has observed that Kant appears unable to decide whether this *sensus communis* "exists as a constitutive principle of the possibility of aesthetic experience or else whether, in a regulative capacity, reason commands us to produce it for more elevated purposes."[19] Kant's inability to explain the precise nature of the common sense on which he bases so much reveals, according to Derrida, "the complicity of a moral discourse and an empirical culturalism."[20] Both the doctrine of reflective judgment comprising the first part of the third *Critique* and the doctrine of teleological judgment comprising the second depend on the possibility of distinguishing between constitutive and regulative principles, so this is potentially a criticism of considerable scope. It is certainly the case that many readings of the *Critique of Judgment* have concluded that it is really a moral discourse disguised as an aesthetics; and there seems to be ample support for the objection of "empirical culturalism" if we examine the ways in which Kant's examples of beauty invariably betray the peculiarities of his own tastes.

Still, it is possible that this "common sense" has a critical function. Of crucial significance here is the question of how *sensus communis* is grounded in the idea of communicability.[21] Kant writes, "We could even define taste as the ability to judge something that makes our feeling in a given presentation *universally communicable* without mediation by a concept" (*Judgment*, 162). Even if a mistake is made in a judgment of beauty such that the judgment fails to be pure and mingles with the concept of the object judged or with the individual's sensations of it, Kant avers that this does not compromise the essential authority on the basis of which a judgment lays claim to universal assent, and nothing else.

If "subjective universal communicability" is the sole achievement of an aesthetic judgment, it could be argued that its preeminence is an expression of the universalist humanism often attributed to the *Critique of Judgment*. Kant states that since every aesthetic judgment is based on "the subjective relation suitable for cognition in general," it must hold true for all people of similar cognitive faculties (*Judgment*, 62); and he makes the consequences of this point quite explicit: "A concern for universal communication is something that everyone expects and demands from everyone else, on the basis, as it were, of an original contract dictated by [our] very humanity" (164). In this sense, community is simply another name for the common (communal, collective) nature of our faculties and the interplay between them, a common contract of universal communicability.

Hannah Arendt seems to support such an interpretation when she argues that it is "the very humanity of man that is manifest in this [*sensus communis*]." She immediately complicates the discussion, however, by considering the implicit theory of language at work, emphasizing that this "extra sense that fits us into a community" can be understood only insofar as we distinguish between communication and mere "expression."[22] "The *sensus communis*," Arendt writes, "is the specifically human sense because communication, i.e., speech, depends on it. To make our needs known, to *express* fear, joy, etc., we would not need speech. Gestures would be enough. . . . Communication is not expression."[23] For her, Kant's communication is the manifestation of "community sense" because what communication actually communicates is first and foremost the fact of community's existence, the fact of our status as communal beings.[24] Prior to transmitting any particular datum, communication communicates the commonality, the co-sharing, that is human existence. In these terms, communication is not the medium through which an individual articulates a specific want or need, but a speech act of an essentially universal nature by which individuals confirm their status as members of humanity.

Arendt bases her interpretation of the third *Critique* on an implicit model of empathy. If in "Idea for a Universal History" Kant argues that human beings anticipate that others are like them and hence expect to be treated antagonistically, Arendt describes this anticipation as productive of mutual comprehension: "Communicability obviously depends on the enlarged mentality; one can communicate only if one is able to think from the other person's standpoint; otherwise one will never meet him, never speak in such a way that he understands."[25] Like Habermas, Arendt conceives of communication in Kant as a teleological process aimed at understanding, an understanding presented as the basis of social harmony. Given the aforementioned uncertainties about the relative degree of optimism or pessimism informing Kant's political thought, it is difficult to object categorically to her approach. Still, Arendt goes a step further when she links Kant's idea of the value of the general communicability of a beautiful object to his "deliberations about a united mankind, living in eternal peace."[26] If the value of the aesthetic object is the basis for peace, that is, if aesthetic experience is the grounds of political stability, then an outright identification of community and communication has again been posited, and what human beings communicate is the value of humankind's peaceful existence, an existence that is nothing if not *beautiful*. Yet should it not at least be conceivable that what communicability enables is misunderstanding as well as understanding, a dearth of recognition rather than the satisfied discovery of oneself in the other? In casting *sensus communis* as a force of universal understanding, Arendt unwittingly renounces the critical function of Kant's aesthetics by blurring the distinction between transcendental and ideological thought. In Derrida's terms, she gives up on deciding whether *sensus communis* is a constitutive or regulative principle.

To grasp the problems in Arendt's analysis, we must remember that an interest in the peculiar modality of a judgment of taste is one of the most distinctive features of the third *Critique*. Kant is explicit that an aesthetic judgment is in essence a demand: "In making a judgment of taste (about the beautiful) we require [*ansinnen*] *everyone* to like the object" (*Judgment*, 57). In the simplest terms, a judgment of taste is a demand for its own universality, or better, it is a demand for a voice, a language, in and through which such a judgment could be articulated. Kant writes:

> We can see, at this point, that nothing is postulated (*postuliert*) in a judgment of taste except such a universal voice about a pleasure unmediated by concepts. Hence all that is postulated is the possibility of a judgment that is aesthetic and yet can be considered valid for everyone. The judgment of taste itself does not *postulate* everyone's agreement. . . . It merely *requires this agreement from everyone. . .* (*es sinnet nur jedermann*). (60)

The aesthetic judgment is a "postulate"—Kant relies on the Latin *postulare*: "to demand, to request"—and what a judgment postulates is "not that everyone *will* agree with my judgment, but that he or she *ought* to" (89, emphasis in original). The judgment demands the necessity of a universality over whose actual existence it has no control. Taste is not self-realizing; it does not create a universality and then install it retroactively as its own condition of possibility, for in that case it would be a cognitive judgment rather than an aesthetic one. In this idiom of universalizability, an aesthetic judgment postulates the possibility of what it demands that it be without being able to confirm that it *can* be what it demands. The voice of common sense has no assurance that it can make itself heard, even, or perhaps especially, by itself.

The communal language of beauty that we *should* all speak is not perfectly autogenerative, and the discourse of taste remains finite and fallible. Given the subjective vicissitudes of an individual's faculties, it is conceivable, Kant acknowledges, that someone could designate an object as "beautiful" without the judgment conforming to the postulate of a universal discourse. In other words, the adjective "beautiful" has no magic of its own; it is a singular instance of reference rather than a divine act of speech. The demand for a universal voice that can say that something is "beautiful" never becomes an imperative and is thus never part of a maxim that can be submitted to a process of universalization in the mode of Kant's categorical imperative. Despite Kant's description of beauty as the symbol of the morally good, his aesthetics remains distinct from his ethics. Acts of taste gain their critical function from the fact that they produce nothing and are directed toward nothing.

Kant is adamant that this demand for a universal voice, a voice of universalizability without universal concepts, is the demand in virtue of which thought and language are to be coordinated—if imperfectly. There is therefore no "pre-established harmony" between empirical subjects endowed with language, as Habermas claims. A judgment of taste is the demand for the possibility of communication, which is in turn identified with the harmony of the faculties that makes cognition possible, but this possibility is never present as a preexisting actuality. In this regard, to confirm its status as cognitive, any instance of cognition must prove its ability to communicate that communication is possible.

Here the contrast with Arendt becomes quite clear. Whereas she presumes that an aesthetic judgment communicates the fact of humankind's community, the fact that this state-of-community is a given, Kant speaks only of *giving* possibilities, not of giving facts that can be taken for granted as data about social or existential conditions. As a result, it is uncertain whether the postulates that comprise the discourse of aesthetic judgments are themselves communicative. As a demand for communicability, a judgment of taste never confirms its ability to transmit concepts or intuitions. It is not, in the language of speech act theory, a constative statement. On the other hand, a judgment of taste does not demonstrate that communication is possible simply by demanding its possibility, i.e., it is not a performative utterance, either. It may well be that all communication depends on the possibility of an aesthetic demand being articulated, but no given demand can ever confirm its own status as such a communiqué; it can never be an example of communication. In this respect, Kant's aesthetic utterances can never be conceptualized as instances of what Habermas calls communicative praxis. These demands are always as much a challenge to the authority of communication as they are a confirmation that it is taking place.

This last point is decisive because an aesthetic judgment is ostensibly supposed to convey communicability as such. If in being articulated it does not *de facto* or *de jure* communicate that communication as possible, then it is not clear how we are to understand the peculiar universalism to which Kant maintains it lays claim. In this respect, we have to look more closely at Kant's term for communication, *Mitteilung*, which is often translated into English as "im-parting" in order to preserve the connotations of the German *Teil*, "part" and *Teilung*, "division." *Mitteilung* is Kant's word for the Latin *communico*, which means "to share" in the potentially adversative senses of "dividing up" and "joining." In imparting, *Mitteilung* at once connects and separates. From this perspective, we can describe more precisely why communicability in the third *Critique* is not governed by the aim of facilitating comprehension or understanding. In contradistinction to what we saw in both Habermas and Arendt, the "common sense" that for Kant makes us all human is not merely a force of joining or uniting, whether as a synthesis that constructs concepts or as a gathering of people's opinions. *Sensus communis* is as much an impetus for a retreat into parts as it is a connection of one person or concept with another person or concept that explains it or allows it to recognize itself in it. In this respect, the *Critique of Judgment* is closer to the model of society as oppositioning in "Idea for a Universal History" than it is to a theory that celebrates the common intellectual traits that make us all human. No longer a passive medium of transport or transmission, communication can be thought of as bringing individuals or the various faculties of the mind together, but only if it is at the same time seen as dividing them and as marking them with a difference from one another that they can never surmount.

What are we to make, then, of the implicit concept of community at work in the third *Critique*? Has Kant moved from a paradigm of individuality to a genuinely collective schema? Does his project lie outside of the liberal democratic tradition, or is it simply another version of a discursive society, at odds with and yet not entirely foreign to Habermas's worldview? To answer these questions, we will turn to one of the most perceptive early responses to the challenges we have considered in the *Critique of Judgment*, Friedrich Schlegel's "On the Concept of Republicanism" (1796). Here, Schlegel tries to link the Kantian idea of community to the highest practical principle of subjective idealism—"the I should be" (*das Ich soll sein*)—through the notion of communicability.[27] He writes:

> By means of the theoretical datum that the human being, apart from the capacity it possesses as a pure isolated individual as such, has the *capacity of communication* in relation to other individuals of its species . . . the pure practical imperative receives a *new specific modification*, which is the foundation and object of a new science. The proposition "*the I should be*" means in this specific case "*the community of humanity should be*" or "*the I should be communicated.*"[28]

We are again close to an identification of Habermas's two key concepts—
"communication is community; community is communication"—with the
crucial difference that Schlegel presents this relationship in the mode of what
ought to be the case. "Community *should* be" means "the I *should* be communicated," which also means, as we now know from Kant, that no human
communiqué, no utterance of "I," can unproblematically communicate this
imperative. Far from the Idealist model of an absolute self that could posit
"I" and "not-I," we have an utterance that cannot even demonstrate that it
belongs to the "I" that posits it. All that can be said is that it *should*.

Schlegel's argument suggests that the language of judgments can never
communicate that communication is possible, even if no political order is
conceivable without the universalizability this communicability *ought* to
make possible. Community is communicability, but there can be no simple
sharing of this fact; there is no way for it to be held in common, as communal knowledge or as the basis for an understanding about what we have
in common with each other. Accordingly, the connection facilitated by
Kant's notion of *sensus communis* is never a gathering of pieces into a broader
frame that would subordinate them as its members. *Sensus communis* heralds
a dividing, an im-parting that parts us in ways that challenge both our integrity as individuals and our relative dependence on or independence from our
larger political formations. This common sense does not make us into parts
of a whole or even prove that the whole is composed of its parts. It parts us
a-part such that we no longer know whether the whole exists because of the
parts or vice versa, much less whether any individual part can communicate
something about its status as a section of a whole. In this respect, Kant's
theory of community is not primarily concerned with an aggregate of people
who enjoy common membership in a larger unit as, for instance, citizens of a
city or state. Rather, Kant conceives of humanity in terms of a dynamic clash
between agents whose interactions are political insofar as they reveal the
parameters of the body politic to be anything but self-evidently available to
cognition or moral evaluation.

Rejecting Habermas's embrace of communication as the motor of a social
praxis predicated on harmonious consensus, the third *Critique* calls for us to
rethink relations between people without assuming that the linguistic facil-
ity we all ostensibly have in common is necessarily the stable grounds for a
commons on which we can stand together and face one another as equals.
Language is an irreducibly social phenomenon that is essential to any model
of community, but it is a source of what Kant terms "discord" as much as it is
a medium that gives shape to our understanding of ourselves or our intersubjective horizons. Like Habermas, Kant is committed to examining the "special kinds of arguments" that constitute our interactions with others. Unlike
his successor, he leaves no doubt that the forces organizing these arguments

are anything but "unforced." In this way, the *Critique of Judgment* invites us to consider democracy as the articulation of differences rather than as a system designed to protect the common traits that supposedly make us the same.

Notes

1. It would be no exaggeration to say that throughout his oeuvre Habermas is in constant dialogue with Kantian thought. In what follows, we will be concerned in particular with two of his explicit discussions of Kant's philosophy: "From Kant's 'Ideas' of Pure Reason to the 'Idealizing' Presuppositions of Communicative Action: Reflections on the Detranscendentalized 'Use of Reason,'" in *Pluralism and the Pragmatic Turn: The Transformation of Critical Theory*, ed. William Rehg and James Bohman (Cambridge: MIT Press, 2001), 11–39, and "Morality and Ethical Life: Does Hegel's Critique of Kant Apply to Discourse Ethics?" in *Kant and Political Philosophy: The Contemporary Legacy*, ed. Ronald Beiner and William James Booth (New Haven: Yale University Press, 1993), 320–36.

2. Unless otherwise stated, quotations from Kant are from the following translations: *Groundwork for the Metaphysics of Morals*, ed. and trans. Allen W. Wood (New Haven: Yale University Press, 2002), "Idea for a Universal History from a Cosmopolitan Point of View," in *On History*, ed. Lewis White Beck (New York: Macmillan, 1963). Page numbers to these translations are included parenthetically in the body of the text.

3. Peter Fenves considers these problems at length in *A Peculiar Fate: Metaphysics and World History in Kant* (Ithaca: Cornell University Press, 1991). On the irony of "To Perpetual Peace," see the final section of Avital Ronell, "Support Our Tropes: Reading Desert Storm," in *Finitude's Score: Essays for the End of the Millennium* (Lincoln: University of Nebraska Press, 1994), 269–91; see pages 285–91.

4. Seyla Benhabib, "Communicative Ethics and Current Controversies in Practical Philosophy," in *The Communicative Ethics Controversy*, ed. Seyla Benhabib and Fred Dallmayr (Cambridge: MIT Press, 1990), 331. Although Habermas often praises Apel's work, one should not take it for granted that their philosophies are simply identical. On the differences between them, see Alexander García Düttmann, "Die Dehnbarkeit der Begriffe: Über Subjektivität, Kritik, und Politik," in *Postmoderne und Politik*, ed. Jutta Georg-Lauer (Tübingen: Edition Diskord, 1992), 57–77.

5. Jürgen Habermas, *The Theory of Communicative Action*, vol. 1, *Reason and the Rationalization of Society*, trans. Thomas McCarthy (Boston: Beacon Press, 1984), 101.

6. Martin Heidegger, in *Kant and the Problem of Metaphysics*, trans. Richard Taft (Bloomington: Indiana University Press, 1990), explores the curious relationship in Kantian moral doctrine between subordinating oneself to the law and subordinating oneself to oneself (107–10).

7. Habermas, "Morality and Ethical Life," 321–22.

8. Ibid., 326.

9. For a decidedly anti-Habermasian approach to Kantian ethics that explores these issues in detail, see Werner Hamacher, "The Promise of Interpretation:

Remarks on the Hermeneutic Imperative in Kant and Nietzsche," in *Premises: Essays on Philosophy and Literature from Kant to Celan*, trans. Peter Fenves (Cambridge: Harvard University Press, 1996), 81–142.

10. Habermas, "From Kant's 'Ideas' of Pure Reason," 14.

11. Ibid., 29.

12. Habermas, "Morality and Ethical Life," 325.

13. Habermas, *Reason and the Rationalization of Society*, 239.

14. Habermas, "Morality and Ethical Life," 323.

15. Jacques Derrida, "Signature, Event, Context," in *Margins of Philosophy*, trans. Alan Bass (Chicago: University of Chicago Press, 1982), 307–30, begins such a reconsideration of the concept of communication through a reading of Edmund Husserl and J. L. Austin.

16. Jean-Luc Nancy, in *The Inoperative Community*, trans. Peter Connor et al. (Minneapolis: University of Minnesota Press, 1991), offers a radically non-Habermasian model of community that takes its point of departure from Martin Heidegger's theory of the essential finitude of *Dasein*. Nancy writes: "Sharing comes down to this: what community reveals to me, in presenting to me my birth and my death, is my existence outside myself. Which does not mean my existence reinvested in or by community, as if community were another subject that would sublate me, in a dialectical or communal mode. *Community does not sublate the finitude it exposes. Community itself, in sum, is nothing but this exposition.* It is the community of finite beings, and as such it is itself a *finite* community. In other words, not a limited community as opposed to an infinite or absolute community, but a community *of* finitude, because finitude 'is' communitarian, and because finitude alone is communitarian" (26–27).

17. Theodor W. Adorno, *Minima Moralia*, trans. E. F. N. Jephcott (New York: Verso, 1989), 80.

18. Citations of the third *Critique* are from *Critique of Judgment*, trans. Werner S. Pluhar (Indianapolis: Hackett, 1987); page numbers to this translation are included parenthetically in the body of the text.

19. Jacques Derrida, "Parergon," in *The Truth in Painting*, trans. Geoff Bennington and Ian McLeod (Chicago: University of Chicago Press, 1987), 35.

20. Ibid.

21. Kant's terms for communication and communicability are *Mitteilung* and *Mitteilbarkeit*, words that share no obvious etymological or lexical association with *sensus communis*, but the Latinate *kommunizieren* was already a standard word in eighteenth-century German, so as in English, the link between community and communication would be evident on the level of the letter as well as on the level of the concept.

22. Hannah Arendt, *Lectures on Kant's Political Philosophy*, ed. Ronald Beiner (Chicago: University of Chicago Press, 1982), 70.

23. Arendt goes on to cite a passage from Kant's *Anthropology* in which he argues that "the only general symptom of insanity is the loss of the *sensus communis* and the logical stubbornness in insisting on one's own sense (*sensus privatus*), which [in an insane person] is substituted for it" (ibid.).

24. Ibid., 72.

25. Ibid., 74.

26. Ibid.

27. Schlegel's argument is in part based on Fichte's "Some Lectures Concerning the Scholar's Vocation." There, Fichte tries to rework Kant's categorical imperative into a statement about the absolute "I," concluding with the claim: "One of man's fundamental drives is to be permitted to assume that rational beings like himself exist outside of him. He can assume this only on the condition that he enter into society (in the sense just specified) with these beings." J. G. Fichte, "Some Lectures Concerning the Scholar's Vocation," in *Early Philosophical Writings*, trans. Daniel Breazeale (Ithaca: Cornell University Press, 1988), 156.

28. Friedrich Schlegel, "The Concept of Republicanism," in *The Early Political Writings of the German Romantics*, ed. Friedrick C. Beiser (New York: Cambridge University Press, 1996), 99–100.

BIBLIOGRAPHY

Adorno, Theodor W. *Minima Moralia*. Translated by E. F. N. Jephcott. New York: Verso, 1989.

Allison, Henry. *Kant's Theory of Taste: A Reading of the Critique of Aesthetic Judgment*. Cambridge: Cambridge University Press, 2001.

———. "Justification and Freedom in the *Critique of Practical Reason*." In *Kant's Transcendental Deductions: The Three Critiques and the Opus postumum*, edited by Eckart Förster, 114–30. Stanford: Stanford University Press, 1989.

Ameriks, Karl. "The Hegelian Critique of Kantian Morality." In *New Essays on Kant*, edited by Bernard den Ouden and Marcia Moen, 179–212. New York: Peter Lang, 1987.

Anderson, Benedict. *Imagined Communities*. London: Verso, 1983. Rev. ed., 1991.

Anderson-Gold, Sharon. *Cosmopolitanism and Human Rights*. Chicago: University of Chicago Press, 2001.

———. "God and Community: An Inquiry into the Religious Implications of the Highest Good." In *Kant's Philosophy of Religion Reconsidered*, edited by Philip J. Rossi and Michael Wreen, 113–31. Bloomington: Indiana University Press, 1991.

Aquinas, Saint Thomas. *Summa Contra Gentiles*. Translated by Pegis et al. Notre Dame: Notre Dame University Press, 1975.

———. *Summa Theologiae*. Translated by the Fathers of the English Dominican Province. New York: Benziger, 1974.

Arendt, Hannah. *The Human Condition*. Chicago: The University of Chicago Press, 1998.

———. *Lectures on Kant's Political Philosophy*. Edited and with an interpretive essay by Ronald Beiner. Chicago: The University of Chicago Press, 1982.

Arendt, Hannah, and Martin Heidegger. *Letters 1925–1975*. Edited by Ursula Ludz. Translated by Andrew Shields. New York: Harcourt, 2004.

Aristotle. *The Politics*. Translated by Carnes Lord. Chicago: University of Chicago Press, 1984.

Ashcroft, Bill, Gareth Griffiths, and Helen Tiffin, eds. *The Post-Colonial Studies Reader*. New York: Routledge, 1995.

Banham, Gary. *Kant and the Ends of Aesthetics*. New York: St. Martin's Press, 2000.

Beiner, Ronald. "Rereading Hannah Arendt's Kant Lectures." *Philosophy & Social Criticism* 23 (1997): 21–32. Reprinted in *Judgment, Imagination, and Politics: Themes from Kant and Arendt*, edited by Ronald Beiner and Jennifer Nedelsky. Lanham, MD: Rowman & Littlefield, 2001.

———. *Kant and Political Philosophy*. Edited by William James Booth and Ronald Beiner. New Haven: Yale University Press, 1993.

———. *Political Judgment*. Chicago: University of Chicago Press, 1983.

Beiser, Fredrick. "Moral Faith and the Highest Good." In *The Cambridge Companion to Kant and Modern Philosophy*, edited by Paul Guyer, 588–629. Cambridge: Cambridge University Press, 2006.

Benhabib, Seyla. *Another Cosmopolitanism*. With commentaries by Jeremy Waldron, Bonnie Honig, and Will Kymlicka. Edited and introduced by Robert Post. Oxford: Oxford University Press, 2006.

———. "Communicative Ethics and Current Controversies in Practical Philosophy." In *The Communicative Ethics Controversy*, edited by Seyla Benhabib and Fred Dallmayr, 330–69. Cambridge: MIT Press, 1990.

Bennett, Jonathan. *Kant's Analytic*. Cambridge: Cambridge University Press, 1966.

Bittner, Rüdiger. *What Reason Demands*. Translated by Theodore Talbot. New York: Cambridge University Press, 1989.

Bourdieu, Pierre. *Distinction: A Social Critique of the Judgment of Taste*. Translated by Richard Nice. Cambridge: Harvard University Press, 1984. Originally published as *La Distinction: Critique sociale du jugement*. Paris: Les Éditions de Minuit, 1979.

Bowie, Andrew. "What Comes After Art?" In *The New Aestheticism*, edited by John J. Joughin and Simon Malpas, 68–82. Manchester: Manchester University Press, 2003.

Boyd, Richard. "How to Be a Moral Realist," in *Essays on Moral Realism*, edited by G. Sayre-McCord, 181–228. Ithaca: Cornell University Press, 1988.

Brandom, Robert. "Some Pragmatist Themes in Hegel's Idealism: Negotiation and Administration in Hegel's Account of the Structure and Content of Conceptual Norms." *European Journal of Philosophy* 7, no. 2 (1999): 164–89.

Brandt, Reinhard. *The Table of Judgments: Critique of Pure Reason A 67–76; B 92–101*. Translated by Eric Watkins. Atascadero: Ridgeview, 1995.

———. *Eigentumstheorien von Grotius bis Kant*. Stuttgart: F. Frommann Verlag, 1974.

Brett, Annabel. *Liberty, Right, and Nature: Individual Rights in Later Scholastic Thought*. Cambridge: Cambridge University Press, 1997.

Brocker, Manfred. *Arbeit und Eigentum: Der Paradigmenwechsel in der neuzeitlichen Eigentumstheorie*. Darmstadt: Wissenschaftliche Buchgesellschaft, 1992.

Buckle, Stephen. *Natural Law and the Theory of Property: Grotius to Hume*. Oxford: Oxford University Press, 1991.

Canovan, Margaret. "Rousseau's Two Concepts of Citizenship." In *Women in Western Political Philosophy*, edited by Ellen Kennedy and Susan Mendus, 78–105. Brighton: Wheatsheaf Books, 1987.

Caruth, Cathy. "The Force of Example: Kant's Symbols." In *Unruly Examples: On the Rhetoric of Exemplarity*, edited by Alexander Gelley, 277–302. Stanford: Stanford University Press, 1995.

Cheah, Pheng. *Spectral Nationality: Passages of Freedom from Kant to Postcolonial Literatures of Liberation*. New York: Columbia University Press, 2003.

Delanty, Gerard. *Inventing Europe: Idea, Identity, Reality*. London: Macmillan, 1995.

Denker, Alfred, and Tom Rockmore, eds. *Kant's Pre-critical Philosophy*. New York: Prometheus, 2001.

Derrida, Jacques. "Parergon." In *The Truth in Painting*, translated by Geoff Bennington and Ian McLeod, 15–147. Chicago: University of Chicago Press, 1987.

————. "Signature, Event, Context." In *Margins of Philosophy*, translated by Alan Bass, 307–30. Chicago: University of Chicago Press, 1982.

Des Chene, Dennis. *Physiologia: Natural Philosophy in Late Aristotelian and Cartesian Thought*. Ithaca: Cornell University Press, 1996.

Digby, Kenelm. *Two Treatises: In the One of Which, the Nature of Bodies, in the Other, the Nature of Man's Mind, is Looked Into*. Paris: Gilles Blaizot, 1644; Facsimile reprint by Garland Publishing, 1978.

Düttmann, Alexander García. "Die Dehnbarkeit der Begriffe: Über Subjektivität, Kritik, und Politik." In *Postmoderne und Politik*, edited by Jutta Georg-Lauer, 57–77. Tübingen: Edition Diskord, 1992.

Eagleton, Terry. *The Ideology of the Aesthetic*. Oxford: Basil Blackwell, 1990.

Edwards, Jeffrey. "Natural Right and Acquisition in Grotius, Selden, and Hobbes." In *Der lange Schatten des Leviathan. Hobbes' politische Philosophie nach 350 Jahren*, edited by Dieter Hüning, 153–78. Berlin: Duncker & Humblot, 2005.

————. "Property and *communitas rerum*: Ockham, Suarez, Grotius, Hobbes." In *Societas Rationis: Festschrift für Burkhard Tuschling zum 65. Geburtstag*, edited by Ulrich Vogel, Burkhard Tuschling, Dieter Hüning, and Gideon Stiening, 41–60. Berlin: Duncker & Humblot, 2002.

————. *Substance, Force, and the Possibility of Knowledge: On Kant's Philosophy of Material Nature*. Berkeley: University of California Press, 2000.

————. "Disjunktiv- und kollektiv-allgemeiner Besitz: Überlegungen zu Kants Theorie der ursprünglichen Erwerbung." In *Recht, Staat, und Völkerrecht bei Immanuel Kant*, edited by Dieter Hüning and Burkhard Tuschling, 121–40. Berlin: Duncker & Humblot, 1998.

Ellis, Elisabeth. *Kant's Politics: Provisional Theory for an Uncertain World*. New Haven: Yale University Press, 2005.

Elshtain, Jean Bethke. *Public Man, Private Woman: Women in Social and Political Thought*, 2nd ed. Princeton: Princeton University Press, 1993.

Eze, Emmanuel Chukwudi. "The Color of Reason: The Idea of 'Race' in Kant's Anthropology." In *Postcolonial African Philosophy: A Critical Reader*, edited by Emmanuel Chukwudi Eze. Oxford: Blackwell, 1997.

Felten, Gundula. *Die Funktion des sensus communis in Kants Theorie des ästhetischen Urteils*. Munich: Wilhelm Fink, 2004.

Fenves, Peter. *A Peculiar Fate: Metaphysics and World-History in Kant*. Ithaca: Cornell University Press, 1991.

Fichte, J. G. "Some Lectures Concerning the Scholar's Vocation." In *Early Philosophical Writings*, translated by Daniel Breazeale. Ithaca: Cornell University Press, 1988.

Figal, Sara Eigen, and Mark Larrimore, eds. *The German Invention of Race*. Albany: State University of New York Press, 2007.

Flathman, Richard A. "Citizenship and Authority: A Chastened View of Citizenship." In *Theorizing Citizenship*, edited by Ronald Beiner, 105–51. Albany: State University of New York Press, 1995.

Friedrich, Rainer. *Eigentum und Staatsbegründung in Kants "Metaphysik der Sitten."* Berlin: de Gruyter, 2004.

Fulda, Hans Friedrich. "Zur Systematik des Privatrechts in Kants *Metaphysik der Sitten*." In *Recht, Staat, und Völkerrecht bei Immanuel Kant*, edited by Dieter Hüning and Burkhard Tuschling, 141–56. Berlin: Duncker & Humblot, 1998.

Gailus, Andreas. *Passions of the Sign: Revolution and Language in Kant, Goethe, and Kleist*. Baltimore: Johns Hopkins University Press, 2006.

Galston, William A. *The Practice of Liberal Pluralism*. Cambridge: Cambridge University Press, 2005.

Garve, Christian. *Versuche über verschiedene Gegenstände aus der Moral und Literatur*. Breslau, 1792.

Gasché, Rodolphe. *The Idea of Form: Rethinking Kant's Aesthetics*. Stanford: Stanford University Press, 2002.

Grotius, Hugo. *The Freedom of the Seas*. 1609. Translated by R. V. D. Magofin. Oxford: Oxford University Press, 1916.

———. *De Jure Belli ac Pacis Libri Tres*. 1625; 2nd ed. 1631. Edited by J. B. Scott. Oxford: Oxford University Press, 1913.

Guyer, Paul. "The Crooked Timber of Mankind." In *Kant's Idea for a Universal History with a Cosmopolitan Aim: A Critical Guide*, edited by Amelie Oksenberg Rorty and James Schmidt, 129–49. Cambridge: Cambridge University Press, 2009.

———. "The Possibility of Perpetual Peace." In *Kant's Perpetual Peace: New Interpretative Essays*, edited by Luigi Caranti, 161–82. Rome: LUISS University Press, 2006.

———. *Kant's Critique of Taste: Critical Essays*. Edited by Paul Guyer. Lanham, MD: Rowman & Littlefield, 2003.

———. "Kant's Deductions of the Principles of Right." In *Kant's Metaphysics of Morals: Interpretive Essays*, edited by Mark Timmons, 23–64. Oxford: Oxford University Press, 2002.

———. *Kant on Freedom, Law, and Happiness*. Cambridge: Cambridge University Press, 2000.

———. "Life, Liberty, and Property: Rawls the Reconstruction of Kant's Political Philosophy." In *Recht, Staat, und Völkerrecht bei Immanuel Kant*, edited by Dieter Hüning and Burkhard Tuschling, 273–92. Berlin: Duncker & Humblot, 1998.

———. *Kant and the Experience of Freedom: Essays on Aesthetics and Morality*. Cambridge: Cambridge University Press, 1996.

———. *Kant and the Claims of Knowledge*. Cambridge: Cambridge University Press, 1987.

———. *Kant and the Claims of Taste*. Cambridge: Harvard University Press, 1979.

Habermas, Jürgen. *Europe: The Faltering Project*. Translated by Ciaran Cronin. Malden, MA: Polity Press, 2009.

———. "From Kant's 'Ideas' of Pure Reason to the 'Idealizing' Presuppositions of Communicative Action: Reflections on the Detranscendentalized 'Use of Reason.'" In *Pluralism and the Pragmatic Turn: The Transformation of Critical Theory*, edited by William Rehg and James Bohman, 11–39. Cambridge: MIT Press, 2001.

———. *The Postnational Constellation: Political Essays*. Cambridge: MIT Press, 2001.

———. "Morality and Ethical Life: Does Hegel's Critique of Kant Apply to Discourse Ethics?" In *Kant and Political Philosophy: The Contemporary Legacy*, edited by Ronald Beiner and William James Booth, 320–36. New Haven: Yale University Press, 1993.

———. *Moral Consciousness and Communicative Action*. Translated by C. Lenhart and S. W. Nicholson. Cambridge: MIT Press, 1989.

———. *The Theory of Communicative Action*. Vol. 1, *Reason and the Rationalization of Society*. Translated by Thomas McCarthy. Boston: Beacon Press, 1984.

———. *Theory and Practice*. Translated by John Viertel. Boston: Beacon Press, 1973.

Habermas, Jürgen, and Jacques Derrida. "February 15, or What Binds Europe Together: A Plea for a Common Foreign Policy, Beginning in the Core of Europe." In *The Derrida-Habermas Reader*, edited by Lasse Thomassen, 270–77. Chicago: University of Chicago Press, 2006.

Hamacher, Werner. "The Promise of Interpretation: Remarks on the Hermeneutic Imperative in Kant and Nietzsche." In *Premises: Essays on Philosophy and Literature from Kant to Celan*, translated by Peter Fenves, 81–142. Cambridge: Harvard University Press, 1996.

Hegel, G. W. F. *Political Writings*. Edited by Laurence Dickey and H. B. Nisbet. Cambridge: Cambridge University Press, 1999.

———. *Lectures on the History of Philosophy*. Translated by E. S. Haldane and Frances Simson. 3 vols. Lincoln: University of Nebraska Press, 1995.

———. *Elements of the Philosophy of Right*. Translated and edited by Allen W. Wood. Cambridge: Cambridge University Press, 1991.

———. *The Encyclopaedia Logic*. Translated by Theodore F. Geraets, W. A. Suchting, and H. S. Harris. Indianapolis: Hackett, 1991.

———. *Werke in Zwanzig Bänden*. Frankfurt am Main: Suhrkamp Verlag, 1979.

———. *Faith and Knowledge*. Edited by H. S. Harris and Walter Cerf. Albany: State University of New York Press, 1977.

———. *Phenomenology of Spirit*. Translated by A. V. Miller. Oxford: Oxford University Press, 1977.

———. *Science of Logic*. Translated by A. V. Miller. New York: Humanities Press, 1976.

———. *Hegel's Logic*. Translated by William Wallace. New York: Oxford University Press, 1975.

———. *Briefe von und an Hegel, Band I: 1785–1812*. Edited by Johannes Hoffmeister. Hamburg: Felix Meiner Verlag, 1952.

Heidegger, Martin. *Kant and the Problem of Metaphysics*. Translated by Richard Taft. Bloomington: Indiana University Press, 1990.

Henrich, Dieter. *Between Kant and Hegel: Lectures on German Idealism*. Edited and translated by David S. Pacini. Cambridge: Harvard University Press, 2003.

———. *The Unity of Reason: Essays on Kant's Philosophy*. Cambridge: Harvard University Press, 1994.

———. *Aesthetic Judgment and the Moral Image of the World*. Stanford: Stanford University Press, 1992.

Hobbes, Thomas. *Leviathan*. Edited by Richard Tuck. Cambridge: Cambridge University Press, 1993.

Honig, Bonnie. *Emergency Politics: Paradox, Law, Democracy*. Princeton: Princeton University Press, 2009.

———. *Political Theory and the Displacement of Politics.* Ithaca: Cornell University Press, 1993.

Ilting, Karl-Heinz. "Hegels Auseinandersetzung mit der Aristotelischen Politik." *Philosophisches Jahrbuch* 71 (1963–64): 38–58.

Ishiguro, Hidé. *Leibniz's Philosophy of Logic and Language.* London: Duckworth, 1972. Second edition, Cambridge: Cambridge University Press, 1990.

Jacobs, Brian, ed. *An Introduction to Kant's Anthropology.* Cambridge: Cambridge University Press, 2003.

Joughin, John J., and Simon Malpas, eds. *The New Aestheticism.* Manchester: Manchester University Press, 2003.

Kagan, Robert. "America's Crisis of Legitimacy." *Foreign Affairs* (March/April 2004): 65–87.

———. *Of Paradise and Power: America and Europe in the New World Order.* New York: Alfred A. Knopf, 2003.

Kant, Immanuel. *Anthropology, History, and Education.* Edited by Robert Louden and Günter Zöller. Cambridge: Cambridge University Press, 2008.

———. *The Cambridge Edition of the Works of Immanuel Kant.* Edited by Paul Guyer and Allen W. Wood. 13 vols. Cambridge: Cambridge University Press, 1992–.

———. *Critique of Judgment.* Translated by Werner Pluhar. Indianapolis: Hackett, 1987.

———. *Critique of Pure Reason.* Edited by Paul Guyer and Allen W. Wood. Cambridge: Cambridge University Press, 1998.

———. *Critique of Pure Reason.* Translated by Norman Kemp Smith. New York: St. Martin's Press, 1965.

———. *Critique of the Power of Judgment.* Edited by Paul Guyer. Translated by Paul Guyer and Eric Matthews. Cambridge: Cambridge University Press, 2000.

———. *Groundwork for the Metaphysics of Morals.* Edited and translated by Allen W. Wood. New Haven: Yale University Press, 2002.

———. *Groundwork for the Metaphysics of Morals.* Translated by Arnulf Zweig. Edited by Thomas E. Hill Jr. and Arnulf Zweig. Oxford: Oxford University Press, 2002.

———. *Groundwork for the Metaphysics of Morals.* Translated by Thomas K. Abbot. Edited and revised by Lara Denis. Peterborough: Broadview, 2005.

———. *Kants gesammelte Schriften.* Edited by the Royal Prussian (later German, then Berlin-Brandenburg) Academy of Sciences (Königlich Preußische Akademie der Wissenschaften). 29 vols. Berlin: Georg Reimer, later de Gruyter, 1900– .

———. *Kritik der Urteilskraft.* Hamburg: Felix Meiner Verlag, 2001.

———. *Lectures on Ethics.* Edited by Peter Heath and J. B. Schneewind. Cambridge: Cambridge University Press, 1997.

———. *Lectures on Logic.* Edited by J. Michael Young. Cambridge: Cambridge University Press 1992.

———. *Lectures on Metaphysics.* Edited by Karl Ameriks and Steve Naragon. Cambridge: Cambridge University Press, 1997.

———. *Metaphysical Foundations of Natural Science.* Translated by J. W. Ellington. Indianapolis: Bobbs-Merill, 1970.

———. *Metaphysische Anfangsgründe der Rechtslehre (Philosophische Bibliotek* edition). Edited by Bernd Ludgwig. Hamburg: Felix Meiner, 1998.

————. *On History*. Edited by Lewis White Beck. New York: Macmillan, 1963.

————. *Opus postumum*. Edited by Eckart Förster. Translated by Eckart Förster and Michael Rosen. Cambridge: Cambridge University Press, 1993.

————. *Perpetual Peace and Other Essays*. Translated by Ted Humphrey. Indianapolis: Hackett, 1983.

————. *Political Writings*. Edited by Hans Reiss. Translated by H. B. Nisbet. Cambridge: Cambridge University Press, 1991.

————. *Practical Philosophy*. Translated and edited by Mary J. Gregor. Cambridge: Cambridge University Press, 1996.

————. *Religion and Rational Theology*. Edited by Allen W. Wood and George di Giovanni. Cambridge: Cambridge University Press, 1996.

————. *Religion within the Boundaries of Mere Reason*. Translated and edited by Allen W. Wood and George di Giovanni. New York: Cambridge University Press, 1998.

————. *Religion within the Limits of Reason Alone*. Translated by Theodore M. Greene and Hoyt H. Hudson. New York: Harper & Row, 1960.

Kelly, Michael, ed. *Encyclopedia of Aesthetics*. Oxford: Oxford University Press, 1997.

Kersting, Wolfgans. *Wohlgeordnete Freiheit: Immanuel Kants Rechts- und Staatsphilosophie*. Frankfurt am Main: Suhrkamp, 1993.

Kneller, Jane. *Kant and the Power of Imagination*. Cambridge: Cambridge University Press, 2007.

————. *Autonomy and Community: Readings in Contemporary Kantian Social Philosophy*. With Sidney Axinn. Buffalo: State University of New York Press, 1998.

————. "Disinterestness." In *Encyclopedia of Aesthetics*. Vol. 2, edited by Michael Kelly. Oxford: Oxford University Press, 1997.

Lange, Lynda. "Rousseau: Women and the General Will." In *The Sexism of Social and Political Theory: Women and Reproduction from Plato to Nietzsche*, edited by Lorenne M. G. Clark and Lynda Lange, 41–52. Toronto: University of Toronto Press, 1979.

Langton, Rae. *Kantian Humility: Our Ignorance of Things in Themselves*. Cambridge: Cambridge University Press, 1998.

La Vopa, Anthony. *Fichte: The Self and the Calling of Philosophy, 1762–1799*. Cambridge: Cambridge University Press, 2001.

Leibniz, G. W. *New Essays on Human Understanding*. Translated by Peter Remnant and J. Bennett. *Cambridge Texts in the History of Philosophy*. Cambridge: Cambridge University Press, 1996.

————. *Philosophical Essays*. Edited and translated by Roger Ariew and Daniel Garber. Indianapolis: Hackett, 1989.

————. *Philosophical Papers and Letters*. Second edition, translated and edited by Leroy E. Loemker. Dordrecht: Reidel, 1969.

————. *Die Philosophischen Schriften von G. W. Leibniz*. Edited by C. I. Gerhardt. 7 vols. Berlin: Weidmann, 1875–90.

Lloyd, David. "Kant's Examples." In *Unruly Examples: On the Rhetoric of Exemplarity*, edited by Alexander Gelley, 255–76. Stanford: Stanford University Press, 1995.

Longuenesse, Béatrice. "Point of View of Man or Knowledge of God: Kant and Hegel on Concept, Judgment, and Reason." In *The Reception of Kant's Critical System in*

Fichte, Schelling, and Hegel, edited by Sally Sedgwick, 253–82. Cambridge: Cambridge University Press, 2000.

———. *Kant and the Capacity to Judge*. Princeton: Princeton University Press, 1998.

Lugones, Maria. "Playfulness, 'World'-Traveling, and Loving Perception." *Hypatia* 2, no. 2 (1987): 3–18.

Lyotard, Jean-Francois. *Lessons on the Analytic of the Sublime*. Translated by Elizabeth Rottenberg. Stanford: Stanford University Press, 1994.

Machiavelli, Niccolò. *Discourses on Livy*. Translated by Harvey C. Mansfield and Nathan Tarcov. Chicago: Chicago University Press, 1996.

Martyn, David. *Sublime Failures: The Ethics of Kant and Sade*. Detroit: Wayne State University Press, 2003.

Marx, Karl. *Grundrisse der Kritik der politischen Ökonomie*. Berlin: Dietz, 1974.

McCumber, John. *Poetic Interaction: Language, Freedom, Reason*. Chicago: University of Chicago Press, 1989.

Mendus, Susan. "Kant: 'An Honest but Narrow-Minded Bourgeois'?" In *Essays on Kant's Political Philosophy*, edited by Howard Lloyd Williams, 166–91. Chicago: University of Chicago Press, 1992.

Menninghaus, Winfried. *In Praise of Nonsense: Kant and Bluebeard*. Translated by Henry Pickford. Stanford: Stanford University Press, 1999.

Michalson, Gordon E., Jr., *Kant and the Problem of God*. Oxford: Blackwell, 1999.

———. *Fallen Freedom: Kant on Radical Evil and Moral Regeneration*. Cambridge: Cambridge University Press, 1991.

Mills, Charles. *The Racial Contract*. Ithaca: Cornell University Press, 1997.

Morrison, Margaret. "Space, Time, and Reciprocity." In *Proceedings of the Eighth International Kant Congress*, edited by Hoke Robinson. Vol. 2, 187–95. Milwaukee: Marquette University Press, 1995.

Nancy, Jean-Luc. *The Inoperative Community*. Translated by Peter Connor, et al. Minneapolis: University of Minnesota Press, 1991.

Nehring, Robert. *Kritik des Common Sense. Gesunder Menschenverstand, reflektierende Urteilskraft und Gemeinsinn—der sensus communis bei Kant*. Berlin: Duncker & Humblot, 2010.

Nietzsche, Friedrich. *Beyond Good and Evil: Prelude to a Philosophy of the Future*. Translated by Walter Kaufmann. New York: Vintage, 1989.

———. *Thus Spoke Zarathustra*. Translated and with an introduction by R. J. Hollingdale. London: Penguin, 1961.

Nussbaum, Martha C. *Women and Human Development: The Capabilities Approach*. Cambridge: Cambridge University Press, 2000.

Okin, Susan Moller. *Women in Western Political Thought*. Princeton: Princeton University Press, 1979.

O'Neill, Eileen. *"Influxus Physicus."* In *Causation in Early Modern Philosophy*, edited by Steven Nadler, 27–56. University Perk: Pennsylvania State University Press, 1993.

O'Neill, Onora. "Political Liberalism and Public Reason: A Critical Notice of John Rawls's *Political Liberalism*." *The Philosophical Review* 106 (1997): 411–28.

den Ouden, Bernard, and Marcia Moen, eds. *New Essays on Kant*. New York: Peter Lang, 1987.

Parkinson, G. H. R. *Logic and Reality in Leibniz's Metaphysics*. Oxford: Clarendon Press, 1965.

Pateman, Carole. *The Sexual Contract*. Stanford: Stanford University Press, 1988.

Pinkard, Terry. *Hegel's Phenomenology: The Sociality of Reason*. New York: Cambridge University Press, 1996.

———. "Historicism, Social Practice, and Sustainability: Themes in Hegelian Ethical Theory." *Neue Hefte für Philosophie* 35 (1995): 56–94.

Pippin, Robert. "Hegel and Institutional Rationality." *Southern Journal of Philosophy* 39 (2001): 1–25.

———. "Hegel, Ethical Reasons, Kantian Rejoinders." In Pippin, *Idealism as Modernism: Hegelian Variations*, 92–128. New York: Cambridge University Press, 1997.

———. "On the Moral Foundations of Kant's *Rechtslehre*." In Pippin, *Idealism as Modernism: Hegelian Variations*, 56–91. New York: Cambridge University Press, 1997.

———. "What Is the Question for Which Hegel's Theory of Recognition Is the Answer?" *European Journal of Philosophy* 8 (2000): 155–72.

Rauzy, Jean-Baptiste. "Leibniz on Body, Force, and Extension." *Proceedings of the Aristotelian Society* 105, part 3 (1995): 363–84.

Rawls, John. *Lectures on the History of Ethics*. Edited by Barbara Herman. Cambridge, MA: Harvard University Press, 2000.

———. "Kantian Constructivism in Moral Theory." In *John Rawls, Collected Papers*, edited by Samuel Freedom, 303–58. Cambridge: Harvard University Press, 1999.

———. *Political Liberalism*. New York: Columbia University Press, 1993.

———. *A Theory of Justice*. Cambridge: Belknap Press of Harvard University Press, 1971.

Reath, Andrews. "Two Conceptions of the Highest Good in Kant." *Journal of the History of Philosophy* 26, no. 4 (1988): 593–619.

Reiss, Hans. "Kant's Politics and the Enlightenment: Reflections on Some Recent Studies." *Political Theory* 27, no. 2 (1999): 236–73.

———. "Postscript." In Kant, *Political Writings*. Second enlarged edition, edited by Hans Reiss, 250–73. Cambridge: Cambridge University Press, 1991.

Revueltas, Juan Cristóbal Cruz. "Philosophy as a Problem in Latin America." In *What Philosophy Is*, ed. Havi Carel and David Gamez, 116–25. New York: Continuum, 2004.

Ripstein, Arthur. *Force and Freedom: Kant's Legal and Political Philosophy*. Harvard University Press, 2009.

———. "Kant's Legal and Political Philosophy." In *A Companion to Kant's Ethics*, edited by T. Hill, 161–78. Oxford: Blackwell, 2009.

———. "Authority and Coercion." *Philosophy & Public Affairs* 32, no. 1 (2004): 2–35.

Ritter, Joachim. "Morality and Ethical Life: Hegel's Controversy with Kantian Ethics." In Ritter, *Hegel and the French Revolution: Essays on the Philosophy of Right*, translated by Richard Dien Winfield, 151–82. Cambridge: MIT Press, 1982.

Robinet, A., ed. *Malebranche et Leibniz: Relations Personelles*. Paris: J. Vrin, 1955.

Ronell, Avital. "Support Our Tropes: Reading Desert Storm." In Ronell, *Finitude's Score: Essays for the End of the Millennium*, 269–91. Lincoln: University of Nebraska Press, 1994.

Rosen, Alan. *Kant's Theory of Justice*. Ithaca: Cornell University Press, 1993.

Rossi, Philip J. *The Social Authority of Reason: Kant's Critique, Radical Evil, and the Destiny of Humankind*. Albany: State University of New York Press, 2005.

Rossi, Philip J., and Michael Wreen, eds. *Kant's Philosophy of Religion Reconsidered*. Bloomington: Indiana University Press, 1991.

Rousseau, Jean-Jacques. *"The Discourses" and Other Early Political Writings*. Edited and translated by Victor Gourevitch. Cambridge: Cambridge University Press, 1997.

———. *Emile: or, On Education*. Introduction, translation, and notes by Allan Bloom. New York: Basic Books, 1979.

———. *On the Social Contract, with the Geneva Manuscript and Political Economy*. Edited by Roger D. Masters. Translated by Judith R. Masters. New York: St. Martin's Press, 1978.

———. *Politics and the Arts: Letter to M. d'Alembert on the Theatre*. Edited and translated by Allan Bloom. Ithaca: Cornell University Press, 1968.

———. *Oeuvres completes*. Vol. 3, *Discours sur l'origine et les fondements de l'inégalité*. Paris: Gallimard, 1964.

Rutherford, Donald P. "Natures, Laws, and Miracles: The Roots of Leibniz's Critique of Occasionalism." In *Causation in Early Modern Philosophy*, edited by Steven Nadler, 135–58. University Park: Pennsylvania State University Press, 1993.

Sassen, Brigitte. "Artistic Genius and the Question of Creativity." In *Kant's Critique of Taste: Critical Essays*, edited by Paul Guyer, 171–79. Lanham, MD: Rowman & Littlefield, 2003.

Schlegel, Friedrich. "The Concept of Republicanism." In *The Early Political Writings of the German Romantics*, edited by Friedrick C. Beiser. New York: Cambridge University Press, 1996.

Schmidt, James, ed., *What Is Enlightenment? Eighteenth-Century Answers and Twentieth-Century Questions*. Berkeley: University of California Press, 1996.

Schneewind, J. B. *The Invention of Autonomy: A History of Modern Moral Philosophy*. New York: Cambridge University Press, 1998.

Schopenhauer, Arthur. *Sämtliche Werke*. Vol. 2, *Die Welt als Wille und Vorstellung*. Edited by Arthur Hübscher. Wiesbaden: Eberhard Brockhaus Verlag, 1972. Translated as *The World as Will and Representation*, by E. F. J. Payne. 2 vols. New York: Dover, 1966.

Schönfeld, Martin. *The Philosophy of the Young Kant*. New York: Oxford University Press, 2000.

Scruton, Roger. "Contract, Consent, and Exploitation: Kantian Themes." In *Essays on Kant's Political Philosophy*, edited by Howard Lloyd Williams, 213–27. Chicago: University of Chicago Press, 1992.

Sedgwick, Sally. "Can Kant's Ethics Survive the Feminist Critique?" In *Feminist Interpretations of Immanuel Kant*, edited by Robin May Schott, 77–101. University Park: Pennsylvania State University Press, 1997.

Selden, John. *Opera omnia*. 1636. London, 1726.

Shell, Susan Meld. "Nachschrift eines Freundes: Kant on Language, Friendship, and the Concept of a People." *Kantian Review* 15, no. 1 (2010): 88–117.

———. *Kant and the Limits of Autonomy*. Cambridge: Harvard University Press, 2009.

———. "Freedom and Faith Within the Boundaries of Bare Reason." In *Freedom and the Human Person*, edited by Richard Velkley, 181–206. Washington: Catholic University of America Press, 2008.

———. "Kant's Conception of a Human Race." In *The German Invention of Race*, edited by Sara Eigen and Mark Larrimore, 55–72. New York: State University of New York Press, 2007.

———. "Kant on Just War and Unjust Enemies." *Kantian Review* 10, no. 1 (2005): 82–111.

———. "Kant as Propagator: Reflections on Observations on the Feeling of the Beautiful and Sublime." *Eighteenth-Century Studies* 35, no. 3 (2002): 455–68.

———. *The Embodiment of Reason: Kant on Spirit, Generation, and Community*. Chicago: University of Chicago Press, 1996.

———. *The Rights of Reason: A Study of Kant's Philosophy and Politics*. Toronto: University of Toronto Press, 1980.

Soni, Vivasvan. "Communal Narcosis and Sublime Withdrawal: The Problem of Community in Kant's *Critique of Judgment*." *Cultural Critique* 64 (2006): 1–39.

Strawson, Peter F. *The Bounds of Sense: An Essay on Kant's "Critique of Pure Reason."* London: Methuen, 1966.

Taylor, Charles. *Modern Social Imaginaries*. Durham: Duke University Press, 2004.

Thorpe, Lucas. "Is Kant's Realm of Ends a Unum per Se? Aquinas, Suárez, Leibniz, and Kant on Composition." *British Journal for the History of Philosophy* 18, no. 3 (2010): 461–85.

———. "The Realm of Ends as a Community of Spirits: Kant and Swedenborg on the Kingdom of Heaven and the Cleansing of the Doors of Perception." *Heythrop Journal* 48 (2010): 1–24.

———. "The Point of Studying Ethics According to Kant." *Journal of Value Inquiry* 40, no. 4 (2006): 461–74.

Tierney, Brian. "Permissive Natural Law and Property: Gratian to Kant." *Journal of the History of Ideas* 62, no. 3 (2001): 381–99.

———. *The Idea of Natural Rights: Studies on Natural Rights, Natural Law, and Church Law 1150–1625*. Atlanta: Scholars Press/Emory University, 1997.

Timmons, Mark, ed. *Kant's Metaphysics of Morals: Interpretive Essays*. Oxford: Oxford University Press, 2002.

Tuck, Richard. *The Rights of War and Peace: Political Thought and the International Order from Grotius to Kant*. Oxford: Oxford University Press, 1999.

———. *Philosophy and Government: 1572–1651*. Cambridge: Cambridge University Press, 1993.

Tugendhat, Ernst. *Self-Consciousness and Self-Determination*. Cambridge: MIT Press, 1986.

Tunick, Mark. "Are There Natural Rights? Hegel's Break with Kant." In *Hegel and the Modern World*, edited by Ardis B. Collins, 219–36. Albany: State University of New York Press, 1995.

Tuschling, Burkhard. "*Rationis societas:* Remarks on Kant and Hegel." In *Kant's Philosophy of Religion Reconsidered*, edited by Philip Rossi and Michael Wreen, 181–205. Bloomington: Indiana University Press, 1991.

Twellmann, Marcus. "*Ueber die Eide.*" *Zucht und Kritik im Preußen der Aufklärung.* Konstanz: Konstanz University Press, 2010.

Velkley, Richard, ed. *Freedom and the Human Person.* Washington: Catholic University of America Press, 2007.

Watkins, Eric. "Kant on Transcendental Laws." In *Thinking About Causes: Past and Present*, edited by J. Machamer and G. Wolters, 100–122. Pittsburgh: Pittsburg University Press, 2007.

———. *Kant and the Metaphysics of Causality.* New York: Cambridge University Press, 2005.

———. "Kant's Model of Causality: Casual Powders, Law, and Kant's Reply to Hume." *Journal of the History of Philosophy* 42, no. 4 (2004): 449–88.

———. "Forces and Causes in Kant's Early Pre-critical Writings." *Studies in History and Philosophy of Science* 34 (2003): 5–27.

———. "From Pre-established Harmony to Physical Influx: Leibniz's Reception in Early Eighteenth-Century Germany." *Perspectives on Science* 6 (1998): 136–203.

———. "Kant's Third Analogy of Experience." *Kant-Studien* 88 (1997): 406–41.

———. "The Laws of Motion from Newton to Kant." *Perspectives on Science* 5 (1997): 311–48.

———. "The Development of Physical Influx in Early Eighteenth-Century Germany: Gottsched, Knutzen, and Crusius." *Review of Metaphysics* 49 (1995): 295–339.

———. "Kant's Theory of Physical Influx." *Archiv für Geschichte der Philosophie* 77 (1995): 285–324.

Weiler, Joseph H. H. *Un'Europa Cristiana: Un saggio esplorativo.* Milan: BUR Saggi, 2003.

———. *The Constitution of Europe: "Do the New Clothes Have an Emperor?" and Other Essays on European Integration.* Cambridge: Cambridge University Press, 1999.

Wellmon, Chad. "Kant and the Feelings of Reason." *Eighteenth-Century Studies* 42, no. 4 (2009): 557–80.

Wilkerson, T. E. *Kant's Critique of Pure Reason: A Commentary for Students.* 2nd ed. Bristol: Thoemmes Press, 1998.

Willaschek, Marcus. "Which Imperatives for Right? On the Non-Prescriptive Character of Juridical Laws in Kant's *Metaphysics of Morals.*" In *Kant's Metaphysics of Morals: Interpretive Essays*, edited by Mark Timmons, 65–87. Oxford: Oxford University Press, 2002.

———. "Why the *Doctrine of Right* Does Not Belong in the *Metaphysics of Morals.*" *Jahrbuch für Recht und Ethik* 5 (1997): 205–27.

Williams, Bernard. *Ethics and the Limits of Philosophy.* Cambridge: Harvard University Press, 1985.

Williams, Howard. *Kant's Critique of Hobbes.* Cardiff: University of Wales Press, 2003.

Wilson, Margaret Dauler. *Leibniz' Doctrine of Necessary Truth.* New York: Garland, 1990.

Wood, Allen W. "Kant and the Intelligibility of Evil." In *Kant's Anatomy of Evil: Interpretative Essays and Contemporary Applications*, edited by Sharon Anderson-Gold and Pablo Muchnik, 144–72. Cambridge: Cambridge University Press, 2010.

———. "The Final Form of Kant's Practical Philosophy." In *Kant's Metaphysics of Morals: Interpretive Essays*, edited by Mark Timmons, 1–22. New York: Oxford University Press, 2002.

———. "The Moral Law as a System of Formulas." In *Architektonik und System in der Philosophie Kants*, edited by H. F. Fulda and J. Stolzenberg, 287–306. Hamburg: Felix Meiner Verlag, 2001.

———. *Kant's Ethical Thought*. New York: Cambridge University Press, 1999.

Woodmansee, Martha. *The Author, Art, and the Market: Rereading the History of Aesthetics*. New York: Columbia University Press, 1994.

Yovel, Yirmiahu. *Kant and the Philosophy of History*. Princeton: Princeton University Press, 1980.

Contributors

RONALD BEINER is professor of political science at the University of Toronto and a fellow of the Royal Society of Canada.

JEFFREY EDWARDS is associate professor in the Department of Philosophy, State University of New York at Stony Brook.

MICHAEL FEOLA is Bennett Boskey Visiting Professor of Political Science, Williams College.

PAUL GUYER is Murray Professor in the Humanities and professor of philosophy at the University of Pennsylvania.

JANE KNELLER is professor of philosophy at Colorado State University.

BÉATRICE LONGUENESSE is professor of philosophy at New York University.

JAN MIESZKOWSKI is associate professor of German and humanities at Reed College.

ONORA O'NEILL is professor emeritus in the Faculty of Philosophy in Cambridge, and was president of the British Academy from 2005–9. She is an independent crossbench member of the House of Lords (Baroness O'Neill of Bengarve).

CHARLTON PAYNE is a Christoph-Martin-Wieland Postdoctoral Fellow at the University of Erfurt.

SUSAN M. SHELL is professor of political science at Boston College.

LUCAS THORPE is assistant professor of philosophy at Boğaziçi University, Istanbul, Turkey.

ERIC WATKINS is professor of philosophy at the University of California, San Diego.

ALLEN W. WOOD is Ward W. and Priscilla B. Woods Professor of Philosophy at Stanford University.

INDEX

EXPERIENCE AND REASON

The Phenomenology of Husserl and its Relation to
Hume's Philosophy

by

R. A. MALL

MARTINUS NIJHOFF / THE HAGUE / 1973

PRINTED IN THE NETHERLANDS

CONTENTS

PREFACE

In this work the author has tried to present a brief exposition of the phenomenology of Husserl. In doing this, he had in mind a two-fold purpose. He wanted on the one hand to give a critical exposition, interpretation and appreciation of the most leading concepts of Husserlian phenomenology. On the other hand, he tried to show that a true comprehensive understanding of Husserl's phenomenology culminates in his teaching of experience and reason.

It is the strong conviction of the author that the central-most teaching of Husserl's phenomenology is the discovery of the "noetic-noematic" correlativity. In the reduced realm of "constituting-intentionality," the distinction between reason and experience seems to vanish, and these two concepts become interchangeable terms.

The present study suffers from one great limitation, and this must be made clear right here in order to avoid any misconception about the author's intentions. The author has not discussed the other important theories of experience and reason. He has undertaken the humble task of giving an account of Husserl's phenomenology of experience and reason.

The bringing in of Hume serves, as would be clear in the course of the book, a two-fold purpose. It tries on the one hand to show the programmatic similarity between the philosophies of these two philosophers. On the other hand, it implicitly maintains that the philosophical continuity from Hume to Husserl runs not so much via Kant, but rather via Meinong, Brentano, Avenarius, James and so forth.

The author's interpretation of Husserl's phenomenology is very sympathetic without being uncritical or orthodox Husserlian.

The author wishes to thank Professors Ludwig Landgrebe (with whom he has worked for a long time, and whose lectures have greatly influenced his philosophical thought) and Gerhard Funke (with whom he has discussed some of the very knotty problems of Husserlian phenomenology). The author is also very grateful to Prof. Heinz Hülsmann who has provided him with much philosophical stimulation, and with whom he has discussed some portions of the work in manuscript. The author would also like to thank Prof. H. L. Van Breda for kind words of encouragement.

The present work has been conceived and completed at the "Husserl-Archiv," Köln, and the author wishes to put on record his gratitude to its members.

R.A.M.

ABBREVIATIONS

References are to the editions of Husserl's Works

C.M.: Cartesianische Meditationen und Pariser Vorträge, hrsg. S. Strasser, 2.Auflage. Husserliana, Band I. (The Hague, 1963).

Ideen I: Ideen zu einer reinen Phänomenologie und phänomenologischen Philosophie. Erstes Buch. Allgemeine Einführung in die reine Phänomenologie, hrsg. W. Biemel, Husserliana, Band III. (The Hague, 1950).

Ideen II: Ideen zu einer reinen Phänomenologie und phänomenologischen Philosophie. Zweites Buch. Phänomenologische Untersuchung zur Konstitution. hrsg. W. Biemel. Husserliana, Band IV. (The Hague, 1952).

Ideen III: Ideen zu einer reinen Phänomenologie und phänomenologischen Philosophie. Drittes Buch. Die Phänomenologie und die Fundamente der Wissenschaften, hrsg. W. Biemel. Husserliana, Band V. (The Hague, 1952).

Krisis: Die Krisis der europäischen Wissenschaften und die transzendentale Phänomenologie. Eine Einleitung in die phänomenologische Philosophie. hrsg. W. Biemel. Husserliana, Band VI. (The Hague, 1962) 2. Auflage.

E.P. I: Erste Philosophie (1923/24) Erster Teil. Kritische Ideengeschichte, hrsg. R. Boehm. Husserliana, Band VII. (The Hague, 1956).

E.P. II: Erste Philosophie. (1923/24). Zweiter Teil. Theorie der phänomenologischen Reduktion, hrsg. R. Boehm. Husserliana, Band VIII. (The Hague, 1959).

Phän. Psy.: Phänomenologische Psychologie. Vorlesungen Sommersemester 1925, hrsg. W. Biemel. Husserliana, Band IX. (The Hague, 1962).

Zeitbewußtsein: Zur Phänomenologie des inneren Zeitbewußtseins (1893–1917), hrsg. R. Boehm. Husserliana, Band X. (The Hague, 1966).

L.U. I: Logische Untersuchungen. Band I. Vierte Auflage. (Halle, 1928).

L.U. II, 1: Logische Untersuchungen. Band II, 1. Teil. Vierte Auflage. (Halle, 1928).

L.U. II, 2: Logische Untersuchungen. Band II, 2. Teil. Dritte Auflage. (Halle, 1922).

F.u.t.L.: Formale und transzendentale Logik (Halle, 1929).

E.u.U.: Erfahrung und Urteil. Untersuchungen zur Genealogie der Logik, 3. Auflage. (Hamburg, 1964).

Philosophie als strenge Wissenschaft. Frankfurt a.M. 1965.

U.M.: Unpublished Manuscripts of Husserl (Husserl-Archiv, Köln).

References are to the editions of Hume's Works

Treatise: A Treatise of Human Nature: Being an Attempt to introduce the experimental Method of Reasoning, ed. by L. A. Selby-Bigge (Oxford, 1960).

Enquiries: Enquiries concerning the Human Understanding and concerning the Principles of Morals, ed. by L. A. Selby-Bigge (Oxford, 1966).

Dialogues: Dialogues concerning Natural Religion, ed. with Introduction by H. D. Aiken. The Hafner Library of Classics, Number five. New York. fourteenth printing, 1966.

Essays: Moral, Political and Literary. Oxford University Press, 1963.

Abstract: An Abstract of a Treatise of Human Nature. Reprinted in: Hume – Theory of Knowledge, ed. by D. C. Yalden-Thomson. Edinburgh, 1951.

CHAPTER I

INTRODUCTORY

The twin concepts of "experience" and "reason" are the most deceitful in the long history of philosophy and there are theories based on them which represent extreme forms of empiricism and rationalism. The rationalism is generally contrasted with empiricism and this contrast depends on the opposition between experience and reason. These problems are as old as the life of philosophy and philosophers have always struggled hard to overcome the traditional opposition between these two concepts. All these attempts ended more or less in either surrendering experience to reason or reason to experience with the unavoidable consequence that the gulf between these two theories could not be bridged. The present work thematizes this age-old problem from anew and hopes to overcome the opposition by a critical but sympathetic exposition, interpretation and analysis of the phenomenology of Hussel.

The work is based on a particular understanding of the phenomenological philosophy which in the first instance is a fruitful method of search and research with endless possibilities. Phenomenology means here the comprehending, clarifying and explaining of the phenomena; and a phenomenon is anything which shows itself in any mode of givenness. The phenomenological philosophy is not a "positional" one with metaphysical convictions and beliefs. It is rather a method of search for the "noetic-noematic correlativity". The phenomenology of Husserl prepares a new way towards an attempt to solve the problem of experience and reason. A comprehensive understanding of Husserl's phenomenology convinces us that it culminates into a philosophy of experience and reason. Such a conviction underlies the present project.

A sheer sensuous experience without any possibility to transcend the immediate given ends as much in a blind alley as a pure a priori reason which idealizes and formalizes everything in order to rule over the world. There is not only a sensuous, but also a rational blindness. A reason which cooperates with practice and remains in lively contact with experience retains its character of "openness" as much as an experience which develops by self-correction and self-modification.

Even our day-to-day experience implies a certain relationship between these two concepts. Neither the "common-sense experience" nor the "concrete reason" can be raised to a fixed and independent dimension. That the experience shows a power to teach is the result of our reflection. This reflection "brings forth" the dynamic structure called "reason" without "creating" it. And reason as the common task of humanity is present at each level of our practice and experience. From the detached level of reflection one gets a better view of the interplay between reason and experience. No experience, not even the most primitive one, is atomic. No reason at any stage of its development is fixed and purely speculative. Husserl's conception of experience is far richer and possesses a greater explanatory power than the atomistic theories. The Husserlian phenomenology of reason dynamizes the concept of reason.

Supposing that experience depends on sensuous perception or that sensuous perception is the "original mode" of experience, we can still remark that this very statement is in principle of a different nature and transcends the limited boundaries of sense. In this act of transcending of the boundaries of sense, reflection has always been at work. At the level of reflection the traditional opposition between experience and reason vanishes, for it is shown that the ability to learn is not foreign either to experience or to reason. Thus neither the classical idea of experience as a bundle consisting of chaotic sensuous impressions nor that of reason as a fixed dimension with certain a priori principles can be upheld.

It goes to the credit of Husserl's phenomenology to have worked out in detail the full implications of relational-intentional view of human consciousness. It does not concentrate exclusively on either the subject of experience or on the object of experience; it studies consciousness as intentional, as directed to objects. Such an intentional character of our consciousness makes our experience intentional-relational in character. Phenomenology is a science of experience and it studies experience at each level of it – perception, imagination, thought and so on. Such a study is "transcendental", for it tries to disclose the structure of consciousness as consciousness.

It is the strong conviction of the author that the central-most

teaching of Husserl's phenomenology is its discovery of the "noetic-
noematic correlativity" which at a phenomenological level of explanation, understanding and justification constitutes all that is there
in the sense of being a phenomenon-correlate to intentional-acts.
Husserl's theory of constitution thus neither implies "creation" nor
does it claim to "create" an objective world purely idealistically from
out of the sheer activities of consciousness. The primacy of our constitutional consciousness consists in the fact that the world needs consciousness in order to be meaningful and not vice versa. And "to be"
for us is to be meaningful. Human consciousness is only the "giver"
of sense to the world and not its "producer" or "creator".

Our exposition and interpretation of the most leading concepts of
Husserlian phenomenology are guided by the one underlying aim that
all of them serve in their own way to work out a philosophy of experience and reason. All the painstaking researches of Husserl aim
at the discovery of an "apodictic" "transcendental" field of experience which is nothing else than the self-experience of transcendental
subjectivity. In the discovery of such a realm of experience the role
of "phenomenological reduction" can hardly be exaggerated.

The Husserlian phenomenological analyses and reflections of the
problems of experience and reason take place at a level which is not to
be confused either with realism or idealism, empiricism or rationalism.
At the level of radical phenomenological reflection the distinction
between experience and reason seems to vanish, for in the reduced
pure realm of intentionality they become interchangeable terms.

To work out the field of an "original experience" is the underlying
motive guiding Husserlian phenomenology, which is like the identical
motivational underlying idea running all through his reflections. The
path of phenomenology of Husserl is thus interpreted as a path in
search of and leading to such a field of original experience. Every experience is, according to Husserl, seeing; and a transcendental original
experience must mean a transcendental seeing, which consists in
self-experience of our intentionality, being nothing else than our
meaning-giving consciousness.

Husserl, of course, would be wrong if he intended through his
transcendental phenomenological analysis of experience and reason
to have furnished a complete solution of the problems of experience
and reason in their day-to-day socio-empirical character. It must not
be forgotten that Husserl's phenomenology is an "eidetic science".

The concepts of experience and reason as introduced here are intimately connected with the concept of a phenomenological reflection as an "iterative-regressive" process which is "endless" but "effective". Since reflection possesses an act-character performed by us and since an act performed is "lived", experienced by us, we rightfully speak of a "reflective experience" which surpasses both reason and experience. We further call this reflective experience "critical", because it is critical both of the naivities and habitualities of experience as well as of reason. Added to this quality of being a "critical reflective experience" it possesses the character of being "comprehensive", because it overcomes the traditional opposition between experience and reason. Thus the new concept of experience introduced here is the concept of a "comprehensive critical reflective experience" (CCRE). Seen from such a level of reflective experience the terms reason and experience, learning and a priori, empiricism and rationalism and so forth are no longer exclusive of each other. Our concept of CCRE is neither introspective-psychological nor sensualistic-empirical; it is not abstract-rational-axiomatic either. It is rather phenomenological in character in the sense of being "bodily given" in the very act of reflection performed by us. Experience in the phenomenology of Husserl does not mean our experience of psychological activities; it is always an act-experience.

Such a CCRE – thanks to its methodological purity – enables us to see the problems of sensualism and empiricism from a necessary distance which provides us with an analytic power to overcome the different types of biases present in empiricism as well as in rationalism. Such a reflection is not and cannot be "positional" in character and it represents the dynamic instance of a perpetual suspension of all naivities. No reason can think without experience; and no experience can prosper without reason. The characteristic common to all reflections performed in the different fields of human inquiry is the quality of its being an act which can always be reactivated in order to show the constitutional relationship between the operations performed and the results achieved.

In the course of his exposition, interpretation and critical appreciation the author has thus come to suggest two fundamental principles. According to the one, the continuity between sense and thought, between "experience" and reason can be established only on the ground of a reflection which can always be reactivated in order to discover the particular "noetic-noematic correlativity". Such a continuity may be termed a "reflective continuity". It was a firm belief of

Husserl that formalization, idealization, axiomatization is a mental accomplishment and can be understood and explained only by discovering the correlative constituting "noetic pole". If Husserl intended to mean that there is a phenomenological continuity between experience and thought in the sense that all that is there at the level of thought can be shown to be there at the level of sense without remainder, then there would be, of course, a "phenomenological discontinuity".[1] Husserl is not repeating Locke in this respect. The problem is whether Husserl's phenomenology could be judged to imply continuity in this sense of denying all differences present amongst phenomena belonging to different types. The continuity, phenomenology may claim to establish, does not and cannot consist in showing that there is nothing "new" at the level of thought; but it is a continuity consisting in our attempt to show how we come to the universal of thought. The concept of reflective continuity as introduced here tries to explain the "origin" of thought-idealities in the acts of reflections performed. The ideal-objective universal of thought can be shown to have its "origin" in pre-predicative experience only in the sense that the former, given the necessary motivations like idealization, formalization, control and prediction, originates "reflectively" in the latter.

Husserl's attempts to describe the process of idealization, axiomatization and formalization no doubt involve an endless process of reiteration (the famous immer wieder) which cannot be broken up. But the production of the thought-idealities might still be shown through a reflective analysis of the motivations leading to an actual break up and thus resulting in the production of idealities. Herein lies the claim to priority and superiority of the phenomenological method in the republic of methods. According to the other principle the theory of a "comprehensive critical reflective experience" avoids the unnecessary narrowness of empiricism as well as the excessive intellectualism of rationalism.

The justification for our bringing in a brief comparison of Husserl to Hume is the all-round programmatic similarity of their philosophies. This similarity does not consist, of course, in the details and in the results achieved, but mainly in their character of belonging to the same "type" of philosophizing, namely a "foundational-constitutional philosophy".

This programmatic similarity may be explicated as follows: Like Husserl's transcendental phenomenology, the philosophy of the human

[1] J. N. Mohanty: *Edmund Husserl's Theory of Meaning*, Foreword.

nature and its principles can hardly be said to belong either to the field of traditional empiricism or to rationalism. Hume's concept of the "vulgar consciousness" developed consequently points to the Husserlian teaching of the "general thesis of the natural standpoint". (Generalthesis der natürlichen Einstellung). The counterpart to Husserl's concept of the world we live in, our life-world (Lebenswelt), is to be found in Hume's concept of the external world whose existence the vulgar consciousness naively takes for granted. Like Husserl and unlike Descartes Hume is not doubting the existence of the world; his investigations serve the purpose to show how we come to "believe" in the continued existence of the world. Husserl tells us very clearly in his "Cartesianische Meditationen" that we must lose the world in order to regain it. The various leading concepts of Husserlian phenomenology like "reduction", "constitution", "Lebenswelt", "transcendental subjectivity" correspond roughly to the guiding principles of human nature, e.g. "fiction", "imagination", "external world", "human nature".

Such a brief reference of Husserlian teaching to that of Hume's lays bare the grounds in the successive self-realization of phenomenology which is, as Husserl maintains, the "secret longing" (geheime Sehnsucht) of Western philosophical thought. Added to this, it also makes us see more clearly the reasons why Husserl speaks with praise of Hume and his achievements. Husserl in a letter to A. Metzger speaks very frankly and acknowledges that he has learnt incomparably more from Hume than from Kant. He still goes further and writes: "I possessed the deepest antipathy against Kant and he (Kant) has not, if I judge rightly, influenced me at all". [2] According to his judgment of his person and philosophy he studied English empiricism repeatedly and he was very far removed from Kantian and German idealism. He himself liked the critical-sceptical point of view. [3]

It would also be evident to a careful reader that philosophico-historical continuity from Hume to Husserl does not run so much via Kant, but rather via Meinong, Brentano, Avenarius, James and so forth.

This programmatic similarity as suggested here has been worked out very briefly and needs further investigations and elaborations. The

---

[2] "Ich habe von Hume unvergleichlich mehr gelernt als von Kant, gegen den ich tiefste Antipathie hatte, und der eigentlich (wenn ich recht urteile) mich überhaupt nicht bestimmt hat". *Philosophisches Jahrbuch der Görres-Gesellschaft*, 62. Jahrgang, 1. Halbband, 4. Sept. 1919, S. 198.
[3] M. Farber: *The Foundation of Phenomenology*, p. 17.

author must also warn the reader, right here in the beginning, in order to avoid any misconception about his intentions: This programmatic similarity must not be stretched too far, for that would involve artificial attempts at arbitrary philosophical interpretation.

CHAPTER II

THE PHENOMENOLOGY OF EDMUND HUSSERL

The phenomenology of Edmund Husserl and the phenomenology in general are not one and the same thing and there is no one way of doing phenomenology today.[1] Even during his life-time Husserl felt such a discrepancy and he very clearly says this in the "epilogue" to his "Ideen". He wishes there that a sharp distinction be made between his phenomenology and the various developments going by the same name.[2]

It has been the firm belief of Husserl that the science of phenomenology represents the "telos" of the history of Western thought from its very beginning. He speaks of a "secret longing" (geheime Sehnsucht) of philosophy in this context and identifies it with phenomenology.[3] To discover the most apodictic realm of experience, a realm of the prime consciousness (das originäre Bewußtsein) is the ultimate goal, the real task of his phenomenology. It is this goal which runs as a binding red tape through all Husserlian literature from the very beginning where it is not very clearly formulated to the end where it is clearly stated.

Husserl was a very passionate researcher and he never hesitated to start always anew in search of an ultimate clarity. This is why his philosophy never did end in an enclosed system. He calls himself a "true beginner".

Husserl's phenomenology has been interpreted variously, and the moment we lose sight of the inner consistency and continuity we artificially divide his philosophy into different periods with no inner harmony of purpose. In spite of the periodical and epoch-making

---

[1] P. Thévenaz: *What is Phenomenology?* Chicago 1962, pp. 37 f.; also *Phenomenology in Perspective*, ed. by F. J. Smith, Martinus Nijhoff, 1970.
[2] *Jahrbuch f. philosoph. und phänom. Forschung*, II, 1930, pp. 549 f.
[3] *Ideen I*, p. 118.

changes in the development of his philosophical thought, we must not mean as if "the" Husserl of the first period, as a mathematician and logician, has nothing to do with "the" Husserl of the second period, engaged in idealistic research. The third period which is a brave attempt at overcoming all the oppositions between realism and idealism, subjectivism and objectivism, rationalism and empiricism, does not represent a sudden change; it is rather present from the very beginning as the very base of phenomenological motivation. It is truer that the later works of Husserl are indispensable to a clear understanding of his earlier works (not vice versa).

Husserl studied the philosophers of the British empirical tradition repeatedly and this he writes in many of his personal letters. Among the precursors of phenomenology, Husserl, of course, mentions the name of David Hume and it goes to the credit of his "Treatise" to have conceived an ultimate foundational science of human consciousness. With James, Husserl shares the dissatisfaction with traditional philosophy as being too abstract and too remote from the field of our lived experiences. But Brentano, Husserl's master, can be taken to be the immediate precursor of the phenomenological movement. We try to outline here in brief the phenomenology of Edmund Husserl who is, in fact, the founder of this movement. We shall try here to explain and clarify some leading concepts of his phenomenology by way of an introduction to it.

Husserl's way of doing philosophical research was to start again and again in order to go beyond the "already reached" in search of a still deeper level of experience. The aim of Husserl's radical philosophical reflection is to show clearly the presuppositions of all sciences, natural as well as social. Husserl gave himself the name of a "true beginner". This way of doing philosophy aimed at a "first philosophy" as a "rigorous science" in the truest sense of the term.

It is true that Husserl was a mathematician, but he never blindly followed the ideal of mathematical sciences. This he makes amply clear in his "Krisis" when he discusses the ideal of Galilean science. Husserl's understanding of mathematical sciences was deep enough not to blind him towards its limitations. Husserl does not belittle the achievements of these sciences; he only maintains that their claim to autonomy is mistaken. The problem haunting Husserl's thought from the publication of his "Philosophie der Arithmetik" to his "Krisis" and other published and unpublished manuscripts was that "of foundation" which is the guiding unitary thread of his whole thought.

When Husserl speaks of science he means something quite different than the ideal of objective science. In order to guarantee the scientific character to any serious human inquiry, the point of departure must be the casting of a philosophical doubt upon the implicit presuppositions of all our habitual thinking – scientific or otherwise. It was a firm belief of Husserl that none of the so-called rigorous sciences using mathematical language can lead us toward an ultimate understanding of our experience of the world we live in. These so-called objective sciences remain subject to naivities.

Since phenomenology wants to establish the ultimate basis of all constitution and foundation, it would be a gross misunderstanding of phenomenology to believe that it is anti-scientific, not caring for empirical observations, analysis and perceptions. As a radical method of philosophical thinking, phenomenology wants just to work out the most original and ultimate ways and means which can always be reactivated in order to trace the meaning of our experience in its multiple contexts and at its different levels.

Once Husserl wrote in a personal letter[4] to A. Metzger that his whole life consisted of nothing else than "in learning to see" and to show the foundational character of such a "seeing". The only ultimate and legitimate source of all evidence lies in this "prime consciousness which presents the given immediately" (das originär gebende Bewußtsein). The character of "immediate given" consists in its being given completely and bodily; it is a "Selbstgebung". Phenomenology strives to get at the "things themselves" (zu den Sachen selbst). These "things" are neither entities out there in the external world nor are they psychological activities of a psycho-physiological ego-consciousness; they are the things in the sense of whatever is "given", that which we "see" in consciousness. This given is what is termed in phenomenology the "pure phenomenon". It is no phenomenon in opposition to a "noumenon" for that would damage the character of the "given", as apodictically and fully given. The question whether this given is true or false, reality or appearance, is immaterial for the phenomenological method. Husserl is a philosopher cutting all ties between psychology and logic on the one hand and between meta-

---

[4] "Ich, dessen ganzes Leben es war, reines Sehen zu lernen und zu üben, und sein Urrecht durchzusetzen, sage: Wer zum reinen Sehen (in arbeitsvoller Erfüllung der Intentionen) durchgedrungen ist, ist des Erschauten in Wiederholung des Erfuellungsprozesses als 'originär gegeben' voellig gewiß. ... Und ich sage weiter hinsichtlich der Methode, der Horizonte, der Arbeitsfelder der Ideen das eine Wort: Siehe!" (*Phil. Jahrbuch d. Görres-Gesellschaft, 62*). 1. Halbband, p. 196.

physics and philosophy on the other. His main aim is to analyse consciousness in order to "found" all that is there in any sense of being-there.

The method of phenomenology is neither a deductive nor an inductive one; it is neither rational nor empirical in the style of the traditional philosophy. Husserl is never tired of repeating that his method consists in "showing", in "pointing" (Aufweis) to what is given. It is this given that is the object of phenomenological elucidation. The whole direction of the phenomenological philosophy is towards the objective in the sense of being "a given" as a correlate to the diverse acts of intentions. This method analyses and studies that which is loved in the act of loving, hated in the act of hating, imagined in the act of imagining and so forth. But we must not misunderstand Husserl as "hypostatizing" these objects; they are no platonic entities. Husserl rejects platonism; nay, he even goes further and is ready to call himself a "positivist", a "radical positivist" on the grounds that all knowledge is based upon and rooted in the given. Husserl criticizes the positivists for their blunder of equating given with the sense-datum, seeing with the sensible. He, of course, credits Hume of having hinted at an immanent possibility of consciousness, but he takes him to task for his sensualistic interpretation of all "impressions". Whether or not Hume's theory of impressions, phenomenologically interpreted, would come very near to Husserl's "Wesensschau" is a difficult problem, but Hume could be made more consequent, if we see in his concept of "impressions" something like the "originäre Anschauungen" of Husserl. [5]

Husserl's phenomenology in search of a radical foundation moves from the reflections in the field of mathematics and logic to the reflections in the field of philosophy of history. In all his radical questionings he follows the dynamism of intentional consciousness. His goal never changes from the "Logische Untersuchungen", where he is trying a new foundation of pure logic and epistemology to the "Cartesian Meditations" where he is busy with the idea of philosophy as the science of absolute foundation. The noetic-noematic correlativity is all-pervasive.

The Husserlian criticism of Descartes centres round the Cartesian terms "ego cogito". Descartes took the cogitations to be isolated entities in the stream of our thought and paid no heed to the most

[5] F. Sauer: "Über das Verhältnis der Husserlschen Phänomenologie zu David Hume", *Kant-Studien*, XXXV., pp. 151 f.

important intentional-relational character of all of our thinking and experience. He failed to make a radical distinction between the act of thought and the object of thinking. W. James was in this regard far more radical than Descartes. F. Brentano had already discovered the "intentional" character of all our mental acts. All experiences as they appear within our consciousness are necessarily referred to the objects experienced. Every thought is thought *of*, for there is no such thing as thought, fear, imagination as such. Although Husserl took the term intentionality from his master Brentano, he nevertheless differed with the latter in the use he made of it. Husserl speaks of intentionality not only in the sense of "intentional relationship" as Brentano did, but also of the "intentionality of consciousness" (Intentionalität des Bewußtseins). The view that different acts may refer to identically the same object is not Brentano's; but it is purely Husserlian.

Husserl's concept of intentionality thus designates the essential relationship between our acts of experiencing and the corresponding objects experienced. Such a character of intentionality of all our "cogitations" leads us to distinguish sharply between the act of thinking, remembering, fearing, imagining and the object thought of, remembered, feared and imagined. These two moments in the life of intentionality are termed technically "noesis" and "noema" respectively and intentionality consists essentially of them.

Husserl went deeper than Brentano in his analysis, for an act is not a psychological activity, but it is an intentional experience. Husserl also talked of a field of intentionality and maintained it to be one of the most important topics of phenomenological research. The phenomenological notion of intentionality radically and fundamentally transforms the traditional data of philosophical problem; the whole life of philosophy is seen from a deeper foundational point of view. Unlike Brentano, Husserl from the very beginning takes intentionality in a wider epistemological, transcendental and even "ontological" (understood in Husserlian way) sense.

Intentionality refers to all acts and does not stand for a thing or entity. It characterizes acts in their essentiality. All "cogitations" are from their very nature intentional and it is wrong to maintain that they get this character of intentionality after being lived as psychical experiences. For Husserl's concept of intentionality the question of transcendence and immanence as understood in the traditional philosophy does not arise at all; intentionality just represents the most essential fundamental way of our human consciousness. It is the very "being" of all consciousness, and the character of our consciousness as social is subordinated to the wider character of intentionality of the same.

But the discovery of the notion of intentionality must not be confused with the banality and common place that all consciousness or knowledge has an object, a content. If Husserl did only this much, he did not do anything. The deeper import of intentionality is rather the destruction of the very notion of a "reality in itself" or of an absolute object. Also the idea of a consciousness closed in on itself (as in Descartes) is destroyed. The Cartesian way of defining consciousness as "cogitations" is not complete, for he fails to clarify the unity of the "cogito" with the "cogitation". This is why Husserl starts a Cartesian meditation all over again. Philosophy is placed in a "new dimension" and this new dimension results from a radical phenomenological attitude, namely that of phenomenological reduction.

The proper object of phenomenology, the essences, the eidos, can be attained by what Husserl terms the technique of "Epoché" which is no Cartesian doubt questioning the existence of the world, but which is only a "suspension", a "bracketing" of it. Husserl is here nearer to Hume than to Descartes, for Hume, too, maintains that the existence of the world cannot be questioned. In his "Enquiry concerning the Principles of Understanding" he says that once you call (Hume means here Descartes and the Cartesians) the world in question, you would be completely at a loss to regain it. With the help of "Epoché", phenomenology only "brackets" the world along with all the philosophical doctrines in order to reach the things themselves (die Sachen selbst). This practice of "bracketing" goes by the name of "eidetic reduction" which suspends all existence and objects. Such a practice is a means to an end.

Since phenomenological analysis does not wish to stop just at the level of our descriptive analysis of the essences intended by consciousness, Husserl discovers and brings in the method of "phenomenological reduction" which is also transcendental, for it opens up a new field in the "transcendental" field. The use of the technique of phenomenological reduction does not deny the existence of the world; it only suspends our belief in it. There is nothing mysterious about this notion. Husserl no doubt admits that there is something artificial (unnatürlich) in this practice. But then any radical step is artificial in face of the vast mass of our dogmatic philosophical thought. Phenomenological reduction involves a radical change in our whole attitude; it is a new radical attitude eliminating the habitual natural attitude. It does not destroy the natural attitude in the very point of departure. To reduce means not to doubt, but to eliminate in order that the uncritically presupposed certainties and objectivities of the natural attitude may now be referred back to a constituting transcendental consciousness as its original accomplishments. The pure field of consciousness discovered after the performance of phenomenological reduction can be studied and explored in its own right and Husserl believes that only such a study would enable us to lay bare the ways and means upon which all our beliefs – scientific or otherwise – are founded. Since there is a correspondence between the features of this reduced realm and the world experienced before, phenomenological reduction does not lose the world. The world now reappears as a phenomenon within this reduced realm of pure consciousness. This technique of reduction has been and can be very fruitfully used in all the different branches of human inquiry.

The being of the world in the reduced sphere of pure givenness does not consist in its mundane existence, but rather in its meaning. In fact, the world is a "cogitatum" intended by the "cogito"; it is an "intentum" of "intention". Thus the consciousness of the world is the consciousness constituting the world and constitution is the act of giving meaning to the world. One must not think here that there are two spheres dividing the whole field of reality. No, there is only one world and the transcendental is rather only another name of a constituting instance which is nothing else but the very intentionality of our consciousness. Phenomenology does not "hypostatize".

It is sometimes maintained that the suspension of all our habits would ultimately lead to some form of "solipsism" or "nihilism". I have annulled, so to speak, not only the world of natural as well as social sciences, but also my own self as a psycho-physiological unit. What then remains? Although much can be (and has been) said about the unlucky choice of the word Husserl makes here, one thing is sure that after the reduction the consciousness is not reduced to a "nihil". The stream of thought is there with all its richness, only that it is now fully pure and given completely. The intentional character of our "cogitations" is not lost. This method only helps to see what is not seen at the natural level, namely the fundamental "noetic-noematic" correlativity.

My perception of this mango tree in my natural attitude corroborates my belief in its real existence in my garden and this belief is the ground of my further judgments about this tree. Now I perform the phenomenological reduction. What I really do is to refrain from believing in the existence of this mango tree. What actually happens is this: The mango tree perceived remains outside the bracketing; but the perception as an act is doubtless an element of our reduced sphere. And, thanks to the Husserlian concept of intentionality, this perception is not "perception as such", without any reference. The intentional-referential character of the perception can never be destroyed, and thus this perception remains a perception *of* ... What I now do is that I am abstaining from attaching to this perception any judgment whether this mango tree really exists or not. It is now not the corporeal thing, the mango tree, to which my perception refers, but the intentional correlate of the preserved act of perception is the mango tree as I perceive it. Thus we see that the whole world is preserved within the reduced sphere of our consciousness only in so far, as it is now the intentional correlate of my intentional conscious life. But these correlates, these intentional objects are now no longer the real existing things of the outer world as they really exist, but the phenomena as they are given in pure intentional consciousness. The real mango tree may undergo all sorts of changes, but the perceived phenomenon "mango tree" remains unaffected by all these changes. What is destroyed is the existing tree in my garden and not the tree as the correlate of my act of perception. No reduction can reduce this fact of correlation.

The "noesis-noema", "cogitare-cogitatum" analysis implied in the intentional-relational explanation of all our experience does not necessarily mean that the "cogitations" are not subject to certain modifications. When I perceive any corporeal thing my act of perceiving suggests to me other possible aspects: the front side, the back side of the object. All these moments are the elements of what Husserl terms "inner horizon". The perceived object as a "noema" can also be systematically explored in that we follow the intentional indications which are lying within the noema itself. Husserl also speaks of an "outer horizon" which means, roughly speaking, the possibility that a perceived object, say the mango tree, may refer to the garden, the garden to a vaster field and so on to the whole world.

We may also talk of noetical modifications which are due to the perceiving act itself. The important distinction made between "originary" and "derived" experience helps us to make the point clear.

Much misunderstanding centres round the Husserlian term "Evidenz". The sense in which this concept is used in Husserlian phenomenology is not mystical; it is no hidden quality of an altogether different occult type of intuitive experience. It is not reserved to certain philosophers as their born privilege. Evidence in phenomenology is the demand to refer back all derived experiences to an originary one. The ultimate evidence consists in seeing which we possess when we experience the reduced realm of pure intentional life.

We have mentioned above the Husserlian concept of constitution. This is one of the most controversial concepts in the phenomenology of Husserl. Husserl is sometimes charged with being an idealist par excellence, for his theory of constitution is just a theory of "production" or "creation" of the world. That such an understanding of constitution does not do justice to Husserl's philosophy will be discussed later. The term "constitution" means that all that is transcendent must be explained, understood immanently as the accomplishment of an intentional consciousness. Here we see how the method of phenomenological reduction prepares the ground for constitution by opening up the field of a pure reduced consciousness.

Our knowledge of an object represents the sedimentations of our previous mental acts which have constituted this object. Every object has its own history. Husserl's theory of constitution is not a fixed scheme blind to all historical factors; it is a "genetic constitution" which takes the historical factor into due consideration and traces back the very constitution of the idea of historicity to the accomplishments of our transcendental subjectivity. In our every day life of natural attitude we are satisfied with the ready-made meanings and operate with them habitually. We do not ask as to how they come to be what they are. Meaning of an object is not a fixed quality of an object; it is rtaher intentional achievement of our consciousness.

Husserl never failed to emphasize the distinction between the empirical and the "eidetical" approach. He calls phenomenology an eidetical science which deals not with existences but with "essences", with "eidos". We have already mentioned above the Husserlian criticism of the British empiricism on this point. Husserl maintains that every sensible, individual object possesses an "essence" (Wesen) which can be "seen", i.e. to say, experienced as acts. Each individual, though a contingent reality, owns "a pure eidos" (ein rein zu fassendes Eidos). Thus there are two kinds of sciences – a factual science resting on the sensible experience and an eidetic science which aims at the "intuition" of essences (Wesen). Because of the all-over importance of "noetical-noematical correlationship" the former is based and founded on the latter. Hume with his theory of the "relations of ideas" was very near to this Husserlian teaching of the "Wesensschau" and Husserl, of course, tries to interpret Hume along this line. The Husserlian "Wesensschau" is no lofty intuition of platonic entities which are metaphysical realities. One does not need to be a mystic to see what Husserl means when he talks of his intuiting, seeing the essences. Seeing is experiencing at a higher transcendental level made acceptable to us through the performance of transcendental phenomenological reduction.

Phenomenology always emphasizes the rôle played by our fancy, our imagination in our philosophical thought. The method which Husserl uses in order to discover the essences is the famous method of "eidetic variation" (eidetische Variation). It consists in our freely imagining an infinite number of possibilities in which an object, say a cube, may exist. This freely varying the object in my fancy helps me to discover what really belongs to the invariant structures of this object. The "eide" of a thing are just the common qualities which remain unchanged through all the different variations. The eidetic variation does not deal with concrete things although it starts from some one particular object. This method of eidetic variation serves also the purpose of finding out the meanings as they are constituted by the intentional acts of our consciousness.

Phenomenology invites us to make a radical attempt to "see" and "live" things from a deeper, more original point of view. It is a practice of seeing ever deeper and deeper. The deepest seeing which is, as mentioned above, the very experience of intentionality, is the true sense of Husserl's "transcendental" experience. It is the most originary one, for it means a return to an apodictic evidence. At this level of experience, consciousness "lives", "experiences" itself as the performer of all acts and as the giver of all sense, the last source of all meaning. At such a level of apodictic foundation, the transcendental "experience" and the "rationality" become interchangeable terms and reason represents an endless task of self-comprehension.

This level of phenomenology is the most radical one, the most positive one and the distinctions between the different "-isms" have no meaning at such a level, for the very understanding of these -isms can be accomplished from such a level.

The discovery of the world of our concrete lived experiences, the familiar world given prior to all reasonings, the life-world (Lebenswelt) shows that the phenomenology of Husserl is not averse to our actual historico-cultural levels of existence. The manifestation of the "Lebenswelt" in the phenomenology of Husserl is the point of culmination of his transcendental phenomenology. Whether, strictly speaking, there can be a science of "Lebenswelt" or not, may be a matter of philosophical discussion, but the life-world is in a sense the most radical foundation of all philosophy.

CHAPTER III

HUSSERL'S APPRECIATION AND UNDERSTANDING
OF HUME

Edmund Husserl has given Hume the credit for being a forerunner of phenomenology and this we read at several places in his philosophical literature. Hume almost enters the domain of phenomenology which is as it were the secret longing of the whole philosophy. Unfortunately, Hume is blinded by the sensualism and fails to discover fully the domain of phenomenology.[1] In spite of this the lesson to be learnt from the failures of British sensualism and empiricism is of far-reaching importance. Husserl tells us clearly that the works of Hume deserve to be studied seriously. In all the expositions and explanations of Hume there are to be found phenomenological insights of great importance. Before thematizing Husserl's own appreciation and understanding of Hume's philosophy it is interesting to note how Husserl's understanding of Humean philosophy develops along the line of his criticism of Kant. Regardless of the truth of Kant's philosophy in itself we must not overlook Husserl's comments, that the Hume – as Kant interprets and understands him – is not the real Hume.[2] Husserl neither belongs to the groups of traditional interpreters[3] of Hume nor does he see Hume through Kant's eyes.

Hume's "Treatise of Human Nature" is in the opinion of Husserl his greatest and most important work. Husserl regrets that the "Treatise" remained without any remarkable effect in the eighteenth century and it never entered the mental range of Kant. It would have been better had Kant been awakened from his dogmatic slumber not through "The Essays", but through his "Treatise". In spite of the sceptical utterances in his book it points to an immanent intuitionism (imma-

---

[1] *Ideen I*, p 118.
[2] *Krisis*, p. 98 ff.
[3] R. A. Mall: *Hume's Concept of Man*, chapt. II, "The Traditional Interpretation of Hume's Philosophy".

nenter Intuitionismus) and implies the idea of immanent transcendental consciousness along with its elementary acts of constitution. The underlying meaning of Hume's "Treatise" does not lie in its "sceptical paradox", but in its attempt towards a transcendental philosophy. [4]

Husserl does not understand the challenge of Hume the way Kant does it. There is no problem for Hume regarding the immediate knowledge from experience and consequently synthetic a posteriori judgments pose no problem for him. The judgments like "I perceive the table", "I perceived it" and "I would perceive it" are not problematic. There is also no problem for Hume regarding the knowledge in the field of the relations of ideas, for it is analytic and depends on the nature of our ideas. The judgment "three plus two is equal to five" is not problematic, for one could easily see wherein the truth of this result lies. The field of knowledge comprising synthetic judgments a priori is problematic, for they refer to objects not given to our immediate experience. [5] They must thus be shown to be in some way related to consciousness.

Hume divides the whole field of knowledge into two classes: the field of the "relations of ideas" and of the "matters of fact". Husserl is primarily interested in the former and he interprets this field of knowledge in the sense of his "Wesenslehre". Whether such an interpretation of Hume's "relations of ideas" corresponds to the intentions of the author may be a matter of philosophical controversy, but for Husserl, the phenomenologist, such an interpretation not only fits in with his plans, but helps him work out a more constructive picture of Hume's philosophical intentions and achievements. That Husserl sees more in Humean distinction between the "relations of ideas" and "matters of fact" is mainly due to his interest in utilizing this for his own teaching regarding the "Wesensschau". The truths of the former class are grounded in the nature of ideas, that means, in the concepts involved. The truths in this field cannot be denied without contradiction; whereas negations of the truths in the field of matters of fact do not necessarily involve contradiction. Husserl here puts the question: What then is the meaning of "a priori" for Hume? Wherein does it consist? True to

---

[4] E.P. I, p. 198.
[5] E.P. I, p. 350 (While criticizing Kant's problem of synthetic judgments a priori, Husserl writes:
"Hume: 1) Kein Problem die unmittelbare Erfahrungserkenntnis (synthetisch 'a posteriori')
2) Kein Problem die Urteile über das, was in bloßen Ideen liegt (analytisch), ...
3) Dagegen problematisch: alle Urteile (synthetisch 'a priori')."

the spirit of Hume's philosophy Husserl maintains that the Humean concept of a priori has nothing to do with the concept of innate ideas. Innate ideas are fictions of metaphysics. The transcendent is not known to us. All that is given to us are the perceptions: impressions and ideas. In such a set-up the a priori can be placed within and not outside the sphere of perceptions. Husserl rightly thinks that if there is an a priori for Hume, it must be immanent (ein immanentes A priori) [6]. Wherein lies such an immanent a priori? For Husserl, this consists in finding the relations which necessarily and inseparably belong to the very essence of ideas. Although Husserl praises Hume for having thought of an immanent a priori, he still criticizes him for his not being very clear in his expositions and explanantions. Hume, according to Husserl, does not distinguish between "ideas" as arbitrary results of phantasy and "ideas" as the general concepts with their conceptually given essences. But Husserl is nevertheless sure that his interpretation and understanding of Hume's teaching regarding the great division between the relations of ideas and matters of fact do justice to his philosophical intentions.

Husserl criticizes Kant for the latter's not being able to understand Hume rightly. Kant, according to Husserl, sees the relations between the ideas as purely analytic and identical judgments. [7] Such an interpretation of Hume's relations of ideas is, in fact, wrong according to Husserl. As Husserl understands Hume, all the identical judgments are the relations between ideas, and not vice versa; all the relations between ideas are not identical. Unlike Kant, Husserl maintains that Hume's theory of the relations of ideas does not imply that mathematical judgments are purely analytic and tautological. [8] Husserl traces back all this misunderstanding of Kant to his (Kant's) failure of not having studied the book "A Treatise of Human Nature".

According to Husserl, the point of departure for the philosophy of Hume is the sphere of impressions and ideas. Hume's philosophy is an immanent philosophy of consciousness. The Humean impressions are what is immediately given to us. This given is the starting point for Hume. Unlike Locke and Kant, Hume does not start with the affections of the objects on the subject. For Hume, there is no duality between the subject and object to start with. But Husserl does not

---

[6] *E.P. I*, p. 351. ("Wenn es ein A priori gibt, so gibt es nur ein immanentes A priori".)

[7] *Ibid.*, p. 353 ("Kant aber gerät auf einen Abweg, indem er Humes Begriff des A priori identifiziert mit seinem Begriff der analytischen Erkenntnis.")

[8] *Ibid.*, p. 352 ff. ("Völlig korrekt ist doch der Ausgangspunkt Humes von den Impressionen und Ideen, wenn er die Berechtigung, so anzufangen, auch nicht klar erörtert.")

fail to note that Hume is not fully justifying his starting point. Hume, as Husserl interprets and understands him, may well be said to start doing philosophy with the "phenomenologically given".[9] Hume is right in dealing primarily with the statements on impressions as such. His theory of the relations of ideas points to a theory of evidence. Kant, according to Husserl, misinterprets Hume on this point in that he identifies his own idea of analytic judgment with Hume's concept of a priori. For Hume, the opposite of matters of fact is possible and can be easily conceived. Hume's theory of "relations of ideas", rightly understood, points to a theory according to which reality consists in its being given subjectively.

Husserl further maintains that the philosophical teaching of Hume already implies the Copernican revolution[10] that unity of experience is rooted in human thought.[11] In the opinion of Husserl, Kant is still subject to Humean scepticism. For Husserl, Hume does not "subjectivize" all forms of intuition and understanding. All the relations between ideas possess an absolute validity and they are as true as our statements of immediate knowledge. These relations are valid not only for a particular class of being, say human beings, but they hold true even of God.[12] The anthropology implied in the philosophy of Hume is more radical than that of Kant.

The absolute necessity is to be found only in the field of relations of ideas. This necessity must not be confused with the general validity to be found in the field of matters of fact. This necessity implies the impossibility to conceive the opposite of a relation of ideas. Such an insight expresses the relationship between the ideas and is rooted in the very nature of these ideas. Husserl in his interpretation and understanding goes further and maintains this necessity to be intuitive and evident. According to Husserl, the problem of Hume is: How does an immanent consciousness transcend the field of its immanence? How does it posit and apprehend the transcendental objects? Husserl maintains that Hume with his theory of the relations of ideas is nearer to the truth and he does not, like Kant, take them simply to be analytic statements showing only logical and formal character. These

---

[9] *Ibid.*, Beilage XV.

[10] H. H. Price in his book *Hume's Theory of the External World* speaks of "a Scottish version of Kant's Copernican revolution", p. 9.

[11] *E.P. I*, p. 354 ("Liegt nicht auch in Humes Lehre die Kopernikanische Umwälzung?")

[12] *E.P. I*, p. 355 ("Wir werden durch Kant nicht vor dem härtesten Skeptizismus errettet, sondern in einen noch härteren als den Hume'schen hineingezogen.") Like Husserl, B. Russell maintains that Kantian philosophy represents "a pre-Humean type of rationalism, and can be refuted by Humean arguments". *History of Western Philosophy*, p. 646.

relations between ideas are truths expressing the pure relationships which are necessarily posited along with the ideas.[13] We see how Husserl is trying to interpret and understand Hume phenomenologically.

It follows from what has been said above that Kant cannot be the continuation and successor of Hume and Hume is not just the precursor of Kant. Husserl believes that the philosophical researches and insights of David Hume are inevitable for the phenomenology and a true critique of knowledge is incomplete without him. Hume occupies a very central position in the history of philosophy and his real intentions have come to bear fruit not so much in Kant, but in the philosophical teachings of Meinong, Brentano, Avenarius, James and Husserl. In point of radicality, the philosophy of Hume surpasses even that of Descartes. The philosophical continuity from Hume to Husserl does not run via Kant.

The observations and comments of Husserl on Hume are not always unitary. Like the psychology of William James, the philosophy of Hume is on the way to a phenomenological philosophy. Husserl's appreciation and understanding of Hume's philosophy are the result of his constant analysis of the latter's philosophy, which he discusses in his books "Erste Philosophie", "Krisis" and in his lectures on Hume. The vast mass of Husserl's unpublished manuscripts also points to a lively interest of Husserl in Hume. Husserl speaks of Hume at several places in his philosophical literature as a genius. Hume was almost treading on the path of phenomenology[14] and his philosophy would have developed into a full-fledged phenomenology, had he not been blinded by a purely sensualistic empiricism. Husserl criticizes Hume for his failure of not having seen and realized the vast constructive possibilities in his discovery of the theory of relations of ideas. Hume was only a forerunner of phenomenology.

Since Hume could not get rid of sensualism completely, his philosophy failed to overcome solipsism and scepticism. Husserl levels Hume's philosophy also as an "As-if" philosophy. Husserl goes further and speaks of the "fictionalism" of Hume, for he thinks that Hume relegates the different concepts of the external world, causality, identity etc. to the fictions of imagination. Thus Husserl's interpretation of Hume has two sides: he praises Hume for his truly phenome-

---

[13] *E.P. I*, p. 359 ("Im Grunde war Hume mit seinen 'relations of ideas' der Wahrheit näher, und alle Vorwürfe Kants sind unklar oder unbegründet.").

[14] *Ideen I*, p. 148.

nological insights and discoveries, but he takes him to task for his blindness of not having seen and worked out the full implications of his discoveries.[15]

Husserl gives Hume the credit of being a ruthless consequent thinker, for he (Hume) ruthlessly shows the negative consequences of the very logic implied in the Locke-Berkeley tradition. It is interesting to note that Husserl's interpretation of the Locke-Berkeley tradition is very similar to that of Hume. Like Husserl, Hume also maintains that this tradition betrays a scepticism.[16] Husserl in his critical historico-philosophical discussion of the British empirical tradition[17] comes to the conclusion that this tradition implies not only a "Schein-empirismus", but also scepticism. Even Hume who generally lays bare the sceptical consequences of the Locke-Berkeley tradition, is said to remain subject to such an "empiricism".[18] In this context Husserl speaks of the formation of prior sceptical forms of phenomenology through Hume. Hume's scepticism, rightly understood, is, according to Husserl, nothing short of a "transcendental phenomenology".

Husserl's interpretation of Humean scepticism is very interesting. He maintains that Hume's scepticism is nothing but the fundamental task put to modern philosophy. This task consists in our attempt to overcome this scepticism in a way which is characteristic of "every radical scepticism." To overcome scepticism does not mean to give a sham explanation of it; scepticism cannot be explained away. A true philosophy has to face scepticism in order to overcome it at a higher radical level. Husserl speaks of seeing the truth of scepticism at such a level which means overcoming of scepticism. The radical transcendental philosophy of Husserl represents such a higher level. Husserl also maintains that Hume's "Treatise" is an attempt towards such a science of philosophy.

Husserl is of the opinion that the psychology implied in Hume's science of human nature is very radical and it can be taken to lay down the foundation of a rigorous science of philosophy. Husserl terms such a psychology a radical science of foundation (radikale Grundwissen-

---

[15] Whether Husserl's interpretation always does justice to Hume's philosophy is difficult to maintain. Husserl seems not to have always given the deserved importance to Hume's theories of the external world, imagination, belief etc.

[16] Hume goes still further and calls Berkeley a sceptic in disguise and the father of all modern scepticism. (*Enquiries*, p. 155).

[17] *E.P. I*, p. 138 ff.

[18] *Ibid.*, p. 135.

schaft)[19]. The "psychologism" of Humean philosophy is essentially of a new type, for it tries to trace back all the sciences to this source of all foundations. This new type of psychology is termed by Husserl a pure "Egologie". Husserl credits Hume of having conceived a systematic science of pure consciousness. Such a science has to deal with the pure given in the field of consciousness; it is a "tabula rasa" psychology, which, by performing a radical suspension of all judgments, would deal only with what is immediately given to our consciousness. Hume's "Treatise", according to Husserl, is an attempt at a universal plan with the elements of constitution; it is the first and the concrete immanent theory of knowledge. The great achievement of "Treatise" does not lie so much in logically showing the sceptical consequences of Locke-Berkeley tradition, but mainly in its conception of an "immanent naturalism" pointing at a "radical psychologism". Although Hume's "Treatise" is interpreted to imply a rigorous foundational science of philosophy in the sense of a pure phenomenology, it still remains sensualistic and empirical. Even as a purely sensualistic and empirical phenomenology the project of the "Treatise" is inevitable for the historical development of a pure phenomenology in the quest for a rigorous science of philosophy.

Husserl wavers from a decision regarding the "as-if character" of Hume's philosophy. He thinks one could hardly ascribe to Hume a view according to which the world, the other persons, etc. are nothing but fictions of our imagination. Husserl also asserts that such an "Unsinn" is not to be found in the works of Hume.[20] On the other hand Husserl maintains that all the different accomplishments (Leistungen) of our intentional life are relegated to fictions by Hume. Husserl goes even further and characterizes Hume as a sceptic who in his transcendental loneliness tries to show that a true nature, an external world and objective knowledge are nothing but illusions; they are fictions arising out of irrational grounds. Since Hume fails to see the fundamental intentional character of our life, his philosophy, in spite of its great discoveries, is termed by Husserl a philosophy of as-if, i.e. to say an "Antiphilosophie".[21] Husserl asks us to learn from the "ingenious mistakes" made by Hume.

[19] *E.P. I*, p. 155 ff. It is unfortunate, Husserl tells us, that Hume has been particularly misunderstood on these points of his philosophy. His theory of human nature was misinterpreted as a general psychology dealing with the human consciousness in the objective world.

[20] *E.P. I*, p. 156.

[21] *E.P. I*, p. 227 Husserl does not take here into account that Hume does not relegate the external world to a fiction; he even does not doubt its existence. *Treatise*, p. 187.

That Husserl studied thoroughly and very carefully only the "Treatise" of Hume is beyond all doubt. Husserl hardly mentions the other works of Hume which are very important for understanding how Hume works out his project roughly and rather one-sidedly outlined in the opening pages of his "Treatise". We know today for certain that Hume's "Enquiries", "An Abstract" and his "Dialogues" throw a different light on his philosophy. Hume in his "Treatise" reacted too sharply against the dogmatic rationalism in the history of philosophy. He reacted still more sharply against the metaphysics of Descartes and went too far in the opposite direction.

In his phenomenological psychology, Husserl speaks of the "Treatise" as an ingenious work comprising the notion of a pure phenomenology. But Hume fails to work out his project into a full-fledged phenomenology, for he lacks the eidetical method. [22]

Husserl calls Hume a "Berkeleyaner" [23], for he thinks Hume, like Berkeley, takes external things to be nothing else than complexes of impressions and ideas. Although Hume's conception of abstraction is not identical with that of Berkeley, still it takes general ideas to be nothing but particular ones, annexed to a certain term, which gives them a more extensive signification. [24] Hume seems, unlike Berkeley, to assign to general names the power which makes particular ideas represent other particular ideas which are similar to them. Although Hume here seems to go beyond Berkeley, he still remains within the framework of an empirical-psychological investigation. Husserl wants Hume to go beyond this psychologocal investigation. Hume fails in the details and in the fundamentals.

In his last great work "Krisis", Husserl speaks with praise of Hume's real achievements. The real Hume is not one who ruthlessly shows the sceptical consequences of the Locke-Berkeley tradition and leads it ad absurdum; the real Hume is one who works out the science of human nature as the foundational ultimate discipline. There is a subtle shade of constant tension lurking between Husserl's understanding of Hume and Kant. In the "Krisis", Husserl moves nearer to Hume and it is not out of place to remark that Husserl's point of departure is not so much the continental rationalism but rather the British empiricism. In a letter to M. Farber, Husserl clearly admits

---

[22] *Phän. Psy.*, pp. 328 f.
[23] *E.P. I*, p. 351.
[24] *Treatise*, Book I, Part I, § VII.

his aversion to Kantianism and to German idealism and his sympathy to British empiricism. [25]

Hume's fictional theory of knowledge means the bankruptcy of all philosophy and science. All the categories of objective knowledge seem to have no foundation. It goes to the credit of Hume to have clearly seen and shown this contradictory character of modern philosophy, but he chooses to play the easy rôle of an academic sceptic rather than to overcome this by fully working out the intentional character of all our life. Hume, according to Husserl, fails to see that his own scepticism is a stepping-stone towards a radical science of philosophy. [26] All the painstaking researches of Husserl may be understood as a struggle against the very spirit of scepticism. Husserl even testifies this view in that he wishes his transcendental phenomenology to be understood as the most radical overcoming of all scepticism. Unlike Kant, Husserl's reaction towards Humean scepticism is positive for he sees it as an important stage in the historical development of a pure phenomenology. Husserl speaks thus of the "ingenious and fruitful mistakes" (geniale und fruchtbare Fehler) of Hume. He sees and discovers in Hume's psychologism a scepticism which can take different forms, including the perspective of a transcendental phenomenological research. It is in this direction in which Husserl's interest for Hume lies.

Husserl does not think it worth the trouble to refute the metaphysical form of scepticism which totally denies the very possibility of true and ultimate metaphysical knowledge. For Husserl, the most pernicious form of scepticism is one that denies the noetic-noematic conditions of knowledge.

A very striking resemblance between the philosophical motivation of Husserl and Hume consists in their incessant attempt at overcoming scepticism, and Husserl credits Hume for having undertaken such an attempt in the form of his programme to work out the most foundational science of human nature. [27]

Husserl's interpretation of the philosophical teachings of Hume has made it clear that the so-called Humean "impressionism", consequently

---

[25] "I liked the critical skeptical point of view", writes Husserl, "since I myself did not see firm ground anywhere. I was always very far removed from Kantianism and German idealism... I have repeatedly studied the English Empiricists ...". M. Farber: *The Foundation of Phenomenology*, p. 17.

[26] *Krisis*, Beilage, XI.

[27] The author feels that both, Hume and Husserl, strictly speaking, fail to give an argumentative refutation of scepticism. Not only that, it is rather difficult to conceive what such an attempt can achieve.

worked out, leads ultimetaly not to a scepticism but to a phenomenology of immanence. [28]

There is no doubt about the fact that Hume lags far behind Husserl
in working out the details of the programme conceived by him, nay,
Hume sometimes even reverts back into sensualism, psychologism and
relativism. Although Hume fails to work out a truly phenomenological
description of his very important concept of "impression" which in
its "liveliness", "strength" and "vivacity" is a counterpart to the
Husserlian concept of "originäre Anschauung", he, nevertheless,
prepares the ground for Husserl's theory of "Wesensschau". Even
Hume's theory of association which leaves much of its mechanistic
colouring to be found in the "Treatise" when he comes to discuss and
develop it in his "Enquiries" points to a phenomenological theory of
the same. [29] Association is no longer mechanical; it represents the most
original way in which our human nature works. The concept of association as developed later expresses something objective, no doubt the
language of Hume remains still very psychological.

Husserl hardly mentions anywhere the Humean concept of association, for his study of the "Treatise" seems to have made him sure that
the Humean concept of association is mechanistic and psychological in
character. Husserl reads and studies most carefully only the "Treatise"
of Hume.

Husserl develops and clarifies further the Humean claim to trace
back everything to the correlative acts present in consciousness. The
type of philosophy Husserl and Hume are engaged in is genetic. Hume
develops his genetic philosophy on the line of "naturalism", whereas
Husserl on the line of "transcendentalism".

In the pages to follow we shall discuss and interpret some of the most
leading tenets and concepts of the phenomenology of Husserl. We
shall also try to show very briefly how some of them are related to
certain concepts in the philosophy of Hume. But the programmatic
similarity between the philosophies of Husserl and Hume should not
blind us to the very sharp and deep-rooted differences in the results
reached. The temperamental differences between these two philosophers
are reflected in their philosophies.

---

[28] F. Sauer: Über das Verhältnis der Husserlschen Phänomenologie zu David Hume,
Kant-Studien, XXXV.
[29] R. A. Mall: *Hume's Concept of Man*, pp. 148 f.

CHAPTER IV

THE THEORY OF THE "GENERALTHESIS DER NATÜRLICHEN EINSTELLUNG" (HUSSERL) AND THE SYSTEM OF THE "VULGAR CONSCIOUSNESS" (HUME)

The most unsophisticated and natural outlook upon life is termed by Husserl the "natural standpoint or attitude" (die natürliche Einstellung). The general-most thesis of this standpoint is called the "general thesis" (General-thesis).[1] Like every thesis this general thesis is also posited by the natural standpoint.

We as human beings in the world find ourselves continually present and standing over against us the one spatiotemporal fact-world. This world I am aware of is for me "simply there". It is an endless world, spread out not only in time, but also in space. Not only things and beings, but even we ourselves belong to it. It is continually "present" for me and I myself am a member of it, Husserl maintains. This fact-world is not confined only to the facts of the world, but it includes with the same immediacy the world of values, of goods and of practical ends.[2]

All our acts of asserting, doubting, rejecting etc. leave standing this one world as the general thesis of our natural attitude. At odd points it may be different than we supposed it to be, but all illusions, hallucinations are appearing at the background of this one world of facts and values. For our naive experience the general thesis is always there prior to all theoretical and practical judgments. No falsification can cancel this world, for all acts of falsifying take place within this very fact-world. This one world of ours having spatial and temporal horizons is the world common to all of us, and this is the world which is taken for granted in all our communications with our fellow human beings. I apprehend the world-about-me and the world-about-other subjects like me as the same world which no doubt differs in its modes of affecting our consciousness differently.

[1] *Ideen I*, §§ 27 f.
[2] *Ibid.*, § 27.

We may briefly characterize the natural standpoint to which this one fact-world is immediately present as follows:

1) Not only things and beings, but we ourselves as human beings belong to this world which is naively supposed to be there as such. The attitude inherent in such a supposition is what is called the natural standpoint;

2) It is the basis of our experiencing ourselves as persons living among others;

3) It is prior to all other attitudes, theoretical as well as practical;

4) It implies a passive acceptance and a belief in the continuous existence of the world;

5) It is a pre-reflective, pre-philosophical attitude of natural human beings imagining, judging, feeling, willing in it. [3]

The main task of the phenomenological reflection is to work out the "science of the natural standpoint". Even the most radical phenomenological reduction does not deny or put in question the existence of the general thesis. Husserl's scientific explanation of this world consists in his proposal to alter this natural standpoint radically. The science of the natural standpoint would know this one fact-world and solve the problems which offer themselves upon its ground from a more radical point of view. This knowing is more comprehensive, perfect and trustworthy.

But the radical way of Husserl is not the Cartesian way of doubting everything. It is only a device of method helping us to see certain points more clearly. [4] The attempt to doubt everything, Husserl says, has its place in the realm of our perfect freedom. The attitude which thematizes the natural attitude is unique, and it does not deny or abandon the thesis adopted in the natural standpoint. There is no change in our conviction regarding the being of the world itself. If we speak of a "phenomenological doubt", we must mean by it the act of doubting the way the world is constituted and not the world itself. It does not ask the question "whether there is a world or not", but it

---

[3] *Ibid.*, § 26.

[4] *Ibid.*, § 31. Hume in his "Enquiry concerning the Principle of Understanding" criticizes Cartesian method of doubt very much in the spirit of Husserlian phenomenology. He writes: "There is a species of scepticism, 'antecedent' to all study and philosophy ,which is much inculcated by Des cartes and others, as a sovereign preservative against error and precipitate judgment. It recommends a universal doubt, ... The Cartesian doubt, therefore, were it ever possible to be attained by any human creature (as it plainly is not) would be entirely incurable ... Not to mention, that, if the external world be once called in question, we shall be at a loss to find arguments, by which we may prove the existence ..." (*Enquiries*, pp. 149 f.)

asks only "how do we come to constitute" the world taken for granted in and by our natural attitude?[5]

It is not the negation, but only the suspension (Aufhebung) of the thesis which interests Husserl as a phenomenologist. This thesis remains as experience intact; we only do not make any use of it. This "not making any use of it" is no privation; it is rather a conscious act indicating a form of consciousness which "transvalues" and modifies the thesis. Through such a transvaluation and modification the status of the thesis becomes that of a "bracketed thesis".

Husserl is not worrying about the doubts as to the reality of the external objects of experience. Even the epistemological theories advocating the impossibility of transcending to objects lying outside the field of immanent consciousness do not disturb him. He is not going to comment on the truth or falsity of the judgment, say, "there is a table before me". This judgment may itself be false, but the "judged" remains to be true. Husserl is interested primarily in that which is "intended", "meant".

Our natural attitude towards the world is thematized in the phenomenological attitude of reflection. The natural attitude consists in naively believing that there is a world existing independent of our consciousness. Such a naive supposition is what is termed by Husserl as the "general thesis" (Generalthesis) of the natural standpoint (der natürlichen Einstellung). All changes take place within this one world of the natural attitude. This one world of our natural attitude common to all of us is given not as an individual object in an act of perception; it is rather taken for granted and lies at the back of all our theoretical as well as practical activities.

The standpoint of natural experience takes for granted that the things we perceive are simply there for us and that they exist continually. Not only the objects, but the other persons are also present within this field of experience as realities. They continue existing even when I cease to take notice of them. Besides, we take for granted not only the world of things and beings as existing independently of us; but even the world of values with all its valuational and practical attributes is presupposed by us in our natural attitude. Thus the general thesis of the natural attitude includes in its scope the world of physical nature, human society, cultural products and all other substrates of our common-sense and scientific thinking. Every actual

[5] *Treatise*, pp. 187 f.

field of perception presupposes the co-presence of other objects in a horizon capable of infinite extension. The world taken for granted in our natural attitude is, in some form or other, always present before us. The perceived points to the depth or fringe of indeterminate reality. This indeterminacy is infinite. Husserl talks of the "misty horizon" which cannot be completely outlined, but which remains necessarily there. [6]

Husserl is not denying this attitude, for a denial would lead to artificiality and would be of no use to philosophy which explains, understands and justifies the world we live in. He, of course, admits that such an attitude needs justification. Husserl, in order to reach a higher level of pure givenness, starts from this attitude as the point of departure. This leads him to his phenomenological attitude which is radical in that it does not naively take the world of things and beings for granted. The natural attitude is "naive" because it simply takes for granted the world. What this attitude leaves out of discussion is the very problem of transcendence.

Husserl characterizes the natural attitude as a "passive belief in being" (passiver Seinsglauben) for it does not reflect on how the world we live in comes to be for us.[7] Not only the natural attitude, but also our theoretical scientific attitude lacks radicality. In comparison to the natural attitude, scientific attitude is no doubt radical, but it is not radical enough because it also presupposes at least part of the existence of nature. Thus there remain assumptions within the scientific attitude which, according to Husserl, must be questioned. Even our different theoretical attitudes fall short of the ideal of phenomenological radicality, for they too posit objectively and try to determine it through judgments. Such an objectivity, Husserl maintains, can only be constituted in and through the acts of our intentional experience.

The general thesis is the essence of the natural attitude. No reduction can deny this fact-world and Husserl very clearly tells us that he does not deny this world as a solipsist. He does not doubt that it is there as a sceptic.[8]

In order to distinguish phenomenological attitude from the natural

---

[6] *Ideen I*, § 27.

[7] Hume, while discussing scepticism with regard to the senses, maintains that no philosophy would ever be able to put the existence of the external world in question. "We may well ask, 'What causes induce us to believe in the existence of body?' but 'tis in vain to ask, 'Whether there be body or not?' That is a point, which we must take for granted in all our reasonings." (*Treatise*, p. 187.)

[8] *Ideen I*, § 32.

attitude, Husserl sometimes calls the former "unnatural" (unnatürlich) reflective attitude. Such a radical phenomenological attitude involves a "reduction" to the field of pure consciousness wherein intentional acts of pure experience constitute the different types of objectivities. Husserl maintains that the pure field of the transcendental subjectivity can be attained only by performing such a reduction which suspends the world of empirical objects and subjects without negating it. What remains is the stream of my "cogitationes" which is immediately and apodictically given. This stream is the real seat of apodictic evidence. Viewed from such a reduced platform the objects of experience include not only the world of factual objects, but also all sorts of possible objects as "noemata" of the "noetic-acts", as the noematic correlates of the noetic acts of our intentional life.

Another drawback of the natural attitude is that it is open to doubt. All that is given in the natural attitude or all that is taken for granted in such an attitude may as well be denied. It is not the actual denial which Husserl here talks of, but only the theoretical possibility of such a denial is not apodictically ruled out. But the pure intentional consciousness we attain after the performance of phenomenological reflection is beyond all doubt. All that is there and can be in any way conceived to be there has to have its correlate in form of intentional acts.

Phenomenological attitude is thus the suspension of all assumptions, theoretical as well as practical. In the light of the naturality of the natural attitude, the phenomenological attitude must appear to be "unnatural". But it is the only device which enables us to reflect on the world in a non-solipsistic, non-sceptical and non-positivistic manner. Husserl warns us that one should always be alert lest one falls back into the old natural attitude with its habits and beliefs.

The general thesis of the natural standpoint is not modified or changed through our acts of doubts and rejection. The world is always there, maybe that it is different than we expected it to be. Thus the concept of the "Generalthesis" is not the sum total of the correlates of our various judgments in our natural attitude; it is rather the world which is all the time there as the substrate of all our actions. All our supposed particular existences may be struck out of it, but the "it" of the world remains unaffected in the sense of the general thesis of the natural standpoint. The different modifications and corrections take place within it without changing this one infinite spatio-temporal horizon.

In the section "of scepticism with regard to the senses", Hume writes: "We may well ask, "What causes induce us to believe in the existence of body?" but 'tis in vain to ask, "Whether there be body or not?" "[9] Expressed in Husserlian terminology it means that the general thesis of the natural standpoint is there in Hume, too. It must be taken for granted in all our reasonings; it is the starting point for our philosophical reflections.

The question thus raised by Hume is a twofold one: (i) why we attribute a "continued existence" to objects, even when they are not present to the senses, and (ii) why we suppose them to possess a distinct existence from our perceptions.

In answering this question Hume criticizes the philosophies of reason and senses, and he ultimately comes to the positive teaching of his philosophy ragarding belief which via imagination carries the mind to the real existence. The "vulgar consciousness" (counterpart to Husserl's natürliche Einstellung) supposes the continued existence of the world. Hume like Husserl does not question the existence of the world; he only accounts for it from a higher level of reflection, namely from the level of the principles of human nature.[10]

Hume is a critic not only of the theory of the vulgar consciousness, but he also criticizes the philosophical theory which fails to establish the continued existence of the external world and thus leads to scepticism and solipsism. He calls the philosophical system the "monstrous offspring".[11]

Hume really asks for the "manner" in which the conclusion regarding the independent continued existence of the world is derived.[12] Hume like Husserl aims at working out the science of the vulgar consciousness.

What programmatically corresponds to the concept of the general thesis of the natural standpoint of Husserl in the philosophy of Hume is his understanding and criticism of the world of the vulgar consciousness. Hume's philosophical teaching consists in his attempt to show the drawbacks of a common-sense philosophy which, according to Hume, fails to establish its claim regarding the existence of the world. Not its claim, but the way it establishes its claim is to be doubted. The British school of common-sense philosophy as represented by Reid, Beattie

---

[9] *Treatise*, p. 187.
[10] N. K. Smith: *The Philosophy of David Hume*, pp. 450 f.; R. A. Mall: *Hume's Concept of Man*.
[11] *Treatise*, p. 215.
[12] *Ibid.*, p. 206.

etc. is shown by Hume to possess no philosophical foundation. The vulgar consciousness operating in such a philosophy naively takes the world for granted. It is this naive acceptance (passive Hinnahme bei Husserl) which is criticized by Hume, and not the existence of the world as such.[13] The existence of the world is beyond all question, for it is the basis of all our actions.

For Hume, the philosophical problem consists in our attempt to show how we come to believe in the existence of the world. Like Husserl, Hume tries to systematize the natural standpoint. But, unlike Husserl, Hume fails to develop a full-fledged theory of reduction and constitution.

The vulgar consciousness falsely identifies the perceptions with the objects; it fails to make a distinction between the two. The attitude guiding such a system of the vulgar consciousness supposes a world of objects without asking how is it accomplished by our human nature. The concept of the world existing independently of our consciousness plays the most important role in the system of vulgar consciousness.

Hume's point of departure is his firm belief that "consciousness never deceives".[14] This Humean expression is in fact very Husserlian. Hume's concept of the "impression of reflexion" also substantiates our view that he is a critic of the natural attitude. The vulgar consciousness lacks the very idea of a scientific explanation and justification.[15] Reflection is foreign to our natural standpoint. For Husserl as well as for Hume, the point of departure for a more radical philosophical reflection is the field of the general thesis of the natural standpoint. Like Husserl, Hume too criticizes Descartes' denial of the existence of the world.

Husserl "brackets", "suspends" the world. He regains and re-establishes it from a deeper radical level of phenomenological reflection which ends in the discovery of the pure constituting field of our intentionality. Although Hume possesses no such device, still he establishes in his own way the truth of the continued existence of the world by working out the different principles of human nature. In doing so Hume generally relegates the world to a fiction for he shows that neither reason nor senses can establish the true opinion of the continued existence of the world. But his relegating the world to fiction does not mean his questioning the existence of it; he rather

[13] *Treatise*, p. 193.
[14] *Enquiries*, p. 66.
[15] N. K. Smith: *The Philosophy of David Hume*, p. 450 f.

uses it as a device to show from his own philosophy of the principles of human nature a deeper and more trustworthy way of approach. In the chapter to follow, we shall try to show that the so-called Humean "fictionalism" (a term Husserl himself uses to characterize Hume's philosophy), interpreted in the sense specified here, is more or less a programmatic counterpart to the Husserlian device of the elimination of the world.

Like Husserl's natural standpoint, the vulgar consciousness which is the Humean counterpart to Husserlian natural attitude fails to understand, defend and justify itself. And a sufficient understanding is provided by the trancendental phenomenology of constitution (Husserl) and by the original principles of human nature (Hume) respectively.

CHAPTER V

THE CONCEPT OF REDUCTION

The meaning of philosophy demands that he who philosophizes must do it radically. The radical attitude consists in the destruction of the presupposition of a world existing independently of us. It is this destruction which leads to the ideal of "presuppositionlessness" (Voraussetzungslosigkeit). Such a radical reflection comes very near to a sceptical one in such a way that the statement "the world is" is my statement. Thus, Husserl in search of his "first philosophy" takes into account the radicality of the sceptical attitude. Husserl is transcendentally motivated in his praise of Humean sceptical attitude.

The intentionality, the will to ultimate responsibility (Wille zur letzten Verantwortlichkeit),[1] reigns supreme in Husserl's concept of a radical science. This science is no ready-made something we start with; we have to work it out. The absolute radicalism (der absolute Radikalismus) involved in the demand of philosophy leads to a "life out of absolute vocation" (Leben aus absoluter Berufung).[2] Radicalism is thus nothing else but a strife towards presuppositionlessness (ein Streben nach Voraussetzungslosigkeit).[3]

The radical self-reflection (Selbstbesinnung) ends in the life of our transcendental subjectivity. The return to the transcendental subjectivity is the return to the original field of all reason (Ursprungsfeld aller Vernunft).[4] The concept of reduction is an important device and serves the purpose of discovering the transcendental field of all constitution. Phenomenology as a transcendental-genetic way of accounting for the phenomena lives in acts of reflections. These reflections lead us to reduction which begins as a reflection of the man in the natural field of life

---

[1] *Phän. Psy.*, p. 345.
[2] *E.P. II*, pp. 11 f.
[3] *F.u.t.L.*, p. 224.
[4] *E.P. I*, p. 28.

(Menschen des natürlichen Lebens).[5] In the beginning it is nothing but our natural reflection in a pre-phenomenological sense. A change of attitude takes place through the performance of Epoché which consists in suspension of the entire natural world. The world thus bracketed remains existent for us; we only refrain from using it as the foundation of our judgments. Thus Husserl's suspension and conviction of the world seem to go together.

One of the most irritating, puzzling and at the same time most important concepts of Husserlian phenomenology is that of "reduction". Husserl is variously interpreted on this point and we can roughly classify the different interpreters into two main groups. In the opinion of the one group, Husserl wanted to show the inseparable unity of the "I" and the "world" by means of the performance of his method of reduction. These interpreters maintain that this inseparable unity between the I and the world cannot be further reduced because it itself is the result of the reduction. The last residuum is not a lonely consciousness, but this unity of I with the world. Mostly the French school of phenomenology and some of the American interpreters of Husserl, e.g. J. Wild, belong to this group. The lonely transcendental subjectivity which claims to be without the world is a sheer abstraction, a result of intellectualization.

The other group is of the opinion that Husserl, no doubt, shows the interrelatedness of the I with the world and vice-versa, still the main aim of this device of reduction is to transcend the world we live in. The phenomenological reduction does not stop at the "Lebenswelt"; it goes further and deeper and discovers the reduced field of pure intentional consciousness. All that is there including the world of common-sense as well as of science is constituted within the pure sphere of intentional acts. The discovery of the universal constitutional correlativity between the noetic and noematic world is the main task of the technique of reduction.

What remains then when the whole world is bracketed? Husserl maintains that it is the world of "eidos" which is the last phenomenological residuum when all has been suspended.[6] The goal of reduction is the winning of a new region of being, and this region of being is nothing else but the pure reduced realm of intentionality. Phenomenology as an eidetic science does not break the unity of the I with the

[5] *Ideen* p. 57.
[6] *Ibid.*, *I*, § 33.

world; it rather "lives" it and "founds" it from a deeper and more original level of reason, of experience. Interpreted in such a way, we could well maintain that the phenomenological reduction transcends even the "Lebenswelt", for our life-world itself is a world constituted by our transcendental intentionality. Thus the phenomenological reduction is extended to the world of natural as well as mental sciences. Even the transcendence of God is suspended. [7] The real transcendental phenomenological domain results thus after "bracketing" all naivities in the fields of epistemology, metaphysics, natural sciences, mathematics and theology. Herein lies the methodological importance of the systematic theory of phenomenological reduction.

The method of reduction is a phenomenological technique within the wider field of phenomenology as a method. Husserl's phenomenology tries to discover the world of essences in the pure field of intentional life of the transcendental subjectivity. The "eidetic" point of view is of central importance to such an undertaking. Husserl's "Ideen" and his "Logical investigations" contain enough materials which help our understanding this method of "eidetic reduction". [8]

Phenomenology as descriptive phenomenology deals with the problem of our empirical consciousness. The researches with regard to the intentionality have established that our empirical consciousness works with intentional acts and their implications. In order to get at the constituting ego Husserl has to eliminate all "positions". What remains after this elimination is the realm of pure activities of the ego. Husserl's theory of reduction eliminates not only the empirical ego; it also suspends the transcendental ego. After the elimination of these two layers of egos, Husserl discovers the third and the deepest layer of the pure constituting ego. [9]

The very first step in the transition from the empirical ego to the transcendental subject is termed "Epoché", "bracketing", "reflection", "reduction". [10] The "transcendental" does not stand for a faculty-consciousness; it is just the name of our act-consciousness which refrains from using the mundane level of our empirical experience. The "transcendent" as eliminated means here the intended content. The discovery of the field of our own experiences (Erlebnisse) is the result of a second reduction which is nothing else than the eidetic one. The most radical

[7] *Ibid.*, §§ 56, 58 and 62.
[8] *Ideen I*, §§ 56 f.
[9] W. Szilasi: *Einführung in die Phänomenologie Edmund Husserls* pp. 59 f.
[10] *Ideen I*, pp. 58 f.

transcendental reduction aims at the discovery of an endless realm of the transcendental pure subjectivity in which all the eliminated is present in the form of transcendental phenomena.[11] The eidetic reduction, as shown above, is followed by another reduction which is called transcendental. Thus the concept of phenomenological reduction includes both the above mentioned forms of reductions.

The point of departure for Husserl's theory of reduction is his radical criticism of our experience at the level of our natural attitude. The radical phenomenological reduction eliminates the very "general thesis" of the natural standpoint as such.[12] The transcendental reduction is elaborately stated first in the "Ideen" in which the world of our natural attitude is eliminated in order to discover the pure realm of consciousness. Husserl tells us very clearly that we start from the natural standpoint, from the world as it stands out there before us. Our I-consciousness as furnished in our psychological experience must be studied in view of the conditions constituting it. The radical performance of the method of phenomenological reduction would set free the vast horizon of transcendentally purged phenomena. It is this field which, according to Husserl, is the proper field of phenomenology (das Feld der Phänomenologie in unserem eigentlichen Sinne.)[13]

In search of the transcendental field of constitution, Husserl must proceed from the psycho-physiological level to the transcendental one. Husserl's technique of eidetic reduction plays the central role in such a transition of attitudes, for it "brackets" the world of natural attitude and abstains from using it as the basis of any judgments. Performing phenomenological reflection we do not stay within the natural field. In such a reflection, our attention is given to acts and the intentional objects referred to by these acts. We move now within the purified field of intentional acts which are apodictically given.[14]

The nature of consciousness is intentional. In his preface to the English edition of his "Ideas", Husserl distinguishes between his own pure psychology contained in his transcendental phenomenology and the descriptive psychology contained in the concept of intentionality as used by Brentano.[15] It is here that Husserl credits Hume for having

---

[11] *Ideen III*, p. 145.

[12] L. Landgrebe: *Der Weg der Phänomenologie*, pp. 44 f.

[13] *Ideen I*, p. 5.

[14] Husserl rightly remarks that Hume failed to develop a theory of intentionality, although he (Hume), Husserl maintains, could have easily done it. Hume's psychology remained, at least partly, fettered to the inherited naturalism, psychologism and empiricism.

[15] *Ideas-General. Introduction to pure Phenomenology*, translated by W. R. B. Gibson, p. 23.

given us the first systematic sketch of a pure phenomenology. The mistake of Hume lies in his sensualistic empiricism which naturalizes the pure consciousness.

The natural world that is reduced and "put out of play" does not disappear altogether from the field of our pure reduced consciousness; it is rather purified and reappears as the phenomena, as the transcendental correlate of our experience of the world. What happens to the world when we perform reduction is no destruction but "suspension"[16] of it. Thus the real meaning of this device of reduction is not denial but "elimination" (Ausschaltung). Phenomenological reduction is nothing but a conscious abstaining from using the world of natural attitude as the basis of our scientific judgments. The bracketed and the eliminated world now no longer influence our phenomenological research. The practice of this method is free from all metaphysical colourings. Phenomenological reduction is no "eccentricity", Husserl tells us in his preface to the English edition of his "Ideas".

In the "Cartesian Meditations", Husserl clearly tells us that we must first lose the world (verlieren) in order to regain it from the most original and apodictic point of view of radical phenomenological reduction.[17] To regain means to show that the world experienced is in fact constituted as an "intentum" of "intention". The field of constituting subjectivity is not empty; it is the very seat of the "noetic-noematic correlativity".

After the performance of phenomenological reduction, I am confronted only with the acts populating the realm of pure consciousness. I do not perceive the objects which were the contents of our natural empirical experience. The way leading to such a field of pure intentional acts is what is termed technically the method of phenomenological reduction. Husserl is no Cartesian; his method is not a method of doubt.

The phenomenological reduction is, in the first instance, a reduction to myself, to the individual consciousness. The radical phenomenological reduction cannot stop before it reaches "rock-bottom of an individual (solitary) ego."[18] This first reduction presents us with myself as "ego-cogito" which expresses itself in the judgment "I am alone", and it must then face the problem of other egos. The constitution of other egos is accomplished by invoking the concept of a

[16] L. Landgrebe: *Der Weg der Phänomenologie*, pp. 82 f.
[17] *C.M.*, p. 183.
[18] M. Farber: *The Foundation of Phenomenology*, p. 531.

mediate intentionality which represents a "coexistence" that cannot be presented in the form of a person. The experience at this reduced solitary level is an experience of an act which makes others "co-present"; it is an act of "appresentation".

The main purpose of the device of reduction is the discovery of an "absolute" and "apodictic" instance of constitution. There must appear a field which contains only the pure given. This field is nothing else than that of pure consciousness of constitution. It is the meaning-giving centre of all performances (Leistungen). This phenomenological "absolute" must not be confounded with the absolute of the traditional philosophy for it is no metaphysical entity fixed for all time to come. It is rather the very original, primordial "flux" (Fluß) of our "cogitationes" within the reduced sphere of pure intentionality[19]. It is not something "hypostatized".

The device of phenomenological reduction is, according to Husserl, the way of a radical reflection. In the reduced realm of transcendental subjectivity, no traces are lost. All the painstaking phenomenological researches take the way of reflection on our intentional acts. Husserl speaks of an "apodictic reduction" (apodiktische Reduktion) and distinguishes it form the transcendental or phenomenological reduction. The former represents a task made possible after the performance of the latter. Husserl maintains that one must possess a pure field of experience before one goes to any type of apodictic criticism[20].

Husserl often uses the term "entdecken" with regard to the achievements of his phenomenological reflections. This points to the fact that within the reduced sphere of transcendental subjectivity the whole field of reality has to be shown as the correlate of the intentional acts. This is accomplished by means of the Husserlian theory of constitution. In the chapter to follow, we shall show how the device of reduction consequently leads to the problem of constitution.

The most radical reflection is the intersubjective reduction.[21] The eliminated world is always there. It is not a world experienced and constituted only by me. The world is as much my world as it is the world of my fellow human beings. The real objectivity of the world is in fact its intersubjectivity. This intersubjective world carries structures which cannot be fully understood if we try to see them in relation only

---

[19] G. Funke: *Phänomenologie – Metaphysik oder Methode?* pp. 34 f.

[20] We see and realize here how the method of reduction serves the purpose of laying bare the last structures of experience. The concept of a pure original experience is essentially related with the performance of phenomenological reduction.

[21] L. Landgrebe: *Der Weg der Phänomenologie*, pp. 89 f.

to my "solus ipse". Thus the world must mean an intersubjective accomplishment (intersubjective Leistung) in the sense of a common horizon of a common experience.

Husserl's teaching is not sceptical when he maintains that the world of the natural attitude is "eliminated". There is no loss of our conviction we cherish with regard to the existence of the world. Husserl distinguishes very sharply his theory of reduction from the method of Cartesian doubt which really seems to doubt the very existence of the world.[22] Hume, in the opinion of Husserl, is more consistent and radical on this point than Descartes. For Husserl, the Cartesian method of universal doubt is in reality an attempt at universal negation.

The performance of the phenomenological reduction leads us to the discovery of the attitude of a "disinterested onlooker" (uninteressierter Zuschauer). This attitude of disinterestedness (Uninteressiertheit) is nothing but the centre of all activity, namely the constituting transcendental pure subjectivity.

Why and how the very possibility of the non-existence of the world is ruled out even when we perform the most radical reduction? The world cannot be lost, for – thanks to the Husserlian concept of intentionality – it is (and remains) in all its variations an intentional (noematic) pole of our noetic acts. If the possibility of the non-existence of the world is accepted by Husserl, he will land in scepticism and solipsism. What then happens to the world in the process of our performing the act of elimination? In what way does the world change its character? All that the world loses is its metaphysical character of existing independently of human consciousness. Reduction is the destruction of the very idea of being which is unconstituted. There is no unconstituted transcendence. The phenomenology of reduction implies a damaging criticism of all forms of naive realism – metaphysical as well as epistemological. Reduction destroys the myth of a reality which is mind-independent. The process of reduction is a twofold process of destruction and foundation; it destroys the world by founding it, i.e. by constituting it. The loss of the world aims at firm gain of it.

In the "Cartesian Meditations", Husserl characterizes his device of "Epoché" as the most radical and universal method which helps us discover the pure field of our consciousness.[23] Whether or not the method of phenomenological reduction fulfills all that is demanded of it is very controversial. Whether phenomenological reduction succeeds

---

[22] *Ideen I*, § 31.
[23] *C.M.*, pp. 60 f.

in providing us with a field of pure phenomena free from all horizon is doubtful. But still as an attitude of man who does not live always naively and naturally the idea of reduction establishes its claim. It results in a total change of attitude which opens up a new vista. But it must not be left unmentioned that Husserl leaves the possibility of a transformation of this method open. [24]

As a method laying bare the level of those intentional acts which constitute all that is there, it is one of the most fruitful methods of philosophy and would claim the central place within the pluralism of philosophical methods. It is not far from truth to define phenomenology as the most radical descriptive science of philosophy with infinite steps of reflections in search of the constitutional noetic-noematic correlativity.

Husserl characterizes the attitude implied in the concept of radical phenomenological reduction as a very revolutionizing one. It brings about a complete "personal metamorphosis" (eine völlige personale Umwandlung). Husserl goes still further and compares it with a "religious conversion" (religiöse Umkehrung). [25] Such a far-reaching and radical conversion brings about a new way of seeing the world of things and beings. Husserl always emphasizes the character of phenomenology which consists in "seeing" ever deeper and deeper. Husserl assures us of having experienced the fate of a philosophical existence. [26]

The performance of reduction leading to pure intersubjectivity is an extension of the first reduction. Such an extension leads to the discovery of a realm of pure psychology, that is to say, to a phenomenology of "empathy" (Einfühlung) wherein the subjectivity of the other is "indexed" (indiziert). Such a phenomenology of sympathetic understanding gets its confirmation in and through the acts of our common social life. The phenomenon of social communication testifies the constitution of a "society of monads" within the pure realm of our subjectivity. We are always in principle our own subjectivity.

Phenomenological philosophy is no doubt a descriptive analysis of the ideal essences intended by our consciousness; but it is also more than that. Such a descriptive phenomenology has itself to be radicalized in order to discover the apodictic realm of all foundations, and pheno-

---

[24] *E.P. II*, p. 80.

[25] *Krisis*, p. 140. (The practice of Yogic-techniques in Indian philosophy of Yoga seems to demand a similar type of radical conversion of attitude, although it pursues a different goal and is motivated differently.)

[26] *Krisis*, p. 17. Husserl writes: "Ich versuche zu führen, nicht zu belehren, nur aufzuweisen, zu beschreiben, was ich sehe".

menology is essentially a radical philosophy of foundations. It is this radicalization which is accomplished by the Husserlian method of radical phenomenological reduction which, in the last run, stands for the deepest and the truest type of self-reflection (Selbstbesinnung). The field that is opened up after the execution of reduction is neither "psychologistic nor metaphysical"; it is "transcendental". In the course of our further discussion we shall see that the term "transcendental" in the phenomenology of Husserl points to that instance of intentionality which is the last and the most original point of contact between the consciousness and the world that is constituted by the consciousness. Reduction is thus not merely a technique without any further and deeper mission. It permits us to go beyond all psychologism and relativism to a realm of apodictic evidence. The discovery of the most original field of experience is what reduction aims at.

The method of phenomenological reduction offers itself necessarily to one who philosophizes phenomenologically. When the impossibility of the decision for the being or the non-being of the world dawns on us, we of necessity take the help of the radicalness implied in the theory of reduction. The only radical ground guaranteeing the impossibility of the non-being, non-existence of the world lies in our original experience that the world is nothing else but an intentional pole, and it gets its meaning, and in this sense its being, from the consciousness.

The moment the world loses its apodictic certainty of being, the radical philosopher is forced to return to a realm of experience which is beyond all doubt and which contains its own justification. Husserl means it sincerely and seriously when he speaks of a total personal change with regard to the attainments of reduction. Herein lies the most lasting sense of Husserl's concept of reduction, and the question with regard to its transformations in particular cases must be left open.

There is hardly any programmatic parallel to the Husserlian concept of reduction in the philosophical literature of Hume. This does not mean the total absence of any programmatic similarity. We have already mentioned that Husserl calls Hume's philosophy a philosophy of "as-if" which relegates all the categories of objective knowledge to mere "fictions of imagination". The personal identity is a "psychological fiction" (die Identität ist eine psychologische Fiktion). Hume thus ends, Husserl comments further, in solipsism. Hume ought to have taken the bull of scepticism and solipsism by the horns.[27]

But Husserl of course credits Hume for having thought of reduction.

[27] *Krisis*, pp. 88 f.

He maintains that Hume, in principle, was very near to the true discovery of a genuine method of reduction, but he misses the goal in that he tries to reduce all the ideas to impressions which are, according to Husserl, only sensuous. Since Husserl thinks that Hume always tries to trace back everything to the sensuous impressions, he labels Hume's attempt at reduction a "nominalistic reduction of all ideas to impressions" (nominalistische Reduktion aller Ideen auf Impressionen). [28] As Husserl fails to take into account Hume's extension of his theory of impressions to the impressions of reflection and thought, he comes to the conclusion that Hume's philosophy is "fictionalistic" in nature. Hume, as we know, speaks of "impressions of reflexions", [29] "impressions of feeling", "impressions of ourselves", "impression or consciousness of person", and tries to modify and extend his teaching regarding impressions which is so very much sensualistic in tone, at least, in his "Treatise" wherein he first of all proposes his theory of impression.

But in trying to bring Husserl's concept of reduction in relation to the so-called "fictionalism" of Hume we are not attempting here a more sympathetic interpretation of Hume's theory of impressions and ideas. Hume's psychology lacks the idea of intentionality, and his fundamental science of man describes in a natural way the various operations of human nature which take the form of the principles of human nature.

Our purpose here is to show that Hume who leads the Locke-Berkeley tradition to its most logical consequences has necessarily to declare the as-if (fictional) character of all the categories of objective knowledge. The similarity we want to show lies in the purpose. Like Husserl's method of reduction, Hume's relegating these categories of objective knowledge to fictions of imagination really prepares the ground for a more original way of showing how they are constituted by the most fundamental principles of human nature. Hume, too, destroys the independence of a world. All the sciences, Hume says clearly, have a relation, greater or lesser, to human nature; and "however wide any of them seem to run from it, they still return back by one passage or another". [30] Human nature is the "capital or center" of all sciences, and no victory can be achieved unless we work out the true science of human nature.

[28] *E.P. I*, Vorlesung 23.
[29] *Enquiries*, pp. 75 f.
[30] *Treatise*, Introduction.

We attempt to interpret Hume on this point in such a way that the positive results of his otherwise fictional theory are similar (at least in programme, purpose and goal) to those of Husserl's theory of reduction. This negative theory of fiction serves the positive purpose which consists in Hume's working out his science of man. Like the reduction of Husserl, Hume's fictional approach discovers the ground of human nature.

Hume's own constructive philosophy of human nature sides neither with the Locke-Berkeley tradition of sensualistic empiricism nor with the rationalism of Descartes. Hume criticizes both the traditions of empiricism and rationalism as implying some form of scepticism as well as dogmatism. Hume very clearly says that the categories like causality, existence, person, identity and so on cannot be established and proved either on the ground of reason or senses. He speaks thus in his "Treatise" of a "scepticism with regard to reason" and of a "scepticism with regard to the senses".[31] This is why Hume relegates the external world and all the other categories of objective knowledge to fiction. It is the "way", "manner" in which these categories are established that is false, and not that which is established. Hume is as much convinced of the existence of the world as Husserl.

Added to this, we must not forget that Hume never fails to show the difference between fiction and belief.[32] Belief is something felt by the mind which distinguishes the objects believed from the fictions of the imagination. Belief is the name of a "manner" in which ideas are felt. He uses the terms like "sentiment", "feeling", "vivacity" in describing the nature of belief. These are also the terms which he uses while describing his impressions. Such a theory of belief and of impression is developed by Hume in his "Enquiries".[33]

We have already mentioned that Husserl tells us in his "Cartesian Meditations" that we must lose the world in order to regain it more truly, more intimately and apodictically. Similarly, Hume's relegation of all certainties to fictions really opens up the new realm of human nature and permits him to see the most original instance of all constitution. This field, opened up after declaring the world of objects to fictions, is neither sensualistic nor rationalistic in the traditional sense of the term; it is rooted neither in the senses nor in the reason, but in the imagination. In the case of Husserl, this new field discovered is

---

[31] *Treatise*, pp. 219 f.
[32] *Enquiries*, pp. 47 f.
[33] *Ibid.*, pp. 47 f.; 62 f.; 75 f.

"transcendental"; for Hume, it is "natural" (understood in the Humean sense of "easy", "genuine", "true"). [34]

Husserl also fails to take into account that when Hume talks of the fictions of imagination, he means by imagination a faculty of feigning, of producing fictions. His own theory of imagination represents the most constructive side of his philosophy. [35] In the chapter to follow we shall be discussing Hume's own theory of imagination.

The result Hume reached is no transcendental philosophy of consciousness as is the case with the phenomenology of Husserl. Hume discovers his philosophy of human nature which is a counterpart to Husserl's philosophy of the transcendental subjectivity. Hume's "naturalism", [36] which consists of the discoveries and descriptions of the guiding principles of human nature, has at least this similarity with Husserl's transcendental phenomenology that it too cannot be categorized as empiricism or rationalism, as realism or idealism.

[34] C. W. Hendel: *Studies in the Philosophy of David Hume*, pp. 310 f.
[35] R. A. Mall: *Hume's Concept of Man*, Ch. on "Imagination".
[36] N. K. Smith: *The Naturalism of Hume*, Mind, 1905.

CHAPTER VI

THE CONCEPT OF CONSTITUTION AND HUME'S IMAGINATION

The operation of phenomenological reduction opens up a realm of all foundations. This apodictic instance of original experience is the pure intentional consciousness of constitution. The concept of constitution is as irritating[1] as the concept of reduction, and it is as important, if not more, as the concept of reduction. It is but natural that Husserl after having discovered the pure reduced realm of pure intentional consciousness must now turn to the task of constituting the world of things and beings eliminated by the phenomenological reduction. M. Farber calls the way "the way out"[2] for it now goes to understand the "bracketed" transcendence.

Husserl's theory of reduction has a twofold result: it results in the discovery of a region of apodictic experience and it opens up the very instance giving sense and meaning to everything we come in contact with. It is the latter one which is the central theme of the theory of constitution. The whole world of things and beings requires the consciousness, not in order "to be" or "to exist" as such, but in order to be meaningful. The phenomenological idealism of Husserl does not deny the real existence of the world. The world we live in is not a world of appearance. It is not the "world's-being-there" that is constituted, but the way of its being meaningful to us is elucidated. That the world exists is beyond all doubt. It is given to all of us as the universal field of our experience.[3]

---

[1] "The idea of constitution", Robberechts writes in his book "Husserl", "is a very irritating one and much ink has been spilled." p. 49. In a similar way, N. K. Smith writes about the Humean concept of imagination as being "very confusing. It has a twofold employment: as the faculty of feigning (fancy) and as signifying the 'vivacity of conception'". *The Philosophy of David Hume*, p. 137.

[2] *The Foundation of Phenomenology*, p. 529.

[3] "Der phänomenologische Idealismus", Husserl writes, "leugnet nicht die wirkliche Existenz der realen Welt (und zunächst der Natur) als ob er meinte, daß sie ein Schein wäre, dem das natürliche und das positiv wissenschaftliche Denken, obschon unvermerkt, unterläge.

At the pure phenomenological level of eidetic search and research it is true to maintain that the world needs consciousness and not vice-versa. But this does not mean that phenomenology is solipsistic or sceptical. Phenomenological theory of constitution (it must be made clear in the beginning) is in our view no theory of "creation" or "production"; it is rather the way to show how the world that exists and in which we find ourselves becomes a meaningful world to us. Constitution is the elucidation of the world as a world "accomplished" (geleistet) by our intentionality.

One must not misunderstand the real purport of Husserl's teaching with regard to his philosophy of constitution. It is not so that our apodictic consciousness has started constituting the world after Husserl's phenomenology has discovered this constitutive quality of it. The acts of constitution have always been there; all that Husserl is doing is to show the world has no other source to get meanings. This constitutional execution of our intentionality is already there as the "intentional accomplishment" of our meaning-giving consciousness. [4] Thus the distinction between "passive" and "active" constitution implies no paradox.

The real intent, the main purpose of constitution consists in its activity of elucidating the life of meaning-giving consciousness. Any constitutional study has to show how we come to this or that meaning of any object or being. To give sense to the world does not mean to "create" or "to produce" it out of nothing; it is also not just a mere reporting of sense which the things and beings show themselves. To constitute is to explain the meaning the world and the other persons have for us.

A true understanding of Husserl's concept of constitution is of crucial importance for the whole phenomenology and there is a lot of difference particularly on this point among the phenomenologists. The vast phenomenological literature of Husserl seems to testify more or less to both the ways of interpreting constitution, as production and as elucidation. But it is the latter sense which tallies with the spirit of Husserl's phenomenology. Here we come to the conclusion that the real meaning of the concept of constitution is not, and cannot be, production or creation; constitution is just the most fundamental and

---

Seine einzige Aufgabe und Leistung ist es, den Sinn dieser Welt, ..., aufzuklären. Daß die Welt existiert, ..., ist vollkommen zweifellos." *Ideen III*, p. 152.

[4] L. Landgrebe: *Phänomenologie und Geschichte*, pp. 30 f.

original way expressing the essential relationship between "intention" and "intentum".

Independent of one's understanding of phenomenological reduction as either discovering the "Lebenswelt" or the transcendental subjectivity, constitution remains the ultimate way of showing how the world is formed (gestalten) by our constituting consciousness. Constitution is neither a "subjective creation" of a metaphysical entity called mind or spirit nor is it just a translation, a reproduction of a world with fixed meanings. The theory of constitution does not imply any hypostatization; not only that, it even denies the independent existence of all metaphysical entities.

The centralmost core of the constitutional problem lies within the correlativity of noesis and noema. Which of the two – noesis or noema – is prior? Do they depend on each other mutually? Is not the noesis more important phenomenologically than noema? Is not every noetic act essentially related to a noematic object? The reduction has taught us the lesson from the discovery of the transcendental subjectivity which is the original most source of all constitutions. This trancendental consciousness is the "absolute", the "first" not only because it means an original experience, but (seen from the point of view of constitution) mainly because it does not need any other reality to have a sense. It is rather the last forum to give sense to all that is. The transcendental subjectivity is the performer of all acts and giver of all sense.

In the "Ideen", the constitutional analyses describe the ways of our consciousness in which the unities, say, of thing, body, soul etc. occur. The fourth and the fifth meditation of "Cartesian Meditations" deal primarily with the problem of constitution of the other, of the intersubjectivity. Husserl shows here that phenomenology, rightly understood, does not end with "solus ipse"; it reaches objectivity through constitution. The other is constituted in me through a system of ordered indications. It is the body of the other which is really present to me and it belongs to the original sphere of my own experiences of my body. This bodily presence of the other indicates the psychical inner life of the other through "appresentation". It is in this way that the other is constituted as a psycho-physical unity. I occupy a place in the space which is my absolute "here" and the other is "there" for me. The other from his own "here" sees the world as I do it from my "here". Husserl tries to show that, in spite of the perspective differences I and the other have from the world, it is one and the same intersubjectively common world which is perceived by both of us.

Thanks to the process of "empathy" we are conscious of such an identity.[5] In understanding myself I understand the other. There is no other way to reach his inner life.

In order to explain this consciousness of identity, Husserl invokes the help of a passive synthesis of association which works as a link between the analogical appresentation of the other and the original presentation of myself. Association is a primordial form of a passive synthesis.[6] The "Cartesian Meditations" deal with the problem of the constitution of a world common to all of us.[7]

Husserl uses the concept of constitution to describe the way our pure absolute ego carries on its task of elucidating the meanings which things and persons possess. But Husserl's philosophy of constitution does not claim to have carried out a constitutional analysis for all particular cases. Husserl's phenomenology of constitution wants to establish the only way we take in our understanding the world. His painstaking phenomenological reflections show that his philosophy is not a closed system with fixed principles laying down in all concreteness the steps any future philosophy has to take.[8] Phenomenology is an unending process of search and research. The constitutional philosophy of Husserl represents a dynamic process taking place within the apodictically given realm of pure intentional consciousness.

Husserl believes firmly that there is nothing which founds the transcendental subjectivity. It is the pure ego which is prior to all beings with meanings. Husserl tells us in his "Krisis" that the intersubjectivity which makes objectivity possible is itself made possible by the absolute ego.[9]

We have already mentioned that the constitutional problem implies a particular type of relationship between the constituting consciousness and the constituted world of things, beings and values. The realm of consciousness is self-sufficient and this self-sufficiency (Selbstgenügsamkeit) means that reality, the world, needs consciousness in order to be real, i.e. to say, to be meaningful. To be is to be meaningful. The terms being, reality, meaning seem to be interchangeable in this context. To talk of a being devoid of all meaning to us is phenomenologically impossible.

Husserl maintains that the transcendental phenomenology, when

[5] *Ideen II*, §§ 46–47.
[6] *C.M.*, p. 142.
[7] *Ibid.*, §§ 55–56.
[8] L. Landgrebe: *Phänomenologie und Geschichte*, p. 31.
[9] *Krisis*, pp. 190 & 259 f.; see also *F.u.t.L.* p. 243.

consistently carried forward, culminates in the philosophy of constitution. The job of the philosophy of constitution is to show that all the
conceivable objects we could ever meet with in experience, in short the
whole real world together with all its categories and likewise all "ideal
worlds" are transcendental correlates. The intentional constitutive
phenomenology implies a psychology in which the life of the pure ego
is made intelligible. This "making-intelligible" consists in constituting
the meaning of all that is present in and to the experience. The constitutional psychology leads thus to an intentional psychology which
works out the system of intentional acts.

But Husserl is very careful and warns us that he should not be understood to mean that the very brute world is reduced to consciousness
without any remainder. It is a great mistake not to see that the
constitutional phenomenology of Husserl is not at all thematizing the
world as a metaphysical substratum of the different philosophical
"Weltanschauungen". It is this very metaphysical substratum which
is destroyed by the Husserlian phenomenology of reduction. There
would hardly be any differences between Berkeley and Husserl if we
take the latter to have "idealized" the matter in the fashion of Berkeley.

The relation between consciousness and the world it is conscious of is
very complex and it can be seen from different points of view. Husserl
no doubt maintains that the being is not just identical with the consciousness. No ego is without the body which relates us with the world.
But Husserl also remarks that in the realm of inner temporality the
being is identical with the inner consciousness of being.[10] It is more
secure to interpret Husserl on such delicate points as meaning that the
being in the sense of a being with meaning has its last source in the
constituting consciousness, for it is this very meaning of being which
is an accomplishment (Leistung) of consciousness. Strictly speaking,
phenomenology has no right to sit in judgment on things which fall –
if there is any such thing at all – beyond the noetic-noematic correlativity.

It is wrong to maintain that Husserl is necessarily led to a philosophy
of subjective idealism. The meaning, the sense that is constituted and
given to the world is not an arbitrary act of an individual psychological
consciousness. The term consciousness, as understood in phenomenology, is not a psychological entity which must receive affection from
outside; it is rather the very dynamic instance of intentional act-

[10] "Denn hier fällt ja das Sein und Innerlich-bewußtsein zusammen." *Zeitbewußtsein*,
p. 471.

execution. Being is no doubt dependent on consciousness, but it is also a transcendent being and "both the dependence of reality and its transcendence towards subjectivity have to be retained if we are to give Husserl's concept of constitution the philosophical value and balance which belong to it".[11] What does this transcendence towards subjectivity mean? It is wrong to speak of transcendence metaphysically, for such a thing does not exist for the philosophy of constitution, which aims at elucidating all transcendence immanently.[12] Since all transcendence is constituted, it is phenomenologically a paradox to speak of a transcendence as such.

When we push the side of dependence unduly far, we not only misinterpret Husserl's constitutional philosophy by relegating it to some type of solipsism, but we also fail to do justice to the very mission of phenomenological reflection which is a constant search for meaning within a dynamic framework of noetic-noematic correlativity. If we, on the other hand, concentrate too much on the side of independence, we are led to a view of consciousness wherein it plays just the passive role, repeatedly reproducing the world. Husserl's phenomenology is an archenemy of any form of "epiphenomenalism". Not only that, we even mistake the very intention of Husserl who never dreams of making consciousness superfluous. But Husserl also does not maintain that consciousness creates the world out of nothing.

It is thus a matter of choice and taste if we call the world of things and beings thus constituted by consciousness a "dream-world". We have at our disposal only this way of constitution; and to maintain that the reality is not constituted at all is nothing but a bad philosophy with metaphysical colourings.

In order to give a just interpretation of Husserl's concept of constitution, we must avoid both the extreme views mentioned above. The way Fink interprets Husserl's concept of constitution leans too much on the side of dependence of all being on consciousness, and consequently this concept, according to him, means "creation", "production" and the like.[13] The constitutional ego neither creates meaning nor does it merely read ready-made meaning. There are no ready-made meanings independent of intentional acts in and through which they are meant.

[11] R. Sokolowski: *The Formation of Husserl's Concept of Constitution*, p. 197.

[12] "Die Herstellung der Lesbarkeit der Welttexte entspricht dem, was Husserl mit Konstitution im eigentlichen Sinne bezeichnet. Ihre Leistung ist, daß alles zunächst Transzendente immanent erfaßt wird." W. Szilasi: *Einführung in die Phänomenologie Edmund Husserls*, p. 91.

[13] E. Fink: *Was will die Phänomenologie Edmund Husserls?* Die Tatwelt, 1934.

To maintain that consciousness, nevertheless, gives meaning to the world means the very way of our being in a position to talk of meaning with regard to all that possesses meaning for us. One should not blackmail Husserlian phenomenology of constitution by bringing in the mythical metaphysical considerations of a being. The minimum amount of conceptualization involved in the phenomenology of constitution is explained by discovering the pure field of original experience.

Without me the world of course means nothing to me, but I am not the creator of the world. Its character of being there for all of us is never put in question by Husserl. It is true that Husserl himself uses the term "erzeugen" while explaining his theory of constitution, and it, of course, holds true in the field of pure mathematics and logic wherein the ideal objects of these sciences may well be said to be "created". Husserl as a mathematician might have been led to think, at least in the beginning, that we could work out the axiomatic character of all other disciplines. But in the course of the development of his philosophy, he develops a theory of "genetic constitution" (genetische Konstitution) which is no longer static but dynamic. There are no fixed patterns of constitution. Every meaning an object possesses has a developing history of its own.

The theory of genetic constitution consists mainly in our dynamic search *for* and *of* the history of the senses of an object. Such a view of constitution overcomes the static character of a purely formalistic concept of constitution. Genetic constitution cannot be "schematized" for all time to come for it tries to show how this or that meaning has been attached to this or that object, and how it has developed slowly but surely from previous senses. The concept of "sedimentation" plays an important role in the theory of genetic constitution.

The pre-predicative encounter thus becomes the source to which different analyses are to be traced back; it is, so to say, a "sense-pit". We can speak of different histories of sense this or that object possesses, for the sense we give to a mental object is traced back to a different historical process than the sense we give to a tree or an animal. The consciousness does not create the sense; it only searches the origin of it. To constitute means thus to trace back the origin of sense to the ultimate point of all references, namely to the field of intentional life of our constituting consciousness.[14]

---

[14] The importance of the genetic constitution in the field of social sciences cannot be overestimated, and it can be fruitfully employed in and by these sciences in order to explain and understand the various historico-cultural products.

This concept of genetic constitution lays bare the character of historical development within the history of a particular object. Thus the previous stages in the meaning-history of an object do represent the conditions for the meaning of the latter stages of the same object. But this does not mean that the fact of our perpetual encounter with the world becomes superfluous. Phenomenology is not averse to the field of our concrete experiences; it only opens up a way to "live" and see them more intimately. We realize more truly and more radically the "involvement-character" of all life after eliminating all our involvements through the practice of phenomenological reduction. From our reduced solitude we 'live' the world as our own constitution. The experience of constitution is the most original one.

The later senses of an object are, no doubt, conditioned, but they are not completely caused or brought forth by the former ones. The constant encounter with the world we live in is and remains the inevitable source. Thus the Husserlian theory of constitution stands for the very concrete analysis we undertake in our search of meaning. To constitute means thus to show the very possibility of how we come to meanings. To constitute means to explicate, to elucidate and to explain. Our subjectivity does not create the meaning it constitutes and understands. Constitution is comprehension.

The process of constitution has no end; it has no beginning either, strictly and phenomenologically speaking. There is always a meaning acquired through the previous constitutional acts. All that happens is historical in character and philosophy is no "positional metaphysics"; it is rather a movement from one event to the other in search of the constitutional acts.[15]

Husserl, no doubt, reaches and also starts with the transcendental subjectivity which provides us with the last ground for the very possibility of constitutional analysis. Facticity of the world is not denied; it is only understood and elucidated from an apodictic point of view. Constitution is the name of the most original relationship of the human consciousness with the world. Phenomenology has no phenomenological interest in anything which is devoid of such a fundamental relationship; nay, there is in fact nothing which is devoid of such a relationship.

The quest for a rigorous science of philosophy is always the last motive of Husserl. The philosophizing ego which is present in all his

---

[15] L. Landgrebe: *Phänomenologie und Geschichte*, pp. 135 f.

experience and knowledge of the world must reflect on itself. It is this self-reflection which in justifying itself justifies the presupposition-lessness of philosophy. Transcendental phenomenology, Husserl maintains, is not a theory, devised as a reply to the historic problem of idealism; it is a science founded in itself. It is a science that stands absolutely on its own ground, and a consequent working out of this science leads to the constitutive problems.

In his time-analysis, Husserl develops a new concept of the "absolute" which he terms the "living flowing present" (lebendig strömende Gegenwart). This living immediate present seems to be the last absolute in the phenomenology of Husserl, for the very stream of our consciousness is now made relative to it. This immediate present is originally and absolutely given (das originär und absolut Gegebene). Husserlian time-analyses are nothing but the phenomenological steps towards building up the very concept of time-horizon. Our consciousness never loses its temporal profile. The flow of time must now be seen in relation to this present which "stretches", so to say, backward and forward giving rise to our sense of a temporal distance, to "specious present".[16] This present possesses two characteristics of "retention" and "protention" and is the very condition for consciousness. Our experience of immanent objects is thus made possible which in its turn shows the way towards the constitution of transcendent objects. In the field of immanence the world is not "doubled" or "duplicated"; it is only elucidated in a way which is beyond all doubt. It is this way which goes by the name of constitution.

The very temporal character of the world thus becomes a correlate of our original time-consciousness. It is here that Husserl speaks of a "Urintentionalität". It is this original and primordial intentionality wherein all constitutional performances take place, and we ourselves as living organic centres along with world-understanding are first constituted in it.

The living immediate present with its twin comets of retention and protention makes the inner experience, the transcendental subjectivity as such, possible which in its turn explains the further constitution of a transcendent world of objects. The Husserlian sense of constitution at this level expresses the most fundamental essential relationship between the "absolute" and the "relative", and the immediate present

---

[16] Husserl's analysis of time is very similar to that of W. James who speaks of the "specious present" and maintains that it is "the original intuition of time". *The Principles of Psychology*, vol. I, p. 642.

is the only true absolute which is the "unconstituted constitutor" of all
that is.

Husserl speaks in this context of "Urevidenz" in the sense of an
original unity without any diversity. This unity, the immediate present,
is not to be contrasted with the temporal multiplicity constituted
later; it is rather the very condition of our possibility to talk of constitution at all.[17] Since it is unconstituted, it first lays bare the ground
from out of which all our various formations and articulations arise.
Phenomenology seems to take here the form of pure reflection.

Such an analysis which Husserl gives here cannot of course be said
to be completely free from all formalism. But the formalism involved
in phenomenology is eidetic in nature. At the level of phenomenological
purity of reflection the "seeing" that really matters has nothing to do
with the material content-side of the meant. What, in all concreteness,
is meant and how it is meant is the problem of genetic constitution.
The constitutional function of the immediate present expresses the
form of all constitution, namely that it is constituted.

If Husserl's phenomenology claims to have explained the material
content-side of the objects meant, then it would be surely wrong, for
that cannot be done unless he is ready to plunge all into a total
subjective creation. Husserl maintains that his transcendental phenomenology overcomes the problem of "transcendental solipsism or of
transcendental intersubjectivity".[18]

The idea of constitution is present in the phenomenology of Husserl
from the very beginning. In the "Philosophie der Arithmetik", Husserl
already tries to explain and understand the mathematical objects,
operations and entities through a constitutional analysis. The sense-
data are intentionally interpreted, and intentionality provides here
the form of analysis. Such a formal structural analysis is to be found
in the "Logische Untersuchungen" wherein Husserl tries to work out
systematically the essence and structure of intentionality. He is in fact
interested in the constitution of objectivity, and the idea of objectivity
is wider than that of logical objectivity. We find thus in his "Logical
Investigations" the "sensation-intention" schema.

The first paradigm of the constitutional philosophy of Husserl is the
constitution of objectivity, of transcendence which, of course, means
"intentum" of the acts of intention. In his lectures on time, Husserl

---

[17] L. Landgrebe: *Phänomenologie und Geschichte*, pp. 30 f.
[18] *Ideas: General Introduction to pure Phenomenology*, translated by W. R. B. Gibson, p. 18
(Husserl's own preface to the English edition).

dynamizes this formal and static concept and comes to his dynamic concept of genetic constitution. Thus the concept of constitution is formed as the phenomenological reflections develop. It now takes the form of a process and overcomes the tension present in the "Ideen" between the two schemata of "noesis-noema" and "genetic constitution". In order to explain the objectivity, Husserl now takes into account the predicative level of our encounter with the world and consequently comes to a clear-cut notion of the "Lebenswelt".

Our very brief survey of Husserl's concept of constitution has established the continuity in the constitutional analyses. It has also shown that slowly but surely the schema of formal static constitution is replaced by the concept of dynamic constitution. The concept of genetic constitution possesses greater explanatory power than that of static constitution, for it allows Husserl to comprehend the character of our life as a process better. Maybe, the later Husserl realizes more and more the character of historicity which seems to be all-pervasive.

Merleau-Ponty criticizes Husserl for the latter's having furnished an "intellectualistic" way of explanation of our knowledge. This might be partly true with regard to the formal static schema of constitution. But this criticism does not apply to the later developments in the philosophy of constitution. Added to this, the criticism of Merleau-Ponty is motivated by his greater interest in the existential and socio-political problems.

It is more appropriate to name the process of constitution by using a neutral term like "to come to be" or "to grow" which brings forth its meaning essentially and avoids successfully both the extremes of creating new meanings or reproducing just the meanings present. Such a term would also do justice to the neutrality of Husserl's "immediate present". Thus constitution means that senses and meanings "come to be" what they are; they become what they are. The phenomenological reflection can help us any time to perform the acts which are responsible for the coming to be of a particular sense. Husserl repeatedly maintains that all that can have meaning for us must have it through us. It is *in me* and *through me* that the world with all its objects becomes a meaningful world.

Husserl's constitutional analysis is the most dominating principle of explanation, understanding and justification in his search of a "first philosophy" which strives for the ideal of presuppositionlessness. Husserl hardly claims that this is the only principle of explanation. If he did, then it would be factually futile and theoretically impotent.

Sokolowski in his book on "The Formation of Husserl's Concept of Constitution" seems to think that Husserl went too far in his constitutional programme. Husserl, according to Sokolowski, wanted to establish subjectivity as the "sine qua non" for the real. Such a charge loses much of its force when we see that Husserl hardly bothers about the real which may be beyond all constitution. Nay, such a real would be phenomenologically meaningless and would mean a piece of metaphysics. Husserl might be charged with an excessive exploitation of subjectivity, but what other way is at our disposal if we strive to discover a basis which contains its own justification. Husserl never mixes up a constitutional phenomenology of reality with a metaphysical philosophy of the same. The charge brought by Sokolowski against Husserl seems to have unknowingly confused between the two.

We have already mentioned that Husserl clearly says the reality of the world cannot be put in question. That the world exists and is the universe of our common experience is beyond all doubt (ist vollkommen zweifellos). It would be futile on the part of Husserl if he maintains the consciousness to be the "sine qua non" for the real. This way of putting the problem is non-phenomenological, for the real without this constitutional contact is a myth of metaphysics.

The most critical question to be put to Husserl is: what is to be understood by the "constitution of the world"? Does it mean that consciousness creates, brings forth or produces the world? Is it not so that I can speak of the world that "it is" only in so far as it is given to us on the ground of the constitutional performances of my consciousness? We have already shown that although an interpretation of constitution as production is not totally baseless, still such an interpretation would reduce Husserl's transcendental phenomenology to some form of "psychologistic and purely subjective idealism". The transcendental phenomenology is opposed "to every form of psychologistic idealism", Husserl writes in his preface to the English edition of his "Ideas".

Merleau-Ponty sees in Husserl's analysis of constitution a lurking ambiguity – ambiguité – which consists, he maintains, in the failure of phenomenological reflection to "overtake" the world of our lived-experiences, the general thesis of our natural standpoint. The shadow of reflection, namely the world, is always a step ahead of reflection and it combats and disobeys the laws of a total production of the world through consciousness.[19] Merleau-Ponty thus concludes that the

[19] Merleau-Ponty: *Das Auge und der Geist*, pp. 45 f.

discovery of the "Lebenswelt" puts in question the theory of constitution as "creation" or "production". This conclusion would be right if we maintain that Husserl really wanted to make consciousness the creator of the world.

All constitution is constitution of meaning (Sinnstiftung); it is really the way to comprehend "something" as "something". The former "something" is not, and cannot be, produced by me; it can only be elucidated by me through the latter "something".

I cannot judge about a thing if it has the character of no-existing-for-me. To exist-for-me means that I have performed acts which bring the thing, say the picture, to givenness. And to be real means, phenomenologically speaking, to exist-for-me; and to exist-for-me means to be constituted. The philosophy of constitution aims at establishing the primacy of "noesis" over "noema", of "intention" over "intentum". The most important function of intentionality is the function of constitution, and the theory of constitution is a description of this function in different regions. All transcendences, whether of the body or of the soul, of the common objective world or of the ideal worlds, of intersubjectivity and so on, are constituted in pure consciousness. The problem of phenomenological constitution is thus the problem of reason in search of evidence. We have tried to show that the concept of constitution is a thoroughly functional concept and must not be confused with any metaphysical-idealistic construction.

We have already stated that Hume's relegating the world to fiction of imagination does not mean putting the existence of the world in question. His conviction in the existence of the world is as strong as that of Husserl. In his criticism of Descartes, Hume, very much in the spirit of Husserlian phenomenology, maintains that once the world is put to question, we shall be completely at a loss to prove its existence. Nevertheless, when Hume declares the world to be a fiction, he does so for he thinks a reason unaided by experience can only create objects and our senses, left to themselves, cannot give rise to the idea of the existence of the world. Hume is motivated to search for a new way of explaining by his thorough criticism of the unwarranted claims of both reason and experience. He speaks thus "of scepticism with regard to reason" as well as "of scepticism with regard to the senses". [20]

Our present comparison between Husserl's concept of constitution and Hume's view of imagination tries to work out and establish the following points:

[20] *Treatise*, pp. 180 f.

1. After the world is reduced to fiction, Hume like Husserl does not leave the question of how we come to believe in the existence of the world unanswered.
2. If neither reason nor senses can explain and justify the transcendence to the world we believe in, there must be some other source of transcending to the world. This source is, in the philosophy of Hume, the principle of imagination.
3. Hume's concept of imagination also suffers from ambiguity which he, of course, admits and he tries to distinguish between his own theory of imagination and the other one which is nothing else than a faculty of feigning or fancy.

The "way-in" for Hume is completed in that he declares the bankruptcy of both the sensualistic as well as rationalistic traditions. Thus arises for him the necessity of a "way-out" which enables him to regain the lost world. Hume speaks of "sceptical solutions" of his doubts. This solution consists in his bringing in the imagination to solve the problem of transcendence. The act of transcendence must be based on a sure foundation and Hume very clearly tells us that if our mind is not able to take this step on ground of reason or senses, it must be induced by some other principle of equal weight and authority.[21] What is this principle? How does it make a transcendence possible? This principle, according to Hume, is the principle of imagination.[22]

Imagination is generally equated with our fancy which produces fictions, and when Hume charges the ancient philosophers with having produced the fictions like substance, soul etc., he of course takes imagination in this sense. But his own view of imagination has nothing to do with the production of fictions for it expresses the "vivacity of ideas". It is the same type of vivacity which accompanies our impressions. Hume very clearly says that "without this quality, by which the mind enlivens some ideas beyond others, we could never assent to any argument, nor carry our view beyond those few objects, which are present to our senses. ... The memory, senses and understanding are, therefore, all of them founded on the imagination, or vivacity of our ideas".[23]

Thus the principle of imagination is invoked in the philosophy of

---

[21] *Enquiries*, pp. 41 f.

[22] Most of the interpreters of Hume – including Husserl – have failed to see the central role played by imagination in the philosophy of Hume.

[23] *Treatise*, p. 265.

Hume not with regard to the fictions, but with regard to the act of belief restoring the lost world. The working of imagination, according to Hume, is as universal as human nature itself. While distinguishing his own concept of imagination from the unsteady imagination, Hume comes to characterize imagination as possessing "the principles which are permanent, irresistible, and universal".[24] The other imagination which does not possess universality and which does harm to philosophy is characterized by Hume to be "changeable, weak and irregular". The foundation of all our thought and action is the imagination in the former sense.

After fixing the nature of his own imagination as nonfictional, Hume goes on to distinguish between "fiction" and "belief". And the world is believed in. Hume asks: "Wherein, therefore, consists the difference between such a fiction and belief?" Hume answers this question in the following way: the distinction between fiction and belief lies in some sentiment or feeling which is attached to the latter and not to the former.[25] Due to the universal qualities possessed by imagination, it "founds" the objectivity of the world. The world is now no longer a world of fiction; it is a world which is believed in and which is the performance of imagination.

The point we want to emphasize here is not so much that Hume's concept of imagination, as interpreted here, has foreshadowed Husserl's concept of constitution, but that the role of imagination in the programme of Hume's philosophy is more or less similar to the role played by the concept of constitution in the philosophy of Husserl. Like Husserl's constitution, the imagination of Hume paves the way towards transcendence which is now no longer unfounded and dogmatic. Like Husserl's constitution, the imagination of Hume does not "produce" the world; it rather shows the way we come to believe in it. Not only the world we believe in is the performance of our imagination, but the other persons are also brought to an immediate awareness through imagination. The idea of the other is converted by the imagination into an impression. "The mind", Hume writes, "passes easily from the idea of ourselves to that of any other object related to us". We are never "solus ipse", for "ourself, independent of the perception of every other object,[26] is in reality nothing".[27] The other is constituted in and through me.

---

[24] *Ibid.*, p. 225.
[25] *Enquiries*, pp. 47 f.
[26] Hume means by "object" here also our perception of other persons.
[27] *Treatise*, pp. 340 f.

CHAPTER VII

THE CONCEPT OF THE "LEBENS WELT" AND THE "EXTERNAL WORLD" OF HUME

Husserl's concept of the "Lebenswelt" (life-world) is to be found implicitly in his theory of the "general thesis" (Generalthesis) of the natural standpoint. But a real terminological fixation along with a conceptual clarification takes place late in the writings of Husserl. "Lebenswelt", as would be seen, includes all the objects, persons and events which we encounter in our experience. All the different worlds divided in regions are appearing as figures at the background of one common life-world. The objects are surrounded by a field which refers to other objects.[1]

The life-world as one world common to all of us seems to have a twofold characteristic: it is immanent in the various worlds, but yet it transcends them all.[2]

The method of reduction opened up a realm of pure experience consisting of constitutional acts of our intentionality. This reduction also helped Husserl to find the solution to his problem of the foundation, the very central mission of Husserl's phenomenology. This leads Husserl to his "first philosophy" in the sense of a philosophy of fundamental principles. The term "first philosophy" at this level expresses what we understand in phenomenology by experience in a non-empirical sense of pure intentionality. It is this phenomenology which is called "radical" in the true sense of the term.

But reduction also shows that our consciousness is essentially

[1] It was the American psychologist and philosopher W. James who in his *The Principles of Psychology* very clearly pointed out that the objects of experience are not isolated impressions as the sensualistic empiricism maintained. The objects as we experience them in our actual perceptions are surrounded by a field of meanings which refer them to other objects. These references are generally forgotten. James called them "fringes". Developed consequently and interpreted phenomenologically, this notion of the "fringes" leads roughly to the Husserlian concept of the "Lebenswelt". *The Principles of Psychology*, pp. 258; 281 f.; 471 f.

[2] J. Wild: *Existence and the World of Freedom*, p. 46 f.

related to the world we live in. The field of our lived-experiences populating our life-world is not brought forth or created after the performance
of reduction; it is always there and reduction makes the importance
of the life-world clear. All that happens is that we now see and live this
world of experience in its meaning. To see the life-world in its meaning
means that it is constituted in a higher experience which is nothing
else but the constituting consciousness. The life-world is not foreign
to the phenomenological reflection; it is rather the manifestation in
which the transcendental phenomenology of Husserl culminates. To
discover the constituting performances of the transcendental subjectivity means to lay bare the ways in which the life-world is constituted.

The concept of the life-world reaches its terminological fixation
clearly in his "Erfahrung und Urteil" and "Krisis". Although the
origin of the idea of the life-world may be traced back to the "Ideen"
wherein Husserl speaks of working out the concept of a natural world,
still the life-world is systematically thematized mainly in the above
mentioned two books of Husserl. The life-world, considered systematically, represents the opposite pole of the so-called objective world of
the sciences. It is the pre-scientific world (vorwissenschaftliche) and
is the foundation of the objective world of the sciences. Irrespective of
the polarity – pre-scientific and the scientific world –, the life-world
is nothing but the most common world appearing to us phenomenologically. And this is the only world we can meaningfully speak of.

Husserl's phenomenology does not create the life-world; it only
founds it radically by discovering the transcendental dimension
wherein it is rooted. The life-world is not only founded transcendentally, but it also founds the world of objective science. Thus there is a
twofold sense of foundation with regard to the life-world.

The life-world, according to Husserl, is the most familiar natural
field of all our actions and thoughts. It is the stage of all our performances, theoretical as well as practical. It is given to us as a
universal field.[3] This universal field means the universal horizon
capable of endless extension. To live is to live already and always in a
life-world. One of the main lines of argument of Husserl's "Krisis" is
its attempt to show that, as over against the dominant tradition of
Western thought, it is the pre-scientific, pre-predicative horizon of the
life-world which is prior to all constructions of the objective sciences

[3] *Krisis*, pp. 145 f.

and is more comprehensive. Such an understanding of the concept of the life-world is corroborated by the independent researches of such thinkers as James, Hume, Merleau-Ponty, Heidegger who all have their own points of departure. The phenomenological investigations of the "Krisis" deal with and discuss the problem of the life-world in relation to its fundamental structures by emphasizing the role played by kinetics. [4]

The life-world is pre-scientific for it is there prior to all theoretical scientific activities; it is the basic premise. Husserl recognizes this life-world as the universal horizon in which we ourselves, our acts and our intentions with all their manifold ramifications have their being. It is in this universal horizon that all the different types of beings appear. It is one and the same world differing in its various modes of givenness.

We all, as scientists or laymen, live in this life-world, and all our diverse questions are put to it. Husserl speaks of the life-world as the "forgotten sense-foundation of natural science" (vergessenes Sinnes-fundament der Naturwissenschaft). [5] Husserl investigates here the so-called "Selbstverständlichkeiten" of Galilei in his "mathematization" of nature. In his criticism of Kant, Husserl speaks of the life-world as the implicit presupposition of Kant's philosophy. [6] The life-world is the most concrete and the most common point of reference. This world has its own unknown structures which are discovered by means of concrete scientific researches. [7]

The very concept of our scientific induction, Husserl tells us, is rooted in the pre-scientific "inductivity" of the life-world. This is what Husserl terms as our "day-to-day induction". [8] He also speaks of a style of causality (Kausalstil) which is a characteristic of the life-world. Our life-world is the realm of evidence which is more original. [9] The life-world is the world immediately present to us, and all our lived-acts, intentions and objects in it are no constructions of a scientific method. The essence of our life-world is thus to be sharply distinguished from the beings whose appearances are just made possible within this life-world; it is a unique world of our lived-experiences and can never be

---

[4] *Ibid.*, §§ 28 and 45–48.
[5] *Krisis*, p. 48.
[6] *Ibid.*, p. 105.
[7] *Ibid.*, pp. 50 f.
[8] *Ibid.*, p. 50. ("Aus der alltäglichen Induktion wurde so freilich die Induktion nach wissenschaftlicher Methode")
[9] *Ibid.*, p. 130.

completely concretely worked out into a set pattern with fixed principles. There seems to be a relationship of "figure" and "ground" between
all our different worlds, including the ideal worlds, and our life-world.
The life-world is the basic world of all our experiences. As the premise
of all our experiences, it is not an object of experience among other
objects. The life-world is the unmoving ground, basis of all our knowledge regarding the movement of our earth. The earth does not move
to our immediate experience; the knowledge that it rotates stems not
from our immediate experience, but from our scientific explorations.
Husserl thus speaks of a "turning round" of "Copernican revolution"
which consists in the insight that all our experiences necessarily presuppose an unmoving ground.

Husserl distinguishes between the life-world and the so-called
"objective world" constructed by the sciences through idealization
and mathematization of nature. The worlds of the different sciences
are ideal constructions and require the life-world as the model-giving
base.[10] The facts populating the life-world are different from the
scientific facts. Whereas the facts of our life-world are immediately
present to us and are given directly to our immediate consciousness,
the scientific facts remain abstract constructions and can be understood
only when we follow the methodological dictates of those sciences.

One of the most intriguing passages in Husserl's "Krisis"[11] is the
passage wherein he discusses the problem of the relativity of the different
worlds, say the world of the Chinese, of the Indians and of the Europeans. All these different worlds are lived by them and consist of lived
experiences. None can be relegated to a sheer abstraction. It is here
that the concept of the life-world as the world common to all of us shows
its weakness. This weakness consists in our not being able to relegate
any of the worlds counted above to a fiction or to a purely private
world. Is then the life-world common to all of us itself a fiction in the
sense that we hardly meet it in our life? It is difficult to answer this
question in the affirmative without doing violence to the spirit of
Husserlian phenomenology. Husserl of course knows and admits that
our worlds differ in so far as we all have our own points of departure
conditioned differently. But when questions are asked regarding the
fictional or non-fictional character of this or that particular world, of
this or that particular culture, these questions themselves are not put

[10] *Krisis*, p. 132. (Husserl hardly shows anywhere how we could distinguish at such a level
between illusion and reality).
[11] *Krisis*, pp. 141 f.

and asked within the limited horizon of any one of the particular worlds. They are asked within the universal field of our common discourse.

It is wrong to maintain that we can arrive at such a universal field by way of abstraction or generalization. This world of common discourse is prior to all such processes and is presupposed by the different worlds belonging to different historico-cultural surroundings. It is truer if we understand the life-world as an accomplishment of a particular situation of our consciousness.[12] Thus the life-world is not just the raw world of uncultivated nature; it is rather the world as shaped and worked out by all of us.[13] The different worlds of the Chinese, Indians and Europeans appear as figures at the background of the universal field of common discourse.

A fictional analysis of the life-world fails to take into account the most important fact that all the different worlds themselves presuppose an unmoving base as the common ground making all our communication possible. It is true that we are objects among other objects within this life-world. But when Husserl speaks of the constitution of the life-world, he brings in his concept of the constituting ego which is an instance of pure theoretical reflection. The disinterested onlooker (der uninteressierte Zuschauer) cannot be hypostatized.

The life-world, as we have already seen, has been superseded under the influence of the modern science inaugurated by Galileo. That which passes by the name of objectivity in the natural objective science is nothing but "superstructure" built on and in the life-world; it is a tissue of ideal constructions. Husserl speaks of "Ideenkleid" in this context. The world of the natural mathematical sciences is a theoretico-logical construction which is, unlike our life-world, given neither to direct experience nor to any other forms of immediate awareness. Husserl repeatedly and rightly tells us that the construction of the universe of objective science involves mental performances, certain specific operations.

Since the life-world is pre-given and is prior to all activities, the universe of objective science requires the life-world in order to get an ultimate clarification. The life-world is the unquestioned presupposition of all scientific practices; our tools used in our experiments form part of our life-world. The concept of the life-world does not include only the actual mundane existence; it is rather the world continually

---

[12] G. Funke: *Phänomenologie – Metaphysik oder Methode?* pp. 140 f.
[13] L. Landgrebe: *Der Weg der Phänomenologie*, p. 49.

present to our experience, and all the different worlds, actual as well as possible, real as well as ideal, are relative to this life-world. When we speak of "nature", "bodies" and so on within our life-world, we do not mean the idealized and formalized nature of the objective sciences but the nature given in direct and immediate experience.

The term "nature" as used here seems to have a threefold meaning: nature of the objective science not given to our immediate experience; nature as given to our immediate experience in our life-world and nature as the structure of passivity of our constituting transcendental subjectivity. Husserl speaks in this context of a "Naturseite" of our transcendental subjectivity.[14]

The life-world is always one and this is an unquestioned foundation of our common experience. The possibility of our communication needs the life-world as the most common field of our discourse.[15]

The life-world is not non-historical; it possesses a historical connotation. The life-world is also relative to a certain society at a given time; it has its own history. It is this historical nature of the life-world which explains the differences between the world of a mythico-magical society and that of our modern society. As mundane existences we are part of the life-world, and this points to a type of naturality which expresses the pre-reductive character of this judgment. But we are also subject with respect to the life-world. It derives its meaning from our collective social mental life. The society of "egos" in their communicative relationship is the absolute foundation of the world.[16]

Our life-world is thus a collective accomplishment and comprises all our diverse cultural products. The life-world is not something static; it is no entity beyond all change and modification. In and through the interplay of our activities it undergoes modification. It is a "geistiger Erwerb" of the different egos in their community. Thus the life-world is historical in character and is dynamically relative to the living community.

In speaking of science as a cultural accomplishment within the realm of the life-world, Husserl mentions the concept of a "practice of theorizing" (theoretische Praxis) which does not differ in principle with the productions of other cultural activities. Since the life-world is the world to which all other worlds are relative, Husserl's phenome-

---

[14] *E.P. II*, p. 506.
[15] A. Gurwitsch: The last Work of Edmund Husserl, *Phil. and pheno. Research*, vol. XVI, pp. 372 f.
[16] *E.P. II*, p. 506.

nological analyses clearly show the hypothetical character of the universe of science as a superstructure built on the universe of our life.

The age-old dogma of the traditional Western philosophy going back to the Greeks is: real scientific knowledge is objective and all other types of knowledge are knowledge just by proxy; in truth, they are opinions and beliefs. Such an assessment of knowledge underrated the importance of the life-world. The life-world was neglected and decried as merely "subjective-relative". This is why there were hardly any attempts to explore our life-world seriously and scientifically. Such a forgetfulness of the life-world is one of the main reasons of the crisis of our modern sciences, Husserl maintains.[17]

Since the life-world is no ideal construction it is hard to thematize it within the methodological sphere of objective science. For the methodology of objective science our life-world is too "opaque" and Husserl realizes this very well. For a systematic exploration of the life-world the phenomenological method of description is the most suitable.

The problem of the life-world, in its wider connotation, includes not only a description of what it is, but also an exploration and a scientific investigation into its invariant structures. Such an investigation results in working out a science of the life-world (Wissenschaft der Lebenswelt). Our exploration with regard to the invariant structures of the life-world really points to the problem of an a priori of the life-world (lebensweltliches Apriori).[18] When Husserl mentions the concept of a science of the life-world, he does not of course mean science of Galilean style in which the life-world would be decried as a purely subjective construction. The science of the life-world aims at working out the constituting moments of the society of our constituting egos.

In order to reach such a systematic exploration of the life-world, we need to perform first of all an "Epoché" concerning the whole field of "objective science". This of course does not mean ignoring the importance of the objective science. The scientific achievements are not denied and while performing such an "Epoché" we do remain interested in the universe of science. All that we aim at is the suspension of this world; we no longer participate in it actively. We refrain from being involved in it. Thus we reach the attitude of "disinterestedness" (Uninteressiertheit) which is no callous indifference. The truth of ob-

---

[17] It is interesting to note that Hume, too, repents the neglection of the problem of the external world. Not only that, philosophers did not think the external world to be an object of any serious scientific exploration. This is why the character of belief remained a mystery to the philosopher who wrongly relegated it to the field of "subjective-relative".

[18] L. Landgrebe: *Phänomenologie und Geschichte*, pp. 148 f.

jective science is not put in question; in the "Epoché", we simply take it for granted. The "Epoché" really puts the very idea of scientific objectivity out of play. Such a practice thus opens the way to work out the idea of objectivity as the performance (Leistung) of the communicative life of transcendental subjectivities.

Such an "Epoché" with regard to the universe of objective science makes it possible that we face the life-world as we experience it within the historico-cultural frame of reality.

In order to work out a science of the life-world we have to show that it is an accomplishment of our constituting subjectivity. The problem of the constitution of the life-world stands in the centre of the phenomenology of Husserl. But our attempt at the constitution of the life-world is beset with troubles. We have already mentioned the pre-reductive character of the naturality which is essential to the life-world. We would hardly ever succeed concretely to reduce the world of our life. But this does not stand in our way, Husserl would tell us, of showing the transcendental-genetic constitution of the life-world. Although such a science of the life-world would not be of Galilean style, still it must admit of certain objective norms, i.e. it must have an objective validity and so on. But this seems hardly possible; it seems also incompatible with the above mentioned historical relativity of the life-world. The different communities are not constituting an identical life-world. The life-world is and remains the last presupposition of all our thoughts and actions. Nevertheless, Husserl strongly maintains that the world we speak and could ever speak of is the world we constitute in the immanence of our socialized life of consciousness.[19]

The difficulty with regard to the science of the life-world must not mislead us. Notwithstanding the relativity, the historical character of the life-world, it of course shows certain invariant structures which may provide us with the framework of such a science.[20] It is this framework of invariant structures within which all the changes, modifications, corrections etc. take place.

The life-world is experienced, prior to all scientific judgments, as "extended" in space and in time. The experienced space and time are not the constructed concepts of objective science; they are given directly. We encounter in the life-world corporeal things, bodies which

---

[19] "Die Welt, von der wir reden und je reden können, von der wir wissen und je wissen können, ist doch keine andere als eben diejenige, die wir in der Immanenz unseres eigenen, einzelnen und vergemeinschafteten Bewußtseinslebens ... konstituieren." *E.P.* I, p. 277.

[20] Husserl presents it as a task to be accomplished, and he does not claim to have worked out such a science fully.

are not the defined bodies of the natural sciences. We have already noted that the life-world shows its own causal style which is character-ised by a typical uniformity, regularity. It has its own "habits" and "habitual forms" of behaviour. The things of the life-world behave similarly under similar circumstances. Another invariant structure of the life-world is its native inductivity which works as the premise for the further development and construction of our infinite scientific induction.

The life-world which shows all these invariant structures is of course all the time "hidden" to us. No cancellation cancels the "it" of the world which must be there as the basis of all cancellations. Husserl says that the life-world is naturally given to all of us as persons within the horizon of our fellow-beings, that means, it is present in each and every connection, communication and relation we have with our fellow human beings. It is present to us as "the" (die) world.[21] It is the most common world presupposed by all the life-worlds differing from society to society, from culture to culture. The life-world is not a world among the other worlds; it is the premise of all of them. Nevertheless, it is difficult to maintain that the idea of science of the life-world can be free from all formalism and abstraction.

The idea of a science of the life-world points in fact to the most radical point of termination in our phenomenological search for an ultimate realm. This realm is the transcendental subjectivity which in its "Tiefendimensionen" constitutes the world.[22] But the phenome-nological reflection does not divide the world into two: the empirical-natural and the transcendental-genetic. All that it does is to compre-hend and elucidate the empirical-natural transcendentally. In other words, this means that the world we live in forms itself in the genesis of the transcendental ego. Thus there is no dualism in the phenome-nology of Husserl. There is no duality of human nature either, for there are no two types of men: one sensuous and the other pure. The reflection teaches us further that man is a "transcendental I" and all the psycho-physical processes and occurrences like stimuli, affections, kinesthesia, impressions, perceptions, acts of will, acts of thought etc. are the transcendental functions. In the "Krisis", Husserl clearly speaks of the identity between the "empirical I" and the transcen-dental one.[23]

---

[21] *Krisis*, p. 124.
[22] L. Landgrebe: *Phänomenologie und Geschichte*, pp. 148 f.
[23] *Krisis*, p. 209.

In his "Krisis", Husserl proposes to work out a science of the life-world, and he speaks of an "exposition of the problem of the science of the life-world". Such a science, he further tells us, can be thematized in a twofold way: the life-world can be explored as a partial problem within the general problem of the objective science and it can also be thematized independently in the sense of a universal problem of philosophy. [24] Husserl himself is more in favour of the latter way of thematizing the life-world.

One could as well invoke the help of the method of the imaginative variation, eidetic variation (eidetische Variation) in order to explore the general structures of the life-world. This method consists in freely imagining diverse possible life-worlds. We are not limited to a particular life-world, although we have to start from some particular life-world. The question whether these possible imagined worlds freely lose their historical character is out of point here for it does not touch the core of our practice. All that we want to arrive at is the working out of a common core which remains unchanged in all of these imagined worlds. We want to know what essentially and necessarily pertains to the life-world as such. It is in this context that Husserl speaks of an "ontology of the life-world" which is radically different from the ontologies of philosophical traditions. This ontology is to be understood as a possible world of intersubjective experience, as a world which can in no circumstances be impossible. The structures and the common characteristics discovered by such an ontology of the life-world hold true to all the various life-worlds, no matter how the latter differ in their historico-cultural set-up. Husserl has pointed out the possibility of such a discipline without exploring it in details.

Our brief exposition of the concept of the life-world has made its relation to the objective world of science clear. The life-world serves as the foundation for the scientific world. The only justification our concept of empirical induction possesses lies in the inductive style of the life-world. [25] How far does the science along with its various activities stem from this pre-scientific style of the life-world and how far does it serve the purposes lying within the life-world? In what particular way is the scientific world to be traced back to the life-world?

All practice, Husserl tells us, implies induction. The induction as practised in the objective sciences is a methodologically purified and

[24] *Ibid.*, pp. 133 f.
[25] *Krisis*, p. 449.

idealized form of the induction to be found in the life-world. [26] Although the achievements of the modern objective sciences seem to have changed our idea of the world by absolutizing its own constructed world, still all these achievements "stream in" (einströmen) the life-world. [27] The life-world is thus shared even by the scientists who first bring out the concept of an exact objective world of science. The crisis Husserl talks of in his book of the same name consists in the failure of the modern objective sciences to see that the world constructed by them represents a "hypothesis". It is wrong to absolutize this world and maintain it to be the only real objective world. Husserl criticizes the concept of objectivity implied in the modern natural and mathematical sciences. Husserl in criticizing the objective sciences really criticizes their conviction that the only objectively real world is the world of the objective science. [28] It is their conviction of autonomy which is criticized by Husserl.

The overcoming of this crisis represents, according to Husserl, a task to establish the original right of the life-world in its relation to the constructed world of the objective sciences. The objective logical evidence has to be traced back to the evidence of the original experience which consists in the character of the life-world as given to us immediately prior to all theoretico-scientific activities, constructions, idealizations and so forth. The model-character of all our scientific theories points to the life-world as the field of all actual as well as possible confirmations. The principle of "falsification", to use Popperian terminology, reigns supreme only in the field of natural sciences; but in the life-world there is the principle of verification through evidence, givenness.

The idea of a science of the life-world, first introduced in the "Krisis" as a postulate, culminates in the science of the transcendental subjectivity which works out its own world-constituting performances (Leistungen). [29] The universe of true being is inseparably related to the universe of possible consciousness. Husserl speaks of the "concretion of the transcendental subjectivity" in relation to the constitution of the world. [30]

---

[26] *Ibid.*, p. 449.
[27] *Ibid.*, pp. 134 and 446.
[28] *Krisis*, p. 127.
[29] L. Landgrebe: *Phänomenologie und Geschichte*, p. 156.
[30] "Das Universum wahren Seins fassen zu wollen als etwas, das außerhalb des Universums möglichen Bewußtseins ... steht, ... ist unsinnig. Wesensmäßig gehört beides zusammen, und wesensmäßig Zugehöriges ist auch konkret eins, eins in der einzigen absoluten Konkretion der transzendentalen Subjektivität." C.M. p. 117.

The fundamental philosophical importance of the life-world cannot be grasped if we remain within the fixed static schema "life-world – objective world of the sciences". It evades such a schema and Husserl himself admits it in his "Krisis".[31]

Hume, while giving a justification for the belief of the vulgar theory of consciousness in the independent existence of the external world, comes very near to the discovery of the relational and horizon-character of all our perception and experience. He takes the example of a letter he gets from his friend who lives far away from him and wants to show that the objects of our perception and experience are not isolated impressions. One object of perception points to the other one and so on. "'Tis evident", Hume writes" I can never account for this phenomenon (the man carrying the letter to him from his friend), conformable to my past experience in other instances, *without spreading out*[32] in my mind the whole sea and the continent between, and supposing the effects and continu'd existence of posts and ferries, ...".[33] Interpreted phenomenologically, this leads us to see the character of the world as an endless horizon. Mere perceptions, Hume maintains, are not themselves the ground of any inference with regard to the continued existence of the world. Our consciousness bestows on the objects perceived a greater regularity, and it is the principle of imagination which is at work in an "oblique manner".[34]

Objects do possess a certain degree of coherence even as they appear to the senses. "But this coherence is much greater and more uniform, if we suppose the objects to have a continued existence".[35] Human nature is active in forming the world through its guiding principles.

We have already noticed that Hume never doubts the existence of the world. The problem is not, he says, whether there is a world or not, for that is a point we must take for granted in all our reasonings and actions. The philosophical problem with regard to the world common to all of us is to show how we come to believe in the world. The naivity of the common sense must be philosophically explained, elucidated and justified.

The external world is taken for granted as the most fundamental basis of our common experience. Like the world of Husserl's natural standpoint, it is the one world common to all of us. It exists prior to

[31] *Krisis*, § 34, e) and f).
[32] italicized by the author.
[33] *Treatise*, pp. 196 f.
[34] *Ibid.*, p. 197.
[35] *Ibid.*, p. 198.

all theoretical considerations. No scepticism, not even the most excessive Pyrrhonian type, can successfully doubt the existence of the world.[36] There is nothing like total scepticism, and whoever has taken the pains to refute such a scepticism has really disputed without an antagonist.

Like Husserl, Hume too maintains that prior to all reasonings we do suppose a world as existing continually and as one which is common to all of us. He also maintains like Husserl that structures exhibited by this world are not as "perfect" as the categories of our objective sciences. But still this world possesses its own habits, and the constancy, coherency, regularity etc. are the typical ways of our common world.[37]

The existence of the one common world can never be called in question, Hume always emphasizes. Like Husserl, he maintains that it is our most familiar world. Not only Husserl, but Hume too points to the pre-given character of this world. Our reasoning, Hume tells us, neither establishes it nor destroys it.[38]

The character of inductiveness which Husserl takes to be one of the invariant structures of the life-world, is also admitted by Hume. Hume speaks in this context of a negative tendency which leads us to think that under similar circumstances things behave similarly. The induction exhibited in the world is not as perfect as the one to be found in the universe of science. The character of abstraction and idealization implied in the practice of the objective sciences is recognized by Hume.

As emphatically as Husserl, Hume takes the history of philosophy to task in that he charges it with having completely neglected the most important problem of our belief in the world. Nobody ever thought it worth the trouble to explore the world scientifically. This world we live in, Husserl maintains, must be studied from the radical point of view which lays bare the correlative character of the world. Hume, in his own way, comes to the conclusion that only the different principles of human nature e.g. custom, habit, belief, imagination etc. can give a true foundation and explanation of the world we believe in.[39] Like Husserl, Hume also is against any attempt to relegate the world of belief (Doxa) to the field of mere subjectivism and relativism. Hume very clearly tells us the ancient and the modern philosophers, just by consulting their fancy, have erected systems and created fictions like substance, golden age, state of nature, etc.

[36] *Treatise*, pp. 180 f.
[37] *Ibid.*, p. 195.
[38] *Ibid.*, pp. 187 f.
[39] R. A. Mall: *Hume's Concept of Man*, chap. on "Imagination".

When Hume demands a systematic scientific exploration of the problem of the world he too does not mean to undertake it in the Galilean style. The bodies, things and other objects in and of the world we experience and live in are not the results of abstraction as is the case with objective sciences.

Hume speaks of "the chief objection against all 'abstract' reasonings" and he takes the case of space and time. These ideas which are experienced by us clearly in common life seem to lead to "absurdity and contradiction" when "they pass the scrutiny of the profound sciences". [40] Hume also is of the opinion that the world of objective science is a constructed one and can be traced back ultimately to the world we experience in common life. The ideas of mathematics are clear and determinate, but they have their own difficulty. [41] The world we experience in common life possesses the character of givenness in and to our experience in opposition to the objects of the abstract sciences which are the results of abstractions and idealizations.

In the opening pages of his "Enquiry concerning Human Understanding", Hume contrasts "the easy and obvious philosophy" with "the accurate and abstruse" and warns against losing all contacts with common sense. This warning of Hume consists in the following words: "Indulge your passion for science, ..., but let your science be human, and such as may have a direct reference to action and society. Abstruse thought and profound researches I (Hume personifies nature here) prohibit, and will severely punish, by the pensive melancholy which they introduce, by the endless uncertainty in which they involve you .... Be a philosopher; but, amidst all your philosophy, be still a man". [42] The real import of the warning contained in these words of Hume hints at the "crisis of the European sciences" of which Husserl speaks in his "Krisis". Hume too, in his own way, is a critic of the conviction of the abstract sciences of autonomy.

Like Husserl's science of the life-world which ends in working out the constituting functions of the transcendental subjectivity, a scientific exploration of the problem of the world, in the philosophy of Hume, points to the most fundamental science of human nature which consists in working out the guiding principles of human nature.

---

[40] *Enquiries*, pp. 156 f. "Whatever disputes there may be about mathematical points, we must allow", Hume writes, "that there are physical points; that is, parts of extension, which cannot be divided or lessened, either by the eye or imagination." *Ibid.*, p. 156 (foote-note).

[41] *Enquiries*, pp. 61 f.

[42] *Ibid.*, p. 9.

CHAPTER VIII

THE SCIENCE OF TRANSCENDENTAL
SUBJECTIVITY AND OF HUMAN NATURE

Husserl is one of the very few philosophers who know no end in the process of radical self-criticism. The ideal of the philosopher is very high and Husserl is convinced to have reached a beginning in his old age, as he writes in his preface to the English edition of his "Ideas".[1]

Phenomenon, in phenomenology, means that which gives itself; it is the "Selbstgebung". The science of phenomenology is a science of phenomena in this sense. The radical phenomenological analysis with all its tedious and painstaking investigations aims at reaching an absolute evidence in the sense of pure givenness. Such an absolute world of givenness justifies itself, presented as the most primary and original experience. We have already mentioned that such an absolute is the transcendental subjectivity itself which needs nothing outside itself to found it; it rather founds everything. What Husserl's phenomenology in the name of a strict science of philosophy wants to achieve is nothing else but the most radical source of apodicticity. It is this instance of apodictic givenness which gives to all activities – scientific or otherwise – their meaning.

The radical method of phenomenological reduction discovers thus neither a psychologistic nor a metaphysical entity; it rather opens up a new field of serious research: the transcendental field. Descriptive phenomenology culminates in transcendental phenomenology.

What Husserl calls his "transcendental-phenomenological idealism" is opposed not only to every form of psychologistic idealism, but also to the traditional forms of idealism and realism. Husserl tells us in his own preface to the English edition of his "Ideas" that every form of current philosophical realism is in principle absurd.[2] Given a deeper understanding of his exposition, one could easily see that Husserl is

[1] *Ideas – General Introduction to Pure Phenomenology*, translated by W. R. B. Gibson, p. 28.
[2] *Ibid.*, pp. 19 f.

giving us a piece of pure self-reflection revealing original self-evident facts. The result of such a self-reflection is that the only absolute worth the name is the transcendental subjectivity. It is the only non-relative which contains its own justification. The world which no doubt exists and can never be put in question is relative in respect of essence to transcendental subjectivity. It is in the transcendental experience (the self-experience of the transcendental subjectivity) that the world gets its meaning as existing reality in the form of an intentional meaning-product of the transcendental subjectivity. Even the "transcendental society of ourselves", Husserl writes, "reveals itself" within my own life of transcendental consciousness. [3]

For Husserl, the transcendental subjectivity is the basis of all performances (Leistungen) which are from their very nature intentional-relational. In his search for such a basis, Husserl discovers in his "Erste Philosophie" the transcendental subjectivity as his absolute starting point. It is the field of absolute experience. The mundane experience is not absolute for it lacks apodictic certainty, i.e., it lacks absolute givenness. Husserl thus maintains that our world-belief (Weltglaube) is nothing else but a "universal preconception of positivity" (universales Vorurteil der Positivität). [4]

What Husserl really understands by this experience of the transcendental subjectivity must be the self-experience. The transcendental subjectivity is a field of our life, of our "I am" (ich bin). As "solus ipse" it does not imply solipsism, for Husserl speaks of an "Urintentionalität" whose constitutional performances and achievements remain "anonymous" (anonym). We need the most radical phenomenological reflection (the transcendental reduction) in order to come to a radical self-reflection (Selbstbesinning) which means the most radical form of self-understanding. This self-understanding is, thanks to the performances of the constitutional intentionality, at the same time a world-understanding.

The absoluteness of the transcendental subjectivity consists in its character of self-sufficiency. This means that the world of things and beings needs consciousness and not vice-versa. Self-sufficiency is also the character of absolute givenness.

The Husserlian criticism of mundane experience (mundane Erfahrung) is the way which leads him to the discovery of the transcendental experience, of the transcendental subjectivity. Any natural

[3] *Ibid.*, pp. 21–22.
[4] *E.P.* p. 461.

psychological reflection moves always within the field of a mundane experience, and such a self-experience presents us always with an "empirical-natural I" (empirisch-natürliches Ich).[5] The discovery of the transcendental field means thus the discovery of the transcendental subjectivity which founds the whole realm of our mundane life-experience. Phenomenological research aiming at an absolute realm of all constitution eliminates the contingent field of mundane experience. The Husserlian criticism of mundane experience is thus the function of uncovering the richer life of our transcendental subjectivity hidden from our natural attitude.[6] Husserl speaks in this context of the "field of a transcendental experience as the theme of a transcendental criticism" (das Feld der transzendentalen Erfahrung als Thema einer transzendentalen Kritik).[7]

But Husserl speaks of another way which leads directly to the field of transcendental experience. This direct approach consists in discovering the transcendental subjectivity from the thought-point of view. This point of view consists in asking the question: Is there any form of experience which is apodictic and which is presupposed everywhere? This presupposition is nothing else but the transcendental experience itself.[8]

The field of transcendental experience Husserl here speaks of is no experience in the sense of the traditional psychology. Husserl never forgets to distinguish over and over again between the "Menschen-ich" and the "transcendental-Ich" meaning thereby our psychological and transcendental ego respectively. It is the latter "I" which is the object of our transcendental experience. The transcendental "I" is in fact a "Ur-ich" which can never be the object of any reflective psychological experience. One must discover the transcendental subjectivity as the field of apodicticity, as the most original field of all performances. This discovery takes place, in the first instance, for one's own self which means "living" the infinite richness of "philosophical solitude" (philosophische Einsamkeit). For such a discovery, we need a special method freeing us from the bondage of our experience at the attached level of our natural standpoint.[9] Unless we put the mundane level of experience out of play, unless we eliminate it, we cannot discover our transcendental subjectivity as the most radical and solid ground of

---

[5] *Ibid.*, p. 78.
[6] L. Landgrebe: *Der Weg der Phänomenologie*, p. 178.
[7] *E.P.*, pp. 75 f.
[8] *Ibid.*, pp. 312–13.
[9] *Ibid.*, pp. 79 f.

all elucidations, explanations and understanding. The mundane experience naively points to the world and operates in it without ever even mentioning the question of "founding" it. The transcendental subjectivity is understood by Husserl in this context as a type of "irreality" (Irrealität) which constitutes all reality. It goes without saying that the "irreality" as used here stands for our transcendental subjectivity, whereas the "reality" means our normal world-experience at the naive natural standpoint. Husserl has already pointed out the "unnatural" character of his phenomenological reduction. For a man involved in the natural attitude the whole field of transcendental subjectivity must appear, to begin with, irreal.

In the most strict sense when there *is* nothing existing for me, I am able to catch hold of my own subjectivity as that "irreality" which founds (and is presupposed by) all reality.[10] Even Kant, according to Husserl, remained subject to an anthropologism and psychologism.[11]

All the painstaking researches of Husserl aim at working out a science of this transcendental subjectivity. Husserl really "works out" such a science and does not "posit" or translate the life of an existing entity. All that Husserl's "science of the transcendental subjectivity" (Wissenschaft von der transzendentalen Subjektivität) may comprise is the pure description of the field of the transcendental experience as specified and presented above. It is a pure description of the constituting life of the transcendental subjectivity. Husserl does not seem to be very sure of the concrete possibility of such a science from the very beginning, for he hardly mentions the possibility of such a discipline in his "Ideen".[12]

The transcendental subjectivity as the realm of all foundations can be understood as the basis of all performances; and a science of it would thus consist in describing these intentional performances (intentionale Leistungen). Wherein consists the life of the transcendental subjectivity? It must consist in acts of constitution, for it is the performer of all acts and the giver of all sense to the world. Although the transcendental subjectivity is known to us in and through the constitutional performances, still as the last apodictic realm of all constitution it is not itself "constituted" in the same sense. Is there then an "auto-constitution" of the transcendental subjectivity? Husserl must admit such a type of self-constitution of the transcendental subjectivity. Such a

[10] *E.P. II*, p. 79.
[11] *E.P. I*, pp. 354 f.
[12] *Ideen I*, p. 175.

self-constitution really takes place within the pure realm of our "living immediate present" (lebendig strömende Gegenwart) with its twin tails of "retention" and "protention". But the trancendental subjectivity of Husserl must not be confused or confounded with something unknown and unknowable, say, with "noumenon" or with any other occult metaphysical entity. [13] It is rather the most concrete instance for it is "lived" and experienced most apodictically, intimately and originally. No experience is as original as the self-experience of the transcendental subjectivity.

The world along with the mundane experience cannot "found" such a science of transcendental subjectivity, for the possibility of its non-being cannot be, in principle at least, denied. Added to this, the world is never given to us outside the fundamental correlativity of noesis and noema. [14] This is the reason why Husserl dispenses with the idea of a science of the world and undertakes to go beyond the world and its sciences. In this "going-beyond", Husserl discovers the field of transcendental subjectivity and works out the possibility of an apodictic science of it. This is the field which "founds" the world and the meaning of it. Husserl speaks of this transcendental subjectivity as "die Stätte jeglicher Sinn- und Seinsbildung" in his "Cartesian Meditations". [15]

There seems to lurk an ambiguity in the Husserlian concept of the science of the transcendental subjectivity. This can be shown by taking into account the problem of phenomenological reduction. We ask here the question: What ultimately is the outcome of the reduction? Is it the "Lebenswelt" or the transcendental subjectivity? Is there any contradiction or paradox in reduction's discovering both the "Lebenswelt" as well as the transcendental subjectivity? Husserl repeatedly tells us that the "Epoché" leads us to the discovery of the anonymous transcendental subjectivity. [16]

We have already shown that there is no paradox if we maintain that the reduction discovers first the "Lebenswelt" and nothing beyond, for the possibility of a science of the "Lebenswelt" ultimately means the concretion (Konkretion) of the transcendental subjectivity itself. A science of the life-world aiming at the discovery of the invariant structures of it – when consequently developed – really points to the science of the transcendental subjectivity which in its turn searches

---

[13] G. Funke: *Zur transzendentalen Phänomenologie*, pp. 39 f.
[14] *C.M.*, p. 57.
[15] *Ibid.*, §§ 7–8.
[16] *E.P. II*, p. 417.

and researches the most "originary" experience of the "noetic-noematic" correlativity. Husserl wants to establish and demonstrate everywhere the genetic-historical-intentional character of all beings which
possess meaning for us.

The phenomenology seems to waver in its ultimate decision with
regard to a philosophy of "being" or of "becoming", although it
sympathizes with the latter. The dynamic and not the static is the key
to solve philosophical problems. This becomes still clearer when we
read the latter Husserl who is more sensitive to the historico-cultural
factors. But this does not mean that he changes the concept of phenomenology. In his own preface to the English edition of his "Ideas", Husserl clearly tells us that there is nothing which he has to take back in
regard to "transcendental-phenomenological idealism". The solipsistic
objection raised against his phenomenological idealism should be
understood, Husserl clarifies, as an objection against the incomplete-
ness of his exposition. [17]

Husserl maintains further that a complete working out of the science
of the transcendental subjectivity is an endless task put to us; and this
task cannot be solved all at once. It is the rationality of the intention
of philosophy itself which presents itself as a task to be solved by
humanity. It is of course right to emphasize that there is no "absolute
beginning" from out of an absolute unchangeable knowledge in the
sense of being purely non-historical. And Husserl seems to have realized
this. He might have modified his idea of absolute beginning in this sense,
and his talk of "the dream of philosophy as an apodictically strict
science dreamt out" [18] might be understood in this context.

But Husserl never doubts the possibility of such a science and the
rationality of it which is and would ever remain the only goal of humanity. Such a goal is nothing short of a total clarification aiming at
the science of philosophy in the sense of presuppositionlessness.
Husserl is not giving up the ideal of a rigorous science of philosophy;
he only now realizes more poignantly than before that such an ideal is
an "endless task" presented to the community of humanity, and only
a team-work could help us realize this goal.

The latter Husserl sees in all clarity that all our ways of reflection
are intimately related to and founded upon historical motivations. [19]

---

[17] *Ideas – General Introduction to pure Phenomenology*, p. 19.
[18] *Krisis*, p. 508. (Philosophie als Wissenschaft, als ernstliche, strenge, ja apodiktisch
strenge Wissenschaft, der Traum ist ausgeträumt.)
[19] L. Landgrebe: *Der Weg der Phänomenologie*, p. 187.

Thus when Husserl speaks of the dream of philosophy as dreamt out, he only expresses his mind that such a science has not yet been realized in all concreteness, and phenomenology represents a great bold beginning in this direction.

If one understands by the term "dream" that Husserl is thinking of a science of eternal truths (ewige Wahrheiten) from out of eternal knowledge, then there would be no doubt that such a dream must be dreamt out. But then the question is whether Husserl ever dreamt of such a science. [20]

The science of the transcendental subjectivity as conceived by Husserl is a task put to us by the very history of philosophy itself. Phenomenology, Husserl always maintains, is the secret longing of the movement of Western philosophical thought. It is a task we put to ourselves; and as a goal to be realized it is the most rational and concrete. Such a historical foundation and motivation cannot be apodictic in the old sense of knowledge of eternal truths which might have their source in an external power. The science of the transcendental subjectivity expresses our readiness, our "decision" (Entschluß) to utilize all historical possibilities in order to realize this goal of rationality. Such a science is the culmination of all our philosophical endeavours. It is this decision towards self-justification and self-understanding which comprises within itself a world-justification and a world-understanding. Herein lies also the true nature of our freedom.

The question regarding the transcendental subjectivity centres round the problem of the purity of a transcendental ego made accessible to us by our transcendental phenomenological reduction. What is this transcendental ego of Husserl? Is it an empirical-psychological I? No, Husserl says for he distinguishes between such an I and the transcendental I. The empirical-psychological I is a part of our mundane existence. Is the transcendental ego then a person, the personal I? No, Husserl maintains for such an I forms part of our surrounding world and lives a mundane life within the realm of our mundane existence. Is this transcendental ego to be identified with the I of the psychological introspection? No, Husserl answers for he maintains that the transcendental ego is neither an object of outer nor of inner psychological experience. This transcendental ego is the ultimate identical performer of all constitutional operations and validities (identischer Vollzieher aller Geltungen). It is an identical ego-pole

[20] A. Gurwitsch: "The Last Work of Edmund Husserl", *Philo. and pheno. Research*, XVI.

passing from one phase of its conscious life to the other retaining the past and anticipating the future. When there is nothing left, then there is this transcendental ego. [21] The living immediate present (lebendig strömende Gegenwart) is the most concrete instance and it surpasses in its purity all other constituted things and beings.

The term transcendental subjectivity is very concrete and meaningful for it is the basis of all meaning-giving activities; nay, it is the very dynamic instance manifesting itself in its acts of constitution. Is this transcendental subjectivity the very being of the subject as such? Is it the pure subject independent of all things? An affirmative answer to such questions is beset with difficulties for the phenomenological concept of constituting intentionality stands for the subject-object going hand in hand. Added to this, the questions asked above seem more or less to hypostatize the transcendental subjectivity. The transcendental subjectivity is, nevertheless, something "unobjective" (ungegenständlich), for it is neither natural nor a psychological subjectivity. It is the very act-instance of constitution; it is the very experience of these acts of constitution. It is the last point of all references which must first be "lived" by us prior to all objectivities.

The transcendental phenomenological reflection thematizes the world and all that the world includes – even the human beings as phenomena – from the point of view of such an instance which, according to Husserl, is the incomparable philosophical solitude (einzigartige philosophische Einsamkeit). Such a solitude is attained only through the performance of the reduction. To confuse or identify such an instance with any of the metaphysical entities of the traditional philosophy is to read too much in Husserl.

But this does not mean that Husserl identifies his transcendental subjectivity with a logical possibility. This constituting instance of transcendental subjectivity is absolutely given and is "lived" by us most intimately. To experience the transcendental subjectivity does not mean any type of mystical or mythical intuitive seeing; it is an intentional experience of the acts performed constantly to constitute the world of things and beings. Transcendental subjectivity is also not an abstraction for it is always already at work in our noetic-noematic correlativity. Husserl speaks of the anonymous nature of the transcendental subjectivity. The science of the transcendental subjectivity is thus the description of the intentional acts which point to their correlates. The trancendental subjectivity is discovering itself constant-

---

[21] *E.P.*, pp. 79 f.

ly in and through the acts of reflection (Akte der Reflexion). [22] In the "Formale und transzendentale Logik", Husserl speaks of all things and beings relative to this transcendental subjectivity. [23]

Wherein consists the absoluteness of the transcendental subjectivity? The adjective "absolute", when attached to the transcendental subjectivity, has nothing to do with the adjectives like eternal, immutable. The transcendental subjectivity is absolute because it is "fully" given; it is absolute because it is completely evident, and it is evident because it is "lived" and experienced as an act which justifies itself. It is absolute because it does not need anything else to be what it is. It is absolute because it is the last instance, the last performer of all acts. When we use the noun "performer", we do not mean any metaphysical or psychological agency or faculty behind it, but only the act-instance which is non-graphic. The absoluteness of the transcendental subjectivity does not consist in an absolute knowledge which, so to say, takes possession of us; it is no external truth overwhelming us. It is the absoluteness of our being placed before an insurmountable facticity pure and simple. [24] It is an act of decision to "found", understand and justify the world by self-understanding and self-justification. It is the very fact of freedom to decide and act in the name of humanity.

Husserl speaks of the transcendental subjectivity as an absolute being in his "Ideen". In his "Cartesianische Meditationen", he holds fast to such a determination of transcendental subjectivity. In his search for an absolute basis, Husserl renounces the idea of the world which cannot furnish us with such a basis, for the possibility of the non-being of the world cannot be denied. Husserl emphasizes the two most important characteristics of his transcendental subjectivity: its "unworldliness" (Unweltlichkeit) and its "unnaturality" (Unnatürlichkeit). The former means its being not an object in the world, whereas the latter points to the radical phenomenological reduction eliminating the natural attitude along with the general thesis. This "unnatural attitude" leads us to the transcendental subjectivity, to the most original experience of self-reflection. [25]

The radical transcendental reflection is the only way to overcome the sceptical reflection radically. If one wants to avoid an "ad infinitum", one must reflect radically transcendentally. [26]

[22] E.P. pp. 79 f.
[23] F.u.t.L., § 103, p. 241.
[24] L. Landgrebe: Der Weg der Phänomenologie, p. 188.
[25] E.P. II, p. 121.
[26] Ibid., p. 418.

The motivational ground for the search of an absolute basis lies in Husserl's conviction that all knowledge, all opinion, all belief regarding our world of things and beings stem from our own experience.[27] Landgrebe maintains that the transcendental I is itself the free subject of an absolute experience; it has not to accept the world naively. It must rather constitute, explain and justify it.[28] This attitude of not saying naively "yes" to the world does not mean a mere "privation" (bloße Privation) expressing indifference; it does not mean to doubt the existence of the world. It only aims at a firmer grasp of the world from a deeper dimension. Husserl speaks of "special motivation" (besondere Motivation) which first of all frees me from my bondage of the world and of myself. This leads us further to the attitude of a "non-participating onlooker" (unbeteiligter Zuschauer) which enables us to describe our self-reflections.[29] Such a radical attitude does not imply negation of the world for we can never stop experiencing the world. The experience that we can never stop experiencing the world takes place more deeply and intimately at the level of an attitude of disinterestedness, of non-participation.

Transcendental subjectivity thus represents the ever present instance of an ultimate noetic-pole which our regressive reflection searches for. It can always be reactivated in our search for the noetic-noematic correlativity. The transcendental ego of Husserl is thus no metaphysical instance which is realized successively or which manifests itself.[30]

When Husserl speaks of the transcendental ego as the "author" of the world, he means our consciousness of meaning-giving intentionality. It is the world-forming (weltmachende) instance. All the so-called sceptical reflections, carried out consequently, culminate in the most radical form of reflection, namely, self-reflection (Selbstbesinnung). According to Husserl, Hume failed to overcome his scepticism because he still remained subject to naturalism.

The performances of the transcendental subjectivity are always at work and our radical reflection uncovers the veil of anonymity (Anonymität) of the transcendental subjectivity. Husserl finds himself at a loss when he tries to give a proper name to this anonymity, for all names from the world of mundane existence are unsuitable and out of place,

---

[27] *Ibid.*, p. 461.
[28] L. Landgrebe: *Der Weg der Phänomenologie*, pp. 196 f.
[29] *E.P. II*, p. 98.
[30] G. Funke: *Phänomenologie – Metaphysik oder Methode?* pp. 176 f.

and they endanger the quality of purity and transcendentality which is essential to it. Husserl remarks that it cannot be "normally" named. In his "Vorlesung zur Phänomenologie des inneren Zeitbewußtseins", Husserl very clearly tells us that we lack all names (uns die Namen fehlen).[31]

Seen from the point of view of our mundane experience, the absolute stream of the transcendental subjectivity (der absolute Fluß der tanszendentalen Subjektivität) is unspeakable and inconceivable.[32] Why can't Husserl give it a name? Why is it beyond all names? Wherein lies its inconceivable character?

The phenomenological reduction leads us to the philosophical solitude. This means concretely that all the "nameable", "speakable", "conceivable" etc. has already been left behind and forms part of the eliminated world. Consequently, when Husserl comes to talk of the transcendental subjectivity, he often uses terms like "Urego", "Ursubjektivität", "Urich", "Urstiftung" and so forth.[33]

In one of his unpublished manuscripts, Husserl speaks of a "timeless consciousness as the primordial performance of worldliness" (zeitloses Bewußtsein als Urstiftung der Weltlichkeit).[34]

The science of the transcendental subjectivity is thus the process of our discovering and describing the most primordial realm of experience. In his "Erste Philosophie", Husserl speaks of an "absolute experience" (absolute Erfahrung) and means by it self-experience of the transcendental subjectivity. The philosophy as strict rigorous science is nothing else but a "systematic self-development of the transcendental subjectivity in the form of a systematic transcendental self-theorizing on the foundation of transcendental self-experience" (systematische Selbstentfaltung der transzendentalen Subjektivität in form systematischer transzendentaler Selbsttheoretisierung auf dem Grunde transzendentaler Selbsterfahrung).[35]

We have tried in our brief exposition and interpretation of the concept of the transcendental subjectivity and of its science to establish the following points:

I. The transcendental subjectivity is neither a sheer formal logical

---

[31] *Zeitbewußtsein*, p. 429.
[32] Although very differently motivated and pursuing different ends, the philosopher, Sanker, of the Vedanta school of Indian philosophy finds himself in a similar predicament in his attempt to name the pure consciousness which he then calls "unspeakable" (anirvacniya).
[33] *Krisis*, pp. 190 f.
[34] U.M., B I, 14, VI., p. 10.
[35] *E.P. II*, Theorie der phänomenologischen Reduktion, 52. Vorlesung, pp. 164 f.

possibility nor a metaphysical or psychological entity. The science of the transcendental subjectivity thus does not mean a formal discipline.

2. The transcendental subjectivity is an ever widening instance which can always be reactivated in our perpetual search for noetic-noematic correlativity. The science of the transcendental subjectivity, therefore, describes these pure acts of constitution.

3. The science of the transcendental subjectivity implies in the last run a phenomenology of reflection; it is transcendental reflective science.

4. In the name of the science of the transcendental subjectivity, Husserl in fact is proposing a philosophy of beginning (his "first philosophy") leading to the constitutive problems.

Although the human nature as conceived and described by Hume is quite different from the transcendental subjectivity of Husserl, still the role it plays in his philosophy is strikingly similar to the role played by the transcendental subjectivity in the phenomenology of Husserl. Our comparison here purports only to show some of these programmatic similarities.

Hume's claim to have found in human nature the most ultimate point of all explanations and justifications is very similar to the conviction of Husserl with regard to the foundational nature of his transcendental subjectivity. Hume's project to work out a fundamental science of human nature equals any epoch-making revolutions in philosophy, and Husserl rightly points out that Hume conceives of a fundamental science of human nature on which all other sciences depend.

To start with, the human nature Hume talks of is no biological nature; it is also not the psycho-physiological nature of man. It is the centre of all performances; it is, to use his own words, "a foundation almost entirely new". [36]

The human nature is given to us in and through the various principles of it which represent the ways it works in order to understand and explain the world. The basis of human nature along with its principles is the most secure foundation of all inquiries. "There is no question of importance", Hume writes in the introduction of his "Treatise", "whose decision is not compriz'd in the science of man". [37]

In proposing a science of human nature, Hume is not going to

[36] *Treatise*, Introduction.
[37] *Ibid.*, Introduction.

imitate the so-called objective sciences of Galilean type. The science of human nature, Hume tells us, would mean a complete change in the system of all other sciences. Husserl very rightly credits Hume of having conceived in his "Treatise" the programme of a pure phenomenology.

Hume's own positive philosophy which is the other side of his scepticism in the sense of a positive working out of the principles of human nature is a counterpart to the transcendental philosophy of Husserl. All the different sciences, Hume tells us, are dependent on the science of human nature, and no progress can be made in the other sciences unless we become perfectly acquainted with this fundamental and foundational science of human nature.

Like Husserl, Hume is interested in working out the most original realm of givenness characterized by "strength", "vivacity". "liveliness" and so on. Hume no doubt fails to describe clearly his own theory of impression fully phenomenologically, still a sympathetic phenomenological reading of his impressions would lead to see their nearness to Husserl's "originäre Anschauungen".

All our investigations, Hume proclaims, must be carried out with the end in view that they should lead us to the centre of all the sciences, namely to the human nature. Hume criticizes the old method of philosophical research as "tedious, lingering method".[38] From the "station of human nature", Hume maintains, we could easily do fruitful researches in all other sciences connected with it. And all the sciences are related with the science of human nature, Hume says. "Even Mathematics, Natural philosophy, and Natural Religion are in some measure dependent on the science of Man".[39]

If we are ready to interpret Hume's theory of impressions phenomenologically by taking into account the impressions of reflections, sentiments, feelings etc., and further, if we are ready to abstract from all perceptions the quality of absolute givenness and liveliness of impressions, then we could very well maintain that the science of human nature is really the description of the field of "original experience". In the name of his science of human nature, Hume thus proposes to work out the most original principles of human nature.[40]

Like Husserl, Hume always traces back the explanation of all the problems to human nature, i.e., to its principles. Provided we inter-

---

[38] *Treatise*, Introduction.
[39] *Ibid.*, Introduction.
[40] R. A. Mall: *Hume's Concept of Man*, pp. 55 f.

pret the different principles of human nature like custom, habit, belief, imagination, sympathy etc. as the different performances of it, we could see in Hume's concept of human nature at least a great programmatic similarity between him and Husserl.

Hume characterizes human nature further by saying that it is the "original constitution" of the human mind. The concepts like originality, immediacy etc. are generally used by Hume in his description of human nature. The human nature is the most original instinct in us, Hume says. [41]

Hume also emphasizes the arbitrary character of human nature and seems to mean thereby that the ways of human nature "founding" all our other inquiries cannot themselves be founded ultimately. Hume speaks thus of the "primary constitution of human nature". [42] Hume, unlike Husserl, fails to show the self-justifying character of human nature.

The human nature, according to Hume, is not something which differs from individual to individual. It is something which is common to all of us. Unlike Husserl, Hume's investigations of human nature are not free from anthropologism and psychologism. Although Hume lags far behind Husserl in his clarification of the concept of human nature and its functions, still he always maintains like Husserl that human nature is what "prevails in the end over any reasoning whatsoever". [43]

Hume, in criticizing the "total scepticism" which produces a total extinction of belief and evidence, only wants to put forward his own "hypothesis 'that all our reasonings concerning causes and effects are derived from nothing but custom; and that belief is more properly an act of the sensitive, than of the cogitative part of our natures' ". [44]

Hume's science of human nature is no metaphysics in the traditional philosophical sense of the term, for Hume always avoids speaking of ultimate, eternal principles in his philosophy. Although Hume emphasizes the character of regularity of human nature, still he is not ready to "hypostatize" it as a Platonic entity. [45]

Like Husserl, Hume too traces back the origin of all the objectivities to the human nature. Real necessity, Hume tells us very clearly, lies in the mind, not outside.

Hume also banished the metaphysical concept of soul not only from

[41] *Treatise*, p. 368.
[42] *Ibid.*, p. 281.
[43] *Enquiries*, p. 41.
[44] *Treatise*, p. 183.
[45] A. Schaefer: *David Hume*, pp. 45 f.

psychology, but also from the field of philosophy. He replaced it, of course in a functional-foundational sense, by his new concept of human nature which is an "abbreviator" for the original ways our human nature works.

The operations of nature are independent of thought and reasoning. Human nature, according to Hume, controls all the different fields of our life, for by an absolute and uncontrollable necessity nature has determined us to judge as well as to breathe and feel. [46] It is the human nature which compels the sceptic to assent to the existence of the world. [47] Nature is not opposed to habit, for habit is nothing but one of the principles of human nature. [48]

While discovering the various principles of human nature, Hume remarks with a sense of regret that the science of human nature has been most neglected. The only science of man is the human nature. Hume speaks of the tortures he suffers due to the confusion, unclarity in philosophy, and his only hope is to bring "a little more into fashion" the most fundamental science of human nature. Hume writes about the original motivation of his philosophy: "I have expos'd myself to the enmity of all metaphysicians, logicians, mathematicians, and even theologians ..., Can I be sure, that in leaving all establish'd opinions I am following truth; and by what criterion shall I distinguish her, even if fortune shou'd at last guide me in her foot-steps? I am confounded[49] with all these questions, and begin to fancy myself in the most deplorable condition imaginable. ... I am uneasy to think I approve of one object, and disapprove of another, call one thing beautiful and another deform'd, decide concerning truth and falsehood, reason and folly without knowing upon what principles I proceed .... This is the origin of my philosophy". [50]

The different principles of human nature represent "the accurate anatomy of human nature". [51] These are the most certain and original principles which Hume wants to proceed upon. The aim of his science of human nature is to work out these principles on which all our knowledge, belief and opinion rest.

Like Husserl's transcendental subjectivity, the human nature of

[46] *Treatise*, p. 183.
[47] *Ibid.*, p. 187.
[48] *Ibid.*, p. 179.
[49] Husserl speaks of a similar philosophical motivation: "Die Qualen der Unklarheit, des hin -und herschwankenden Zweifels habe ich ausreichend genossen. Ich muß zu einer inneren Festigkeit kommen." Husserliana, Bd. II, Preface.
[50] *Treatise*, pp. 264 f.
[51] *Ibid.*, p. 263.

Hume is discovered by working out its principles. As Husserl takes the help of various operative concepts, e.g. Epoché, reduction, constitution etc. in order to clarify the constitutional nature of the transcendental subjectivity, so does Hume who describes human nature in that he discovers its principles. There is a sense in which the foundation of all foundations, namely, the human nature, cannot itself be founded.

For Husserl as well as for Hume, we cannot go beyond the transcendental subjectivity and human nature respectively. Although Hume is far behind Husserl in working out the transcendental character of experience, still he maintains that no human inquiry "can go beyond experience, or establish any principles which are not founded on that authority".[52] When Hume speaks of experience with regard to the principles of human nature as it is the case in the lines quoted above, he does not mean experience in a sensualistic-empiristic sense. It is an experience to be understood in the sense of an evidence characterized by the qualities like "strength", "liveliness", "vivacity" "immediacy" and so on.

Hume failed to extend his theory of impressions to his theory of human nature. He was, as Husserl rightly maintains, only a forerunner of phenomenology.

[52] Treatise, Introduction.

CHAPTER IX

EXPERIENCE

The appeal to experience (in the sense to be specified below) is the central demand of the phenomenology of Husserl, and his phenomenology, of course, fulfills this demand in its own way. Husserl is a great critic of all those mathematical-formal systems of thought with a claim to autonomy.[1] Real autonomy can be reached only in the realm of experience which is full of phenomena in the sense of being "bodily given" (Selbstgebung). The formal-logical-mathematical evidence has to be traced back to the most original one which is given in the absolute realm of experience. Husserl's phenomenology of experience does not end with his description of pre-predicative experience; it culminates in his philosophy of "transcendental experience".

The traditional British empiricism failed completely to do justice to the relational-intentional character of all our experience. More than Hume, James and Brentano, Husserl emphasizes the 'intentional'-relational character of all experience not in the sense of psychological activities but in the sense of acts "lived" at a purely phenomenological level. The phenomenological theory of experience goes deeper, is more radical, wider and possesses a greater explanatory power. All the objects of our experience at the empirical level of our mundane existence are given within the most fundamental 'noetic-noematic' correlativity of an experience which is "originary" in the sense that it is this level of experience which bestows meaning on everything. The intentional experience cannot be understood as chopped up in psychical bits of atomic activities. Intentional experience is an experience of act-performances as radiating from a centre (transcendental subjectivity) in different ways towards the constitution of different ranges of objects in so very many different ways. To discover thus the most apodictic

---

[1] *Krisis*, p. 144.

realm of experience is the task of phenomenology, and all the manifold operational devices performed by the radical phenomenological reflection serve to discover the most originary experience. The path of phenomenology may well be interpreted as a path in search of and leading to the pure field of an "original experience". [2] Such an original experience is the self-experience of our intentionality as the meaning-giving instance. In the centre of the concept of Husserl's theory of experience lies the notion of "seeing" (Anschauung), and at the most radical level of self-seeing of constitutional intentionality reason and experience seem to lose all their enmities and become interchangeable terms.

We have already mentioned that experience consists in seeing; a transcendental experience must thus consist in a transcendental seeing which can only be made possible after the performance of phenomenological reduction. When we search for an original transcendental seeing we demand a return to an original evidence which consists in seeing that which is 'bodily given'. This seeing at the transcendental level is apodictic for consciousness experiences, "lives" itself in the "cogito". It is also the most originary because this experience "lives" itself as the performer of all acts and as the giver of all sense; it is the last traceable source of the meaning for the world of things and beings. Thus the concept of phenomenological experience possesses not only evidence; but it is also apodictic. It is at this transcendental level of experience where we most intimately experience how consciousness is essentially (intentionally) tied to the world which is already pre-given in our experience and is the object of all our experiences at the level of our mundane existence. We can never stop experiencing the world; but this fact naively taken for granted in our natural attitude is essentially understood and explained when we, instead of remaining at the level of natural attitude, reflect on the intentional acts as such. Such a reflection results in a new attitude in relation to the world of our mundane experience. It also opens up a new field of experience in that it brings to light a new consciousness which is no formal-logical ego but a "concrete ego" lived by us. Any discussion of Husserl's theory of experience has to take into account the two levels of it: the pre-predicative level of experience, the mundane experience (mundane Erfahrung) and the original transcendental experience (transzendentale Erfahrung).

[2] Landgrebe rightly maintains that the 'path of phenomenology' is the problem to discover the field of the "original experience" (originale Erfahrung). "The problem of an original experience" is also the sub-heading of his book *Der Weg der Phänomenologie*.

In his "Formale und transzendentale Logik" Husserl speaks of 'pure phenomenology of experience as such' (reine Phänomenologie der Erlebnisse überhaupt) and hints at a theory of experience which points to the character of the ultimate given, the most 'positive'. The real positive consists, according to Husserl, in its character of being apodictically given. Husserl's theory of experience is intimately connected with his theory of the phenomenological reduction, and the performance of the latter discovers the field of "positivities" which are most "originary" in the sense of being bodily present in the reduced realm of intentional consciousness. If positivism means our attempt to "found" all sciences upon the most "positive", that is to say, upon that which can be originally seen and "lived", then the phenomenologists are, according to Husserl, the real positivists[3]. The phenomenological criticism of the so-called positivistic theories of experience aims at two things. First, it shows the naivities involved in them, and secondly it attempts to overcome them by radicalizing the ordinary level of our experience. Husserl, starting from a higher predicative level of judgments, goes regressively back to the 'empirical judgments'. These empirical judgments are called "Erfahrungsurteile" for the individuals of empirical judgments are given through experience.[4] The individual judgments cannot be taken to be purely pre-predicative for to judge means to predicate. There is no pre-judgmental level of predication; but there is surely a pre-judgmental level of experience called in phenomenology the pre-predicative level.

Husserl always emphasizes that the discovery of the transcendental field of an original and apodictic experience can be made only in stages, and his theory of pre-predicative experience with all its characteristics, e.g. induction, anticipation, general causality etc., is one of the stages on the road to transcendental experience. The slogan "back to experience" really means back to this level of transcendental experience which represents a pure level of transcendental radical phenomenological reflection.

Husserl's "Erfahrung und Urteil" purports to give a foundation to logic by way of tracing back the origin of predicative judgments to pre-predicative experience.[5] Formal logic with all its predications replaces the concrete substrates by an X. Husserl tries to show that the actual world given to experience remains at the back of our pre-

[3] *Ideen I*, § 20.
[4] *F.u.t.L.*, § 84, § 87.
[5] *E.u.U.*, Einleitung.

predicative experience. The pre-predicative experience is defined in terms of the given at this level.[6] The evidence to be found at this pre-predicative level "founds" the evidence of logic. The theory of formal logic, Husserl maintains, ignores the foundational evidence and remains thus subject to certain naivities.[7]

The concept of evidence is the soul of Husserl's theory of experience, and he speaks of the various stages of evidence (Stufen des Evidenz-problems). The most original evidence means the self-givenness of the object, its being bodily present (selbst da, leibhaft da) in opposition to a mere individual representation of it.[8] This is why Husserl maintains that the so-called objective world of science is not and cannot be given to our immediate experience. It is the "Lebenswelt" which is full of evidences. All the evidences of our judgments must thus be traced back to this original evidence wherein the object itself is bodily present. Husserl's theory of experience distinguishes between different forms of givenness, and to each of these forms corresponds a form of experience.

When Husserl speaks of "Erfahrungsurteile" he of course clearly admits that there is a certain degree of idealization in them.[9] Even the lowest stage of our experience unmistakably shows structures which are idealized further in terms of the universally common judgments.[10] Such a way of "founding" formal logic is more or less foreign to Anglo-American logicians, like Russell, Carnap and so on. Carnap even maintains in his "Der logische Aufbau der Welt" that all statements can be reduced to formal ones. Such a reduction lacks the original evidence-character to be found at the pre-predicative level of experience. Husserl criticizes in this context the formal logic as a mere play with symbols, and such a practice leads to an identification of logic with syntax. Of course, Husserl's project is not to work out a theory of formal logic; he is interested in the "logic of meaning", and such a logic must be founded on intentional act-experiences which constitute meaning.[11] Husserlian logic is concerned with meanings; and Husserl's "Logische Untersuchungen" and the "Formale und transzendentale Logik" do not provide us with a system of logic

[6] *Ibid.*, pp. 36 f.
[7] *Ibid.*, p. 3.
[8] *Ibid.*, pp. 11 f.
[9] *Ibid.*, p. 58.
[10] *Ibid.*, p. 59.
[11] Even Carnap seems to modify his previous opinion in his *Introduction to Semantics* when he writes: "I no longer believe that a logic of meaning is superfluous." p. 249.

but with a systematic 'meta'-logic. Husserl builds up his logic not on conventions but on intuitions.

It is wrong to speak of pre-predicative judgments in the Husserlian theory of pre-predicative experience. Husserl defines experience in terms of those individuals which are bodily given.[12] The evidence of experience is the last evidence to which all other higher and more idealized forms of evidence have to be traced back. Thus a theory of predicative judgments presupposes (and is founded upon) a theory of pre-predicative experience.[13] It is this pre-predicative experience - consciousness which is the starting point for Husserl in his "Erfahrung und Urteil".

Experience in the widest sense includes the following points:
1) the bodily self-giving character of individual objects;
2) all the different modalities of this self-givenness (Selbstgebung) along with the different forms of belief in the existence of being such as possibility, anticipation, supposition etc.;
3) the modality of "as if";
4) the apperceptive extension by way of analogy as in the case of understanding the unknown in some mode of the known.[14]

Experience is in the first instance perception, Husserl tells us. It is also remembering; and in a certain sense it is also expectation. Such an experience is credited by Husserl to possess the knowledge of the past as past and of the future.[15]

Husserl develops his theory of pre-predicative experience a step further in that he works out its original structure of possessing the quality of certainty. All beings of experience are, in the first instance, pre-given to us with such a certainty.[16] This certainty is nothing else than the certainty to be found in the "general thesis" of the natural standpoint. The different acts of doubts, correction, modification and so on come later; they rather presuppose the existence of the general thesis. Experience possesses the essential structure of horizon because it implies anticipation, induction, and cognizance (Mitwissen, Vorwissen). Our life-world experiences possess, Husserl tells us, a native inductive character. The anticipatory structure of experience allows us to understand the "new" in some mode of the already known and cognized. Husserl speaks in this context of an "indetermined definiteness". The course of future

---

[12] *E.u.U.*, p. 21; *F.u.t.L.*, pp. 181 f.
[13] *E.u.U.*, pp. 21 f.
[14] U.M., II, p. 84.
[15] *E.P. II*, p. 84.
[16] *E.u.U.*, p. 23.

experience is open; but it is determined in the sense that it is already anticipated. But this anticipation, although incompletely determined, is not completely vacuous for in the absence of it the very possibility of experience would be in danger.[17]

Husserl speaks of induction which belongs to the very essence of experience and cannot be separated from it (zu jeder Erfahrung gehörige und von ihr untrennbare Induktion).[18] Induction as experience or experience as induction consists thus in its anticipatory character, and Husserl speaks of an "original induction" or anticipation" (ursprüngliche Induktion oder Antizipation). No experience is closed to itself; it shows its structures of "retention" and "protention". Experience possesses an "inner" and an "outer" horizon; and both can be explicated and determined more and more as the process of experience develops. When we speak of the transcendence of experience we mean this structure of horizon. The concept of horizon makes the process of experience an open one. Husserl speaks of the "transcendence of sense" (Sinnestranszendenz) and this character of experience points to its nature of being a guide to life.[19]

The world pregiven in our "passive doxa" represents the lowest level of experience. It is the experience we always start with. Husserl terms this the "plain experience" (schlichte Erfahrung). All experience in this regard, Husserl maintains, is natural for it is valid mediately for all the world-objects.[20] It is here that Husserl makes the distinction between the "plain experience" (schlichte Erfahrung) and the "founded experience" (fundierte Erfahrung).[21] The former represents the last stage to which our predicative evidence in the process of "founding" has to be traced back. This stage of experience includes the evidence of our experience of the life-world. But it is wrong to maintain that such an experience can be reached without the performance of reflection. If Husserl so intended, then he would be wrong, for to discover the structures of experience is the job of reflection on the experience. Any theory of experience has to conceptualize.

In "Erfahrung und Urteil" Husserl characterizes this level of "schlichte Erfahrung" by pointing out its habitualities which represent the typical directions of such an experience.[22] Husserl identifies here

---

[17] *Ibid.*, p. 27.
[18] *Ibid.*, p. 28.
[19] Buck: *Lernen und Erfahrung*, p. 57.
[20] *E.u.U.*, p. 29.
[21] *Ibid.*, p. 54.
[22] *Ibid.*, p. 52.

habitualities and acquisitions for both of them mean our abiding possession of knowledge.[23] When Husserl speaks of the "crisis" of the sciences in his "Krisis" he means the underrating of this experience under the influence of the objective science of Galilean style.

Husserl repeatedly speaks of experience when he discusses the problem of the "Lebenswelt". What does he mean by the experiences in the life-world? The Lebenswelt is full of evidence. We are led to the discovery of the life-world through the stages of pre-predicative evidence and pre-reflective experience. The life-world is a pre-scientific world. Our experiences in the life-world are being characterized by their being given to us prior to all scientific activities. Husserl further characterizes the life-world experience as follows: it is familiar (altvertraut), certain and the premise of all constructions. Our life-world experience is the basis of all verifications. The results of all the sciences stream in the experience of the life-world. But such a structural analysis of life-world experience is the result of our reflection.

In "Erfahrung und Urteil" Husserl tells us that the vast mass of idealizations, formalizations, and axiomatizations of the mathematical sciences has eclipsed the life-world, and the only way to regain it is to analyse and dismantle these veils of idealizations (Abbau der die Lebenswelt verhüllenden Idealisierungen).[24] In his attempt to lay bare the field of life-world experiences Husserl invokes the help of Epoché which suspends all the so-called objectivities of the science.

The life-world experiences have their own habitualities, typicalities, and regularities. Husserl solves the problem of identification by invoking the help of these typicalities present at the level of our pre-predicative experience.[25] But this explanation does not suffice to explain our notion of identification in the field of objective science. The concept of an exact identification is an idealization; and it represents a transformation of the "vague typicalities" of the life-world experiences. Whether the exactness of the objective science can be shown to have its origin in pre-predicative experience is beset with troubles. Mohanty speaks of a "certain phenomenological discontinuity" between sense and thought.[26] A continuity may be shown only on the ground of a reflection which joins the method of an endless reiteration with

---

[23] *Krisis*, Beilage XX; *Phän. Psy.*, pp. 462 f.; *C.M.*, p. 102; *Ideen II*, § 29 and *E.u.U.*, § 25.
[24] *E.u.U.*, § 10.
[25] *Krisis*, p. 29.
[26] J. N. Mohanty: *Edmund Husserl's Theory of Meaning*, p. 145.

the various motivations present in the production of the thought-idealities.

The concept of the world as given in our pre-predicative experience entails the concept of an endless horizon. This concept of horizon implies, as mentioned above, the possibility of further explication, determination (inner horizon) and anticipation of other objects (outer horizon). There is nothing entirely unknown; and all experiences, actual as well as possible, belong to "the world" given to us in our pre-predicative experience. Husserl's concept of world is not a Kantian totality of all objects; it is a world with open horizon-character.

The concept of association, phenomenologically speaking, means that something points towards some other thing. All experiences entail the moment of expectation. Every concrete experience is thus the fulfilment of a prior expectation. Husserl's theory of experience avoids the errors committed by the phenomenalistic or physicalistic theories of experience. Since phenomenology is the destruction of all atomistic theories it cannot take the help of psychological principles in order to explain the character of the world which is always passively pregiven to us prior to all activities of thought. It also does not take the help of logical principles for constructing the world out of the elements. Phenomenology, in order to describe the character of the given, introduces the notions of horizon, pre-cognition (Vorwissen), inductivity, associativity, habituality and so forth.

Any comprehensive understanding of Husserl's theory of experience must not stop with the description, exposition and interpretation of the field of pre-predicative experience. The concept of phenomenological reduction opens up a new field of experience which is more intimate to us than our experience at the mundane level of existence. The world of mundane experience can be doubted, for it is not given apodictically. The realm opened up by the phenomenological reduction is the apodictically given field of pure intentionality. The experience at this level is termed by Husserl "transcendental". The object of the transcendental experience is the transcendental ego. Husserl tells us very clearly in one of his unpublished manuscripts that the "experiential evidence" (Erfahrungsevidenz) [27] of the transcendental ego is "lived" by us. This transcendental ego, transcendental subjectivity is to be found only in a reflective attitude; it is the subject of reflection and lives its life in and through the acts of reflections. The transcendental experience is

---

[27] U.M., A V, 5. pp. 3 f.

in fact an experience of the reflective character. In the name of his pure phenomenology Husserl gives us a theory of experience which lays bare the fundamental structures of the life of consciousness including the real, the intentional, the appearing, the appeared, the evidence and the fulfilment. It is this theory of experience which Husserl terms in his "Logische Untersuchungen" a pure phenomenology of experiences. Husserl does not distinguish between a "pure phenomenology" and a "pure or phenomenological psychology".[28] The device of reduction presents thus a phenomenological criticism of experience. Such a criticism consists of the following steps:

1) the first phenomenological reflection must take the road to transcendental pure phenomenology in such a way that it reaches transcendentality from naturality;

2) a criticism of positive sciences belonging more or less to the natural standpoint belongs in this place;

3) this Husserlian criticism of experience does not intend to show the possibility of the non-being of the world. This is also the reason why Husserl criticizes the Cartesian way;

4) Husserl's criticism of experience takes the form of an analysis of the essence of "consciousness of something". Husserl hopes thus to discover a region of being which is absolute as such. What is this region? It is not the world of the natural attitude; it is rather the field of the transcendental subjectivity itself. The consciousness does not lose its being even when the Epoché reigns supreme. This region of consciousness is not and cannot be the region of mundane existence, for Husserl's criticism of mundane experience aims at discovering the ultimately real field in such a way that it shows that all that is there is dependent on this region of transcendental subjectivity for its being meaningful;[29]

5) Husserl thus gets to his theory of transcendental original experience through the description of the ways in which all being becomes meaningful for us, i.e. to say, the ways in which the constituting subjectivity gives meaning to the world of things and beings;[30]

6) the "I" as the performer of all pure experiences, i.e. to say, of all intentional relationships to intentionally immanent objectivity is not the psycho-physiological I existing in space and in time. This

[28] *Phän. Psy.*, p. 217.
[29] *Ideen III*, Nachwort; *Ideen I*, § 49.
[30] *Krisis*, pp. 363, 214 and 154.

pure I is the dis-interested onlooker; it is the subject of experience at a pure transcendental level. The return to such an I, to the pure experiences means to speak of experience in a "new sense". This new sense is nothing else than the transcendental sense of experience;

7) all the anticipated as the correlate of possible experiences, of "experienceabilities" (Erfahrbarkeiten) is rooted in the fact of this self-givenness; and it is this fact which bestows a solid style on all possible experiences. The conception of possible experience does not mean a vacuous logical possibility.[31]

Every experience is possible only through the mediation of the already known, because even the so-called entirely unknown or new can be understood as "something" (etwas). Even our practical behaviour (Handeln) realizes the new on the ground of the already known. The new is already anticipated as known within our project to produce effects. Husserl speaks of a "known practical possibility" (bekannte praktische Möglichkeit) to be realized. This realization takes place in and through the actual behaviour performed.[32] Practical behaviour is thus for Husserl an act of cognition. The I of the pure acts is always occupied with the world and all that is worldly in a special way. To be occupied means to be occupied with "something" (sich beschäftigen mit etwas).[33]

The immediate givenness, the self-givenness of the object under consideration is the central point in Husserl's theory of experience. In his search for the most apodictic point of all certainty, Husserl eliminates the world of mundane experience and reaches thus the realm of transcendental subjectivity which is experienced in our original experience.[34] The principle of all principles is the statement "I am" ("ich bin" das wahre Prinzip aller Prinzipien).[35] The world with all its perceptual experiences at the mundane level is given only "inadequately"; only the "I am" with all its richness of noetic-noematic correlativity is given fully and adequately.

The transcendental subjectivity as the ultimate constitutional noeti-

---

[31] *Ideen I*, p. 112. Husserl writes there: "Die Erfahrbarkeit besagt nie eine leere logische Möglichkeit ..."

[32] U. M. B. I 14 VI, p. 9. Husserl writes there: "Handeln erzielt auf Grund von schon Seienden neue Seiende, aus schon Bekanntem Neues, das Neue ist im Vorhaben der Erzeugung doch schon im voraus antizipiert als bekannt ... Die Handlung führt aus, bringt zur Selbstgebung und macht wirklich bekannt, was schon in Antizipation bekannt ist."

[33] *Ibid.*, p. 1.

[34] *E.P. II.*, pp. 41 f.

[35] *Ibid.*, p. 42.

cal pole bestows meaning on the world, including our mundane experiences (mundane Erfahrung). The level of mundane experience is
founded upon transcendental experience. Husserl terms this new type
of experience a kind of "theorizing", of "thinking" (eine neue Art des
Erfahrens, des Denkens, des Theoretisierens).[36]

This new type of theorizing is what Husserl understands by original
experience. Everything has its origin in this experience. The concept
"to originate" is more or less metaphorical. But origination does not
and cannot mean a total explanation of the idealities of thought without
remainder; it is rather an endless task to be realized in the course of
future philosophical reflections. The factor of motivation active in the
field of abstract thought must not be forgotten. A complete original
explanation of the universal of thought includes an analysis of the
peculiar scientific motivation present in the Galilean science. It is this
motivation which breaks the endless process of reiteration present in
the process of phenomenological reflection.

It is a grave misunderstanding to try to hypostatize this theoretical
reflective level of transcendental original experience. Many interpreters
of Husserl have thus been misled to criticize him of being too intellectualistic in his theory of experience. But Husserl himself tells us very
clearly that this experience is no negation of our mundane experience;
it only opens up a new plane from where we see, explain and justify
our mundane existence more deeply and intimately. The transcendental
original experience is in the last run nothing else than an experience of
reflection.

Transcendental experience is the self-experience of transcendental
subjectivity which manifests itself as the constitutional instance of
consciousness. This means, in other words, a pure phenomenological
description of the multiple ways of transcendental constitution. The
transcendental phenomenology of Husserl is thus the description of the
life of transcendental subjectivity.[37] The whole eliminated and bracketed world of our natural as well as scientific attitude is present here as
a "noematic-correlate" of noetic acts of constitution.

The problem as to what type of evidence is involved in transcendental experience is very complex. Ultimately, it is the evidence to be
found in the radical phenomenological reflection. All experience is
traced back to an immediate "seeing". The problem of an absolute
original transcendental experience entails thus an original absolute

[36] *Krisis*, pp. 154 f.
[37] *Krisis*, p. 263.

transcendental seeing. Husserl speaks in this context of an "absolute Anschauung".[38] He maintains that we do "live" the absolute transcendental ego; we "live" it absolutely for we experience it as the performer of all acts and as the giver of all sense to the world.

The transcendental plane of experience is nothing mystical; it is no field of bare logical possibilities. It is the most concrete and actual field of experience in the sense that the "meaning-giving intentionality" is lived in all apodicticity. In other words, this experience is nothing else than the experience of our consciousness that gives meaning. It is the most radical experience for no reduction can eliminate this consciousness. The absoluteness of this experience is not rooted in our knowledge of absolute and eternal truths. Such an understanding would be non-phenomenological for it involves "hypostatization".

There is in the beginning, Husserl tells us, an act prior to all methodological reflections.[39] Husserl speaks of the passivity as the lowest level of activity, as the level of "I-activities". At this level of "first beginning" (der erste Anfang), the transcendental I is "passively active". But Husserl seems to admit in his "Phänomenologische Psychologie" that there is something incomprehensible in the first beginning. It is this incomprehensible (unbegreiflich) which occasions the "first stroke" (unbegreiflicher Anstoß). First of all there are definite impressions (definitive Empfindungen), affections (Affektationen) on our I demanding I-reactions and I-activities (Ichakte).[40] Such a beginning is beyond all motivations; it is also beyond all genesis. This is perhaps the reason why it is "incomprehensible" (unbegreiflich). The eternity, perpetuity is not temporal; it is something removed from time. It is the original temporality of the absolute inner consciousness in its native timeless present.[41] Thus the "anonymous", timeless and nameless transcendental subjectivity is nothing else than this present which is itself eternal. In opposition to the stream of life which has a beginning and an end, the life of transcendental subjectivity is without any beginning and end.[42]

[38] *E.P. II*, p. 367.

[39] *Krisis*, pp. 159 f.

[40] *Phän. Psy.*, p. 487.

[41] Wittgenstein explains the concept of eternity in a similar way. He writes in his "Tractatus Logico-Philosophicus", 6, 43.11: "Wenn man unter Ewigkeit nicht unendliche Zeitdauer, sondern Unzeitlichkeit versteht, dann lebt der ewig, der in der Gegenwart lebt."

[42] U.M. B I 22 I, p. 15. We may suggest here the following three ways to explain the first beginning: 1) we always start with "acquisitions" and "habitualities"; 2) the timeless eternal transcendental subjectivity occasions it, and 3) there might be some external power as the cause of the first beginning. Husserl's phenomenology sympathizes with the second possibility and herein lies the origin of his "idealism".

It is safer to interpret Husserl's concept of transcendental original experience as the reflective experience of an instance which is the last point of all references. Merleau-Ponty seems to replace this eternal instance by his concept of "corporeality" starting always with "acquisitions" and "traditions". Merleau-Ponty's criticism of Husserl might be right if Husserl is taken to have given a corporeally concrete beginning. We have already seen that Husserl's transcendental experience is just the dynamic instance of a radical reflection, and this instance can always be reactivated. Husserl maintains that we always find the absolute beginning in us. We must not forget the functional character of the transcendental experience of Husserl. Such an understanding of his original transcendental experience avoids successfully the "regress ad infinitum" which the concept of corporeality starting always with acquisitions fails to avoid. Unlike Merleau-Ponty's philosophy of corporeality, Husserl's transcendental constitutional phenomenology attempts to constitute even the world of acquisitions.

The concept of transcendental original experience is thus nothing else than the experience of reflection consisting of our pure descriptions of the life of transcendental subjectivity. This is the "Archimedean point" (archimedischer Punkt) Husserl is in search of.[43]

Experience understood and interpreted transcendentally-genetically, intentionally-genetically guarantees authentically the being of all that is there for us. This is why Husserl speaks of changing over to philosophical universality from the psychological one. Husserl says, "I always take the world for granted and keep it as my supposition". But then he asks, "is it not I which assumes?".[44] Views would always differ concerning the question whether the I or the "Lebenswelt" represents the "real first" in Husserl's phenomenology.

The Humean analysis of experience takes place primarily at the level of mundane existence, and a comparison between Husserl's and Hume's theory of experience can take place only at this level. Husserl's concept of pre-predicative experience has much similarity with Hume's concept of experience.

Like Husserl, Hume too emphasizes the inductive, anticipatory and associative character of all our experiences.

Husserl rightly says that Hume tries to discover the most "original impressions" (Urimpressionen) of all ideas.[45] Such a tracing back to the

---

[43] *E.P.*, pp. 40 f.; *Phän. Psy.*, p. 339.
[44] "Ich halte die Welt", Husserl writes in his "Erste Philosophie, II", "vorausgesetzt und halte sie noch jetzt in Setzung. Aber bin ich es nicht, der da setzt ...?" p. 448.
[45] *Krisis*, p. 377.

original impressions results in Hume's theory of the different leading principles of human nature.[46]

Hume's "impressionism", if phenomenologically interpreted, would come very near to Husserl's theory of "originäre Anschauungen". Even Hume's impressions are marked out by their qualities of "givenness", "liveliness", "strength", "force" and so forth. But Hume fails to work out his theory of ideas into a full-fledged theory of "Wesensschau". Hume could not discover the "noetic-noematic correlativity" of our acts.

Our perceptions – impressions and ideas – are the materials of our experience. Hume in his "An Abstract of a Treatise of Human Nature" describes a perception by the quality of its being present to the mind "whether we employ our senses, or are activated with passion, or exercise our thought and reflection".[47] This implies that Hume admits the existence of the "impressions of reflections". His theory of experience does include the act of reflection as an operation in it. The coming to be of what we call "experience" is not due to a mechanical process of mechanically putting the isolated impressions together. Experience is the result of the activities of our mind.

When Hume speaks of the "impressions of reflections", he of course means our acts of reflecting on our common sense experience, and philosophy is, Hume maintains, nothing else but a systematization of the results of our reflections on our common life. Thus the Humean theory of experience is not so much a "psychological theory" speaking of psychological elements only; it is rather a descriptive account of experience.[48] The different principles of human nature like custom, habit, belief etc. are not purely psychological operations. Hume's "naturalism" takes these principles to be "easy, natural and true" principles of human nature.

That Hume's teaching with regard to experience is not atomic can be seen clearly when we take his theory of belief into account. Belief possesses an "immediateness" and attends experience. Belief is different from fiction; and it brings the objects believed nearer to the impressions. Experience is thus synthetic in character.[49] Our knowledge, our belief in causality arises from "observation and experience".[50]

Like Husserl, Hume's concept of experience is intimately connected

[46] R. A. Mall: *Hume's Concept of Man*, pp. 41 f.
[47] *Hume – Theory of Knowledge*, ed. by D. C. Yaldon, p. 249.
[48] A. P. Cavendish: *Hume*, pp. 34 f.
[49] An Abstract, pp. 259 f.
[50] *Treatise*, p. 82.

with the concept of "Doxa". Hume in explaining the nature of experience emphasizes not only the important factors of "remembering" and the relations existing between the objects thus remembered, but he also stresses the factor of a "regular order"[51] in it. The regularity, the uniformity of nature belongs to the very essence of experience; and in the absence of these factors "all experience becomes useless, and can give rise to no inference or conclusion".[52]

Like Husserl, Hume emphasizes the anticipatory character of experience in that he talks of extending our past to the future. He clearly tells us that we habitually conclude that nature of the "unexperienced" from that of the experienced. There is nothing entirely unknown, for the unknown has to exist in some mode of the known. In explaining the problem of causality, Hume makes it amply clear that we extend the past to the future. He even speaks of an impression of causality which is produced in an "oblique" manner. This manner is the way imagination works in Hume's philosophy. The principle of causality as a universal principle of transition is rooted in the universality of imagination.[53]

A complete understanding of Hume's theory of experience must thus take into account not only the impressions and ideas as its constituting elements, but also the principles of belief, imagination, induction, anticipation, association and so forth.[54] It is wrong to identify experience exclusively with impressions. Hume, too, admits the complex nature of experience[55] and seems to point to its relational character. The particular isolated perceptions themselves do not constitute the experience.[56]

The distinguishing feature of experience is the manner in which the perceptions are ordered; not the perceptions as such, but their relations are important for experience.[57] Experience is, Hume says, one of the guiding principles of human life.

Hume is really giving us a criticism of experience when he asks for the reason why the past should be a guide for the future. His theory of experience verges on the discovery of a transcendental explanation of our mundane experience. Although the authority of the experience

---

[51] *Ibid.*, p. 87.
[52] *Enquiries*, p. 38.
[53] *Treatise*, pp. 225 f.
[54] R. A. Mall: *Hume's Concept of Man*, pp. 41 f.
[55] W. H. Walsh: *Reason and Experience*, p. 115.
[56] C. W. Hendel: *Studies in the Philosophy of David Hume*, p. 508.
[57] *Treatise*, pp. 87 f.

is unquestionable, still it is legitimate, Hume writes, to ask for the principles "which give this mighty authority to experience".[58] The principles Hume here asks for are in fact the different principles of human nature. We can readily accept, Hume tells us, that our past experience gives us the knowledge of the objects perceived. But the question Hume is asking is: "But why this experience should be extended to future times, and to other objects ...?"[59] In explaining this "why" Hume abandons the psychological as well as the logical way of describing experience; he introduces the notions of inductivity, habituality, belief, associativity and anticipation. Hume speaks of "association of impressions".[60] Hume's theory of experience does include the active moments in it.

The explanation of experience takes place at a reflective level; and Hume does conceptualize in his attempt to explain the nature of experience. Since Hume lacked the Husserlian device of phenomenological reduction, he failed to discover the pure transcendental field of experience phenomenologically.

If we emphasize the "inductive sense" of experience of Hume's theory of experience we come to recognize the principles of human nature which are themselves not experienced at the mundane level. The "epistemic sense" of Hume's experience is restricted to his demand of tracing back the origin of all ideas to the originally given impressions with their liveliness and strength. It is the "inductive sense" which is nearer to Husserl's theory of pre-reflective experience.

Although Hume failed to develop in all clarity the theory of impression as the "original seeing" (originäre Anschauung) of Husserl, still his programmatic approach is similar to that of Husserl. Both of them are trying to give a genetic explanation of experience. This genetic explanation is not to be confused either with the psychological or with the logical. Hume's concept of the "natural" seems to be the counterpart of Husserl's concept of the "transcendental".

Like Husserl, Hume too tries to explain the origin of all exactness of our thought in the sphere of our experience in such a way that he speaks of our "imagining a perfect standard" of, say, equality liable to no change and correction. Hume brings in the principle of imagination while examining the foundation of mathematics because "the imagination, when set into any train of thinking, is apt to continue,

[58] *Enquiries*, p. 36.
[59] *Ibid.*, p. 33.
[60] *Treatise*, pp. 383 f.

even when its object fails it, and like a galley put in motion by the oars, carries on its course without any new impulse".[61] The phrase "even when its object fails it", if developed consequently and phenomenologically, points to scientific facts which, according to Husserl, are not given to our immediate experience. Hume of course fails to develop the notions of idealization, formalization, axiomatization and so forth which are at work in the process of our objective thought producing idealities.

Simply to have a sense perception is not "ipso facto" to have experience. In reasoning from experience Hume clearly shows the complex constitution of experience. In his "Treatise", Hume describes the nature of experience by mentioning the factors of observation, memory, constant conjunction, regular order, in short the notions which point to the factors constituting experience.[62] Hume, it is true, refers every idea to the impression from which it might be derived. But, as we have seen, further explanation is required in order to explain the nature of experience. This further explanation consists in Hume's attempt to discover the principles of human nature.[63] In order to "reason" from experience we need more than the particular present facts. The real challenge of Hume's scepticism consists in his asking for the reason of our extending the past to the future. Hume, in other words, asks by what reason we can pretend to extend the order of the phenomena observed in the past to the future. This challenge of Hume is still a deadlock in philosophy; and the presumptive character of our extending past to future subsists.

[61] *Treatise*, p. 198.
[62] *Ibid.*, p. 87.
[63] C. W. Hendel: *Studies in the Philosophy of David Hume.* pp. 505 f.

CHAPTER X

REASON

The concept of reason is overloaded with all sorts of meanings ranging from reason as a god-like faculty to reason as a fixed entity endowed with a priori principles constituting all experience, actual as well as possible. Such a concept of reason is dynamized in the phenomenology of Husserl; and a phenomenological understanding of reason has to take into account its redefinition in phenomenology. The concepts reason, rationality get a new type of meaning in the phenomenological reflection.

No principles can be fixed for all time to come; and reason as an "eternal faculty" must give way to "reason-in-the-making", to a reason on the way to its self-realization. Reason thus leaves its character of fixity, eternity etc. and becomes a process. The absoluteness of reason in the sense of an absolute knowledge cannot be accepted today. All understanding is historical in nature and so the history of reason goes hand in hand with the history of the whole humanity. The process of the self-realization of reason represents the process of philosophy, and since such a realization means an endless task, philosophy itself is a task to be realized.

Pure phenomenology is a search for the "eidos", "essences" and not for the existence or being. It is "Wesensforschung" and no "Daseinsforschung".[1] While searching for the clarification of the concept of reason, Husserl is really trying to discover the real essence of humanity. The real being of humanity is, according to Husserl, its being in relation to a "telos", and the real philosopher's job is to realize this telos ever more and more. This telos is the telos of complete clarity and reason consists in an original evidence. As officials (Funktionäre) of humanity philosophers cannot neglect the gradual realization of the

[1] *Ideen I*, p. 59.

goal reason.[2] Husserl tells us very clearly in the opening pages of his "Krisis" that such a realization of reason is the very purpose (Vorhaben) of his reflections in this book.

In order to understand the course of the development of Husserl's phenomenology, we must keep in mind the fact that he is ceaselessly struggling to reach the ideal of "presuppositionlessness" (Voraussetzungslosigkeit). This ideal he seems to have reached and found in the very idea of rationality as a goal (Zweck), as a task (Aufgabe) to be realized continuously through approximation.

Complete clarification is an endless task. We do not start with it, but rather we reach it. The painstaking reflections and investigations of Husserl in his "Krisis" aim at working out phenomenology of reason which takes reason not only as a means, but also a goal to be realized. The phenomenological reason dives deeper and is to be distinguished from reason to be found at the level of mundane existence.[3]

Husserl often mentions the first and the foremost discovery of the Greek mind in this respect, but in conformation to the spirit of his phenomenology he grasps and defines reason in a new way. Reason, for phenomenology, is a process of development pointing to a goal to be realized in the course of our philosophical development. In the concrete execution of the realization of this goal, our reason shows its real nature of being a "teleological unfolding". Such an unfolding of reason is no theoretical possibility, but it is our ultimate freedom to act and to risk the fulfilment of this fundamental "intentionality". But this fulfilment of reason is not the realization of a possibility already determined by some other external power; it is rather a possibility to be worked out, to be undertaken, to be seen.[4] Phenomenological reason, as would be made clear, is an open one. It does not consist in construction, but in seeing.

Phenomenology treads on a middle path in that it disregards neither our experience nor reason; it only radicalizes both of them. The call of phenomenology "to the things themselves" (zu den Sachen selbst) really points to the most radical and active level of our constituting intentionality. This call means the process of our perpetual discovery of the deeper operations and performances (Leistungen) of our most original constitutional consciousness. The science of phenomenology is neither empirical nor rational in the traditional sense of the term;

---

[2] *Krisis*, p. 15.
[3] G. Funke: *Phänomenologie – Metaphysik oder Methode?* pp. 107 f.
[4] L. Landgrebe: *Phänomenologie und Geschichte*, p. 165.

it is rather the most radical "positivism" in the sense of showing us the most positive, the ultimately given. The most positive is the intentionality itself. Such a constituting intentional consciousness is the stage of "presuppositionlessness". Reason is the "experience", the "seeing" of this prime intentionality.

The science of phenomenology as rationalism aims at objective truth in the sense of the things given apodictically. The most positive which Husserl is in search of, in the world of things and beings with which our normal natural thought has to do. Such a world is taken for granted as existing independently of our consciousness. It is this very presupposition of an independent world that stands in the way of a science of presuppositionlessness. Phenomenology can reach rationality only through a radical approach opening up the field of presuppositionlessness.

Husserl is of the opinion that it is not only the 18th century empiricism that implies scepticism, but even the rationalism is not free from such a scepticism.[5]

The objectivism of the rational as well as of the empirical type is to be rejected for it is still subject to naive presupposition of a world existing as such.

Reason as a task (Aufgabe) is to be worked out and completed. It is like a dynamic force manifesting itself through the evolutionary process of history. But the phenomenological reason is no "absolute idea" of Hegel prefixed in its steps; it is rather the goal of humanity set by itself in all freedom. Reason is rather the very freedom we human beings possess to act and to justify. It is not a freedom borrowed or given by grace. It is a freedom of self-realization, of self-justification. Such a self-justification includes world-justification.

The rationality of reason lies in our radical decision to "found" humanity, i.e. to say, to set the goal humanity has to realize. This goal, this task of reason need not be always explicit. Husserl speaks of a "latent teleology" (verborgene Teleologie).[6] A reason that is latent in philosophy must be brought to full clarification which is nothing else than the self-realization of reason through reason. The discovery of reason is a process manifesting itself at each level of our practice. The

---

[5] *Krisis*, pp. 13 f. Husserl writes: "... daß der Rationalismus des 18. Jahrhunderts, seine Weise, die geforderte Bodenständigkeit des europäischen Menschentums gewinnen zu wollen, eine Naivität war."

[6] *Krisis*, pp. 16 ff. "Wir versuchen, durch die Kruste der veräußerlichten "historischen Tatsachen" der Philosophiegeschichte durchzustoßen, deren inneren Sinn, ihre verborgene Teleologie, befragend, aufweisend, erprobend."

concepts of rationality and philosophy seem here to be interchangeable terms.

In his "Philosophie als strenge Wissenschaft", Husserl criticizes the "naturalists" for their "naturalizing" reason; he also praises them for their zeal in favour of exactness. But they formalize this concept of exactness. This central notion of exactness – misunderstood by the natural scientists as exactness of the objective science (exakt natur-wissenschaftlich) – leads, consequently developed, to the phenome-nological concept of reason which does not consist in "creating" or "producing" as the mathematical reason, but in acts of seeing.

Husserl writes that the very idea of science conceived in its "ideal completion" (ideale Vollendung)[7] is identical with reason.

Husserl does admit the Greek definition of man as endowed with reason, but he does not take reason to be solely an equipment of knowledge. According to Husserl, the traditional epistemology has always distinguished between the epistemological and the genetic origin and has thus failed to realize the character of epistemological reflection as "historical revelation" (historische Enthüllung).[8] Episte-mology is nothing else but a "unique historical task" (eigentümliche historische Aufgabe);[9] it consists in our perpetual search of the acquisition, origin and revelation of the history of being at any given time.

The idea of reason pervades all our activities; no practice is devoid of reason. This can be true only when reason no longer remains a fixed entity. The phenomenological reason understands the living movement of history as a going-together of the "original sense-constitution" and "sense-sedimentation" (ursprüngliche Sinnbildung und Sinnsedimentie-rung).[10]

Rason is not an equipment like eyes and ears which are there to fulfill their functions of seeing and hearing respectively. If it were so, then it would be a fixed faculty with prefixed principles. As life and history, so also reason is in the process of making. The process of the evolution of reason must be understood in the sense of an ever better self-realization. The concept of phenomenological reason must not be confused with the concept of reason as a generalizing faculty; reason is no faculty to be accounted for. It is neither inductive nor deductive;

---

[7] *Philosophie als strenge Wissenschaft*, p. 16.
[8] *Krisis*, p. 379.
[9] *Ibid.*, p. 379.
[10] *Ibid.*, p. 380.

it is a reason full of evidence, and this evidence of reason is present even at the level of "doxa".

Phenomenological reason does not copy the mathematical reason. Unlike the latter it does not consist in construction. It does not formalize; it does not create either. It is a reason which shows itself as a task and is clearly seen and "lived" as such. The constitutional transcendental subjectivity always remains in a lively contact with the world we live in; it only "experiences" it at a deeper level.

Like the mathematical reason, phenomenological reason does not aim at a total control of all it surveys. It is no faculty of an arbitrary determination. Husserl makes this very clear in his critical discussion of the development of mathematical-natural sciences of Galilean style.[11] The mathematical reason is obsessed with the passion of ruling the world; it "mathematizes" the world of primary as well as of secondary qualities and replaces the real world by the world it thus constructs. It is this reason with the unlimited passion for ruling that ends in a blind alley in its attempt to comprehend and explain the world we live in.[12] Husserl does not criticize its praise-worthy achievements, but only its unwarranted claim to autonomy.

The phenomenology of Husserl makes reason stand for something practical, historical, genetic, intersubjectively objective, in short, for a process in lively touch with the human life and history. The false objectivism can be overcome only through a transcendentally subjective objectivism. There is no absolute transcendence, for every act of understanding implies the constitutional performance of our consciousness.

But reason also determines the goal from which the human practice is attracted like a magnet. The goal of humanity is the goal of reason. Thus reason, no doubt, determines, controls and gives a sense of direction, but it does not predetermine life and history. There is a relation of mutual cooperation between reason and practice. Human practice occasions the coming to be of reason to itself without being its producer. There is no reason entirely detached from the practice.

In order to understand Husserl's concept of reason we must not forget to consider his theory of "self-reflection" (Selbstbesinnung). He often emphasizes the central importance of the twin processes of self-reflection and "self-responsibility" (Selbstverantwortung) in order to show the real nature of reason not only as a process, but also as a goal

[11] *Krisis*, pp. 18 f.
[12] L. Landgrebe: *Der Weg der Phänomenologie*, p. 133.

never to be lost sight of. Reason is a performance to be carried out endlessly. This endless and perpetual performance-character of reason points to its being an endless task of humanity. Husserl writes very clearly in his "Krisis" that philosophy is the self-reflection of reason (menschheitliche Selbstbesinnung der Vernunft).[13] Humanity in her creative freedom is nothing else but reason itself.

The phenomenological reason is always on the way towards self-comprehension; it is the endless movement of "self-clarification" (Selbsterhellung).[14] Reason, phenomenologically considered, cannot be speculative in character; it must remain open both as a means and as an end. Such an understanding of reason cannot allow any distinction between "theoretical", "practical" and "aesthetic" reason.[15] Wherever such a distinction is made, it is bound to be artificial.

Reason, according to Husserl, is the essence of humanity. It signifies that which human being as human being in his innermost being aims at; it is what satisfies him utmost. Reason is the apodictic telos (apodiktisches Telos) which is present in all our acts and purposes. To come to know and realize this telos is nothing else than our self-realization in the form of philosophy.

In the process of our self-understanding which implies our understanding of the history and of the world we live in, we realize the life of our reason as standing for the ideal of autonomy. Humanity in her prime intentionality is itself reason. The life of reason consists of the endless acts of self- and world-constitution. The autonomy of our reason points to our task of necessarily giving meaning to the world; phenomenological reason is essentially intentional.

In order to bring forth the autonomous creative side of reason, Husserl generally uses the verb "gestalten" which means "shaping", "forming" or "giving a direction". It is this act of "gestalten" which represents in all concreteness the endless task which humanity has freely laid to herself. Phenomenological reason is no gift from some external power; it is rather the very meaning-giving style of life. In the process of the realization of the goal called reason, we are no passive onlooker, for no realization can take place unless we do our best to reach this goal. Husserl asks the philosophers to act in the name of and for the sake of the whole humanity. Reason points to what we "teleologically ought to be" (Teleologischsein und Sein-sollen).

[13] *Krisis*, p. 269.
[14] L. Robberrechts: *Husserl: Eine Einführung in seine Phänomenologie*, pp. 34 f.
[15] *Krisis*, pp. 275 f.

The two following convictions of Husserl are always at work in his philosophy: one, the legitimate idea of an "absolute foundation", and the other, that this idea must be the idea of philosophy. Since "eternal truths" are not what philosophy can achieve, Husserl maintains that it must be rooted in experience.[16]

But we should not deduce from what has been said above with regard to the teleological character of reason that phenomenological reason predetermines the very end of history and denies the appearance of any novelty. Such a contention would amount to an ontological, if not to a religious, confession regarding the character of reason. Husserlian faith in reason is not Cartesian, for Husserl does not bring in the notion of the "divina veracitas" as Descartes did. Of course there is no ultimate verification of reason, but this is because the reason as a task cannot be realized all at once. The goal of complete rationality is, as mentioned above, "presuppositionlessness", a stage of complete self-understanding. Such a stage cannot be substantial, and there is no way of experiencing substance. Husserl is very Humean on this point.

Phenomenology as an open method of search and research realizes this goal step by step in that it discovers the fundamental "noetic-noematic" correlativity. Husserl's act of synthesizing these two streams of noesis and noema is surely not free from all abstraction. The reason as a task is rooted in the very history of thought of Western culture.[17]

What is this task, this goal, this end of rationality we always strive to reach? Wherein lies the very teleological character of reason? How and in what way this reason manifests itself? The very process of history is a witness to the presence of reason in it.[18] Husserl calls reason as the progressive element 'of' and 'in' history. The reason is historical not as a result of history, but as a motivation of it. History does not bring forth reason; it manifests the life of reason. Phenomenological reason is no objectified something; it does not consist of abstract ideas and their relations. It has nothing in common with the Humean reason in the field of the "relations of ideas". But phenomenological reason differentiates itself also from the common sense reason, for it does not live in sheer convictions. Husserl speaks of a

[16] Q. Lauer: *Phenomenology – Its Genesis and Prospects*, Ch. 7. "A universal Phenomenology of Reason".

[17] Husserl limits his inquiry historically to the analysis of the European thought-life and its various manifestations, and the question must be left open whether the Greek idea of rationality can be taken to be the ultimate point of all orientations in all cultures and for the whole humanity. Husserl himself seems to leave this question open in wait for the verdict of future events.

[18] *Krisis*, p. 386.

continuous unbroken sense of a goal-directed philosophy (Zwecksinn der Philosophie)[19] and takes this sense to be the very meaning of teleological reason which identifies the practice we call philosophy. In the absence of such a rational direction, we could hardly talk of the "Selbigkeit" of philosophy.

In the opening pages of his "Krisis", Husserl speaks of an "absolute reason" (absolute Vernunft) from which the sense of the world stems (aus der die Welt ihren Sinn hat). To lose faith in reason is, according to Husserl, thus to lose faith in humanity. Husserl's faith in reason really means his strong conviction that reason is our task and its realization our sacred duty. Husserl may rightly be said to have a boundless faith in reason; he may be criticized on this point, for the self-realization of reason suffers (and has suffered) great set-backs and takes a very zigzag way; but as an endless task to be realized, it is no doubt something very real. There is no practice at any level of our life which might be entirely devoid of a sense of goal which ever remains an ideal something to be attained. Reason does not negate "Doxa"; it only "founds" it from a deeper and truer level. Not in the field of "Doxa", but in the field of reason, clarity reigns supreme.

The real being for Husserl consists in an ideal goal which is reason as our task.[20] Even in our daily life we realize the character of the real being as an end we strive to achieve. Phenomenological reason is characterized by this quality of striving (Streben).

In the actual course of our historical development, reason comes to realize itself better. The ideal of complete clarity implying the stage of presuppositionlessness was misinterpreted in the modern mathematical sciences. These sciences replaced this ideal by a purely formal clarity to be found in the ideas and concepts constructed by them. This deviation taking place in the mathematical sciences is exemplified by Husserl choosing the key-figure of Galileo. The unusual success of these sciences tempted the scientists to "mathematize", "idealize", "formalize" and "axiomatize" the whole world, not only of "secondary qualities", but also of "primary qualities". In this context, Husserl tries to show that the Euclidean Geometry, instead of accounting for the world we live in, is, on the other hand, accounted for by it.[21]

What Husserl severely criticizes in the so-called objectivistic and

---

[19] *Ibid.*, p. 512.

[20] *Ibid.*, p. 11. ("Überall ist wahres Sein ein ideales Sein, eine Aufgabe der Vernunft").

[21] Husserl hardly mentions the non-Euclidean geometries which point to a complete axiomatization and formalization. They represent an extra burden to his conviction that all the idealities of thought can be traced back to experience.

positivistic sciences are not their achievements, but their claim to autonomy ranging from the method to the construction of a world. The method of science, instead of explaining the world, is itself explained by the methods which express the typical character of the life-world. Husserl's "Krisis" aims at a restoration of the original right of the world as the instance of foundation.

All that is, exists for Husserl as the "noematic-correlate" of the various "noetic-acts". The discovery of this correlative structure of all our intentional acts is one of the most important contributions of Husserl's "Ideen". Even the mathematical sciences have to be understood as the performances (Leistungen) of our constitutional consciousness. The modern mathematical sciences forget such a transcendental motive and remain subject to so many naivities. It is here that Husserl praises the attempts of Hume and Descartes who try in their own way to restore back this transcendental motive in all our inquiries.

Both the worlds of our common-sense experience and of mathematical sciences have to be referred back to the intentional acts of constitution of our consciousness; they are "cogitata" of our "cogitationes" and derive their meaning from the performances (Leistungen) of our consciousness. It goes to the credit of Husserl to have shown in all clarity and radicality the universal character of constituting intentionality. The Husserlian concept of reason is intimately connected with this constituting meaning-giving consciousness; nay, it is this very consciousness itself. The realm of the transcendental subjectivity as the most apodictic one is the realm of reason. The Husserlian reason manifests itself in and through the performances of this transcendental subjectivity that does the act of "founding" the world. If we choose to speak of our "experience of reason", we may well do it, for at this level reason itself is "experienced", "lived" as the founding intentionality itself.[22]

In order to bring out the process-character of reason we must go further into the structure of human practice in its relation to our "Lebenswelt" which is pre-given and which is full of evidence. This life-world which is our starting point is itself thematized in our radical phenomenological reflection. Such a reflection shows not only the presence of reason at all the different levels of our practice, but it also lays bare the developing character of reason. Husserl's "rationalism" is historically situated and is teleological in nature. It retains its identity in spite of the various forms of rationalism from Plato to modern positivism.

All practice starts with a dialogue with the life-world. This primitive unreflective dialogue is the object of radical phenomenological reflection, and reason is, so to say, the gradually evolving result of this intercourse between radical reflection and pre-reflective practice. Reason emanates itself when reflection sets in order to "found" the practice. The famous notion of the "disinterested observer" (unintressierter Zuschauer) is not comprehending a ready-made rationality – for there is no such thing –, but it itself establishes the rationality. Phenomenological reflection gives phenomenological reason its personality, for prior to all reflection this reason is "latent" in our practice. No human practice at any level of its development is entirely devoid of rationality, for corresponding to the different levels of practice there are different stages in the life-history of reason. Human rationality is thus a matter of more or less. It does not pose a problem to be solved; it represents rather a goal to be realized. Phenomenological reason is no metaphysical reason, for there is nothing hidden behind it which might be unknown and unknowable. Phenomenological reason neither hypostatizes nor is it itself a hypostatization.

But reason meets a certain level of rationality reached in our practice. It thus no doubt starts from an already present level of rationality, but it never takes this or that stage of it to be a fixed substantial reason. Reason as the process of absolute clarification cannot identify itself with any of the reached stages in its own life-history. Phenomenological reason is an open reason, for it neither dogmatizes any level of rationality nor does it predetermine the end of history. Reason is a "comprehending reason" (begreifende Vernunft). The structure we call reason is in the making. In order to give a new and more justified explanation to our practice, reason thematizes it always from anew. Reason is thus to be defined as the process in which practice and reflection alternate giving rise to ever new philosophical problems. The self-comprehending phenomenological reason is an open reason also because it does not possess any closed system of principles fixed for all time to come. This openness of reason is also brought to light by our process of reflection. Reason has to remain an open structure, for the reflection is an endless process of reiteration.

Phenomenological reason is essentially "intentional" and it provides with the very norm for the identity of philosophy. It is the self-same reason which manifests itself in all the different forms of our philo-

sophical development. Reason is thus the identical intention of philosophy.[23] In the last paragraphs of the "Krisis", Husserl speaks of a
"conversion", a type of change-over, of our theoretical reason into an
"apodictic-rational attitude".[24] The real rationality consists in an
attitude and Husserl may be rightly criticized here for his neglecting
the reason we are confronted with in our day to day life. But then the
problem is whether Husserl ever claimed to have furnished a concrete
existential analysis of our life. Reason for Husserl is its own teleological
destiny.[25] Phenomenological reason is no fixed possession of man; it
is rather the most radical insight in the necessity of our task to give
sense to the world. It is a universal and radical self-understanding of
man in the form of a universal responsible science. Such a science is
nothing else than philosophy itself.[26] For Husserl, the practising
phenomenologist, this meant a task of supreme importance involving
a total personal conversion wherein Husserl seems to have lived the
"fate of a philosophical existence in its full earnestness".[27]

The intentional reason is not exhausted through the acts of our
understanding. The gradual fulfilment of the intention of philosophy,
i.e. to say, of reason takes place in various "experiments which have
to be dared and undertaken by us".[28]

In sum: phenomenological reason is neither an absolute faculty
endowed with infallible fixed a priori principles nor is it purely speculative in character. Although it criticizes the traditional forms of
rationalism and of intellectualism, still it does not surrender itself to
anti-rationalistic tendencies. The reason of Husserl is as much against
the dualistic prejudice of Descartes as against the Kantian limitation
of all science and knowledge, for it aims at a rigorous universal science
of philosophy as an endless task to be realized gradually. The "proto-
intention" (Urintention) of philosophy is reason itself. The autonomy
of reason aiming at a complete clarity manifests its teleological
destiny which actualizes and realizes itself in historical process.

The phenomenology of Husserl is a new grand defence of reason
without its "deification". Phenomenological reason is dynamic; and

---

[23] *Krisis*, p. 394.
[24] *Ibid.*, p. 269.
[25] A. Gurwitsch: "The Last Work of Edmund Husserl", *Philo. and pheno. Research*, XVI &
XVII (1956 and 1957).
[26] *Krisis*, p. 346.
[27] *Ibid.*, p. 17.
[28] Placed within the context of social-research this would amount to our working out
different "strategies" as proposals for actual realization within our concrete socio-political
life.

it rightly replaces the static reason as a faculty (Vermögen) by a dynamic concept of reason which is essentially practical, historical and teleological in nature. It is an open reason comprehending itself. There is nothing "eternal" about it; it is opposed to a reason as a closed system of eternal truths.

Phenomenological reason possesses thus both the characteristics of "growth" as well as of a "telos", of a task whose identity remains unchanged. There is no disparity between the two views, the two sides of the reason if we understand it in the following way: It is one and the same reason discovering and realizing its own nature from the twin directions of process and task. The "process-character" of reason attempts to fulfil the "task-character" of it; the "task-character" of reason is gradually fulfilled in the historical process.

It is this very idea of rationality as an endless task of the whole humanity which Husserl's phenomenology defends and not its different forms which represent the different stations on the zigzag road of the self-comprehension of reason.

Husserl's concept of reason seems thus to stand for the ideal of complete clarity which can only be realized gradually. If Husserl intended to imply that such a stage might be reached in all concreteness, then he would be facing many difficulties. Supposing, humanity had reached such an ideal stage; how could we identify it for what it is? It is difficult, if not impossible, to work out a satisfactory criterion establishing the identity between the ideal reached and the ideal we wish to reach. It was also not the intention of Husserl to maintain that such a stage could be reached soon. The last years of his life witnessing the barbarous acts of throwing over board all that is human must have made him see how far a complete stage of self-realization of reason still is.[29]

Philosophy, Husserl tells us, is an occupation consisting in our attempt to go beyond that which is reached. Phenomenological reason manifests itself in and through this occupation called philosophy. Philosophers, according to Husserl, are the officials (Funktionäre) of humanity working for the realization of the intention of philosophy. True and authentic philosophy is nothing else but the true and authentic rationalism. Husserl writes: "Denn von neuem betone ich: wahre und

---

[29] In a latter to A. Metzger, Husserl writes: "... ich bin nicht zum Fuehrer der nach 'seligem Leben' ringenden Menschheit berufen – im leidensvollen Drang der Kriegsjahre habe ich das anerkennen muessen, mein daimonion hat mich gewarnt. Vollbewußt und entschieden lebe ich rein als wiss. Philosoph (ich habe daher keine Kriegsschrift geschrieben ...)". *Philo. Jahrbuch der Görres-Gesellschaft*, 62. Jahrgang, I. Halbband, p. 196.

echte Philosophie bzw. Wissenschaft und wahrer und echter Rationalismus ist einerlei".[30]

Husserl of course does not claim that philosophy has reached this
ideal with him. But he no doubt maintains that his phenomenology is
the true historic form of rationalism, and that he has established the
ultimate primacy of reason in man's historical life.

In the opening section "of scepticism with regard to reason", Hume
shows the mistakes committed by the dogmatists as well as by the
sceptics.[31] Hume's own position is above this controversy between the
sceptics and the dogmatists. Although these two antagonists are otherwise very dissimilar to each other, still they are one with regard to a
false view of reason. Both of them agree that reason is something like
a sovereign faculty. The dogmatists defend such a sovereignty of
reason, whereas the sceptics deny it. Both are wrong for, as Hume
says, they fail to discern the real vital issue which lies not in the controversy whether reason possesses the sovereignty or not, but in trying
to show the functions and limitations of reason. The reason operating
in the field of the "relations of ideas" is no doubt to "be consider'd as a
kind of cause, of which truth is the natural effect", still it has its own
limitations which consists in the fact that it cannot furnish any
information outside the narrow field of the "demonstrative sciences".[32]

Since the field of matters of fact and existence is of vital concern to
us, it is not reason, but "belief" which possesses the ultimate sovereignty. "Reason is", Hume tells us, "and ought only to be the slave of the
passions".[33] When we talk of the subordination of reason to the
passions in Hume's philosophy, we mean the subordination of this
dogmatic and sceptical reason. Hume is a critic of an analytic a priori
reason. Like Husserl, he does not criticize the achievements of such a
reason in the fields like geometry, mathematics, but only its claim to
an ultimate sovereignty, including the field of matters of fact and
existence.

To a very great extent, Hume himself is responsible for the misunderstanding of his view of reason. "All reasonings may be divided
into two kinds, namely, demonstrative reasoning, or that concerning
relations of ideas, and moral reasoning, or that concerning matter of fact
and existence".[34] The first kind of reasoning is analytic in character

---

[30] *Krisis*, pp. 200–201.
[31] *Treatise*, p. 180 f.
[32] *Ibid.*, p. 180.
[33] *Ibid.*, p. 415 f.
[34] *Enquiries*, p. 35.

and consists in the relations of the ideas compared. "That three times five is equal to the half of thirty, expresses a relation between these numbers".[35]

When we seek to extend our knowledge by means of inference, we make use of a synthetic process which is very similar to our instinctive propensities. Hume seems to call such a reason "reason in general".[36] We shall see further down that Hume roundly declares reason to be a wonderful and unintelligible instinct in our souls.

Hume's use of reason is thus beset with ambiguities and it needs clarification. He uses it primarily in two senses: reason in the field of the "relations of ideas",[37] and reason in the field of matters of fact and existence. Reason as a wonderful instinct in our souls relates to the latter sense.[38] Reason in the field of relations of ideas is "analytic" and is exhausted by the relations between the ideas. Hume's own view of reason seems to sympathize with the reason in the field of matters of fact and existence.[39]

A complete view of reason involves taking into account Hume's theory of belief, of knowledge and of imagination. Hume tells us clearly that what we generally call reason is nearer to our "sentiments" and "feelings".[40] Like Husserl, Hume, too, is a critic of all abstract reasonings.[41]

Reason as opposed to experience is, for Hume, a false reason. Reason as distinguished from experience cannot give rise to the idea of causality. Hume tells us clearly in his "Enquiry Concerning the Human Understanding" that an "un-experienced reasoner" is no reasoner at all.[42] Reason in order to be useful must cooperate with experience. The philosophico-historical continuity from Hume to Husserl seems to have been broken off with Kant, for neither Husserl nor Hume maintains the sharp and unbridgeable gap between reason and experience.

Like Husserl and unlike Kant, Hume also does not accept the view of reason as a faculty endowed with fixed a priori principles. Hume further says that such an a priori reason would be unable to help us in our life. In the opening pages of his "Enquiry Concerning the Human Understanding", Hume distinguishes between "the easy and obvious

[35] *Ibid.*, p. 25.
[36] N. K. Smith: *The Philosophy of David Hume*, p. 100 and p. 288.
[37] *Treatise*, p. 180.
[38] *Ibid.*, p. 179.
[39] *Enquiries*, pp. 43 f. (foot-note).
[40] N. K. Smith: *The Philosophy of David Hume*, pp. 288 f.
[41] *Enquiries*, p. 156.
[42] *Enquiries*, pp. 43 f.

philosophy" and "the accurate and abstruse". He recommends the cultivation of the former rather than of the latter for the "abstruse philosophy, being founded on a turn of mind, which cannot enter into business and action, vanishes when the philosopher leaves the shade".[43] Abstract reason, Hume maintains, seems to have enjoined only a momentary reputation. The view of reason Hume is proposing includes an appeal to common sense.

To reduce life to exact rules is, according to Hume, not only painful, but also a fruitless occupation.[44] The distinction made by philosophers between reason and experience "is, at bottom, erroneous, at least, superficial".[45]

In his "Dialogues", Hume speaks of reason as a structure which lies very deep in our nature. He compares this structure with our instinct.[46] Reason, Hume maintains further, arises from the principle of "generation". All these Humean statements with regard to the nature of reason refer to reason in the synthetic sense and point to its character of being an incomprehensible process.

The synthetic sense of reason consists in its being an "experimental reason", a term used by Hume himself. This experimental reason is the ordering, designing and creative agency. It is no discursive faculty of reason "à la Kant".

Hume's own view of reason thus comes very near to a type of genetic explanation of the concept of reason. Reason is not something like fixed dimension liable to no change; it develops in that human practice, human history develops. There is a tendency even in Hume's philosophy to replace the speculative, abstract and pure reason by an "experimental experiential reason".

While emphasizing the role of reason in the field of the matters of fact and existence, Hume brings his concept of reason nearer to that of imagination. The universal principled imagination of Hume seems to replace his reason in its reflective instrumental role.

The following points seem to be of importance for our comparison:

1) Hume while criticizing an abstract, a priori, fixed and speculative reason prepares the ground for a phenomenological treatment of the same.

2) Like Husserl, Hume too maintains that reason as a fixed dimension

---

[43] *Ibid.*, pp. 6 f.
[44] *Essays*, p. 183.
[45] *Enquiries*, pp. 43 f.
[46] *Dialogues*, pp. 49 f.

(Vermögen) not only fails to overcome scepticism, but rather remains susceptible to scepticism.[47]

3) The reason described as a wonderful and unintelligible instinct in our souls points to what Hume terms "experimental reason". This experimental reason cooperates with experience and guides it. Hume already anticipates the process character of reason in close touch with the process of history.

4) Hume's view that there is no opposition between reason and experience implies a dynamic concept of reason.

5) Hume in characterizing reason as an incomprehensible, "wonderful and unintelligible instinct" does not bring in the concept of a "divine reason" (he is far from accepting such a view of reason); he rather points, but very vaguely, to the means and task-character of reason. Such a character of reason cannot be comprehended in one simple act of actualization. Reason is situational, historical and practical.

[47] It may not be out of point to remark that the position taken by Husserl and Hume in their "transcendental phenomenology" and "the science of human nature" respectively is outside and above the empiricism-rationalism controversy.

CHAPTER XI

EXPERIENCE AND REASON

In this and the chapter to follow we shall attempt to give a critical interpretation and appreciation of Husserl's philosophy of experience and reason. In doing so, we shall emphasize the reflective character of phenomenology more than its transcendental and purely descriptive characters. We hope thus to develop a "comprehensive" and less transcendental theory of a "critical reflective experience". In doing that we could hardly avoid a brief recapitulation of what has been said above on experience and reason.

Reflection is used in all serious philosophical discourses. No theory can be completely free from conceptualization; and this holds true to our consideration of the problems of experience and reason. Not only reason, but even the coming to be of experience points to certain factors, say, interpretation, induction, anticipation, reflection and so on. These factors themselves are "experienced" at a higher reflective level.

In the course of our investigation we have been able to establish the underlying conviction running through this work, namely the conviction that Hume's concepts of experience and reason are more similar to those of Husserl than to those of Kant. The philosophico-historical continuity from Hume to Husserl runs not via Kant, but rather via Meinong, Brentano, Avenarius, James etc.

Experience is to be understood as a process of perpetual contact with the world of things and beings; and the end of this process cannot be precalculated and prefixed. The concept of a "possible experience" is something like positing our past into the future. Thus experience is a process in becoming in which it marches forward by way of induction, anticipation, modification and even self-correction.[1] Because of these

---

[1] W. James maintains that experience is such a process that it "undoes her own work, and for an earlier order substitutes a new one." *The Principles of Psychology*, vol. II, p. 620.

factors of experience we speak of the habitualities of experience which allow us to conceive the future events. That the unknown presents itself in some mode of the already known is the result of our reflection. From the strategic point of view such an anticipatory character of experience is very important.

Even the origin of the concept of "negation" and of "negative judgments" can be shown to lie in our experiences of something being different from the anticipated. All anticipations expressed in any form of judgments have to be verified through experience. The most common characteristic of all forms of experience is "seeing" (Anschauung)[2] which takes place at different levels. Experience itself needs to be verified for the preconceived has to be actualized in concrete forms of experience.

Reason is to be understood not as fixed dimension with a priori principles; it is no reservoir of eternal truths. Reason is rather to be understood dynamically as an endless act of learning from experience through the mediation of reflection on life. Reason as endowed with eternal principles is "too speculative" to be tuned with experience and life. Our observations here aim at making experience agree with reason and vice-versa. The mutual dependence between reason and experience is very complex; and this complexity results from the fact that neither experience nor reason can be raised to fixed dimensions. The mistake of dogmatic rationalism consists in its making reason stand for a fixed faculty; whereas the sensualistic empiricism does a similar type of fixation with regard to experience.

As an act of learning, reason is dependent on experience; for experience is the material to be reflected upon. Reason learns from experience in order to guide the latter. In the absence of reason, as specified here, there is hardly any experience, for it needs reflection in order to show its own structures.

The birth of reason seems to be a later one depending on the performance of our act of reflection. The primary original mode of experience is, no doubt, sensuous perception; but reflection is the only dynamic factor of conceptualization which is needed in order to work out the structures of experience. The view of reflection as specified here avoids the twin mistakes of surrendering experience to reason and reason to experience.

The term experience as used here includes not only our direct contacts with the sensuous objects, but all sorts of "givenness", including

[2] *Krisis*, p. 464.

the given at the level of reflection. The term "given" has a manifold meaning[3] and can stand for something fully independent of the human mind, or for some sensuous content. It may also mean our experience on the non-reflective level. The sense in which we use this term "given" here points to our reflective experience. A pure method of reflection brings out the structures of experience and reason. Experience should also include the different modes like anticipation, expectation, induction, probability and so forth. Understood in this wide sense, experience may be interpreted to include even our experiences of "things-being-different-than-expected". Thus, the experiences of failure disappointment, deception, disagreement and so on form part of the stream of experience. The very possibility of falsification thus points to an experience which serves as the base of our act of falsifying. To falsify means to possess the experience of "not this, but that". Since experience includes its own modifications and corrections, there cannot be any total negation of experience.

The dispute between experience and reason is as old as our philosophical thinking. It was the Greeks who first of all distinguished the two paths of "Doxa", belief or opinion and of "episteme" or knowledge. This bifurcation became a traditional acquisition of the history of philosophy. The truth, it was maintained, can be reached only by means of "episteme"; the path of "Doxa" leads to falsity. Such a distinction was particularly emphasized by Parmenides in opposition to Heraclitus who sought the truth not in an absolute unchangeable being, but in the becoming. Thus Plato relegated the world of change to a world of appearance and credited only the world of ideas with reality. Since "being" in opposition to "becoming" is the real, the philosophers of being either denied the world of becoming or made it entirely dependent on the world of "episteme".

The implicit presupposition or conviction underlying such an argumentation was an unwarranted fixation of reality. Reality was conceived to be unchangeable, one, eternal and so forth. Parmenides talks of the path of "Doxa" as the forbidden one for it leads to darkness (falsity). The whole development of Western metaphysical thought has been taking place within and at the background of such a bifurcation of paths. The various forms of empiricism and rationalism testify to this.[4]

[3] J. Wild: "The Concept of the Given in Contemporary Philosophy", *Phil. and phen. Research*, vol. I (1940) pp. 70 f.
[4] L. Landgrebe: *Phänomenologie und Geschichte*, pp. 154 f.

This very presupposition or conviction has become questionable today; and we no longer believe that the changeable cannot be real simply because it changes. The static has been replaced by the dynamic; and "a Heraclitus" is today more actual than "a Parmenides" or "a Plato", "a Hume" and "a Husserl" more important than "a Hegel" or "a Kant". The philosophical thought must learn to see that all that is has become what it is. Mere ideal constructions ranging from metaphysical to axiomatic ones cannot solve the problems which demand a different type of clarity than that which an abstract reason is able to give. The phenomenological method of reflection is more suited to solve the problem lying between experience and reason.

The course of experience, as mentioned above, cannot be entirely predetermined. The future course of experience can be worked out in certain modes of itself. In this working out of the future course of experience the factor of reflection plays the most important role. Our reflective analysis has to take into account the historical factors which shape our experience. Wherein lies the historical character of experience? The character of experience as "historical" means that the preconditions of any historical situation cannot be predetermined completely. The thought-forms are generally taken to be underived from experience; but they are the forms with which our experience largely agrees. Such an abstract analysis forgets that the only forms which could not be the results of experience must be those with which experience disagrees. The continuity between sense and thought, between experience and reason is neither logical nor psychological; it is rather a continuity which is grounded in reflection. We shall discuss this point in the next chapter.

The concept of eternal truth thus gets a new meaning. As an ideal construction it no doubt retains its truth. One can even go further and maintain that at least in part the motivations to such constructions are present in our experience. These constructions are hypostatized by our wishful metaphysical thinking which then, instead of starting from experience, starts from reason.

Philosophy is a foundational science in the sense that it reflectively searches and researches the descriptive, explanatory and justificatory grounds of the phenomena (understood in the phenomenological sense). It thus represents an endless process; and its whole life consists of reflections. In addition to this, the conviction that reality itself is in the making makes our attempt to search for eternal truths still more futile. To philosophize means thus not so much to "find" as "to search".

We have learnt that, according to Husserl's phenomenology, reason is the task to be realized by philosophy; it is the "telos" of philosophy. Supposing that this telos of philosophy undergoes no change and the different forms of its realization in the history of philosophy are nothing but stepping-stones towards a complete realization of this goal, still there seems to be present in it a conviction which is very near to some sort of hypostatization. That there is such a teleology may well be admitted even from the point of view of experience; but then it must not be hypostatized in any way for that would mean cutting all relations with experience. That there is such a "telos-reason" must not be raised to a "dogma". All that we could, strictly speaking, maintain is that philosophy aims at such a telos of complete clarification, but we could hardly foresee how it would look in actualization. That this telos may itself vary from time to time and may undergo modifications and corrections is a point not to be lost sight of. The history of philosophy testifies to our observation.

Husserl's view of reason goes a bit too far in emphasizing the ideal of reason as a telos beyond all change and modification. Although Husserl does not make reason purely speculative and emphasizes its character of openness, still he makes it reside at too high a transcendental level of his phenomenology. We prefer the dynamic concept of reason which is open and comprehends the world and itself. The self-comprehending reason of Husserl thus remains in living touch with the process of reflection. Philosophy as reflection never loses its actuality.[5]

The role played by reflection in our context of experience and reason is of central importance. Reason as the "experience of reflection on the experience" is nothing else but experience of experience at a higher level of our reflective consciousness. The function of such a reason is to learn from and give guidance to experience.

Husserl's transcendental phenomenology seems to have two sides: (i) the transcendental ego "exists" absolutely and can be described only transcendentally and reflectively; and (ii) the purely descriptive

---

[5] The concrete socio-political relevance of philosophy as reflection lies in its attempt to discover models or strategies to be realized in real concrete historical situations. It should work out not only practicable models, but should also suggest the means of realization. A reflection residing at a very high transcendental level and living its life of pure theoretical acts fails to orient itself socially. The character of "reflectivity" necessarily bears the stamp of "sociability" and vice-versa.

character which is healthier and nearer to experience and reason in their relation to the life and the world we live in. Husserl's phenomenology has certain programmatic similarities with the movement called "linguistic analysis", but the latter is not transcendental in approach. What is of enduring importance for our philosophical research today is not so much the transcendental phenomenological project of Husserl, but rather his purely reflective procedure.[6] Such a procedure can be fruitfully applied to different problems of philosophy.

The dispute between experience and reason has also been amply displayed by the two rival theories of empiricism and rationalism in philosophy. The main problems of philosophy have received answers mainly from these two sides. The empiricists' answer consists in their argument that all knowledge is based upon experience. But their mistake lies in their unnecessarily narrowing down the scope of experience; they limit experience to sense-experience only. They also fail to see the important role played by reflection in philosophy. The act of reflection itself may be experienced at a higher level of givenness. Empiricism modified in this way may well claim to be a very healthy approach in philosophy. Rationalists, on the other hand, maintain reason or intellect in itself to be the only true source of knowledge. They maintain further that the truths of reason are superior to those of experience. Reason is made to be a "reservoir" of a priori certain principles beyond all changes. Such a reason is too abstract, speculative and intellectualistic to be harmonized with our experience. Empiricism subordinates reason to experience; whereas rationalism does just the opposite of it. Both of them are thus in the wrong. They are too static to show a dynamic point of contact between them.

The act of reflection thematizing all convictions enables us not only to see the mistakes of rationalism as well as of empiricism; but it also paves the way to overcome their so-called opposition in that it makes reason a factor in experience in such a way that this factor of reason develops with the process of reflection.

We attempt here to work out an instance which is comprehensive of both experience and reason in such a way that it not only shows the process-character of experience as well as of reason, but explains them. Such an instance is that of a pure phenomenological reflection. It is pure not because it points necessarily to the transcendental phenomenological dimension, but because it leaves the mundane level of our experience and studies it from a sensually detached point of view. This

---

[6] M. Farber: *The Foundation of Phenomenology*, pp. 540 f.

reflective instance functions as our reason learning from experience; it is experience experiencing itself reflectively.

The dispute between experience and reason seems to be without any foundation, and the distinction made between them becomes superfluous when we take the mediating role of reflection into account. There are two types of naivities which must be avoided in philosophy: It is as naive to wish to determine everything for all time to come just as to take everything for granted without any critical reflection. As reason cannot be identified with a fixed faculty with a priori principles, so also experience cannot be equated with mere sense-perceptions. Experience without reflection is blind and cannot transcend the boundaries of sense-perceptions; reason without reflection is too speculative and static a faculty to do justice to experience.

Reason as a "reflective learning" from experience guides our life. Such a reason is free from all fixed a priori principles. The concept of possible experience cannot be determined on the ground of the native forms of our reason; it can only be anticipated on the ground of the structural moments within experience, e.g. induction, expectation, anticipation, association and so forth. We need not necessarily perform the transcendental phenomenological reduction in order to arrive at such a concept of experience and reason. We are also not determining the concepts reason and experience terminologically and arbitrarily for that would lead either to artificiality or constructivism. The structures reason and experience are shown to arise from our practice of reflection on the mundane existence.

Kant in opposition to Husserl and Hume determines the concepts of reason and experience. He also starts from a particular concept of experience, namely experience in the field of natural sciences.

If rationality of philosophy represents the goal of a complete clarification, then we must not forget that even this ideal itself is constituted by an act of reflection. How else could we constitute it? Husserl's concepts of reason and experience are not completely free from all ambiguities. At the radical transcendental level these two concepts do not only lose all their opposition, but they seem to be interchangeable terms. Such a mutual merging of the two concepts fails to do full justice to our day-to-day life-experiences. The domain of our concrete experiences is not so much neglected by Husserl's transcendental phenomenological reduction; it is rather explained only "eidetically". This is the point where many analysts part company with Husserl's programme which, in spite of so many differences, has

much in common with their programme. Although both these pro-
grammes share a great respect for the ordinary language, the phenomenologist goes further and explains it transcendentally. A complete
detachment from the actual life-experiences seems to be very artificial
for an analyst; whereas a phenomenologist must perform this device
in order to reach the pure reduced field of constituting consciousness.[7]

Husserl tries to overcome the so-called chasm between experience
and reason in that he, at the transcendental level, does not separate
the two, for they both mean a transcendental seeing which consists of
the pure original self-experience of the transcendental subjectivity.
Husserl credits experience in that he maintains that it represents our
immediate contact with the objects. The reason, he praises, is the very
telos of philosophy and must be realized gradually.

We want to emphasize not so much the pure transcendental-phenomenological character of experience and reason, but rather their
character of learning and guiding which results from reflection. The
stream of experience is made the object of reflection, and the result of
such a reflection is the reason as a factor in experience. Such a reflection is not contrary to experience, for the act of reflection itself
can be experienced at a higher level. Our concept of reflection emphasizes that aspect of Husserlian reason which, though not created by
practice, is occasioned by it.

The reason that reigns supreme in the field of mathematical sciences
can be understood as a faculty of construction busy with projects; it is
our constructive projective capacity that transforms the world of
lived-experiences into vacuous but already defined constructs and
axioms. But these transformations fail to explain the world they
themselves are founded upon. They rather try to replace world-facts
by scientific-facts.[8] Such a reason is an abstract faculty aiming at
controlling the world. It creates the world it is busy with. The mistake
of such a reason lies in its excessive claim to an universal autonomy.
As an instrument for explaining the world of life, this mathematical
reason must be replaced by what we have termed here "learning
reason".[9]

The reason consists thus in the perpetual exposition, understanding,
interpretation and justification of the world given in experience.
Reason learns the art of such an exposition through reflection. Thanks

---

[7] J. Wild: *Existence and the World of Freedom*, pp. 102 f.
[8] *Ibid.*, pp. 60 f.
[9] L. Landgrebe: *Der Weg der Phänomenologie*, Chap. VI.

to such an instance of "reflective experience" that reason and experience cooperate with each other in such a way that reason learns from experience and experience is guided by reason.

On the level of our natural, unreflective attitude our life goes on well as if there were hardly any problems to be solved. It is true that philosophical problems of and about life consist not so much in the unreflective attitude, but rather in our reflective approach to it. The natural experience that naively gets its verification as well as modification and correction does not bother about the structures of experience. It is reflection which thematizes such an experience at a higher level of experience. Reflection teaches us that neither experience nor reason can be raised to fixed dimensions liable to no change. There is no closed system of reflection, and every philosophy of reflection must remain open to new results of reflection.

What is then the meaning of a rational explanation? It consists in our reflection on the unreflective life with the goal to guide it. All decisions, in order thus to be rational, must show the character of reflection. "Philosophical decisions are nothing", Hume writes, "but the reflections on common life, methodized and corrected".[10]

No theory of experience and reason can predetermine the future course of life; all that it can do is to anticipate the course of future experience. There are things and events which are new to our experience which extends the past to the future. Husserl speaks of "residuum", "naturality", "passivity" which really means admitting that all that is cannot be understood only in terms of consciousness without remainder.[11] There are real novelties which experience does experience in the course of its future developments. The experience of the unexpected, unanticipated is one of such novelties. Merleau-Ponty speaks of an "insubordination of things" in their relation to human consciousness.[12]

Our exposition of experience which emphasizes the important role played by reflection cannot be interpreted as implying sensualistic empiricism. The character of reflection purges experience of its limited sensualistic horizon. The way we describe reason cannot be taken to be dogmatic for reason is made to stand for a dynamic process of learning from experience. Our phenomenological-reflective analysis of the twin concepts of experience and reason points to a "reflective empiricism"

[10] *Enquiries*, p. 162.
[11] Merleau-Ponty: *Das Auge und der Geist*, pp. 66 f.
[12] *Ibid.*, p. 115.

as well as to a "reflective rationalism"; for it thematizes experience and reason from a purely reflective point of view which is not the case with the traditional theories of empiricism and rationalism.

Reflection as a dynamic process of perpetual suspension of all naivities and "hypostatizations" does not relegate them to "mere nothing"; it rather enables us to see their origin, meaning and justification. The act of reflection enables us to see the process-character of both experience and reason. Reflection is the dynamic instance of control. It is reflection that makes reason guide experience and makes experience provide reason with content. Reflection is the go-between empiricism and rationalism.

We have already mentioned above the different modes of experience, e.g. induction, anticipation, modification, correction, all of which belong to experience. Thus the flowing stream of experience does not consist only of positivities, but also of negativities which are experienced. In the sense of a reflective givenness there is hardly any negative experience, for something is always "lived" facing the subject living it.

The life as an "unreflective practice" is given in the beginning. It is spontaneity pure and simple. Such a life knows no reflection and expresses the pre-reflective level. The experience on this stage is unreflective, too. This unreflective or pre-reflective experience possesses certain invariant structures which work as habitualities. These habitualities seem to guarantee a smooth flow of life. The reflection sets in whenever and wherever there are upsets and irregularities in the smooth run of this unreflective life. Thus reflection provides the very basis for further learning which in the form of a developing reason takes the role of a guide to our experience. The experience which is guided by reason is not and cannot be fully determined by reason; it rather occasions further conformation, modification and correction of our reason. And this process goes on endlessly. The following schematic representation makes our point clear:

Life .... Experience .... Reflection ....
.... Reason .... Experience ....
.... Reflection .... Reason .... and so on.

We have emphasized the character of openness not only of our experience but also of our reason. This openness of reason is in fact not primary; it is rather derived and secondary for it is derived from the original insight in the endless character of our philosophical reflection.

Reflection is thus above both experience and reason, and it comprises both of them. The reason thus manifests itself as a function within the realm of experience. Whitehead speaks of the function of reason as consisting in its promoting life.[13] Reason is also a component part of experience in the sense that it is shown to develop from out of experience when reflection sets in.

The concept of reflection, as specified here, serves to solve the problem of experience and reason in the following way:

1) It shows that neither experience nor reason can be raised to fixed dimensions;

2) It thus dynamizes the twin concepts of experience and reason;

3) It overcomes thus the traditional opposition between experience and reason in that it shows that experience is not just only sense-perception and reason is not a fixed faculty endowed with a priori principles;

4) It is the mediating instance between experience and reason and paves the way for a solution of this age-old problem of the opposition between experience and reason.

5) The solution consists in showing their mutual cooperation. Reason learns from experience and guides the latter. Experience gives herself to reflection so that reason may be born out of it.

---

[13] "Reason is a factor in experience which directs and criticizes the urge towards the attainment of an end realized in imagination but not in fact". A. N. Whitehead: *The Function of Reason*, p. 5.

CHAPTER XII

TOWARDS A THEORY OF "COMPREHENSIVE, CRITICAL AND REFLECTIVE EXPERIENCE"

No theory can be worked out without taking into account the central role played by reflection. A theory of language is the result of the reflection on the language. The theory of science thematizes the sciences with regard to their presuppositions, methods, results etc. from a higher level of reflection. Every theory thus implies necessarily a meta-stage of reflective investigations.

A theory of experience must thus thematize the course of our experience reflectively. To theorize means to use the method of reflection (in the sense to be specified below). The act of reflection is a performance we undertake in order to explain, understand and justify the objects of the field we reflect on.

When we speak here of "reflective experience", we mean that the act of reflection performed by us is itself a stuff of experience. At the level of our mundane experience we do not differentiate between the experience of material objects and the experience of activity. But when we go to work out a theory of experience we have to include the act of reflection which thematizes the mundane level of our experience within the field of our reflective experience. Experience comes thus to self-consciousness in reflective experience. Not reason but reflection thematizes experience. From a higher dynamic level of reflective experience we are in a position to observe the interplay between reason and experience. Reason as a factor in experience might be hypostatized along with the hypostatization of our mundane experience, but the level of reflective experience is beyond all hypostatization. It is the very instance of perpetually theorizing the fixations made uncritically at the level of our mundane existence.

We speak here of a theory of "comprehensive critical reflective experience" (CCRE) and hope to show that such a concept of experience would be able to avoid the undue narrowness of the sensualistic-empirical concept of experience, on the one hand, and the excessive intellectualism and transcendentalism attached to this concept on the other. It is as much a mistake to "materialize" and identify experience with isolated sense-data as to "formalize" and "transcendentalize" it.

The concept of experience our theory introduces and works out is "reflective" because it reflects on, i.e. to say, thematizes the mundane level of our experience. It is "critical" because it does not take for granted and use as the basis of further judgments the uncritical naive claims of our experience made at the level of mundane existence. It is "comprehensive" because the reason is shown to be a factor in such an experience. It is comprehensive also because it tries to open up a way towards an empiricism which without degenerating into reductionism proposes to establish the continuity between experience and reason.

There is a sense in which we can speak of the continuity between sense and thought. Provided we take into account all the various motivations which are implicitly or explicitly active in the so-called objective sciences, we might see how the sense lives in the life of the thought. The way to show and establish the continuity cannot mean any demonstrative proof; it can mean only a reflective continuity (in the sense to be specified below).

Husserl's contention to show and establish the origin of the ideal objective universal of thought in the pre-predicative experience has been variously interpreted and criticized.[1] Mohanty has rightly pointed out the concept of "origination" is to be understood in a metaphorical sense. The process of idealization is an endless process of reiteration, and it is maintained that such a process cannot be completed "so as to result in the real production of the idealities".[2] Such a reading of the problem of the origin of thought in experience leads rightly to the conclusion that there is some type of "phenomenological discontinuity".

The intention of Husserl's phenomenology is to show that the exact objectivity is a performance of method (exakte Objektivität ist Leistung der Methode).[3] Husserl maintains that the objective and absolutely unchangeable knowledge of truth is itself an endless idea (eine unendliche Idee).[4]

---

[1] J. N. Mohanty: *Edmund Husserl's Theory of Meaning*, p. 144.
[2] *Ibid.*, p. 145.
[3] *Krisis*, p. 359.
[4] *Ibid.*, p. 373 (foote-note).

In order to grasp the full meaning of what Husserl intends when he speaks of the origin of the idealities in experience, we must briefly mention the distinction he makes between "to reactivate" and "to deduce". The original evidence which is to be reactivated cannot be identified with "the evidence of the axioms" (Evidenz der Axiome).[5]

Husserl maintains further, while trying to show the genesis of thought in experience, that the science of geometry is only a so-called deductive science; it is not fully deductive. He speaks of the fundamental law which is absolutely evident: The premises must be reactivated to the last stage of evidence so that the evidence of deduction may continue with it further and go on constructing and deducing idealities.[6]

The sciences are no ready-made heritage (ein fertiges Erbe)[7] in the form of well documented sentences; they are rather productive developments of sense-constitution (Sinnbildung) which has at its disposal the previous sedimentations.

The process of deduction follows in its development the formal-logical evidence. But without our ability to "reactivation" (Vermögen der Reaktivierung) leading to the original activities hidden in the fundamental concepts of the so-called purely deductive sciences, geometry would be a tradition empty of all meaning. Husserl speaks of the "what" and "how" of the prescientific materials in the absence of which we would not even be in a position to think of the sense which geometry might have for us.[8]

The theoretical-genetic motivation aiming at showing the origin of the deductive evidence in original evidence has been forgotten under the influence of the practical success of the applied geometry (praktischer Erfolg der angewandten Geometrie).[9] Husserl speaks in this context of the "dangers of a scientific life" (Gefahren eines wissenschaftlichen Lebens)[10] which surrenders itself completely to logical activities. The alienation lying within such a practice of the deductive sciences results into and favours the conviction of the objective science to autonomy.

If there is any sense in speaking of a "phenomenological continuity"

---

[5] *Ibid.*, p. 375.
[6] *Krisis*, p. 375.
[7] *Ibid.*, p. 375.
[8] "Die Deduktion in ihrem Fortschreiten folgt der formallogischen Evidenz, aber ohne das wirklich ausgebildete Vermögen der Reaktivierung der in den Grundbegriffen verschlossenen ursprünglichen Aktivitäten, ..., wäre die Geometrie eine sinnentleerte Tradition ..." *Ibid.*, p. 376.
[9] *Ibid.*, p. 376.
[10] *Ibid.*, p. 376.

between experience and thought, then it must be a transcendental-genetic sense-constitution (Sinnstiftung). Husserl differentiates between the heritage-continuity lying within the deductive sciences and that pointing to our ability of reactivation. The heritage of methods to construct ever new idealities logically goes on without any break, whereas the ability to reactivate the original sources of meaning for the latter has failed to transmit itself.[11] Thus the continuity Husserl's phenomenology claims to establish means our ability to reactivate the meaning-giving sources (Sinnquellen). It belongs also to the sense of the continuity not to forget that the real production of the idealities results under the conviction that there are pure deductive sciences. It is this very conviction which is criticized by Husserl. Husserl speaks of the deductive science as implying in the first instance only a demand. And this demand, Husserl maintains further, can be justified by our ability to reactivate the most original evidence. It is this ability to reactivation which is expressed by the pretended claim of the objective science to search for the truth.[12]

It follows from what has been said above that the problem of continuity between experience and thought can be established only by taking into account the role played by our reflective experience. Thus the much discussed and debated problem of the continuity as well as discontinuity is attacked here from a reflective point of view. The emergences of real differences at the thought-level cannot be denied, and if Husserl's phenomenology is understood to deny this there is of course a discontinuity. But Husserl is not a Lockean to claim that there is nothing in the thought which was not previously in the sense.

In order to explain the emergence of the real differences, we need a theory or reflection which, no doubt, does not deny the real differences, but which certainly maintains that there is a certain "reflective continuity" between the life of our experience and that of our thought. The method of reflection is a way of theoretical practice and it is limited not only to phenomenological but can be used in other disciplines too.

Reflection, as understood here, consists of our act-performances in which the manifold occurrences are analysed. It is the method of our "conscious analysis" as such.[13] It is the only method that helps us explain the different conceptualizations and idealizations to be found

[11] *Krisis*, p. 376.
[12] *Ibid.*, p. 377.
[13] *Ideen I*, pp. 147 f.

in the different fields of human inquiries. The experience that is analysed here is the experience of our reflective act-performances.

The method of reflection, to begin with, suspends all matter-of-course, all naivities and all the so-called objectivities to be found in the different branches of human inquiry. These naivities are not just explained away but shown to be the correlates of the acts of reflection performed.

The reflection, performed in all concreteness, in the field of natural and mathematical sciences differs from one undertaken in the field of social sciences. Still both the performances are reflective in character because they are thematizing the matter-of-course at a higher level. Thus there corresponds to every type of givenness a certain form of our reflective experience.[14] Any critical reflective method must remain open, for it consists of acts searching and researching the noetic-noematic correlativity everywhere. Reflection opens the way to the problems of constitution. And the constituting function of our consciousness is all-pervasive.

The method of reflection is no construction; it does not claim to have given an ultimate solution. It is no metaphysical reflection, for it is non-positional. It does not start with any position of its own which it must defend. The most important job of reflection is to look for problems and their solutions where other dogmatic and semi-dogmatic sciences do not see any problem.

The method of reflection is not a speculative one, for it does not create the objects it deals with. The act of reflection is thus neither merely logical-axiomatic nor dogmatic-rational; it is also not sensualistic in character. It is a higher form of reflective experience in which all the reflections mentioned above are themselves thematized and reflected upon.[15] Reflection is consciousness' own method expressing itself not only in human thought but also in human language. Reflection is the constitutive feature of consciousness.

Any philosophy of reflection has to remain an open process for the very process of reflection is open in character. The question regarding an "ultimate logic of reflection" cannot be answered affirmatively for such a logic points to a goal which can be reached only approximately.[16] This is why every attempt to establish an absolute closed system of a

---

[14] *F.u.t.L.*, § 60.
[15] *E.P. II*, pp. 109 f.
[16] G. Frey: *Sprache: Ausdruck des Bewußtseins*, p. 38.

philosophy of reflection is futile for it betrays so many metaphysical traits it remains subject to.[17]

We have already mentioned that the concept of reflection we introduce here is "non-positional" which means that it does not take up any position dogmatically. Since it consists of acts of suspension it cannot itself be positional, i.e. to say, it cannot claim a position for itself beyond all suspension. This does not mean that it is self-destructive. As an act-instance it is outside the opposition "positional and anti-positional" (not non-positional). Thus there is something artificial in the attempt to lay down the fixed number of our steps of reflection. The process of reflection is an unending one in the sense of an "iteration" which means our ability to reactivate and to repeat an act of reflection. Such a process of iteration can be continued ad infinitum, at least theoretically. And as a non-positional reflection, it possesses no motivation to break the process in order to end in the real productions of systems or idealities. This "unending iteration", Husserl says, is nothing else but the "unlimitedness of perceptual field" (Unabschließbarkeit des Wahrnehmungsfeldes).[18] It is this field which is reflectively thematized resulting into what we call the unending character of our reflection.

The process of reflection is an open one also because it does not "absolutize" any conclusions reached, not even its own. There are naivities not only in the field of mundane experience. Husserl speaks of "the naivities of the higher stage" (Naivitäten höherer Stufe) which consist in the "absolutization" of the methods used and the results reached.

The reflective experience in the sense of a reflective consciousness needs and comprehends the level of our non or pre-reflective consciousness. The consciousness we have at this higher level of reflection is beyond the reach of our experience we have at our mundane level. The question whether there is an "absolute reflection" in the sense of not being in need of any material must be answered in the negative. There is as little an absolute reflection as there is a human existence without any reflection. It is always some type of matter of course which sets the reflection going.

Our concept of the CCRE is not without consequences for the problem of "learning" put within the context of experience and reason. The most formal and general schema of all human inquiries is: "thought

---

[17] H. Wagner: *Philosophie und Reflexion*, Preface.
[18] U.M., A V. 16.

searches truth". We have already mentioned that reason represents the learning-process or moment from experience. This is made accessible to us at a higher level of reflection. On the basis of this learning, reason guides experience. But experience in its onward march occasions modification or correction of what has been learnt. Reason must thus always be in the process of making. There is no fixed reason for there is no fixed learning. There are no ultimate and finally absolute criteria of a learning which might be said to be beyond all modification or correction. If we have learnt to the effect that no further learning is needed, then learning loses its character of being a process. Not only that, but all our inquiries would then be nothing else but a futile and constant repetition. This would mean that the future is just a point to point elongation of the past. That we never end to learn points to the fact that there do exist novelties. No learning makes further learning superfluous.

We learn not only in the sense of augmentation of knowledge, of control and correction, but we learn also in the sense of improving our very criteria of knowledge, truth and so on.[19] There is a general, but no final learning.[20]

The so-called "negative experiences" in the sense of modification, correction, disappointment of our anticipation affect the process of experience "positively", for they bring about better ways, i.e. to say, more rational ways of explanation, understanding and justification. They extend and enrich the field of what has been learnt.

The reason thus is no eternal faculty with fixed a priori principles, it is a "limited reason" which learns from experience, guides it, makes mistakes and needs correction and development. Any "critique" of reason has to be thus a "critique" of such a reason. Since reason cooperates with experience and remains – thanks to the process of reflection – in a living touch with it, its so-called a priori principles are more or less the lasting insights gained from experience through reflection. Reason is also not completely passive for the moment of reflection is active. Reason is only seemingly independent of experience; it is only apparently pure. Reflection teaches us the seat of all evidences is no longer reason.

All our statements in the different fields of human inquiry are related to the process of reflection in which they are rooted and by which they are thematized. There is thus a "fundamental relevance"

---

[19] P. Krausser: *Kritik der endlichen Vernunft*, pp. 193 f.
[20] Dilthey: *Gesammelte Werke*. Bd. VII, pp. 86 f.

possessed by reflection, for all our conceptual knowledge represents the results reached through the performance of reflection. This knowledge reached is what we term "theory" and the concrete process of experience resulting from this theory is called "practice". Our different "strategies" as suggested models put for realization betray both the sides of theory and practice. The concept of reflection is thus comprehensive of both theory and practice.

We may thus speak of the "primacy of reflection" in human inquiries. The primacy of reflection consists in the perpetual practice of reflective suspension of all matter-of-course. The demand for an absolute point we should arrive at or we should start from is itself a piece of metaphysics.

Reflection is no problem to be solved; it is also not a question to be answered. It is just a way, the way to solve problems. Reflection is thus not a theory itself, but it is the very way to work out theories. The reflective experience as specified above is the most original experience in the sense that it represents the purest form of the most immediate givenness. It is the very dynamic source of all our explanation, description and justification. Reflection is the only critical remedy for all the metaphysical diseases.

The concept of reflective experience as advocated here does not side either with the traditional empiricism or with the dogmatic rationalism. It does not subordinate either reason to experience or experience to reason. As the most critical instance it is neither introspective-psychological nor sensualistic-empirical; it is also no abstract rational or axiomatic process. It is rather "phenomenological" in the strict sense of a method of "pointing to".

Since the method of reflection is allied neither with empiricism nor with rationalism, it possesses the needed distance for a fair treatment of the problems of philosophy which have generally been seen either from the point of view of rationalism or from that of empiricism.

We may characterize our concept of the CCRE point by point in the following way:

1. It is no concrete sensuous contact between the subject and object. It is an immanent perception.
2. It is an act performed at a deeper and higher level thematizing the lower level of our mundane experience.
3. As an act performed, it is "lived", i.e., experienced by us. It is a form of reflective experience under which other lower forms of experience are given.

4. It is the most dynamic instance of perpetual suspension of all matter of course to be found in the different fields of human inquiry.

5. It serves thus the most important philosophical purpose by opening the way to the problems of constituting function. It discovers in all concreteness the "noetic-noematic correlativity" and shows that all that is, corresponds to some form of reflective experience.

6. It is thus neither "positional" nor "anti-positional"; it is "non-positional" which means the act of positing the being of all that is reflected upon.

7. It is the very instance leading to a view of experience which is comprehensive of both reason and experience as they are generally understood in the traditional philosophy. It is the instance which overcomes the so-called age-old controversy, dispute and opposition between reason and experience.

8. It makes reason and experience cooperate with each other in that it shows that reason as an instance of learning from experience is a factor in experience and experience is there to be reflected upon. Reason and experience are not contrary but complementary to each other in the process of learning.

9. It is an open process not only because of the unlimitedness of the field it perpetually thematizes, but also because it never "absolutizes" its own results. Strictly speaking, it does not aim at fixed results.

10. Experience and reason, left to themselves, fail to establish any conclusion. Both need the process of reflection in order to be able to cooperate with each other.

11. It is a critical instance criticizing not only the unwarranted assumptions and "absolutizations" of the different sciences, but also the undue claims of reason and experience.

No reason thinks without experience; no experience is without reason. The dynamic instance of a comprehensive, critical reflection as the needed "go-between" accomplishes the ensemble of reason and experience resulting in a fruitful dialogue between them.

The following schematic representation of the different modes of reflection brings out clearly the relationship between them:

REFLECTION

positional			non-positional

formal-axiomatic	metaphysical-dogmatic

logical calculus	closed systems without internal contra-diction

various metaphysical systems		various philo-sophies of Being	the different "Weltan-schau-ungen" and re-ligious systems

negative side	positive side
Insight into the necessarily im-perfect character of all concretely performed reflec-tions	Insight into the poten-tial character of end-lessness of reflection (an endless iteration)

BIBLIOGRAPHICAL REFERENCES

The list of the primary sources containing the original works of Husserl and Hume has been mentioned in the note on Abbreviation at the beginning of the book. The list given below includes only the names of such works as have been directly or indirectly alluded to in the course of the book.

Aguirre, A. F., Natürlichkeit und Transzendentalität. Der skeptisch-genetische Rückgang auf die Erscheinung als Ermöglichung der Epoché bei Edmund Husserl, Dissertation, Köln, 1968.
Avenarius, R., *Der menschliche Weltbegriff*, Leipzig, 1912.
Avenarius, R., *Kritik der reinen Erfahrung*, 2 Bände. Leipzig, 1921.
Biemel, W., "Die entscheidenden Phasen der Entwicklung von Husserls Philosophie", *Zeitschrift für philosophische Forschung*, XIII, 1959.
Blanshard, B., *Reason and Analysis*, London, 1942.
Brentano, F., *Psychologie vom empirischen Standpunkt*, Hamburg, 1955.
Brentano, F., *Von der Klassifikation der psychischen Phänomene*, Hamburg, 1959.
Buck, G., *Lernen und Erfahrung. Zum Begriff der didaktischen Induktion*, Berlin/Köln, 1967.
Carnap, R., *Introduction to Semantics*, Cambridge, Mass., 1942.
Cavendish, A. P., *David Hume*, London, 1969.
Dewey, J., *Experience and Nature*, London, 1929.
Diemer, A., *Edmund Husserl. Versuch einer systematischen Darstellung seiner Phänomenologie*, Meisenheim a. G., 1956.
Dilthey, W., *Gesammelte Schriften*, Leipzig-Berlin, I–VIII.
Eley, L., *Die Krise des Apriori in der transzendentalen Phänomenologie Edmund Husserls*, The Hague, 1962.
Fink, E., "Operative Begriffe in Husserls Phänomenologie", *Zeitschrift für philosophische Forschung*, XI, 1957.
Fink, E., "Was will die Phänomenologie Edmund Husserls?" *Die Tatwelt*, 1934.
Frey, G., *Sprache – Ausdruck des Bewußtseins*, Stuttgart, 1965.
Funke, G., *Zur transzendentalen Phänomenologie*, Bonn, 1957.
Funke, G., *Phänomenologie – Metaphysik oder Methode?*, Bonn, 1966.
Gadamer, H. G., *Wahrheit und Methode. Grundzüge einer philosophischen Hermeneutik*, Tübingen, 1960.
Gurwitsch, A., "The Last Work of Edmund Husserl", *Philosophy and Phenomenological Research*, XVI, 1956 and XVII, 1957.
Gurwitsch, A., William James' Theory of the 'Transitive Parts' of the Stream of Consciousness, *Philosophy and Phenomenological Research*, III, 1943.

Habermas, J., *Erkenntnis und Interesse*, Frankfurt a.M., 1968.
Held, K., *Lebendige Gegenwart. Die Frage nach der Seinsweise des transzendentalen Ich bei Edmund Husserl, entwickelt am Leitfaden der Zeitproblematik*, Haag, 1966.
Hendel, C. W., *Studies in the Philosophy of David Hume*, New York, 1963.
Hohl, H., *Lebenswelt und Geschichte. Grundzüge der Spätphilosophie E. Husserls*, Freiburg/München, 1962.
Hülsmann, H., "Der Systemanspruch der Phänomenologie Edmund Husserls", *Salzburger Jahrbuch für Philosophie*, Band. VII, 1963.
Hülsmann, H., "Epoché und Existenz", *Salzburger Jahrbuch für Philosophie*, Band. IX., 1965.
James, W., *The principles of Psychology*, 2.Vols. Dover Publication, Inc., 1950.
Juhos, B., "Negationsformen empirischer Sätze", *Erkenntnis*, VI, 1936.
Kern, I., *Husserl und Kant*, Haag, 1964.
Krausser, P., *Kritik der endlichen Vernunft. Diltheys Revolution der allgemeinen Wissenschafts- und Handlungstheorie*, Frankfurt, a.M., 1968.
Kuspit, D. B., "Fiction and Phenomenology", *Philosophy and Phenomenological Research*, XXI, 1968.
Kydd, R., *Reason and Conduct in Hume's Treatise*, London, 1946.
Landgrebe, L., *Der Weg der Phänomenologie*, Gütersloh, 1963.
Landgrebe, L., *Phänomenologie und Geschichte*, Gütersloh, 1967.
Landgrebe, L., *Phänomenologie und Metaphysik*, Hamburg, 1949.
Langen, Th., *Merleau-Ponty's Critique of Reason*, London, 1966.
Lauer, Q., *Phenomenology – Its Genesis and Prospect*, New York, 1965.
Mall, R. A., *Hume's Concept of Man. An Essay in philosophical Anthropology*, Calcutta/New York, 1967.
Mall, R. A., "Husserl's Ctiticism of Kant's Theory of Knowledge", *The Journal of the Indian Academy of Philosophy*, vol. I, 1967.
Merleau-Ponty, M., *Das Auge und der Geist*, Hamburg, 1967.
Merleau-Ponty, M., *Phänomenologie der Wahrnehmung*, Berlin, 1966 (übersetzt von R. Boehm).
Metzger, A., "Ein Brief Edmund Husserls von 1919 an A. Metzger", *Philosophisches Jahrbuch der Görres-Gesellschaft*, 62.Jahrgang.
Mohanty, J. N., *Edmund Husserl's Theory of Meaning*, The Hague, 1964.
Mohanty, J. N., "The Concept of Phenomenology", *The Journal of the Indian Academy of Philosophy*, vol.IV, 1965.
Murphy, A. E., *The Use of Reason*, New York, 1943.
Paci, E., *Die Lebensweltwissenschaft*, Symposium sobre la nocion Husserliana de la Lebenswelt, Mexico, 1963.
Peursen, C. v., *Phänomenologie und analytische Philosophie*, Köln, 1969.
Price, H. H., *Hume's Theory of the External World*, Oxford. 1963.
Price, H. H., *Thinking and Experience*, London, 1953.
Robberechts, L., *Edmund Husserl. Eine Einführung in seine Phänomenologie*, übersetzt von K. Held, Hamburg, 1967.
Santayana, G., *The Life of Reason*, New York, 1959.
Sauer, F., "Über das Verhältnis der Husserlschen Phänomenologie zu David Hume", *Kant-Studien*, XXXV.
Smith, N. K., *The Philosophy of David Hume*, London, 1960.
Smith, N. K., "The Naturalism of Hume", *Mind*, 1905.
Szilasi, W., *Einführung in die Phänomenologie Edmund Husserls*, Tübingen, 1959.
Seebohm, Th., *Die Bedingungen der Möglichkeit der Transzendentalphilosophie. Edmund Husserls transzendentalphilosophischer Ansatz dargestellt im Anschluß an seine Kant-Kritik*, Bonn, 1962.

Sokolowski, R., *The Formation of Husserl's Concept of Constitution*, The Hague, 1964.
Schaefer, A., *David Hume: Philosophie und Politik*, Meisenheim a.G., 1963.
Schutz, A., "Das Problem der transzendentalen Intersubjektivität bei Husserl", *Philosophische Rundschau*, Bände 5–6. 1957/58.
Thévenaz, P., *What is Phenomenology?*, Chicago, 1962.
Wagner, H., *Philosophie und Reflexion*, München, 1959.
Walsh, W. H., *Reason and Experience*, Oxford, 1947.
Waelhens, A. De, *Phénoménologie et Vérité*, Louvain, 1965.
Whitehead, A. N., *The Function of Reason*, Princeton, N. J., 1929.
Wild, J., *Existence and the World of Freedom*, Princeton, Hall, N.J., 1963.
Wittgenstein, L., *Tractatus Logico-philosophicus*, Suhrkamp, Frankfurt a.M.
Yolton, J. W., The Concept of Experience in Locke and Hume, *Journal of the History of Philosophy*, 1963.

INDEX